The Norroena Society

THE ODINIST EDDA

Sacred Lore of the North

The Odinist Edda

Sacred Lore of the North

The Norroena Society may be contacted via Facebook or Twitter, or by email at:

norroenasociety@gmail.com

or visit our website at:

www.norroena.org

ISBN: 978-0692249529

ISBN: 0692249524

Published in the United States of America

First Edition 2014

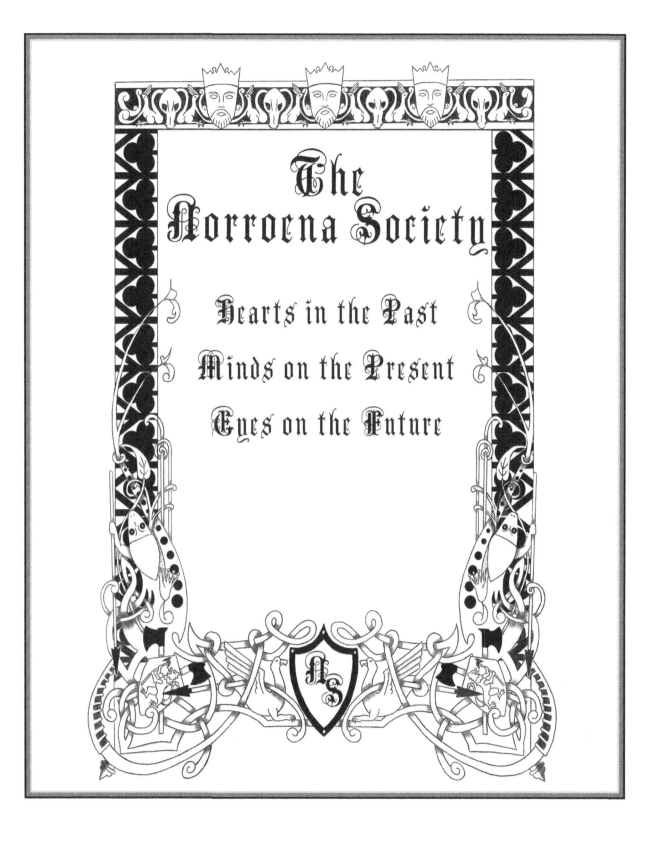

The Norroena Society

Hearts in the Past

Minds on the Present

Eyes on the Future

Table of Contents

The Odinist Edda..**V**

    Introduction...xi

    About The Odinist Edda xviii

The Ur Age 1

    I.   Ginnungagap 1
    II.   Yggdrasil..1
    III.   Audhumla..3
    IV.   Jormungrund...4
    V.   Odin 5
    VI.   Runes 10
    VII.   Idavoll 12
    VIII. Grotti 13
    IX.   Ymir 15
    X.   Alfar 16
    XI.   Ljosalfar 19
    XII.   Asgard 21
    XIII. Vanaheim 24
    XIV. Goddesses 25
    XV.   Thurses 27

The Golden Age 31

    XVI. Aesir..31
    XVII. Ivaldi..36
    XVIII. Hnossir..37
    XIX. Ask and Embla 38
    XX.   Heimdall..43
    XXI. Jarl 54

The Silver Age 58

    XXII. Gullveig...58
    XXIII. Jormungand 65
    XXIV. Hel 65
    XXV. Valhall...75
    XXVI. Niflhel 80
    XXVII. Ydalir 85
    XXVIII. Mjodvitnir 87
    XXIX. Kon 89
    XXX. Utardloki 91
    XXXI. Egil 99
    XXXII. Geirrod 101
    XXXIII. Thrym 106
    XXXIV. Sleipnir..109

XXXV.   Sif 110
XXXVI.   Hrungnir 112
XXXVII.   Byrgir 116
XXXVIII.   Sunna 121
XXXIX.   Vartari 123
XL.   Niflungs 124

The Copper Age 129

XLI.   Idun 129
XLII.   Leikin 129
XLIII.   Groa 131
XLIV.   Fimbulwinter I 136
XLV.   Hrafnagaldur 141
XLVI.   Odainsacre 143
XLVII.   Folkwanderung 145
XLVIII.   Ull 148
XLIX.   Volund 148
L.   Hod 149
LI.   Nanna 151
LII.   Hild 154
LIII.   Baldur 159
LIV.   Sinmara 171
LV.   Skadi 176
LVI.   Hringhorni 179
LVII.   Vali 181
LVIII.   Vafthrudnir 185
LIX.   Grougaldur 189
LX.   Svarinsmound 193
LXI.   Od 201
LXII.   Menglodum 203
LXIII.   Gambantein 214
LXIV.   Fjolsvid 218
LXV.   Breidablik 224
LXVI.   Alvis 225
LXVII.   Gerd 228
LXVIII.   Fenrir 237
LXIX.   Folkvig 238
LXX.   Hadding 248
LXXI.   Gudorm 259
LXXII.   Hunwar 265
LXXIII.   Asmund 267
LXXIV.   Singastein 273

The Iron Age 277

LXXV.   Gleipnir 277
LXXVI.   Hymir 279
LXXVII.   Harbard 283
LXXVIII.   Loki 287
LXXIX.   Eggther 295
LXXX.   Har 295

The Varg Age 307

    LXXXI. Fimbulwinter II...307
    LXXXII. Ragnarok 307
    LXXXIII. Gimle 310

Appendix: The Hugrunes 312

Glossary 329

Index 406

The Odinist Edda

Introduction

In the age of innocence, the age of peace and plenty, when our ancestors lived without vice or villainy, there came the first lore. The Gods sent to their proteges a divine teacher, an immortal among mortals, who would bring all the necessary implements to build a culture and a civilization. At first the lore was simple and direct; telling of the creation of worlds, of mankind, and the Gods' conflict with the powers of Chaos. As time passed more and more stories developed, detailing the complex and beautiful natures of these benevolent deities, the Aesir and Vanir, while explaining their relations to one another and their dealings with the world.

At the core of this very ancient tradition, reaching back many thousands of years, lies the epic chain of events, beginning with Ginnungagap and ending with Ragnarok and the subsequent renewal. The chain is a sacred institution that lies within the cultural and religious expressions of the people of the North that has existed since the time of the earliest Indo-Europeans. The idea of *cohesion*, so important in many hierologies, resounds in the tales of the Odinist pantheon as part of the necessary logic behind the skaldic heritage. As new stories would arise, new episodes would be added to the epic as they fit into the chronological order of events. At the same time, local customs and beliefs could form that would *not* be deemed appropriate for the greater body of lore, and so would remain within the town or community it developed in. Eventually, the stories would be recorded, although in a severely corrupted form, in a treatise that would forever label them as *Edda*. Although the text was composed three hundred years after the conversion to Christianity, for those who honor the ancient deities, this would become a holy term.the most commonly accepted definition of *Edda* comes from the Old Norse language, where it means

"Great-Grandmother," representing the idea of elders telling the sacred tales to their descendants. In ancient times, these were told as part of an oral tradition, where storytellers would pass the narratives down through the generations. To know and understand the lore was a sacred responsibility, one that gave its keepers prominent positions within their tribes or clans. The diligence with which this duty was upheld is evidenced by the survival of the customs themselves, which evolved over centuries, embodying the cultural manifestations of the folk will. The pre-Christian poems of what would be known as the *Poetic* or *Elder Edda*, along with those of the elaborate and enigmatic skaldic discipline, would act as the primary representatives of this ancient inheritance.

Then, in the midst of this cultural evolution, there came a foreign invader upon Northern soil. Christianity began its campaign of forced conversion that would take centuries to complete, while the old ways started fading out early on. It was only by chance that the fragments of Odinist lore were able to survive as a product of church propaganda. In order to convince the masses to convert, Christian leaders had to explain why these people had been worshipping "false gods" for millennia. To the uneducated peasants the answer was easy: their ancestors had been tricked by demons into deifying them, causing the folk to turn away from the "true faith." However, the learned nobility had established their lineage through the pantheon, and valued their familial relationship with the Gods as part of their royal heritage. The nobles were, by far, the most important part of the church's conversion tactics, for they would convert their subjects to the new faith, and they could make war if they were not pleased. Therefore, a more appropriate response was needed for their concerns, which would have to coincide with that given to the lower classes. Thus, the euhemerist movement began. The Christian clergy told the heathen nobles that their Gods and Goddesses were actually human kings and queens who had achieved such repute among their people, they were eventually elevated to divine status. An elaborate doctrine was created to back up this claim, including the complete reformation of the old lore to fit this new idea. The Teutonic deities became heroic Trojans, and a false etymological relationship between "Asia" and "Aesir" was developed. In the end, this plan would backfire, since the actual recording of the traditions themselves would be valued most, while lies about human Aesir from Troy would be all but forgotten.

Many years later, during the Germanic Renaissance of the late 19th century, scholars all over Europe would collect, translate, and piece together the fragments as best they could, in order to form a coherent system of lore from Northern Europe. During this era, modern mythological research was born. Although often falsely classified as "Norse," these stories represent an ancient body of religious beliefs that were once celebrated from Austria to Iceland, and beyond. The most prominent scholar of this Renaissance was, without a doubt, Jacob Grimm, the German linguist who gathered popular traditions and stories remaining from the North's heathen past, and meticulously researched every detail, pioneering the field of investigating these customs in his work *Deutsche Mythologie* ("Teutonic Mythology"). Following Grimm was Swedish poet and author Dr. Viktor Rydberg, whose *Undersokningar i Germanisk Mythologi* ("Researches Into Germanic Mythology") and *Fädernas Gudasaga* ("Our Fathers' Godsaga") would be the most thorough, yet most underrated texts ever written on the ancient ways. These latter books have served as a template for the present volume.

Shortly thereafter, in Australia, 1936, Alexander Rud Mills established the Anglecyn Church of Odin, officially heralding the rebirth of the Odinist or Asatru religion. At the time, it seemed as though this new awakening of an old path would be quite prolific. However, with the coming of World War II and false allegations made by an overly paranoid Australian government, many of the early Odinists were led to concentration camps, and the light of Odin would remain dim for the time being.

It would not be until the late 1960s, when Danish born Else Christensen, inspired by Mills' work, would relight the flame of Odinism among the Gods' descendants in America and Canada. Her group, the *Odinist Fellowship*, worked diligently in spreading the word that the old faith was indeed born again, this time for good. Earning the name "Folksmother," Else was a true force to be reckoned with, for her strong will and life-long dedication to Odinic beliefs would help set the stage for many to follow in her footsteps. Although still facing persecution (in her 80s Else was falsely imprisoned and deported from the U.S. due to her success with the *Odinist Fellowship*), these defenders of the faith will always be remembered and honored within the Odinist Nation.

From there, the message grew like wildfire, with organizations cropping up all over the Western world, and individuals finding the path on a daily basis. In America, there would be the *Asatru Free Assembly* (to become the *Asatru Folk Assembly*) and the *Asatru Alliance*, from England the *Odinic Rite* would spread across the globe, whereas the *Asatruarfelag* in Iceland would become the first nationally recognized Asatru organization in modern times.

To this day, the faith still faces opposition from those who would make false accusations based on outdated misconceptions. In spite of this, the religious revival continues to evolve and move forward in ever more positive directions. The celebration of European ethnicity may seem threatening to some, but should be recognized as the beautiful and uplifting experience we Odinists know it to be. The Odinist religion is, by all means, an esoteric belief system, only because it embodies the cultural values of the peoples of the North. In this way, it is no different than other ethnic religions found in India, Japan, Africa, Native America, and elsewhere.

Our people were great explorers and adventurers who tread upon almost every land on earth. Their admiration and desire to learn of other cultures was a staple of their way of life, exemplified by certain rites of passage where youths would set off to see the world. Long before such tolerance and acceptance of others became a trend of modern society, Northern sailors traveled from one end of the globe to the other, without leaving any trace of imposition or disrespect towards those they encountered. Archaeological evidence shows them to have been peaceful traders among the nations they fared, though their fierce defense of their homelands was legendary. Odinists today would emulate our ancestors' attitudes in honoring other peoples, while at the same time demanding that our way of life is not devalued or attacked simply because of its place of origin.

As more and more people answer the call of their ancestral Gods and Goddesses, more projects, institutions, and groups will arise. Everywhere the faith is practiced, believers seek legitimacy and recognition within the countries they reside, which has proven to be no easy feat. Many forces have opposed this religion since the first Christian set foot on Teutonic soil. Yet, this is the true testament to the power and strength of the folk will, and of the customs themselves. Without forced conversions, without exorbitant amounts of funds and resources to advertise and campaign with, without the backing of mainstream society, Odinism has survived, and now thrives once again. The voice of Odin's Nation will be heard, and the Gods and Goddesses of our folk will be honored among all the nations of the West, taking their rightful place as our divine patrons.

As stated, the academia began the Odinic revival in the late 19th century. Some claim that certain secret societies at the time were practicing Odinist customs in Germany and elsewhere, which included many of these intellectuals. While we greatly value the contributions made by mainstream scholars over the past 120 years, the time has come for this movement to break away from our dependence upon these institutions. No longer should outsiders be allowed to dictate the shape of the lore or the beliefs we adhere to, when in many cases these do not reflect the best interests of the Odinist nation. Among the folk are those who can and will create texts by and for members of the faith, manifesting every cultural aspect that would be used in its celebration. As the necessity for the work of mainstream academia wanes, it is up to the community at large to seek out texts and materials that reflect the needs and values of the Odinist religion. Not that we would discourteously reject any attempts to aid us in our revival, nor would we ignore good information when it presents itself, no matter who wrote it. It is the strong reliance upon non-Odinist scholars that holds us back from achieving our maximum potential. Odinism is one of the only religions in the world that finds members placing academics outside the community upon a pedestal, according them the same prominence as religious leaders. As if adopted into some sort of pantheon or canon, these scholars' writings have become gospel to many.

It is time to begin a new era, where traditions can be coalesced as part of the evolution of the religious movement, rather than merely co-opted from the work of outsiders. This is a part of our sacred heritage, and as such must be expressed in a body of lore that comes from the nation itself. The first thing that must be done is to accept that it *can be* done, *is* being done by Odinists all over the world.

One of the most beautiful aspects of Odinic beliefs is the lack of a sanctified dogma, which has come to be greatly valued among believers. There are no sects to represent various interpretations or differences in viewpoints, and it is widely accepted that no two Odinists will think alike. While we appreciate these differences, there is little tolerance towards those who would place negative, disrespectful, or immoral connotations upon the practice of the religion.

For the most part, however, our take on the customs will differ, and few of us would have it any other way.

It is in following with the spirit of this idea that The Odinist Edda was written. The purpose of such a massive undertaking, which is the culmination of over ten years of work, and thirty years of combined research between several scholars, is not to develop a strict authority on what Odinist lore should and should not be. Although it was put together to be a sacred text, rather than just another "mythology" book, the sanctity of the work is in re-establishing holy story-telling traditions in the form of the Teutonic epic. Like a great puzzle, the fragments of lore have been pieced together, cleansed of Christian elements, and presented as a source for Odinists to enjoy as part of our legacy.

Before the age of Bibles and Korans, tales of the worlds' religions were shared over hearths or near children's beds. The lore was not a concrete rule of divine law that had to be maintained, word for word, at all costs. Rather, it was a vibrant, fluid development that constantly changed and evolved, while keeping in line with what had come before. Although the stories themselves are sacred, what's more important are the lessons one walks away with, the true inspirations of the Gods and Goddesses. The *inspiration* is the holy experience in reading or hearing the lore, and remains so to this day. Our connection to the divine should not be considered any less potent than it was among our ancestors, so we should not shy away from contributing to the traditions now. In fact, it should be considered our duty to do so. The Odinist Edda is an attempt to live up to this obligation. The idea is to try to keep the heathen customs intact, never harming that which we are confident is part of the ancient ways, then building upon them, filling in gaps when needed, using in-depth research and logical conclusions to do so.

There will be those who will scoff at this, who will claim that the sources we have are enough. Why? Because they are old? Because they came from Iceland or Scandinavia or Germany? When the Christians changed the lore to fit their purposes, they did so on a whim, without any regard for the importance it held as part of Northern European heritage. It was demonized and mutilated to coincide with an evangelical agenda to rob the heathen Teutons of their past, and to degrade the legacy of their forefathers. Well, now we take it back! Now we reclaim our ethnic birthright, now we call out to the heavens, to the Odinist martyrs who died by Christian swords, and let them know that they did not die in vain, that their children's children's children woke up and took back what is rightfully ours.

However, we are the only ones who can do this. The power is in *our* hands. Only *we* can choose what customs we will hand down to our descendants. Only we can decide what stories we will tell, what rites we will practice. At least now we have the choice, we are no longer imprisoned by a tarnished and confused inheritance from those of a religion completely and utterly opposed to our own. Only by accepting the power within ourselves, to take our destiny within our own hands, can we truly take our rigthful place as the children of Odin.

About The Odinist Edda

As stated, the purpose of this work is to present a purely Odinic record of the lore of our ancestors, in a way that more closely reflects the original, pre-Christian epic. The years of work put into this have culminated in the formation of dozens of investigations and hundreds of theories, based on the close scrutiny of every line of our sources. Using a strict methodology focusing on the epic's analysis, while examining details as they fit into the larger puzzle, has allowed us to strip away many of the corruptions and misunderstandings surrounding these stories. Because of this, a more concise body of Odinist tales can be illustrated.

It must be understood that such a text is not meant to be simply read, like a novel. As with the research that led to its creation, the idea is to take the reader on a journey into the hearts of our forefathers to find greater wisdom and understanding in the lore and poetry they passed down to their descendants. We study diligently the heritage of our past and take what we will from it, learning the inspirations of the divine. For this reason, we have tried to retain the original wording of the sources as much as possible (even though these are translated into English), and avoided the tendency to 'interpret' passages unless this was absolutely necessary.

The length and complexity of such an undertaking is rewarded by the fact that so many of our records have been condensed in an easy to understand format, using the most important information for our religious use. Simply looking through the hundreds of endnotes contained within the first edition of The Ásatrú Edda can give an idea of the many volumes one would need to read, and the thousands of hours one would otherwise have to spend searching for bits and pieces scattered through a plethora of writings. Still, to put this all together in forming the sacred Teutonic epic may require a change in the very way many of us even look at these ancient tales.

For instance, it will be noticed that some stories here are drastically altered from their popular forms, while some accounts are missing and entirely unrecognizable narratives are presented. Tales famously attached to one character, such as Sigurd, are here given to another (in this case Hod). These are not errors, nor are they based upon simple, fly-by-night theories that cannot be backed up with sound research. If we are to seek a body of lore that truly manifests our Odinist heritage, we have to remain detached to the Christianized and mutilated sources that have been handed down to us. If we hold on to them, they will always act as the sole proprietors of our ancestors' legacy, even though their original purpose was to annihilate everything our forefathers stood for.

The ancients sought to pass the lore down through the generations, all the way to us today. Sadly, this did not happen. With the coming of Christianity, so much was lost, but these traditions are being revived all over the world, and will continue to be resurrected as time passes. We can save our hierology, to an extent . . . We may never see a text that perfectly recreates the stories as they were before the conversion, but that is not really the point. As our faith renews itself, new customs are born, new ideas are formulated and coalesced, and new wisdom is shared that only accentuates our heritage, building something we can call our own. We pick up the pieces of our charred past, then move forward in a way that would make our ancestors proud.

The Ur Age

I. Ginnungagap

1. In the earliest age, what is was not, there was no sand, nor sea, nor cool waves. The earth did not exist, nor the sky above. There was a mighty chasm, Ginnungagap; but grass grew nowhere.

2. It was many ages before the earth was created that Niflheim was made, and in its midst lies a spring or well called Hvergelmir, resting atop the Nidafjoll. From there flow the rivers Svol, Gunnthro, Fjorm, Fimbulthul, Slid and Hrid, Sylg and Ylg, Vid, Leipt, and Gjoll. Gjoll lies next to Helgates and Leipt is so holy sacred oaths are sworn upon it. All of these rivers are known collectively as Elivagar. Hvergelmir flowed north of Ginnungagap, enveloping Niflheim in mist and cold.

3. First, there was that world in the southern region which is called Sokkdalir or Utgard, in Helheim. It is bright and hot. That area is flaming and burning and was impassable for those that were foreigners there and were not native to it. Also in Helheim the fountain of warmth and strength giving liquids, called Urdarbrunn, is to be found. There was no sun to shine.

4. Between these two regions lies the well of wisdom, Mimisbrunn, where Ginnungagap once was. When the Elivagar rivers came so far from their source, the kvikadrops hardened like a slag of cinders running from a furnace, and became ice. When this ice began to solidify and no longer run, kvikadrops spewed out and froze into icy rime. Then, layer by layer, the ice grew within Ginnungagap.

5. That part of Ginnungagap, which reached into the northern regions, became filled with thick ice and rime. Inside the gap there was mist and wind-whipped rain. But the southern part of Ginnungagap grew light because of sparks and glowing embers flowing from Helheim. Sparks flew from the south-world: the fire gave life to the ice.

6. Just as coldness and all things grim came from Niflheim, the regions close to Helheim in the south were hot and bright, but Ginnungagap was as mild as a windless sky. Thence in each direction there arose a holy fountain which would bring life into the worlds.

II. Yggdrasil

1. In the darkness a golden seed was formed which fell into Mimisbrunn. From this seed

sprouted the mighty ash, Yggdrasil, the World-Tree, which sent out roots through the wells of the three powers and its countless interlacing root-threads were the foundation on which Jormungrund rests. During lengthy world-ages the tree's trunk lifted itself ever higher and sprouted branches over each other, on which the various worlds, after the creation was complete, would have their foundations. Yggdrasil's Ash is the most excellent of trees. From the spreading of its golden root-threads, the fountains it grew from then became surrounded in gold.

2. It is radiant and shining, yet to human eyes it is invisible. To those who can see it, it is an immense tree, said to be the biggest and the best. Its branches spread through the eight winds over all the worlds and extend across the sky. Three roots support the tree and they are spread very far apart across Jormungrund, where each is fed by the sacred fountains. The first is in Helheim, in the south, and beneath that root is the holy well of warmth, Urdarbrunn. The second root stands over the central well called Mimisbrunn, or Odroerir, where Ginnungagap once was. The third root extends over Niflheim, and under that root is the well of cold, Hvergelmir; but Nidhogg gnaws at this root from below. The wells are so large a person could live in them. The trunk and branches

of Yggdrasil are silver-white, as are its roots; but its root-threads, foliage, and fruits are red-gold.

3. From its fruit, which shall be borne on fire to pregnant women, shall that come out which was held within; so it is with the Manna Meotod. These fruits contain the essence of youth, which the Gods bite into when they grow old. They all become young again, and so it will be right up to Ragnarok. The fruits, the Manna Meotod, are laden with Yggdrasil's saps, drawn from the powers of the holy wells, and thus have many wonderful uses, but must be sanctified by the divine for their various purposes.

4. A hundred thousand kinds of plants have arisen from Yggdrasil's seed, and all trees have originated from it. Even godly powers lied within it.

5. The mead of the three fountains sustains the tree, which then returns these saps to Jormungrund. Thence come the dews that fall into the dales, forever green it stands over Urdarbrunn. Many creatures and beings survive throughout the ages on this drink alone, for it has strange, nourishing qualities.

6. An eagle sits in the branches of the ash, and it has knowledge of many things. Runes are risted on the eagle's beak. Between its

eyes sits the hawk called Vedurfolnir. Odin once spoke of the tree in such a manner:

7. The squirrel is named Ratatosk,
   which has to run
   in Yggdrasil's ash;
   from above he must carry
   the words of the eagle,
   and repeat them to Nidhogg below.

8. There are also four harts,
   which nibble from
   its crown with bent backs;
   Dainn and Dvalin,
   Duneyr and Durathror.

9. More serpents lie
   under Yggdrasil's ash,
   than a weak minded fool would think:
   Goin and Moinn—
   they are Grafvitnir's sons—
   Grabak and Grafvollud,
   Ofnir and Svafnir,
   will, I think,
   ever gnaw at the branches of that tree.

10. Yggdrasil's Ash
    suffers hardship
    greater than men know of;
    its trunk is rotting,
    and Nidhogg gnaws beneath.

11. The cock sitting in Yggdrasil, all-glittering with gold, is called Vidofnir; he stands in the clear air on the limbs of the tree.

12. The ash is exceedingly high and precious to all. No man knows from what root it springs: and few can guess what shall make it fall, for fire nor iron will harm it. With its sturdy trunk it offers a stubborn resistance, though it is attacked by many a man or beast.

III. Audhumla

1. When the kvikadrops of the Elivagar from Hvergelmir and the warm winds of Helheim met in Ginnungagap, they thawed and dripped. There was a quickening in these flowing drops and life sprang up, taking its force from the power of the heat. From Elivagar sprayed kvikadrops, which grew until they became an Etin, and he was named Ymir. The Hrimthurses call him Aurgelmir, and from him are their generations descended.

2. When he slept he sweated. There grew under his left arm a male and a female, who were named Mimir and Bestla. From them came a family of Etins who are beautiful and friendly. But foot begat with foot the strange, three-headed son of the wise Etin. Countless winters before earth was formed, Bergelmir was born; Thrudgelmir was his father, Aurgelmir-Ymir his grandfather. From them came the clans of Hrimthurses, descended from Aurgelmir-Ymir.

3. Next it happened that as the icy rime dripped, the aurochs called Audhumla was formed. Four rivers of milk ran from her udders, and she nourished Ymir. Audhumla licked the blocks of ice, which were salty. As she licked these stones of icy rime the

first day, the hair of a man appeared in the blocks towards the evening. On the second day came the man's head, and on the third day the whole man. He was called Buri, and he was beautiful, big, and strong. By drinking Audhumla's fertile milk he begat the son Bur.

IV. **Jormungrund**

1. Jormungrund is the most ancient land, which was inhabited and decorated long before the other worlds. Originally it was divided by three realms, each separate from the other.

2. First, there is Niflheim, which lies north of the Nidafjoll. Here is the gloomy, muddy, and cold land of frost, which is shrouded by mist and fog. Hvergelmir rests atop the Nidafjoll, the mountain region which serves as the boundary between it and the southern realms.

3. Next, there is that land which is owned by Mimir, called Glasisvellir or Okolnir. This is a place of indescribable magnificence, with flower fields and groves that are never ravaged by frost or winter. Here is also where Mimir's hall is located. That wonderful hall that the Aesir call Brimir's hall, was owned by Mimir. After his birth, Mimir became the guardian of the central well, Odroerir, or Mimisbrunn, and the root of Yggdrasil borne out of it. Because this well bore Ygg-

drasil's seed, the great ash is called Mimameid as well. Hidden in the glorious well of Mimir lies all knowledge, and wisdom and intelligence are also hidden there. He is full of wisdom because each morning he drinks of his mead from the Gjallarhorn. It is from him and his well that the runes and Galdur have their origin. Glasisvellir is separated from the south by the river Gjoll.

4. Finally, there is the southernmost region, called Helheim. There arose from the sea, Urdarbrunn, which stands under the tree, three maidens who were fostered by Mimir and Bestla. They were given the names Urd, Verdandi, and Skuld, and together they are known as Norns. Urd rose from the well. They are Norns who shape necessity. They established laws, allotted life to the sons of men, and pronounced urlag. These maidens shape men's lives, and runes are risted on the Norns' nail. In the starry sky they weave the Web of Wyrd, whose threads would spread across all lands. These threads are called urlagthreads. The Norns became guardians over Urdarbrunn, as well as Yggdrasil's southern root extending over it. There the Gods have their place of judgment, which lies within the handsome hall that stands under the ash beside the well, which is called Gimle or Vingolf. This hall is the most beautiful of them all and is

brighter than the sun. It will remain standing when both heaven and earth are gone, and good and righteous men will inhabit that place through all ages.

5. Each day the Norns take water from the well and pour it up over the ash so that its branches may not wither or decay. That water, or mead, is so sacred that all things that come into the spring become as white as the membrane called the skin, which lies on the inside of the eggshell. Two birds nourish themselves in Urdarbrunn. They are called swans, and from them comes the species of bird with that name. The Norns have wolves for steeds, and because of this wolves are called "The Norns' Dogs."

6. The mead from Hvergelmir is filled with a hardening substance that allows Yggdrasil to endure throughout the ages, in spite of its many afflictions. Its mead is called Svalkaldur Saer. The mead of Urdarbrunn is called Urdar Magn, which gives Yggdrasil warmth and strength. Mimisbrunn produces a drink known as Sonar Dreyri, which includes the creative force and wisdom to keep the great ash thriving.

V. <u>Odin</u>

1. Bur, son of Buri, took as his wife the woman called Bestla. She was the daughter of Ymir, sister of Mimir, and with Bur she had three sons. One was called Odin, another Vili-Lodur, and a third Ve-Hoenir. It is our belief that this Odin and his brothers are the rulers of heaven and earth. Lodur became the ward of the sky and protector of time. Hoenir became an administrator of blot, the first godi, whose name, Ve, designates a sacred enclosure. As such he would become the one who is able to choose the lot-wood. Hoenir is called Odin's Table Companion or Comrade or Confidant and Inn Skjota As and Langifot and Aurkonung. Both of these brothers became the progenitors and jarls of the Vanir. Lodur was thought to be proud and bold, Hoenir gentle and kind.

2. Odin is the highest and oldest of the Gods. He rules in all matters, and, although the other Gods are powerful, all serve him as children do their father. We know that Odin is his name, and this is what we call the one whom we know to be the greatest and the most renowned. He lives through all ages and governs all things in his realm. He decides all matters, great or small. He and his brothers made heaven, earth, and the skies, and everything in them. Most important, they created man and Odin gave him a living spirit, called ond, that will never die, even if the body rots to dust or burns to ashes.

3. At this time the oldest Gods lived peacefully and happily in the evergreen realms of

Jormungrund with Mimir, the Norns, and other members of the noble Etin race of Ymir's arms. Odin knew that he had many great deeds to perform for the worlds, yet he was still young and inexperienced, and knew that he did not have the power to do what needed to be done. One drink from Mimisbrunn could help him; but Mimir, the well's deep-minded guardian, refused him the drink before he would prove himself worthy through self-sacrifice. Then Odin gave himself as the sacrifice for his life task, which he described in his own words:

4. I know that I hung
   on the wind-tossed tree
   nine nights,
   wounded by my spear,
   given to Odin,
   myself given to myself;
   on that tree
   of which no one knows
   from what root it springs.

5. No one gave me bread,
   nor a horn of drink,
   I peered downward,
   I took up the runes,
   wailing I learned them,
   then fell down thence.

6. I obtained nine Fimbulsongs
   from Bolthorn-Ymir's, Bestla's father's,
   celebrated son, Mimir,
   and I got a drink
   of the precious mead
   drawn from Odroerir.

7. Then I began to quicken,
   and to become wise,
   and to grow and to prosper;
   each word I sought
   resulted in a new word;
   each deed I sought
   resulted in a new deed.

8. You will find runes,
   and explained characters,
   very powerful characters,
   very potent characters,
   which Fimbulthul-Mimir drew,
   and the oldest Powers made,
   and Odin risted.

9. By Odin for the Aesir,
   by Dainn-Brokk for the Alfar,
   and by Dvalin-Sindri for the Dwarves,
   Asvin-Mimir risted runes for the Etins,
   some I risted myself.

10. Do you know how to rist them?
    Do you know how to interpret them?
    Do you know how to draw them?
    Do you know how to prove them?
    Do you know how to pray?
    Do you know how to blot?
    Do you know how to send?
    Do you know how to consume?

11. It is better to not pray
    than offer too much;
    it is better to not send
    than blot too much.
    So Thund-Odin risted
    before the origin of men,
    this he proclaimed
    after he came home.

12. I know those songs
    which kings' wives do not know,
    nor sons of men.
    The first is called Hjalp,
    for it will help you against strifes and cares.

13. For the second I know,
    what the sons of men require

who will live as leeches.

14. For the third I know,
    if I have great need
    to restrain my foes,
    I deaden the weapon's edge:
    neither my adversaries,
    nor arms nor wiles harm at all.

15. For the fourth I know,
    if men place
    bonds on my limbs,
    I sing so
    that I can walk;
    fetters spring from my feet,
    and chains from my hands.

16. For the fifth I know,
    if I see a shot from a hostile hand,
    a shaft flying amid the host,
    it cannot fly so swift,
    that I cannot stop it,
    if only I get sight of it.

17. For the sixth I know,
    if one wounds me
    with a green tree's root,
    also if a man
    declares hatred to me,
    harm shall consume them sooner than me.

18. For the seventh I know,
    if I see a lofty house
    blaze over those inside,
    it shall not burn so furiously
    that I cannot save it,
    that song I can sing.

19. For the eighth I know,
    what to all is
    useful to learn,
    where hatred grows
    among the sons of men:
    I can soon set it right.

20. For the ninth I know,

if I stand in need
to save my ship in the water,
I can calm
the wind on the waves,
and lull the sea.

21. For the tenth I know,
    if I see Tunridur
    doing mischief in the air,
    I can work so
    that they will forsake
    their own forms
    and their own minds.

22. For the eleventh I know,
    if I am to lead those in battle,
    whom I have long held in friendship,
    then I sing under their shields,
    and with success they fare
    safely to the fight,
    safely from the fight,
    safely on every side they go.

23. For the twelfth I know,
    if I see a hanged man's
    corpse in a tree,
    then I can so rist
    and draw in runes,
    so the man shall walk
    and talk with me.

24. For the thirteenth I know,
    if I sprinkle water
    on a young man,
    he shall not fall,
    though he comes into battle:
    that man shall not sink before swords.

25. For the fourteenth I know,
    if I have to name the Gods,
    Aesir and Alfar,
    in the society of men,
    I know them all well,
    few can do this unskilled.

26. For the fifteenth I know,

7

what the Dwarf Thjodreyrir sang
before Delling's door:
power to the Aesir,
victory to the Alfar,
and wisdom to Hroptatyr-Odin.

27. For the sixteenth I know,
if I wish to possess
a modest maiden's favor and affection,
I change the heart
of the white-armed damsel,
and wholly turn her mind.

28. For the seventeenth I know,
that that young maiden
will reluctantly avoid me.

29. For the eighteenth I know,
that which I never teach
to maid or wife of man,
(all is better
what only one knows:
this is the song's closing)
save her alone
who clasps me in her arms.

30. Odin is the cleverest of all, and from him all others learned their arts and accomplishments; and he knew them first, and knew many more than other people. It was from the drink he received from Mimir's well that he gained such wisdom. But now, to tell why he is held in such high respect, we must mention the various causes that contribute to it. When sitting among his friends his countenance is so beautiful and dignified, that the spirits of all are exhilarated by it, but in war he appears dreadful to his foes. This comes from his being able to change his skin and form in any way he likes. He can be recog-

nized by the fact that no dog, however fierce, will attack him.

31. Another cause is that he converses so cleverly and smoothly, that all who hear believe him. He speaks everything in verse, such as that composed, which we call the skaldcraft. He and the Gods are called Ljodasmiths, for from them that art of song came into the Northern lands.

32. He is called Aldafather in our language, but he has many other names, which he once spoke of:

33. I am called Grim,
I am called Gangleri,
Herjan and Hjalmberi,
Thekk and Thridi,
Thund and Ud,
Helblindi and Har,

34. Sad and Svipal,
and Sanngetal,
Herteit and Hnikar,
Bileyg, Baleyg,
Bolverk, Fjolnir,
Gaut and Grimnir,
Glapsvid and Fjolsvid.

35. Sidhot, Sidskeg,
Sigfather, Hnikud,
Allfather, Valfather,
Atrid and Farmatyr;
I have never been called
by one name,
since I have gone among men.

36. I am called Grimnir
at Geirrod's,
and Jalk at Asmund's,
and Kjalar

when I drew Kjalki-Vagnhofdi,
Thror at the Thing,
Vidur in battles,
Oski and Omi,
Jafnhar and Biflindi,
Gondlir and Harbard with the Gods.

37. Svidur and SVidir
I was called at Sokkmimir-Surt's,
and beguiled that ancient Etin,
at the time when I
became the slayer
of Mjodvitnir-Fjalar's son.

38. I am now named Odin,
I was called Ygg before,
before that, Thrund,
Vak and Skilfing,
Vafud and Hropt,
with the Gods, Vidur and Jolf,
Ofnir and Svafnir,
all which I believe
to be names of me alone.

39. Odin's other names are: Arnhofdi, Alda-gaut, Asgaut, Audun, Bruni, Dresvarp, Dorrud, Eylud, Farmagud, Feng, Fimbultyr, Forni, Frarid, Geigud, Geirlodnir, Gestum-blindi, Geirolnir, Ginnar, Gizur, Gondul, Herfather, Hjarrandi, Hlefrey, Hlefod, Hrammi, Hrani, Hvatmod, Jolfud, Jolnir, Jormun, Lodung, Hrafnagud, Njot, Olg, Sid-grani, Sigdir, Sveigdir, Svidud, Svolnir, Tveggi, Thriggi, Thrasar, Thropt, Thunn, Valthognir, Valtyr, Veratyr, Vidir, Volsi, Yrung, As, Blindi, Hangatyr, Sigtyr, Gauta-tyr, Hangagud, Hangi, Haptagud, Hergaut, Herjafather, Hertyr, Mimsvin, Havi, Haptsoenir, Vidhrimnir, Vidar, Ennibratt,

Hjorvard, Karl, Sigurhofund, Sigrun, Sigtryg, Vegtam, Rognir, Valgaut, Svidar, Gagnrad, Yggjung, Thunn, Raudgrani, Sig-mund, and Wralda.

40. Odin is a majestic figure; his forehead is high, his eyebrows strongly drawn, his facial features noble, and his gaze thoughtful and brooding. Driven by his thirst for knowledge, he sank one of his own eyes into Mimisbrunn, and thus is one-eyed. He appears with this handicap to human beings, when he wants them to know who he is, usually wearing a wide-brimmed hat, and wrapped in a loose blue cloak. In his own hall, however, among the Gods and Einher-jar, he seems handsome and without defect and although heavy in thought, he seems so gentle that all look gladly into his awe-inspiring face. His beard extends down over his chest.

41. Often he travels so far from Asgard that he passes many seasons on his journeys. His two brothers, Hoenir and Lodur govern the realm when he is absent.

42. Odin can make his enemies in battle blind, or deaf, or terror-struck, and their weapons so blunt that they can cut no more than a willow wand. On the other hand, his warriors rush forward without armor, as mad as dogs or wolves, biting their shields, and are as strong as bears or wild bulls, and kill

people at a blow, but neither fire nor iron hurts them. These are called Berserks, as well as Ulfhednar.

43. Odin can transform his shape: his body lies as if dead, or asleep; but then he will be in the shape of a fish, or serpent, or bird, or beast, and be off in a twinkling to distant lands upon his own or other people's business. This practice is called Skipta Litum and Utiseta. With words alone, through the power of Mimir's runes, he can quench fire, still the ocean in tempest, and turn the wind to any quarter he desires. Sometimes he even calls the dead out of the earth, or sets himself beside the burial mounds; whence he is called the Draug Allvald, and Haug Drottinn.

44. Odin knows finely where all missing cattle are concealed under the earth, and understands the songs by which the earth, the hills, the stones, and mounds are opened to him; and he binds those who dwell in them by the power of his word, and goes in and takes what he pleases. His enemies dread him; his friends put their trust in him, and rely on his power and on himself.

45. He gives the food on his table to his two wolves, Geri and Freki. He himself needs nothing to eat. For him, wine is both drink and food. The wolves have runes risted on their claws. Two ravens sit on his shoulders, to whom he taught the speech of man, and they tell all the news they see and hear into his ears. Their names are Hugin and Munin. At sunrise he sends them off to fly throughout the worlds, and they return at the evening meal. Thus he gathers knowledge about many things that are happening, and so people call him Hrafnagud. As Hugin and Munin fly each day over Jormungrund, he fears that Hugin may not return, yet he is afraid more for Munin.

46. Odin has the gift of prophecy, as does his wife, and through this learning he knew what he had to do through the ages for the benefit of the worlds. In all such things he is pre-eminently wise. He taught all these arts in runes, and songs which are called Galdur, and therefore the Gods are called Galdursmiths.

47. Odin consecrates oaths. Pray to Herjafather-Odin for his favor on a journey: he gives and grants gold to his followers. He gave to Hermod-Od a helm and coat of mail, and Sigmund received a sword from him. He gives victory to his sons, but riches to some; eloquence to the great, and wisdom to others, fair winds to the sailor, song-craft to skalds, he gives valor to many a warrior.

VI. <u>Runes</u>

1. The holy knowledge of runes was originally in Mimir's possession. He, however,

did not intrinsically hold this knowledge, but gathered it from the well of wisdom that he guarded under the World-Tree's central root. Through self-sacrifice in his youth, Odin received a drink from it and nine rune-songs, called Fimbulsongs, that contain secret, beneficial powers. Among the Fimbulsongs, the following should be noted:

2. Sigrunes that are sung when one goes to meet an opposing army. Then the warriors raise their shields level with their upper lips and sing in low tones, so that their many voices blend together in a dull roar, like breakers on the shore. If they hear Odin's voice join in with their own, then they know that he will grant them victory.

3. Olrunes that are used to purify drink and keep one protected from those who would mix their mead with treachery.

4. Bjargrunes that ease a child's entry into the world and allay sorrow and worry.

5. Brimrunes that cleanse the air of harmful beings and give power over wind and wave when sailors need to be rescued from distress at sea, and power over fire when it threatens men's homes.

6. Limrunes that grant curative power.

7. Malrunes that return the power of speech to the mute and silenced.

8. Hugrunes that aid in knowledge and wisdom. Hugrunes are of various types and comprise both earthly and spiritual wisdom. Men and women, highborn and lowborn, have sought after them. So too Limrunes, which are handed down within some noble families.

9. Each type of runes have their various uses in prayers and songs to the Gods. Here are the runes the sons of men have:

10. **Fehu** is kinsmen's strife
    and flood's fire
    and serpent's path.

11. **Uruz** is moor's ranger
    and Buri's liberator
    and Etin's nourisher.

12. **Thurisaz** is women's torment
    and cliff-dweller
    and Vardruna's husband.

13. **Ansuz** is Aldagaut
    and Asgard's jarl
    and Valhall's leader.

14. **Raido** is horseman's joy
    and swift journey
    and horse's toiling.

15. **Kenaz** is bright flame
    and sun of houses
    and beacon on the mound.

16. **Gebo** is king's duty
    and lord of friendship
    and adornment of maids.

17. **Wunjo** is wholesome home
    and lack of sorrow
    and laughter's kinsman.

18. **Hagalaz** is cold grain

and sleet-shower
and serpent's sickness.

19. **Nauthiz** is bondmaid's grief
and hard condition
and toilsome work.

20. **Isa** is river's bark
and waves' roof
and bane of the doomed.

21. **Jera** is mankind's profit
and good summer
and thriving crops.

22. **Eiwaz** is strong bow
and brittle iron
and Etin of the arrow.

23. **Perthro** is recreation source
and giver of omens
and home of lots.

24. **Elhaz** is antlered beast
and fierce defender
and hunter's game.

25. **Sowilo** is clouds' shield
and shining glory
and destroyer of ice.

26. **Tiwaz** is one-handed As
and wolf's leavings
and prince of hofs.

27. **Berkano** is leafy twig
and little tree
and fresh young shrub.

28. **Ehwaz** is prideful beast
and prince's joy
and source of comfort.

29. **Mannaz** is man's joy
and earth's augmentation
and ship's adornment.

30. **Laguz** is eddying streams
and wide kettle
and land of fish.

31. **Ingwaz** is ancient hero
and Freya's husband
and changer of urlag.

32. **Dagaz** is Skinfaxi's lord
and Natt's child
and Delling's son.

33. **Othala** is fathers' land
and inherited property
and cherished heritage.

34. Measures were taken in the early days to spread these beneficial runes among all races of beings. Odin spread them among the Aesir; Mimir's sons Dainn-Brokk and Sindri-Dvalin spread them among the Alfar and Dwarves. Through Heimdall they would come to men. The good gift is blended with holy mead and sent far and wide. Thus, they are with the Aesir and with the Alfar, some are with the wise Vanir, and some among the children of men. Nor had the Etins been spared a share. They too took part in the primeval peace compact, and Mimir sent them runes, which formed the basis of that knowledge found among the clans of Jotunheim, and afterwards put to ill use by them.

VII. <u>Idavoll</u>

1. The Aesir met on Idavoll, built lofty hofs and horgs, set up forges, fashioned treasures,

created hammers, tongs, and anvils, and with these they made all other tools. Following this, they worked metal, stone, wood, and great quantities of gold, such that all their furniture and household utensils were of gold.

2. Allfather-Odin would assign rulers who would judge with him people's urlag and oversee the arrangement of the worlds. This was to be done at Idavoll, within Urd's realm. The Gods' first task was to build the Thingstead where twelve seats were placed, including Allfather's throne. That building is the best and largest in the worlds. Outside and inside everything seems to be made of gold, and the place is called Gimle or Vingolf. This sanctuary belongs to the Norns, and it is exceptionally beautiful.

VIII. Grotti

1. Gods and Etins came together and created an enormous mill, called Grotti. It was also called Skerry Grotti and The Mill of the Storm. Its foundation rests on the Nidafjoll, encircling the Hvergelmir well, which is the mother well to all the waters of the worlds. The waters come from Hvergelmir, and they return after a completed cycle. These rivers are:

2. Sid and Vid,
   Saekin and Eikin,
   Svol and Gunnthro,
   Fjorm and Fimbulthul,
   Rhine and Rennandi,
   Gipul and Gopul,
   Gomul and Geirvimul:
   they wind around
   the Gods' dwellings.
   Thyn and Vin,
   Tholl and Holl,
   Grad and Gunnthrain.

3. One is called Vina,
   a second Vegsvin,
   a third Thjodnuma;
   Nyt and Not,
   Nonn and Hronn,
   Slid and Hrid,
   Sylg and Ylg,
   Vid and Von,
   Vond and Strond,
   Gjoll and Leipt;
   these two fall near men,
   and fall hence to Hel.

4. Kormt and Ormt,
   and the two Kerlaugs.

5. Through a channel going through the ocean's bottom through the earth, the perpetual relationship between Hvergelmir and the ocean is maintained. Under this channel, the millstone is placed on its foundation in such a way that the eye of the moveable stone stands midway over the well. Because of this, the water swells through the eye of the millstone to and from Hvergelmir. Ebb comes to the sea when the water rushes down through the millstone's eye; flow comes to the sea when the water thrusts up again through the same opening. The revolv-

13

ing millstone causes the Maelstrom that is dreaded by sailors. One will see the Grotti-Mill after traversing the land of frost, reaching thus the Hvergelmir well, where the water of the ocean flows back to this mysterious fountain. This deep, subterranean abyss wherein the ebbing streams of the sea are swallowed up to return and which with the most violent force draws the unfortunate seamen down into the Underworld. Here is the unfathomably deep eddy, which we call the Navel of the Sea. Twice a day it swallows the waves, and twice it vomits them forth again. Often, we are assured, ships are drawn into this eddy so violently that they look like arrows flying through the air, and frequently they perish in this abyss. But sometimes, when they are on the point of being swallowed up, they are driven back with the same terrible swiftness.

6. The mill can grind out whatever the grinder prescribes. One can grind riches, grind happiness and wealth in abundance on the wishing-mill. Here shall no one harm another, nor harbor malice, nor bring to bane, nor strike with sharp sword, even if he found his brother's slayer bound. Nine Etin-maids turn Grotti's moveable millstone. In the beginning, however, they happily ground luck, plenty, artistry, wisdom, gold, and peace. Occasionally other Giantesses will

join them in turning the mill. Here is the song they sung:

7. "We grind riches for the worlds,
  we grind happiness
  and wealth in abundance
  on the wishing-mill.
  May they sit on riches,
  may they sleep on down,
  may they wake to joy:
  then we have ground well!

8. "Here shall no one harm another,
  nor harbor malice,
  nor bring to bane,
  nor strike with
  sharp sword,
  even if he found
  his brother's slayer bound."

9. At this time the Gods chose Lodur to be the attendant of the mill. Lodur supervises the mill's regular motion and under him stand the nine Etin-maids pushing the mill-handles. The mill-servants not only turn its moveable stone with these handles, but also the starry vault. It is the movement of the starry vault which Lodur has to supervise. Because of this he is called Gevar, the ward of the atmosphere.

10. The World-Mill, Grotti, is also the origin of the sacred friction-fire, which produces the holiest flame. Fire had been discovered before then, and was used ever since the beginning; but there are many kinds, and the purest and most excellent did not come until Grotti's stones rubbed against each other.

Up until that point this fire had been hidden in the elements, without revealing itself before the eyes of the Gods; but it was now brought forth by the friction.

11. It was this holy flame of Grotti that gave birth to the brightest God, Heimdall. In ancient times he was born endowed with wonderous might, of divine origin: the nine Etin-maids gave birth to the gracious God at the world's edge. Gjalp did bear him, Greip did bear him, Eistla bore him, and Eyrgjafa, Ulfrun bore him, and Angeyja, Imd, and Atla, and Jarnsaxa. Because Lodur is the mill's caretaker and the nine Etin-maids who turn Grotti created him through their labor with the mill-handles, Heimdall is said to be their son. This action made the mill the worlds' first fire-auger.

IX. Ymir

1. Ymir killed Audhumla in his thirst and hunger for the nourishing juices and food her body, filled with fertile saps, could provide. Because of this, the sons of Bur killed the Etin, with blood surging from his wounded neck. When he fell, so much blood gushed from his wounds that with it they drowned all the race of Hrimthurses except for one, Bergelmir, who would later suffer the same Wyrd as Ymir. Audhumla now rests within the Nidafjoll until the day of Ragnarok, when she shall issue forth.

2. The Hrimthurses were not completely destroyed, for their souls survived in their land of birth, Niflheim, which would become their haunt. There they built themselves a hall and during the course of time became dangerous neighbors to Mimir's realm. To the race of Hrimthurses belong the spirits of disease, who also reside in Niflheim. Among them are the Gifur, Tram, Morn, Topi, Opi, Tjosul, and Otholi. The realm they established in Niflheim is one of the two Jotunheims. The other would be built in the farthest north of Midgard.

3. Bur's sons, Odin, Hoenir, and Lodur, took Ymir and moved him to the middle of Ginnungagap and made from him the world. With the blood that gushed freely from the wounds, they made the lakes and the sea. The earth was fashioned from the flesh, and mountain cliffs from the bones. Because of this, he is called Leirbrimir and Aurgelmir. They made stones and gravel from the teeth, the molars, and those bones that were broken. Trees and plants were made from his hair. By fashioning that sea around, they belted and fastened the earth. Most men would think it impossible to cross over this water.

4. The limbs of Ymir were laid on the Grotti-Mill and ground up. The kind of meal thus produced was the soil and sand, which the

sea has cast upon the shores of Midgard since the earliest dawn of time and with which the bays and strands have been filled, to eventually become green fields. From Ymir's flesh were the oldest stores of soil derived, those which covered Midgard's stone grounds when Odin and his brothers raised them from Ymir's blood. The soil was fertile because it was saturated with Audhumla's milk and flesh, and thus would Midgard be covered with vegetation.

5. After Ymir's flesh was transformed into soil this was done to Thrudgelmir's and after him to Bergelmir's flesh. Countless ages before the earth was formed was Bergelmir born, after his father was laid on the mill. Bergelmir's limbs are ground by the mill in our present age.

6. The earth is circular around the edge and surrounding it lays the deep sea. On these coasts, in the northeast, the sons of Bur gave lands to the clans of Etins to live on, which would also be known as Jotunheim. The drowned Hrimthurses had not all the same deformities. They had reduced with every generation. Among Bergelmir's children and grand-children is there to be found such beings who were well formed and less savage than their strange-headed fathers. Odin himself showed compassion to these younger Etins and let them save themselves from the

waves of Ymir's blood upon the shores of this Jotunheim, which they and their descendants thereafter settled. Further inland, Odin and his brothers built a fortress wall around the world to protect against the hostility of the Etins. As material for the wall, they used the eyebrows of the Etin Ymir and called this stronghold Midgard.

X. Alfar

1. Mimir married a Giantess named Sin-mara, who was among the noble race of Etins, born of Ymir's arms. Together, they had twelve sons and twelve daughters, renowned for their beauty. The sons are called Njars or Brisings and the daughters Ostaras. From these children are the Alfar descended.

2. Next, the Gods took their places on their thrones. They issued judgments in Idavoll and remembered where the Dwarves had come to life in the soil under the earth, like maggots in flesh. The Dwarves emerged first, finding life in Ymir's flesh. They were maggots at that time, but by a decision of the Gods they acquired human understanding and assumed the likeness of men, living in the earth and rocks. They were created by Mimir and his son, Durin [Surt]. For this reason they are often called their sons. Thus, the Dwarves and Alfar are both considered to be Mimir's progeny, and are named here:

3. Nyi and Nidi,
    Nordri and Sudri,
    Austri and Vestri,
    Althjof, Dvalin-Sindri,
    Nar and Nain,
    Niping, Dainn-Brokk,
    Bifur, Bafur,
    Bombur, Nori,
    An and Anar,
    Ai, Mjodvitnir-Fjalar.

4. Veig and Gandalf,
    Vindalf, Thrain,
    Thekk and Thorin,
    Thror, Vitur, and Litur,
    Nyr and Nyrad,
    Regin and Radsvid.
    Now I have rightly
    told of the Dwarves.

5. Fili, Kili,
    Fundin, Nali,
    Heptifili,
    Hannar, Sviur,
    Frar, Hornbori,
    Fraeg and Loni,
    Aurvang, Jari,
    Eikinskjaldi.

6. Uni and Iri,
    Ori and Bari,
    Billing and Bruni-Volund,
    Bild, Buri,
    Var and Vegdrasil,
    Dori, Uri,
    and Delling,
    the cunning Alf.

7. There were Draupnir,
    and Dolgthrasir,
    Haur, Haugspori,
    Hlaevang, Gloi,
    Skirfir, Virfir,
    Skafid, Alf,
    Yngvi, Thjodreyrir,
    Duf, Andvari,

Har, Siar.

8. Fjalar and Frosti,
    Finn-Ivaldi and Ginnar,
    Heri, Hugstari,
    Hljodolf, Moinn:
    that above all shall,
    while mortals live,
    be accounted
    the progeny of Lofar-Mimir.

9. Other Dwarves are: Berling, Blovur, Dolgthvari, Bofur, Dulin, Duri, Fal, Gjolp, Gloni, Grer, Grim, Hledjolf, Hlevarg, Loinn, Oin, Skavaer, Vigg, Nid, Olnir, Eitri, Galar, Horr, Ingi, Rekk, Vali, Blain, Dari, Gud, and Solblindi.

10. From full horns the sons of Mimir drank the pure mead of Mimisbrunn, and became, just as their father and in their father's service, personal powers of creation, supervisors of nature, and great smiths who forged grass and plants and wonderful ornaments of fire or gold or other elements. Among their creations are the beautiful horses of the Gods:

11. Glad and Gyllir,
    Glaer and Skeidbrimir,
    Silfrtopp and Sinir,
    Gisl and Falhofnir,
    Gulltopp and Lettfeti,
    on these steeds the Aesir
    ride each day
    when they go to pronounce dooms
    at Yggdrasil's ash.

12. Other horses are: Hrafn and Sleipnir, splendid horses, Val, and Tjaldari was there, I heard Goti and Soti mentioned, Mor and Lung with Mar, Vigg, and Stuf. Blak is able to carry a thane; I also heard Fak mentioned, Gullfaxi and Jor with the Gods. There is a horse called Blodughofi, and they say he bears the mighty Atridi-Frey.

13. Dag rides Drosull-Skinfaxi, Dvalin-Sindri rides Modnir, Hjalmther Hod, and Haki Fak. The slayer of Beli [Frey] rides Blodughofi, and the prince of the Hadding-jas [Kon] Skaevad, Vestein Val and Vifil Stuf, Menthjof Mor and Morgin-Delling Vak; Ali-Od on Hrafn. Bjorn-Hod rides Blak and Bari-Berling [Bjar], Kort, Atli Glaum and Adils-Ull Slungnir, Hogni Holkvir and Harald Folkvir, Gunnar Goti and on Grani, Sigurd.

14. Only Mimir's direct descendants, the Alfar, were allowed to drink of the mead. The Dwarves that were created by him and Durin were not given permission to partake in the holy potation, but rather were taught their arts by Mimir's sons. This would later cause enmity within their ranks.

15. For those who take pleasure in good drink, plenty will be found in the hall called Brimir. It stands at the place called Okolnir or Glasisvellir, the beer-hall of the Etin who is called Brimir-Mimir. Another stands on Nidavoll, north of Idavoll, a hall of red-gold for Sindri's race, the splendid hall they made of red-gold is also called Sindri. In this hall good and virtuous beings will live. Among them are Mimir's daughters, the Goddesses of Night, and Natt herself is the highest and most beautiful of them. Bodvild is another, and there are ten more.

16. These twelve women are also Goddesses of Dawn; one sees them riding on red-colored horses, wearing red outfits and all their riding gear shines with gold. As stated, Natt is far lovelier than the others, and her sisters are in attendance of this great Goddess. As Goddess of the Dawn, she herself is known as Ostara. When they put their horses to graze, the women set up a splendid tent, with stripes of alternating colors and embroidered everywhere with gold. The points of the tent are ornamented with gold, and on top of the pole that stands up through the tent, there is a great golden ball.

17. Natt is black and swarthy like her kinsmen, the Svartalfar. She was first married to the man called Naglfari, or Lodur; their son was named Aud, or Njord. They also bore Mani and Sol together, who in turn had the daughters Nanna and Sunna. These maids shall ride on their parents' course when the Powers die. Next, Natt was married to Anar, or Hoenir. Their daughter was named Jord

or Frigga. Finally, she married Delling, who is from the family of the Gods. Their son is Dag, and he is as bright and beautiful as his father's people, the Ljosalfar. From these lines came the divine clans of Aesir, Vanir, and Alfar, and because of this Natt is known as the Mother of the Gods. The Alfar were given a land in the eastern part of Mimir's realm, which is called Alfheim. The people called the Ljosalfar live there, but the Svartalfar live down below in the earth. They are different from the Ljosalfar in appearance, and far more so in nature. The Ljosalfar are more beautiful than the sun, while the Svartalfar are blacker than pitch.

18. As protection against the Hrimthurses in Niflheim, the Gods and Mimir arranged for a watch at Hvergelmir's well on the border of the Nidafjoll. The jarl chosen for the watch was Ivaldi, who was given powerful weather runes to keep the frosts and mists of the northern lands at bay.

XI. Ljosalfar

1. Then Bur's sons took Ymir's skull and from it made the sky. They raised it over the earth and under each of the four corners they placed a Dwarf. These are called Austri, Vestri, Nordri, and Sudri. Then they took embers and sparks shooting out from Sokkdalir and flying randomly. These they placed in the middle of Ginnungaheaven,

both above and below, to light up heaven and earth. They fixed places for all these elements. Some were placed up in the heavens, whereas others, which had moved about under the heavens, they found places and established their courses. Before this Sol did not know where she had mansions, stars did not know where they had stations; Mani did not know what might he had. It is said that, from then on, times of day were differentiated and the course of years was set.

2. There are nine worlds and nine heavens. It is said that a second heaven lies to the south of ours. It is called Andlang. Still further up, there is a third heaven called Vidblain. We believe that this region is in heaven, but now only the Ljosalfar live there. The stream is called Ifing, which divides the earth between the Etins and the Gods: it shall flow openly throughout all time. No ice shall be on that stream. Nine heavens on high are listed. The nethermost is Vindblain, it is Heidornir and Hreggmimir. The second heaven is Andlang, the third Vidblain. Vidfedmir is the fourth, Hrjod, and Hlynir is the sixth; Gimir, Vetmimir. Skatyrnir stands higher than the clouds, it is beyond all worlds.

3. Then the Gods all went to their Things-eats in Idavoll. There they gave names to Natt and Nidjar, they named Morgin-Delling and Middag-Dag, afternoon and evening, to

reckon the years. The beneficent Powers also made Ny and Nid to count years for men.

4. Then Allfather-Odin took Natt and her son Dag. He gave them two horses and two chariots, crafted by the Dwarves, and placed them in the sky to ride around the earth every twenty-four hours. Natt rides first with the horse called Hrimfaxi. He draws each night forth over the beneficent Powers and from his bit he lets drops fall every morning, whence comes the dew in the dales. People call the dew, which falls to the earth, honey-dew, and bees feed on it. From their honey comes the mead of men. Dag's horse is called Skinfaxi, and with its mane it lights up all the sky and the earth, drawing forth the bright day over humankind. That steed is counted best among our people. His mane always sheds light. Delling's son urges on his horse, well adorned with precious stones; the horse's mane glows above Midgard, the steed draws Dvalin-Sindri's playmate, Dag, in his chariot. The Gods decided at Idavoll that Natt and Dag would alternately travel through Jormungrund's eastern horse-doors, near Delling's home, into the Upphimin, and return through these gates in the west, where Billing had his land allotted to him.

5. Mundilfari-Lodur's children with Natt, Mani and Sol, were made to journey each day around heaven, to count years for men.

Dwarves forged their chariots of fire and gold. Sol was made to drive the horses that draw the chariot of the sun, which the Gods, in order to illuminate the worlds, had created from burning embers flying from Sokkdalir. These horses are red in color and are called Arvak and Alsvid, who shall wearily drag up the weight of the sun. In order to cool them, the Gods placed two bellows under their shoulders, which are called Isarnkol. A shield was placed before Sol, which is called Svalin. If it fell from its place, mountains and oceans would burn. The ancient Powers risted holy runes on this shield, on Arvak's ear, and on Alsvid's hoof.

6. Sol got on her chariot for the first time and drove up into the newly created heaven. Now that the sons of Bur had lifted up the lands, they who fashioned glorious Midgard, Sol shone from the south on the stones of the abode; then the ground grew green with leeks. Sol, Mani's companion, from the south cast her right hand across the horse-door to heaven.

7. Sol moves fast, almost as if she is afraid. And she cannot go faster on her journey even if she were afraid of her own death. But it is not surprising that she moves with such speed. The one chasing her comes close, and there is no escape for her except to run. Skoll is the wolf's name that chases

the fair-faced Goddess to the Varnwood. He frightens her, and he eventually will catch her.

8. Mani guides the path of the moon and controls its waxing and waning. His shining chariot is drawn by a white horse. His path lies beneath Asgard, and stands firm within the sky. Carrying the thorn-rods called limar, he is the lord of the Heiptir, and it is to him that one must pray against their hateful vengeance. The moon itself is sometimes a silver ship floating in the Ifing river, and because of this Mani is called Nokkvi.

9. Another wolf is called Hati, he is Hrodvitnir-Fenrir's son, and he is also called Managarm. He runs in front of Sol, trying to catch Mani. And this will happen. Until then, he shall follow the bright maid of heaven.

10. At each horizon of Jormungrund there are horse-doors, which the Ljosalfar ride through on their journey to and from the sky. Near the eastern horse-door lies Delling's hall, in Alfheim, where he gives aid to Natt and her kinsmen. Near the western horse-door is Billing's domain, who does the same. Delling is the jarl of the Ljosalfar and lord of the dawn; Billing rules over twilight. Delling is Natt's husband and father of Dag. The dawn is a reflection of Midgard's eastern horizon from Delling's

home. It can only be seen when Natt leaves the Upphimin and before Sol and Dag have come forward. When Natt completes her journey under the Upphimin and the red light of dawn appears, the Dwarf Thjodreyrir sings before Delling's horse-door: "Power to the Aesir! Victory to the Alfar! And wisdom to Hroptatyr-Odin!"

11. The twilight is a reflection of Midgard's western horizon from Billing's domain, in Vanaheim. Here he leads the Varns, warriors who safeguard the Ljosalfar and provide them lodging each night.

12. From the equinox, it is autumn until the sun sets in the position of none. Then it is winter until the equinox. Then it is spring until the moving days. Then it is summer until the equinox. Haustmonth is the name of the last month before winter, Gormonth is the name of the first one in winter, then it is Frermonth, then Hrutmonth, then Thorri, then Goi, then Einmonth, then Gauksmonth and Seedtide, Eggtide and Twimonth, Solmonth and Selmonth, Heyannir, and finally Kornskurdarmonth.

XII. Asgard

1. Next, the Gods made a stronghold for themselves in Yggdrasil's branches, and it was called Asgard. There the Gods live together with their kinsmen, and as a result, many events and happenings have taken

place both on the earth and in the sky. There are many halls in Asgard. Holy is the land lying near the Aesir and Alfar.

2. The first hall is Bilskirnir, what would later be called Valhall, lying in the district known as Gladsheim. The hall lies in the center of Asgard, and was built around Yggdrasil's bole, which penetrates the roof. So says the story that Odin let the great hall be built in such a way, that Yggdrasil stood therein, and the limbs of the tree blossomed far out over the roof of the hall, while below stood the trunk within it. The golden leaves of Glasir-Yggdrasil stand before Sigtyr-Odin's hall. That is the most beautiful tree among Gods and men. The hall is so high that one can scarcely see over it, and its roof is covered with golden shields like tiles.

3. The next dwelling is where the kind Powers have decked the hall with silver; it is called Valaskjalf, which Odin acquired for himself in days of old. Inside this hall is Hlidskjalf, as this throne is called. When Allfather sits in this seat, he sees through all worlds and into all men's doings. Moreover, he understands everything he sees.

4. Many other halls would be built as the Gods grew in number.

5. Odin built the massive wall that stands around Asgard. It is called Gastropnir, and he built it from Leirbrimir-Ymir's limbs; he

supported it so strongly that it shall stand as long as the world. The wall's gate is called Thrymgjoll; it was made by the three sons of Solblindi-Ivaldi: a fetter fastens every way-farer, who lifts it from its opening. The gate is also called Valgrind, which stands in the plain, holy before the doors: that gate is ancient, but only a few know how it is closed with lock.

6. Yggdrasil expands over Asgard, which is thus visible to the Gods, and its upper leaf-abundant branches are filled with hanging fruits. Higher up than this is the place in the region of the worlds where all of the waters of heaven are collected–the evaporation from the sea and the lakes and from Yggdrasil's crown. The water found there is filled with a substance called Vafur or Ofdokkum Ognar Ljoma; wise craftsmen made it out of the flaming light of the flood [gold]. This gives the thunderclouds their metallic color. It can ignite and then becomes Vafurfires: quick, flickering, zig zag flames that strike their target with a conscious accuracy. A river streams down from Eikthyrnir, the stag over Bilskirnir, which, with its Vafur-evaporating billows pours out a protective moat around Asgard. If the Vafurmist ignites over the river, it resembles the whirling of a fire-torrent. Thrymgjoll is also the drawbridge that leads over the river.

7. Gomul and Geirvimul wind around the Gods' dwellings. These rivers swirl down with such headlong violence that animals normally lose the strength to keep afloat and are drowned. First, they run in a trickle from the pinnacles of the mountains, then dash down steep precipices to the rocks below, multiplying the thunder of their waters as they plunge into deep valleys; though they rebound continually from one obstructing boulder to another they never lose any of their hustling speed. As they surge and churn down the whole length of this channel they create a foaming whiteness everywhere, but when they have shot from the canyon between the cliffs they spread their flow more spaciously and form Asgard from a rock that lies in their path. The ridge, sheer on both sides, projects from the water and is so clustered with different kinds of trees that from a distance they screen the rivers from view.

8. The Gods built a bridge from Jormungrund to the sky and it is called Bifrost. It has great strength, and it is made with more skill and knowledge than other constructions. Everyday the Aesir ride up over Bifrost, which is also called Asbridge. Bifrost is the best of bridges, and on its head are holy runes risted. The bridge's ends lie near the northern and southern horse-doors of Jormungrund. Thund-Ifing roars, Thjodvitnir's [Heimdall's] fish [Bifrost] rests in the flood. The river-current seems too strong for wading to the hosts of the slain. The Hrimthurses and Bergrisar would go up into Asgard if Bifrost was crossable by everyone that wanted to go. There are many beautiful places in heaven and everywhere there has divine protection around it.

9. The Gods extended their land fortifications over the level ground. When they leave Asgard, they reach the outer land before Bifrost by the drawbridge, Thrymgjoll. This connection with the gateway of their fortress they regulate with ropes; as though operating on some revolving hinge it would now lay a road across the river, at other times, drawn up from the hidden cables controlling it, it guards the entrance.

10. Odin was born with warlike thoughts and an inclination to intervene, to be adventurous, and to make a real effort into his actions. This disposition would be transferred onto his descendants, who were all, even the mild Baldur, born as Gods of battle and victory. The days would come when the destructive powers would threaten the worlds and it would then be necessary to have in Yggdrasil's high crown, with a view in all directions that danger would come from, a

world-protecting watch of battle-ready hero-Gods.

XIII. <u>Vanaheim</u>

1. As Asgard was built for Odin and his descendants, the Aesir, the Vanir continued to settle Jormungrund, establishing Vanaheim for Odin's brothers in its western district. With Natt, Lodur became the father of Njord, and Hoenir became father of Frigga, from whom the Vanir are descended. Hoenir was the jarl of the Vanir. While Njord lived in Vanaheim he had taken his own sister, Frigga, in marriage, for that was allowed by their law; and their children were Frey, Freya, and the daughters Hlif, Hlifthrasa, Eir, Thjodvarta, Bjart, Blik, Blid, and Frid. But among the Aesir it is forbidden to intermarry with such near relations.

2. Njord, prince of men, made himself a dwelling in Noatun; he is guiltless of sin, and rules over the high-timbered horg. Over hofs and horgs he rules by the hundreds, yet was not born among the Aesir. He rules over the movement of winds, and he can calm sea and fire. One invokes him in seafaring and fishing. He is so rich and prosperous that he can grant wealth in lands or valuables to those who ask for his aid. It is believed that Njord rules over the growth of seasons and the prosperity of the folk.

3. Frigga is the foremost Goddess. She owns the dwelling called Fensalir, and it is splendid in all ways. She knows the urlag of all, though she herself says nothing.

4. Njord's children, Frey and Freya, are beautiful and powerful. Frey is the most splendid of the Gods. He controls the rain and the shining of the sun, and through him the bounty of the earth. It is good to invoke him for peace and abundance. He also determines men's success in prosperity. In ancient times the Gods gave Alfheim to Frey as a toothfee. He was also given rule over the Grotti-Mill with Lodur. On Frey's behalf, his servants Byggvir and Beyla attend the grist, while Lodur supervises the mill's regular motion. Frey is the boldest rider of all the exalted Gods. He makes no maid, no wife of man weep, and loosens all from bonds. Frey owns the horse called Blodughofi. He is also called Argud and Fegjafa.

5. Freya is the most splendid of the Goddesses. She has a home in Asgard called Folkvang, and there she decides the choice of seats in the hall. She chooses half of the slain each day, and half belong to Odin. Wherever she rides into battle, half of the chosen-slain belong to her. Her hall, Sessrumnir, is large and beautiful. It is said that if the door is closed and bolted, no one

can enter this hall against her will. Next to Sessrumnir is Lyfjaberg, and long has it been the joy of the sick and wounded: each woman becomes healthy, although she has had a year's disease, if only she ascends the mount.

6. When she travels, she drives a chariot drawn by two cats. She is easily approachable for people who want to pray to her, and from her name comes the title of honor whereby women of rank are called Frovur or ladies. Freya became so celebrated that all women of distinction are called by her name, whence they now have the title Frua; so that every woman is called Frua, or mistress over her property, and the wife is called Husfru or Husfreya. Odin loves Freya very much, and she is the fairest of all women.

7. Freya is white as snow and the blue of her eyes she won from the rainbow. Her hair, which is as fine as spiderweb, shines like the beams of midday. If her lips unlock, then birds hush and leaves rustle no more. Through the strength of her look, the lion stretches down before her feet and the serpent holds back his poison. Her food is honey and her drink is Yggdrasil's dew gathered in the bosoms of blooms. Freya has nine beauties, where her daughters have inherited

but one each, at most three. But even if she were ugly, she would be dear to us.

8. Every summer, in which men offer to Njord's nine daughters at the holy place, no evil can happen that is so severe that they cannot help them out of their distress.

9. The Vanagods, that mild race of Hoenir, are also the equivalents of their father and have his inclination for peaceful actions. Their duty is to maintain the regular consistency of the laws of time with the course of the worlds; the Aesir are to defend it against enemies. In that lies the true difference between these divine families. It is because of the Vanir, who see to the regular motion of the starry heavens and the tides, that the balance between the years, the moon phases, and night and day divide the course of time. It is the Vanir who attend to the successful growth of seeds and the bounty of the year's crops, and it is they who connect men and women with bonds of love and see to it that the chain of generations joins, link after link. But where a powerful intervention and defense is necessary, the Aesir will appear there. However, the Vanagods will also display valor when it is necessary.

XIV. <u>Goddesses</u>

1. There are twelve Aesir whose nature is divine. The Goddesses are no less sacred, nor are they less powerful. Those of the Ae-

sir are called Asynjur, those of the Vanir are called Vanadisir. Frigga-Jord is the highest of the Goddesses. She would become Odin's wife.

2. A second Goddess is Saga-Idun. She lives at Sokkvabekk, which is a large dwelling, identical to the moon.

3. A third is Eir, the best of physicians.

4. A fourth is Urd. She is a maiden, and women who die as virgins serve her.

5. A fifth is Fulla. She too is a virgin, and she goes about with her hair loose and a gold band around her head. She carries Frigga's casket, looks after her footwear, and shares secrets with her. She is Frigga's sister.

6. Freya, along with Frigga, is the most noble. She married the man called Od. Their daughter, Hnoss, is so beautiful that from her name comes the word for a treasure that is exceptionally handsome and valuable. Their other daughter is Gersemi. Od went traveling on distant paths while Freya remained behind, crying tears of red-gold. Freya has many names, because she gave herself different names as she traveled among unknown peoples searching for Od. She is called Mardoll and Horn and Gefn and Syr. Freya owns Brisingamen. She is called Vanadis, Thrungva, and Skjalf.

7. The seventh Goddess, Sjofn, is deeply committed to turning the thoughts of both men and women to love. The word for lover, *sjafni*, is derived from her name.

8. The eighth Goddess is Lofn. She is so gentle and so good to invoke that she has permission from Allfather-Odin or Frigga to arrange unions between men and women, even if earlier offers have been refused and unions have been banned. From her name comes the word *lof*, meaning permission as well as high praise.

9. The ninth is Var. She listens to the oaths and private agreements that are made between men and women. For this reason, such agreements are called *varar*. She takes vengeance on those who break trust.

10. The tenth, Vor, is so knowledgeable and inquires so deeply that nothing can be hidden from her. Hence, the expression that a woman becomes *vor* ("aware") of what she learns.

11. The eleventh is Syn. She guards the doors in the hall and locks out those who ought not to enter. She is also appointed to defend cases that she wants to see refuted at the Thing. From this situation comes the expression that a *syn* ("denial") is advanced when something is refused.

12. The twelfth, Hlin, is appointed to guard over people whom Frigga wishes to protect

from danger. From her name comes the expression that he who escapes finds *hleinir* ("peace and quiet").

13. The thirteenth, Snotra, is wise and courtly. From her name comes the custom of calling a clever woman or man *snotr*.

14. The fourteenth is Gna. Frigga sends her to different worlds on errands. She has the horse named Hofvarpnir which rides through the air and on the sea. Once some Vanir saw her path as she rode through the air, and one of them said:

15. "What flies there?
   What fares there
   or moves through the air?

16. She replied:
   "I fly not,
   though I fare
   and move through the air
   on Hofvarpnir,
   the one whom Hamskerpir begot
   with Gardofa."

17. From Gna's name comes the custom of saying that something *gnaefir* (looms) when it rises up high.

18. Sol and Natt, whose natures have already been described, are counted among the Goddesses.

19. Rind, the mother of Vali, is counted among the Goddesses.

20. Other Goddesses are Groa, Hlif, Hlifthrasa, Thjodvarta, Bjart, Blik, Blid,

Frid, Sigyn, Sunna, Nanna, Sif, Skadi, Modgud, Bodvild, Alveig, Auda, Sinmara, Roskva, Thrud, Gerd, and Ilm.

21. There are also the lesser disir who watch over men, whose natures will be described further on.

XV. Thurses

1. The Hrimthurses have one abode together in Niflheim, while the Etins who die and go there have many courts. In the upper Jotunheim the Etins continued to grow in number.

2. To the north is Jotunheim, the savage territory lacking civilization and swarming with strange, inhuman races; a vast stretch of sea separates this from the opposite shores of Midgard and, since navigation there is hazardous, very few have set foot upon it and enjoyed a safe return. This precipitous land resounds with a thundering din of storms that sounds as if they are deluging rocks. Cattle race about in droves along the seaboard. If they are harmed, monsters fly to the shore filling the forests with their howls and attacking their assailants. Etins armed with massive clubs will wade out into the sea, keeping the intruders from sailing away before they atone for the murdered cattle with blood. Jotunheim is a region of everlasting cold, spread with deep snows, for it does not experience the sun's vigor even in summer. Abounding in trackless forests, it is

incapable of producing crops and is haunted by animals uncommon elsewhere. There are many rivers, whose courses are churned into the foam of roaring rapids by the reefs embedded in their channels.

3. The Etin Fornjot had three sons: Hler, or Aegir, Logi, and Kari, each of whom maintain the destructive forces of their respective element. Aegir was also called Gymir, and his wife Ran is also known as Gullveig or Aurboda, who came from the family of Bergrisar. Gerd is one of their daughters, and she is one of the most beautiful women. Gymir-Aegir's Urcold vala often carries the ship amid breaking billows into Aegir's jaws. She is a she-wolf of the deep, and is among the Haffrus. She had been forced into fearful waters, the cold depths. The Aesir later discovered that Ran-Gullveig had fashioned a net in which she caught everyone that went to sea, designed after the net created by Loki just before his capture. Ran-Gullveig is immorality. But sea-crest-Sleipnir [ship], spray-driven, tears his chest, covered with red-paint, out of white Ran-Gullveig's mouth.

4. How shall sea or Aegir be referred to? By calling it Ymir's Blood, Visitor to the Gods, Husband of Ran-Gullveig, Father of Aegir's daughters, whose names are Himingloeva, Dufa, Blodughadda, Hefring, Unn, Hronn, Bylgja, Bara, and Kolga; Land of Ran-Gullveig and of Aegir's daughters and of ships and of terms for sea-ship, of keel, stem, planks, strake, of fish, ice; Sea-Kings' Way and roads, no less Ring of the Islands, House of the Sands and seaweed and skerries, Land of Fishing-Tackle and of sea-birds, of sailing wind.

5. How shall wind or Kari be referred to? By calling it Son of Fornjot, Brother of Aegir and Logi, Breaker of Tree, harmer and slayer or dog or wolf of tree or sail or rigging. Kari's son is Jokul, and he is the father of Snaer. Snaer's children are Thorri, Fonn, Drifa, and Mjoll.

6. How shall fire or Logi be referred to? By calling it Brother of Kari and Aegir, slayer and damager of tree and houses, the Undoing of Half and the Sun of Houses.

7. There is one counted among the Aesir whom some call Slanderer of the Gods, the Source of Deceit, and the Disgrace of All Gods and Men. Named Loki or Lopt, he is the son of the Etin Farbauti. His mother is named Laufey or Nal, and his brothers are Byleist and Helblindi.

8. Farbauti is the Etin of hurricanes and thunder. The hurricane's cloud bursts and heavy showers, which through the swollen torrents wed themselves to the sea, gave rise to Helblindi. The hurricane's whirlwind

gave rise to Byleist. A lightning strike from the storm brought Loki into the world. The violence in Farbauti's character did not demonstrate itself on the surface of Loki's character at first. It was only later, when he was laid down in a cave of torture for his crimes that this came about.

9. Loki is pleasing, even beautiful to look at, but his nature is evil and he is undependable. More than others, he has the kind of wisdom known as cunning, and is treacherous in all matters. He constantly placed the Gods in difficulties and often solved their problems with guile. His wife is Sigyn and they have two sons together.

10. Near the mill-handles of Grotti, the Hrimthurse Bergelmir, or Hrimnir, before he was slain, had a daughter with Imd, one of the Giantesses who turn the mill. In the earliest age she was at the mill, kissing the thrall-wenches. Her name is Gullveig, and she is Loki's equivalent and Heimdall's counterpart. In the core of her being she is even more dreadful than Loki himself. Although she was brought forth by Hrimnir and Imd, she would be slain by the Gods three times. They burned her three times, three times burned, and three times born oft and again. One of her other parents is Vidolf, for all the valas are from Vidolf; all the vitkis are from Vilmeid, all the seidberends are

from Svarthofdi-Surt; all the Etins come from Ymir. Gullveig is also called Heid, Aurboda, Angerboda, Ran, Ividja, Jarnvidja and Hyrrokin. Bergelmir-Hrimnir had a son named Hrossthjof, who is Gullveig's brother. Both of them share the gift of prophecy.

11. At the far northern end of Jormungrund sits an Etin named Hraesvelg. He has the shape of an eagle, and when he beats his wings to take flight, the winds blow out from under them. Thus, come the winds that blow over all men.

12. Svasud is the name of the father of Sumar. He is a man so content that from his name comes the expression "it is *svasligt*" referring to what is pleasant. The father of Vetur is alternately called Vindloni and Vindsval. He is the son of Vasad. These are cruel and cold-hearted kinsmen, and Vetur takes his nature from them. Yearly they both, Sumar and Vetur, shall forever journey, until the Powers perish.

13. I shall tell the names of the Etins: Ymir, Gang[Egil] and Mimir, Idi [Slagfin], and Thjazi [Volund], Hrungnir, Hrimnir, Hraudnir, Grimnir, Hvedrung, Hafli, Hripstodi, Gymir [Aegir]. Hardverk, Hrokkvir and Haustigi, Hraesvelg, Herkir and Hrimgrimnir, Hymir and Hrimthurse, Hval, Thrigeitir, Thrym, Thrudgelmir, Thistilbardi. Geirrod, Fyrnir, Galar, Hrim,

Oflugbardi, Gjolp, Gilling, Thrivaldi, Fjolverk, Geitir, Flegg, Blapthvari, Fornjot, Spretting, Fjalar [Suttung], Stigandi, Somur [Sumar] and Svasud, Svarang, Skrati, Surt [Durin], and Storverk, Saekarlsmuli, Skaerir, Skrymir [Fjalar], Skerkir, Salfang, Oskrud and Svart, Ondud, Stumi, Alsvart, Aurnir, Am and Skalli. Kott, Osgrui and Alfarin, Vindsval, Vidgymnir, Vipar and Vafthrudnir, Eldur and Rangbein, Vind, Vidblindi, Vingnir, Leifi. Beinvid, Bjorgolf and Brandingi, Dumb, Bergelmir, Dofri and Midjung [Volund], Nati, Logi, Kari, Jokul. Frosti, Snaer, Thorri, Nor, Gor, Hrossthjof, Koll, Vidolf, Vilmeid, Hengjankjopt, Beli, Starkad, Alsvid, Eggther, Hati, Hrod, Hrym, Aurgrimnir, Gylling, Gyllir, Mornir, Skrimnir, Grepp, Haki, Jari, Lodin, Beitur, Glam, Glaumar, Glaumvor, Gusir, Hloi, Kyrmir, Skram, Skrog, Vornir, Ornir, Heidrek, Leidi. Eimgeitir, Im, Hringvolnir, Viddi, Vingrip, Vandill, Gyllir, Samendil , Kaldgrani, Etin, Ogladnir, Grimling, Offoti, Ganglati and Helregin, Durnir-Surt, Hundolf, Baugi, Hraudung, Fenrir, Hroar, and Midi. Now there have been listed the names of very powerful Thurses.

14. I shall list the names of the Giantesses: Grid and Gnissa, Gryla, Bryja, Glumra, Geitla, Grima and Bakrauf, Guma, Gestilja, Grottintanna. Gjalp, Hyrrokkin [Gullveig], Hengjankjapta, Gneip and Gnepja, Geysa, Hala, Horn and Hruga, Hardgrepa, Forad, Hryggda, Hvedra and Holgabrud. Hrimgerd, Haera, Herkja, Fala, Imd, Jarnsaxa, Ima, Fjolvor, Morn, Amgerd, Simul, Svivor, Skrikja, Sveipinfalda. Oflugbarda and Jarnglumra, Imgerd, Ama and Margerd, Atla, Eisurfala, Leikin, Munnharpa and Myrkrider. Eistla, Eyrgjafa, Ulfrun and Angeyja. Leirvor, Ljota and Lodinfingra, Kraka, Vardruna and Kjallandi, Vigglod, Thurbord. Goi, Hundla, Sela, Gunnlod, Keila, Sivor, Hyndla, Yma, Brana, Buseyra, Greip, Hvedna, Hyrja, Kleima, Mana, Nefja. We wish to name Ryg last, and Rifingafla.

15. The Gods would defend the worlds against these Thurses and their violent storms. The Aesir would be responsible for cleansing the air of the forces of Chaos that bring harm to Midgard's lands and people. From the Gods came the pure, beneficial powers of nature that oppose those of the Etins.

The Golden Age

XVI. <u>Aesir</u>

1. The newly created Midgard, adorned with vegetation, now lied in the prime of its existence, and was a sight that pleased the eyes of the Gods. The powers of Jotunheim that inflict the earth with frost and drought, with whirlwinds and floods, restrained themselves and left Midgard in peace, since they were not strong enough to dare attack the Gods' creation. The Etins who got to rescue themselves from Ymir's sea of blood upon the shores of Jotunheim were still few in number and were treated kindly by the Gods. Nothing disturbed the regular course of the world-establishment. The seasons succeeded one another in steady time, the Grotti-Mill stood erect on its foundations; the soil that it ground was abundantly mixed with gold, and it was turned round during songs of blessing. The North Star stood in the uppermost heaven of the world-age and the vault of heaven did not have the sloping position it afterwards acquired.

2. To safeguard the peace in the worlds it was decided that all races of beings would enter into an alliance and exchange hostages. Njord is not of the Aesir family. He was brought up in Vanaheim, but the Vanir sent him as a hostage to the Aesir. As Frey's father, he is the progenitor of the race of Ynglings. Divine beings who did not originally belong to Asgard, but were adopted into Odin's clan, and thus became full citizens within the bulwarks of the Asaburgh, still retain possession of the lands, realms, and halls which are their odal and is where they were reared. After he became a denizen in Asgard, Njord continued to own and to reside occasionally in the Vanaburgh Noatun beyond the western ocean. All of his children were adopted into Asgard as well; Frey and Freya became prominent among the Aesir.

3. Odin made a vow that he would marry the most beautiful woman he knew of, and was told that his brother Hoenir had a daughter of incomparable beauty, named Frigga, Njord's sister. A messenger was sent to Vanaheim to ask Hoenir for Frigga's hand, but he refused. Upon the messenger's return, when Odin asked his tidings, he said:

4. "We have had our labors
but have not performed our errand;
our horses failed
on high mountains;
afterwards we had to ford
a swampy lake;
then Svafnir-Hoenir's daughter,

adorned with rings,
whom we would obtain,
was denied us."

5. Odin commanded them to go a second time, and through much effort they obtained Frigga for him. They were married and from this family come the kindred we call the Aesir. They live in Asgard and the realms that belong to it; each member of this family is divine. Odin can be referred to as Allfather, since he is the father of all the Gods and men and of everything that has been accomplished by his power. With Frigga he had his first son, and this is Asathor. He has strength and might, and because of this, he defeats all living creatures.

6. Thor is the foremost among the Aesir. Called Asathor and Okuthor, he is the strongest of all Gods and men. He rules at the place called Thrudvang, and his hall is called Thrudheim. Holy is the land, which I see lying near the Aesir and Alfar; but Thor shall dwell in Thrudheim until the Powers perish. Thor is also called Atli and Asabrag. He is Ennilang and Eindridi, Bjorn, Hlorridi and Hardveur, Veur, Vingthor, Sonnung, Veud, and Rym. With the Giantess Jarnsaxa he had the son Magni, and he would later have Modi and Thrud, the Valkyrie, with Sif. No one is so wise that he can recount all of Thor's important deeds.

7. Thor was brought up in Jotunheim by a jarl named Vingnir, and when he was ten years old, he received the stone hammer, Vingnir's Mjollnir. So great is his beauty that, when he is among other people, he stands out as elephant ivory does when inlaid in oak. His hair is more beautiful than gold. By the time he was twelve years old, he had acquired his full strength. Then he was able to lift from the ground ten bearskins, all in a pile. Next, he killed his fosterfather, Vingnir, and his wife Hlora or Glora. Afterwards, he traveled widely through many lands, exploring all parts of the worlds, and on his own overcame all manner of Berserks and Etins, as well as many beasts. Thor bears ill will towards Etin women.

8. Odin's second son is Baldur, and there is much good to tell about him. He was born in Glasislund. He is the best, and all praise him. One plant is so white that it is likened to Baldur's brow. It is the whitest of all plants, and from this you can judge the beauty of both his hair and his body. He is the wisest of the Gods. He is also the most beautifully spoken and the most merciful, but it is a characteristic of his that once he has pronounced a judgment it can never be altered. He once owned that hall which is called Glitnir, but now he lives at the place

called Breidablik. It is in Odainsacre, and no impurity may be there, as is said:

9. It is called Breidablik,
   where Baldur has
   made a hall for himself,
   in that land
   where I know there are
   the fewest perils.

10. Baldur was sent to Mani to be raised on the moon.

11. Hod is the name of one of the Gods. He is Baldur's twin brother and Odin's third son. He is a great hunter and is immensely strong. Greater is his strength than his growth: well can he wield swords, and cast forth spears, shoot shafts, and hold shields, back horses, and do all the great deeds that he learned in the days of his youth. As a stripling Hod surpassed his foster-brothers and contemporaries in his immensely sturdy physique, not to mention his talent for a variety of skills. He was as knowledgeable and deft in swimming, archery, and boxing as any youth could be, for strength and training together made him a champion. His richly endowed mind made him outstrip his unripe years. No one was a more expert harpist or lute-player, as well as which he was dexterous in the whole art of psaltery, lyre, and fiddle. By performing in difffferent modes he could excite in men's hearts whatever emo-

tions he wished: joy, sorrow, pity, or hatred, and by delighting or dismaying their ears could capture their minds. A particular mode of song, Hadarlag, is named after him.

12. Hod was a handsome youth, but thoughtless in character: violent, easily moved, easily led, and passionate with raging emotions. His behavior once depended on whose influence he was under at the time. For a while, he allowed Baldur to lead him and made himself worthy of praise; thereafter he allowed Gullveig and Loki to influence him, and he committed deeds he deeply regretted.

13. Baldur almost always had Hod near him. They were inseparable friends, and Baldur's gentleness worked to calm Hod's raging temperament. It is said that when Hod was a boy, he was so impulsive, wanton, and mischievous and so easily fell under Loki's influence that Odin thought it best to send him away to be taught by Mimir. Mimir accepted the duties of teacher of the handsome Asason and instilled rich character in him. The boy was willing to learn, and became skilled in poetry, song, the art of the smith, and many sports. Mimir taught Hod all manner of arts, the playing of Tafl, the lore of runes, and the talking of many tongues. Hod flourished and, before reaching his teenage years, had gained unusual physical strength. But his impulsiveness and his violence were not

easily quelled. He engaged in mischief, especially when he was in the smithy. Once, when Sindri had been scolding him, the boy took Draupnir's renowned smith by the hair and dragged him out over the threshold. On another occasion, when he was ordered to work at the forge but did not want to, he hit the anvil so hard with his sledgehammer that the anvil burst into pieces. But by degrees, Mimir, in his wisdom succeeded in taming his temper, if not his impulsiveness, and when his teacher sent him back to Asgard a fair, courteous youth, trained in many sports, Odin received him with much love, and he was well accepted by all of his relatives in Asgard. Then he was allowed to join his brother Baldur to be fostered by Mani.

14. Tyr is the name of another of Odin's sons. He is the boldest and most courageous. For men of action, he is good to invoke. The expression goes that a man is *Tyhaustur* if he is the type who advances out in front, never losing his courage. Tyr is so wise that a clever person is said to be *Tyspakur*. It is a mark of his daring that when the Aesir tried to lure the wolf Fenrir in order to put the fetter Gleipnir on him, the wolf would not trust the Gods to free him until finally they placed Tyr's hand as a pledge in the wolf's mouth. Then, when the Aesir refused to free him, the wolf bit off the hand at what is now

called the *Ulflidur*. Because of this, Tyr is one handed, and men do not think of him as a peacemaker.

15. Odin fathered Tyr with a beautiful Giantess, who was a friend of the Gods and was also one of those found in Jotunheim. Tyr's mother was married to the Etin Hymir, and allowed Tyr to remain as foster-son in Hymir's odal during his early years.

16. One is called Vidar, Valfather's mighty son; he is the silent God. The Giantess Grid was the mother of Vidar inn Thogli. He has a thick shoe and is nearly as strong as Thor. The Gods rely on him in all difficulties. Vidar may be called Inn Thogla As, Possessor of the Iron Shoe, Enemy and Slayer of Fenriswolf, the Gods' Avenging As, Fathers' Homestead Inhabiting As, and Son of Odin, Brother of the Aesir. Vidar's spacious Landvidi is overgrown with branches and high grass: there the son will descend from the steed's back to boldly avenge his father.

17. Odin exchanged pledges of mutual friendship with Mimir, which were never broken by either of them. Odin gave Mimir the Gjallarhorn as a pledge. All kinds of staves were engraved and painted on the horn: the long heath-fish [serpent] of Haddingland [Hel], unharvested ears of grain, and animals' entrances. When one, incapable of restraining his greed, stretches uncon-

trollable hands towards the horn, it will lengthen into a serpent and take the life of its bearer, if he is not meant to touch it. Mimir became the Gods' friend and the worlds' benefactor through voluntary action. He acquired Odin's friendship because he let him drink of his mead.

18. Odin demanded and received oaths of loyalty from the Alfar, among whom Ivaldi and his sons were jarls. It was decided by the Gods that Volund and his brothers would take charge of the upbringing of Frey.

19. Odin's sons were fostered in Jotunheim. These young Gods were of fierce temperament, stalwart in their early manhood, preeminent in their physique, famous as the conquerors of Etins, renowned for triumphs over the powers of frost, and rich with their spoils.

20. In return, the Etins gave hostages–the Etin-maid Gullveig and the Etin-youth Loki. Both of them got to stay in Asgard where Gullveig was taken into Frigga's household as her maidservant. When one desires to have a child, they pray to the Gods with heart and soul that they might have one. And so it is said that Odin hears their prayer, and Frigga no less heeds their petition: so she, never lacking for all good counsel, would, at that time, call to her casket-bearing maid, Hrimnir's daughter Gullveig, and set an ap-ple in her hand, and bid her to carry it to her devotees. Gullveig would take the apple, put on a feather-guise, and would fly to Midgard till she found them and would drop it into the lap of those who had prayed for it, and upon eating of it the woman would soon grow big with child, for these are the fruits of Yggdrasil, the Manna Meotod. These duties were conferred upon all of Frigga's maids.

21. Loki was not a big man, but he early on developed a caustic tongue and was alert in trickery and unequalled in that kind of cleverness that is called cunning. He was very full of guile, even in his youth, and for this reason he was called Loki the Sly. He set off to Odin's home in Asgard and became his man. Odin always had a good word for him whatever he did, and often laid heavy tasks upon him, all of which he performed better than expected. He also knew almost everything that happened, and he told Odin whatever he knew. Odin and Loki mixed their blood together and vowed to never taste mead unless it was offered to them both. Almost immediately, Loki began plotting against the Gods. At this time, he married the Goddess named Sigyn, who became very devoted to him. They had two sons together.

XVII. Ivaldi

1. Ivaldi was one of the Dwarves created by Durin in the Ur Age, and then King Vilkin and Queen Rusila, one of the finest female warriors and one of the Haffrus, raised him. They were rulers of the Alfar who dwelled south of the Elivagar. Ivaldi was married to Sunna, daughter of Sol, and with her had the daughters Idun, Auda, and Alveig. Idun was the youngest of Ivaldi's elder children. With the Giantess Greip he had the illegitimate sons Volund, Egil, and Slagfin.

2. Clad in armor smithied by Volund, Ivaldi was the great spear-champion, who despised all other weapons of attack, and was also called Geirvandill. He was the Gods' sworn protector of the Hvergelmir fountain and the rivers that spring from it; most especially the Elivagar rivers, which separate Jotunheim from the other realms. He would later become the great folk-hero and protector of Svithjod. His sons inherited these positions. Ivaldi is a kinsman of Heimdall, and was the first of the race of Skilfings and Ylfings.

3. In ancient times a mighty fortress was built for Ivaldi as an outpost against the powers of frost. It is called Yset, and lies within the land called Ydalir, located in the northernmost part of Alfheim, just south of the Elivagar. This became the odal of the Ivaldi clan, passed down generation after generation. The land is described as rich in gold, and *Yseturs Eldur* [Yset's Fires] is a kenning for gold.

4. Ivaldi's sons also learned powerful Fimbulsongs from Mimir, which allowed them to keep the cold and frost of Niflheim at bay. Volund learned the art of the smith at Mimir's hearth and became a most excellent artisan, renowned throughout all the worlds. Egil and Slagfin also learned the art of the smith, but mainly served as Volund's assistants in the creation of their wondrous items.

5. Egil became the greatest archer ever known, and was also called Orvandill. One of the greatest feats he performed with his bow was shooting an apple off of his son's head. Egil had three arrows, fashioned by him with Volund's help, which always return to his quiver. He, like the other descendants of Ivaldi, was famous for running on skis, and owned a pair that could ride on water as well as on land, and, when necessary, could become a shield and used in war. This shield had images of a wild boar and a bear carved on it, both of which are symbols of Egil. After his father, Egil became the great defender of Hvergelmir and the Elivagar, and was much feared by the beings in Jotunheim.

6. Slagfin was most beloved by the Gods, and became close friends with several of

Odin's sons. With his sister, Idun, he was raised in the home of Mani.

7. In the Ancient Age, Ivaldi's sons were the devoted friends of the Gods, and were the decorators and protectors of the creation. They smithied ornaments, and at their outpost by the Elivagar they defended the worlds against Jotunheim's powers of frost. They were endowed with pleasing qualities–profound knowledge of the mysteries of nature, intelligence, strength, beauty, and with faithfulness towards their beloved. In times of adversity, the brothers were firmly united.

XVIII. <u>Hnossir</u>

1. It was during the the Golden Age that the Dwarves and Alfar forged splendid treasures for the Gods that adorn Asgard and were given for their benefit and defense. All that the Gods needed or desired of golden ornaments, weapons, or utensils were forged for them at the smithy of Mimir's sons or that of Ivaldi's sons.

2. Thor was given his wonderful items by the great smiths. He has two male goats, called Tanngnjost and Tanngrisnir. He also owns the chariot that they draw, and for this reason he is called Okuthor. He, too, has three choice possessions. One is the hammer Mjollnir. Hrimthurses and Bergrisar recognize it when it is raised in the air, which is not surprising as it has cracked many a skull among their fathers and kinsmen. His first hammer was stone, but later he would receive an iron hammer from Mimir's sons. His second great treasure is his belt, Megingjard. When he buckles it on, his strength doubles. His third possession, the Jarngreips, are also a great treasure. He cannot be without these when he grips the hammer's shaft. Baldur's ship was called Hringhorni, and it is the greatest of all ships. For Njord they forged the best of battle-axes, which can break any lock.

3. There were four Dwarves of the Brising clan, the sons of Mimir, called Sindri-Dvalin, Brokk-Alfrik, Berling-Bari, and Grer. It chanced one day that Freya went to Mimir's smithy and found it open, and the Dwarves were forging a gold necklace, Brisingamen, which was almost finished. Freya was charmed with the necklace, and the Dwarves with Freya. She asked them to sell it, offering gold and silver and other costly treasures in exchange for it. The Dwarves replied that they were in no need of money, but each one said that they would give up his share of the necklace for her love and favor, which she agreed to. And at the end of four nights, they handed it to Freya. She went home to Sessrumnir and kept silent about it as if nothing happened.

4. For several of the Goddesses the smiths made falcon and swan-guises. Freya owns a falcon-guise made by these artists. Among the extraordinary treasures was also the Tafl game made of gold, which the Gods played with during the age of peace. The Tafl game plays by itself, when someone challenges it. But the most important of the primeval artists' gifts to the Gods were the rejuvenating apples, the Ellilyf Asa. These are the fruits of Yggdrasil, specially prepared for this purpose, for their youthful essence has various uses. Volund was the smith who created the feather-guises and prepared the apples. Ivaldi's sons are beautiful, gold-forging youths that shake down Yggdrasil's mature fruit. The apples were presented to Idun, Ivaldi's daughter, who had been adopted among the Asynjur. When they are in her custody, they possess their power, but when in the hands of others they do not. The Gods are greatly dependent on Idun's care and good faith. In her private wooden box she keeps the apples which the Gods bite into when they begin to grow old. They all become young again, and so it will be right up to Ragnarok.

5. The smiths also introduced the art of mead brewing. At this time, there were four types of mead–those of the three fountains of Jormungrund, and that which was brewed for the Gods. The Gods' mead comes from the leaves of Yggdrasil and is therefore not as powerful as the purest meads of the subterranean wells. Two more types of mead would later be created–that of the Byrgir fountain, and the mead of men.

XIX. <u>Ask and Embla</u>

1. The Powers all went to their Thingseats, the high-holy Gods to consider thereon: to find who should raise the race of men out of Brimir-Ymir's blood and Blain-Ymir's limbs. There Modsognir-Mimir had become the most esteemed of all the Dwarves, but Durin-Surt the second. They, the Dwarves, fashioned many human forms from earth, as Durin commanded.

2. The sons of Bur were once walking along the seashore of Aurvangaland, which borders the sea of Joruvellir, and found two trees. These trees rose from the seeds of Yggdrasil. After the twelfth Yulefest their forms had grown up from the earth in such a manner that their arms rested, behind on their shoulders, and one joined to the other so they were connected together and both alike. And the waists of both of them were brought so close and connected together that it was not clear which was the male and which was the female. The three Aesir, mighty and venerable, came to the world from their Thing; they found on the land the

powerless Ask and Embla, without urlag. They had no ond, they had no odur, neither la nor laeti, nor litur goda. The sons of Bur lifted the logs and created people from them.

3. When they were born, they stood naked and bare, unsheltered against the rays of the sun. When they came naked, Odin-Wralda fed them with his breath, to the end that mankind should be bound to him. Both of them changed from the shape of trees into the shape of humans, and the breath went spiritually into them. Odin gave them ond, gave them breath and life; Hoenir gave them odur, gave them consciousness and movement; Lodur gave la with laeti and litur goda, gave them form, speech and hearing and sight. As soon as they were ripe, they took joy and pleasure in the dreams of Odin-Wralda. The Gods gave them clothing and names. Odin gave his garments to the two tree-people: they seemed like heroes to themselves when they got clothes. The naked man is embarrassed. The man was called Ask and the woman, Embla. From them came mankind, and they were given a home behind Midgard's wall.

4. When Bur's sons created us, they, in their wisdom, lent us sense, memory, and many good traits. Herewith might we consider their creatures and their laws. Thereof might we teach and thereof might we speak, all

and only for our own well-being. Had they given us no sense, so should we know of nothing and we should be more helpless than a jellyfish, which is driven through ebb and through flood.

5. Ask and Embla had no other people to ask for help, and no one could lend it to them. Then Odin went to them and wrought in their minds inclination and love, fear and dread. When he and his brothers gave child to the parents of the human race, they also gave them Malrunes; thus they laid speech upon all tongues and upon all lips. The Gods had given this gift to the folk, so that they might understand each other, what one must avoid and what one must seek in order to find happiness and to keep it in all eternity.

6. Odin then established by law that all dead men should be burned, and their belongings laid with them upon the pile, and the ashes be cast into the sea or buried in the earth. Thus, said he, everyone who comes to Valhall will come with the riches he had with him upon the pile; and he would also enjoy whatever he himself had buried in the earth. For men of consequence a mound should be raised to their memory and a standing stone for all other warriors who had been distinguished for manhood. On Winter Day there should be a blot for a good year, and at Midwinter for a good crop; and the third blot

should be on Summer Day, for victory in battle, called the Sigurblot.

7. Then Odin said to Ask and Embla: "Be human! Be the parents of the world! In devotion, you were created as perfect beings. In complete devotion, do the law's work, think good thoughts, speak good words, do good deeds, and worship no Thurses!"

8. Both of them first thought this: that one of them should please the other. And the first deed done by them was this: when they went out they washed themselves thoroughly. And the first words spoken by them were these: that Bur's sons had created Midgard and all prosperity whose origin and effect are from the manifestation of righteousness.

9. Ask and Embla looked roundabout, their inclination chose the best and they sought shelter under a protecting tree. But rain came and caused them to become wet. However, they had seen how the water dripped off the slanting leaves. Now they made a roof with slanting sides, they made it of sticks. But storm and wind came and blew rain under it. Now they had seen that the trunk gave protection, afterwards they went and made a wall of turf and sod, the first on one side and further on all sides. Storm wind came back yet wilder than before and blew the roof away. But they did not complain about the Gods nor against the Gods, but instead made a reed roof and laid stones thereupon.

10. And they had gone thirty days without food; and after the thirty days they went forth into the wilderness, came to a white-haired goat, and milked the milk from the utter with their mouths. Afterwards, in another thirty days and nights they came to a sheep, fat and white-jawed, and they slaughtered it. They ate its flesh and made clothes from its hide. Then they made an axe of stone, chopped down a tree with it, and made a house of wood.

11. Now they bore twelve sons and twelve daughters, at each Yuletide, two. Having found how hard it is to labor alone, they taught their children how and wherefore they did thusly. These wrought and thought together. In this wise there came homes in which they could dwell, even though they were still nomadic at this time. This place, the area where they were created, was called Lund.

12. Whatever happened with the first human pair is repeated to a certain extent in every human. Both of the trees Ask and Embla came from had sprouted up from seeds which the World-Ash, Yggdrasil, dropped to the earth. The circumstances are the same with their descendants.

13. There are six elements which make up humans: the ond, which is Odin's gift; the odur, which is Hoenir's gift; the litur goda and la with laeti, which are Lodur's gifts; the earthly matter, which is called lik; and a vegetative force. The latter two were found in Ask and Embla while they were still trees, and they are found in the fruits growing on Yggdrasil, which are carried by Hoenir's winged servants to those who would be mothers.

14. Litur, Lodur's gift, is the name of old with which the inner body is designated. The appearance of the body depends on the condition of the litur. If the litur is beautiful, the body is as well, and if the litur is altered, the body is altered. There are found people who can exchange their litur with one another for a short time; from this, one then acquires the other's appearance without altering their odur and ond. La with laeti, Lodur's second gift, is the way in which a conscious being moves and acts, granting them warm blood and mannerisms.

15. The elements in every human sprout, bloom, and ripen into apples on the massive World-Ash's branches. Yggdrasil is the Preparer of Humans. When such a fruit as this ripens, it falls down into Fensalir, which is Hoenir's land and his daughter Frigga's odal. There the fruits that do not go unno-

ticed still lie. The storks, who are Hoenir's birds–because of this he is called Langifot and Aurkonung–see them and fly with them to women who yearn to caress the small hands of a child. As shown, Frigga also has a hand in this. Lodur, the lord of the sacred fire and the fire-auger, bears them on fire into the mother's womb and there gives them what he gave to Ask and Embla: the ability to move, warm blood, and the image of the Gods. These gifts allow them to procreate.

16. Hoenir gives them the odur and Odin the ond. Odur is that material which forms the kernel of human personality, its ego, whose manifestations are understanding, memory, fancy, and will. Ond, the spirit, is that by which a human being becomes a participator in the divine also in an inner sense, and not only as to form.

17. But Hoenir does not send humans the odur he thinks is best. Countless souls await their birth into life, and must be selected individually and have mothers chosen for them. The choice is made by the Goddess of urlag, Urd, who, because those who want to be mothers are so numerous, must have many of the lesser norns to help her perform this service. These are the norns who come to each person at birth to decide the length of one's life, and these are related to the

Gods. Of many births the norns must be, nor are they of one race: some to Gods, some are kin to Alfar, and some are Dvalin-Sindri's daughters. The norns decide the urlag of men in a terribly uneven manner. Some people enjoy a good and prosperous life, whereas others have little wealth or renown. Some have a long life, but others, a short one. The good norns, the ones who are well born, shape a good life. When people experience misfortune, it is the bad norns who are responsible.

18. To the mother who one of these norns has selected for a child-soul, this is sent through Hoenir, or even Frigga. Every human comes into the world in this manner: a fruit from Yggdrasil, transformed by a threefold divine power and delivered by Urd to the mother's womb receives, wherein it lands, the life status and the urlag it has to experience. A shooting star means a baby will be born. Urd also gives the child a guardian for its entire life, a lesser norn, also known as a fylgja or hamingja or a dis. Women who die as virgins shall serve Urd in the next life.

19. Over three mighty rivers comes Mogthrasir-Mimir's maidens, the sole hamingjas who are in the world, though nurtured by Etins. These are the maidens, so wise in their hearts, which travel over the ocean. Once the idisi [disir] set forth, to this place and that; some fastened fetters, some hindered the horde, some loosened bonds from the brave: "Leap from the fetters! Escape from the foes!" When a child comes into the world a fylgja rises out of Jormungrund, up over the western horizon, and glides across the sea to seek her ward in Midgard. She follows him through his life unseen, knows his thoughts, whispers into his conscience, urges him on and warns him in his dreams. She counsels him to good, and warns him against evil, speaking to him in his sleep; thus she is also called a draumkona. She calls to him: "Be not the first cause of a murder! Do not excite peaceful men against yourself! Promise me this, charitable man! Aid the blind, do not scorn the lame, and never insult a Tyr robbed of his hand!"

20. The fylgja is beautiful, brilliant, strong, tall, graceful, and noble, with white arms and a high bosom. She represents our good thoughts, good words, and good deeds. The fylgja of the unjust is also beautiful, but when he meets her after death, she is accompanied by an Underworld hound with a list of his evil thoughts, words, and deeds. There are three types of fylgjas: Mannsfylgjas, Kynsfylgjas, and Aettarsfylgjas.

21. It is most perilous, if your foot stumbles, when you go to battle. Guileful disir stand on either side of you, and wish to see you fall. However, a fall is good luck at the beginning of a journey. I believe those cut off from their disir are doomed. One foresees his death when his fylgja appears before him, riding on a wolf. There she may offer to attend him.

22. Ask and Embla's descendants multiplied in the fertile Aurvangaland. Yet they did not know how to use fire, they had no seed corn to sow, they did not understand how to bring ore up from out of the earth, much less how to forge such things. They did not know of social bonds or laws, other than those Odin had established, nor of any other Gods than the three who created their first parents. However, they did not need many laws in the beginning, because they were honest and good-natured. But they were also easily led and there would come a time when an evil temptress would appear among them. Thus, in order to cultivate and strengthen their good dispositions, to enlighten them, and bind them to the Gods with holy bonds, the Powers decided that the humans would be sent a guide and teacher.

XX. Heimdall

1. Heimdall, God of the pure and holy fire, was chosen to be teacher of the humans soon after he was born. His father, Lodur, initiated the voyage to Midgard and prepared him for it. Heimdall is counted among the Vanir because he, through his nine mothers at Grotti's turning rods, was brought into the light of day on Jormungrund's outer western zone, on the other side of the world-sea, where the Vanir live.

2. For this important mission, the child had to be equipped with strength, wisdom, and fortitude. Because of this, he was allowed to drink the same three liquids that water Yggdrasil's roots, namely those in the three subterranean wells.

3. The first drink the child received was from Urdarbrunn, which gave him might from its strengthening elixir. After this, he was taken to Mimisbrunn, and obtained a drink of the mead of wisdom and inspiration. From there, the child journeyed to the Hvergelmir well to drink of its cold, hardening waters. Thus the boy was empowered with Urdar Magn, with Svalkaldur Saer, and Sonar Dreyri.

4. By the strand of Vanaheim, a boat was made in order for Heimdall to travel to Midgard. The boat was decorated with gold rings and other ornaments, and the boy was laid in it, while he, after receiving the drinks, slept. Next to him was laid the fire-auger with which the holy Needfire could be

obtained, and placed around him were tools that would be needed for all types of crafts, plus weapons and ornaments.

5. Heimdall came on a ship propelled without rowers, sleeping on a sheaf of grain, which had been placed at his head, to the Aurvangaland, to the birthplace of waters. He was a boy of tender age, entirely unknown to the inhabitants of that land; yet they received him and nourished him with care. The natives of the district received him as one who had been miraculously sent to them. Because he had arrived with the sheaf of grain, they called him Skef.

6. So Heimdall-Skef grew up with that folk and was still a youth when he became their teacher and instructor in agriculture and all sorts of crafts, in Aefinrunes and Aldrunes. When he came to manhood, they finally elected him to be their ruler and called him Rig. He was the one born who was greater than all, the boy empowered by Urdar Magn; he was declared a ruler, mightiest and richest, allied by kinship to all princes.

7. Heimdall, the one born on the other side of the atmosphere, knower of all wisdom and all sciences, came to be asked questions. An immortal among mortals, a guest among men, a companion of humans, they listened to him as to a father. The first thing he taught his children was self-control; the other was love of virtue, and when they had developed, he taught them the worth of freedom. For without freedom, he said, are all other virtues good only to make you into slaves, your heritage to everlasting shame.

8. Heimdall taught the humans how to plow and bake, to craft and forge, spin and weave, rist runes and read. He taught them how to tame domestic animals and to ride, to erect sturdier buildings and tie family and social bonds. He taught them to establish stable dwellings around hearths on which fires would burn because of him, for he is the friend of the homestead. In this manner, there came houses with steps, a street, and Barnstokks protecting against the sun's rays. At last they built a burgh, called Lund, and all others followed. He then taught them how to use the bow, the axe, and the spear to hunt and to defend themselves against the wild animals of ancient times.

9. So our ancestors began to grow and to learn, and to teach their knowledge and understanding to future generations. What Heimdall taught is sacred to men, and the implements he brought are eternally honored and revered. While later technologies would replace those given to the most ancient forefathers, Heimdall's tools shall always be remembered in tradition and ceremony.

10. The sacred lore of the runes, which Heimdall taught as much to the humans as is useful to know, was originally in Mimir's possession. This holy art, which came to mankind from the Gods, is called Galdur. In ancient times arrangements had already been made to spread the knowledge of Galdur among all beings.

11. He instructed the humans in the decrees of the Norns for an honest life, taught them what true freedom is, and how the people aught to live in love, in order to win blessings from the Gods. From this lore came the Nine Virtues: Honesty, Honor, Wisdom, Generosity, Kindness, Courage, Loyalty, Independence, and Piety. He also taught the first law, which we call the Runelaw.

12. When he felt they were ready, Heimdall called his children together in Aurvanga-land. There he gave them the law, the Runelaw, and said: "Let it be your pathfinder, so that nothing shall ever go ill for you." Here is the law:

13. **Fehu** ᚠ
Be neither a thief, nor a miser.

14. **Uruz** ᚢ
That which you send out shall return to you, so do no harm and work for the order. When you err, make amends; when you are wronged, seek reparation.

15. **Thurisaz** ᚦ

Be courageous and bold, and never shrink from a challenge. In your lives face the decrees of the Norns with a strong and valiant heart.

16. **Ansuz** ᚨ
Journey on the Paths of Power with respect and devotion for the Gods and the ideals, institutions, and traditions that represent their divine might.

17. **Raido** ᚱ
One must be careful when traveling about, retaining our standards of nobility and using wisdom in unfamiliar situations. In the company of others be modest and polite, as well as patient with those who are not.

18. **Kenaz** ᚲ
The journey for wisdom, knowledge, and awareness is an eternal one. Those who will honor the Gods accept the challenge of this quest sincerely and without expectation.

19. **Gebo** ᚷ
Be kind and compassionate, helpful and charitable. To your neighbor offer hospitality, generosity, and friendship. May they return it.

20. **Wunjo** ᚹ
Be happy and free, enjoy life to its fullest, and allow others to do the same, but be temperate in pleasing the senses, and recognize that certain aspects of human nature must be denied.

21. **Hagalaz** ᚺ
Understand that the forces of nature are innately neutral, and work neither for, nor against you. He who holds what *should* shall ever regret what *is*.

22. **Nauthiz** ᚾ
From necessity one gains strength, courage, and insight. The simple life most often

brings forth what a person truly needs–health and happiness. Live for this and scold not those who are lacking in embellishments.

23. **Isa** |
Only the disciplined can be truly strong, and only the strong can be disciplined. One must *understand* in order to walk upon the Paths of Power, and one must learn and train to understand.

24. **Jera**
Be responsible and industrious. Never shirk from obligated duties. Life is rewarding for those who will toil for its benefits.

25. **Eiwaz**
Give honor to your ancestors and have care and respect in your treatment of the bodies of the dead. Give the praise to them that you hope to have after death.

26. **Perthro**
He is wise who will listen to good advice, and noble who will scorn bad. Hear the counsels of the Gods and Norns and learn. Those who hear them clearly must not take lightly their duty in sharing providence.

27. **Elhaz**
The strong must protect the weak, most especially by never becoming the cold-hearted coward who would oppress or harm them.

28. **Sowilo**
Be always a peacemaker, willing to help others settle their own disputes, and acceptant of the aid to resolve your own. You shall fight only when all else fails.

29. **Tiwaz**
Be honest and true, except when to punish a lie for a lie, and keep all promises, oaths, and vows at all costs.

30. **Berkano**
Keep strong to your marriage obligations, and be wise in the upbringing of children.

31. **Ehwaz**
Be sincere and faithful to those who are your true friends. Know who are your friends and who are your enemies: give gifts and protection to the former, and cunning to the latter.

32. **Mannaz**
The bonds of blood are sacred, and unwavering loyalty to family and folk is demanded. Family devotion is manifested by helping them in any circumstance and avenging them in death.

33. **Laguz**
Flow around obstacles and blockages, parting and rejoining, but always flowing with the gravity of one's own urlag. Water is incremental and tireless, as are Heimdall's children.

34. **Ingwaz**
Find happiness in the arms of another; seek joy in the adventures of sexual pleasure. However, you must not defile yourself with the ignoble behaviors of perversion, sexual violence, or promiscuity.

35. **Dagaz**
Exist in harmony with the divine order by living in accordance with the law as set by the Gods and Norns. Strive for nobility and live so that you have an honored name and a judgment of approval over your death.

36. **Othala**
The best thing you can do for your children is work for a greater tomorrow and hand them down a legacy of wisdom and nobility. Teach your children what is right and watch the seed become a mighty tree!

37. Then Heimdall told them: "All regulations that last an age, that is a century, may, upon the advice of your leaders and by the common will, be written upon the walls of the burghs; when they are written upon the walls, then they are law, and it is our duty to hold all of them in honor.

38. "Whenever a law is made or a new rule set down, so must it be decided to the common need, but never to the profit of particular persons, nor of particular clans, nor of particular states, nor of anything else which is particular.

39. "If there is any evil wherefore no laws are set down, so one must call a Thing. There one judges after Odin's wisdom, spoken to us so we may rightly judge over all. If all do this, your judgments shall never come out wrong."

40. By Heimdall the humans got to know the names of the Gods and their various duties. He allowed them to raise horgs and hofs, evoked the Needfire with the fire-auger, which is the only one worthy enough to burn in the Gods' service, and dictated prayers and holy songs, which ever since then rise to the Powers from the lips of humans. Thus, he taught human beings how to pray and to blot, and gave them poetry and inspiration. He bears oblations to the Gods for whosoever supplicates. Heimdall bestows a blessing on each pious man, and opens wide the doors for him. His fire carries blots to the Gods, as well as brings the higher elements of men to Helheim after they die. He is the herald of all the Gods, the offering bearer, and lord of sacred rites.

41. The land Heimdall established as his realm was called Svithjod, named after Odin-Svidur. Before the bad time came, Svithjod was the most beautiful land in the world. The sun rose higher and there was seldom frost. On the trees grew fruits and nuts, which are now lost. Among the grass seeds there was barleycorn, oats, and rye, but also wheat, which looked like gold and which one could bake under the sunbeams. Years were not counted, for one year was as blithe as another. The land was closed in on the one side by Odin's sea, whereupon no folk but ours neither might, nor could travel.

42. Disease did not afflict mankind and livestock, drought did not beset the plant kingdom, and the means of nourishment were inexhaustible. Thurses did not show their evil, the air was neither too hot, nor too cold for the comfort of life. A father standing by his son, like him, resembled a fifteen year old youth.

43. Heimdall went on his way along a certain sea-shore [Joruvellir], and came to a

village, where he called himself Rig. In accordance with this saga is the following:

44. In ancient days, they say,
    the strong and active,
    aged and wise As
    known as Rig
    went along green paths,
    wending his way.

45. He went forward
    on the middle-way
    and came to a dwelling.
    The door stood ajar,
    he went in,
    on the floor was a fire,
    a hoary man and his wife
    sat there by the hearth,
    Ai and Edda,
    dressed in clothes.

46. Rig would give
    counsel to them both,
    and sat himself
    in the middle seat,
    having the domestic pair
    on either side of him.

47. Then Edda took
    a loaf from the ashes,
    heavy and thick,
    and mixed with bran;
    she laid more than this
    on the middle of the board,
    broth was set
    on the table in a bowl,
    there was boiled calf,
    a most excellent food.

48. Rig would give
    counsel to them both,
    then he rose up,
    prepared to sleep;
    he laid himself down
    in the middle of the bed;

the domestic pair lay
on either side of him.

49. There he stayed
    three nights together,
    then departed
    on the middle-way.
    And so nine months
    were soon passed by.

50. Edda bore a son:
    they sprinkled him with water,
    wrapped his dark
    skin in cloth
    and named him Thrall.

51. His skin was wrinkled,
    and rough on the hands,
    his knuckles knotted,
    his fingers thick,
    his face ugly,
    his back twisted,
    and his heels big.

52. He grew up
    and thrived well,
    then he began
    to prove his strength,
    he bound bast ropes,
    and carried loads,
    bore home faggots,
    the whole day long.

53. Then a woman with crooked legs
    came to their home,
    her soles were dirty,
    her arms sunburned,
    her nose was flat,
    her name was Thy.

54. She sat herself
    in the middle seat,
    the son of the house
    sat beside her,
    they whispered and laughed,
    and prepared the bed,

Thrall and Thy,
till the day was through.

55. They lived happily,
and had children,
I believe their names were:
Hrin and Fjosnir,
Klur and Kleggi,
Kefsir, Fulnir,
Drumb, Digraldi,
Drottur and Hosvir,
Lut and Leggjaldi,
they built fences,
manured fields,
tended swine,
kept goats,
dug turf.

56. Their daughters were
Drumba and Kumba,
Okkvinkalfa,
and Arinnefja,
Ysja and Ambat,
Eikintjasna,
Totrughypja
and Tronubeina.

57. Rig went on,
in a direct course,
and came to a house,
the door stood ajar,
he went in,
on the floor was a fire,
man and wife sat there
busy with their work.

58. The man was planing wood
for a weaver's beam;
his beard was trimmed,
a lock on his forehead,
his shirt tight;
a chest stood on the floor.

59. His wife sat by,
wielding her distaff,
with outstretched arms,

prepared for clothing;
a hood was on her head,
a smock over her breast,
a kerchief round her neck,
and brooches on her shoulders.
Afi and Amma owned the house.

60. Rig would give
counsel to them both;
he rose from the table,
prepared to sleep;
he laid himself down
in the middle of the bed,
the domestic pair lay
on either side of him.

61. There he stayed
three nights together.
And so nine months
were soon passed by.
Amma bore a child,
they sprinkled him with water,
and called him Karl;
she wrapped him in a cloth,
his face was ruddy,
his eyes twinkled.

62. He grew up,
and thrived well;
he tamed oxen,
made plows,
built houses,
constructed barns,
made carts,
and drove the plow.

63. In a wagon they brought
a bride for Karl,
dressed in goatskins,
with dangling keys;
her name was Snor,
she sat under a veil;
they prepared a home,
and exchanged rings,
they decked the bed,
and formed a household.

64. They lived happily,
    and had children;
    these were named
    Hal and Dreng,
    Held, Thane, and Smith,
    Breidurbondi and Bundinskeg,
    Bui and Boddi,
    Bratskeg and Segg.

65. Their daughters were known
    by other names:
    Snot, Brud, Svanni,
    Svarri, Sprakki,
    Fljod, Sprund, and Vif,
    Feima, Ristill:
    thence have come
    the race of Karls.

66. Rig went thence,
    in a direct course,
    and came to a hall,
    the doors faced south,
    standing wide open,
    a ring was on the door-post.

67. He went in,
    there was straw on the floor,
    a couple sat
    facing each other,
    Fadir and Modir,
    playing with their fingers.

68. The husband sat,
    and twisted string,
    bent his bow,
    and prepared arrow-shafts;
    but the Husfreya
    looked at her arms,
    smoothed her veil,
    straightened her sleeves.

69. There was a brooch on her breast,
    and a cap on her head,
    her train was broad,
    her gown was blue;

her brow was brighter,
her breast fairer,
her neck whiter
than driven snow.

70. Rig would give
    counsel to them both,
    and sat himself
    on the middle seat,
    having the domestic pair
    on either side of him.

71. Then Modir took
    a broidered cloth
    of white linen
    and covered the table.
    Then she took
    thin cakes
    of snow-white wheat,
    and laid them on the table.

72. Then she set out
    on the table,
    full vessels
    adorned with silver,
    game and pork,
    and roasted birds;
    there was wine in a crock,
    the cups were ornamented.
    They drank and talked
    till the day was gone.

73. Rig would give
    counsel to them both;
    then he rose,
    prepared the bed;
    the domestic pair lay
    on either side of him.

74. There he stayed
    three nights together,
    then departed
    on the middle-way.
    And so nine months
    were soon passed by.

75. Modir bore a son,
    they wrapped him in silk,
    sprinkled him with water,
    and named him Jarl.
    His hair was light,
    his cheeks bright,
    his eyes piercing
    as a young serpent's.

76. There at home
    Jarl grew up,
    he brandished shields,
    fastened the string,
    bent the bow,
    shafted arrows,
    hurled javelins,
    wielded spears,
    rode horses,
    unleashed hounds,
    handled swords,
    and practiced swimming.

77. Out of the forest
    came the fast-traveler,
    came the fast-traveler,
    and taught him runes,
    he gave him his own name,
    declared him his son,
    he told him to take hold of his odal,
    his odal,
    his ancient homes.

78. Then Jarl rode on
    through the dark forest,
    over cold mountains,
    till he came to a hall.

79. He shook his spear,
    he brandished his shield,
    he spurred his horse,
    he drew his sword,
    he raised strife,
    and reddened the field,
    he killed warriors
    and conquered lands.

80. Then he ruled alone
    over eighteen halls,
    he gained wealth
    and gave to all,
    stones and jewels
    and slender horses,
    he offered rings,
    and shared arm-rings.

81. His messengers went
    by wet paths,
    and came to the hall
    where Hersir-Danp dwelt;
    there they found
    a slender maiden,
    fair and elegant,
    her name was Erna-Drott.

82. They asked for her hand,
    and brought her home,
    she married Jarl,
    dressed in linen;
    they lived together,
    and thrived well,
    they had children,
    and lived happily.

83. Bur was the eldest,
    Barn the second,
    Jod and Adal,
    Arfi, Mog,
    Nid and Nidjung.
    They learned games;
    Son and Svein
    swam and played Tafl.
    One was named Kund;
    Kon was the youngest.

84. The sons of Jarl
    grew up there,
    they broke horses,
    curved shields,
    cut arrows,
    and shook spears.

85. But Kon the Young

had knowledge of runes,
Aefinrunes,
Aldrunes.
He also knew well,
how to deliver men,
blunt sword-edges,
and subdue the ocean.

86. He learned bird-song,
and how to quench fire,
to soothe and comfort,
and drive away sorrow,
he had the strength and energy
of eight men.

87. He rivaled Rig-Jarl
in runes;
practiced cunning,
and proved superior,
he sought and soon
won the right
to be called Rig,
and to know runes.

88. The young Kon rode
through swamps and forests,
he hurled darts
and tamed birds.

89. Then sang a crow,
sitting alone on a bough:
"Why do you, young Kon,
tame the birds?
You should rather
ride on horses,
and overcome armies.

90. "Dan-Jarl and Danp,
skilled in
navigating ships
and wielding swords,
have more precious halls
and a better odal
than you."

91. Heimdall sanctified and established the three classes: the Thralls, the Karls, and the Jarls. All three were honored with divine birth, yet at the same time they were human. They were made by him into kinsmen and were consequently obligated to treat other kindly and fairly. Because of this they are called "Heimdall's Holy Children."

92. Humans lived peaceably under the laws given by Heimdall for religion and custom, under the protection of Jarl's authority as judge. No man harmed another, even if he came upon the killer of his father or brother, whether they were free or bondsmen. There were neither thieves nor robbers, and for a long time a gold ring lay untouched on Jalangsheath. Heimdall became the progenitor of the royal families that later became famous, who were called Skjoldungs, Skilfings or Ynglings, Hildings, and Budlungs. As the first Teutonic patriarch, he is also called Ygnvi.

93. Heimdall lived for a long time among our forefathers and subjected himself to the common Wyrd of humans– to grow old and die. He had it arranged that his body would be carried down to the bay where he landed as a child, and placed in the boat he had arrived in. It was during the winter time. Before he died he called his children to him and said:

94. "I am the child of nine mothers, I am the son of nine sisters. This mortal vessel I am not," he declared, "and I will return whenever the times have need. Not the self-reflected flower, I go the seed and grow and fruit, life after life. To my shining ship bear me, when this time is done."

95. Some transformed, he said, through time, some in the lust of combat, then released; some transformed by kindred minds blended to Powers, and, "I transform through you. Though I die many times to be with you. Some for power, some for perfection, some for their amber sheen, but I transform that you transform, as darts against the gathering gloom. Once I was bended at care," said Rig-Heimdall, "then let it go in my best bow's release. In my quietest stealth and bravest position, took the field of valor. While others held the shield, I held also the sword."

96. Heimdall taught Jarl and Kon how to use the fire-auger, and they were the first humans to use its pure flame. Then he struck up the foddik and said:

97. "Upon Jarl have I put all my hope, therefore must you take him to be your ruler. Follow my advice, then he and all pious folk who follow him shall remain my children; then shall the foddik, which I have struck up for you, never go out. The light there shall everlastingly enlighten your brain, and you shall then remain free, even from unfree powers, as your sweet rain streams from the salt water of the endless sea."

98. Sturdy Skef-Heimdall
    fared forth
    at the fated moment
    to the Gods' shelter.
    Then they bore him
    over to ocean's billow,
    loving clansmen,
    as late he charged them,
    while the winsome Rig
    wielded words,
    the beloved leader
    who long had ruled....

99. A ring-adorned vessel
    rocked in the roadstead,
    ice-flecked, outbound,
    atheling's barge;
    there they laid down
    their darling lord
    on the breast of the boat,
    the breaker-of-rings,
    the mighty one by the mast.
    Many a treasure
    fetched from afar
    was freighted with him.

100. I have known no ship
    so nobly adorned
    with weapons of war
    and weeds of battle,
    with breastplate and blade:
    on his bosom lay
    a heaped hoard
    that hence should go
    far over the flood
    floating away with him.

101. They loaded
    the lordly gifts,

the thane's huge treasure,
no less than those
who in former times
had sent him forth,
a suckling child,
alone on the seas.

102. High over his head
they hoist the standard,
a gold-woven banner;
they let billows take him,
gave him to the ocean.
Their spirits were grave,
their mood mournful.
No man is able
to say in truth,
no son of the halls,
no hero beneath heaven—
who harbored that freight!

103. By his wishes, Jarl succeeded Rig-Heimdall as jarl and judge in Aurvangaland.

104. Heimdall's boat returned to Vanaheim. Here he was stripped of his aged human form and turned into a radiant young God. Odin received him in Asgard and into his family circle.

105. He is called Hviti As and is powerful and sacred. He excels in physique and spirit-edness. He has a remarkably beautiful head of hair, locks of such radiance that it shines like silver. He is called Son of Nine Mothers, Vord Goda, Loki's Enemy, Recoverer of Freya's Necklace. He is also known as Vindler, Hallinskidi, and Gullintanni, as his teeth are gold. His horse is called Gulltopp. There is a place called Himinbjorg, and there they say it is Heimdall who rules over the holy hof: there the watchman of the Gods gladly drinks the good mead in his comfortable home. This hall lies near the northern bridge end of Bifrost.

106. He is the watchman of the Gods and sits at the end of Jormungrund, to the north of Niflheim. There he keeps watch over the Bifrost bridge against the Etins. He needs less sleep than a bird, and he can see equally well by night or by day a distance of a hundred leagues. He hears the grass growing on the earth and the wool on sheep, as well as everything else that makes more noise. Heimdall was chosen by Mimir to be Gjallarhorn's guardian. The head is referred to as Heimdall's sword, and the sword became his favored weapon.

XXI. <u>Jarl</u>

1. When Jarl was a youth he won repute among his father's huntsmen by defeating a huge beast, a remarkable incident which foretold the quality of his bravery in the future. He had asked the guardians who were bringing him up conscientiously for permission to go and see the hunting, when he encountered a bear of unusual size. Although weaponless, he managed to bind it with the belt he used to wear and then gave it to his companions to kill. During the same period he is reputed to have overcome individually

many champions of tested courage, among whom Atli and Skat had wide renown.

2. Already at fifteen he had grown to such a stature that he presented the perfect specimen of manhood, and so forceful were the proofs of his talent that he was given the name Skjold, and kings of the Danes assumed from him the common title of Skjoldungs, who are the royal family of Denmark. He was also called Dan Mikillati, and from him Denmark took its name. Skjold-Jarl's boldness, then, outstripped the full development of his strength and he fought contests which someone of his tender years would scarcely have been allowed to watch. He would become the leader of the warriors of Aurvangaland.

3. Under the patronage of Rig-Heimdall, Skjold-Jarl's duty was to defend Svithjod from the Etins of the north, and because of this he was also called Borgar. Not only was he notable for feats of arms, but also in affection for his fatherland. He continued to spread the custom of Heimdall's holy fire, and introduced beneficial laws, earnestly performing anything which could improve his country's condition. He looked after his jarls, giving them incomes when they were at home, as well as the booty won from the enemy, for he would maintain that soldiers should have their fill of money and the glory

go to their leaders. All men's debts were settled from his own treasury, as if he vied with other rulers' courage through his own bounty and generosity.

4. He used to attend the sick with remedies and bring kindly comfort to persons in deep distress, bearing witness that he had undertaken his people's welfare rather than his own. Where men had abandoned themselves to an emasculated existence, undermining their sobriety by debauchery, he energetically roused them to pursue merit in an active career.

5. So his age and virtue increased. As has been told, Jarl, or Skjold, was married to Erna, who was also called Drott. She was a daughter of king Danp, also called Hersir. One day two smiths had come to king Danp's realm, and they each forged a sword for him. The king then destroyed the first sword, called Hviting, in capricious trials of the iron's strength and resiliency. The second smith was angered by this, and foretold that his sword, Lysing, would cause the death of the king's most famous grandson.

6. When Drott's father had reached extreme old age, he learned that his daughter might be taken from him, so he fashioned a cave and had her placed within it, first granting a suitable retinue and providing sustenance for a long period. He also committed to the

cave, along with other gear, the sword Lysing, to keep the curse from coming true, and so that his enemy would be unable to use weapons that he was aware that he could not handle himself. So that the cavern should not rise up too obviously, he made its hump level with the solid earth.

7. Skjold-Jarl had been struck by Drott's great beauty, so he had messengers go and ask for her hand. The messengers learned that Skat, who was also called Hildur, was also courting her and Danp feared that he was going to steal her away.

8. As soon as he heard that Danp's daughter had been shut up in a far-off hiding place, Skat-Hildur bent all his wits and energies to finding her. Eventually, while he was personally conducting a search along with others, he half fancied that he could detect a murmuring noise underground. Gradually working his way nearer, he grew more convinced that it was the sound of a human voice. When he had given orders for the earth beneath their feet to be dug down to solid rock, a cavity was suddenly revealed where he could see a warren of winding passages.

9. The servants who tried to defend the covered entrance were cut to pieces and the girl dragged out of the hole along with the other prizes which had been stored there; all ex-

cept the sword, Lysing, for with admirable foresight, Drott had stowed it away in an even more secret place. Hildur-Skat compelled her to submit to his lust, and she bore him a son, named Hildigir or Hildibrand, progenitor of the Hildings. From this a battle was waged in which Danp lost his life.

10. In the meantime, Skjold-Jarl, comprehending that Skat-Hildur had forcibly taken Danp's daughter Drott to his bed, robbed him of his partner and his life, and married Drott himself. His messengers then took her to his home. She was no unwilling bride, since she considered it proper to take her father's avenger in her arms. While the girl mourned her father, she could not bring herself to submit with any pleasure to his murderer.

11. Jarl reigned long, and in his days were good seasons and peace. His son was the first called king (*konungr*) in the Danish Tongue. His descendants always afterward considered the title of king the highest dignity. Kon was the first of his family to be called king, for his predecessors had been called *drottnar*, after his mother, Drott, and their wives were called *drottningar*, and their court *drott*. Each of their race was called Yngvi, or Yngvin, and the whole race together Ynglings. Jarl lived to a very great age before his son, Kon, succeeded him. It is

said that Jarl died in his bed in Uppsala, and was transported to Fyrisvellir, where his body was burned on the riverbank, and where his standing stone still remains.

12. The earliest clan, the Skjoldungs, was thought to have greater wisdom, greater strength, and more influence on the Gods than the godar of later times. For many generations noble families have traced their lineage back to Jarl and, through him, to Rig-Heimdall himself. Skjoldungs, Budlungs, Hildings, and Ylfings are all descended from these royal lines, who spread themselves out all over Midgard.

13. Many years later, when Jarl descended to Hel, he lived there in communion with Heimdall, with whom he would become estranged due to his pride. This lasted nine years, after which they were permanently reconciled. Jarl remained the ward of Rig, and took part in several of the God's adventures.

The Silver Age

XXII. Gullveig

1. Gullveig was beautiful, like Loki, and like him was adopted in Asgard as a hostage from Jotunheim. During Jarl's reign, Gullveig began to prepare for her activities in Midgard. Gullveig-Heid and Hrossthjof were of Hrimnir's race. Her father, Hrimnir-Bergelmir, had grown weary from not being able to ravage the land of men, so she went to visit him, traveling down Bifrost to Niflheim. When she saw him lying dormant, she said:

2. "Stand up father! I will incite a war in the world, whereby Odin and the other Gods will suffer agony and anxiety. In the war, I shall spew so much poison on the pure men and on the beasts of burden that they shall not live. I will kill their souls. I will torment the waters, I will torment the plants, torment Heimdall's fire, torment all of creation."

3. She boasted that she had created the Seid, with which she could bring about her horrible plans. By means of this one could know beforehand the predestined urlag of men, or their not yet compelled lot; and also bring on the death, ill-luck, or bad health of people, and take the strength or wit from one person and give it to another. But after such witchcraft follows such weakness and anxiety, that it is not thought respectable for men to practice it; and therefore only evil women are brought up in this art.

4. From her words, Hrimnir became joyous and anxious for the corruption that was to come.

5. Spiteful towards the Gods, Gullveig went out from Jotunheim and came to Midgard to call on whatever evil sleeps in the hearts of the earthly beings. Up until then, the humans were taught to revere the Gods as children to their parents and follow their commands as sons and daughters, which is to say—willingly and devotedly, although not without faults and lapses. Up until then they had sought knowledge in the runes the Gods gave them; but when they needed special revelations in difficult circumstances, then they would see signs, whose foreboding properties were revealed to them by the Gods. They also listened to words of inspiration on the lips of noble and pure women.

6. She went into the land of Svithjod, carrying with her the evil Seid. They called her Heid, when she came to houses, the wise, prophetic vala, who blessed gandurs; who

practiced Seid, by Seid sent Leikin, she was always sought after by evil women. She allured residents of Midgard to desire evil things, and for the fulfillment of their wishes to turn to the unmentionable dark powers who, originating from Chaos, brood in the depths of evil Etins' hearts and give power to such evil arts, which she practiced and apprenticed out. From her Seidhall she sang the words with which evil humans ever since understood to lay misfortune on otherwise wholesome things, to seize others' gold for themselves, to strike the unaware with mental aberration, defects, disease, and death. So she gave, when an evil wish had been incited, power for this to bring about secret harm and ruin. Mistrust and fright, strife and conflict, hate and vindictiveness, theft and robbery grew up behind her, wherever she roved.

7. From Gullveig's Seid came the Nine Vices, to counter the Nine Virtues brought to us by Heimdall. These vices are: Murder, Perjury, Adultery, Sacrilege, Greed, Thievery, Treason, Slander, and Cruelty. Her evil arts, which involve an invocation of evil powers meant to increase one's strength and intended to harm humans and plants, stand against the Fimbulsongs, which Mimir sent the Gods, and against all the holy knowledge Heimdall taught to the humans. Those who practice Seid are enemies of the Gods; they are worse than the serpents, wolves, and other creatures that seek to harm Yggdrasil's roots. They destroy one-third of the earth's crops, and one-third of pious men's good thoughts, good words, and good deeds.

8. Her activities began the corruption of the Gods' creation, which would change the worlds forever. The Golden Age was spoiled by the arrival of Gullveig from Jotunheim. Situated in the northeastern-most regions of Jormungrund lies a forest, which was once called Gaglwood, for its trees were made of copper or bronze. After the introduction of the Seid it was called the Ironwood , for the trees became iron. The troll women who are called Jarnvidjas live in that forest. Gullveig is among them, and she is thus called Jarnvidja and Ividja. She is eventually banished to a marsh there by the Gods, along with her vile progeny.

9. The Ironwood is also called Myrkwood and Wolfdales, and is a mysterious land in which the wolf conceals himself. This frost-stiffened wood waits and keeps watch above a lake, called Wolfsea; the overhanging bank is a maze of tree-roots mirrored in its surface. At night there, something uncanny happens: the water burns. And the lake's bottom has never been sounded by the sons of men. On its bank, the heather-stepper

halts: the hart in flight from pursuing hounds will turn to face them with firm-set horns and die in the wood rather than dive beneath its surface. That is no good place. When wind blows up and stormy weather makes clouds scud and the skies weep, out of its depths a dirty surge is pitched towards the heavens.

10. Then the Powers all went to their Thingseats, the high-holy Gods to consider thereon: who had filled all the air with evil? To discover this, Odin sent the Goddess named Gefjon, also called Nyhellenia, to see what was happening in Midgard. He had seen from Hlidskjalf that the trouble seemed to be centered in southern Svithjod, so this is where she was sent.

11. By this time, an Etin named Gylfi had overcome Jarl's forces and, with Gullveig's assistance, taken over lands in this region. The area was ravaged by winter cold, and became the place where Gullveig began to focus her activities. It is said that Gylfi offered a traveling woman, in return for the pleasure of her company, a piece of plowland in his realm as large as four oxen could plow in a day and a night. But this woman, who was Gefjon, was of the Aesir. She took four oxen from Jotunheim in the north. They were her own sons by an Etin, and she yoked them to the plow, which dug so hard

and so deep that it cut the land loose. The oxen dragged this land westward out to sea, stopping finally at a certain channel. There Gefjon fastened the land and gave it the name Zealand, and afterwards she settled and dwelt there. The place where the land was removed has since become a body of water in Svithjod now called Logrinn, and in this lake there are as many inlets as there are headlands in Zealand.

12. Gefjon gladly dragged from
Gylfi the land beyond value,
Denmark's increase,
steam rising from the swift-footed bulls.
The oxen bore eight
moons of the forehead and four heads,
hauling as they went in front of
the grassy isle's wide fissure.

13. Nyhellenia-Gefjon established a burgh in this land, and began to investigate. It had come to pass that Jarl's wife, Drott, had died, and as the first Folkmodir, she was adopted into Asgard and became an Asynja. Upon an island near Zealand, there is the burgh Valhallagara, and on its walls the following saying is written: "read, learn, and watch." Gefjon dwelt in this burgh. Gullveig roamed among the folk under the name Heid, as well as Syrhed, and obtained great influence over the minds and hearts of the folk. To counteract this influence Nyhelle-

nia-Gefjon began reinforcing the wisdom that Heimdall had established among men.

14. Gullveig-Heid was full of guile; her countenance was beautiful and her tongue quick, but the advice she gave was ever in obscure words. Therefore, she was called Kalta by the seamen, but the land dwellers thought that this was an honorary name.

15. When Drott had died, she named three successors for the title of Folkmodir. In the final will of the late mother, Rosamuda stood first, Nyhellenia-Gefjon second, and Gullveig-Heid third. Gefjon put no thought to this, for she only wished to perform her duty in discovering the source of the corruption. However, Gullveig was deeply offended. Displaying her Etin nature, she would be honored, feared, and prayed to, but Gefjon would only be loved.

16. Finally, all the seamen of Denmark came to ask Nyhellenia-Gefjon for her grace, which wounded Gullveig, for she wished to excel above her. So the folk would have great esteem for her watchfulness, she made herself a flag with a cock on it.

17. Then Gefjon saw this flag and decided to make her own, trying to antagonize the maid she now suspected of evil. A herd dog and an owl were placed upon Gefjon's flag.

18. She said, "The hound watches over his master and the owl over fields, so they are not wasted by mice. But the cock has friendship for no one, and through his wantonness and pride he is often the murderer of his next of kin."

19. Of course, these words were meant solely to entice Gullveig, for we believe the cock to be a sacred bird, which is the special foe of demons and the powers of darkness. Each morning it wakes the world with its song.

20. When Gullveig saw that her work came out wrong, she went from bad to worse. She allied herself with foreign enemies and slowly exposed her true nature even more. From all her misdeeds, she became no better. As she saw that the seamen shrank more and more away from her, she would then win them through fright. When the moon was full and the sea stormy, she then leapt over the wild waves, calling to the seamen that they should all be lost if they did not worship her. Furthermore, she blinded their eyes, thereby they held water for land and land for water, and from this many ships were lost with man and mouse. Her nine daughters with Aegir-Gymir, the nine waves who cause many a ship to sink, dragged them down.

21. Upon the first war feast, when all her land dwellers were armed, she let hogsheads of beer be poured, and in that beer she put

magic drink. When the folk were altogether drunk, she climbed up upon her steed, leaning forward with her head against her spear, dawn could not be more beautiful. When she saw that all eyes were fixed upon her, she opened her lips and said:

22. "Sons and daughters of Heimdall, you know well that in recent times we have suffered much harm and failure, for the seamen no longer come to trade with us, but you do not know how this came to be. Long have I held myself back on this matter, though now I can no longer. Hear me then friends, so you might now know and afterwards may you bite. On the other side of the sea, they are making good on their own and they can do well without us. Our goods and trade have made us prosper, and the Folkmodir has wanted us to maintain this. But Nyhellenia has bewitched all the folk; yes, bewitched friends, just as she has all of our cattle, which lately have fallen dead. Thus must be said, if I were no maid, I should well know, I would burn the witch in her own nest."

23. When she had spoken the last word, she sped herself toward her burgh, but the drunken folk were so inspired they were unable to watch over their judgment. In mad boldness they fared to Valhallagara and meanwhile, after night fell, they went loose upon the burgh just as boldly. Though again Heid-Gullveig missed her goal: Nyhellenia-Gefjon and her handmaidens and the foddik were all saved through the alert seamen.

24. When she returned, Nyhellenia-Gefjon saw how Kalta had destroyed her famous burgh. The seeds of mistrust had been planted into the minds of the folk, so there then came some princes and godar to where the burgh once was and asked Nyhellenia where her odal lay.

25. Nyhellenia-Gefjon answered, "I bear my odal in my bosom; what I have inherited is love for wisdom, right, and freedom; if I lose them, so am I like the least of your slaves. Now I freely give advice, but after this I should sell it."

26. The gentlemen went away, and all called out, laughing, "Your obedient servants, wise Hellenia." Though with this they missed her intention, and the folk that loved her and followed her used this as a name of honor. When they saw they had missed their shot, then they accused her and said that she had bewitched the folk, but the people of that land knew this to be an insult.

27. Once, they came and asked, "If you are no witch, then what do you do with the fruits you always have with you?"

28. Gefjon answered, "These fruits are the symbol of Urd's counsel, in which our fu-

ture lies hidden and that of all mankind. Time must brood them out and we must watch them and make sure no harm comes to them."

29. The godar said, "Well said, but what purpose does the dog in your other hand serve?"

30. Nyhellenia answered, "Has the herdsman no sheep dog to hold his flock together? What the dog is, in the service of the shepherd, am I in the Aesir's service. I must watch over Heimdall's children."

31. "That we like," said the godar, "but what is the significance of the owl which always sits above your head; is that light-shy animal perhaps a token of your Seid workings?"

32. "Nay," answered Nyhellenia-Gefjon, "he helps me remember that there is a sort of person dwelling around the world who, even as he, makes their homes in hofs and in caves, who roots about in the gloom. Though not as he, to help us from mice and other plagues, but to plan ruses, to rob people of their wits until they take hold over them so as to make slaves of them and to suck their blood like the Draug." This owl has runes risted on its beak.

33. The godar replied, "Once they came with a band of folk, and a plague has come over the land; they said we are all to make offerings to the Gods so that the plague may

be prevented. Will you not help us to still the pain of the inflicted, or have you yourself brought the plague over the land with your art?"

34. "Nay," said Gefjon, "but I do not know any of the Gods who are evil-doing; therefore I cannot ask if they will become better. I know that because Odin-Wralda is good, he therefore does no evil."

35. "Whence comes evil, then woe?" asked the godar.

36. "All evil comes from you and from the stupidity of the people who let themselves be taken by you," Nyhellenia replied.

37. "If the Gods are so confounded good, why has evil not been eliminated?" asked the godar.

38. Nyhellenia-Gefjon answered, "Heimdall has brought us upon the way and time must do the rest. Before all disasters, is advice and help which Odin wants us to seek ourselves so that we shall become strong and wise. If we will not, then he lets us struggle out our bewilderment so that we may learn what follows after wise and after stupid deeds."

39. Then a prince said, "I think it would be better to prevent that."

40. "It may well be," answered Nyhellenia, "then when the people become tame as sheep, you and the godar would not only

want to guard them but shear them and lead them to the slaughter. Furthermore, our Godhead wants nothing more from us than that we help each other; but he also wants everyone to be free and wise."

41. "That is also our desire, which is why our folk chooses its princes, jarls, advisors, and all bosses and leaders from the wisest of the good men so that everyone does his best to become wise and good. Insodoing, we shall at once learn and teach people that being wise and doing wisely alone lead to happiness." "That is like a judgment," said the godar, "but if you mean that plague comes through our stupidity, would Nyhellenia be so good as to teach us something of that new light which she is so proud of?"

42. "Yes," said Nyhellenia-Gefjon, "the raven and other birds come only to fall upon foul carrion, but plague not only likes foul carrion, but also bad custom-habits and captivity. If you will now take the plague from this place and keep it away, then you must do away with the captivity and it shall be pure within and without."

43. "We believe that your judgment is good," said the godar, "but tell us how we should impart it to the people who are under our authority?"

44. Then Nyhellenia-Gefjon stood up from her seat and said: "The sparrows follow the sower, the people their good princes, therefore you should begin by making yourselves pure, so that you may direct your gaze, both inward and outward, without becoming ashamed of your own mind. But instead of making the folk pure, you have invented foul festivals during which folk drink beer and wine so long, that they are at last like swine, which root in the slime so that they may atone for your foul lusts."

45. The folk began to howl and to mock. Therefore, she did not dare to spin any more arguments. Now everyone should believe that they had called the folk together to drive her from the land. Nay, instead of chiding her, they declared through all nations that it had pleased Allfather-Odin to send his wise daughter, Gefjon, or Nyhellenia, among the people, from over the sea, with a cloud, to give them good advice so that all who heard her should become rich and happy.

46. The folk were so pleased with Nyhellenia's wisdom it was decided that she should become the Folkmodir. She was married to Jarl-Skjold, and they dwelt at Hleidra. Later she returned to Asgard to rejoin the ranks of the Asynjur.

47. Gullveig was captured by the Gods and brought before the Thing in Asgard. Gylfi was forced back into Jotunheim by Jarl's armies, supported by Odin and other deities.

Gylfi made a peace with them, for he believed that he did not have the strength to oppose the Gods and the humans of Svithjod. Odin and Gylfi had many tricks and enchantments against each other, but the Aesir were always superior.

XXIII. <u>Jormungand</u>

1. The Gods were appalled at the consequences Gullveig's Seid would have if allowed to continue to spread. They had gathered at their Thingseats, the high-holy Gods, to pass judgment on her. She was sentenced to die by fire, so the Gods raised Gullveig on spears in Odin's hall, and burnt her. It was difficult for the flames to touch her. Loki ate the heart, which laid in the embers, and he found the woman's heart half-burnt; Lopt-Loki was soon with child from the woman, and thence came Jormungand among men. This monster seems the most deadly of all, which sprang from Byleist's brother.

2. Loki traveled to Jotunheim and gave birth to Jormungand by Gnipalund on Thorsnes. And when the Gods realized Jormungand was being brought up in Jotunheim, and when the Gods traced prophecies stating that from him great mischief and disaster would arise for them, then they all felt evil was to be expected from him, to begin with because of his mother's nature, but still worse because of his father's.

3. Then, Allfather-Odin sent Gods to seize Jormungand and bring him to him. And when they came to him he threw the serpent into the deep sea which lies around all lands, and this serpent grew so that it lies in the midst of the ocean encircling all lands and bites on its own tail. Broad ground, wrapped round by the deadly-cold serpent [Jormungand], lies beneath the spruce [man] of holm-fetter's [Jormungand's] path [gold, hence the sea].

XXIV. <u>Hel</u>

1. Urd, the Goddess of urlag, is also the Goddess of death. Because she determines the urlag and length of every human's life, she also determines their death. She who lays the lots of life, lays the lots of death. She and her sisters reign over the past, present, and future; she reigns over and gathers under the scepter of her realm the generations of the past, present, and future. As the Goddess of death and ruler of Jormungrund, she is also called Hel. Hel is both the name of the realm of bliss in Jormungrund, and its queen.

2. When one is about to die, their fylgja will appear before them, right before she departs for Hel to prepare a feast for them. One may dream before their death that these women shall come to them, heavy and drooping, and choose them as their companion; so it may

happen that these are their fateful women. At this point, some may consider what sort of dwelling they will obtain in the land of the dead when the breath leaves their body, or what reward was earned by a ready devotion to the Gods. By Hel's summons, one will be called away to Odin's Thing, and they must obey the decrees of the Norns. Each evening the maids of Hel call the dying to their home, for there is a time when every man shall journey hence to the otherworld, to stay in Hel's high hall.

3. The fylgja hears of it before anyone else when her mistress, Urd, has announced the doom of death against her favorite. She then leaves, which can be perceived in dreams or by revelations in other ways, and this is an unmistakable sign of death. But if the death-doomed person is not a niding, whom she in sorrow and wrath has left, then she by no means abandons him. They are like members of the same body, which can only be separated by nid. The hamingja or fylgja travels to Hel, her land of birth, to prepare an abode there for her favorite, which is to belong to her as well. It is as if they enter into a spiritual marriage. The fylgja meets her chosen after their third night's separation from the body. It takes three days before they leave for the Underworld. At the same time, one may join their spouse or lover from Midgard in their home there, if they are worthy of such.

4. The dead should fare to the Helthing well dressed and ornamented. Warriors carry their weapons of defense and attack, often still covered in the blood of their enemies. Women and children carry ornaments and objects that were cherished by them. Images of these objects that kinsmen and friends lay on the pyre follow the dead as evidence before the judges that they enjoyed the survivors' esteem and affection. The appearance of the gathered at the Thing of the dead shows how careful the survivors observe the law that commands respect for the dead and care for the remains of the deceased. Special shoes should be given to them, called Helshoes. Let a man ride to the Thing washed and fed, although his garments are not too good; of his shoes and breeches let no one be ashamed, nor of his horse, although he does not have a good one.

5. Many die under conditions that make it impossible for kinsmen to observe these caring duties. Then strangers should take the place of family. The condition in which the dead arrive at the Thing shows best if pious dispositions are prevailing in Midgard; for noble hearts take the divine law to heart. Render the last service to the corpses you find on the ground, whether they have died

from sickness, or are drowned, or are dead from weapons. Make a bath for those who are dead, wash their hands and their head, comb them and wipe them dry, before you lay them in the coffin, and pray for their blissful slumber.

6. Their nails should be clipped. At Ragnarok it will happen that the ship Naglfar will loosen from its mooring. It is made from the nails of dead men, and for this reason it is worth considering the warning that if a person fares to Hel with untrimmed nails he contributes crucial material to Naglfar, a ship that both the Gods and men would prefer not to see built. Naglfar, the largest ship, is owned by Muspel-Loki.

7. It is our custom that he who gives an heir-ship-feast after kings or jarls, and who enters upon the heritage should sit upon the foot-stool in front of the high-seat, until the full bowl, which is called the Bragarfull, is brought in. Then he should stand up, take the Bragarfull, make solemn vows to be ful-filled afterwards, point to the four corners with the horn, and thereupon empty the beaker. Then he should ascend the high-seat which his father had occupied; and thus he comes into the full heritage after his father.

8. Do not mourn too much for the loss of a loved one, for such tears can be cruel to those dead, for each one falls bloody on their heart, ice-cold and piercing, and full of sorrow. Such will cause them to be covered with the dew of sorrow, and will bring them back to visit their lamenting kinsman or woman to allay their sadness. One can also wake the dead with prayer, which is best done at night, for all dead warriors are more powerful in the darkness of night than in the light of day. It is said that the dead are easier to summon and listen more closely to earth-ly life once night has set in. Malrunes will give speech to the dead, so they will walk and talk with you. Besides the power of sor-row and prayer, there is a third means of bringing the dead back. This is conjuration; but conjuring the dead is a nid, which makes the transgressor yield to the wights of pun-ishment.

9. The earthly death consists of the earthly matter, the la and the lik, being separated from the person's higher elements and stay-ing behind on Midgard. The dead who have fared to Jormungrund are made up of ond, odur, and litur. If one is sentenced to a sec-ond death at Gimle, the ond and the litur go-da will be separated from him at the Na-gates. Then there remains only the odur; and this receives a litur that corresponds with the condition of the odur. The higher elements return to the Gods, traveling to the after-world; whereas the lower elements are

spread across the earth, returning to the waters, to the plants, and to all that lives.

10. It is our belief that the higher the smoke of the pyre rises in the air, the higher he will be raised whose pile it is; and the richer he will be, the more property that is consumed with him. Because the litur can be damaged in the flames of the pyre, an offering is made so that the fire will consume it, rather than the litur. This offering is customarily a goat.

11. The appearance of the outer body depends on the condition of the litur; that is, of the inner being. Beautiful women have a joyous fair litur. An emotion has influence upon the litur, and through it upon the blood and the appearance of the outer body. A sudden blushing, a sudden paleness, are among the results of this. Litur also signifies a hama, a guise or earthly garb which persons skilled in magic can put on and off. The form seen when one travels towards Hel is none other than the litur, which shows distinctly what the dead one has been in the earthly life, and what care has been bestowed upon his dust. The washing, combing, dressing, ornamenting, and supplying of Helshoes of the dead body has influence on one's looks when they are to appear before their judges.

12. When the dead return from Hel they can be either good or evil, depending on the nature of the person who dies. When they are good, they are called Hollarwights, when they are bad, Owights. The higher elements can return from the afterworlds if they are called forth, but only conjuration can raise the Owights. Then they are evil and dangerous, but the Hollarwights are honorable and benevolent and work for the benefit of their folk, which is why they are good to have around. For this reason people will often have family grave-mounds, where the ashes of the dead should be kept, near their home. Preceding important events in the clan, these wights gather and confer among themselves.

13. Odin has decreed that all dead men should be burned, but circumstances may arise where burial may be necessary. The elements of the dead one entombed in the grave-mound will continue their interaction with one another for a long while, forming a kind of entity that preserves his personality and qualities, because these were permeated with ond and odur in mortal life. Thus, the grave-mound contains a doppelganger of the person who has gone down to the kingdom of death. These doppelgangers are called Haugbuis and Draugs. Draug actually designates a tree-trunk cut off from its roots; the Haugbui is called this because he is separated from his root of life, the odur, and by de-

grees, slowly pays its debt to nature, going on to meet its dissolution.

14. It might also happen that the lower elements, when abandoned by odur and ond, become a doppelganger in whom the vegetative and animal elements exclusively assert themselves. Such a creature is always tormented by animal desire of food, and does not seem to have any feeling or memory of bonds tied in life. In such cases, it is thought that the lower elements of the deceased consigned to the grave were never in his lifetime sufficiently permeated by his odur and ond to enable these qualities to give the corpse an impression of the rational personality and human character of the deceased. In one of this sort, the vegetative element, united with his dust, still asserts itself, so that hair and nails continue to grow as on a living being, and the animal element, which likewise continues to operate in the one buried, visits him with hunger and drives him out of the grave to suck the blood of surviving kinsmen. The dead are burnt to protect survivors from such beings, but if buried, graves are built and rites spoken over the dead to keep the Haugbuis from leaving the grave, to prepare a peaceful, uninterrupted sleep for them, and thus protect the survivors from affliction by them.

15. Once a person has died, their higher elements remain around the corpse for three days, and attend their own Helfare. All will have a guide that will lead them to Hel, which appears before them right before their death, carrying their summons to the Helthing. Foremost among them are the Valkyries, beautiful maidens with contemplative faces. Wherever a battle takes place, they appear fully armed there on their horses, though some wear feather guises, and with their spear shafts point out the champions whom Odin and Freya have selected for their halls, and they carry the fallen to Jormungrund, and from there on Bifrost to Asgard.

16. Urd sends maidservants of a very different sort to the inhabitants of Midgard who are not among the heroic dead, each by the nature of their death. To those who surrender to the burden of years comes the Goddess who is the handmaiden of the bent and stooping. This kind-hearted Goddess removes the burden which Elli puts on men, and which gradually gets too heavy for them to bear. Children have their guides, who are motherly, tender, and kind. To those who were snatched away by plague or other epidemics come Leikin and the beings of Niflhel who resemble her, and those who die of disease are carried away by the correspond-

ing wights of disease to the Helthing to be judged by the Gods.

17. One must travel to the uppermost north, into Jotunheim, to get to Jormungrund. The entire road there is said to be fraught with peril and is almost impassable for mortals. You must sail across the ocean, which girds the earth, putting the sun and stars behind your back, journey beneath the realm of night, and finally pass into the regions which suffer perennial darkness without a glimmer of daylight. From there, in the midst of Jotunheim's monstrous horde, you will find the passage towards Hel.

18. To begin with, all of the dead travel a common path, called the Helway. They are directed on the same traveled road, and the same Helgate opens itself daily for the multitudes of spirits who wait for different lots. The key that opens the gate is called Gylling. Women and children; youths, men, and the elderly; those who were busy in the peaceful arts and those who stained weapons with blood; those who lived in accordance with Odin's and Urd's decrees and those who broke them– they all have to take the same course. They come on foot and on horse, for the horse that was cremated with its master afterwards brings the hero down to Hel. Those burned with their ships will ride the wooden horse to Hel. Beautifully adorned Valkyries, the mild being who helps the old-aged, the kind spirit-guides of children, or the black and white Leikin and the gloomy wights of disease lead them there. They gather outside the eastern Helgates, one of the four situated at each point of Jormungrund.

19. The cords of Hel
were tightly
bound round my sides;
I would rend them,
but they were strong.
It is not easy to go free.

20. I alone knew
how on all sides
my pains increased.
Each eve the maids of Hel
called me to
their home.

21. I saw the sun,
true star of day,
sink in its roaring home;
but I heard
Hel's grated doors
heavily creaking on the other side.

22. I saw the sun,
beset with blood-red streams:
then I was quickly declining from this world.
In many ways
she appeared mightier
than she was before.

23. I saw the sun,
and it seemed to me
as if I had seen a glorious God:
I bowed before her
for the last time,
in the world of men.

24. I saw the sun:
     she beamed forth so
     that I seemed to know nothing;
     but Gjoll's streams
     roared from the other side,
     mixed with much blood.

25. I saw the sun,
     with quivering eyes,
     appalled and shrinking;
     for in great measure
     was my heart
     dissolved in sickness.

26. I saw the sun,
     seldom sadder;
     I had almost declined from the world:
     my tongue had
     become like wood,
     and all was cold without me.

27. I saw the sun,
     never again,
     since that gloomy day;
     for the mountain waters
     closed over me,
     and I went, called from torments.

28. The high road in Jormungrund first goes west through deep and dark dales. At one place the dead have to go across a mile wide heath that is overgrown with thorns and has no trails. Then it is good to have Helshoes as protection for the feet. Because of this, a dead man's relatives should not neglect to bind Helshoes to the body before it is burned. Thus, it is cutomary to bind the Helshoes to men, so that they shall walk on to Valhall. It is certainly true that these shoes, just like everything else placed with the dead, such as clothes, weapons, and ornaments, are burned up with the body. Everything in creation, even those things crafted by humans, has an inner substance and an inner form, and it is the inner being of the objects laid on the pyre that follows the dead to Hel. The care the survivors have for the dead is reckoned by these goods, and if they have Helshoes they come across the heath with well-kept feet. If they do not have them, and in their lives they have been unmerciful towards those who have walked the thorny paths of life, then they do not get across it without torn and bloody feet. But for the merciful, who lack Helshoes, there are some hanging from a tree which grows from where the thorny path begins. They walk along a path worn by long ages of travelers.

29. After this the dead come to a river with rushing water in which sharp-edged irons fill its torrents. The bed of this stream forms a natural boundary between the human and the afterworlds. This is the river Gjoll, here much mixed with the blood of the unmerciful, which divides Jormungrund's northerly and southerly regions, flowing east to west. Foot-wide boards float there, where no bridge is to be found. The boards give support when the feet of the merciful step on them, and carry them over the river un-

harmed. The planks represent their good thoughts, good words, and good deeds. They slip away from the feet of the unmerciful, who fall into the river and wade through it in severe pain. Although they are terribly cut-up by the irons, they appear without a mark on them from this when they come up onto the other strand.

30. On the other side the dawn begins and the green regions lie in the break of day with the Gjoll river flowing through them. Having advanced further, they again stumble on the river of blue-black water, swirling in headlong descent and weapons of various kinds are spinning in its swift eddies. Again the dead must cross this river, but here they travel over the Gjallarbridge. The bridge is roofed with shining gold, and the maiden guarding it is named Modgud. Once over the bridge, they come to a fork in the road. One path goes north to Mimir's realm, one south to Urd's fountain. Here is Gimle or Vingolf, where the Helthing is held to pronounce judgments over the dead.

31. All of this walking takes place in unbroken silence. The tongues of the dead are cold and numb and do not make a sound. Neither can their footsteps be heard, for they have the litur of dead men. Their horses, when they arrive on such, noiselessly touch their hooves to the ground of the kingdom of the dead. The gold-laid bridge rumbles only under the hooves of the steeds of the Valkyries.

32. Our ancestors called the funeral proceedings Helfare, to honor the commencement of the journey to Urd's domain, which lasts nine nights. The path of the dead leads them over mountains and through valleys, towards the Thing where they will be judged by the Gods, so during this time we pray for their safe voyage and good judgment before the court.

33. When the dead reach the Thingstead they sit in long rows in front of the holy ring of the stones of justice. Here they are awaited by their fylgja, who went before them to Hel and now sit beside their ward. Unfortunate is the one who has no fylgja at the Helthing, where the judgments are passed that have eternal validity.

34. Your cattle shall die,
    your kindred shall die,
    you yourself shall die,
    but the fair fame
    of him who has earned it
    never dies.

35. Your cattle shall die,
    your kindred shall die,
    you yourself shall die,
    one thing I know
    which never dies:
    the judgment on each one dead.

36. The third root of Yggdrasil extends to the south, and beneath that root is the holy well, Urdarbrunn. There the Gods have their places of judgment. Every day the Aesir ride down there on Bifrost, and come through the southern Helgates into Urd's realm, when they cross several rivers to their destination. The Aesir ride on their steeds each day when they go to pronounce dooms at Yggdrasil's ash. Thor rides across the sky, while Mani's path thunders beneath him, then he walks to the Thing, wading the rivers Kormt and Ormt, and the two Kerlaugs. Thor must wade these waters each day, when he goes forth to pronounce dooms beneath the ash-tree Yggdrasil; for the Asbridge-Bifrost is all on fire, the holy waters boil.

37. When the Gods have arrived from Asgard, dismounted from their rides, and taken their judges' seats, the proceedings begin. The dead are now in their places, and we may be sure that their guides have not been slow on their journey to the Thing. The Aesir sit as judges in the south at Urdarbrunn.

38. Odin sits in the high-seat and the other Aesir sit on Thingseats on each side. Before them sits the dead in their rows; they are pale and have the marks of the death they endured. They have to listen to the legal proceedings and receive their judgment in silence, provided they do not have Malrunes, which give them the power to speak and defend themselves against any charges. You must know Malrunes, if you do not wish that the mighty one, Odin, shall requite you with consuming woe for the injury you have caused. You must wind, weave, and place together all those runes in that Thing where the host of people go into the full judgments.

39. It very rarely happens that someone has these runes; if such is the case, he gets to step up onto a rostrum that was built for this purpose and state what he can in his defense. But no one does this other than those who are abandoned by their fylgja, and because of this do not have any solicitors at the Thing. The others do not need to speak, as little as they are capable of it, because every fylgja defends their ward. She is a benevolent witness for him, and also the most reliable before the court, because she knows all of his thoughts, motives, and deeds. It is rarely required that she speak, for her presence next to the dead is a proof in and of itself that he is not a niding.

40. Urdar Ord is Urd's judgment, which must come to pass, no matter whether it concerns life or death. No one may deny Urd's judgment, however lightly spoken. Those who are to join their ancestors in the lands of bliss are given the judgment called

Lofstirr, whereas the judgment of the damned is called Namaeli.

41. The Gods judge human faults and frailties leniently. During their time of learning they have made mistakes as well. Those who have come to the Thing can expect a good judgment if they went through life free from deceit, honorable, helpful, and without fear of death– if they observed respect for the Gods and their hofs, and tended to the duties of kindred and to the dead. Thus, they must have followed the laws given to us by the Gods, and lived by their virtues.

42. I sat in the Norns' seat
for nine days,
thence I was mounted on a horse:
there the Giantess' sun
shone grimly
through the dripping clouds of heaven.

43. Without and within,
I seemed to traverse all
the nine netherworlds:
up and down,
I sought an easier way,
where I might have the readiest paths.

44. Those who are declared worthy of bliss by the Thing receive a taste of the mead before they leave, which removes every mark that remains on the dead, and restores their warmth of life. Their bodies again become corporeal, their tongues loosen, their life-force is enhanced, their strength increased, and it grants them the ability to forget their sorrows without obliterating dear memories or making one forget that which can be remembered without longing or worrying. Odin will hand them to drink in Mimir's Gjallarhorn, a cool, bitter drink, to forget their past afflictions. This drink is made from the liquids of the Underworld fountains. They shall drink the Dyrar Veigar, though they have lost life and lands; here stands the mead, the Skirar Veigar, prepared for the dead. Thus this drink is a mixture of the liquids from the wells that maintain Yggdrasil's life, the same as was given to Heimdall in preparation for his trip to Midgard, which keeps them alive through the ages. The blessed dead have the morning dews that fall near Urdarbrunn as their nourishment.

45. When those who have the Lofstirr pronounced over them leave the Thing, they are accompanied by their fylgja to their beautiful home, which these maidens have put in order for their wards. All men who are righteous shall live in that place called Gimle or Vingolf in the green worlds of the Gods. Children shall go to Mimir, who owns the field of ancient fathers in Glasisvellir. But evil men go to Hel, where they are judged, and from there into Niflhel, which is below the ninth world.

46. They are eager to see the many wonders of the glorious regions and to visit kinsmen and friends who have gone before them to their final destination. The fylgja escorts her chosen on joyous paths, called Munways that are the home of the honey-ships [flowers]. There they see rich nobles dressed in colorful robes; passing these by, they eventually come upon the sunny region, which produces vegetation, where they will spend their afterlife. Here the inquisitive can participate in the Leita Kynnis, where one seeks out and converses with ancestors and progenitors, and learn the remarkable urlag of their family, indeed of all the ancients, told by those who actually saw what they speak of.

47. Each morning the soot-red cock in Hel's halls crows in the Underworld. In honoring the Thing and those declared honorable by it, he calls out: "Rise, you men, and praise the justice which is most perfect! Behold the demons are put to flight!"

XXV. <u>Valhall</u>

1. Because of the evil Seid Gullveig had brought to men, the age of war came, and with it heroes fought against nidings, Etins, and other terrible beings. These noble men and women are honored by the Gods if they are held worthy of Valhall's glory. The brave heroes are chosen to become Einherjar

after they die, while all others either go to Hel or Niflhel.

2. Gladsheim is the land where the golden-bright Valhall stands spacious; each day Hropt-Odin selects there the men who die by weapons. Valhall is the sacred stead, which rests on top of a mountain, called Sigtyrsberg. Here the mighty Yggdrasil rises from Valhall's roof, with its red-gold foliage. It is easy for him to recognize, who comes to Odin and beholds the hall; its rafters are spears, it is roofed with shields, and breastplates are strewn on its benches. It is easy for him to recognize, who comes to Odin and beholds the hall; a wolf hangs before the western door, an eagle hovers over it. The wolves who pace back and forth, guarding the tree's foliage, are called Freki or Gif and Geri, if you wish to know: they watch the watchers until the Powers perish. They, the twin dogs, were strictly told to not sleep at the same time, when they were given the watch; one sleeps at night, the other by day, so no wight can enter, if they come.

3. The sword fallen who are escorted by the Valkyries to the Helthing, are met by their fylgja and receive the Dyrar Veigar. If one fallen by the sword lacks his fylgja he must step down from the saddle and sit down on the bench of the dead, for he is certainly a niding, and if he cannot defend himself with

Malrunes he is sentenced to the suffering of Niflhel, with the judgment of Namaeli. The honorable warrior, after receiving the drink, sets out from the Thing to visit his kinsmen on the fields of bliss and to look at the wonders there, until the time comes for him to journey to Asgard. They travel west over Vindhelm's Bridge, Bifrost. Then the Aesir are there before them, and when they hear the rumble of Bifrost under the arriving riders, then Hermod-Od and Bragi go to meet the princes, the ones arriving in Valhall who are considered heroes. Warriors and jarls who die of natural causes also come to Valhall.

4. In this hall, Odin gives a welcome to all his friends, and all brave warriors should be delivered to him. Odin will show himself to them before any great battle, and sings under the shields of those he will give victory. To some he gives victory; others he invites to himself, and both of these are reckoned to be fortunate. "You shall now see Odin, come to me if you can!" is his invitation to all warriors.

5. All those who fall in battle or live heroically are his adopted children. He assigns them places in Valhall and they are known as Einherjar. All those worthy men that have fallen in battle, or who have lived as heroes since the beginning of the world have now come to Odin. There is a pretty large number there, and many more have yet to arrive, and yet there will seem too few when the wolf comes.

6. Freya is the most glorious of the Asynjur. She has a dwelling in Asgard called Folkvang, and wherever she rides to battle she gets half the slain, and the other half goes to Odin. Folkvang is the place where Freya directs the sittings in the hall Sessrumnir. Each day she chooses half of the fallen, but Odin the other half.

7. There will never be such a large number in Valhall that the meat of the boar Saehrimnir will not be sufficient for them. It is cooked each day and is whole again by evening. The cook is called Andhrimnir and the pot Eldhrimnir. By Andhrimnir, in Eldhrimnir, is Saehrimnir boiled, the best of meats; but few know what the Einherjar eat. The heroes abide in the vast Valhall, drink of costly cups with the Aesir, and are sated with Saehrimnir at Odin's feast.

8. Odin does not have the same fare as the Einherjar. He gives the food that stands on his table to his two wolves, Freki and Geri. He himself needs no food: wine is both meat and drink for him. Geri and Freki are fed by the triumphant Herfather-Odin; but Odin, the famed in arms, ever lives on wine alone.

9. The goat that stands over Odin's hall is called Heidrun, which bites from Laerad-Yggdrasil's branches; she fills the vat with the fair clear mead; that drink shall never fail. The goat Heidrun stands on top of Valhall and eats the leaves of that most famous tree. From her udders streams the mead that daily fills the vat that is so large that from it all the Einherjar satisfy their thirst. That goat is especially useful to them, and the tree she eats from is remarkably good. Even more notable is the stag called Eikthyrnir, which stands over Odin's hall, and bites from Laerad-Yggdrasil's branches; drops fall from his horns into Hvergelmir, whence all waters rise.

10. There are five hundred and forty doors, I believe, in Valhall. Eight hundred Einherjar will fare at once from each door, when they go to war with the wolf. One can surely say that it would be remarkable if everyone were unable to pass in and out freely. There are five hundred and forty floors, I believe, built in Bilskirnir-Valhall. Of all the roofed houses known, is this one the greatest. In truth, it is no harder to find places for people inside than it is to enter it.

11. Large crowds of people are at Valhall. They are men who met their death by the sword, or lived heroically, and present an everlasting display of their destruction; they are trying to equal the activity of their past lives. Each day the cock Salgofnir-Vidofnir, also called Gullinkambi, awakens heroes. Over the Aesir crows Gullinkambi, which wakes the heroes with Herjan-Odin. After they dress, they put on their war gear. Then they go out to the court and battle, the one attacking the other. Such is their sport. When it comes time to eat, they ride home to Valhall and sit down to drink. All the Einherjar in Odin's halls fight together each day; they choose their victims, and ride from the conflict; they drink beer with the Aesir, eat their fill of Saehrimnir, then sit in harmony together.

12. And in the evening when they are about to start the drinking, Odin has swords brought into the hall, and they are so bright that light shines from them, and no other light is used while they sit drinking. Everything there is magnificent to look at. The wall-panels are hung with splendid shields. There is also strong mead there, and great quantities to drink.

13. Inside Valhall there are many apartments and many people, some engaged in games, some are drinking, and some are armed and fighting. Songs are sung, with Odin's son Bragi as the head singer, for he is the best of skalds.

14. There are maidens whose duty it is to serve in Valhall, who, with the Gods, delight in song and harp-playing. They bring drink and see to the table and ale cups. These women are called Valkyries. They are sent by Odin to every battle, where they choose which men are to die, and they determine who has the victory. Gunn and Rota and the youngest Norn, named Skuld, always ride to choose the slain and to decide the outcome of a battle. The Valkyries wear helmets and carry shields.

15. Hrist and Mist bring Odin the horn, Skeggjold and Skogul, Hlok and Herfjotur, Hild and Thrud, Goll and Geironul, Geirdriful, Geiravor, Hrund, Svipul, Thogn, Hjalmthrimul, Sangrid, Thrima, Geirahod, Svava, Gunnthorin, Hjordrimul, Randgrid and Radgrid, and Reginleif, these bear beer to the Einherjar. The Valkyries, far traveled, are ready to ride over Goth-thjod: Skuld bears a shield, Skogul is next, then Gunn, Hild, Gondul, and Geirskogul. Now are enumerated Herjan-Odin's maidens, the Valkyries ready to ride over the earth.

16. These beautiful battle-maidens carry out Urd's death judgments, the Urdar Ord, and carry the dead warriors to Hel. They also protect the heroes they favor. Skuld herself personally brings some, who may bypass the Thingstead at Urdarbrunn, to Valhall. When these great warriors are chosen, the Valkyries pronounce: "Now we must ride to the green world of the Gods to tell Odin that a mighty king is coming there to see him."

17. These southern disir from Urd's realm fly through the air and over the waters; the helmed maids come from heaven above to increase the clash of arms. As Natt arrives at Delling's door, the Valkyries leave for battle, their horses shake themselves, and from their manes dew runs into the deep dales, hailed down onto lofty trees, thence come harvests to men. When the sun-bright daughters of the south arrive, a ray gleams from Logafell, and from that ray lightning flashes. Then, in the field of air comes the helmed band of Valkyries: their corslets sprinkled with blood, and beams of light shine from their spears. Occasionally they will sing during the battle, and this is their song:

18. Blood rains
from the cloudy web
on the broad loom
of slaughter.
The web of man,
grey as armor,
is now being woven;
the Valkyries
will cross it
with a crimson weft.

19. The warp is made
of human entrails;
human heads

are used as weights;
the heddle-rods
are blood-wet spears;
the shafts are iron-bound;
and arrows are the shuttles.
With words we will weave
this web of battle.

20. The Valkyries go weaving
with drawn swords,
Hild and Hjordrimul
Sangrid and Svipul.
Spears will shatter,
shields will splinter,
swords will gnaw
like wolves through armor.

21. Let us now wind
the web of war,
which the young king
once waged.
Let us advance
and wade through the ranks,
where friends of ours
are exchanging blows.

22. Let us now wind
the web of war,
and then follow
kings to battle.
Gunn and Gondul
can see there
the blood-spattered shields
that guard kings.

23. Let us now wind
the web of war,
where the warrior banners
are forging forward.
Let their lives
not be taken;
only the Valkyries
can choose the slain.

24. Lands will be ruled
by new peoples

who once inhabited
outlying headlands.
We pronounce kings
destined to die;
now the jarls
are felled by spears.

25. The defeated men
will suffer a grief
that will never grow old
in the minds of men.
The web is now woven
and the battlefield reddened;
the news of disaster
will spread through lands.

26. It is horrible now
to look around,
as a blood-red cloud
darkens the sky.
The heavens are stained
with the blood of men,
as the Valkyries
sing their song.

27. We sang well
victory songs
for young kings;
hail to our singing!
Let him who listens
to our Valkyrie song
learn it well
and tell it to others.

28. Let us ride on horses
hard on bare backs,
with swords unsheathed,
away from here.

29. Those who have become immortal look down on the mortals and protect their children here on earth. In Midgard's atmosphere, through the entire airspace they travel, and where one prepares blot and invokes

them, there come the holy, faithful, wise fathers with help and blessings for their children. They bring power, wealth, and descendants; they hear, help, and console; and they fight bravely and heroically in battle.

XXVI. <u>Niflhel</u>

1. When the first Hrimthurses had to abandon the fields populated by Bur's sons, they received an abode corresponding as nearly as possible to their first home, and, as it seems, is identical to it, except that Niflheim now, instead of being a part of Chaos, is an integral part of the order, and is the extreme north of Jormungrund. As a part of this order it is also called Niflhel.

2. Because of Gullveig's Seid and the corruption of mankind, it was necessary for the Gods to create a realm where nidings could be punished for their awful crimes. This place of the damned was built in the cold Niflheim and was called Niflhel. Within Niflhel lies the Nastrand where the caves of punishment lie. It would be decided at the Helthing whether or not the dead shall suffer the penalties that await them in this dreary land. Lies meant to harm others receive a long, expansive retribution; perjury, murder, adultery, defaming of hofs, opening of grave-mounds, treason, and villainy are all punished with unmentionable terrors. To the niding Odin has said: "Much did you lose when you lost my help, of all the Einherjar's and Odin's favor. Ygg-Odin shall now have your corpse; your life is now run out: the disir are angry with you! You shall now see Odin at the Thing!" Malevolent vengeance awaits souls, and only recompense can spare their lot.

3. When the judgment over the nidings is pronounced, they have to walk to meet their terrible Wyrd. Their former fylgja weeps when they see their departure; these norns bewail the nair, and continue to feel sorrow and sympathy for them to the last. The cords of Hel are tightly bound around their sides, and they are too strong to break. It is not easy to go free. They are driven along their way by the Heiptir, who, armed with limar, unmercifully lash them on hesitating heels. Invoke Mani against the Heiptir.

4. Their path from Urd's well goes north through Mimir's realm. It is arranged so that they should have to see the regions of bliss before their arrival in the world of torture. Thus they get to know what they have forfeited. So their course leads them over the Leipt river, by whose shining, clear, very sacred waters solemn oaths are customarily sworn. It flows between glittering fields with flowers that never whither and crops that are never cut– over this river past Breidablik, the radiant stronghold, where Baldur

and Nanna live with Lif and Leifthrasir; past Hoddgoda, a fortress with several Underworld rivers winding around it, where Mimir collected treasures for a coming world-age; past Mimir's well that is ornamented with a nine-fold gold trim, in which Yggdrasil's lowest, leaf-abundant branches are reflected, and in which its middle root immerses its silver-white root-threads; past the fortress of Mimir's twelve sleeping sons, and past the halls of Natt and her sisters.

5. Without and within
   I seemed to traverse all
   the nine netherworlds:
   up and down,
   I sought an easier way,
   where I might have the readiest paths.

6. Of what is to be told,
   which I first saw,
   when I came to the worlds of torment:
   scorched birds,
   which were souls,
   flew numerous as gnats.

7. From the west I saw
   Von's serpent fly,
   and obstruct Glaevald-Mimir's street;
   he shook his wings,
   far around me the earth
   and heaven seemed to burst.

8. I saw the stag of the sun
   coming from the south,
   he was led by two together:
   his feet stood on the earth,
   but his horns
   reached up to heaven.

9. Riding from the north I saw

the sons of Nidi-Mimir,
they were twelve in all:
from full horns
they drank the pure mead
from Baugregin-Mimir's well.

10. The wind was silenced,
    the waters stopped their course;
    then I heard a terrible noise:
    fickle-wise women
    ground earth for food
    for their husbands.

11. These dark women
    turned bloody stones
    in sorrow;
    their bleeding hearts hung
    out of their breasts,
    tortured with great suffering.

12. The sound of the Hvergelmir well's surge and the motion of the Grotti-Mill is much stronger as they approach the southern slope of the Nidafjoll. The procession goes up into this mountain range through valleys and gorges, where the rivers flowing from Hvergelmir seek their paths to the south. It leaves Hvergelmir and the Grotti-Mill behind and sets across the bordering waters of Hraunn-Elivagar. Behind there rises Niflhel's black, perpendicular mountain walls. Moving on, they see in the near distance a gloomy, decayed place looking most of all like a misty cloud. Niflhel is a sunless region, a land that knows neither stars nor the light of day, but is shrouded in everlasting night. Stakes raised at intervals along bat-

tlements display the severed heads of men. Before the gates, called Nagates, they find wolves of uncommon savagery keeping vigilant watch over the entrance. Howling and barking from the gate-keeping wolves of Niflhel betokens the arrival of the damned.

13. At the Nagates, the dead are given a deadly drink, called Eitur, and here die dead men from Hel. Just as those blessed with Lofstirr receive the Dyrar Veigar, the damned must drink this poison to die their second deaths in Jormungrund, and thus become a corpse for the second time. This poison is said to come from the veins of the demons in Niflhel and restores their bodies, but only so they can feel the torments that await them. It is the mead much mixed with venom, which forebodes evil. The Eitur does not loosen the speechless tongues of the damned. They suffer their agonies without uttering a sound, and in Niflhel only the torturing demons speak. However, when the wights of torture so desire, and force and egg them on, they can produce a howl.

14. Their second death consists of the ond, which they received from Odin before their birth and is the most precious element of humans, flying away from them, to return to the Asagod himself. With it flies the litur goda, which Lodur gives to every human; it is the finer body made in the image of the Gods and gives its outer physical coat the form that it bears in the earthly life. With their inner body leaving them the damned soul receives another covering, whose appearance reproduces its wickedness and is always ugly, often monstrously harsh to behold. Now they are nair, the damned who are conscious and capable of suffering, and have been condemned to a punishment which is not to cease so long as they are sensitive to it.

15. Now winged monsters, the bands of Niflhel's birds of prey, the one who gnaws at the World-Tree, Nidhogg, the eagles Ari and Hraesvelg and their equals fly in dense flocks to the south and alight on the rocks around the Nagates. These open on creaking hinges, and when the damned come through them the winged demons fall upon the offering selected for them, press them under their dagger-sharp wings, and fly with their terrible screeches through Niflhel's misty atmosphere to the rooms of torture appointed for them.

16. The gate-entry stands high above them, but they make their way to the lofty point of access. Within, black, misshapen specters throng the region, and you can hardly tell which is more frightful, the sight or the sound of these gibbering phantoms. Everything is foul, so that the rotting filth assails

the visitors' nostrils with an unbearable stench.

17. The regions over which the demon hordes fly are simply terrible to behold. This is Niflhel, home of the Hrimthurses, the dead Underworld Etins, and the wights of disease. At Jormungrund's northern horse-door, under the outermost root of the noble tree, Giantesses and Etins, dead men, Dwarves, and Dokkalfar dwell. It is here that the offspring of Ymir's feet live, the monstrously born and monstrously bearing primeval Etins, or rather their souls wrapped in a ghostly body similar to their earthly one. They do not speak; they only shriek and stare with wild eyes. They live together in a great hall, while the members of the younger Etin race live in courts scattered over stinking, marshy lands, through which a river, flowing from Hvergelmir to the north, seeks its path in muddy beds. From the east this river falls through the venom dales, with swords and daggers, its name is Slid.

18. It is here in Niflhel that demons of restless uneasiness, mental agony, convulsive weeping, and insanity have their homeland; Topi and Opi, Morn, and Otholi, increase torment and tears, while Tramar shall bow them to the earth. It is here that the wights of disease live with their queen, Loki's daugh-

ter, Leikin. The atmosphere is perpetually filled with mist.

19. However, this dreary land is only the forecourt of the true place of torture. An abyss leads from there down into nine enormous caves of punishment situated below Niflhel. From the abyss rises a repulsive steam and the river Slid spews dark, slimy masses of water down its slope. It is in this abyss that Nidhogg and the other flying demons plunge with their offerings. Before they deliver them they bore their beaks, jaws, and claws into their limbs and tear them to shreds; but these grow together again: a third death is not given to the damned. After this, they are divided between caves of torture in accordance with the mortal nids they have committed.

20. I saw many a man
go wounded
on those ember-strewn paths;
their face seemed
to me all reddened
with reeking blood.

21. There Nidhogg sucks
the corpses of the dead,
the wolf tears men.

22. He gorges on the feast
of cowards' corpses,
stains the rulers'
homes with blood.

23. Goin shall sooner
pierce me to the heart,

and Nidhogg
suck my brains,
Linn and Langbak
tear my liver,
then I will abandon
my steadfastness of heart.

24. In Nastrand
 you shall be given to Nidhogg.

25. I saw many men
 gone down into the earth,
 who might not have holy blots;
 stars of Chaos
 stood above their heads,
 painted with deadly characters.

26. I saw those men
 who harbor much envy
 at another's fortune;
 bloody runes
 were painfully engraved
 on their chests.

27. There I saw men,
 many unhappy,
 they were all wandering wild:
 this he earns
 who is infatuated
 by this world's vices.

28. I saw those men
 who had in various ways
 acquired others' property:
 in crowds they went
 to castle-covetous,
 and bore burdens of lead.

29. I saw those men
 who had bereft
 many of life and property:
 strong venomous serpents
 passed through the chests
 of those men.

30. I saw those men

who would not observe
the holy days:
their hands were
firmly nailed
to hot stones.

31. I saw those men
 who had uttered
 many false words of others:
 Hel's ravens
 miserably tore their eyes
 from their heads.

32. Swear no oath
 if it is not true,
 horrible limar
 fall heavy on broken faith:
 accursed is the oath-breaker.

33. The sons of mortals,
 who wade in Vadgelmir,
 will get a cruel retribution;
 for they have uttered
 false words against others,
 long shall they be tortured with limar.

34. You will not get to know
 all the horrors
 which Hel's inmate's suffer.
 Pleasant nid
 end in painful penalties;
 pains ever follow pleasure.

35. The nine realms of punishment consist of nine enormously vast mountain-grottos, joined to each other through openings broken into the mountain walls and obstructed by gates that have guards standing outside of them who by shape and conduct represent the nids of the nidings they watch. The cave of punishment located in the farthest north is called Nastrand because one can fare to

Amsvartnir's sea, through a gate in its northern wall. In a forecourt outside the court there guards Dokkalfar who maintain a fire from which the smoke eddies into the immensely long hall that is built into the cave of torture. The cave mouth is unsightly, the door-posts in disrepair, the walls black with filth, the ceiling dingy and the floor infested with serpents, everywhere offensive to the eye and mind.

36. On Nastrand is a large and unpleasant hall, and its doors face north. It is also woven out of serpents' bodies like a wattled house, and the serpents' heads all face inside the house and spit poison so that rivers of venom flow along the hall, and wading those rivers are oath-breakers and murderers. The hall stands far from the sun on Nastrand, with doors opened to the north; venom-drops fall through the roof-holes. The hall is made from the backs of twined serpents. There wade through heavy streams, perjurous men and murderers; the waste water of the venom falls on him who seduces another's wife. The serpents fly from every direction and spit over them. The phrenetic demons hover above and cast their venomous spittle everywhere on those beneath. The venom can remove limbs as if they had been sliced off with a sword, but the nair always regrow them. Being hanged, with a

wolf tied to one's body, is a method of punishment reserved for murderers of kinsfolk.

37. The hall, completely ruinous within and thick with a vile, powerful odor, is crammed with everything which could disgust the eye or mind. The door-posts smeared with age-old soot, the walls plastered with grime, the ceiling composed of spikes, the floor and walls crawling with serpents and spattered with every kind of filth. The bloodless apparitions of monsters squat on the iron seats, which are railed off by a netting of lead, while fearful porters are stationed to keep watch at the threshold. Some of these, shrieking, wield rows of clubs, while others play an ugly game of tossing a goat-skin to one another.

XXVII. Ydalir

1. The term *gotnar* comes from the name of a king called Goti, whom Gotland is named after. He was called after one of Odin's names, for this was derived from Gaut, for Gautland or Gotland was called after this name of Odin, while Svithjod is from the name Svidur. This is also one of Odin's names. At that time all the mainland that he ruled over was known as Hreidgotaland, and all the islands Eygotaland. These are known as the realm of the Danes and the realm of the Swedes. Goti is another name of Jarl-Skjold, from whom the Skjoldungs are de-

scended. They are kings of Denmark, and what was then called Hreidgotaland is now called Jutland. Jarl's residence and the lands he ruled over were in what is now called Denmark, but was then known as Gotland. Kon inherited this realm after his father's death.

2. Svidur is also another name of Ivaldi, and his realm, Greater Svithjod, was rich in gold, its northernmost rivers flowing on beds of golden sand. Ivaldi was the first ruler of Greater Svithjod, which the Swedes lived in the southernmost part of. North of them, Ivaldi rules a clan of skiers, the Skridfinns. For this reason he is called Finnking. He was a mighty drinker, and as skillful with the spear as his son Egil was with the bow.

3. Ivaldi protected Midgard from the powers of frost in Jotunheim, leaving Ydalir, in Alfheim, in the charge of his sons Egil, Volund, and Slagfin. There they protected Hvergelmir and the regions of bliss from the powers dwelling in Niflheim. Collectively, Ivaldi's clan is known as Niflungs.

4. Frey was six years old when Njord offered him to the sons of Ivaldi to be raised in Ydalir. Since he had been given Alfheim as a toothfee in his infancy, he would rule over this land when the time came. Volund, Egil, and Slagfin were entrusted with the protection of their king, and were given authority

to govern the realm under him. With their abundant physical and intellectual gifts, their minds and strength were more than equal to the task.

5. The danger posed by Jotunheim did not seem great, as long as the leader of the border patrol that had been established to guard against the Etins, namely Ivaldi and his sons, upheld the oaths of loyalty that they had sworn to the Gods. These Alf-princes were entrusted to watch the whole length of the waterway that flows up from Hvergelmir to the surface of the earth, and divides Midgard from Jotunheim.

6. Their sisters, daughters of Ivaldi and Sunna, were also their wives, and thus they were also united by family ties to the powers that defend the welfare of Yggdrasil and provide the inhabitants of Midgard with harvests. Volund fell in love with his sister Idun and together they had the daughter Skadi. Skadi travels on skis, carries a bow, and shoots wild animals. She is called Ondurgod or Ondurdis, for she later became an Asynja.

7. Of the three sons of Ivaldi, Volund spent most of his time in his smithy, where he forged divine ornaments and treasures, and brewed holy mead, thereby benefiting the cause he had sworn to serve. Frey, his foster son, often stayed with him. Therefore, the duty of safeguarding Hvergelmir and Mid-

gard fell mainly to his two brothers, Egil and Slagfin. Egil particularly distinguished himself by his untiring and brave service as a watchman.

8. Egil's first wife was named Groa. She lived with him in Yset, a well guarded, pleasantly furnished fortress, decorated with gold, located by the Elivagar, in Ydalir. Groa was the wise housewife of Egil, who is knowledgeable of law, of blots and sacred songs, of the Galdur and the runes. She is not Egil's sister, but rather is the daughter of the Alf-ruler Sigtryg and is a sister of Sif. Groa and Egil once found two small children lying in a dyke, a little boy and a little girl. They took the children home and adopted them as their own. The boy was named Thjalfi, and the girl Roskva. Later, Egil and Groa had the son Od, who would become close to his foster-brother, Frey.

9. Thor, who often visits the borderlands to keep an eye on the Etins, was Egil's good friend, and was accustomed to staying with him on such visits. Groa often stayed in Thor's home, Thrudvang, whenever Egil made forays on the Elivagar and on the coast of Jotunheim, alone or with his army of Alfar. Egil had eight-hundred Alfar under him, who were fishermen and warriors. Thor travels from Asgard to Yset in his chariot drawn by the goats Tanngnjost and Tan-

ngrisnir. At Egil's the evening is passed with song and mead. At dawn, Thor leaves Egil to battle Etins. He travels on foot, with a basket on his back: in it there is no better food; in peace he eats before he leaves the house, and is sated on herring and goat-meat. The herring are caught by Egil's fishermen, and the goat-meat comes from Thor's goats, which he can slay one night, then resurrect with his hammer the next day. While there, Egil gives the horn-strong goats care. Sometimes Egil rides with Thor in his chariot.

10. Slagfin married his sister Auda and shared in many of his brothers' adventures. Auda is also called Hladgud Swanwhite.

XXVIII. Mjodvitnir

1. The sacred mead of wisdom originally belonged to Mimir. From an unknown depth it rises in Jormungrund directly under Yggdrasil, whose middle root is watered by the precious liquid. Only by self-sacrifice, after prayers and tears, was Odin permitted to take a drink from this fountain. The drink increased his strength and wisdom, and enabled him to give order to the world situated above the lower regions. From its middle root, the World-Tree draws liquids from the mead-fountain, which bless Asgard with the beverage, and bless the people of Midgard with a fructifying honeydew. But this is not

the purest mead, for only that can be found in each of the Underworld fountains.

2. Mimir had the Dwarf Durin working with him during the first ages of creation, and Durin had a son who was very dear to him, named Fjalar. Mimir's sons were allowed to drink of the mead, but it is believed that Durin's sons were not, only Mimir's naturally born children were allowed to drink. Fjalar had desired to drink of Mimir's mead, but it was strictly forbidden unless he could prove himself worthy. Out of jealousy, Durin enticed his son to steal some of the mead and hide it away. And this he did. Fjalar took the stolen mead to a secret location and with it created the Byrgir fountain.

3. Mimir is the wisest of all beings, so it did not take him long to realize that someone had taken some of the mead who did not deserve it, and he knew who that someone was. When he confronted Fjalar, he refused to tell Mimir where he had hidden the mead. Then Durin came to his son's defense, which caused conflict between him and Mimir, and thus their friendship ended forever.

4. This caused a division among the divine clans, for many Alfar and Dwarves supported Durin and Fjalar, and thus they could no longer remain in Mimir's realm. Durin and many of his sons were banished by the Norns to Utgard, also called Sokkdalir,

where they dwell until Ragnarok. The home they established there is called Hnitbjorg. They allied themselves with the Etins and Durin even became one of their jarls, and is thus also called Surt. Fjalar is also called Suttung and Mjodvitnir or Midvitnir.

5. There are a multitude of beings from the Alf and Dwarf races who now work, as they had before, on the upkeep of the world and promote the blossoms and vegetation under Frey's supervision. The Alfar are fair and benevolent, yet quick to take offense and, if they are offended, are extremely vindictive. They take revenge by launching invisible arrows called Alfskot, which cause sickness. Or, if someone is intrusive towards them when they wish to not be disturbed, such as when they dance the ring-dance on moonlit nights, it can happen that the Alf, whom he has come too close to will breathe on him; he then has received the Alf-blast. These Alfar, who dwell in Midgard and work for its upkeep, are called Landwights.

6. In some mountains there are Dwarves found who mine veins of ore and forge with them. One type of Dwarf keeps themselves in the yards of humans and promotes the year's crops, not on the ground itself, but inside the barns where they multiply the harvested crops and ripen them. Such a Dwarf comes to every newly built dwelling

and remains there if he finds his stay pleasing. And pleasing it will be to him if there reigns harmony, goodwill, diligence, and kindness towards the domesticated animals. For his work he only demands a small milk offering every Yule. Otherwise, if he is seen, he prefers it if they do not speak to him or make pretense of him. In some lands he is called the Tomte.

7. We can hear the Nixi strike his harp on the sea during a storm, and, at times, from the rivers and streams, the Stromkarl can be heard on summer nights playing on a stringed instrument. In ancient times they were doomed by the Norns to wade in the water.

XXIX. Kon

1. It was time's morning,
   eagles screeched,
   holy waters fell
   from the heavenly mountains,
   then the mighty Kon
   was born
   by Borghild-Drott
   in Bralund.

2. It was night,
   norns came,
   they who did shape
   the urlag of the nobleman;
   they proclaimed him
   best among the Budlungs,
   foremost among the Skjoldungs,
   and most famed among princes.

3. With might they twisted
   the urlagthreads,

so that he will settle
burghs in Bralund;
they arranged the golden thread,
and fastened it directly
beneath the moon's hall.

4. In the east and west
   they hid the ends,
   the jarl should rule
   between there;
   Neri-Mimir's kinswoman
   set one thread
   northward and bade it
   hold forever.

5. There was one cause
   of alarm to the Ylfing [Jarl],
   and also for her
   who bore the loved one;
   a hungry raven
   cawed to another raven
   in the high tree:
   "Hear what I know!"

6. "Skjold-Jarl's son stands
   in a coat of mail,
   one day old,
   now the day has come,
   his eyes are sharp,
   like those of the Hildings,
   he is a friend of wolves:
   we shall thrive!"

7. Drott thought she saw
   a dayling in him,
   the people expected
   plentiful harvests,
   the jarl himself
   left the battle
   to give the noble leek
   to the young lord.

8. They named him Kon,
   and gave him Hringstadir,
   Solfjol, Snaefjol,
   and Sigarsvellir,

Hringstadir, Hatun,
and Himinvangar,
an ornate sword,
to Svein's brother.

9. The highborn youth
grew up
in joyous splendor,
in the care of kinsmen.
He paid and gave
to his Huskarls,
nor spared the jarl
the blood-stained sword.

10. Kon's amazing genius was so reminiscent of his father, Skjold-Jarl's, that he was immediately believed to be treading in the same virtuous footsteps. Endowed with outstanding gifts of body and mind, the young man advanced himself to such a pitch of fame that his descendants acknowledged his greatness by making his name in the most ancient Danish poems synonymous with royal nobility. When Kon was born, norns came to him, and said that in time he would become the most renowned of all kings, especially since he was the first to bear this title. Whatever contributed towards hardening and sharpening his strength he practiced ardently and tirelessly. From swordsmen he carefully copied methods of parrying and thrusting. He handled all types of weapons with skill. But his favorite weapon was the club. Kon is also called Halfdan, foremost of the Skjoldungs; famed were the wars led by

the jarl, his deeds seemed to soar to the corners of heaven.

11. Kon was held in such high esteem by the Swedes that he was believed to be the son of Thor, accorded divine honors by the people, and judged worthy of public libations. Through him the families of Jarls get the right of precedence before the other classes, Karls and Thralls. Thor is their progenitor. While all classes trace their descent from Heimdall, the nobility trace theirs from Thor, and through him from Odin.

12. Kon had knowledge of runes, great strength, and courage. He composed poetry in the native manner fluently and eloquently, and was no less renowned for his warrior prowess than his sovereignty. His generosity made him love to strew gold about him. He was also extremely handsome, and easily provoked the love of women with his countenance.

13. Skjold-Jarl had a relative by the name of Hagal, who was also his closest friend. He sent Kon to him to be raised. Hagal had a son, Hamal, the same age as Kon. Kon and Hamal played as boys together, grew into young men together, and swore eternal friendship to each other. They were the handsomest men in Midgard. In appearance, they were so alike that it was difficult to say which one was Kon and which was Hamal.

But they differed in that Kon was eloquent, and Hamal reserved, Kon quick to make a decision and carry it out, Hamal more thoughtful and considerate, but also brave when carrying out resolutions. It is hard to gather whether Kon reaped more renown through his own heroism, or that of his comrade-in-arms.

14. When Kon had become the strongest hero among all of his contemporaries, it is no wonder that he was admired more than most, and was sung of from generation to generation. He, in whom genius and beauty, strength and generosity are united, seemed perfect to many. However, Jarl, Kon's father, was better than him in the eyes of some, for the latter loved peace and strived, more than anyone else, to strengthen the ties of harmony. Kon loved war and adventure. But he was the right man for the time that had come. Peace was gone for all time from Midgard.

15. Kon is also called Helgi, Gram, Rig III, and Mannus.

XXX. <u>Utgardloki</u>

1. The beginning of this business is that Okuthor set off with his goats and chariot and with him the As called Loki. In the evening they arrived at Egil's house and were given a night's lodging there. During the evening Thor took his goats and slaugh-

tered them both. After this, they were skinned and put in the pot. When it was cooked Thor sat down to his evening meal, he and his companion. Thor invited Egil and Groa and their children to share the meal with him. Egil's son was called Thjalfi, his daughter Roskva. Then Thor placed the goatskins on the other side of the fire and instructed Egil and his household to throw the bones on to the goatskins. Thjalfi, Egil's son, enticed by Loki, took hold of the goat's ham-bone and split it open with his knife and broke it to get at the marrow.

2. Thor stayed the night there, and in the small hours before dawn he got up and dressed, took his stone hammer, Mjollnir, and raised it and blessed the goat skins. Then the goats got up, they had not fared long before one of Hlorridi-Thor's goats lay down half-dead before the car; there the pole-horse was lame in his leg; but the false Loki was the cause of this. Thor noticed this and declared that Egil or one of his people must have not treated the goats' bones with proper care. He realized that the ham-bone was broken.

3. There is no need to make a long tale about it, everyone can imagine how Egil felt when he saw his friend Thor making his brows sink down over his eyes; as for what could be seen of the eyes themselves. Thor

clenched his hands on the shaft of the hammer so that the knuckles went white, and Egil and all his household cried out fervently, offering to atone with all their possessions. Then Thor's wrath left him, and he calmed down and accepted from them in settlement their children Thjalfi and Roskva, and they then became Thor's bondservants, and they have attended him ever since. Now have you heard– for who among them who know the lore of the Gods can more fully tell?– what recompense he got from Egil: he paid for it with both of his children.

4. Thor left the goats behind there, and from then on he would always walk on his way to face Etins, leaving his goats behind in Yset. He journeyed south towards Sokkdalir or Utgard, where Surt and his clan had been banished after stealing some of Mimir's mead. He traveled down the Elivagar, and when he came to land he went ashore. With him were Loki, Thjalfi, and Roskva. After they had traveled a little while they came to a large forest. They continued walking that whole day until dark. Thjalfi, who was faster than anybody else, carried Thor's food bag. They were low on supplies.

5. When it became dark they looked for a place to spend the night and came across a very large hall. At one end was a door as wide as the hall itself, where they sought quarters for the evening. But in the middle of the night there was a powerful earthquake; the ground heaved under them and the house shook. Thor stood up and called to his companions. They searched and found a side room on the right, towards the middle of the hall, and they went in. Thor placed himself in the doorway, and the others, who were scared, stayed behind him further inside. Thor held the hammer by the handle, intending to defend himself. Then they heard a loud noise and a roaring din.

6. At sunrise, Thor went outside and saw a man lying in the forest a short distance from him. The man snored heavily as he slept, and he was not little. Thor then thought he understood the noise he had heard during the night. He put on his belt of strength, and divine power began to swell in him. But just at that moment the man awoke and quickly stood up. It is said that for once Thor was too startled to strike with the hammer. Instead, he asked the man his name, and the other called himself Skrymir [Fjalar].

7. "And I do not need," he said, "to ask your name. I know you are Thor of the Aesir. But, have you dragged away my glove?"

8. Skrymir reached out and picked up his glove. Thor now saw that during the night he had mistaken this glove for a hall. As for the side room, that was the glove's thumb.

Skrymir asked if Thor wanted to have his company on the journey, and Thor said yes. Then Skrymir took his food bag, untied it, and started to eat his breakfast. Thor and his companions did the same thing elsewhere. Skrymir next suggested that they pool their provisions, and Thor agreed. Skrymir tied together all their provisions in one bag and threw it over his shoulder. He went during the day, taking rather large strides. Later, towards the evening, Skrymir found them a place for the night under a great oak tree. Skrymir then told Thor that he wanted to lie down to sleep, "but you take the food bag and prepare your evening meal."

9. Next, Skrymir fell asleep, snoring loudly, and Thor took the food bag, intending to untie it. There is this to tell, which may seem unbelievable, but Thor could not untie a single knot, nor was he able to loosen any of the straps. None was any looser than when he started. When Thor realized that his effort was being wasted, he became angry. Gripping the hammer Mjollnir with both hands, he strode with one foot out in front to where Skrymir lay and struck him on his head. But Skrymir awoke and asked whether a leaf from the tree had fallen on his head, and whether they had eaten and were preparing to bed down. Thor then replied that they were getting ready to go to sleep. Then they

moved to a place under the oak, and it can truly be said that it was not possible to sleep without fear.

10. In the middle of the night Thor could hear that Skrymir was sleeping soundly, the forest thundering with the sound of his snoring. Thor stood and went over to him. He quickly raised the hammer and with a hard blow struck Skrymir at the midpoint of his skull. He felt the hammer sink deeply into his head. But at that instant Skrymir awoke and said: "What now? Has some acorn fallen on my head? What's new with you, Thor?"

11. Thor quickly moved back and said that he had just awakened, adding that it was the middle of the night and there was still time to sleep. Then Thor resolved that, if he could get close enough to strike a third blow, he would arrange matters so that this meeting would be their last one.

12. Thor now lay awake watching for Skrymir to fall asleep. A little before dawn, hearing that Skrymir was sleeping, Thor stood up and, running towards Skrymir [Fjalar], raised his hammer and, with all his might, struck Skrymir on the temple. The hammer sank up to its shaft, but then Skrymir sat up, brushed off the side of his head, and asked:

13. "Are there birds sitting in the tree above me? It seemed to me as I awoke that some leaves or twigs from the branches had fallen on my head. Are you awake Thor? It is time to get up and get dressed. You don't have a long way to go to reach the stronghold, which is called Utgard. I have heard you whispering among youselves that I am no small man, and you will see still larger men if you go to Utgard. Now I will give you some good advice: do not go arrogantly. The retainers of Utgardloki-Fjalar will not tolerate bragging from such a small fry as you. Your other choice is to turn back, and in my opinion that would be the best thing for you to do. But if you intend to continue, then head for the east. My path now leads me northward to those mountains that you can now see."

14. Skrymir took the food bag and threw it on his back. He turned sharply and headed north into the forest, leaving the others. In this parting, there is no report that the Aesir mentioned that they were looking forward to meeting him again.

15. Thor and his companions continued on their journey, traveling until midday. Then they saw a fortress standing on a plain, and it was so big that in order to see over it they had to bend their necks all the way back. They approached the fortress, but the front entrance gate was shut. Thor went to the gate and tried to open it, but after struggling to open the stronghold, they finally had to squeeze between the bars. Entering in this way, they saw a large hall and approached it. The door was open, and inside they saw many people sitting on two benches; most of them were rather large.

16. They went before the king, Utgardloki [Suttung-Fjalar], and greeted him, but he took his time in noticing them. Then he said, grinning through his teeth: "News travels slowly from distant parts, but am I wrong in thinking that this little fellow is Okuthor? Surely there is more to you than meets the eye. Tell me, companions, in what skills do you think you are capable of competing? No one can stay here with us who does not have some skill or knowledge greater than other men."

17. Then he who stood at the back of the group, the one called Loki, spoke up: "I have a skill in which I am ready to be tested. No one here in the hall will prove quicker than I at eating his food."

18. Utgardloki-Fjalar answered, "That will be an accomplishment, if you are up to it, and feats such as that will be put to the test." Next he called out to the end of the bench to the one called Logi and told him to come forward onto the floor and pit himself

against Loki. Then a trough filled with meat was brought in and set on the hall floor. Loki placed himself at one end and Logi at the other. Each began to eat as fast as he could, and they met in the middle of the trough. Loki had eaten all the meat from the bones, but Logi had not only eaten the meat but also the bones and even the trough. To everyone it seemed that Loki had lost the contest.

19. Then Utgardloki asked in what the youngster could compete. Thjalfi replied that he would run a race against whomever Utgardloki-Fjalar chose. Utgardloki-Fjalar called that a fine sport, but said that Thjalfi would have to be very quick if he intended to win. Utgardloki-Fjalar made it clear that the matter would quickly be put to the test. Next Utgardloki-Fjalar stood up and went outside where there was a good running course over the flat plain. He called a little fellow named Hugi to come to him and ordered him to run a race with Thjalfi. They ran the first race, and Hugi was so far in the lead that he turned around at the end and faced his opponent.

20. Then Utgardloki-Fjalar said, "Thjalfi, you will need to exert yourself more if you are to win the contest. Yet it is true that no one else has come here who seemed to me faster on his feet than you."

21. Then they began the race a second time. When Hugi came to the end of the course he turned around, but Thjalfi was behind him by the distance of a longbow shot.

22. Utgardloki-Fjalar then said: "I think Thjalfi knows how to run a good race, but I have no faith that he will win. Now comes the test; let them run the third race." When Hugi reached the end of the race and turned around, Thjalfi had not even reached the midpoint of the course. Everyone then said that the contest was over.

23. Utgardloki-Fjalar asked Thor what feat he wanted to show them, as so many tales were told about his exploits. Thor answered that he would most like to pit himself against someone in drinking. Utgardloki-Fjalar said that this contest could easily be arranged. He went into the hall and called to his cupbearer, telling him to bring the feasting horn from which his retainers usually drank. The cupbearer quickly brought the horn and placed it in Thor's hand.

24. Then Utgardloki-Fjalar said, "It is thought that drinking from this horn is well done if it is emptied in one drink. Some drain it in two, but no one is such a small-time drinker that he cannot finish it in three."

25. Thor eyed the horn, and it did not seem to be very large, although it was rather long.

He was quite thirsty and began to drink, swallowing hugely and thinking that it would not be necessary to bend himself over the horn more than once. When he had drunk as much as he could, he bent back from the horn and looked in to see how much drink remained. It seemed to him that the level in the horn was only slightly lower than it had been before.

26. Utgardloki-Fjalar then said, "Good drinking, although not all that much. I would not have believed it if I had been told that Asathor would not have drunk more, but I know that you will drain it in a second drink."

27. Thor gave no reply but put the horn to his mouth and resolved to take a larger drink. He struggled with it as long as he could hold his breath and noticed that he could not lift up the bottom of the horn as well as he liked. When he lowered the horn from his mouth and looked in, it seemed to him that the level had gone down even less than it had in the first try, although there was now enough space at the top of the horn above the liquid to carry the drink without spilling it.

28. Utgardloki-Fjalar asked, "What now, Thor? Are you going to be so brave that you will take one sip more than is good for you? It seems to me that if you want to take a third drink from the horn, then it will have to be the biggest. But among us here, you will not be known as a great man, as the Aesir call you, unless you give a better account of yourself in other contests than it seems to me you are doing in this one."

29. Then Thor grew angry. Placing the horn to his mouth, he drank with all his might, continuing as long as he could. When he looked into the horn, he could see at least some difference. Then he gave the horn back and would drink no more.

30. Utgardloki-Fjalar said, "Clearly your strength is not as great as we thought, but will you still try your hand in other contests? It is obvious that you are not going to succeed here."

31. Thor replied: "I will make a try at still another game. But, when I was home among the Aesir, I would have found it strange if such drinks were called little. What sort of contest will you offer me now?"

32. Utgardloki-Fjalar replied: "Here among us, little boys do something that is thought a rather small matter: they lift my cat off the ground. But I would not have thought it possible to propose such a thing to Asathor if I had not already seen that your strength is much less than I thought."

33. Now, a grey cat, and a rather large one, jumped out onto the floor of the hall. Thor

approached it, and, placing his hand under the middle of the belly, started to lift up the cat. But as much as Thor raised his hand, the cat arched its back. When Thor had reached as high as he could, one of the cat's paws was lifted off the ground. Beyond this effort, Thor could do no more.

34. Then, Utgardloki-Fjalar said, "This contest has gone as I expected it would. The cat is rather large, whereas Thor is short and small compared with the larger men among us here."

35. Thor replied, "Although you call me little, let someone come forward and wrestle with me! Now I am angry!"

36. Utgardloki-Fjalar looked over the benches and replied, "Here inside, I do not see any man who would find it dignified to wrestle with you." Then he went on, "But wait, first let us see. Call my nurse, the old woman Elli, to come here, and let Thor wrestle with her, if he wants to. She has thrown to the ground men who seemed to me to be no less strong than Thor."

37. Next, an old woman walked into the hall. Utgardloki-Fjalar said she should wrestle Asathor. The story is not long to tell. The match went this way: the more Thor threw his strength into the grappling, the more steadfastly she stood her ground. Then the old crone showed her skill. Thor lost his foot

and the contest grew fiercer. It was not long before Thor fell to one knee. Then Utgardloki-Fjalar intervened. He told them to stop the contest, saying that there was no need for Thor to challenge others to wrestle in his hall. By then, it was late at night. Utgardloki-Fjalar showed Thor and his companions to places on the benches, and they were treated well for the rest of the night.

38. In the morning, at first light, Thor and his companions stood up, dressed, and prepared to leave. Utgardloki-Fjalar then came in and had a table set for them. There was no lack of hospitality as to food or drink. When they finished eating, they turned to leave. Utgardloki-Fjalar stayed with them, accompanying them as they left the fortress. At their parting, Utgardloki-Fjalar asked Thor how he thought the trip had gone and whether Thor had ever met a man more powerful. Thor replied that he could not deny that he had been seriously dishonored in their encounter: "Moreover, I know that you will say that I am a person of little account, and that galls me."

39. Then, Utgardloki-Fjalar replied, "Now that you are out of the fortress, I will tell you the truth, for, if I live and am the one to decide, you will never enter it again. On my word, I can assure you, that you would never have been allowed to enter if I had known in

advance that you had so much power in you, because you nearly brought disaster upon us. I have tricked you with magical shape-changings, as I did that first time when I found you in the forest. I am the one you met there. And when you tried to untie the food bag, you were unable to do it, because I had fastened it with iron wire. When you struck me three times with the hammer, the first was the least, yet it was so powerful that it would have killed me had it found its mark. But when you saw a flat-topped mountain near my hall with three square-shaped valleys in it, one deeper than the others, these were the marks of your hammer. I had moved this flat-topped mountain in front of your blows, but you did not see me doing it. It was the same when your companions contested with my retainers. And so it was in the first contest undertaken by Loki. He was very hungry and he ate quickly. But the one called Logi was wildfire in itself, and he burned through the trough no less quickly than the meat. When Thjalfi ran against the one called Hugi, that was my thought, and Thjalfi could not be expected to compete with its speed. When you drank from the horn, you thought it was slow going, but on my word that was a miracle I would never have believed could happen. The other end of the horn, which you could not see, was

out in the ocean. When you come to the ocean you will see how much your drinking lowered it. This is now known as the tides."

40. Utgardloki-Fjalar, had still more to say: "I thought it no less a feat when you lifted the cat. Truly, all those who saw you raise one of the cat's paws off the ground grew fearful, because that cat was not what it seemed to be. It was the Midgardswyrm, which encircles all lands, and from head to tail, its length is just enough to round the earth. But you pulled him up so high that he almost reached the sky.

41. "It, too, was a real wonder that you remained on your feet for so long during the wrestling. You fell no more than on to one knee, as you struggled with the crone Elli, and no one accomplishes that after reaching the point where old age beckons, because no one overcomes Elli, or old age. As we part, I can truthfully say that it would be better for us both if you never come again to meet me. Next time, I will defend my stronghold with similar or other trickery, so that you will not get me into your power."

42. When Thor heard this account, he gripped his hammer and raised it into the air. But, when he was ready to strike, Utgardloki was nowhere to be seen. Then Thor returned to the fortress, intending to destroy it. There he saw a broad, beautiful plain, but no

stronghold. Then, turning back, he journeyed until he came once again to Thrudvang. In truth, it can be said that from then on he was determined to find a way to confront the Midgardswyrm, and later on that happened.

43. Thjalfi would take part in many of Thor's adventures, and became renowned for his bravery, sharing in the Asagod's glory. He is invoked as an ally of Thor, and became a representative of cattle-driving and agriculture, and is a defender of migrants, colonizers, and settlers. Thjalfi shows farmers where to go, and is prayed to when searching for a home or a place to settle. As a warrior and cattle-driver, he carries a prod and an axe. His sister, Roskva, plays an important role in Thor's adventures as well.

XXXI. <u>Egil</u>

1. Egil had become a great champion and had earned widespread reputation for his deeds in defending the Elivagar from the powers of frost. To those who saw the signs of the times, it was clear that the Etins were growing bolder and more dangerous every year. Often Egil would ski out onto the stormy, mist-enveloped, and enchanted Elivagar to spy on the doings of the Etins. Egil was hardly less talked of among the Etins than Thor. It vexed them that this son of Ivaldi, who in stature and strength was by no means superior to the largest among them, had for three whole years now attacked with impunity the coastal regions of the land of the Hrimthurses and killed many of its tenants with his sure-hitting arrows.

2. Running on skis over the crusty snowfield, he was out where they least wanted him and made it impossible to catch him in pursuit, so long as he did not come across Hrungnir on Gullfaxi. This had not happened because his boldness was kept in check by his carefulness, and he let no superior come too close to him before he laid an arrow on the bowstring.

3. However, the Etins would have perhaps finally got him into their possession, if he did not have his supporters among them. The mother of Ivaldi's sons was the Giantess named Greip. Through her they stood in kinship with a powerful family in Jotunheim, which Isung and the later renowned maids Fenja and Menja belonged to. Isung was Egil's kinsman and had received him and given him lodging when he once came shipwrecked, floating on the keel of his overturned ski-boat, to Isung's court by the shore during one of the storms that the Hrimthurses raised on the Elivagar to drown him.

4. He had successfully defied these storms, and successfully conducted himself through

the mist, which his enemies spread out over the water to confuse his course.

5. Now, it so happened that the Etin named Koll learned of Egil's deeds and decided that he would meet him in combat. He cruised about, combing various parts of the seas, until he lit upon Egil-Orvandill's fleet. In the midst of the ocean there was an island held by each of the warriors, who had moored their ships on different sides. The leaders were attracted by the delightful prospect of the beaches; the beautiful vista from off-shore encouraged them to view the woods of the interior in spring and wander among the glades and remote expanses of the forest. Their chance steps led Koll and Egil-Orvandill to an unwitnessed meeting.

6. Egil-Orvandill took the initiative and asked his opponent how he wanted to fight, stressing the most superior method was one which exercised the sinews of the fewest men. He thought that single-combat, called Einvigi, was more effective than any other type of contest for securing the honors of bravery, since a person must rely on his own valor and refuse any other man's aid. Koll, admiring such courageous judgment in a young man, replied:

7. "As you allow me a choice, I vote whole-heartedly for an encounter that only needs the work of two men, free from the usual pandemonium. Certainly this is reckoned to require more fortitude and leads to a speedier victory. On this our verdicts concur spontaneously. As the conclusion remains in doubt, we must each of us make a concession to common decency; rather than give rein to our natural tempers we should observe our obligations to the dead. Hatred is in our hearts; make room in them for compassion, the proper successor to harshness in the end. Though difference of opinion divides us, we share the same universal laws, and these join us together, however much resentment now sunders our spirits. Let our sense of duty then make this stipulation, that the victor should conduct the last rites of the vanquished. All men agree that these embody the final humane courtesy, for no pious individual has ever shirked them. Each side must relax his rigor and cordially carry out this service, let malice depart after the one has met his Wyrd, let death lull the feud. Although hate came between us alive, there is no demand for one to continue persecuting the other's remains, which is a mark of severe cruelty. It will be a glorious token for the conqueror to celebrate a rich Helfare for his victim, for whoever pays the last rites to his dead enemy enlists the good will of his successor, overcomes the survivor by a

kindness in exerting his benevolence towards the departed.

8. "Another, no less lamentable disaster sometimes occurs to the living, when part of the body is maimed. I believe in being just as ready to help a man in this case as when he has breathed his last. Fighters often suffer loss of limbs where life is still intact, and this is commonly reckoned worse than any fatal casualty; death takes away the recollection of everything, whereas the living man cannot overlook the devastation of his own body. One must therefore give support to such a mutilated individual. A suitable reparation then for the injured ought to be ten marks of gold. If it is a duty to sympathize with another's misfortunes, how much more is it to pity one's own? Everyone takes thought for his own condition, and if anyone is negligent in this he is a self-murderer."

9. Each gave his word of honor on this point and they fell to battle. They were not deterred from assailing each other with their blades by the novelty of their meeting, or the springtime charm of that spot, for they took no heed of these things. Egil's emotional fervor made him more eager to set upon his foe than defend himself; consequently, he disregarded the protection of his shield and laid both hands to his sword. This daring had its results. His rain of blows deprived

Koll of his shield by cutting it to pieces; finally, he carved off the other's foot and made him fall lifeless. He honored their agreement by giving him a regal Helfare, constructing an ornate tomb and providing a ceremony of great magnificence. After this, he hounded down Koll's sister Sela, a warring Giantess and accomplished marauder herself.

10. In his ski-boat, he expected new adventures with everything the Etin powers could send out: cold, hail, mist, and darkness. Never had Egil been worse off. He worked restlessly to keep the boat over the water, and he drifted right through the waves and ice-floes toward the coast of Midgard. Howling troll-monsters surrounded him on all sides; with blows from his oar and strikes of his sword, he had to ward off their efforts to overturn his small craft, the cold was ever more overpowering to him, his limbs began to stiffen. For a time he was missing from Yset.

XXXII. Geirrod

1. An Etin named Hraudung had two sons, one named Agnar, the other Geirrod. Agnar was ten, and Geirrod eight winters old. They both rowed out in a boat, with their hooks and lines, to catch small fish; but the wind drove them out to sea. In the darkness of night they were wrecked on the shore, and

went up into the country, where they found a cottager, with whom they stayed through the winter. The cottager's wife brought up Agnar, and the cottager, Geirrod, and gave him good advice. In the spring the man got them a ship; but when he and his wife accompanied them to the strand, the man talked apart with Geirrod. They had a fair wind, and reached their father's place. Geirrod was at the ship's prow: he sprang on shore, but pushed the ship out, saying, "Go where an evil spirit may have you!" The vessel was driven out to sea, but Geirrod went up to the town, where he was well received; but his father was dead. Geirrod was then taken for king, and became famous among the Etins.

2. Once it had befallen Loki, having gone flying for fun with Frigga's falcon-guise, that out of curiosity, he had flown into Geirrod's court and saw a great hall there, and he alighted and looked in through the window. But Geirrod looked out at him and ordered that the bird should be caught and brought to him. The person sent got with difficulty up on to the wall of the hall, it was so high. Loki was pleased that it caused him trouble, and planned to delay flying up until the man had performed the whole of the difficult climb. But when the fellow came at him, he beat his wings and jumped hard afterwards, and found his feet were stuck. Loki was cap-

tured there and brought to the Etin Geirrod. And when he saw his eyes, he had a feeling it must be a person and demanded that he answer him, but Loki remained silent. Then Geirrod locked Loki in a chest and starved him there for three months. And when Geirrod took him out and demanded that he speak, Loki said who he was, and to redeem his life he swore Geirrod oaths that he would get Thor to come to Geirrod's court so they could ambush him.

3. The father [Loki] of the sea-thread [Midgardswyrm] set about urging the feller [Thor] of the life-net of the Gods of the flight-ledges [Etins] to leave home. Lopt-Loki was a mighty liar. The deceitful mind-teaser [Loki] of the war-thunder's Gaut [Thor] declared that green paths led towards Geirrod's wall-horse [house].

4. The brave Thor did not need to be asked often by the vulture-path [Loki] to make their journey; they were eager to oppress Thorn-Ymir's descendants [Etins], where the tamer of Gandvik's [Elivagar's] girdle [Thor], mightier than the Scots of Idi-Slagfin's dwelling [Etins], again set forth from Thridi's [Valhall] towards Ymsi's kindred [Etins].

5. Rognir of the battle [Thjalfi] was quicker to join the swift mover of armies [Thor] on the expedition than the arm-burden [Loki] of

the Goddess of Seid [Gullveig]. I recite Grimnir's [Odin's] lip-streams [poetry]. The maiden-betrayer of the halls of the shrill-crier [Thor] stretched the palms of the soles [feet] onto Endil -Egil's moor [Elivagar].

6. And the battle-Vanir walked, until the prime diminisher [Thor] of the maidens [Giantesses] of the enemy of the Frid of the heaven-shield reached Gang's [Ymir's] blood [the river], when the agile, quick-tempered averter of Loki's mischief [Thor] wished to oppose the bride [Gjalp] of the sedge-buck's kinsmen.

7. And the honor decreaser [Thor] of the Nanna of the pommel of the sea [Giantess] crossed on foot the icy, swollen streams, which tumble around the lynx's ocean. The furious scatterer [Thor] of the scree-villain [Etin] made fast progress over the broad way of the stick-path [river], where mighty streams spewed poison.

8. There they pushed shooting-serpents [spears] into the net-forest [river] against the loud wind of the forest [current]. The slippery, round bones [rocks] did not sleep. The banging files [spears] jangled against the pebbles, while the mountain's falling-roar [cascade] rushed, beaten by an ice-storm, along Fedja's [the river's] anvil [rock].

9. Vimur is the name of the river that Thor waded when he was on his way to Geirrod's court, which is also called Elivagar. And when Thor got to the middle of the river, it rose so much that it washed up over his shoulders. Then Thor spoke this:

10. "Do not rise now, Vimur, since I desire to wade you into the Etin's courts. Know that if you rise then the divine strength in me will rise up as high as heaven."

11. The promoter [warrior] of the whetstone land [battlefield] let the mighty swollen ones [waves] fall over him. The man [Thjalfi], who benefited from the belt of might [Megingjard], knew no better course of action. The diminisher [Thor] of Morn's children [Etins] threatened that his power shall grow unto the hall's roof [heaven], unless the gushing blood [water] of Thorn-Ymir's neck would diminish.

12. The glorious, battle-wise warriors, oath-sworn Vikings [Einherjar] of Gaut-Odin's dwelling [Valhall], waded hard, while the sword-fen [river] flowed. The wave of the earth's snow-dune [river], blown by the tempest, rushed forcefully at the increaser [Thor] of the room-dwellers [Etins] of the land of the ridge [mountain], until Thjalfi, accompanying the friend of men [Thor], flew into the air of his own accord onto the sky-lord's [Thor's] shield-strap [shoulders]– that was a great feat of strength! The widows [Giantesses] of the Mimir of mischief

[Etin] caused a violent stream, strident with steel. Grid's toppler [Thor] carried the battle-tree [Thjalfi] across the bumpy land of the porpoise [the river].

13. The deep-acorns of hostility [hearts] of the men, who firmly opposed disgrace, did not miss a beat at the surge of the current of Glammi's haunt [the river]. The brave son of the isthmus [Thor] was not threatened by the terror of the fjord-trees [the river]; Thor's valor-stone [heart] did not tremble from fear, and neither did Thjalfi's.

14. Then Thor saw up in a certain cleft that Geirrod's daughter Gjalp was standing astride the river and she was causing it to rise, by urinating in it. Then he took a great stone up out of the river and threw it at her, and said:

15. "At its outlet must a river be stemmed."

16. He did not miss what he was aiming at, and at that moment, he found himself close to the bank, with the warriors on his belt and Thjalfi on his shoulders, and managed to grasp a sort of rowan-branch, called Gridarvol, and thus climbed out of the river. Hence comes the saying that Thor's salvation is the rowan.

17. A flock of the cliff-foes [Etins] of the shield [Aesir] of the ever-burning fire made a din of the sword's hoard [battle] against the tighteners of Gleipnir [Aesir], before the crossers of the deep, the destroyers [Thor and Thjalfi] of the nation of the sea-shore [Jotunheim], were able to conduct the bowl [helmet]-play of the hair-parting of Hedin [battle, Hedin= Hod], against the kin-British of the cave [Geirrod's Etins].

18. The skerry-nation of the cold wave of the foe-Svithjod [Etins] fled, and hurried into their sanctuary, accompanied by the crusher [Thor] of the ness-people [Etins]. The Danes of the flood-rib of the outlying sanctuary [Etins] admitted defeat, when the kinsmen [warriors] of Jolnir-Odin's fire-shaker stood resolutely.

19. When Thor got to Geirrod's, he and his companions were first of all shown into a goat-shed as their lodging. When the warriors, endowed with minds of valor, entered the house of Thorn [the cave, Thorn= Ymir, hence Etin], there was a great din among the Cymry of the cave of the circular wall [Etins]. Inside there was a single seat to sit on and it was Thor who sat on it. Then he realized that the seat was lifting under him up towards the roof. The peace-reluctant slayer [Thor] of the reindeer of the Lister of the peak [Etins] was put in a fix there, on the dire, grim hat of the brow-moon [head] against the rafters of the rock-hall [cave], Thor pushed Gridarvol up into the rafters and pressed himself down hard on the seat.

Then there was a great crack accompanied by a great scream. Under the seat it had been Geirrod's daughters Gjalp and Greip, and they were crushed against the rocks of the plain [floor] of the rock-hall [cave]. The hull-controller of the hovering chariot of the thunderstorm [Thor] broke the ancient keel of the laughter ship [backs] of both cave-maidens [Giantesses].

20. Then Geirrod had Thor called into the hall for games. There were great fires there along the length of the hall. Jord-Frigga's son [Thor] taught an unusual lesson, but the men of the lair of the land of the fjord-apple [Etins] did not cease their ale-feast. And when Thor came into the hall opposite Geirrod, Geirrod, the frightener of the elm-cord, Sudri's kinsman, picked up with tongs a glowing lump of molten iron, cooked in the forge, and threw it at the mouth of Odin's grief-thief [Thor]. The oppressor [Thor] of the kinfolk of evening-running women [Etins] opened wide the mouth of his arm [hand] at the heavy, red morsel of the tongs' seaweed [the molten lump]. With his Iron Gloves [Jarngreips] Thor, the swift hastener of battle, Throng-Freya's old friend, greedily drank [caught] the raised drink of the molten lump in the air with the swift mouths of his hands [palms], when the hissing cinder took flight from the hostile breast of the grip [hand] of the ardent lover [Geirrod] of Hrimnir's maiden [Gullveig], towards the one who strongly misses Thrud [Thor]. Thor raised the molten lump into the air, while Geirrod ran into the shelter of an iron pillar for protection. Thor flung the molten lump and it crashed into the pillar and through Geirrod and through the wall and so into the ground outside. The hall of Thrasir-Geirrod shook, when Heidrek-Geirrod's broad head was brought underneath the ancient leg of the wall of the floor-bear [pillar]. The splendid stepfather of Ull [Thor] struck the harmful brooch [the molten lump] with great force down through the middle of the girdle of the villain [Geirrod] of the tooth [rock] of the way of the fishing line [river].

21. The furious one [Thor] slaughtered the descendants of Glaum [Etins] with his bloody hammer [Mjollnir]. The slayer [Thor] of the frequent visitor of the hall of the stone-Goddess [Etin] was victorious. Lack of Thjalfi's support did not hamper the pole of the bow, God of the chariot [Thor], who inflicted grief upon the Etin's bench-mates.

22. The worshipped Hel-striker [Thor], with the Alf [Thjalfi], slew the wood-calves of the subterranean refuge from Alfheim's gleam [Etins] with the easy crusher [Mjollnir]. The Rogalander of the Lister of

the falcon-lair [Etins] were unable to harm the firmly supportive shortener [Thjalfi] of the lifespan of the men of the rock-king [Etins].

23. Well have you, cleaver apart of Thrivaldi's nine heads [Thor] held back your steed with the notorious Etin-feast drinker [Geirrod]. Thor, you broke Leikin's bones, you pounded Thrivaldi, you cast down Starkad, you stood over the dead Gjalp. There was a clang on Keila's crown, you broke Kjallandi completely, before that you slew Lut and Leidi, you made Buseyra bleed, you halted Hengjankjapta, Hyrrokkin-Gullveig died previously, yet was the dusky Svivor's life taken earlier.

XXXIII. Thrym

1. Angry was Vingthor,
when he awoke,
and his mighty
hammer was missing;
he shook his beard,
scratched his head,
the son of Jord-Frigga
felt all around him.

2. These are the words
that he spoke first:
"Listen, Loki,
to what I now say,
which no one knows
anywhere on earth,
nor in heaven above:
the As' hammer is stolen!"

3. They went to the fair
Freya's dwelling,

and these are the words
that he spoke first:
"Will you, Freya,
lend me your feather-guise,
so that I may
seek my hammer?"

4. Freya said: "I would give it to you
even if it were made of gold,
I would entrust you with it,
even if it were made of silver."

5. Then Loki flew,
and the feather-guise whirred,
until he went
beyond the land of the Aesir,
and came within
the realm of the Etins.

6. Thrym sat on a mound,
the lord of Thurses,
braiding gold collars
for his dogs,
and combing the manes
of his horses.

7. Thrym said: "How fare the Aesir?
How fare the Alfar?
Why have you come
to Jotunheim alone?"

8. Loki said: "Ill fare the Aesir.
Ill fare the Alfar.
Have you hidden
Hlorridi-Thor's hammer?"

9. Thrym said: "I have hidden
Hlorridi-Thor's hammer,
eight leagues
beneath the earth;
and no man shall
bring it back again,
unless he bring me
Freya to be my wife."

10. Then Loki flew,

106

and the feather-guise whirred,
until he went
beyond the realm of Etins,
and came within
the land of the Aesir.
There he met Thor,
in the middle court;
these are the words
that he spoke first:

11. "Have you had success
    as well as toil?
    Tell me from the air
    your long tidings.
    Often, from him who sits,
    are the tales defective,
    and he who lies down
    utters falsehood."

12. Loki said: "I have had
    toil and success:
    Thrym has your hammer,
    the lord of Thurses;
    and no man shall
    bring it back again,
    unless he brings him
    Freya to be his wife."

13. They went to find
    the fair Freya;
    these are the words
    that he spoke first:
    "Freya, put on
    the bridal veil,
    for the two of us
    must drive to Jotunheim."

14. Then Freya was full of wrath,
    and foamed with rage;
    all the halls of the Aesir
    trembled beneath her:
    the famed Brising's necklace
    burst into pieces:
    "I would be known
    as the lewdest of women,
    if I drive to Jotunheim

with you."

15. Then all the Aesir went
    straight to the Thing,
    and all the Asynjur,
    to hold council;
    and the mighty Gods
    deliberated on how
    they might get back
    Hlorridi-Thor's hammer.

16. Then Heimdall,
    the Whitest As, spoke,
    well could he foresee,
    like other Vanir:
    "Let us clothe Thor
    in bridal linen,
    let him have
    the famed Brising's necklace.

17. "Let keys jingle
    by his side,
    and a woman's dress
    fall around his knees,
    but on his chest
    place precious stones,
    and set a pretty coif
    on his head."

18. Then Thor,
    the mighty As, said:
    "The Aesir will call
    me womanly
    if I let myself
    be clad in bridal linen."

19. Then Loki,
    Laufey's son, spoke:
    "Shut up, Thor!
    Refrain from such words:
    soon the Etins
    will inhabit Asgard
    unless you get
    your hammer back."

20. Then they clad Thor

in bridal linen,
and with the noble
Brising's necklace,
let keys jingle
by his side,
and a woman's dress
fall around his knees:
and on his chest
placed precious stones,
and sat a pretty coif
on his head.

21. Then Loki,
    Laufey's son, said:
    "I will go with
    you as a servant:
    the two of us
    will drive to Jotunheim."

22. Then the goats
    were driven homeward,
    and hurried to the traces;
    they had to run fast;
    the mountains burst,
    the earth burned with fire;
    Odin's son
    drove to Jotunheim.

23. Then Thrym,
    the lord of Thurses, said:
    "Rise up, Etins!
    Put straw on the benches;
    now they bring me
    Freya to be my wife,
    Njord's daughter,
    from Noatun.

24. "Bring gold-horned cattle
    here to our court,
    all-black oxen,
    for the Etin's joy.
    I have many treasures,
    many ornaments,
    it seemed to me
    that I lack Freya alone."

25. They came early
    in the evening,
    and beer was brought forth
    for the Etins.
    Thor alone devoured an ox,
    eight salmon,
    and all the sweets
    that were set for the women.
    Sif's consort [Thor] drank
    three measures of mead.

26. Then Thrym,
    the prince of Thurses, said:
    "Where have you seen
    a bride eat more voraciously?
    I have never seen
    a bride eat so much,
    nor a maid drink more mead."

27. The wise serving-maid
    sat close by,
    who answered well
    to the Etin's words:
    "Freya has not eaten
    for eight nights,
    so eager was she
    for Jotunheim."

28. He looked beneath the veil,
    wanting to kiss her,
    but jumped back
    the length of the hall:
    "Why is Freya's gaze
    so piercing?
    Methinks that fire
    burns from her eyes."

29. The wise serving-maid
    sat close by,
    who answered well
    the Etin's words:
    "Freya has not slept
    for eight nights,
    so eager was she
    for Jotunheim."

30. In came the Etin's
    luckless sister,
    she dared to ask
    for a bride-gift:
    "Give me the red-gold
    rings from your hands,
    for you to gain my love,
    my love and all my favor."

31. Then Thrym,
    the lord of Thurses, said:
    "Bring the hammer in
    to consecrate the bride;
    lay Mjollnir
    on the maiden's lap;
    unite us, each with the other,
    by the hand of Var."

32. Hlorridi-Thor's heart
    laughed in his heart,
    when the fierce-hearted one
    recognized his hammer.
    First he killed Thrym,
    the lord of Thurses,
    then he crushed all
    of the Etin's kin.

33. He killed the Etin's
    old sister,
    she who had demanded
    a bride-gift;
    she got a blow
    instead of shillings,
    a strike from the hammer
    for many rings.

34. And so Odin's son got his hammer back.

XXXIV. Sleipnir

1. There came a certain builder to the Gods. He offered to construct in three seasons a fortress so solid and trustworthy that it would be safe against Bergrisar and Hrimthurses even if they entered Midgard. As his payment he asked for Freya in marriage, but he also wanted the sun and moon.

2. Then the Aesir, consulting among themselves, arrived at their decision. Their agreement with the builder was that he should have what he requested, if he completed the fortress in one winter. But if any part of the fortress was unfinished on the first day of summer, he would lose his part of the bargain. No other man was to help him in this work. When stating these conditions they agreed to let him have the use of his horse, called Svadilfari. Loki was the one who made this decision after the matter was placed before him.

3. On the first day of winter the builder began to erect the fortress, and during the night he used his horse to haul in stones. The Aesir were amazed at the size of the boulders the horse could drag; the horse's feat of strength was twice that of the builder's. But good witnesses and many oaths had sealed the bargain, because the Etin did not think it safe to be without a truce among the Aesir if Thor should return. At that time, Thor was in the east hammering on trolls. As the winter passed, the building of the fortification steadily advanced, until it became so high and so strong that it was unassailable. With only three days left before summer, the work

had progressed right up to the stronghold's entrance.

4. Then the Gods sat on their thrones of Wyrd and sought a solution. They asked one another who had been responsible for the decision to marry Freya into Jotunheim and to destroy the sky and the heavens by taking the sun and moon and giving them to an Etin. And it became clear, as in most other things, that the one who had advised in this matter was Loki Laufeyarson, the one who counsels badly in most matters. They told him that he could expect a bad death if he failed to devise a plan for the builder to lose his wager. They attacked Loki, and when he became frightened, he swore oaths that, whatever it cost him, he would find a way to keep the builder from completing his part of the bargain.

5. That same evening, as the builder drove out with his stallion Svadilfari to gather stones, a mare leaped from a forest and, neighing, ran up to the horse. When the stallion recognized what manner of horse this was, he became frantic and broke free from his harness. He galloped towards the mare but she raced ahead of him into the forest. Behind them came the builder, trying to grab hold of his horse. Because the horses ran all evening and night, the work was delayed.

6. The next day, there was less work done than previously. When the builder saw that the work would not be finished, he flew into an Etin's rage. Once the Aesir realized for certain that they were dealing with a Bergrisi, they no longer respected their oaths. They called upon Thor, who came immediately, and the next thing to happen was that the hammer Mjollnir was in the air. In this way Thor repaid the builder his wages, but not the sun and moon. Rather, Thor put an end to the Etin's life in Jotunheim. He struck the first blow in such a way that the Etin's skull broke into small pieces, and so Thor sent him down into Niflhel. But Loki's relations with Svadilfari were such that a while later he gave birth to a colt. It was grey and had eight feet, and this is the best horse among Gods and men.

7. Sleipnir is the best of all horses; Odin owns him, and he has eight legs. Runes are risted on Sleipnir's teeth. The horse has such magnificent strength and rapid hooves that it can cross any river, no matter how violent, vanquishing its roaring tide without fatigue. It can also leap over any wall, no matter how high, even if it is composed of Vafurfires.

XXXV. <u>Sif</u>

1. The Goddess Sif is a daughter of Sigtryg, also called Kiarr, and is Groa's sister. She would later become the wife of Egil, and

they would have the son Ull, then she would marry Thor. But before any of this, Loki Laufeyarson cut off all of Sif's hair for love of mischief. At the time it was thought to be a severe disgrace for a woman to have all of her hair cut off. When Thor learned of this he grabbed hold of Loki and would have broken every bone in his body had Loki not sworn to find a way to get the Dokkalfar to make hair from gold for Sif, which would grow like any other hair. Then Loki went to those Dwarves called the sons of Ivaldi, and they made the hair, Skidbladnir, and Odin's spear, called Gungnir.

2. Then Loki wagered his head with the Dwarf called Brokk-Dainn on whether his brother Sindri-Eitri would succeed in making three precious things as good as these were. And when they got to the workshop, Sindri put a pig's hide in the forge and told Brokk to work the bellows and not stop until he took out of the forge what he had put in. But as soon as Sindri left the smithy and the other began to pump air, a fly landed on Brokk's hand and bit him. Brokk continued, nevertheless, to work the bellows as before, and kept on until the smith pulled the work from the forge. It was a boar with bristles of gold.

3. Next, Sindri put gold on the forge. He asked the other to work the bellows and not stop pumping until he returned. Then he left. The fly returned and settled on Brokk's neck, and this time it bit twice as hard. Still, Brokk continued to pump until the smith took from the forge a gold ring, the one called Draupnir.

4. Then the smith placed iron in the forge, telling the other to pump air with the bellows. He said that his work would be ruined if the bellows failed. This time the fly landed between Brokk's eyes, biting his eyelids. Finally, with blood flowing into his eyes, he was unable to see. So, as quickly as he could, he took his hand from the bellows on the down stroke and swatted the fly away. At that moment the smith returned and said that everything in the forge had barely escaped ruin. Then he took a hammer from the forge, and entrusting all the treasures to his brother Brokk, he asked him to go to Asgard to settle the wager.

5. When Brokk and Loki arrived and displayed their treasures, the Aesir took their places on the thrones of Wyrd. Odin, Thor, and Frey were to be the judges, thus settling the matter. Loki gave to Odin the spear Gungnir; to Thor, the hair for Sif, and to Frey, Skidbladnir. He then described the characteristics of each of the treasures: the spear, Gungnir, had runes risted on its point. It always pierces cleanly through, never

stopping during the thrust; the hair would grow fast to the skin as soon as it came on to Sif's head; and Skidbladnir will receive a fair wind whenever its sail is raised, no matter where it is going. The sons of Ivaldi, in days of yore, created Skidbladnir, best of ships, for shining Frey, Njord's noble son. Powerful magic is called upon before something like it is crafted. That ship is so large that it can accommodate all the Aesir, along with their weapons and their war gear. The ship is made of so many different pieces and with so much cunning that, when it is not being used to travel on the sea, it can be folded up like a piece of cloth and placed in a pouch. It was built with the finest craftsmanship. But Naglfar, the largest ship, is owned by Loki-Muspel.

6. Brokk then brought out his treasures. He gave the ring to Odin, saying that every ninth night eight rings of equal weight would drip from it. To Frey he gave the boar, remarking that night or day it could race across the sky and over the sea better than any other mount. Furthermore, night would never be so murky nor the worlds of darkness so shadowy that the boar would not provide light wherever it went, so bright is the shining of its bristles. He is Hildisvini, also called Gullinbursti and Slidrugtanni, who was made by the two skillful Dwarves,

Dainn-Brokk and Nabbi-Sindri. Then Brokk gave the hammer to Thor, and said that with it Thor would be able to strike whatever came before him with as mighty a blow as he wished, because the hammer would never break. And if he decided to throw the hammer, it would never miss its mark, nor could it ever be thrown so far that it would not find its way back home to his hand, and if he liked, it is so small that it could be kept inside his shirt. There was, however, one defect: the handle was rather short.

XXXVI. Hrungnir

1. Once, when Thor had gone into the east to fight trolls, Odin rode Sleipnir into Jotunheim and came to an Etin named Hrungnir. Hrungnir asked who it was that wore a golden helmet and rode through the sky and over the sea on such a fine horse. Odin said he would wager his head that no horse in Jotunheim was its equal. Hrungnir answered that Sleipnir was a good horse, but let on that he himself had a horse that took far bigger strides, and "this horse is named Gullfaxi."

2. Losing his temper, Hrungnir jumped onto his horse and raced after Odin, hoping to repay him for his bragging. Odin galloped so fast that he stayed ahead of the Etin, always just over a hill. But Hrungnir was in such an

Etin-fury that he passed through the gate of Asgard before he realized it.

3. When he arrived at the hall doors, the Aesir invited him to drink. Walking into the hall, he demanded the drink. Then Thor's usual drinking vessels were brought out, and Hrungnir drained them all. The greatest mead-horns in Valhall are placed before Thor. When Hrungnir became drunk, there was no end to his boasting. He said he would lift up Valhall and take it to Jotunheim, bury Asgard, and kill all the Gods except Freya and Sif, whom he wanted to take home with him. When Freya went to serve him, he vowed that he would drink all of the Aesir's ale.

4. When the Aesir grew tired of Hrungnir's boasting they called on Thor, who quickly entered the hall, his hammer raised in the air. Enraged, he asked who had allowed the cunning Etin to drink there. Who had granted Hrungnir permission to be in Valhall, and why should Freya be serving him as though he were feasting among the Aesir? Then Hrungnir answered, his eyes showing no friendship for Thor. He said that Odin had invited him to drink and that he was there on Odin's safe conduct. Thor said he would regret the invitation before he left. Hrungnir replied to Asathor that there was little renown in killing him weaponless, but Thor

would find it a greater test of courage if he dared to fight him on the border at Grjotunagard.

5. "It was very foolish of me," said Hrungnir, "that I left my shield and whetstone at home. If I had my weapons here, we would now be testing each other in a duel; but as matters stand, however, I lay on you a charge of cowardly betrayal if you choose to kill me when I am weaponless." Thor wanted on no account to miss the opportunity to take part in a duel, because no one had ever challenged him before.

6. Hrungnir now went back the way he had come, galloping as fast as he could until he reached Jotunheim. There among the Etins his trip became famous, not least because a contest had been arranged between him and Thor. The Etins felt that there was much at stake in who would gain the victory, for it seemed to them that they would have little hope against Thor if Hrungnir was killed, since he was their strongest.

7. The Etins then fashioned a man from clay at Grjotunagard. He was nine leagues high and three leagues wide under the arms. They could not find a heart that was suitably large for him until they took one from a mare, but his heart became unsteady as soon as Thor arrived. Hrungnir had a heart that was famous. It was made of hard stone with three

sharp-pointed corners just like the carved symbol called Hrungnirsheart. His head was also made of stone, as was his shield, which was wide and thick. Holding his shield in front of him, he stood waiting at Grjotuna-gard for Thor. He had a whetstone for a weapon, and it rested ready on his shoulder. He was not a welcoming sight. Standing terrified at Hrungnir's side was the clay Etin, called Mokkurkalfi. It is said that, on seeing Thor, he wet himself.

8. Thor, accompanied by Thjalfi, went to the dueling ground. Thjalfi ran ahead to where Hrungnir stood and said to him: "You stand unprepared, Etin, holding your shield in front of you. Thor has seen you. He is traveling underneath the earth and will come at you from below."

9. Hrungnir then shoved his shield under his feet and stood on top of it, grasping the whetstone with both hands. He saw flashes of lightning and heard enormous claps of thunder. The terror of Etins [Thor] made a visit to the mound of Grjotun [Grjotuna-gard]. The son of Jord-Frigga [Thor] drove to the game of iron [battle] and Mani's path thundered beneath him. Wrath swelled in Meili-Baldur's brother [Thor].

10. All the hawks' sanctuaries [skies] found themselves burning because of Ull's stepfa-ther [Thor], and the ground all low was bat-tered with hail, when the goats drew the temple-power of the easy chariot [Thor] forward to the encounter with Hrungnir. Svolnir-Odin's widow [Frigga-Jord, i.e. the Earth] practically split apart.

11. Baldur's brother [Thor] did not spare there the greedy enemy of men [Hrungnir]. Mountains shook and rocks smashed; heaven burned above. I have heard that the watcher [Hrungnir] of the dark bone [rock] of the land [sea] of Haki's carriages [ships] moved violently in opposition when he saw his warlike slayer.

12. Hrungnir saw Thor in his divine rage. Swiftly flew the pale ring-ice [shield] beneath the soles of the rock-guarder [Etin]. The Bonds [Gods] caused this, the ladies of the fray [Valkyries] wished it. The rock-gentleman [Hrungnir] did not have to wait long after that for a swift blow from the tough multitude-smashing friend [Thor] of hammer-face-troll [Mjollnir].

13. Thor was rushing towards Hrungnir, but when still at a long distance away, he raised his hammer and threw it at Hrungnir. The Etin, using both hands, lifted his whetstone and threw it towards Thor. The whetstone struck the hammer in mid flight and broke in two. One part fell to the earth, and from it come all whetstones. The other part pierced Thor's head so that he fell to the ground.

And the hard fragment of the whetstone of the visitor [Hrungnir] of the woman of Vingnir's people [Etins] whizzed at ground's [Frigga-Jord's] son [Thor] into his brain-ridge [head], so that the steel-pumice, still stuck in Odin's boy's [Thor's] skull, stood there spattered with Eindridi-Thor's blood.

14. But the hammer Mjollnir landed right in the middle of Hrungnir's head. It smashed his skull into small pieces, and he fell forward, landing on top of Thor with his leg lying across Thor's neck. The life-spoiler [Thor] of Beli's bale-troops [Etins] made the bear [Etin] of the noisy storms' secret refuge [mountain fastness] fall on the shield-islet. There sank down the gully-land [mountain] prince [Etin] before the tough hammer and the rock-Dan-breaker [Thor] forced back the mighty defiant one.

15. Meanwhile, Thjalfi attacked Mokkurkalfi, who fell in such a way that it is hardly worth a story. Roskva's brother [Thjalfi] stood enraged, Magni's father [Thor] had struck a victorious blow. Neither Thor nor Thjalfi's power-stone [heart] shakes with terror.

16. Thjalfi then went to Thor, intending to lift Hrungnir's leg off him, but he could not move it. When they learned that Thor had fallen, all the Aesir came and tried to lift the leg, but they could not budge it. Then Magni, the son of Thor and Jarnsaxa, arrived; he was three winters old at the time. He flung Hrungnir's leg off Thor and said, "It is a great shame, father, that I came so late. I imagine that I would have killed this Etin with my fist, had I met him."

17. Thor stood up and, greeting his son warmly, declared that he would become powerful. "And," he said, "I want to give you the horse Gullfaxi," which Hrungnir had owned.

18. Then Odin spoke. He said that Thor was wrong to give so fine a horse to the son of a Giantess, instead of Thor's own father.

19. Thor then returned home to Thrudvang, and the whetstone remained stuck in his head. Then the seeress called Groa arrived, the wife of Aurvandill the Bold, otherwise known as Egil. Olgefjun [Groa] began to enchant the red boaster of being rust's bale [whetstone] from the inclined slopes [head] of the wound-giving God's [Thor's] hair. She sang her spells over Thor until the whetstone began to loosen. When Thor felt that, he expected the whetstone would soon be removed. Wanting to please and reward Groa for her healing, he told the story of his return from the north, and how he had waded across the river Elivagar, carrying Aurvandill-Egil southwards from Jotunheim

on his back in a basket. He recounted that one of Aurvandill-Egil's toes had stuck out from the basket and had frozen. Thor broke it off and threw it up into the heavens as a token, making from it the star called Aurvandilstoe. Thor added that it would not be long before Aurvandill-Egil returned home. Then Groa became so happy that she couldn't remember any of her magic, and the whetstone got no looser but remained lodged in Thor's head. And it is offered as a warning that one should not throw a whetstone across a floor, because then the whetstone in Thor's head moves.

XXXVII. Byrgir

1. One day in Ivaldi's kingdom, Svithjod the Cold, in the woods near his own stronghold, the spring called Byrgir was discovered. This was the store of mead that had been hidden by Fjalar before, which had been stolen from Mimir's fountain. Ivaldi had kept the discovery a secret and, when night had fallen, he sent his two youngest children, the girl Idun-Bil and the boy Hjuki-Slagfin–who were still living with him– and a pail to fetch this mead and carry it home.

2. But the children never returned. The moon had come up while they were at the well, where Mani had spotted them. He and Ivaldi were not friends. In earlier times,

Ivaldi had carried away Mani's daughter, Sunna, and married her without her father's consent.

3. Mani would now avenge his daughter's theft. He took the children Hjuki-Slagfin and Idun-Bil from the earth while they were walking from the Byrgir well. They were carrying between them on their shoulders the pole called Simul and the pail called Saeg. Idun looked up at the moon and said:

4. "Little man who goes yonder and beholds house after house! Drink this mead with us! We would like to know you, but we cannot get to you."

5. These children follow Mani, as can be seen from the earth. He took the mead as well. Mani treated them tenderly, for they were his daughter's children. Idun had received the rank of Asynja.

6. Ivaldi was very bitter about the loss he had suffered. That Mani took his children could be seen as just compensation, but that he also robbed him of the mead, this was too great a price, and filled Ivaldi with thoughts of revenge. He could see the moon-chariot from his high fortress in Svithjod the Cold every day as it traveled its path. He planned an ambush for it and attacked it with fire at night, and robbed it of its mead store. Slagfin defended his foster-father and in this conflict he received a wound clean to the

thigh-bone from his father. From then on Slagfin bore the names Geldur, Hengest, and Jalk.

7. Ivaldi abandoned his post, where he protected the Elivagar from Hrimthurses, thereby breaking the oath that he had sworn to the Gods. And so that the mead would not fall into their hands again, he quickly carried it down to Fjalar's realm, Sokkdalir, and returned it to the one who had originally stolen the mead and created the Byrgir fountain. The mead was kept in the farthest depths of his mountain halls, in Hnitbjorg, where Fjalar put it in the charge of his daughter, Gunnlod. It was arranged that Ivaldi would marry Fjalar's daughter Gunnlod and that they would own the mead together. Ivaldi had thus for all time made himself into an enemy of the Gods. He left Fjalar to ally himself with Jotunheim's Etins, but would return on the determined day and celebrate his wedding with Gunnlod.

8. Odin was not ignorant of what had happened in the darkness down there in Fjalar's realm. His ravens Hugin and Munin daily fly over Jormungrund, and they not only see what occurs in its beautiful and bright regions, they also spy on that which happens in the misty Niflheim and in Sokkdalir, where Fjalar rules. There and in Niflheim are the ravens exposed to dangers, and Odin

fears that it could go badly for them, but so far their wisdom has protected them, and every evening they have returned to Valhall, sat on Asafather-Odin's shoulders and spoke in his ear what they had found out. It was through them that Odin got to know where Ivaldi had hidden the mead and when his marriage with Gunnlod would take place. There lives in Fjalar's realm day-shy Dwarves who perform bond-services for him and his clan. One of them was Fjalar's door-watcher. He promised to Odin that he would help in the adventure, which he now went to try.

9. Odin set out from home to seek out the ancient Etin, in Sokkdalir. The day had come when Ivaldi would celebrate his marriage with Gunnlod. Fjalar's kinsmen were gathered in his illuminated halls, and guests, belonging to the clan of Hrimthurses, had come there from Jotunheim. A golden chair for the expected bridegroom was placed in front, opposite Fjalar's seat of honor at the drinking table. The Bridal would also be a celebration of the alliance between Ivaldi and the powers hostile to the Gods. It brought great joy among them and they now believed they had a good chance of overthrowing the Aesir and destroying Midgard. The watch the Gods had established by Hvergelmir was abandoned by Ivaldi and

Ivaldi himself was a mighty champion, well suited to lead the hordes of Jotunheim into battle.

10. The bridegroom came at a good time. The doors were opened which separated the intense lighting inside the Etin's halls from the darkness that broods over the depths of his dales, and in stepped the stately Ivaldi who was greeted and led to his golden chair.

11. But the guest of honor was not who he seemed to be. He was Odin, who had assumed Ivaldi's form. Odin had climbed down into Suttung-Fjalar's gloomy chasm and walked over the devious paths in Sokkdalir. Odin had no difficulty in finding his way through the darkness, for he had Heimdall as his companion, who can see a hundred leagues in front of him through the darkest night. Heimdall had brought his fire-auger, which has the drilling and splitting power of lightning when its owner places it against the base of mountains. When they reached Hnitbjorg the Gods separated. Heimdall went up onto the roof of the fortress. He can hear the slightest sound, so he could also hear all that went on down there. The day-shy hall-guardian who stood outside the doors of Hnitbjorg, saw Odin coming through the darkness, and opened the door for him.

12. Then a merry feast was celebrated there. The bridegroom was cheerful and verbose and the guests had never heard a man who put his words so well and had so much to relate that was worth listening to. Little did Odin get there by silence; in many words he spoke to his advantage in Suttung-Fjalar's halls. But it was necessary for him to express himself with great caution at the same time, for an imprudent word was dangerous and he could lose his head. Caution was not so difficult to exercise in the beginning, but it became harder later on.

13. During the feast's proceedings, the bridegroom was to be honored by having his drinking horn filled with the liquids from Byrgir's well. On the golden seat, Gunnlod gave Odin a draught of the precious mead. She took a horn full of the mead and gave it to him, to bind him to her.

14. Then the wedding proceeded, and Odin and Gunnlod swore the oath of faithfulness to each other on the holy ring.

15. The joyous feast was continued, and the horns were filled frequently, especially the bridegroom's. Ivaldi was not only known as the great spear-champion, but also as a drinking champion, equal to Hrungnir and coming closest to Thor in this sport. Because of this he was also called Svidur, SVidir, or Sveigdir. In order to present himself to eve-

ryone as Ivaldi, Odin had to drink a lot, more than he could. He once spoke of this:

16. The heron of oblivion,
    which steals one's wit
    hovers over the sumbel.
    I was fettered
    with this bird's feathers
    in Gunnlod's dwelling.

17. I was drunk,
    I was very drunk,
    at that cunning Fjalar's;
    it's the best sumbel
    when each gets home
    retaining sense and reason.

18. It was no longer easy for Odin to weigh his words, and over his lips now came such that the less drunk among the guests thought it strange for these words to be uttered by Ivaldi, and later in the night they contemplated this after the feast was finished, and they became suspicious.

19. The banquet was at last concluded, and Odin and Gunnlod departed to the bridal chamber. From there a path went through the mountain to the room where the precious Byrgir mead was stored. Gunnlod showed Odin this treasury, and Heimdall, who listened above there and heard what they said, set the fire-auger to its roof. Gunnlod had given her husband her whole soul, her fervent love, and took the vows she swore to him with devout solemnity. Rati-Heimdall's mouth, which struck the rock, made room

for Odin's passage, and gnawed a space in the stone; above and below were the paths of Etins.

20. But Allfather-Odin would not leave from there without a struggle. His careless words bore fruit: a brother of Gunnlod had been kept awake by the thoughts the words aroused in him, and he burst into the mountain chamber where Odin and Gunnlod were, just as Odin was ready to escape. Odin had to fight and kill him. Odin was called Svidur and SVidir at Sokkmimir-Fjalar's, and beguiled that ancient Etin, at the time when he alone became the slayer of Midvitnir-Fjalar's famous son. It is doubtful that he could have left from the Etin's court, had Gunnlod not aided him–he won the heart of that good woman, whom he took in his embrace.

21. Then Odin turned himself into the form of an eagle and flew as hard as he could. He came out, and flew in eagle-guise with Byrgir's mead in the pail Saeg up through the bored passageway that Heimdall's fire-auger had opened, from Fjalar's misty world to the bright regions to the gleaming Asgard. The mead was the drink, which Odin bore from Surt's Sokkdalir.

22. When Suttung saw the eagle's flight he got his own eagle shape and flew after Odin. And when the Aesir saw Odin they put their

containers out in the courtyard, and when Odin came in over Asgard he dumped the mead into the containers, from Saeg, but it was such a close thing for him that Suttung-Fjalar might have caught him. Odin gave Suttung-Fjalar's mead to the Aesir and to those men who know how to make poetry. From the well changed litur he had reaped great advantage: few things fail the wise, for the mead has been brought up to men's earthly dwellings.

23. On the following day the Hrimthurses came to learn of the high-union, in the hall of the high-union; they asked about Bolverk-Odin: were he back among the Gods, or had Suttung-Fjalar destroyed him? Suttung-Fjalar was deceived, his sumbel stolen, and Gunnlod cried for her lost kinsman.

24. Ivaldi, the true bridegroom, arrived at Fjalar's castle not long after Odin. But he never made it inside. He came to Hnitbjorg, where there was a stone as big as a large house. As he entered he cast his eye upon the stone, and saw that a Dwarf was sitting under it. Ivaldi ran towards the stone. The Dwarf stood in the door and called to Ivaldi-Sveigdir, told him to come in, and he should see Odin. Ivaldi ran into the stone, which instantly closed behind him, and Ivaldi-Sveigdir never came back. The day-shy hall guard of Durnir-Surt's descendants deceived

Sveigdir-Ivaldi when he, the dauntless son of Dulsi, ran after the Dwarf into the rock, and when the shining Etin-inhabited hall of Sokkmimir-Surt's kinsmen yawned against the jarl. Some say that Ivaldi was crushed under the boulders that were tossed down from the mountain.

25. The mead is kept in the ship-like, silver chariot of the moon, and was thus returned to Mani. It has the quality of not being diminished when one drinks from it. Odin was invited to partake of the moon-ship's mead, and he goes there often, after he finishes his day's work, as the chariot slowly sinks toward the western horizon. It is called Sokkvabekk, over which cool billows in soughing sounds flow; there Odin and Saga-Idun, joyful each day, drink from golden goblets. Idun is Byrgis Argefn, and is also called Olgefn. The skalds pray that she may be gracious to them, and ask if the noble Bil-Idun will favor them.

26. From Odin's union with Gunnlod was born a son, Bragi. He is renowned for wisdom and especially for eloquence and command of language. He is especially knowledgeable about poetry, and because of him poetry is called *bragr*, and from his name a person is said to be a *bragr* [chief] of men or women who has eloquence beyond others, whether it is a woman or a man. Idun is his

wife. Bragi is the best of skalds, and runes are risted on his tongue. He is called the Inventor of Poetry and Inn Sidskeggja As. It is from his name that the expression "*Skegg-bragi*" comes for someone who has a big beard. Bragi was allowed to drink of the Byrgir mead, which gave him the power of speech and eloquence. Thriggi-Odin's kinsmen's find, the one that had been kept secret, was in time's past carried from Jotunheim into Nokkvi-Mani's ship, where Bragi, unharmed, refreshes himself.

27. Mani is lord of the Heiptir, and he keeps the limar with which these maidens of revenge are armed. Thus he is also called Eylimi. Because Ivaldi, the drink-champion and mead-thief, attacked and burnt the moon, his punishment in the afterlife was that he would never see the realms of bliss, in Asgard or Hel. Instead, he remains on the moon, and there he carries Mani's bundle of limar until Ragnarok.

XXXVIII. <u>Sunna</u>

1. Once Ivaldi had rebelled against the Gods it was determined that his wife, Sunna, must be procured from her husband's lands so she would not fall into the hands of the Etins.

2. Almost from her cradle she displayed such true modesty that she had her face perpetually veiled to prevent her fine looks arousing anyone's passions. She was kept apart from others in Ivaldi's home, stayed under very close supervision, and was given two poisonous serpents to rear, intending that these reptiles should act as her protectors when they had eventually grown to full size. No one could easily pry into her bedroom when entry was blocked by such a dangerous barrier. It was decreed that anyone who tried to get in unsuccessfully should at once be decapitated, and have his head impaled on a stake.

3. Heimdall, believing that the more perilous an enterprise the more brilliant it was, and wishing to bring Sunna back among the Gods, declared himself a suitor. He was told to subdue the creatures which kept guard by the girl's room, for now that Ivaldi was dead it was decided that only their vanquisher should enjoy her embraces. To aggravate their ferocity towards him, he wrapped his body in a pelt wet with blood. Draped in this he soon approached the confining doors where, grasping a bar of red-hot steel in a pair of tongs, he thrust it down the serpent's gaping throat and laid it lifeless on the floor. Next, as the other serpent swept forward in a rippling glide, he destroyed it by hurling his spear straight between its open fangs. Heimdall brought Sunna back to her father, Mani, and asked for her hand, but Mani answered

that he would only take as his son-in-law the man his daughter had chosen freely and genuinely.

4. As the girl's mother, Sol, was the only one to grudge the suitor's petition, she examined her daughter's heart in an intimate conversation. When the princess warmly praised her wooer's excellence, the mother abused her bitterly, saying she had lost all sense of shame and had been won by baited looks. She had not formed any proper judgment of his virtue, but, gazing with an unprincipled mind, had been tickled by his enticing appearance.

5. Once Sunna had been prevailed upon to despise the young God, she changed into a man's clothing and from being a highly virtuous maiden began to lead the life of a savage marauder. Many girls of the same persuasion enrolled in her company by the time she chanced to arrive at a spot where a band of Vikings were mourning the loss of their leader, who had been killed in fighting. Because of her beauty, she was elected their jarl and performed feats beyond a woman's courage.

6. Heimdall undertook many fatiguing voyages in her pursuit until, during winter, he came across a fleet of Svartalfar. At that time of year the running waters solidified so that a vast pack of ice gripped their vessels and, however strongly they rowed, they could make no progress. Since the prolonged cold guaranteed the prisoners a fairly safe footing, Heimdall ordered his men to test the frozen bight of the sea after putting on brogues; if they dispensed with slippery shoes, he said, they could dash over the icy surface with a better balance. As the Svartalfar supposed they had prepared their heels for a speedy flight, they came in to do battle; however, they could only make a lurching advance, for the smoothness beneath their soles gave their feet an unsteady hold. Since the Danes with Heimdall were able to move across the ice-bound deep more securely, they crushed their adversaries, who could only totter along.

7. After this victory, they steered towards Finland. It so happened that when a party was sent into a narrow gulf to scout, they discovered the harbor occupied by a handful of ships. Sunna had sailed before them with her fleet into the same confined inlet. Immediately she caught sight of unfamiliar craft in the distance, and with rapid rowing she shot off to encounter them, judging it wiser to burst on an enemy than lie waiting for him. Though his companions were warning him not to attempt a larger number of vessels with his own, Heimdall replied how intolerable it would be if anyone reported to

Sunna that his purposeful course was upset by a few boats in his path; it would be wrong to let such a petty circumstance tarnish the fine record of their enterprises. The Danes were filled with astonishment when they found what graceful, shapely-limbed opponents they had.

8. When the sea-fight had started, young Heimdall leapt on to Sunna's prow and forced his way up to the stern, slaughtering all who resisted him. His comrade Borgar-Jarl struck off Sunna's helmet, but seeing the smoothness of her chin, realized that they ought not to be fighting with weapons but with kisses; they should lay down their hard spears and handle their foes more persuasively. Heimdall was overjoyed when, beyond all expectation, he had presented to him the girl he had sought tirelessly over land and sea despite so many perilous obstacles. He laid hands on her more lovingly and compelled her to change back into feminine clothing; afterwards Mani gave Sunna in marriage to Heimdall-Glen. The God-blithe bedfellow of Glen will step to her divine sanctuary with brightness; then the good light of grey-clad Mani shall descend.

XXXIX. <u>Vartari</u>

1. The day had now come when Odin, Frey, and Thor had to pronounce their verdict in the case between Sindri and Loki. The real question was whether Loki had lost the case and thus had to forfeit his head to Sindri or not. Before the appointed time, Sindri's brother Brokk appeared at the Thingstead of the Gods, Glitnir, to take Loki's head on the spot should the verdict allow it. Mimir and his Underworld artists did not like Loki. They knew that he desired the fall of the Gods, the devastation of Yggdrasil, and the ruin of the worlds.

2. The verdict must be supported by an unbiased and precise comparison between Sindri's work and Volund's. If Volund's were better than Sindri's, then Loki won the bet. If the opposite were true, he had lost.

3. Brokk was a well-spoken advocate for his brother's work. But neither Volund nor any other son of Ivaldi appeared to testify before the Thing. They had not been privy to the bet. They never dreamed of competing with Sindri or allowing a judgment to be passed on the treasures they gave to the Aesir in reverance and friendship.

4. Their decision was that the hammer was the best out of all the precious things and provided the greatest defense against the Hrimthurses, and they decreed that the Dwarf had won the stake. Then Loki offered to redeem his head; the Dwarf said there was no chance of that.

5. "Catch me then," said Loki.

6. But when Brokk tried to catch him, he was far out of reach. Loki had some shoes with which he could run across sky and sea. Then the Dwarf told Thor to catch him, and he did so. Then the Dwarf was going to cut off Loki's head, but Loki said the head was his, but not the neck. Then the Dwarf got a thong and a knife and tried to pierce holes in Loki's lips and was going to stitch up his mouth, but the knife would not cut. Then he said it would be better if his brother Al was there, and as soon as he spoke his name the awl was there, and it pierced the lips. He stitched the lips together, and it tore the edges off. The thong that Loki's mouth was stitched up with is called Vartari.

7. Loki's lips were soon free again, but the scars from Sindri's awl never went away. Thus his mouth took on an ugly sneer befitting a mocker. From that day forward, Loki's good looks were spoiled.

8. Shortly, the judgment on the works of Ivaldi's sons were known in all worlds and their enemies were filled with malicious glee. But Sindri himself felt no joy in his victory. He had been defrauded of his prize, and he knew that the judgment would have dangerous consequences. Sindri knew Volund's temperament and his power, for Volund had once been an apprentice in Sindri's smithy.

XL. Niflungs

1. Frey had been staying with his foster-father, Volund, when the news came to the Ivaldi sons that Odin had caused their father's death and that Volund's forgings were compared with Sindri's and had failed.

2. Volund and Egil met to talk, but said nothing to each other. Nor did they want weregild from Odin for their father's death. Volund, as usual, was friendly to his foster-son and hid their newfound anger from him. But the magnificent, gold-stitched tapestries in the brothers' halls were taken down and among the best of the gold ornaments and weapons, which shined on their walls, were gradually removed. Their previously filled treasure chamber was now emptied. They fled to the dark regions beyond the Nidafjoll. Those treasures that were not recovered by famous heroes in a later time still lie in caverns and mountain-halls, where they are brooded over by serpents, or immersed in deep stream beds, where they are watched by wights who hold on to nearby rocks in the river or strand ridges. Because Ivaldi and his sons are known as Niflungs and Gjukungs, their treasure is known as the Niflung Hoard; hence gold is called Niflung treasure or inheritance.

3. The Gods began to think that the Ivaldi sons had reason to be dissatisfied with them.

Njord, whose son was in Volund's possession and care, was worried. He consulted with Odin about what should be done, and it was decided that Volund would be honored by a tying of bonds of kinship with the Gods. Njord would ask his daughter Skadi to be his wife, and she would thus be elevated to an Asynja. In this way the Gods would make up for the judgment that was pronounced over Volund's forgings and show how they valued him. They would give compensation for Ivaldi's death, even though he broke his oath to them and had caused his own ruin.

4. Njord sent messengers, selected among the Vanir who followed under him, to Volund. The messengers were to deliver Njord's marriage request, but they never returned. Volund was vexed to meet this obstinate demand for a suit. In a cruel endeavor to check this impudent wooer's ardor, he rushed the envoys off to execution. While they waited for the messengers to return, Odin decided to seek out Volund himself, accompanied by Hoenir and Loki.

5. The visit would be made in all simplicity, and without bringing any attention to them in the world. Odin did not put his golden armor on Sleipnir's back, but he and his companions dressed themselves in the custom of ordinary travelers and subjected

themselves to the same conditions. So they came to Ydalir. Here they wandered for a long time in peaceful dales between snow-capped mountain peaks, but they could not find the way to Yset. Volund had a sharper eye on the Gods than they on him, was as great a sorcerer as he was an artist, and was equally proficient with the evil Seid as with the holy Galdur. He arranged it so that the three Gods traveled to many caverns, but never to the right one. At a certain place he had an ambush planned, and he finally directed the travelers' course there. It was by a well in an oak-covered valley, where it seemed inviting to rest. There he laid down a magical instrument that he had forged, which looked like an ordinary pole or stick.

6. Odin, Loki, and Hoenir had traveled across mountains and wilderness, where they found little food. The lady-wolf [Volund] flew noisily to meet the commanders of the crew [Gods] no short time ago in an old-one's [eagle's] form. When the Gods came down into a certain valley, they saw a herd of reindeer and took one of them, the one called a talhreinn, and set it in an earth-oven. Long ago the eagle alighted where the Aesir put their meat in an earth-oven. The Mountain-Tyr [Volund] of Byrgis Argefn [Idun] was not found guilty of cowardice. And when they thought the meat must be

ready, they opened the earth-oven and it was not cooked. The talhreinn was quite hard between the bones for the Gods to cut. And a second time, when they opened the oven after some time had passed, it was still not cooked. As they began asking each other what could be the cause, they heard a voice from above in an oak tree under which they were standing. The one who was up in the tree said that he was the reason the food remained uncooked in the oven. Looking up they saw an eagle sitting there, and it was not small.

7. They asked: "Why do you cause this, ornament-giver of the Gods, concealed in a guise?"

8. The much-wise corpse-heap-wave [blood]-gull [eagle] began to speak from an ancient fir. Hoenir's friend [Loki] was not well disposed to him. The eagle said: "If you will grant me my fill of the reindeer, then the oven will cook."

9. They agreed to this. The mountain-wolf [Volund] asked Step-Meili [Hoenir] to share out to him his fill from the holy table. The raven-God's [Odin's] friend [Loki] had to blow on the fire. Then the eagle glided down from the tree and landed on the oven. The Rognir [Volund] of the winged cars [feather-guises] of land-whales [Etins] let himself drop down where the guileless defenders of the Gods were sitting. The gracious lord of earth [Odin] bade Farbauti's son [Loki] quickly share the bow-string Var's [Skadi's] whale [reindeer] among the fellows. But the cunning, unyielding opponent of Aesir [Volund] thereupon snatched up four reindeer-parts from the place for a spread feast. The first thing he did was eat the reindeer's two thighs and both of its shoulders. And the hungry father of swords [Volund] was then eating the yoke-bear horribly at the roots of the oak– that was long ago. This angered Loki, who picked up a large pole and swung with all his strength. The deep-minded war-booty withholding God [Loki] struck the mightiest enemy of earth [Volund] down between the shoulder with the pole.

10. Recoiling from the blow, the eagle started to fly, but one end of the pole was stuck fast to the eagle's body, with Loki hanging on the other end. So the burden of Sigyn's arms [Loki], whom all the Powers eye in his bonds, got stuck to the Ondurgod's [Skadi's] fosterer [Volund]. The pole clung to the powerful haunter of Jotunheim [Volund], and the hand of Hoenir's good friend [Loki] to the end of the rod.

11. The eagle flew so low that Loki's feet were dragged on the ground, striking stones, gravel, and trees, and he thought his arms would be pulled from their sockets. The bird

of blood [eagle], happy with its booty, flew a long distance with the wise God [Loki], so that the wolf's father [Loki] was about to rip in two. Then Thor's friend [Volund] tired out, for Lopt-Loki was heavy– he who journeyed with Midjung's [Volund's] mate [Idun, hence Loki], could now sue for peace. He called out, begging the eagle for mercy, but the bird answered that Loki would not be saved unless he swore an oath that he would find a way to lure Idun, with her apples, out of Asgard. The scion of Hymir's race [Volund, who joins the Etins] instructed the crew-guider [Loki], crazy with pain, to bring him the maid who possessed the Ellilyf Asa [Idun]. When Loki agreed, he was set free and returned to his companions. Nothing else is said to have occurred during this trip before they reached home.

12. In Asgard, Odin had nothing good to report about the journey. So Njord decided to go there himself. Baldur and Hod offered to accompany him. They armed themselves, climbed into their saddles, and set out. The purpose of the journey was not war, but reconciliation. For this reason Njord did not want to be accompanied by Thor, or Tyr, or any of the other Aesir, as they were quick to strike. Admittedly, Hod had been violent by nature in his early childhood, but under Baldur's influence he had become peaceable

and was counted among the Gods called Ljonar, of whom Baldur was foremost.

13. The three Gods came to Volund's fortress, but found it empty. They then rode to Egil's fortress by the Elivagar. To their surprise, they noticed that here and there in the distance Jotunheim's inhabitants peered out at them. Previously, the Etins had never come over the Elivagar to the coasts of Ydalir. But the watch of the sons of Ivaldi on these waters had ceased, thus allowing the Etins to come, as many as wanted to, into the land that the Aesir had created for the race of man. Njord and his companions quickened their ride and soon caught sight of whom they sought: Volund. He was accompanied by Egil and the third brother, Slagfin. They were on their way to Jotunheim. The three brothers stopped when they saw the Gods approach and Volund yelled, "What do you want?" Njord responded that he wanted peace with his son's guardian and foster-father, with the Gods' good friend and gift-giver. "No peace," cried Volund, "without revenge!"

14. Njord then inquired as to where Frey was. Volund told him that his son had been delivered to the Etins. "Damn you, who has broken sacred oaths!," was Njord's reply. Volund then said, "Damn the oath itself, you unjust judges, you incompetent Gods!"

15. "We are done with words," yelled Hod, "now weapons will talk. Treacherous sons of Ivaldi, will you stand and fight?" At this, Egil stepped forward and challenged Njord. "You of low-birth, you thrall!," shouted Hod. "Do you dare challenge one of Asgard's finest?"

16. Egil was then challenged by Hod to prevent Njord from encountering an ignoble person. As Hod was attaching an arrow to the string of his bent bow, a shaft shot by Egil suddenly pierced the cord at the top. It was succeeded by a fellow arrow, which dug into the knuckles of his fist. A third appeared and struck the arrow fitted to his bow-string. Egil, intentionally using his talent for long-range archery to merely hit his foe's weapon, tried to discourage the champion from his purpose by indicating that he could easily do the same to his body. Nevertheless, Hod's nerve was not in the least diminished; he despised hazard to his person and entered danger with spirit and expression unaltered, seeming neither to make any acknowledgement of Egil's skill nor remit any of his usual valor. Quite undeterred from his intent, he fearlessly devoted himself to the duel. Both combatants were wounded and withdrew.

17. Now behind the sons of Ivaldi appeared a number of their new allies, a host of dreadful Etins who belonged to Beli's clan, whose heads were like hounds. Volund had surrendered Frey to them. They came in a fog and mist that obscured the whole area. The sons of Ivaldi fled and vanished into the haze. Hod possessed a dog of unusual savagery, a horrifying, vicious brute which was a terror for people to live with, for it had quite often killed a dozen men unaided. The creature was a pet of the Etin Offoti and would guard his herd while it was grazing. Hod unleashed his hound, set it on his adversaries, which caused them to fall back. But Ivaldi's sons were gone, and it was then that the Gods knew that their errand was lost. In sorrow, they rode back to Asgard.

18. Before the sons of Ivaldi continued on their way, they laid hands on one of Egil's arrows and swore they would never work again in the service of others, and that their freedom may be regarded as established, which they confirmed in their accustomed way on the arrow, uttering certain words of their country in confirmation of the fact.

19. Then they traveled on to the Ironwood.

The Copper Age

XLI. Idun

1. At the agreed time, Loki lured Idun out through Asgard into a certain forest, saying that he had found some apples that she would think worth having, and told her she should bring her apples with her and compare them with these. Then Volund arrived in eagle-guise and snatched Idun and flew away with her to the Ironwood .

2. But the Aesir were badly affected by Idun's disappearance and soon became grey and old. The bright-shield-dwellers [Etins] were not unhappy after this, now Idun was among the Etins, newly arrived from the south. All Ingi-Frey's kin [Aesir] became old and grey in their assembly; the Powers were rather ugly in form.

XLII. Leikin

1. There was an Etin named Grepp, who desired to have Freya as his bride, but when he realized his attempts would be ineffective he bribed a woman to become Freya's attendant and secure her friendship. Eventually, she found a cunning excuse for departing the palace, Sessrumnir, and inveigled Freya far from her home. Soon after, Grepp rushed on her and carried her off to his narrow den on a mountain ledge. Grepp belonged to Beli's clan, who had already obtained Freya's brother, Frey.

2. Then the Powers all went to their Things-eats, the high-holy Gods to consider thereon: who had filled all the air with evil? Or had given Od's maid [Freya] to the Etin race? There was no doubt that an Etin had taken the Goddess, and they knew someone would have had to betray her for this to happen. They discovered the culprit. It was an Etin-maid whom Freya had adopted into her royal household, and they made yet another discovery: that the treacherous Etin-maid was Gullveig reborn. Furthermore, they learned that Gullveig had continued spreading the evil Seid, and indeed had taught Freya herself this evil art, for Njord's daughter Freya first taught the Aesir the Seid, as it was put in use and fashion among the Vanir as well. Gullveig had also used this art to enchant Freya so she could be subdued by Grepp.

3. Thor then caught Gullveig and gave her a death-blow with his hammer; once more the witch's corpse was held over a flame. Yet once again it happened that her Urcold heart

was only half-burnt. Loki ate the heart, which laid in the embers, and half-burnt he found the woman's [Gullveig's] heart; Lopt-Loki was soon with child from the woman, and thence came Leikin among men.

4. Loki traveled to Jotunheim and gave birth to Leikin by Gnipalund on Thorsnes. And when the Gods realized Leikin was being brought up in Jotunheim, and when the Gods traced prophecies stating that from her great mischief and disaster would arise for them, then they felt all evil was to be expected from her, to begin with because of her mother's nature, but still worse because of her father's.

5. Then Allfather-Odin sent Gods to seize Leikin and bring her to him. When she appeared before him, he had Thor throw her down into Niflheim and made her rule over nine worlds. She had the power to dole out punishments to those who are sent to her, and they are nidings who have committed serious crimes. She has there an enormous dwelling, with walls of immense height and huge gates. Her hall is called Eljudnir, her dish is Hungur, her knife is Sult, her slave is Ganglati, and Ganglot is her maidservant. The threshold over which people enter is a pitfall called Fallandaforad, her bed is named Kor, and her bed curtains are named Blikjandabol. Thor broke Leikin's bones,

and she is half-black and half flesh-colored, and is easily recognized from this. She has a stooping gait and is rather fierce-looking.

6. Leikin is a kveldrider. The horse she rides is black, untamed, difficult to manage, and ugly-grown. It drinks human blood, and is accompanied by other horses belonging to Leikin, black and bloodthirsty like it. They are intended for those persons whom Leikin causes to die from disease, and whom she is to conduct to Hel, the realm of Urd. Her horse is three-legged, and its appearance brings sickness, epidemics and plagues. These diseases are extremely dangerous, but are not always fatal. When they are not fatal, the convalescent is regarded as having ransomed his life with that tribute of loss of strength and of the torture which the disease caused him. He has thus given death a bushel of oats, that is, its horse. Leikin rides in the time of a plague on her three-legged horse and kills people.

7. Leikin brings the doom of the Norns, and the summons to Gimle to those who die of disease. When famine or pestilence is at hand it is said that Leikin is out riding her three-legged horse. When a bright spot, called Urd's Moon, appears on the wall, it forebodes the breaking out of an epidemic.

8. In Niflheim, the wights of disease made Leikin their queen. Her realm is Niflhel, and

she serves Urd in distributing justice to nid-ings. Her many brothers are called the Ban-ings.

XLIII. Groa

1. There was a king whose name was Kon, also Halfdan the Old, who was the most re-nowned of all kings. He held a great blot at Midwinter and made an offering in order to be granted that he might live in his kingdom for three hundred years. But the reply he got was that he would live no longer than one human life, but that there would be three hundred years during which there would be neither female nor non-noble male in his line of descent. He was a great warrior and went far and wide through eastern lands. He fared skillfully with all weapons, but his fa-vorite weapon was the club.

2. One day he was walking through a tract of shady woodland when he tore up by its roots an oak which blocked his path, and by simp-ly stripping off its branches shaped it into a hefty cudgel. Armed with this weapon, he composed a short song:

3. "See! This rough block which
    I bear with my proud head
    will bring gashes and death
    to other heads.
    Never a more fearful
    token shall scourge
    Jotunheim's people
    than this leafy weapon of wood.

4. "It will split the haughty sinews
    of their bulging necks,
    crush their hollow temples
    with its bulk of timber,
    a club which will tame
    our country's madness;
    nothing shall be more
    lethal to the Etins.

5. "Breaking bones,
    dashing through
    their mangled limbs,
    its torn-off stump
    will thrash
    their wicked backs."

6. When Egil fled with his brothers to the Wolfdales he left behind his wife, Groa, and asked her to go to her father, Sigtryg, who was a jarl among the Alfar and friend of Ivaldi's sons. Sigtryg had his stronghold in Greater Svithjod, where Svarinsmound now lay.

7. When the Ivaldi sons stopped watching the Elivagar, there came many Etins over to the northernmost Midgard and put up resi-dence there. Thor made a journey there in order to either drive away or kill these dan-gerous settlers, and Kon got to follow his Asa-Father on the journey. When he chanced to learn that Groa, the daughter of Sigtryg, was married to Egil, who had allied himself with the Etins, he cursed such an unwanted connection of divine blood and began a war, intending to oppose the exer-tions of monsters with a truly heroic brav-

ery. On entering Gotland he put on goat-skins to intimidate anyone who appeared in his path; accoutred thus in an assortment of animal hides, with a terrifying club in his right hand, he impersonated an Etin. Groa met him as she happened to be riding to the forest-pools to bathe, a small group of handmaids attending her on foot. Kon and Hamal met the women, right and fair and worthy to look on, who rode in exceeding noble array; but Groa far excelled them all. Thinking it was her husband, but at the same time experiencing a feminine concern at his strange dress, she flung up her reins and, with her whole body trembling, began, in the words of our native poetry, like this:

8. "Can it be the Etin,
loathsome to the king,
shadowing the middle
of the road with his steps?
Yet bold warriors
have frequently concealed
themselves beneath
the pelts of beasts."

9. Then Hamal spoke:
"You, maiden, who ride
upon the steed's back,
exchanging words with me,
tell us your name,
and from what lineage
you take your birth."

10. She replied:
"Groa is my name,
my father of royal
blood, resplendent,

dazzling in arms.
But you two disclose
what man you are,
or whence your are sprung."

11. The other answered:
"I am Hamal,
valiant in warfare,
ferocious and terrible
to enemy peoples,
often wetting
this right hand
with foreigners' life-blood.

12. Then Groa said:
"Tell me, what leader
draws up your battle-line?
For whom do you carry
the standards of war?
What jarl
prepares you for action?
Under whose eye
do you wage your strife?"

13. Hamal responded:
"Blessed by the God of war,
never deflected
by force or fear,
Kon guides our troops.
No blazing fire,
ruthless sword, or
heaving billows
ever dismayed him.
Under his generalship,
lady, we raise our
golden standards."

14. Groa answered him:
"Retrace your steps,
reverse your direction.
Otherwise Sigtryg
will crush you all
with his militia.
Fastening you tightly
to a terrible stake,
he would noose your throats,

deliver your bodies
to the stiffening knot,
savagely staring,
would thrust your corpses
to the greedy raven."

15. <u>Again Hamal spoke:</u>
"First, Kon will
put him in Hel,
add him to the shades,
before death closes
his own eyelids,
will send him whirling
to the dreaded Niflhel.
We are not worried
by his encampments.
Why then, mistress,
do you threaten us with
gloomy funerals?"

16. <u>Groa replied:</u>
"Again I shall ride
to visit the well-known
halls of my father,
lest I should rashly
view your brother's
advancing columns.
But turn back now,
I beg you, and stave off
your final Wyrd."

17. <u>To which Hamal answered:</u>
"Return joyfully,
daughter, to your father,
and do not pray
for our swift decease,
letting the anger
pound through your heart.
A stubborn woman,
harshly refusing
her wooer at first,
will often yield
when the plea is repeated."

18. Then Kon, brooking silence no longer,
rounded on the girl, and by giving a harsher

tone to his words imitated the hair-raising
voice of an Etin:

19. "Let not the maiden
fear a savage ogre's brother.
When I draw near,
let her not grow pale.
Sent here by Grepp,
I shall not lie within the embrace
of any female,
except with her consent."

20. <u>To which Groa replied:</u>
"What woman in her senses
wants to be an Etin's whore?
What girl would enjoy
his gargantuan touch,
bear to be a demon's wife,
knowing the monster-breeding seed,
wish to find a ferocious Thurse
sharing the nuptial bed with her?

21. "Who would stake
her finger on thorns?
Who would give
warm kisses to mud?
Who would join
her smooth body,
unjustly fitted,
to bristly limbs?

22. "When nature wholly
cries out against it,
you cannot crop
true love's repose.
Ill-framed to match
with mammoth bulk
is the love that women
are wont to feel."

23. <u>Kon retorted:</u>
"Many times
this conquering arm
has tamed the necks
of mighty monarchs.
This overpowering

right hand
has beat down
their swelling pride."

24. "Take this red-glowing
gold from me,
that by this gift
a lasting pact
of firm faith
may be struck between us,
helping to consolidate
our marriage."

25. At these words he threw off his disguise and revealed the natural grace of his countenance. His true appearance brought almost as much pleasure to the Goddess as his false trappings had instilled her with alarm. He did not forget to ply her with love gifts, and encourage her to mate, which his beauty had provoked in her.

26. Traveling further he learned from those he met that he would be waylaid by the road by two brigands. When they rushed eagerly forward to rob him, he dispatched them with a single blow. Afterwards, not wishing to appear to have conferred a benefit on enemy territory, he tied their dead bodies to planks and stretched them upright in such a way that they seemed to be standing. Those they had preyed on whilst they were alive would still be menaced in appearance by their corpses. Even after death they should be fearsome, and obstruct the way no less in semblance than they did in deed. Men agree

that by such an extraordinary action after slaying the robbers, he showed that he had worked in his own interest, not that of Sigtryg's people, whom he now opposed.

27. Kon carried Groa to Jarl's court. Thor approved of this act, seeing as Egil had become the Gods' enemy and because it was to the advantage of Midgard that a Goddess of vegetation would be there. But Sigtryg, Groa's father, did not approve of it, and this brought about a conflict between him and Kon.

28. Because he had heard from soothsayers that Sigtryg could only be vanquished by gold, he immediately fastened a stud of gold to his wooden mace. Armed with this, he launched a war against Sigtryg and became master of his wishes. There he killed Sigtryg in Einvigi. Kon, chief among men, slew Sigtryg with the gold-studded club. Hamal gave a more lavish favor to this feat by singing thus:

29. "Fierce Kon,
wielding his
splendid club, steelless,
with only a tree-trunk,
used its aid instead
of the sword stroke,
repelled the
king's lances.

30. "Pursuing urlag
and the will of the Gods,
he hammered the fame

of the powerless Alfar,
till he put their
ruler to death,
crushed by the
inflexible gold.

31. "Pondering on his
martial trade,
he bore in his clasp
the flashing oak,
triumphant
he flung
with his glittering scourge
their leader sprawling.

32. "Him whom the Norns
forbade to be
slaughtered by steel,
he cleverly beat
with hard gold,
handling no blade;
for Kon wielded
metal more potent.

33. "Henceforth the fame
of this precious object
will spread in
ever-widening orbit,
for which its inventor
may claim the glory,
the peak
of distinction."

34. Od was brought to Kon's abode with his mother, Groa. His heart filled with thoughts of revenge for the slaying of his grandfather and the taking of his mother. However, to avoid stirring his stepfather's suspicions by behaving intelligently, he pretended to be an imbicile, acting as if his wits had gone quite astray. This piece of artfulness, besides concealing his true wisdom, safeguarded his life. Every day he would stay near his mother's hearth, completely listless and unwashed, and would roll himself on the ground to give his person a coating of filth. His grimy complexion and the refuse smeared over his face grotesquely illustrated his lunacy. Everything he said was the raving of an idiot, everything he did smacked of a deep stupor. Need I go on? You would not have called him a man so much as a ridiculous freak created by Wyrd in a madcap mood.

35. After destroying Sigtryg, the Alf ruler, Kon desired to strengthen his possession of his empire won in war. When Svarin, governor of Gotland, was suspected of aspiring to the throne, he challenged him. Then Svarin's brothers, six born in wedlock and nine from a concubine, sought to avenge his death in an unequal contest, but they were annihilated.

36. A year after this Groa bore with Kon a son, who had the name Gudorm. However, she always felt like a stranger in Kon's home. She suffered from the thought of being married to the man who was her father's bane, and her heart yearned for Egil. After the lapse of a few years, she was sent away by Kon because of this, and she set out with her young son Od back to Greater Svithjod, where she waited for Egil's return. Frosty

nights, snow storms, and hail showers would come, but not Egil. Then the Goddess of vegetation languished away and died. On her death bed she told her son, Od, that if he needed her help he should go to her grave and call on her. Her remains were laid in a tomb built in a mountain rock with walls, a roof, and a door of heavy boulders.

37. For his eminent achievements, Kon's father, Jarl, now extremely old, allowed him to participate in rule, thinking that, rather than exercise supreme power alone in the decline of his life, it was more useful and sensible to share it with his own blood. Now Hring, a nobly-born Zealander, decided that one of them was unripe for honor and the other had now outrun the course of his strength; he pleaded the untrustworthy years of both and incited the majority of the Danes to revolt, maintaining that a boyish and a senile mind were equally unfit for royal power. They fought him and they obliterated him, proving to people that no one's age should be thought a disqualification for manliness.

XLIV. <u>Fimbulwinter I</u>

1. After the arrival of Ivaldi's sons in Jotunheim, the first Fimbulwinter began. The second comes right before the destruction of the worlds. There were three times three winters with great battles taking place throughout the world. Far behind the outermost district in Jotunheim, in the remotest north, near the edge of the earth-disk and by Amsvartnir's sea, over which eternal darkness broods, lies a land to which the Ivaldi sons directed their course. Its dales stretch between glacier covered mountains that are overgrown with trees of the sort that thrive in the darkness and cold of the renowned Ironwood. Black precipices gape down into unknown depths. In one of them is a ravine that leads down into Niflheim in Jormungrund.

2. Here in a passage of the dales, which are called the Wolfdales, Volund and his brothers set up their dwelling and smithy in the house called Brunnacre, in Thrymheim, by a water called Wolfsea. Here they could safeguard themselves against any pursuit, and what they were doing could not be seen from Asgard's lookout tower, Hlidskjalf.

3. Volund had two reasons for staying in this inhospitable land. He was as proficient as Gullveig, and even more so than she, in all the secrets of the Seid and was lord over all of its powers, even though he had no desire to use them up until then. He and his brothers had been taught by Mimir how to control weather to keep the darkness and mist of Niflheim from entering the southern realms of Jormungrund, and as such were the ones who conquered the clouds rising, storm-

foreboding, from the abyss. Now Volund would use these powers to send frost and storms over the worlds and make Midgard uninhabitable. This was his first intention. His second was to forge a sword, in which he would place all of his skill; an irresistible sword that would bring the hammer forged by Sindri to shame, kill Thor, and annihilate Asgard's dominion. He became known as Thjazi, that arrogant Etin, whose daughter was Skadi.

4. Egil and Slagfin traveled on skis and hunted the wild animals that were capable of living in this region of the worlds. Volund worked all day with his Seid-tools and his forge. When strikes of the hammer from the smithy did not echo against the gloomy passages of the dales there was heard the sound of Volund's chanting: a strange, somewhat dismal song that filled the hearts of the wild animals with agony, while frosty nights, worse than any other, made them tremble under their furs from the cold. Then Volund stood on a cliff with his face directed to the south and he shook a cloth, similar to a sail, or he scattered ashes into the air or performed other feats, and then the air darkened in front of him with frosty mists that condensed into a giant cloud and drifted out over Jotunheim and the Elivagar to Midgard, over whose fields it unloaded snowstorms,

hail showers, and devastating whirlwinds. Then hard gusts from the white mountain-range teased apart and wove together the storm-happy daughters of Aegir-Gymir, bred on frost.

5. His song penetrated down into Niflheim in Jormungrund and gripped the nine Etin-maids, who turn Grotti and the starry heaven, with delirium. Two strong Thurse-maids, Fenja and Menja, had joined them and set the mill at a furious pace so that all depths of the earth trembled. Rock fragments soared from the mill-stone, which were cast high up from the sea, the earth's mountains spit fire and smoke, the raised mechanism of the mill was shaken and the starry heaven acquired the sloping position it has held ever since. Fenja and Menja once sang:

6. "Hard was Hrungnir,
and his father,
yet Thjazi-Volund was
stronger than they,
Idi-Slagfin and Aurnir-Egil
are our kinsmen,
brothers of the Bergrisar
from whom we are born.

7. "Grotti had not come
from the grey mountain,
nor yet the hard stone
from the earth,
nor would the mountain-maid
be grinding
if anyone knew
her race.

8. "Nine winters
we were playmates,
beneath the earth
our power grew,
we maidens constantly
performed mighty works,
we ourselves moved
the table-mountain from its seat.

9. "We rolled the stone
over the Etin's house,
so that because of it
the earth shook,
so we hurled
the whirling rock,
the heavy stone,
so we could make it."

10. Even as the wild horse shakes his mane after he has thrown his rider in the grass, so did the earth shake her forests and mountains. Streams spread over the fields. The sea seethed. Mountains spewed toward the clouds, and what they spewed, the clouds flung back upon the earth. First, the earth slanted northwards and sank down lower and lower. Then, the low marks of Midgard were buried under the sea. Forests were heaved up and played in the winds. The year after frosts came and lay the land under a white blanket of snow, followed by storm-winds rising out of the north, with moving mountains of ice and stones. Every year Midgard yielded fewer crops, bad harvest followed bad harvest. Wights of hunger and disease came with the blizzards and laid waste to man and beast.

11. Svithjod fell under the control of an Etin named Snaer, and he had the daughter Mjoll, who flies swiftly through the air. Fornjot had the son Kari, whose son is Jokul, and he is the father of Snaer. Snaer's children are Thorri, Fonn, Drifa, and Mjoll. Fornjot's ugly sons began first to send snow. Under Snaer's reign the harvest was ruined by the severely bad weather, and foodstuffs began to run short; then the populace was painfully tormented by famine. Whether it was because the ground had had insufficient rainfall or had been baked too hard, the seed lay dormant and the fields bore only sparse crops. The region, starved of food, was worn down by the weary famine, nor was there any help available to make the provisions adequate and stave off hunger.

12. Volund's song penetrated, like heavy wing-beats, all the way up to Asgard and filled this region with dread. The sun-chariot's and the time-measuring moon's beams had difficulty making their way through the mist-filled depths down onto the earth.

13. Scarcely one day passed over the course of many years when Volund was not alternating between the work in his smithy and moments of singing his dreadful song. It penetrated through the earth and turned its waters into waste. Year after year the fields

of Midgard sprouted shorter straw and thinner ears of corn, and that which was left to harvest was ravaged every so often by the frosty nights. The humans performed blots in vain to the Gods and began to question their power.

14. Through the reduction of the liquids in Urd's and Mimir's holy wells during these years, Yggdrasil's northern branches were all the more barren of buds and leaves. With Frey and Freya in the possession of the Etins, with Groa dead, and Idun missing from Asgard, the powers of growth were weakened to the point where they could not defend the worlds from the Fimbulwinter.

15. One morning, Ivaldi's sons found by the shore three women sitting and spinning flax. By them lay their swan-guises, for they were Swanmaids. These were Idun, who had joined her sisters on the strand, Auda, another daughter of Ivaldi, and Sif, daughter of Sigtryg. When Loki lured Idun out of Asgard and was taken by Volund, she happily joined her brothers, whom she had longed after, especially Volund, whom she had loved since childhood. She was already in the Wolfdales when her sisters arrived. When Sif came to the Wolfdales, she carried a message to Egil that Groa could not come. He would later discover that she had died. The brothers took them home with them.

Egil had Sif, Slagfin Auda, and Volund Idun. The three maids flew from the south through Myrkwood-Ironwood, young Swanmaids, fulfilling their urlag. One of them pressed Egil into her white embrace, the second was Auda, she laid her head on Slagfin's chest, but the third, their sister, laid her arms around Volund's white neck. Then the Ivaldi sons wore the Swanrings.

16. In this way, these Swanmaids, who adorned Midgard's meadows with flowers, were now missing from Asgard. The hearts of these Goddesses were transformed: they now desired victory for the Ivaldi sons, the destruction of Midgard, and Asgard's ruin. These Goddesses dwelt in the Wolfdales, descended from the upper branches of Yggdrasil. They suffered as the snow fell, confined as they were in the cold lands of Niflheim, for they were used to better abodes back home, and disliked being shrouded in night. They were grieving in the Wolfdales, having exchanged their swan-guises for wolf-skins to keep warm, they changed their dispositions, delighted in guile, shifted their shapes. Thus they became Myrkriders.

17. Loki offered his services as a milkmaid to Volund and joined him and his brothers as they began their work against the Gods. Loki would often return to Asgard whenever it suited his malevolent purposes.

18. Volund's smithy was now a workplace of magical instruments. There hung a long rope of twined bast with which knots were made at even distances. In every one of them a storm-wind was bound. For every week that passed he untied a knot and released the bound wind and sent it with his song to the south, saturated with snow-clouds and hail. In this manner he endured the weeks he spent in the Wolfdales, and he figured that when all the knots of the rope were untied Midgard would be transformed into an ice-covered desert, devoid of humans.

19. Volund had forged an arm-ring out of gold, similar to the ring Draupnir that was forged by Sindri in the respect that other rings, although not as many, dropped from it. The ring is called Andvaranaut, and it can multiply wealth for the one who holds it. The ring, finished ninety nights after Volund's arrival in the Wolfdales, drops two more rings every nine nights. This armlet is of amazing weight. It is a Lindring, and will turn into a serpent and fall with the poisoned tips of its fangs upon the man who puts it on and is not supposed to have it. It and the rings it drops are magical instruments and have the shapes of serpents.

20. Volund worked daily on the sword of revenge. The sword was called Gambantein, and Volund applied all of his artistry, all of his secret knowledge, to its preparation. He tempered the blade in the poisonous waves of rivers in Niflhel and etched runes of certain victory into the invincible steel. He hammered vengeance and hate, woe and misfortune into its grain, sharpened the poisonous edge as sharp as Vafurfires, cleaned its surface with the radiance of the sun, and risted evil runes onto it. The sword had been forged so that it would grant unconditional victory to Volund or one of his relatives, but ruin for anyone else who availed himself of it. This sword is rich in victory and is a good and excellent work of the wonder-smith, fitted with a golden hilt. It was engraved all over and showed how war first came into the world and the flood that destroyed the clan of Hrimthurses. In pure gold inlay on the sword-guards there were rune markings correctly incised, stating and recording for whom the sword had been first made, and ornamented with its scrollworked hilt. This slender, sign-marked sword fights of itself against the Etin race, if it is a wise man who owns it. The sword can assume the form of the tusk of a rare beast, its ends edged with gold. This sword, hardened in the blood and venom of serpents, burns like a pyre when one fares through the dark forest. The smith covered its destructiveness with eye-

capturing beauty, and nevertheless it seemed to never be finished. Every day Volund found something new to do to it.

XLV. <u>Hrafnagaldur</u>

1. Allfather-Odin works,
   Alfar separate,
   Vanir know,
   Norns reveal,
   Ividja-Gullveig gives birth,
   men endure,
   Thurses wait,
   Valkyries yearn.

2. The Aesir suspected
   an evil scheme,
   wights [Ivaldi's sons] confounded
   the weather with magic;
   Urd was appointed
   Odroerir's keeper,
   powerful to protect it
   from the mightiest winter [Fimbulwinter].

3. Hugur [Hugin] then disappears,
   seeking the heavens,
   men's ruin is suspected,
   if he is delayed;
   Thrain's thought
   is an oppressive dream,
   Dainn-Brokk's dream
   was thought enigmatic.

4. The Dwarves' powers
   dwindle, the worlds
   sink down
   towards Ginnung's abyss;
   often Alsvid
   fells from above,
   often he gathers
   the fallen again.

5. Earth and sun
   cannot stand firm;
   malignant winds
   do not cease;

hidden in the glorious
well of Mimir
lies all knowledge;
know you yet, or what?

6. The curious Goddess
   dwells in dales [Wolfdales],
   descended from
   Yggdrasil's ash;
   of Alfar kin,
   Idun was her name,
   youngest of Ivaldi's
   elder children.

7. She suffered,
   and snow fell,
   was confided under
   the old-tree's trunk;
   used to better
   abodes back home,
   she disliked staying
   at Norvi-Mimir's daughter's [Natt's].

8. The victory-Gods see
   Nauma-Idun grieving
   in the wolf's home [Wolfdales];
   given a wolf-skin,
   she clad herself therein,
   changed disposition,
   delighted in guile,
   shifted her shape.

9. Vidir-Odin selected
   Bifrost's guardian [Heimdall]
   to inquire of whatever
   the bearer of Gjoll's sun [Urd]
   knew of
   the world's affairs;
   Bragi and Lopt-Loki
   bore witness.

10. They sang sorcery,
    they rode wolves,
    Rognir-Volund and Regin-Egil,
    against the world's house;
    Odin listens

in Hlidskjalf;
he watched the travelers'
distant journey.

11. The wise one [Heimdall],
the child of Gods
and his road companions,
asked the server of mead [Urd]
if she knew the origin,
duration, and end
of heaven, of Hel,
of the world.

12. She did not speak her mind,
nor was Gefjun-Urd able
to utter a word,
nor express any joy;
tears trickled
from the skull's shields [eyes],
the mighty one
is powerless.

13. As from the east,
out of Elivagar,
comes a thorn from the field
of the rime-cold Etin,
with which Dainn-Brokk
smites all men
of glorious Midgard
every night.

14. Actions are numbed,
the arms slump,
dizziness hovers over
Hviti As' sword [Heimdall's head],
stupor dispels
the wind of the Giantess [thought],
the mind's workings
of all mankind.

15. Thus the Gods perceived
the state of Jorun-Urd,
swollen with sorrow
when no answer came forth;
they grew more persistent
as response was denied,

but all their words
were to no avail.

16. The leader of the
expedition went forth,
the guardian of Herjan-Odin's
Gjallarhorn [Heimdall];
he chose as his companion
the kinsman of Nal-Laufey [Loki],
Grimnir-Odin's poet [Bragi]
guarded the ground.

17. Vidar-Odin's thanes
arrived at Valhall;
borne by
both of Fornjot's sons [wind and wave];
they walk in
and greet the Aesir,
already at Ygg-Odin's
merry ale-feast.

18. "Hail to Hangatyr-Odin,
the happiest As,
may you preside over
the mead at the high-seat!
Sit, Gods, in delight
at the sumbel;
may you, with Yggjung-Odin,
enjoy eternal bliss!"

19. Seated on benches
at Bolverk-Odin's bidding;
the clan of Gods
were sated with Saehrimnir;
at the tables Skogul
gave out the mead
in Mimir's horns
from Hnikar-Odin's vat.

20. Much was asked
during the banquet
of Heimdall by the Gods,
of Loki by the Goddesses,
whether the woman [Urd] spoke
prophecies or wisdom;
all day they asked,

until twilight approached.

21. They deemed it bad
that their futile errand,
of little glory,
had gone wrong;
it would prove hard
to find the play they needed
to get an answer
from the woman.

22. Omi-Odin answers,
all listened:
"Night is the time
for new advice;
think until morning
so that each is able
to provide counsel
for the Aesir's benefit."

23. The wolf's tired
food supply [Sol]
ran along the eddies
of Rind's plains;
the Gods left
the feast and saluted
Hropt-Odin and Frigga,
as Hrimfaxi ascended.

24. Delling's son [Dag]
urged on his horse,
well adorned
with precious stones;
the horse's mane glows
above Mannheim [Midgard],
the steed drew Dvalin's playmate [Dag]
in his chariot.

25. At Jormungrund's
northern horse-door,
under the outermost root
of the noble tree,
Etins and Etin-maids,
dead men, Dwarves,
and Dokkalfar
went to their couches.

26. The Gods arose,
Alfrodul-Sol ran,
Njola-Natt advanced
north towards Niflheim;
Ulfrun's son [Heimdall],
the mighty horn-blower
of Himinbjorg,
lifted Argjoll [Gjallarhorn].

XLVI. <u>Odainsacre</u>

1. Mimir, the guardian of the well of wisdom in Jormungrund, saw that terrible suffering afflicted the humans. Their morals and customs constantly deteriorated under the influence of Gullveig's Seid. Mimir did not want Ask and Embla's offspring to be destroyed by famine and nid.

2. Upon the world the evil winters were about to fall that would make snow-flakes fall thick, even a mile deep on the highest tops of mountains.

3. Mimir gathered his sons Uni and Iri, Ori and Bari, Var and Vegdrasil, Dori and Uri; together they would make a Holt within Glasisvellir, a mile wide on every side of the square. They made that which is seen within the castle of the Asmegir. There they brought the seeds of sheep and oxen, of men, of dogs, of birds, and of red blazing fires. They made a Holt, a mile wide on every side of the square, to be an abode for men, for oxen and sheep. There, in the land

of the rosy dawn, they planted the magnificent grove, called Odainsacre.

4. There they made waters flow in a bed a mile long; there they settled birds, on the green that never fades, with food that never fails. There they established dwelling-places, consisting of a house with a balcony, a courtyard, and a gallery. Breidablik is the hall that was built for Baldur in that land, in which I know exists the fewest crimes. Within this hall is a room, richly adorned, and there stands a beautiful table with delicious food in silver dishes, and mead in golden goblets. There are also splendid beds. Here stands the mead, the Skirar Veigar, prepared for Baldur; shields are spread over, and the Asmegir are waiting impatiently. They decorated the hall, surrounded it with a wall of Vafurfires, and set before it a gate as well-made as the one in Asgard. That Holt they sealed up with a golden ring [of fire], and they made a door, and a window self-shining within. The wall is difficult to approach and surmount. One can wring off the head of a cock and throw it within the enclosing barrier; immediately the bird, resurrected, will give proof by a loud crow that it has truly recovered its breathing. Delling, the cunning Alf, is watchman at the gate.

5. There they brought the seeds of men and women, of the greatest, best, and finest on this earth. The mead from the well of wisdom had given Mimir a vision of the future, after the end of the ages, and for that future he would preserve an undefiled human couple. In Midgard, he sought out two innocent and ordinary children, Lif and Leifthrasir, and took them to Odainsacre, which is also called Hoddmimis Holt. Lif and Leifthrasir are hidden in Hoddmimis Holt. They have morning dew for food, and from them springs mankind after Ragnarok.

6. There Mimir and his sons brought the seeds of every kind of tree, of the highest of size and sweetest of odor on this earth; there they brought the seeds of every kind of fruit, the best of savor and the sweetest of odor. And they continuously made pairs of them, in order that these beings may live in the Holt. Therewith is this land covered in flowers and plants, and those who partake in their delight will forget their past.

7. And there will be no humpbacked, none bulged forward there; no impotent, no lunatic; no one malicious, no liar; no one spiteful, none jealous; no one with decayed tooth, no leprous to be pent up, nor any of the brands wherewith Leikin stamps the bodies of mortals. Within the wall will never come sorrow or suffering, never handicap or sickness, never age or death.

8. In the largest part of the place they made nine streets, six in the middle part, three in the smallest. To the streets of the largest part they brought a thousand seeds of men and women, to the streets of the middle part, six hundred; to the streets of the smallest part, three hundred.

9. What are the lights that gave light in the Holt which Mimir made? There are uncreated lights and created lights. The one thing missing in Odainsacre is the sight of stars, the moon, and the sun, and a year seems only a day. But the Holt is adorned with days and beams of light and waters. Under the tree clothed with goodly leaves where he drinks with the Gods, Mimir, lord of the realm, tends these ancients sires with love. Every fortieth year, two are born to every couple, a male and a female. And thus it is for every sort of cattle. And the men in the Holt which Mimir made live the happiest life.

10. Baldur would eventually come to them and become their teacher and leader, who would show them the pure worship of the Gods and the precepts of morality, and in accordance with these they are to live a just and happy life. At this point they eagerly awaited his arrival.

XLVII. Folkwanderung

1. Midgard was being ravaged by the terrible cold Volund produced. The distinctions between summer and winter disappeared altogether, and it seemed as if winter would reign every month of the year. The land closest to the southern shore of the Elivagar, where Egil's fortress stood, became covered with glaciers and sheets of ice, which the rays of the summer sun did not melt. The Alfar that lived there, who had been Volund's assistants and Egil's and Thjalfi's comrades migrated, proceeding south toward the Swedes. The Etins then set out across the Elivagar in boats and settled on the abandoned meadows. There they made their homes beneath the roofs of glacier-covered mountains. Here, where Midgard's herds had died of hunger, their black oxen and gold-horned cattle grazed well, because, like Audhumla, they licked sustenance from the rime-frost and scratched up nourishing mosses from drifts that covered the valley-paths.

2. In Svithjod, whose southernmost tip was called Aurvangaland, now dwelt many clans, descended from Ask and Embla, all speaking the same language and following the same customs. South of the Swedes and by Joruvellir, which stretches along Aurvangaland's southern coast, lived the Goths,

Danes, Herules, Gepides, Vinili, also called Longobards, Angles, Tyirings, Vandals, and other clans. Until then they had all lived in harmony, regarding themselves as what they were: branches of one and the same family tree. As long as they had been spread out over the north, the land had been good, beautiful, and plentiful.

3. But with the Fimbulwinter came need, first for the Swedes, who lived farther north than the others. Frey and Freya no longer promoted fruitfulness and fertility. The Swanmaids no longer provided the fields and meadows with Yggdrasil's fructifying honeydew. Herds decreased, while bear and wolf packs grew, and worst of all, the wolves, in need of food, closed their jaws on the folk. There came poverty and want in through the windows; hunger spread his wings and struck down upon the land; strife leapt proudly over the street and onward into the houses.

4. Dwarves, led by Sindri, came forth from Svarinsmound and conferred with the jarls of the Swedes. All the Swedes took part in their deliberation, and so resolved to leave the land of their forefathers and go south. If they could not win better fields through peaceful agreements, they would take them by the sword, and thus they often entered into battle. The Skandians who were desir-

ous after the land of their forebears, came to Denmark. Upon a bright night they all came. Now they said that they had a right upon the land, and fought over this. The Swedes pushed down against the Goths, and they against the Danes, and they against the Herules, and the other clans. The push from the north to the south became greater every year, for every year the Fimbulwinter and the unmelting ice-fields consumed a greater portion of the inhabitable country. The Dwarves in Sindri's band, who came forth from Svarinsmound, attacked and took Aurvangaland, as far as Joruvellir. Etins, including Fjalar and Frosti, also joined in this battle to aid Ivaldi's sons in bringing ruin to Midgard.

5. At this time, Jarl lived in Aurvangaland, reigning as its jarl and judge. He was the son of Heimdall, who as a child had come to the land bringing holy fire, beneficial runes, a sheaf of grain, as well as tools and weapons. Jarl had now grown old. After a long and commendable service, he had gained much experience. He recalled from his childhood and youth the happy times of the The Golden Age, free from vice, strife, crime, and need. His adult years had witnessed humanity's Silver Age, and the moral decline of his people. In his later days, he experienced the onset of the Fimbulwinter and the beginning

of the Copper Age, which reminded him of the prophecy spoken by ravens at his son's birth. When they saw the newborn Kon, they declared that the age of peace was over.

6. Kon was held in such high esteem that he was thought to also be the son of great Thor. When the sons of Ivaldi had ceased watching the Elivagar, many Etins had crossed over into the northernmost parts of Midgard and settled there. Thor went to drive off or slay these dangerous newcomers, and Kon accompanied his divine father on the trip. They made many excursions against the Etins who had taken the land in northern Midgard. Many Etins and warring Giantesses met their deaths, but as a whole, this mattered little, since others took their place. As good as Thor's iron hammer was, with it he could not hinder the ever-advancing sheets of ice that covered the mountain-plains. Even in the summertime, the valleys were covered in snow.

7. And now the great Folkwanderung happened, after the Swedes had begun to push southward, Kon had something to do other than follow Thor on excursions against the Etins. The first wave of folk that flowed from the north had set another in motion, and the second a third, and so on, so that wave after wave surged against Aurvangaland, the cradle of our people, where Jarl

had lived for so long and had happily been the law-giver and judge of the folk.

8. Now, on the border of Aurvangaland, mighty battles were fought in which Kon and Hamal performed many feats. But the old Jarl saw that resistance was futile in the long run, as long as the powers of Fimbulwinter raged behind the more northerly clans and compelled them to push onward. They had to do this, or die of starvation. And since all these clans were related and traced their pedigree from Aurvangaland, Jarl did not want to see them destroy one another in this brotherly feud. Thus, he decided to proceed south with his people as well.

9. So it happened, and many clans united under him to win land on the other side of the North Sea. Kon commanded all these clans; their jarls raised him on their shoulders and elected him king. Nothing was able to withstand them. Beneath them, south of the sea, they placed the extensive land, where sailable rivers sought paths between deep, lush forests, and rich pasture lands.

10. They won, and divided among themselves, a kingdom, which in the west had the mighty Rhine river as its border, and in the south a wooded highland, which lay in the shade of one of the highest mountains in Midgard, now called Mont Blanc. In the east, the realm stretched far into an unending

tableland with many rivers that make their way down to the Black Sea. Thus was fulfilled the Norns' prophecy that Kon would have a kingdom, extending in the east and west, as far in these directions as they had stretched the golden threads in the warp of his weave; but to the north there extended only a single thread, and if it did not hold, the cradle of the Teutonic people and the holy graves of the forefathers would forever remain in the power of the forces of frost and the enemies of the Gods.

XLVIII. Ull

1. The Ivaldi sons had children with their Swanmaids. Volund and Idun had already conceived Skadi, and Slagfin had fathered Gunnar, Hogni, and Gudrun with Auda. These children joined them in the Wolfdales. Gunnar particularly excelled, under the tutelage of his father, in playing the harp. When he played, the harp would gain a voice as if it were a man, and not even the swan could make a sweeter sound.

2. While they were in the Wolfdales, Sif conceived the son Ull with Egil. He is such a good archer and skier that no one can compete with him. He is also beautiful in appearance and has a warrior's accomplishments. He is a good one to pray to in the Einvigi. He is also called Onduras, Bogaas, Veidias, and Skjaldraras. It is said that instead of sailing a ship he is able to cross the seas on his skis, which he had engraved with runes, and which skims the waves that rise before him as swiftly as with oars. These skis can also be used as a shield, and thus the shield is also called Ull's Ash-Ship, Ull's Boat or Ship, or Ull's Ash. Oathrings are consecrated in Ull's name.

XLIX. Volund

1. The Swanmaids who stayed in the Wolfdales with Ivaldi's sons lived there through seven winters, but on the eighth they were seized with longing, and on the ninth they were parted by urlag, the maidens yearning to fly through the Myrkwood-Ironwood, the young Valkyries fulfilling their urlag. The storm-terrible Volund came home from the hunt, Slagfin and Egil found their house deserted; they went in and out, and looked around. Egil went east after Sif, and Slagfin west after Auda; but Volund remained alone in the Wolfdales. Each were joined by their children. Volund set red-gold with precious gems and closed the Lindrings well together; and so he waited for his bright consort, if she would return to him.

2. Loki was in the Underworld for eight winters, milking cows as a maid. He used many wiles in women's ways with the Myrkriders, whom he lured from their husbands. After this he returned to the realms of

the Gods to continue his malevolent schemes.

3. Slagfin, who had little interaction with the Etins, took the shortest path to the south through Jotunheim. He finally came to Alfheim and was glad to be home again with Auda. Egil took a detour to the east, perhaps to avoid the districts of Jotunheim, perhaps also enticed by the unknown regions he would wander through. He traveled through the remotest plains of the Ironwood, and there came across a great deal of strangeness. He had to travel many devious paths and search over many bodies of water, before he again saw his family's odal and encountered Sif in Alfheim.

L. Hod

1. Baldur and Hod had grown up with Mani, Nanna's father, though for a while Hod was sent to Mimir because of his temperament. Both of them are different in nature but have much love for each other. Baldur is calm and mild, Hod is impetuous and hot-tempered. They are equals in courage and gallantry. They are also very different in appearance, although both are exceptionally handsome.

2. Both are great sportsmen. No rider or charioteer has ever reined a fiery horse better than Baldur, and never has a ship's captain led his craft through storming waves with a surer hand than Baldur in his ship Hringhorni. Hod distinguished himself above most others as an archer and wrestler. Mani's foster-sons were hardly inferior to Bragi in poetry.

3. Hod was a great hunter, who sought out and slayed monsters throughout the worlds. He had learned that the treasure left by the Ivaldi sons, the Niflung Hoard, had fallen into the hands of an Etin named Fafnir, who lay on Gnitaheath in the form of a serpent. But that gold Volund had owned was cursed, and would be the bane of whomever possessed it, no one shall gain from this wealth. Fafnir also had an Aegishelm, at which all beings are terror-stricken. Hod went up to the Gnitaheath, and there found the track that Fafnir made when he crawled to get water. Then Hod made a great trench across the path, and took his place therein. When Fafnir crawled from his gold, he blew out venom, and it ran down from above on Hod's head. But when Fafnir crawled over the trench, Hod thrust his sword into his body to the heart. Fafnir writhed and struck out with his head and tail. Hod leapt out of the trench, and then each looked at the other. Fafnir said:

4. "Youth, oh youth!
   Of whom, then are you born?
   Say whose son you are,

who redden your bright blade
with Fafnir's blood,
and struck your sword to my heart."

5. Hod concealed his name, because it is believed, since ancient times, that the words of a dying man have great power if he curses his foe by his name.

6. He said: "I am called Gafugt Dyr,
  I go abroad
  a motherless man;
  I had no father,
  as others have,
  and I ever live alone."

7. Fafnir: "If you had no father,
  as others have,
  by what wonder were you born?
  (Though you hide your name
  on the day of my death,
  you know you are lying)."

8. Hod: "I think my race
  is unknown to you,
  and so am I myself;
  my name is Hod,
  I am Harbard-Odin's son,
  who smote you with the sword."

9. Fafnir: "Who drove you on?
  Why were you driven
  to make me lose my life?
  The bright eyed youth
  had a bold father,
  for you are bold in boyhood."

10. Hod: "My heart drove me,
  my hand fulfilled,
  and my shining sword so sharp;
  few are keen
  when old age comes,
  who are timid in boyhood."

11. Fafnir: "If you might grow
  among your friends,
  one might see you fight fiercely;
  but you are bound,
  and taken in battle
  and prisoners are prone to fear."

12. Hod: "You blame me, Fafnir,
  since I am far
  from my father's kin;
  I am not bound,
  though taken in battle,
  you have found that I live freely."

13. Fafnir: "You see hatred
  in all that I say,
  yet alone do I tell the truth;
  the glistening gold
  and the glow-red hoard,
  and the rings shall be your bane."

14. Hod: "Someone shall ever
  hold the hoard,
  till the destined day shall come;
  for there is a time
  when every man shall
  journey hence to Hel."

15. Fafnir: "The Wyrd of the Norns
  you will find before the headland,
  you weak-minded fool;
  you shall drown in the water
  if you row against the wind,
  all danger is near to death."

16. Hod: "Tell me then, Fafnir,
  for you are known as wise,
  and you know much:
  who are the norns
  who are helpful in need,
  and choose mothers for descendants?"

17. Fafnir: "The norns must be
  of many births,
  nor are they of one race:
  some to Gods,

some are kin to Alfar,
and some are Dvalin-Sindri's daughters."

18. Hod: "Tell me then, Fafnir,
for you are known as wise,
and you know much:
what do they call the holm
where all the holy Gods
and Surt shall meet in swordplay?"

19. Fafnir: "It is called Oskopnir,
where all the Gods
shall seek the play of swords;
Bilrost-Bifrost breaks when
they cross the bridge,
and the steeds shall swim in the flood.

20. "I wore the Aegishelm
to frighten men,
while I lay guarding my gold;
I seemed mightier
than any man,
for I never found a fiercer foe."

21. Hod: "No man hides
the Aegishelm
when he faces a valiant foe;
often one finds,
when he meets the foe,
that he is not the bravest of all."

22. Fafnir: "I spewed venom
when I lay by the bright
hoard my father had;
(there was none so mighty
as dared to meet me,
and weapons nor wiles I feared)."

23. Hod: "Hateful serpent,
your hissing was great,
and showed your hard heart,
but the sons of men have
hatred for him
who owns the helm."

24. Fafnir: "I counsel you, Hod,

to heed advice,
and ride home from here;
the glistening gold,
the glow-red hoard,
and the rings shall be your bane."

25. Hod: "Your counsel is given,
but I shall go
to the gold hidden in the heath;
and you, Fafnir,
shall fight with death,
lying where Hel-Urd will have you."

26. So Hod killed Fafnir, then wiped the blood from his sword. He rode along Fafnir's trail to his lair, and found it open. The gate-posts and the gates were of iron. Of iron, too, were all the beams in the house, which was dug down into the earth. There Hod found a mighty store of gold, and he filled two chests with it. He took the Aegishelm and a golden mail-coat and the sword Hrotti, and many other precious things.

LI. Nanna

1. Now it happened that Baldur, son of Odin, was stirred at the sight of Nanna bathing and then was gripped by an unbound passion. The sheen of her graceful body inflamed him and her manifest charms pierced his heart, for there is no stronger incitement to lust than beauty. Baldur went to Mani and demanded his daughter Nanna's hand. Baldur and Nanna were united, and loved each other greatly. Hod wished that he could have

a wife like her, as beautiful and affectionate as she was. But Hod alone would never have come up with the evil idea of taking Nanna for himself.

2. One morning Hod traveled on one of his hunts to the Ironwood , situated in the eastern Jotunheim, into whose ghastly interior nothing mortal dare tread. He hunted alone there the whole day, but went astray so that he could not find his way back. Darkness fell, and it looked as if it would be an unpleasant night. He wandered from his path in a mist and came upon the retreat of a certain forest-maiden, tall and beautiful to look at. She was a troll-woman who rode a wolf with serpents for reins, and said her name was Gondul [Gullveig]. She offered to attend him and gave him lodgings for the night. She gave him a strong drink that clouded his mind, reawakening his violent, impulsive passions. She spoke of Nanna in such a way as to fan his unconscious desire for her into a raging fire.

3. At the Bragarfull Hod bound himself with a vow to possess Nanna, the beloved of his brother, Baldur. Gondul gave him a coat of mail as pledge of the agreement between them and as a necessity in the battle into which his decision would lead him. In the morning when he woke, he found that the dwelling had vanished and that he was standing alone and unsheltered in the center of a plain beneath the open sky. But the coat of mail he had received proved that the night's conversation had happened, and was not just a bad dream. He left the Ironwood, regretting his vow so deeply that he could not face Baldur or return to Valhall, so he wandered through the wild paths to Jotunheim to join the enemies of the Gods so he could seek to fulfill the promise he had to keep.

4. Baldur and Hod were once united, neither would be without the other, until they were driven into a frenzy for Nanna, she was destined to be their undoing. Because of that fair maid, neither of them cared for games or joyous days, they could bear nothing else in their minds other than that bright form. The gloomy nights were sad to them, they could not enjoy sweet sleep: but from that anguish rose conflict between the faithful friends.

5. Thereafter, for some time, Hod bore weapons against his own kindred, because he had made the vow to take Nanna from Baldur by force. Baldur defeated him in battle, so that he was forced to flee to his foster-father Mani, who gave him sanctuary. A second time they engaged in a sharp struggle, with Hod and his Etin army on one side and the Gods on the other, which terminated when Hod fled.

6. When Slagfin discovered that Hod had acquired the the Niflung Hoard he took up arms against him as well in order to secure his family's treasure. But he was killed in this conflict by Hod's bow, and was set upon the pyre by Hod built from his ship, then attended with handsome Helfare rites. Not only did Hod consign his ashes to a fine burial-mound as befitted him, but, beyond this, respectfully honored him with abundant ritual. In doing so, he valiantly paid tribute to his slain foster-brother.

7. Then one day, Hod left the Etins and began wandering through a forest to find Baldur. Then his brother appeared before him.

8. Baldur said: "You are welcome, Hod!
  What new tidings
  can you give
  since we last met?
  Why have you left Asgard, prince,
  and now have come alone
  to find me?"

9. Hod: "I am guilty
  of a much greater crime.
  I have chosen
  a royal daughter,
  your bride,
  at the Bragarfull."

10. Baldur: "Do not accuse yourself;
  the words uttered
  by us both while drinking
  will prove true.
  I have foreseen
  that I shall die soon;
  then may such befall,
  so must it be."

11. Hod: "You said, Baldur,
  that Hod well deserved
  great gifts from you,
  and your good will.
  It would seem better
  to redden your sword,
  than to grant peace
  to your foes."

12. Baldur first conquered his brother with weapons, but with goodness and kindness in the end. He escorted his brother back to Asgard, where he forgave, excused, and consoled him. Hod was welcomed back into Asgard, and to appease the situation between him and Baldur, their father, Odin, came to Hod and offered him the chance at a bride as good as Nanna. He said to him:

13. "Bind the gold rings
  together, Hod,
  it is not kingly
  to harbor fear,
  I know a maid,
  there is none so fair,
  rich in gold,
  if you can get to her.

14. "Green are the paths
  that lead to Hogni,
  and his urlag shows
  the way to the wanderer;
  the folk-king has
  a fair daughter,
  which you may buy
  as a bride, Hod.

15. "A hall stands high
  on Hindarfjoll,
  it is encircled with

Ofdokkum Ognar Ljoma;
wise craftsmen
once made it out
of the flaming
light of the flood [gold].

16. "A battle-maid
sleeps on the mountain,
Vafurfires
blaze about her;
Ygg-Odin pricked her
with the Sleepthorn,
for she felled the
fighter he wished to save.

17. "There you may see
the helmed maiden,
who rode forth from
the fight on Vingskornir;
the victory-bringer
shall not break her sleep,
yet you shall, Hod,
so the Norns have set."

18. Then Odin let his son borrow Sleipnir so he could ride forth on his quest.

LII. Hild

1. Hild was the daughter of Hogni, son of Slagfin. It is said that Hod exchanged oaths of friendship with Slagfin's sons, and that his alliance with Hild would thus compensate for their father's death.

2. Hod rode up the Hindarfjoll, until he came across a building on the mountain. There he saw a bright light, as if a fire were burning, which blazed up to the sky. The Vafurfires flared up to the skies, the earth quivered with awful fire; of the folk-warders few would dare to ride through the fire unflinchingly. Hod urged Sleipnir with his sword: the fire was quenched before the young God, the flames bated before the bold one.

3. Inside he saw a warrior lying asleep, completely armed, wearing helmet and mail-coat. He first took the helmet off the warrior's head, and saw that it was a woman. Her coat of mail was tight on her, as if it had grown to her body. With his sword he slit the armor from the neck down, and then both sleeves, and took it off of her. She then awoke, sat up and, on seeing Hod, said:

4. "What slit my armor?
How was my sleep broken?
Who has cast the
heavy bonds from me?"

5. Hod: "Odin's son
has just now
ripped the raven's perch
with Hod's sword."

6. She said: "Long have I slept,
long was I oppressed with sleep,
long are mortals' sufferings!
Odin is the reason
that I could not
cast off my slumbering state."

7. Hod sat down and asked her name. She then looked up to the sky and cried out:

8. She said: "Hail Dag!
Hail Dag's sons!
Hail Natt and Nipt!

Look down upon us
with benevolent eyes
and give victory to the sitting!

9. "Hail the Aesir!
Hail the Asynjur!
Hail the bounteous earth!
Words and wisdom
give to us
and healing hands in life!"

10. She said her name was Hild, and she was a Valkyrie. She said that two kings had made war on each other, one of whom was named Hjalmgunnar. He was old and a great warrior, and Odin had promised him victory. The other was Agnar, a kinsman of Auda, whom no divinity would patronize. Hild overcame Hjalmgunnar in battle. In revenge for this Odin pricked her with a Sleepthorn, and declared that thenceforth she should never have victory in battle, and should be given in marriage. "But I said to him, that I had bound myself by a vow not to espouse any man who could be made to fear." She had also vowed to wed only that man who dared to ride through the Vafurfires. Hod replied by imploring her to teach him wisdom, for she had knowledge from all the worlds.

11. She said: "You will probably have more knowledge in things than I do; yet I will teach you. Indeed, and gratefully, if there is any of my wisdom that will in any way bring you pleasure, either of runes or of other matters that are the root of things. But now let us drink together, and may the Gods give us a good day, so you may win favor and fame from my words, and that you may hereafter notice what we speak together."

12. Then Hild filled a horn and bore it to Hod, giving him the Minnihorn to bind him to her. Then she said:

13. "I bring you ale,
O oak-of-battle,
it is mixed with might
and with bright glory:
it is full of song
and honorable speech,
of potent incantations,
and joyous discourses.

14. "Sigrunes you must know,
if you will have victory,
engrave them on your sword's hilt;
some on the sheath,
some on the guard,
and twice name the name of Tyr.

15. "Olrunes you must know,
if you wish that another's wife
will not betray your trust
if you confide in her.
They must be risted on the horn,
and on the back of the hand,
and Nauthiz on the nails.

16. "A cup must be blessed,
and guarded against peril,
and a leek cast in the liquor:
then I know that you
will never have mead
mixed with treachery.

17. "Bjargrunes you must know,

if you will help,
and loose the child from women:
they must be risted on the palm
and clasped round her joints,
and pray to the disir for aid.

18. "Brimrunes you must know,
    if you will have your
    sailing steeds float securely:
    they must be risted on the prow,
    and on the helm-blade,
    and etched with fire on the oars.
    No surge shall be so towering,
    nor waves so dark,
    that you will not come safe from the sea.

19. "Limrunes you must know,
    if you would be a leech,
    and would know how to heal wounds.
    They must be risted on the bark,
    and on the leaves of trees,
    of those whose boughs bend eastward.

20. "Malrunes you must know,
    if you do not wish that
    the strong one [Odin] shall requite
    you with consuming woe
    for the injury you have caused.
    All those runes must you
    wind, weave, and place together
    in that Thing [Helthing] where the host
    of people go into the full judgments.

21. "Hugrunes you must know,
    if you will be a
    wiser man than every other.
    Those interpreted,
    those risted,
    those devised by Hropt-Odin,
    from the sap
    which had leaked
    from Heiddraupnir-Mimir's head,
    and from Hoddropnir-Mimir's horn.

22. "He stands on a rock,
    with Brimir's sword [Mimir's head],

he has a helm on his head.
Then will Mimir's head speak
its first wise word,
and utter true sayings.

23. "They are, it is said
    risted on the shield
    which stands before the shining God,
    on Arvak's ear,
    and on Alsvid's hoof,
    on the wheel which rolls
    under Rognir-Volund's car,
    on Sleipnir's teeth,
    and on the sledge's bands.

24. "On the bear's paw,
    and on Bragi's tongue,
    and on the wolf's claws,
    and the eagle's beaks,
    on bloody wings,
    and on the bridge's head,
    on the midwife's hand,
    and on the healing's track.

25. "On glass and on gold,
    on amulets of men,
    in wine and in wort,
    and in the welcome seat,
    on Gungnir's point,
    and on Grani's breast,
    on the Norn's nail,
    and the owl's beak.

26. "All were erased
    that were inscribed,
    and mixed with the holy mead,
    and sent on distant ways:
    they are with the Aesir,
    they are with the Alfar,
    some with wise Vanir,
    some human beings have.

27. "Those are Bokrunes,
    those are Bjargrunes,
    and all Olrunes,
    and precious Meginrunes,

for those who can,
without confusion or corruption,
turn them to his welfare.
Use them, if you understand them,
until the Powers perish."

28. Then Hod said: "Surely no wiser woman than you may be found in all the worlds, teach me more of your wisdom!"

29. She answered: "It is seemly that I do according to your will, and show you more beneficial counsels, for your prayer's sake and your wisdom. Now you shall choose, since a choice is offered to you, keen armed warrior, my speech or silence: think it over in your mind. All evils are meted out."

30. Hod said: "I will not flee, though you know I am doomed, I was not born a coward, I will receive all your friendly counsels, as long as life is in me."

31. Hild: "This I counsel first:
that toward your kinsmen
you think yourself blameless.
Do not take hasty vengeance,
although they raise up strife:
that, it is said, benefits the dead.

32. "This I counsel second:
that you swear no oath
if it is not true.
Horrible limar
fall heavy on broken troth:
accursed is the oath-breaker.

33. "This I counsel third:
that at the Thing you do not
contend with a foolish man;
for an unwise man

often utters worse words
than he knows of.

34. "All is vain
if you keep silent;
then you will seem a coward,
or else truly accursed.
Doubtful is a servant's testimony,
unless you get a good one.
On the next day
let his life go forth,
and so reward men's lies.

35. "This I counsel fourth:
if a nefarious witch
lives by your route,
to go on is better
than to lodge there,
though night may overtake you.

36. "The sons of men
need searching eyes
when they have to fight fiercely:
often evil women
sit by the wayside,
who deaden weapons and valor.

37. "This I counsel fifth:
although you see fair women
sitting on the benches,
do not let their kindred's silver
have power over your sleep.
Entice no woman to kiss you.

38. "This I counsel sixth:
although among men pass
offensive tipsy talk,
never quarrel
with drunken warriors:
wine steals the wits of many.

39. "Brawls and drink
have been a heartfelt sorrow
to many men;
to some their death,
to some calamity:

many are the griefs of men!

40. "This I counsel seventh:
if you have disputes
with a daring man,
it is better for men to fight
than to be burnt
within their home.

41. "This I counsel eighth:
guard youself against evil,
and eschew deceit.
Entice no maiden,
nor wife of man,
nor incite them to wantonness.

42. "This I counsel ninth:
render the last service to
the corpses you find on the ground,
whether they have died from sickness,
or are drowned,
or are dead from weapons.

43. "Make a bath
for those who are dead,
wash their hands and head,
comb them and wipe them dry,
before you lay them in the coffin,
and pray for their happy sleep.

44. "This I counsel tenth:
that you never trust
the oaths of a foe's kinsman,
whose brother you have slain,
or felled his father:
there is a wolf
in a young son,
though he is gladdened with gold.

45. "Do not think strifes and fierce
enmities to be lulled,
no more than deadly injury.
A prince does not easily acquire
wisdom and fame in arms,
who shall be foremost of men.

46. "This I counsel eleventh:
that you look at evil,
whatever course it may take.
It seems to me the prince
may not enjoy a long life;
fierce disputes will arise."

47. Hod said: "A wiser mortal does not exist, and I swear that I will have you, for you are after my heart."

48. She answered: "I will have you above all others, though I have to choose among all men."

49. And this they confirmed with oaths to each other. The battle-strengthener [Hod] engages himself to Hild, the ring is broken as a gift. The ruler of the host [Hod] moves under Hogni's daughter's [Hild's] tent. Hod's beloved [Hild] prepares a bed for most helmet-harmers [warriors]. The lady [Hild] of the Hjadningas [Hod's followers] receives a mund, a sword famous for slaying.

50. At the same time, Slagfin's beloved, Auda, was betrothed to Forseti, Baldur's son with Nanna, to further honor the slain Ivaldi son. Baldur owned the hall Glitnir, the Thing of the Gods, and was their settler of disputes. Forseti later inherits this hall and his father's role as arbitrator. Glitnir is the hall with golden pillars, and its roof is set with silver. There dwells Forseti throughout all time, and settles all disputes. All who

come to him with legal difficulties leave reconciled. That hall is the best place of judgment known to the Gods and men.

LIII. Baldur

1. At this time, Baldur had become incessantly tormented at night by phantoms that caused him to fall into such an unhealthy condition that he could not even walk properly. For this reason, he took to traveling in a chariot or carriage. Indeed, his feet suffered a blight, and Baldur the Good dreamed great dreams boding peril to his life. Urd appeared to him in a dream standing at his side, and declared that soon she would clasp him in her arms.

2. Baldur's horse is called Falhofnir, and it is said to have the ability to produce fountains by tramping on the ground. Several fountains, named after Baldur, were formed in such a manner, since springs rise up under this horse's hooves. Thus, Baldur is the defender of springs and wells. Baldur-Fal and Odin went to Varnwood, then was the foot sprained on Baldur's foal. Then sang over him Sinhtgunt-Nanna, Sunna her sister, then sang over him Frigga, Fulla her sister, then sang over him Odin, as best he could: Bone-sprain, like blood-sprain, like limb-sprain: bone to bone; blood to blood; limb to limb; like they were glued.

3. All the Aesir
went to the Thing,
and all the Asynjur
gathered together,
and the mighty Gods
discussed why
Baldur had
baleful dreams.

4. His sleep was most
afflicting to that God,
his good dreams
seemed to be gone.
They asked the Etins,
wise seers of the future,
whether this might not
forebode calamity?

5. The responses said that Ull's kinsman [Baldur], dearest of all, was destined to die: that caused grief to Frigga and Svafnir-Odin, and to the other Powers. Now although Odin is regarded as jarl of the Gods, he would constantly approach seers, soothsayers, and others whom he had discovered strong in the arts of prediction, with a view to prosecuting vengeance for his son. Hrossthjof, son of Hrimnir and brother of Gullveig-Heid, foretold that Rind, daughter of Billing, must bear him another son, who would take reprisal for his brother's killing; the Gods had destined that their colleague should be avenged by his future brother's hand.

6. But they came up with a plan: that they would send messages to every being, to solicit assurance to not harm Baldur. It was decided to request immunity for Baldur from

all kinds of dangers, and Frigga received solemn promises so that Baldur should not be harmed by fire and water, iron and all kinds of metal, stones, the earth, trees, diseases, the animals, the birds, poison, and serpents. All species swore oaths to spare him, Frigga received all their vows and compacts. The oath was as follows:

7. "All wights, all Vanir, watch over Baldur! May he not meet death by a brother's hand, nor by the hand of one who is not related to him, not by human hand. This I transfer, all oaths provide to him welfare and longevity. All divine beings that are in heaven, on earth, in the air, in plants, in animals, and in water, to him you should dispatch lasting life of many years. The hundred other ways to die he shall avoid."

8. An unusually delicious drink was made for Baldur, which had been devised to increase his vigor. The three holy meads were used, whose liquid provided a potent preparation for Baldur to drink, given to him by three Goddesses. From this, and the oath, Baldur regained his strength, and forgot his past afflictions. His body thus possessed a holy strength impermeable to steel.

9. When the oaths were made and confirmed, it then became an entertainment for Baldur and the other Aesir that he should stand up at the Thing and all the others should either shoot at him or strike at him or throw stones at him. But whatever they did he was unharmed, and they all thought this a great glory. But when Loki Laufeyarson heard about this he was not pleased that Baldur was unharmed. He went to Fensalir to Frigga, changed into the form of a woman. Then Frigga asked this woman if she knew what the Aesir were doing at the Thing. She said that everyone was shooting at Baldur, and moreover that he was unharmed. Then Frigga said:

10. "Weapons and wood will not harm Baldur. I have received oaths from them all."

11. Then the woman asked: "Have all things sworn oaths not to harm Baldur?"

12. Then Frigga replied: "There grows a shoot of a tree to the west of Valhall. It is called mistletoe. It seemed too young to demand the oath from."

13. Immediately afterwards, the woman disappeared. Then Loki took the mistletoe and plucked it, then he returned to the Wolfdales. He entered Volund's smithy, expecting payment for his services as a milkmaid. He spoke his piece and asked Volund to fashion an arrow from the mistletoe, such as Hod himself would make, and instill it with the quality of sure death for whomever it struck. This Volund did. Mistelteinn, as the arrow was called, became Volund's sec-

ond Gambantein. The mistletoe thus became
a dangerous arrow of pain.

14. Valfather-Odin fears
    something defective;
    he thinks the hamingjas
    may have departed;
    he convenes the Aesir,
    craves their counsel;
    at the deliberation
    much is devised.

15. Odin rose up,
    the lord of men,
    and laid the saddle
    on Sleipnir,
    thence he rode down
    to Niflhel,
    he met a dog
    coming from Hel.

16. It was blood-stained
    on its breast,
    on its slaughter-craving throat,
    and nether jaw.
    It bayed and
    barked loudly
    at the Galdurfather [Odin]:
    long it howled.

17. But no dog,
    however fierce,
    would attack him.
    He is the one
    whom no dogs
    would harm;
    Garm is
    the best of dogs.

18. Odin rode on–
    the ground rattled–
    till he came
    to Hel's lofty house.
    Then Ygg-Odin rode
    to the eastern gate,

where he knew
the vala's grave was.

19. He began chanting
    Galdur to the seeress,
    looked towards the north,
    applied potent runes,
    pronounced a spell,
    demanded an answer
    until she was compelled to rise,
    and with deathlike voice, she spoke:

20. "What man is this,
    unknown to me,
    who has made me travel
    the troublesome road?
    I was buried in snow
    and beaten by rain,
    and drenched with dew;
    long have I been dead."

21. Odin: "My name is Vegtam,
    I am Valtam's son;
    tell me of Hel:
    for I am from earth.
    For whom are the benches
    covered with rings,
    and the gold beautifully
    scattered through the room?"

22. Vala: "Here stands the mead,
    the Skirar Veigar,
    prepared for Baldur;
    shields are spread over,
    and the Asmegir
    are waiting impatiently.
    By compulsion I have spoken,
    I will now be silent."

23. Vegtam: "Do not be silent, vala!
    I will question you
    until I learn
    all that I wish to know.
    Tell me who will be
    Baldur's slayer,
    and steal the life

from Odin's son?"

24. Vala: "Hod will send his
glorious brother here to Hel,
he will be the slayer
of Baldur,
and steal the life
from Odin's son.
By compulsion I have spoken,
I will now be silent."

25. Vegtam: "Do not be silent, vala!
I will question you
until I learn
all that I wish to know.
Tell me who shall
bring vengeance on Hod,
and raise Baldur's slayer
on the pyre?"

26. Vala: "Rind bears Vali
in the western halls;
he will slay Odin's son
when one night old.
He will not wash his hands,
nor comb his hair
before he has borne
Baldur's slayer to the pyre.
By compulsion I have spoken,
I will now be silent."

27. Vegtam: "Do not be silent, vala!
I will question you
until I learn
all that I wish to know.
Tell me, who are the maidens
who weep at will
and cast their neck-veils
to the sky?"

28. Vala: "You are not Vegtam,
as I had thought,
you are Odin,
lord of men!"

29. Odin: "You are no vala,

nor wise woman,
but rather are the mother
of three Thurses."

30. Vala: "Ride home, Odin!
And be happy in mind,
for never again shall
any man visit me,
until Loki escapes
from his bonds,
and the day of the all-destroying
Ragnarok comes."

31. Allfather-Odin then went to Mimisbrunn and asked for one drink from the well, but he did not get this until he gave one of his eyes as a pledge. From the well's inspiring liquids he realized that he was not going to be satisfied until he spoke to Urd herself, who knows the urlag of all beings, and understood how he could get her to speak her prophecy. Odin went to her, then laid treaures from Valhall at her feet and asked her about the prophecies she hears from the roar of her well and from the sweeping of Yggdrasil's crown. Then she sang the following song:

32. Hear me, all you
holy children,
high and low
of Heimdall's sons.
You, Valfather-Odin, wish
that I speak well
of ancient tidings of men,
the remotest I remember.

33. I remember Etins,
born early on,

who fostered me
long ago.
Nine worlds, I remember,
nine Ividjas,
the glorious mead-tree
was below the earth.

34. In the Ancient Age,
where Ymir dwelt,
there was no sand nor sea,
nor cool waves.
The earth did not exist,
nor the sky above—
there was a mighty chasm—
and grass grew nowhere.

35. The sons of Bur lifted
up the lands,
they who fashioned
the splendid Midgard.
Sol shone from the south
on the stones of the abode;
then the ground grew
green with leeks.

36. Sol, Mani's companion,
from the south cast
her right hand
across heaven's rim.
Sol did not know
where she had mansions,
stars did not know
where they had stations,
Mani did not know
what might he had.

37. Then the Powers all went
to the Thingseats,
the high-holy Gods
to consider thereon:
They gave names to
Natt and Nidjar,
they named Morgin-Delling,
and Middag-Dag,
afternoon and evening—
to reckon in years.

38. The Aesir met
on Idavoll,
built lofty
hofs and horgs,
set up forges,
fashioned treasures,
created tongs
and made tools.

39. They played merrily
with Tafl in their court;
they had all
bounties of gold,
until three came,
Thurses' daughters,
powerful maidens
from Jotunheim.

40. Then the Powers all went
to their Thingseats,
the high-holy Gods
to consider thereon:
to find who should raise
the race of men
out of Brimir-Ymir's blood
and Blain-Ymir's limbs.

41. There Modsognir-Mimir had
become the most esteemed
of all the Dwarves,
but Durin-Surt the second.
They, the Dwarves,
fashioned many human
forms from earth,
as Durin-Surt commanded.

42. Until three Aesir,
mighty and venerable,
came to the world
from their Thing,
they found on the land
the powerless
Ask and Embla,
without urlag.

43. Ond they had not,
    odur they had not,
    neither la nor laeti
    nor litur goda.
    Ond gave Odin,
    odur gave Hoenir,
    Lodur gave la with laeti
    and litur goda.

44. An ash I know,
    Yggdrasil its name,
    the great tree is watered
    with white liquid:
    thence come the dews
    that fall into the dales,
    forever green it stands
    over Urdarbrunn.

45. Thence come maidens,
    much knowing,
    three from the sea,
    which stands under the tree;
    one is named Urd,
    Verdandi the second—
    they scored on the wood–
    Skuld the third.
    They established laws,
    allotted life to
    the sons of men,
    and pronounced urlag.

46. I remember the first
    folkvig in the world;
    when the Gods had raised
    Gullveig on spears,
    and they burned her
    in Har's hall,
    three times burned,
    and three times born
    oft and again,
    yet still she lives.

47. They called her Heid-Gullveig,
    when she came to houses,
    the wise, prophetic vala,
    who blessed gandurs;

who practiced Seid,
by Seid sent Leikin,
she was always sought out
by evil women.

48. Then the Powers all went
    to their Thingseats,
    the high-holy Gods,
    to consider thereon:
    who had filled all
    the air with evil?
    Or had given Od's maid [Freya]
    to the Etin race.

49. There alone was Thor
    swollen with anger–
    he seldom sits
    when he hears such things–
    and the oaths were broken,
    the words and bonds,
    every powerful pact
    between the Powers.

50. Then the Powers all went
    to their Thingseats,
    the high-holy Gods
    to consider thereon:
    if the Aesir should
    pay compensation,
    or if all the Gods
    should atone with gold.

51. Odin threw his spear
    into the host of the hof;
    then came the first
    war in the world;
    broken was the bulwark
    of the Asaburgh,
    through combat-foresight were
    the Vanir able to tread its fields.

52. She [Urd] sat out alone
    when the ancient one [Odin] came.
    The Aesir's glory [Odin]
    looked into her eyes:
    "What do you ask me?

Why do you tempt me?
I know everything Odin,
where you hid your eye."

53. I know where Odin's
   eye is hidden,
   deep in the wide-famed
   well of Mimir;
   Mimir drinks mead
   from Odin's pledge [Gjallarhorn]
   each morn:
   know you more or what?

54. Herjafather-Odin chose
   necklaces and rings for her
   in exchange for prophetic songs
   and knowledge of prophetic staves.
   Fully she knew the future,
   further on she could see.
   She saw far and wide
   over all the worlds.

55. She knows that Heimdall's
   horn is hidden
   under the high,
   holy tree;
   she sees a river flow,
   with violent torrents,
   from Valfather-Odin's pledge.
   Know you more or what?

56. She saw Valkyries,
   far traveled,
   ready to ride
   to Goth-thjod:
   Skuld bore a shield,
   Skogul was next,
   then Gunn, Hild, Gondul
   and Geirskogul.
   Now are enumerated
   Herjan-Odin's maidens,
   the Valkyries ready
   to ride over the earth.

57. I saw of Baldur,
   the blood-stained God,

son of Odin,
   his urlag hidden.
   There stood full-grown,
   high above the plain,
   slender and fair,
   the mistletoe.

58. The stem,
   so slender it seemed,
   became the awful, woeful shot,
   which Hod eagerly released.
   Baldur's brother
   was born early,
   and one night old
   slew Odin's son.

59. Neither washed his hands,
   nor combed his hair,
   before he sent Baldur's bane
   to the pyre.
   But Frigga wept
   in Fensalir
   for Valhall's woes.
   Know you more or what?

60. She saw lying
   under Hveralund,
   one shaped like
   the insidious Loki,
   there Nidhogg sucks
   the corpses of the dead,
   the wolf tears men.

61. Vali's death-bonds
   were twisted there,
   most rigid bonds
   made from entrails,
   Sigyn sits there,
   for her consort's sake,
   she is not happy.

62. A river falls from the east,
   through venom dales,
   with swords and daggers,
   its name is Slid.

62. In the north there
    stood on Nidi-Mimir's plains a
    hall of gold
    for Sindri's race;
    another stood
    on Okolnir,
    the beer-hall of the Etin
    who is called Brimir-Mimir.

63. She saw a hall standing
    far from the sun
    on Nastrand,
    the doors opened to the north;
    venom-drops fell
    through the roof-holes.
    The hall is made from
    the backs of twined serpents.

64. There she saw wade
    through heavy streams,
    perjurous men
    and murderers;
    the waste-water of
    the venom-troughs
    falls upon him who
    seduces another's wife.

65. To the east in the Ironwood
    lives the ancient Giantess,
    and there fosters
    the brood of Fenris.
    Of them all
    one shall certainly,
    equipped in troll-guise,
    rob the moon.

66. He gorges on the feast
    of cowards' corpses,
    stains the Gods'
    homes with blood.
    The sun becomes black
    summers thereafter,
    every wind is furious.
    Know you more or what?

67. There sat on a hill,
    striking a harp,
    the Giantess' watch,
    the joyous Eggther;
    by him crowed,
    in the Gaglwood,
    the bright-red cock,
    Fjalar is his name.

68. Over the Aesir
    crowed Gullinkambi,
    which wakens heroes
    with Herjan-Odin.
    Another crows
    in the Underworld,
    the soot-red cock
    in Hel-Urd's halls.

69. Garm bays wildy
    at Gnipacave,
    his bonds will break
    and the wolf Freki will run.
    Fully do I know the future,
    further on I can see
    the twilight and fall
    of the godly Powers.

70. Brother may become
    brother's bane,
    life between siblings'
    sons spilled,
    hardship is in the world,
    much whoredom,
    axe-age, knife-age,
    shields are cloven,
    wind-age, wolf-age,
    before the world succumbs,
    no man
    dare spare another.

71. Mimir's sons spring up,
    the Wyrd of creation
    is forebode by the blare
    of the old Gjallarhorn.
    Loud blows Heimdall—
    the horn in the air!
    Odin speaks

with Mimir's head.

72. Standing Yggdrasil's
    ash quakes,
    the old tree trembles,
    and the Etin gets loose;
    all are frightened
    on the Helways,
    before Surt's spirit [fire]
    swallows him [the Etin].

73. Garm bays wildy
    at Gnipacave,
    his bonds will break,
    and the wolf Freki will run.
    Fully do I know the future,
    further on I can see
    the twilight and fall
    of the godly Powers.

74. Hrym steers from the east
    and lifts his shield before him;
    Jormungand coils
    with Etin's wrath,
    the serpent makes the waves swell,
    and the eagle screeches,
    Nidfol tears into corpses,
    Naglfar is loosened.

75. A ship comes from the east,
    the hosts of Muspel
    come over the ocean,
    Loki is pilot.
    All of Fifl-Loki's sons
    come with Freki,
    Byleist's brother [Loki]
    travels with them.

76. What is with the Aesir?
    What is with the Alfar?
    Jotunheim is in an uproar!
    The Aesir are at the Thing;
    outside the stone doors,
    the groaning Dwarves,
    the wise ones of the precipice.
    Know you more or what?

77. Surt fares from the south
    with the scourge of branches [fire],
    then Valtivi-Frey's sword
    shines like the sun.
    Crags are sundered,
    Giantesses sink;
    men tread the path of Hel,
    and heaven is cloven.

78. Then a second sorrow
     is at hand for Hlin-Frigga,
    when Odin fares to
    fight with the wolf,
    and Beli's brilliant
    bane [Frey] with Surt.
    Then will Frigga's
    beloved fall.

79. Then comes Sigfather-Odin's
    mighty son,
    Vidar, to battle
    with his chosen monster.
    With his hands, his sword,
    he will pierce the heart
    of Hvedrung-Loki's son.
    Then is his father avenged.

80. Then comes the strong
    son of Hlodyn-Frigga,
    Vidar's brother [Thor],
    the bane of wolves.
    Odin's son walks
    to battle with the serpent.
    In his rage he will
    slay the serpent.

81. Fjorgyn-Frigga's son
    walks nine feet
    before he must boldly
    collapse from the poison.
    Dead men clear lands
    of all people.

82. The sun blackens,
    the earth sinks into the sea.

The many stars fall
from the heavens;
fire gushes
against Yggdrasil,
the flames leap high
against heaven itself.

83. Garm bays wildly
at Gnipacave,
his bonds will break
and the wolf Freki will run.
Fully do I know the future,
further on I can see
the twilight and fall
of godly Powers.

84. She sees rise up,
a second time,
earth from the ocean,
greenery of the eddying fountains;
cascades fall
and the eagle flies over,
he who spies fish
from the mountain.

85. The Aesir meet
on Idavoll,
where they speak
of the immense World-Tree,
each one is reminded
of their remarkable urlag,
and Fimbultyr-Odin's
ancient runes.

86. Then once again
the wondrous
game of Tafl
is found in the grass,
that which was owned
in time's morning
by a divine prince,
and Fjolnir-Odin's family.

87. Unsown acres
will grow,
all evil is remedied

and Baldur returns.
He and Hod, chosen
Gods and kinsmen, inhabit
Hropt-Odin's victory-home [Valhall].
Know you more or what?

88. Then Hoenir is able
to choose the lot-wood,
and the sons of the two
brothers [Baldur and Hod] inhabit the
spacious Vindheim.
Know you more or what?

89. She sees a hall
more fair than the sun,
covered in gold,
standing on Gimle:
there shall the virtuous
multitudes dwell
and complete happiness
is enjoyed forever.

90. And then shall come
to the doom of the world
the great Godhead [Odin]
who governs all.
He settles strife,
sits in judgment,
and lays down laws
that will always last.

91. There comes the dark dragon
flying from beneath,
the glistening serpent,
from Nidafjoll.
Nidhogg, flying over the plain,
bears a corpse
on his wings.
Now she will descend.

92. The Asafather listened and was not
afraid of the Norns' judgment over him. To
fare joyously until one meets their bane is
what he recommends to men, and would do

this himself; plus, dying on a battlefield befit him. His troubled mind had found some peace, since he had found out that he and Baldur, who was the best side of him, would return and govern a new world. Because of his tragic tale, Baldur is said to be the God of lamentations.

93. When Hod was a youth, his father, Odin, sat him down in Valhall and spoke wisdom to him, which he speaks of here:

94. It is time to talk
from the sage's seat,
by Urdarbrunn
I sat silently,
I saw and meditated,
I listened to men's words.

95. I heard runes spoken of,
and of things divine,
nor of risting them were they silent,
nor of sage counsels,
at Har's hall,
in Har's hall,
I thus heard say:

96. I counsel you, Loddfafnir-Hod,
to heed advice;
you will profit, if you take it.
Rise not at night,
unless to explore,
or would fare to the outhouse.

97. I counsel you, Loddfafnir-Hod,
to heed advice;
you will profit, if you take it.
You should not sleep
in the embrace of an enchantress,
so that she will not enclose you in her arms.

98. She will make it so

that you care little
for the Thing or prince's words;
meal's and men's merriment
will not please you,
and you will go to sleep sorrowful.

99. I counsel you, Loddfafnir-Hod,
to heed advice;
you will profit, if you take it.
Never entice
another's wife
into secret converse.

100. I counsel you, Loddfafnir-Hod,
to heed advice;
you will profit, if you take it.
If you have to travel
by land or sea,
provide yourself with plenty of food.

101. I counsel you, Loddfafnir-Hod,
to heed advice;
you will profit, if you take it.
Never let
a bad man
know your misfortunes,
for from a bad man
you will never receive payment
for a kind heart.

102. I saw a wicked woman's
words mortally
wound a man;
a false tongue
caused his death,
and most unrighteously.

103. I counsel you, Loddfafnir-Hod,
to heed advice;
you will profit, if you take it.
If you know you have a friend
whom you can trust fully,
go to visit him often;
for the way that no one treads
is overgrown with brushwood
and high grass.

104. I counsel you, Loddfafnir-Hod,
    to heed advice;
    you will profit, if you take it.
    Find a good man
    to hold in friendship,
    and learn to make yourself loved.

105. I counsel you, Loddfafnir-Hod,
    to heed advice;
    you will profit, if you take it.
    Never be
    first to quarrel
    with your friend.
    Care gnaws the heart,
    if you can disclose
    your whole mind to no one.

106. I counsel you, Loddfafnir-Hod,
    to heed advice;
    you will profit, if you take it.
    You should never
    exchange words
    with a weak-minded fool.

107. For from an ill-conditioned man
    you will never get
    a return for good;
    but a good man will
    bring you favor
    by his praise.

108. There is a mingling of affection,
    where one can tell
    another all his mind.
    Everything is better
    than being with the deceitful.
    He is not another's friend
    whoever says as he says.

109. I counsel you, Loddfafnir-Hod,
    to heed advice;
    you will profit, if you take it.
    Even in three words
    do not quarrel with a worse man:
    often the better yields,
    when the worse strikes.

110. I counsel you, Loddfafnir-Hod,
    to heed advice;
    you will profit, if you take it.
    Be not a shoemaker,
    nor a shaftmaker,
    unless it is for yourself,
    for a shoe if ill-made
    or a shaft if crooked,
    will call evil down on you.

111. I counsel you, Loddfafnir-Hod,
    to heed advice;
    you will profit, if you take it.
    Wherever you know of harm,
    regard that harm as your own;
    and give your foes no peace.

112. I counsel you, Loddfafnir-Hod,
    to heed advice;
    you will profit, if you take it.
    Never find joy
    in evil,
    but let good bring you pleasure.

113. I counsel you, Loddfafnir-Hod,
    to heed advice;
    you will profit, if you take it.
    Do not look up
    in a battle,
    (the sons of men become
    like swine),
    so men may not enchant you.

114. I counsel you, Loddfafnir-Hod,
    to heed advice;
    you will profit, if you take it.
    If you would induce a good woman
    to pleasant converse,
    you must promise fair,
    and hold to it:
    no one turns from good, if it can be got.

115. I counsel you, Loddfafnir-Hod,
    to heed advice;
    you will profit, if you take it.
    I bid you to be wary,

but not over-wary,
at drinking be most wary,
and with another's wife;
and thirdly,
that thieves do not trick you.

116. I counsel you, Loddfafnir-Hod,
to heed advice;
you will profit, if you take it.
Never treat
a guest or traveler
with insult or ridicule;
they often know little,
who sit within,
of what race they are who come.

117. The sons of men bear
vices and virtues
mingled in their hearts;
no one is so good
that no failing attends him,
nor so bad as to be good for nothing.

118. I counsel you, Loddfafnir-Hod,
to heed advice;
you will profit, if you take it.
Never scorn
the grey-haired speaker,
oft do the old speak good;
often from shriveled skin
come skillful counsels,
though it hang with the hides,
and flap with the pelts,
and is blown with the bellies.

119. I counsel you, Loddfafnir-Hod,
to heed advice;
you will profit, if you take it.
Do not berate a guest,
nor push him away from your gate;
treat the poor well,
they will speak well of you.

120. Strong is the bar
that must be raised
to admit all.

Do give a penny,
or they will call down on you
every ill on your limbs.

121. I counsel you, Loddfafnir-Hod,
to heed advice;
you will profit, if you take it.
Wherever you drink beer,
invoke the power of earth;
for earth is good against drink,
fire cures ailments,
the oak for constipation,
a corn-ear for sorcery,
elder for domestic srife.
Invoke Mani against the Heiptir,
the biter is good for bite-injuries;
but runes against calamity;
let fluid absorb fluid.

122. You will long lack
these songs, Loddfafnir-Hod,
yet it may be good,
if you understand them,
profitable if you learn them.

LIV. Sinmara

1. When it became obvious that the Aesir were in no position to stop the Fimbulwinter, Urd informed Mimir that he had the right and the duty to step in. It was told to Mimir, lord of the Njars, that Volund remained alone in the Wolfdales, and he ordered him to be seized. Mimir and his eldest sons, Sindri among them, mounted their horses, well armed. So the twelve sons of Mimir, excellent in their talents, prepared to leave, and likewise his twelve daughters, renowned for their beauty. Mimir's queen, Sinmara, with their daughters, the Ostaras,

Goddesses of dawn and the night, sat in their saddles, following them. These night-Goddesses are led by Ostara-Natt herself, while the sons, the Brisings, are also called Njars. The help of the Ostaras was necessary for this trip. So they rode over Nidafjoll's precipitous, damp mountain passes, past the Grotti-mill and the Hvergelmir well, down into the gloomy Niflheim, and from there, up through the passage that leads to the Wolfdales.

2. Arriving there they arranged themselves so that the Ostaras formed a ring around the men. By this means, the entire troop advanced, appearing to the naked eye as a dark mist that drifted over the valley-path. Their aim was to surprise Volund, whose sword of revenge made him invincible. The men traveled at night, in studded mail-coats, their shields glistened in the moon-sickle's light; but it was as if the moonlight only played on the mist. They arrived at Volund's smithy late in the evening, remaining near the gable as darkness enveloped them.

3. They jumped from their saddles
   at the house's gable,
   thence they went in
   through the hall;
   they saw the rings
   bound on the bast-rope,
   seven hundred of them,
   which the warrior owned.

4. And they took them off,
   and they put them on,
   all save one,
   which they bore away.

5. The storm-terrible came
   home from the hunt,
   Volund was gliding
   on the long path;
   he went to the fire
   to roast bear's flesh;
   soon the brushwood,
   and the arid fir,
   the wind-dried wood,
   blazed before Volund.

6. Sitting on the bearskin,
   the Alfar's companion
   counted his rings:
   one was missing.
   He hoped that
   Ivaldi's daughter [Idun] had it,
   the young Swanmaid,
   and that she had returned.

7. He sat for a long time,
   until he fell asleep,
   and then he awoke,
   bereft of joy:
   on his hands he felt
   the heavy rope
   and round his feet
   fetters were clasped.

8. Volund: "Who are the mighty,
   who have bound Byrr-Volund
   with bonds,
   and have fettered me?"

9. Then Mimir,
   lord of the Njars, cried out:
   "Where did you, Volund,
   chief of Alfar,
   get our gold that
   is here in the Wolfdales?
   That gold was not

on Grani's path,
I thought our land was
far from Niflheim."

10. Volund: "Auda and Idun
were Ivaldi's daughters,
and Sif was
born of Sigtryg.
I think we had
more treasures
when we were at home
as a whole family."

11. Mimir's cunning queen [Sinmara]
stood outside;
then she went
into the house,
stood on the floor
and quietly said:
"There is hate in him,
who came from the forest."

12. Mimir gave his daughter Bodvild the gold ring, Andvaranaut, which had been taken from the bast-rope in Volund's house and has the miraculous hidden power of increasing its owner's wealth. Mimir himself bore the sword that had belonged to Volund, called Gambantein. Mimir's sons tried to copy the wondrous weapon, the result of which was the sword Tyrfing, which they gave to Lodur. But this sword, as great as it was, did not have nearly the might of Volund's Gambantein.

13. Sinmara: "He bears his teeth,
when he sees the sword
and recognizes
Bodvild's ring:
the glow in his eyes

is as threatening as a serpent's.
Let his sinew's strength
be severed,
and then put him
in Saevarstod."

14. This was done. He was hamstrung and then put on a certain small island near the shore, called Saevarstod. There he forged for Mimir all sorts of precious things. No one was allowed to go to him, except Mimir.

15. Volund said: "The sword shines
on Mimir's belt,
that which I whetted
as skillfully as I could,
and which I tempered,
as seemed to me most cunningly.
That bright blade
is taken from me forever;
never shall I see it
borne into Volund's smithy.

16. "Now Bodvild wears
my bride's ring
of red-gold,
and I can do nothing about it."
He sat and never slept,
and worked with his hammer;
he forged wondrous
works for Mimir.

17. The two young
sons of Mimir,
ran in at the door to look,
in Saevarstod.
They came to the chest,
they asked for the keys—
their ill Wyrd was sealed
when they looked in.

18. There were many necklaces and treasures,
which appeared to be

made of red-gold
to those youths.
"You two come alone,
come tomorrow,
so that gold
shall be given to you."

19. He told the boys to return after the fresh snow had fallen, and to walk backwards towards the door when they arrived. He did this so, when he was suspected of their disappearance, he could clear his name by showing the tracks leading from his door.

20. "Do not tell the maidens,
nor the folk of your household,
nor to anyone,
that you have come to me."
It was early
when one brother
called to the other brother:
"Let's go see the rings!"

21. They came to the chest,
then asked for the keys—
their ill Wyrd was sealed
when they looked in.
He cut off the heads
of those children,
and buried their bodies
beneath the bellows' pit.

22. But he set their skulls
in silver,
beneath the hair,
and gave them to Mimir;
he made precious stones
out of their eyes,
and gave them to the cunning
queen of Mimir.

23. But he made breast-ornaments
out of the teeth

of the two,
and sent them to Bodvild.

24. Then Bodvild
praised the ring:
she brought it to Volund,
when she had broken it:
"I dare tell no one of this,
except for you."

25. Volund: "I will repair
the fractured gold,
so that it will seem
better to your father
and much more beautiful
to your mother,
and the same as before
to you yourself."

26. He then brought her beer,
so that he might
succeed the better,
as she fell asleep on her seat.
"Now I have avenged
all the wrongs done to me,
excepting one,
which demands a more terrible vengeance."

27. "I wish," said Volund,
"that I were on my feet,
which Mimir's men
have deprived me the use of."

28. Laughing, Volund
rose in the air:
Bodvild left
the island weeping,
fearful of his escape,
and her father's wrath.

29. Mimir's cunning queen
stood outside;
then she went
into the house,
but Volund sat down
to rest on the wall:

"Are you awake,
lord of the Njars [Mimir]?"

30. "I am always awake,
joyless, I lie to rest,
when I call to mind
my children's death:
my head is cold
to me, your counsels are cold,
now I wish
to ask this of Volund:

31. "Tell me, Volund,
chief of Alfar,
what has become
of my brave boys?"

32. Volund: "First, you swear
oaths to me,
by ship's bulwark,
by shield's rim,
by the steed's shoulder,
by the sword's edge,
that you will not
harm Volund's wife,
although I have a wife
whom you know,
or I have a child
within your hall.

33. "Go to the smithy,
which you have made,
there you will find the bellows
sprinkled with blood:
I severed the heads
of your boys,
and buried their bodies
beneath the bellows' pit.

34. "But I set their skulls
in silver,
beneath the hair,
and gave them to Mimir;
I made precious stones
out of their eyes,
and gave them to the cunning

queen of Mimir.

35. "I made breast-ornaments
out of the teeth
of the two,
and sent them to Bodvild;
and now Bodvild
the beautiful daughter
of you both
is big with child."

36. Mimir: "You have never said words
that saddened me more,
or for which I would
more severely punish you.
There is no man so tall
that he can pull you down,
or so skillful
that he can shoot you down,
from where you
float up in the sky."

37. Laughing, Volund
rose in the air,
but Mimir remained,
sitting in sorrow.

38. Then Mimir,
lord of Njars, said:
"Rise up,
best of my thralls!
Tell Bodvild,
my fair-browed daughter,
to come speak to her father
in bright attire."

39. "Is it true, Bodvild,
what has been told to me,
that you and Volund
sat together on the isle?"

40. Bodvild: "It is true, Mimir,
what has been told to you,
that Volund and I
sat together on the isle,
in an unlucky hour:

it should not have been!
I could not
strive against him,
I might not
prevail against him."

41. Protected by Mimir's oath, Vidga, the son of Volund, the enemy of the Gods and of the world, grew up in the stronghold of Sinmara, in the care of the family that protects Yggdrasil and is united by family ties and friendship to the Gods. Vidga was heir to the sword of revenge and was obligated, if Volund fell in his battle with the Gods, to avenge his father's death. Thus was his destiny if he ever found Gambantein, the sword of revenge, in his power.

LV. Skadi

1. Volund flew to Thrymheim, in the Wolfdales, with the eagle-guise he had created on Saevarstod. In the valleys between its ice-covered mountains, he expected to find Idun and their daughter, Skadi, and he found them there. Inside Brunnacre, Volund had built expensive halls, which were decorated with his unparalleled works of art. Their doors opened on the Wolfsea, which his songs kept free of ice. Here, inside the mountain hall, he intended to live with Idun through the centuries. The Aesir, bereft of the Ellilyf Asa that Idun alone possessed, would continue to age and the reins of the worlds would fall from their enfeebled hands. This was the plan that Volund now laid.

2. Then the Aesir held a Thing and asked each other what was the last that was known about Idun, and the last that had been seen was that she had gone outside Asgard with Loki. They found Olgefn-Idun's flowing corpse-sea [blood] hound [wolf, thief, i.e. Loki] and bound the thief, that tree of deceit who had led Olgefn-Idun off. Loki was thus arrested and brought to the Thing, and he was threatened with death and torture. "You shall be trapped, Loki," the angry one [Thor] said, "unless by some scheme you bring back the renowned maid, enlarger of the Fetters' [Gods'] joy."

3. Being filled with terror, he said he would go in search of Idun in Jotunheim if Freya would lend him her falcon-guise. And when he got the falcon-guise, he flew north to Jotunheim and arrived one day at Volund's; he was out at sea in a boat, but Idun was at home alone. Loki turned her into the form of a nut and held her in his claws and flew as fast as he could. The trier of Hoenir's mind [Loki] tricked back the Aesir's girlfriend [Idun] with the help of a hawk's flight-skin.

4. When Volund got home and found Idun was not there he got his eagle-guise and flew after Loki and he caused a storm-wind by

his flying. With deceitful mind the father of swords, the Regin of the motion of the feather-leaf [Volund], directed the storm-wind against the hawk's offspring [Loki in falcon-guise].

5. When the Aesir saw the falcon flying with the nut and where the eagle was flying, they went out to the wall around Asgard, then prepared to ignite the Vafurfires. When the falcon flew in over the burgh, it let itself drop down by the wall. The Gods raised the Vafurfires and sharpened their javelins, and the eagle was unable to stop when it missed the falcon. Then the eagle's feathers caught fire and his flight was ended. The son [Volund] of Grepp's wooer [Ivaldi] is scorched. There is a sudden swerve in his travel. Then the Aesir were close by and killed Volund within the Asgates, and this killing is greatly renowned. The spears of the Gods had cut through the air, and enraged, Volund rushed through the swirling Vafurfires in uncontrollable flight, wounded with spears, and fell with wings on fire down against the wall. The eagle-form dropped away together with smoke and sparks, and the Aesir saw Volund himself. He attempted to stand on his lamed legs to fight to the death, but Thor swung Mjollnir against his skull, and the mighty one fell dead, his head crushed.

6. But Skadi, Volund's daughter, took helmet and mail-coat and all weapons and went to Asgard to avenge her father. But the Aesir offered her atonement and compensation, the first item of which was that she was to choose herself a husband among the Aesir and choose by the feet and see nothing else of them. Then she saw one person's feet that were exceptionally beautiful and said:

7. "I choose that one; there can be little that is ugly about Baldur."

8. But it was Njord of Noatun. Baldur's feet had previously been damaged.

9. It was also in her terms of settlement that the Aesir were to do something that she thought they would not be able to do, that was to make her laugh. Then Loki did as follows: he tied a cord around the beard of a certain nanny-goat and the other end round his testicles, and they drew each other back and forth and both squealed loudly. Then Loki let himself drop into Skadi's lap, and she laughed. Then the atonement with her on the part of the Aesir was complete.

10. It is said that Odin, as compensation for her, did this: he had Thor take Volund's eyes and throw them up into the sky, and made two stars out of them. He threw into the wide-wind's basin [sky] the Ondurdis' [Skadi's] father's eyes, above the dwelling of the multitude of men.

11. So Njord married Skadi, Volund's daughter. Skadi wanted to live in the home that her father had owned up in the mountains at Thrymheim. But Njord wanted to be near the sea. They came to an agreement that they would stay nine nights in Thrymheim, and the next three nights at Noatun. But when Njord returned to Noatun from the mountain, he said:

12. "Hateful for me are the mountains,
　　I was not there long,
　　only nine nights.
　　The howling of wolves
　　sounded ugly to me
　　after the song of swans.

13. "Why did I linger
　　in the shadows,
　　enfolded by
　　rugged hills,
　　not following
　　the waves as before?

14. "The challenging howl
　　of the wolf-pack,
　　the ungovernable
　　ferocity of beasts,
　　cries of dangerous brutes
　　ever raised to heaven,
　　snatch all rest
　　from my eyes.

15. "The mountain ridges
　　are desolate to hearts
　　bent on sterner schemes.
　　The unbending cliffs
　　and harsh terrain
　　oppress those whose
　　souls delight in
　　the high seas."

16. His wife loved the life of the countryside and therefore, sick of the morning choir of sea-birds, revealed in these words how much contentment lay for her in roving the woodland tracks. Thus said Skadi:

17. "I could not sleep
　　on the sea-beds
　　for the screeching of the bird.
　　That gull wakes me
　　when he comes each morning
　　from the wide sea.

18. "The chant of the birds torments me
　　lagging here on the shore,
　　disturbing me with their jabber
　　whenever I try to sleep,
　　and I hear the ceaseless roar
　　and fury of the tide
　　as it takes away the gentle
　　repose from my slumbering eyes.

19. "There is no relaxation at night
　　for the shrill chatter of the sea-mew,
　　dinning its stupid screech
　　into my tender ears,
　　for it will not allow me
　　to rest in my bed or be refreshed,
　　but ominously caws away
　　in dismal modulations.

20. "For me there's a safer
　　and sweeter thing—
　　to sport in the woods.
　　How could you crop
　　a more meager share
　　of peace in light
　　or darkness than by tossing
　　on the shifting deep?"

21. Then Skadi went up to the mountains and lived in Thrymheim, as is said:

22. It is called Thrymheim
where Thjazi-Volund lived,
the mighty Etin.
But now Skadi,
the fair bride of the Gods,
lives in her father's house.

23. Because she still lives in the Wolfdales, Skadi is called the Hlodyn of Myrkwood or Myrkmark, and is also considered to be one of the Jarnvidjas of the Ironwood .

LVI. <u>Hringhorni</u>

1. Loki came to the Thing of the Gods, where they were throwing and shooting at Baldur, since it did him no harm. Hod stood at the edge of the circle of people. Loki spoke to him, asking: "Why aren't you shooting at Baldur?"

2. Hod replied, "Because I have no weapon."

3. Then Loki said, "You should be behaving like the others, honoring Baldur as they do. Shoot this arrow at him."

4. Hod took the Mistilteinn and, following Loki's directions, shot at Baldur. The shot went right through Baldur, who fell to the ground dead. This misfortune was the worst that had been worked against Gods and men. Baldur's death left the Gods speechless and so weak that they were unable to muster the strength to lift him up in their arms. They all looked at one another, and all were of a sin-

gle mind against the one who had done the killing. But no one could take vengeance because the place was deeply revered as a sanctuary. When the Aesir first tried to speak, all they could do was weep, and no one could form words to tell the others of their grief. Odin suffered the most from this misfortune. This was because he understood most clearly how grievous the loss was, and that the death of Baldur meant ruin for the Aesir.

5. For the eldest, Baldur, an unexpected deathbed was laid out, through his brother's doing, when Hod bent his horn-tipped bow and loosed the arrow that destroyed his life. He shot wide and buried a shaft in the flesh and blood of his own brother. That offence was beyond redress, a wrong footing of the heart's affections; for who could avenge the prince's life or pay his weregild?

6. The Aesir took Baldur's body and carried it to the air-sea, Ifing. Baldur's ship was called Hringhorni, and it was the greatest of all ships. The Gods would launch it and use it for Baldur's Helfare pyre. It is said that Odin leaned over and whispered something into his dead son's ear, before he was laid on the pyre, but what he said has never been reported, neither to Gods or men. The Aesir were reckoned eleven in number, when Baldur was laid on the pyre. Baldur's body was

179

carried out onto the ship, and when his wife, Nanna, daughter of Nep-Mani, saw this, her heart burst from sorrow and she died. She too was carried onto the Helfare pyre, which was then set on fire. Next, Thor stood up and blessed the pyre with Mjollnir.

7. Many kinds of beings came to this cremation. First to be mentioned is Odin. Far-famed Hroptatyr-Odin rode to the mighty broad pyre of his son. Frigga was with him, as were the Valkyries and his ravens. Valkyries and ravens accompanied the wise victory-tree [Odin] to the drink of the holy offering [Baldur's Helfare pyre]. Frey rode in his chariot. It was drawn by the boar called Gullinbursti or Slidrugtanni. Battle-skilled Frey rode in front to Odin's son's pyre with Gullinbursti, and governed hosts. Splendid Heimdall rode to the pyre raised by Gods for the fallen son [Baldur] of the strangely wise raven-tester [Odin], on his horse, Gulltopp. Freya drove her harnessed cats. Odin laid the gold ring Draupnir on the pyre. It had the characteristic that, every ninth night, eight gold rings of equal weight dripped from it. Baldur's horse, with all its riding gear, was led onto the pyre, and burned with him.

8. A strong northern wind blew from Jotunheim. The pyre lit and its sails raised, Hringhorni drifted out onto Ifing-Thund, the sea of air, and the Aesir remained on shore until the ship, engulfed by flames, had sunk behind the horizon.

9. It ferried Baldur and Nanna to Jormungrund's western gate. Here they were received by the powers of the Underworld and were guided through the glittering fields to Mimir's Holt, Odainsacre, and the castle Breidablik in the land of the rosy dawn. There Baldur and Nanna were expected by Lif and Leifthrasir, the children who will remain in Hoddmimis Holt until the renewal of the worlds. The halls were adorned with tapestries and golden ornaments; on the table before the high-seat stood a drinking bowl, covered with a shield, in which the strength-giving liquids of the three Underworld wells were blended. It is the drink that is extended to the blessed dead to erase the marks of the earthly death and gives them the ability to enjoy the life of bliss, completely free from care. This would be the second time Baldur was allowed to partake in this drink. The shield was removed and when they arrived, they were welcomed with the drink of clear strengths.

10. Baldur and Nanna are to remain in the subterranean Breidablik until the renewal of the worlds. Lif and Leifthrasir, and their offspring, are with them and are fostered by them to be the parents of an untainted race of man.

LVII. <u>Vali</u>

1. Frigga wept in Fensalir for Valhall's woes. Morning after morning, Odin wakes to remember that his child is gone. He gazes sorrowfully at his son's dwelling, the banquet hall bereft of all delight, the windswept hearthstone; the horsemen are sleeping, the warriors underground; what was is no more. No tunes from the harp, no cheer raised in the yard. Alone with his longing, he lies down on his bed and sings; everything seems too large, the steadings and the fields. Such was the feeling of loss endured by Odin after Baldur's death. He was helplessly placed to set right the wrong committed, yet could not punish the killer with the law of blood-revenge himself. But how would Baldur's death be avenged? In Asgard, all were convinced that Hod had not meant to kill his brother, and no one mourned that event more than he. Should Hod, who was innocent, be killed? Should the blood of the Asafather's blood be shed once more, and the death of one son result in that of another? No one could advocate that; no one wanted to lift his hand against Hod. Nor were the Gods able to discern one another's innermost thoughts. In this, as in all similar cases, it was their duty as judges to not turn a blind eye to the culprit's past history, but to investigate whether there was something that

could have motivated the deed. When Loki selected Hod as Baldur's killer, this was exactly what he had in mind. The Aesir must place importance in there being sufficient reason for Hod to have acted with ill-intent: Hod had of course once been Baldur's enemy and had coveted his wife.

2. For this reason, justice, in its severity, demanded that a brother's slayer be punished by death, because in a case such as this, weregild could not be imposed. What fine would be sufficient for the God of summer and the prince of righteousness? The Norns' runes, which sanctify blood-revenge, are not cut on the water's surface or on the heath's drifting sand, and are not easily mocked.

3. Knowing this, Odin muffled his face beneath a hat so that his features would not be recognized and went to Samso, to the western halls of Billing, to offer his services as a soldier. Billing is Delling's brother, is the Alf of twilight and lord over the Varns, who protect Sol and Mani from the wolves Skoll and Hati, who shall pursue them across the sky until Ragnarok. Billing made Odin a general, who proved himself worthy of such rank in excursions against the Etins. On account of his skillful conduct in battle, Billing admitted him to the highest rank in his friendship, honoring him no less generously

with gifts than decorations. After a brief lapse of time, Odin beat the enemy's line into flight single-handed and, after contriving this amazing feat, returned to announce it. Everybody was astounded that one man's strength could have defeated such countless numbers. Relying on these achievements, Odin whispered to Billing the secret of his love for his daughter, Rind. Uplifted by the other's friendly encouragement, he tried to kiss the girl and was rewarded with a slap across the face.

4. Neither the indignity, nor the distress at the insult kept him from his purpose. Next, to avoid feebly dropping the quest which he had begun so enthusiastically, he put on foreigner's clothing and once more sought his patron. It was difficult for anyone meeting him to discern his true countenance, because he had disguised his usual appearance. He made out that his name was Hropt and that he was a practiced metal-worker. By undertaking the construction of various bronze shapes with the most beautiful outlines, he so recommended his skill in workmanship that Billing awarded him a large lump of gold and commissioned him to fashion ornaments for his womenfolk. So he hammered out many trinkets for feminine adornment, and at length presented the girl with a bracelet more painstakingly finished than the rest, and several rings executed with equal care.

5. But none of his services could bend her disdain. Whenever he wished to offer her a kiss she boxed his ears. Presents from someone undesirable to us are unacceptable, while those of friends give much greater pleasure; so it is that at times we rate the value of a gift by its giver. The obstinate girl was quite certain that the sly old fellow was searching for an opening to exercise his lust by a pretense of generosity. His nature was sharp and resolute, so that she recognized some trickery was afoot beneath his admiration and that his plying her with offerings meant that secretly he was up to no good. Her father attempted to browbeat her for refusing the match, but, finding the idea of sexual union with an elderly man loathsome, she claimed that over-early embraces were not suitable for a girl of tender years, and by pleading immaturity lent support to her rejection.

6. Odin, however, had found by experience that nothing served eager lovers more than a tough persistence, and although he had been humiliated by two rebuffs he altered his looks a third time and approached Billing, claiming unparalleled competence in military arts. It was not merely desire which led him to take such trouble, but a wish to elim-

inate his discredit. Gifted sorcerers have the ability to change their aspect instantaneously and present different images of themselves; they are experts at reproducing the qualities as well as the normal appearance of any age group. Consequently, the old veteran would give an admirable display of his professional skills by riding proudly into combat along with the most courageous, having made himself look young and handsome. Despite this tribute the young woman remained inflexible. The mind cannot easily move to a genuine regard for someone whom it has once heartily disliked.

7. Odin then went to her bower and sat in the reeds awaiting his delight. That discreet maiden was body and soul to him. He found Billing's lass on her bed, the slumbering, sun-white maid. A prince's joy seemed nothing to him, if he could not live with that form. He revealed his true form to her, and she said: "You must come later in the evening, Odin, if you would win the maid over; all will be disastrous unless we alone should know of such misdeed." He returned, thinking to love at her wise desire; he thought he would obtain her whole heart and love. When he came to her next, the warriors were all awake, guarding her door, with lights burning and bearing torches: thus was the way to pleasure closed. But in the morning,

when he came again, all the household was sleeping; he found the good damsel's dog alone, tied to the bed. Later, when on one occasion, just before departing, he wanted to snatch a kiss from her, she gave him such a shove that he was sent flying and banged his chin on the floor. Immediately he touched her with a piece of bark inscribed with runes and made her like one demented.

8. Still, he did not shrink from pursuing his plans (for confidence in his greatness had puffed up his hopes), and so this indefatigable wayfarer journeyed to Billing a fourth time, after putting on girl's clothing, and took on the guise of a vala. Once more received at the court, he proved himself not only anxious but even rather pushing. Because he dressed like a woman, that is how he was perceived. He called himself Vaka and said he was a female physician, giving warrant to his claim by his great readiness to help in such matters. At length he was enlisted in Billing's queen's entourage and acted as his daughter's attendant. He used to wash the dirt from her feet in the evenings and, as he rinsed them, was allowed to touch her calves and upper thighs.

9. Rind was still sick from Odin's runes. Looking around for suitable treatments, she called upon the hands she had once cursed to save her life, and employed a person she had

always disdained to preserve her. He closely examined her symptoms and then declared that she must take a certain medicine to counteract the disease as swiftly as possible; unfortunately, this prescription would taste so bitter that unless the girl allowed herself to be tied down she would not be able to bear the potency of the cure. The elements of her distemper must be expelled from her innermost fibers.

10. Once her father had heard this she was laid on the bed, bound, and ordered to submit passively to everything her doctor applied. Billing was quite deceived by the female form which old Odin wore to disguise his persistant scheming, and it was this which enabled a seeming remedy to become a license for his pleasures. Her physician stopped attending on her and seized the opportunity to make love, rushing to wreak his lust before he dispelled her fever, and finding that where in sound health she had been antagonistic, he could now take advantage of her disposition. Thus, Ygg-Odin won Rind with Seid.

11. Rind bore Vali in the western halls of Billing. Baldur's brother was born early, and one night old slew Odin's son, Hod. He neither washed his hands, nor combed his hair, before he sent Baldur's bane to the pyre. Vali showed himself worthy to avenge his own brother: for he slew the slayer. He was, at first, disturbed by the revelation that he had to kill Hod, who was also his brother, but Rind sang a Galdur-chant over him so he could shake from his shoulders what seemed vexing to him. It was with the sword of Baldur himself that Vali performed this act of revenge. He is called the Son of Odin and Rind, Step-son of Frigga, Brother of the Aesir, Baldur's Avenging As, Enemy of Hod and his slayer, and Father's Homestead-Inhabiter. He is bold in battles and a very good shot.

12. Hod arrived in Hel to face the judgment of the Gods. Fortunately for him, he knew the Malrunes, which were given to him by his wife, Hild, so that Odin would not requite him with consuming woe for the injury that he had caused. There he wound, weaved, and placed together those runes in the Thing where the hosts of people go into the full judgments. Charged with the murder of his brother Baldur, he demonstrated before the judges that the slaying was unintentional, although it might seem deliberate, because he made war on Baldur and wanted to take his wife. Baldur received him in Odainsacre, where they live together. Baldur and Hod will return from Hel after Ragnarok and will live in Valhall once the worlds are renewed.

LVIII. <u>Vafthrudnir</u>

1. <u>Odin</u>: "Counsel me, Frigga,
   for I long to go
   to Vafthrudnir to visit;
   I have great desire, I say,
   to contend in ancient lore
   with that all-wise Etin."

2. <u>Frigga</u>: "I would counsel you,
   Herfather-Odin, to stay at home
   in the Gods' dwellings;
   because no Etin is,
   I believe,
   as mighty as Vafthrudnir."

3. <u>Odin</u>: "Much have I journeyed,
   much experienced,
   much received from mighty Gods;
   but this I would like to know:
   how it is
   in Vafthrudnir's halls."

4. <u>Frigga</u>: "May you fare safely,
   return safely,
   be safe in your journeys;
   may your wit aid you,
   when you, father of men,
   shall speak with the Etin."

5. Then Odin went to
   prove the lore
   of the all-wise Etin.
   He came to the hall
   which Im's father owned.
   Ygg-Odin went right in.

6. <u>Odin</u>: "Hail, Vafthrudnir!
   I have come to your hall,
   to see you;
   for I would like to know,
   if you are a
   cunning and all-wise Etin."

7. <u>Vafthrudnir</u>: "What man is this
   that speaks to me,
   here in my lofty hall?

You shall never leave
from this place
if you are not wiser."

8. <u>Odin</u>: "My name is Gagnrad,
   from my journey I
   have come to your halls thirsty,
   needing hospitality,
   and a kind reception,
   for I have fared far, Etin!"

9. <u>Vafthrudnir</u>: "Why then, Gagnrad,
   do you speak from the floor?
   Take a seat in the hall;
   then it shall be proven,
   which of us knows the most,
   the guest or the ancient speaker."

10. <u>Gagnrad</u>: "A poor man who
    comes to a rich man should
    speak usefully or hold his tongue:
    I think that too much
    talk brings him no good,
    who visits a stern man."

11. <u>Vafthrudnir</u>: "Tell me, Gagnrad,
    since you would prove
    your wisdom on the floor:
    what is the name of the steed
    that draws forth each day
    over humankind?"

12. <u>Gagnrad</u>: "He is called Skinfaxi,
    who draws forth the bright Dag
    over humankind;
    among the Hreidgoths he is
    accounted best of steeds.
    His mane always sheds light."

13. <u>Vafthrudnir</u>: "Tell me, Gagnrad,
    since you would prove
    your wisdom on the floor:
    what is the name of the steed,
    which from the east draws
    Natt over the beneficent Powers?"

14. <u>Gagnrad</u>: "He is called Hrimfaxi,
    who draws each night forth
    over the beneficent Powers.
    From his bit he lets
    drops fall every morning,
    whence comes the dew in the dales."

15. <u>Vafthrudnir</u>: "Tell me, Gagnrad,
    since you would prove
    your wisdom on the floor:
    what is the name of the stream
    which earth divides
    between the Etins and the Gods?"

16. <u>Gagnrad</u>: "The stream is called Ifing,
    which earth divides
    between the Etins and the Gods:
    it shall flow openly
    throughout all time.
    No ice shall be on that stream."

17. <u>Vafthrudnir</u>: "Tell me, Gagnrad,
    since you would prove
    your wisdom on the floor:
    what is the name of the plain
    where Surt and the Gods
    shall meet in combat?"

18. <u>Gagnrad</u>: "The plain is called Vigrid,
    where Surt and the gentle Gods
    shall meet in combat;
    it is a hundred leagues
    on every side.
    That plain is decreed to them."

19. <u>Vafthrudnir</u>: "You are wise, O guest!
    Approach the Etin's bench,
    and sitting let us talk together:
    we will pledge our heads
    in the hall, guest!
    He wins whose wisdom is greater."

20. <u>Gagnrad</u>: "Tell me first,
    if your wit suffices,
    and if you know, Vafthrudnir!
    Whence came the earth,

    and the high heaven,
    wise Etin?"

21. <u>Vafthrudnir</u>: "The earth was created
    from Ymir's flesh,
    the rocks from his bones,
    the heavens from the head
    of the ice-cold Etin,
    the sea from his blood."

22. <u>Gagnrad</u>: "Tell me secondly,
    if your wit suffices,
    and if you know, Vafthrudnir!
    Whence came Mani,
    who passes over mankind,
    and likewise Sol?"

23. <u>Vafthrudnir</u>: "He is called Mundilfari-Lodur,
    who is Mani's father,
    and also Sol's:
    each day they must
    journey around heaven,
    to count years for men."

24. <u>Gagnrad</u>: "Tell me thirdly,
    if your wit suffices,
    and if you know, Vafthrudnir!
    Whence came Dag,
    who passes over people,
    and Natt with Nid?"

25. <u>Vafthrudnir</u>: "He is called Delling,
    who is Dag's father,
    but Natt was born of Norvi-Mimir;
    beneficient Powers
    made Ny and Nid
    to count years for men."

26. <u>Gagnrad</u>: "Tell me fourthly,
    if your wit suffices,
    and if you know, Vafthrudnir!
    Whence came Vetur,
    and warm Sumar first
    among the wise Gods?"

27. <u>Vafthrudnir</u>: "He is called Vindsval,

who is Vetur's father,
and Svasud Sumar's;
they shall both
journey yearly forever,
until the Powers perish."

28. Gagnrad: "Tell me fifthly,
if your wit suffices,
and if you know, Vafthrudnir!
Who was the first Etin,
fashioned in ancient times,
and the eldest of Ymir's sons."

29. Vafthrudnir: "Countless winters
before earth was formed,
Bergelmir was born;
Thrudgelmir was
his father,
Aurgelmir-Ymir his grandfather."

30. Gagnrad: "Tell me sixthly,
if your wit suffices,
and if you know, Vafthrudnir!
Whence first came Aurgelmir
among the Etin kin,
wise Etin?"

31. Vafthrudnir: "From the Elivagar
sprayed kvikadrops,
which grew till they became an Etin;
but sparks flew
from the south-world:
the fire gave life to the ice."

32. Gagnrad: "Tell me seventhly,
if your wit suffices,
and if you know, Vafthrudnir!
How he [Ymir] sired children,
the bold Etin,
since he knew no Giantess?"

33. Vafthrudnir: "A son and a daughter
are said to have grown
under the arm of the Hrimthurse;
foot begat with foot
the strange-headed son

of the wise Etin."

34. Gagnrad: "Tell me eighthly,
if your wit suffices,
and if you know, Vafthrudnir!
What do you first remember,
or earliest know?
For you are an all-wise Etin."

35. Vafthrudnir: "Bergelmir was born
countless ages
before the earth was formed.
The first thing I remember
is when he was
laid on the mill."

36. Gagnrad: "Tell me ninthly,
if your wit suffices,
and if you know, Vafthrudnir!
Whence comes the wind,
that passes over the ocean,
itself invisible to man?"

37. Vafthrudnir: "He is called Hraesvelg,
an Etin in eagle's guise,
who sits at the end of heaven:
it is said that the wind
that passes over all men
comes from his wings."

38. Gagnrad: "Tell me tenthly,
since you know the urlag
of the Gods, Vafthrudnir!
Whence came Njord among
the Aesir's kin?
He rules over hofs
and horgs by hundreds,
yet was not born among the Aesir."

39. Vafthrudnir: "Wise creators made him
in Vanaheim,
and gave him as a hostage
to the Gods.
At the fall of the world
he will return to the wise Vanir."

40. <u>Gagnrad</u>: "Tell me eleventhly,
    since you know the urlag
    of the Gods, Vafthrudnir!
    What do the Einherjar do
    in Herfather-Odin's halls,
    until the Powers perish?"

41. <u>Vafthrudnir</u>: "All the Einherjar
    in Odin's halls
    fight together each day;
    they choose their victims,
    and ride from the conflict;
    drink beer with the Aesir,
    eat their fill of Saehrimnir,
    then sit in harmony together."

42. <u>Gagnrad</u>: "Tell me twelfthly,
    since you know the urlag
    of the Gods, Vafthrudnir!
    Of the Etins' runes,
    and of all the Gods',
    say what is truest,
    all-knowing Etin!"

43. <u>Vafthrudnir</u>: "Of the runes of the Etins
    and all the Gods
    I can speak truly,
    for I have been
    in every world:
    I visited nine worlds
    below Niflhel,
    here die dead men from Hel."

44. <u>Gagnrad</u>: "Much I have traveled,
    much I have tried,
    much I have tested the Powers:
    what human persons shall
    still live when the famous
    Fimbulwinter has been in the world?"

45. <u>Vafthrudnir</u>: "Lif and Leifthrasir,
    they are concealed
    in Hoddmimis Holt.
    They have morning dews
    for nourishment,
    thence are races born."

46. <u>Gagnrad</u>: "Much I have traveled,
    much I have tried,
    much I have tested the Powers:
    whence comes the sun
    in that fair heaven,
    when Fenrir has devoured this?"

47. <u>Vafthrudnir</u>: "Alfrodul-Sol shall
    bear a daughter
    before Fenrir swallows her.
    The maid shall ride
    on her mother's course
    when the Powers die."

48. <u>Gagnrad</u>: "Much I have traveled,
    much I have tried,
    much I have tested the Powers:
    who are the maidens,
    so wise in her heart,
    that travel over the ocean?"

49. <u>Vafthrudnir</u>: "Over three mighty
    rivers comes
    Mogthrasir-Mimir's maidens,
    the sole hamingjas
    who are in the world,
    though nurtured by Etins."

50. <u>Gagnrad</u>: "Much I have traveled,
    much I have tried,
    much I have tested the Powers:
    which of the Aesir
    will rule over the Gods' possessions,
    when Surt's fire shall be quenched?"

51. <u>Vafthrudnir</u>: "Vidar and Vali will
    inhabit the Gods' holy hofs,
    when Surt's fire shall be quenched.
    Modi and Magni will
    possess Vingnir's Mjollnir
    at the end of the battle."

52. <u>Gagnrad</u>: "Much I have traveled,
    much I have tried,
    much I have tested the Powers:

what will be the
end of Odin's life,
when the Powers perish?"

53. <u>Vafthrudnir:</u> "The wolf will devour
the father of men;
Vidar will avenge him:
he will cleave his
cold jaws,
in conflict with the wolf."

54. <u>Gagnrad:</u> "Much I have traveled,
much I have tried,
much I have tested the Powers:
what did Odin say
in his son's ear,
before he was laid on the pyre?"

55. <u>Vafthrudnir:</u> "No one knows that,
what you said in your
son's ear in ancient times;
with dying mouth I
have spoken my ancient sayings,
I have now contended
with Odin in knowledge:
of all beings you are ever the wisest."

LIX. <u>Grougaldur</u>

1. Od and Ull were both sons of the champion, Egil, but were born of different mothers. Ull's mother, Od's step-mother, is Sif. Egil and his son, Ull, had encountered considerable adventures on their journey from the Wolfdales; but nevertheless, they came unscathed to Ydalir and again found Sif, who lived there with Egil and Groa's son, Od. Some years passed, during which Egil remained at home with his family. In these years, the lively archer felt more need for rest than adventure, and his thoughts were not always happy.

2. Sif pondered many things. The Swanmaid was saddened by the destruction that had befallen the world because of Volund, and she noticed how Egil brooded about his broken oath and the severed bonds of friendship with the Gods. Sif is prophetic and a vala by nature, and Urd provides her inspirations and prompts her decisions.

3. One day, Sif summoned Od to stand before her. She told him that since he was now fully grown, he should go out and do something worthy of praise. Od replied that he intended to fight Kon, who had stolen his mother, Groa, from Egil, then rejected her, yet he was troubled, because he had spent his first years under Kon's roof and had always been closely watched by him. Under Kon's roof too, he had a half-brother, named Gudorm, who was also Groa's son. Sif said that she shared his apprehension, although he should avenge his mother, but for now wanted to advise him differently. Sif commanded Od to seek out and find the maiden whose heart had long been longing– to find Freya and her brother Frey.

4. Od did not refuse. He was ashamed to. But to him it seemed far beyond his ability, and he suspected that his step-mother Sif did not have his best interests in mind. In the

past, he thought he had noticed that Sif favored her own son Ull. Yet that had never disrupted the friendship between him and his half-brother, for Ull always deferred to Od and looked up to him.

5. When night had fallen, Od went to Groa's grave-mound on the hill. He had heard that the dead are easier to summon and listen more closely to earthly life once night has set in. He stood before the grave-door, crying out:

6. "Wake up, Groa!
   Wake up, good woman!
   I wake you at the gates of death!
   If you remember,
   you told your son
   to come to your grave-mound."

7. Groa: "What now troubles
   my only son?
   What affliction are you burdened with,
   that you call your mother,
   who has become dust,
   and has left the Underworld?"

8. Od: "The cunning woman,
   whom my father has embraced,
   has put a cruel play before me;
   she told me to go
   where none may fare,
   to find the Menglodum [Frey and Freya]."

9. Groa: "Long is the journey,
   long are the ways,
   long are men's desires.
   If you will wait
   for a favorable outcome,
   the Norns will guide your path."

10. Od: "Sing to me

good songs, mother,
to protect your son!
For I fear that I fare
towards my death,
and I seem too young in years."

11. Groa: "First, I will sing to you
    one that is thought most useful,
    which Rind sang to Rani-Vali:
    that you can shake from your shoulders
    what seems vexing to you:
    let you direct yourself.

12. "A second I will sing to you,
    if you have to wander
    joylessly on the ways:
    may Urd's songs
    protect you on every side,
    wherever you see disgrace.

13. "A third I will sing to you,
    if the mighty rivers,
    Horn and Rud,
    threaten your life,
    may they flow down to Hel,
    and ever be diminished for you.

14. "A fourth I will sing to you,
    if foes are ready to attack you
    on the dangerous road,
    their hearts shall fail them,
    and will be in your power,
    and their minds will turn to peace.

15. "A fifth I will sing to you,
    if bonds are placed
    on your limbs,
    I will let Leifnir's Fire
    be sung over them,
    the locks will fall from your arms,
    and the fetters from your feet.

16. "A sixth I will sing to you,
    if storms on the sea
    have might unknown to man:
    wind and water

shall do you no harm,
and shall offer you calm passage.

17. "A seventh I will sing to you,
if frost threatens you
on a high mountain,
the deadly cold
shall not injure your flesh,
nor draw your body to your limbs.

18. "An eighth I will sing to you,
if you meet Natt
on the Niflways,
may the dead woman
have no power
to do you harm.

19. "A ninth I will sing to you,
if you exchange words
with the weapon-honored Etin [Mimir];
words and wisdom
shall be in abundance
as you speak into Mimir's heart.

20. "Now go to wherever
danger awaits
and no harm shall obstruct your wishes;
I have stood at the door
of stone, held firm in the floor,
while I sang songs to you.

21. "My son, bear hence
your mother's words,
and let them dwell in your heart;
for you shall have much fortune
in your life,
if you are mindful of my words."

22. The next morning, Od received word that Ull wanted to follow him and that their parents would allow it. Egil took his sons to one of his hidden treasures and let them choose helmets, coats of mail, and swords.

He took them to a playing field daily and trained them in all sports, of which he himself was master, and taught them many fine tricks with which a resolute and fit warrior could conquer a stronger opponent. When they had attained the level of expertise Egil desired, he determined their day of departure. He also gave them shields that could be transformed into skis and boats.

23. Ull was then dispatched by his father to find out what had been happening in the meantime at home. When he saw smoke rising from his mother's hut, he approached the outside wall and stealthily glued his eye to a small opening. Looking inside, he spied his mother stirring an ugly-looking cauldron of stew. He looked up and also saw hanging aloft from a thin rope three serpents, from whose jaws putrid saliva dripped steadily to provide liquid for the recipe. Two of them were pitch-black, the third had whitish scales and was suspended a little higher than the others. This last had a knot tied to its tail while its fellows were held by a cord round their bellies. Because he reckoned the business smacked of sorcery he kept quiet about what he had seen, rather than have people think he was accusing his mother of practicing Seid. He was unaware that the serpents were harmless or how much power was being cooked in that brew.

24. Afterwards, Egil and Od came up, and catching sight of the smoke from the house, entered to take their places for a meal. When they were seated at the table and her son and step-son were just about to eat, Sif pushed towards them a bowl of food, of two different shades; half of it looked pitch-black flecked with splotches of yellow, the other half whitish, for the different hues of the serpents had made the pottage multicolored. They had each only tasted a single morsel when Od, sizing up the dish not from its colors but from the feeling of strength inside him, turned the bowl as quickly as he could to transfer the darkish part of the concoction, prepared with the stronger juice, to his own side, and gave Ull the paler portion which had been offered to himself. Thus he dined more favorably. To prevent his motive for the change being detected he said, "That's how the stern becomes the prow when the sea grows rough." It required some mental agility in the man to use a figure of speech about sailing to cover up his purposeful action.

25. So Od, now refreshed by his meal of good omen, achieved through its internal workings the most authoritative human wisdom. This potent feast generated in him a bulk of knowledge beyond credence in all subjects, so that he was even skilled in understanding the speech of wild animals and cattle. For he was not only expert in man's affairs, but could interpret the way animal noises conveyed sense and indicated their feelings. Besides this, his conversation was so gracious and refined that whatever he chose to discourse upon was embellished by a string of witty maxims.

26. Once Sif had come up to them and realized the dish had been reversed so that Od had consumed the preferable share, she lamented that the fortune designed for her son had passed to her step-son. Soon, amid her sighs, she began to beg Od, on whom she, Ull's mother, had heaped such an unusual wealth of good luck, never to refuse aid to his brother. By eating a single tasty morsel he had clearly attained the peak of reason and eloquence, not to mention the facility for continual success in combat. She added that Ull would have almost the same degree of prowess and in the future would not entirely miss the feast intended for him. Another piece of advice was that if they were in utterly desperate circumstances they could get help quickly by calling her name; she admitted that she relied partly on her supernatural power, for she wielded within her a divine force, being in a way an associate of the Gods.

27. Od replied that he was naturally drawn to stand by his brother; it was a shameful bird which fouled its own nest. But Sif was more distressed by her own negligence than aggravated by her son's ill-luck; in ancient times a practitioner suffered great embarrassment if he were cheated through his own inventiveness.

28. Then she herself, accompanied by her husband, escorted the departing brothers to the harbor. They embarked together in a single ship.

LX. Svarinsmound

1. With the terrible Volund dead, the power of Fimbulwinter was finally broken. To Midgard there now came years promising life and prosperity. The ice-sheet that had covered the great northern islands melted under the warmth of the sun's rays. It was as lively now on the enormous glacier plains, as it had been silent before. Countless rivulets babbled there and united into brooks that dug ever-deeper beds and with collective force became streams and rivers that surged to the sea between walls of ice, glistening green. More and more the ice-sheets retreated. Every year, greenery appeared earlier in the valleys and stayed longer. Winter began approaching its appointed limits and contended itself with the months it had originally been allotted. Some species of trees, which had been reduced during the Fimbulwinter to bushes or tendrils that crept along the earth under the snow, began to rise with trunks and crowns, and many that died out found successors through seeds that wind and wave carried to the north.

2. At first, the change was slow, but became wonderfully accelerated by an event in the world of mankind. The clans of folk south of the sea in the great kingdom Kon ruled were called together by him to the Thing. He asked them if they believed, as he did, that the holy land, whose womb held their fathers' graves, ought to be conquered and reclaimed. The gathered warriors of the folk signaled their approval with shouts and the clash of weapons. Each clan that had migrated drew up a host of warriors, strong in numbers, commanded by one who belonged to their noblest clan, the Skjoldungs. The Budlungs, Hildings, and Lofdungs, each with their escort of warriors, united under Kon's banner. These clans, along with several others that are renowned in Midgard, joined with Jarl's. They were the descendants of the noblest in Aurvangaland when Heimdall arrived there with the sheaf of grain. A fleet was equipped and the host disembarked to the land just named. The Swedes, and the Alfar living among them, who resided there, did not want to join the

host and push north. They refused to exchange their old lands around lake Vaeni, because, of course, the forces of winter still ruled there. So the jarls of the Swedes gathered their forces to repulse those of Kon. Foremost among these jarls were those of the Skilfing or the Yngling clan who had also joined with Jarl's. These kings had a battle on the ice of the Vaeni lake.

3. They met Egil at the gate of his burgh, and announced the coming of war to the prince. He stood outside, wearing a helmet, noticed the speed of his kinsmen, and asked them why they looked so angry. They then told him of the warriors moving toward them to fight. He then said: "Let bridled steeds run to the divine Thing, but Sporvitnir to Sparinsheath; Melnir and Mylnir to Myrkwood; let no man stay behind of those who can wield swords. Summon Hogni to you, and the sons of Hring, Atli and Yngvi, Alf inn Gamla; they will gladly engage in war; let us warmly welcome Jarl's sons!" It was a whirlwind, when the flashing swords clashed together at Frekastein: Kon was always foremost in the host where men fought together; fierce in battle, disdaining flight; the jarl had a valiant heart. Then helmed maids came from heaven above—they increased the clash of arms and protected Kon. Three fylkings of nine maidens came, although one led them, a bright maid with helmed head. Their horses shook themselves, and from their manes, dew ran into the deep dales, hailed down onto lofty ones, thence came harvests to men.

4. The struggle was fierce, but yielding to superiority, the Swedes had to abandon Aurvangaland and head north. In astonishment, they noticed that their retreat was followed by spring and flowers and flocks of migratory birds. The ice-sheet weakened as they marched north. In the distance before them blew clouds that sent lightning bolts into the melting glacier. It was Thor who thundered there and made it unpleasant for the immigrants from Jotunheim to remain any longer. One could see Etins abandoning their new homes, treading away over the snowfields with their herds of black cattle. And as soon as the snow had melted, the Swedes followed, with Kon's fylkings behind them pushing them on. On Moinnsheath, the Swedes stopped for a time and sought to check their relatives from the south. It was a bloody battle, in which the exploits of the Swedes awakened Kon's admiration. They fought not only against human beings, but also against Gods and Wyrd, and thus had to yield.

5. Among the Swedes, the Hilding Hildigir was one of the noblest. Kon had heard that

the sword Lysing, which had been hidden with his mother before he was born, was the only one by which Hildigir could be slain. He obtained the sword and returned to the battle. Hildigir had been challenged by the Danish champions to combat them; but when he observed they were putting Kon forward, knowing this was his half-brother, he set fraternal loyalty before considerations of valor and announced that he would not join battle with a man who had so little testing, where he himself was famed as the vanquisher of seventy men-at-arms. He therefore ordered Kon to find his own level by less difficult experiments and pursue objects equal to his strength. He furnished these suggestions not because he doubted his own courage, but through a desire to keep himself blameless, for he was not only very brave, but also had the knack of blunting swords by magic. Although he remembered that his father had been overthrown by Kon's, he felt two impulses: desire to avenge his father and affection for his brother; he decided it was better to back out of the challenge than to become involved in an abysmal crime.

6. Kon demanded a substitute and, when a swordsman appeared, he slew him. Soon even the enemy voted him triumphant for his gallantry and popular acclaim judged him the bravest there. In the next day's contest, when two men attacked him, he cut down both; on the third day he overcame three, on the fourth he encountered and subdued four and on the fifth demanded five. Having overwhelmed these, he kept increasing the number of his opponents and victories in similar fashion until the eighth day arrived and he took on eleven at once and laid them all in the dust. Once Hildigir perceived that the record of his own achievements was rivaled by the other's magnificent prowess, he could no longer hold from meeting. As soon as he realized that Kon, who held Lysing, which was impervious to spells, had dealt him a mortal wound, Hildigir cast his weapons away, lay down on the earth, and addressed his brother in these words:

7. "I should like the hour
to roll by in conversation;
stop the sword-play,
rest on the ground a little,
vary the time with talk
and warm our hearts.

8. "Time remains for our purpose.
Different destinies
control our twin fates;
death's lottery brings
one to his appointed hour,
while processions and glory
and a chance to live
the days of better years
await the other.

9. "The omens distinguish us
in separate roles.
Danish territory bore you,
Svithjod me.
Once Drott's maternal breast
swelled for you;
I too sucked milk
from her teat.

10. "Her lawless children have
dared to clash with wild
weapons, and have fallen;
brothers sprung from noble
blood rush to slaughter
each other, until,
craving the summit,
they run out of time and win
an evil doom;
desiring the scepter they combine
their deaths to visit
the Underworld river together.

11. "By my head stands fixed
a Swedish shield,
adorned with a bright
window of varied reliefs,
ringed by paneled
pictures of wondrous art.

12. "There a multicolored
scene depicts princes
destroyed, champions
overthrown, wars too and
the remarkable work of
my right arm;
in the midst,
strikingly engraved and painted,
there stands the likeness
of my son, whose course of life
this hand brought to
its boundary."

13. "He was my only heir, the one
concern of his father's mind,
given by the Gods
to comfort his mother.

Bad is the fortune that heaps
unprosperous years on the happy,
jostles laughter with grief
and plagues the courageous.

14. "It's a mournful, miserable
task to drag out a
downcast life, draw breath
through gloomy days
and deplore
what the future may hold.

15. "Whatever foreknown links are
fastened by the Norns,
whatever the mysteries
of divine reason sketch out,
whatever events are foreseen
and held in the sequence
of urlag, no change in our
fleeting world will cancel."

16. After he had spoken, Kon condemned his brother's hesitation in leaving so long the confession of their fraternal bond. He answered that he had kept silent to avoid being judged a coward if he refused to fight, or a niding for actually doing so. Before he died, he asked his brother to wrap him in his mantle. Kon wept and spread his cloak over his brother's body.

17. While this was happening, Thjalfi, often in Thor's company, campaigned in the islands of the northern seas, cleansing them of the trolls and Etins that had taken up residence there during the Fimbulwinter, making them uninhabitable for humans, and brought new settlers. He joined Thor in combat on the isle of Hlesey against Berserk

brides. Like Gullveig, these Giantesses were most evil and had seduced the folk with their evil arts. Thjalfi fought them in a river which blocked the way for the migrant bands. They were she-wolves, and hardly women. They crushed Thor's ship, that he and Thjalfi rode in, which Thor had secured with props, threatened the Asagod with iron clubs, then drove Thjalfi away.

18. They say that when a migrant band, pursuing their way with their leader, came to a certain river, and were forbidden by Giantesses to cross to the other side, Thjalfi fought with the strongest of them, swimming in the river, and killed her and won for himself the glory of great praise and a passage for the migrants. For it had been previously agreed between the two armies that if the Giantess should overcome Thjalfi, the migrants would withdraw from the river, but if she herself were conquered by Thjalfi, as actually occurred, then the means of crossing the stream should be afforded to them.

19. Before Thjalfi arrived on the island of Gotland, it regularly sank into the sea at sunrise and rose up again at sundown. Thjalfi bore the Needfire around the island, thereby stabilizing it. The settlers that followed him were of the tribe of Goths. Thjalfi had a son named Hafdi, who married a Goddess named Hvita Stjarna. They, in turn, had

three sons who populated Gotland. Goths also dwelt in Gotaland, south of the Swedes, and on the peninsula that has been called Jutland ever since. This entire kingdom was called Hreidgotaland. The Danes lived on the fertile islands outside Aurvangaland, while south of them dwelt the Angles, Saxons, and many other related folk.

20. Mimir's sons, Bari and Brokk, set out to cleanse the North Sea of monsters who had taken up residence there during the Fimbulwinter. When the going was heavy in those high waves, Bari was the strongest swimmer of all. Each of them swam holding a sword, a naked, hard-proofed blade for protection against the whale-beasts. But Brokk could never move out farther or faster from Bari than Bari could manage to move from him. Shoulder to shoulder, they struggled on for five nights, until the long flow and pitch of the waves, the perishing cold, night falling, and winds from the north drove them apart. The deep boiled up and its wallowing sent the sea-brutes wild. Bari's armor helped him to hold out; his hard-ringed chain mail, hand-forged and linked, a fine, close-fitting filigree of gold, kept him safe when some ocean creature pulled him to the bottom. Held fast and wrapped in its grip, he was granted one final chance: his sword plunged

and the ordeal was over. By his hands, the fury of battle had finished off the sea-beast.

21. Time and again, foul things attacked them, lurking, and stalking, but they lashed out, gave as good a they got with their swords. Their flesh was not for feasting on, there would be no monsters gnawing and gloating over their banquet at the bottom of the sea. Instead, in the morning, mangled and sleeping the sleep of the sword, they flopped and floated like the ocean's leavings. From now on sailors would be safe, the deep-sea raids were over for good. Light came from the east, and the waves went quiet; they could see headlands and buffeted cliffs. Often, for undaunted courage, Wyrd spares the man it has not already marked. However it occurred, Bari's sword had killed nine sea-monsters. Such night-dangers and hard ordeals have rarely been heard of, nor of ones more desolate in surging waves. But worn out as they were, they survived, came through with their lives. The ocean lifted and laid them ashore, they landed safe on the coast of Finland.

22. Eventually, the Swedes had to retreat as far as Svarinsmound, the very place that their jarls and the Alfar had gathered and decided to migrate at the beginning of the Fimbulwinter. This, as a result, pushed Jarl and his people along with so many others southward, and caused his son Kon to found his great kingdom on the other side of the sea. There was now no reason for the Swedes to continue the war. The beautiful meadows they had once inhabited around the sea, rich in islands and bays, were green again with forests reflecting along the seashore, and with reverence they looked upon their forefathers' grave-barrows and their family mounds again. This was their native land, and here Kon bade them to stay. They intended to do this, but considered it a lesser honor to accept peace from his hand than to compel him to retreat by force. Egil came from the north, joined the Swedes, and encouraged them to reject the offer of peace. At Svarinsmound, Egil hoped to kill the man who had robbed him of Groa.

23. While this took place, Thor came across Sif in the northern part of the world, and betrothed himself to her. When Egil found out that he had lost his beloved, he decided to follow in his brothers' footsteps and marry his sister, Alveig, who had not yet found a husband, and fought in battle as a Valkyrie. But Alveig secretly loved Kon, and when she found out that Egil had betrothed himself to her she rode with Valkyries through the air and over the sea in search of Kon. Kon was at Logafell, warring against the Swedes. Being over-fatigued with the con-

flict, he was sitting under the Arastein, where Alveig found him, and running to him threw her arms around his neck, and, kissing him, told him her errand. Alveig sought the joyous prince, and quickly grasped Kon's hand; she kissed and addressed the helmeted king. Then the jarl's mind was turned to the lady. She declared that she had loved Jarl's son with her whole heart, before she had seen him.

24. Kon returned to battle, and, upon hearing a false message that he had perished, Alveig returned to Ydalir and accepted her union with Egil. When Kon had heard of this, he sailed to Ydalir so rapidly that he arrived before the wedding's date. On the first day of the celebrations, prior to making for the palace, he asked his companions not to stir from the watch-points he had assigned them until their ears detected the distant clash of swords. He came upon the wedding at night, having assumed a disguise. Being asked what gift he brought, he professed skill in healing. Finally, when all were soaked with carousal and the festivities were at their rowdiest, fixing his gaze on the girl, he disclosed the depth of his displeasure in this song, vehemently cursing the woman's fickleness and boasting to the full his own bravery:

25. "Alone against eight I launched the darts of death, I dispatched another nine swinging my sword back, after I had taken life from Svarin for claiming unjust honor, fame he had never merited; often I dipped my gory blade in foreign blood, wet from the slaughter, nor stood aghast at the clash of swords or bright glint of a helmet.

26. "But wickedly casting me off, she cherishes another's vows, wild Signi-Alveig, detesting the old pact, conceives an irregular passion, making herself a token of female frailty.

27. "She entices princes in order to trap them, dishonors them, most of all rejecting the upright; she remains steadfast with one, but ever-wavering gives birth to divided, ambiguous emotions.

28. "Leaving my father's scepter, I never feared woman's false fabrications or subtle female cunning, when I subdued in battle one alone, then two, three, and four, and soon five followed by six, seven, eight together, then eleven single-handed.

29. "I didn't think that she must be marked with a stain of dishonor,

unfaithful to her
promises, fraudulent
in her agreements."

30. Alveig replied: "In frail control
of affairs, my unsure
mind was confused,
fearful, changeable, drifting.
Your fame, borne on varying
reports, was fleeting
and uncertain;
it seared my wavering heart.

31. "I feared that your youthful
years had perished under the sword.
Could I alone resist
my elders and governors when
they would accept no denial,
pressing me to marriage?

32. "The warmth of my love
remains and shall remain
united and matched to yours;
my promise has not
swerved and will gain
opportunities you can rely on.

33. "I still have not deceived
you in my undertaking,
even though I couldn't,
by myself, reject the
innumerable pressures of
my advisors, nor withstand
the stern bidding to
accept the marriage bond."

34. Kon then challenged Egil to a sword-fight, declaring that the other would have to win before he had his wishes. Egil replied that night-combats were for monsters, daylight suited human beings. So that he could not offer the time as an excuse for dodging battle, Kon pointed out that the brightness of the moon turned night into day. Thus, Egil was forced to contend with him, the banqueting hall became an arena, and by laying the villain in the dust, Kon changed the wedding into a Helfare. Not satisfied with annihilating only one, he proceeded to massacre the majority of the guests. As the party was staggering back drunkenly to make a counter-attack, Kon's attendants arrived on the scene and cut them down. Kon rushed through the host of his foes, and many men fell there. Seizing the prospective wife from among her bridesmaids, he laid low many of the guests before he carried her off aboard his ship. The others saved themselves through flight.

35. The following day the battle took place at Svarinsmound. Many fell on both sides, and among the fallen were Alf-warriors that once had clung with Thjalfi to Thor's belt, Megingjard, as he waded through the Elivagar. The battle ended in such a manner that the Swedes were induced to accept peace. They too now honored Kon as king over all of the people who spoke the ancient language and had received Heimdall's runes, meaning the Teutonic people. And since spring growth followed his conquest, they, like other folk, gave Kon, the adopted son of Thor, divine honors after death.

36. When Kon had completed his successful campaign in the north, he then married Alveig, first among women. Together they had eighteen sons, and nine of them were born together. Their names were as follows: one was Thengil, who was known as Thengil of men; second Raesir, third Gram, fourth Gylfi, fifth Hilmir, sixth Jofur, seventh Tiggi, eighth Skyli or Skuli, ninth Harri or Herra. These nine brothers became so renowned in warfare that ever since their names have been treated in all records as honorific titles, equivalent to the name of a king [Konung] or the name of Jarl. Kon and his wife had a further nine sons, and the foremost of all of them was named Hadding. From the line of Jarl came all the great clans of the north; hence came Skjoldungs, hence came Skilfings, hence came Odlungs, hence the Ynglings, hence come the free-born, hence the high-born, the noblest men that live in Midgard.

LXI. Od

1. While Od and Ull sailed towards their destination, Kon cunningly concealed his fleet and sailed on to encounter them. A naval battled ensued, which led to Egil's sons being surrounded. In the battle, Od had fought heroically seeking revenge for his father's death; but he was captured and brought before his former stepfather. Kon spoke kindly to him, bade him to be his son and to accept a kingdom under him. Od replied that he would not allow himself to be bribed by his father's murderer. He also said that if Kon did not kill him now, he would kill Kon later. He rejected the offer of being spared under conditions of servitude, for he could not bear to set life before liberty. He preferred death to submission, not being so greedy for existence that he would turn from free man into slave, or, in a new role, dance attendance on one whom the Norns had recently made his equal. Bravery does not know how to buy its safety at the price of disgrace. He was therefore removed in fetters to a neighborhood where wild beasts roamed, to suffer a death unsuitable for so majestic a spirit. Kon had him bound to a tree in these woods and left him to his Wyrd.

2. The bonds with which Kon had tied Od did not hold against the Galdur-song that Groa had sung over her son. Od breathed on them and they fell away.

3. But the freedom he won thereby was no consolation. He thought his life had little value, since his father had fallen and he himself had been conquered by his invincible killer. It was Od's duty to avenge his father's death. But how was it possible for him to exact revenge on the powerful Kon, who

was Thor's son and was under his protection?

4. Then he met with Mani, who told him how he could achieve what he had set out to do. Only Gambantein, the sword of Volund, Od's uncle, could be used to defeat Kon, and possibly Thor as well. Mani told Od that, shut away behind the severest barriers was the sword that could deal Kon his Wyrd, which belonged to Mimir, who also possessed the ring Andvaranaut, which had been given to his daughter Bodvild. Sinmara kept the sword in an iron-chest, secured with nine magical locks, but she would only give him the sword if he could sever the urlag-threads that bound Volund's son, Vidga, to avenge his father. Vidga was borne by Bodvild, and raised in Mimir's home. If he had to war against the Gods for killing Volund it would cause much discord in the worlds. By accepting this Wyrd himself, Od, as Volund's kinsman, would save Vidga from the horrible repercussions of such an act. Mani then gave him the silver-sickle of Vidofnir, which could be used to cut the threads. Vidofnir offered the sickle, for he was severely distressed by swarthy Sinmara's constant sighs.

5. The approach to Mimir's realm was pathless, beset with obstacles, and hard of access to anyone, inasmuch as the greater length of the route was perpetually invested by devastating cold, for he would first have to venture through Niflheim. Mani therefore gave Od instructions to yoke a team of reindeer to his chariot so that he could speedily cross over the hard-frozen mountain ridges of Nidafjoll. When he reached his destination, he must erect his tent away from the sun so that it caught the shade of the cave where one of Mimir's sons lived. But the tent's shadow should not touch the cave in return; otherwise the unusual patch of darkness it cast might drive the Dwarf back from the entrance. In this way the ring and the sword would be within his grasp, the one accompanied by material prosperity, the other by success in fighting; both spelt a great boon to their possessor.

6. That was Mani's advice. Od followed his directions to the letter and, when he pitched his tent as dictated, he devoted the nights to his anxieties, the days to hunting. But through either season he remained very wakeful and sleepless, allotting the divisions of night and day so as to devote the one to reflection on events, and to spend the other in providing food for his body. Once, as he watched all night, his spirit drooping and dazed with anxiety, the Dwarf cast a shadow on his tent. Od supposed that it was Mimir's son, clad in a Hulidshelm, which makes its

wearer invisible to the naked eye. The helm could conceal the wearer, but not his shadow. Od went for him with his spear, felled him with a lunge, and bound him while he was still powerless to get away. Then, in the most dreadful words, he threatened him with the worst, and demanded the sword and ring. The Dwarf was not slow to buy his safety with the required ransom. Everyone sets life before property, for nothing is dearer than breath to mortal creatures. He took Od to Mimir's burgh, over the paths through Niflheim's putrid bogs, and it took a brave heart to endure the sights to behold there. Yet, the Grougaldur, through which Urd herself spoke, protected the traveler and repelled danger when he met the ghosts of Hrimthurses and the terrible wights of disease that wander Niflheim's marshes.

7. Od climbed over Nidafjoll and, with wonder, he saw the enormous mill, Grotti, the rumble of whose workings he had heard far in the distance. He saw the roaring Hvergelmir well, and climbed down into Mimir's ever-green kingdom. Mimir and his kinsmen received him hospitably and let him see the many wonders in that region. He was allowed to see, but not set foot in, Breidablik, where Baldur dwells with Nanna and the Asmegir. He also had a conversation with Mimir in which he, to his joy, displayed great wisdom.

8. So Od used the silver-sickle he had obtained from Mani to cut the urlagthreads that bound Vidga to avenge Volund against the Gods. Because of this, Sinmara gave him Gambantein, with which he assumed Volund's legacy and the duties of his heir.

LXII. Menglodum

1. Od returned to meet back up with his brother Ull. Now they would travel across the Elivagar into Jotunheim. There they found the Etin court, sought lodging for the night, and were well received, for they were Volund's nephews. All Etins considered Volund a jarl at the time, and honored his memory.

2. Nevertheless, neither brother dared to speak of Frey and Freya. That would arouse suspicion. But they had a clue. They knew that Frey and Freya dwelt among the Etins of Beli's clan, one of the most wicked in Jotunheim, and they learned that this clan lived far away, near the northern edge of the sea in a labyrinth of confusing, mist-enveloped skerries.

3. Ultimately, they reached the archipelago where Beli's clan lived. Many times during the years, Njord and other Gods had wandered these waters in the ship Skidbladnir, seeking his son and daughter in vain, bat-

tling hail-storms that darkened the air, sea-monsters that clung to the ship's hull and would drag it into the deep, and Etins that cast boulders from sea-cliffs with their slings.

4. Volund's nephews could proceed here much better than the Aesir could. Up to this point, the storm-dispatcher's [Volund's] kin had been well received by Jotunheim's inhabitants. This was also the case with Beli's clan, but in their own characteristic manner. Od and Ull reached a harbor near their abode, but the very instant Od stepped from the boat he inadvertently tripped and fell to the earth. He interpreted the stumble as boding well and predicted that after this weak start more favorable events would ensue.

5. The three brothers who were given the common name of Grepp were conceived together and delivered all at the same time so that their sharing of one name bore witness to a simultaneous origin. One of them was guilty of taking Freya from Asgard with Gullveig's help. When this Grepp heard of Od's arrival, he hurried to the coast. He understood that Od was more eloquent than other men and wished to test him with sharp, cunningly chosen words. He would overcome all his opponents not so much by clever language as by bullying them with a flow of insolence. He therefore started the argument with abuse and attacked Od as follows:

6. Grepp: "Who are you, you fool?
On what silly errand?
Whence and whither
are you bound?
What route, what pursuit,
what father and family?

7. "Those men have special strength,
their guardian deity royal,
who have never strayed
away from their own dwellings.
There are few people who warm
to a deed wrought by a rascal,
and the acts of detestable
fellows rarely please."

8. Od: "Egil is my father,
my characteristic a fluent
tongue, and prowess ever
my life-long love.
Wisdom was my only desire,
and so I scanned the different
manners of men as I
traveled through many lands.

9. "A blockhead, unrestrained
and unseemly in his emotions,
cannot conduct his affairs
with due moderation.
Sailing tackle outstrips
the pull of rowers;
gales ruffle the seas,
but a drearier breeze the earth.

10. "Oars cleave the wave,
falsehood the land;
the latter is vexed
by men's mouths,
but hands weigh
hard on the other."

11. Grepp: "You are crammed full of

disputes, they say, as a cock
with filth, stinking of
low-breeding and accusations.
It is hard to bring a case
against a buffoon,
who thrives on a dance of words,
without expressing a meaning."

12. Od: "By heaven, brainless talk,
unless I am much mistaken,
often rebounds on the head
of him who uttered it.
Through the righteous dispensation
of the Gods, words poured forth
with too little wit
return to plague the deliverer.

13. "As soon as we first detect
a pair of suspicious wolf's ears,
we believe the creature
itself is lurking near.
No one thinks we should
trust a person of empty faith,
one whom report pronounces
guilty of treason."

14. Grepp: "Impudent lad, night-owl,
who have lost your way in the darkness,
you shall pay the price
for such indiscretion of speech.
Those unhallowed words,
which you belch out in your madness,
you shall grieve for when
your death makes amends.
Your lifeless, bloodless body
shall provide a feast for crows,
a morsel for beasts,
the carrion of ravenous birds."

15. Od: "The predictions of the coward and
the hardened cravings of the vicious
were never contained
within proper bounds.
He who cheats the Gods
and hatches lewd designs
will be a snare to his

comrades and himself.
Whoever nurses a wolf in
her home is generally thought
to be fostering a thief,
a murderer of her own household."

16. Grepp: "I never, as you believe,
took advantage of the Goddess [Freya],
but protected her when
she was young and vulnerable.
Thus my odal increased,
for possessing her brought me
rewards, power, wealth,
and good advice."

17. Od: "See! Your pressing
anxiety indicts you.
Independence is safer where
the mind remains untainted.
He is deceived who wants
a servant for his friend;
a menial often
damages his master."

18. Grepp was lost for a deft reply and, setting spurs to his horse, withdrew. Reaching home, he filled the palace with a tempestuous fit of yells and, shouting that he had been defeated, urged all his warriors to gather their weapons, intending to avenge his misfortune in the vocal contest by force. He swore he would stretch flat with eagles' talons this line of newcomers. The jarl, on the other hand, suggested he should reflect a while on his wrath; hasty schemes very often misfired, nothing could be carried out both quickly and warily, and frantic ventures mostly turned against their devisers. Lastly, it was improper for a few men to be attacked

by a great swarm. The clever individual was one who could throw a curb on his rage and interrupt his violent impetuosity in time. In this way, the jarl forced the Etin to be thoughtful in his impulsive anger. Even so, the fury of his over-excited mind was not entirely recalled to discretion; as a prize-fighter in wars of words, who had scant success in his latest controversy, and had been denied armed retaliation, he demanded that at least revenge by way of Seid should be at his disposal.

19. Having obtained his request, he set off again for the shore with a chosen bevy of vitkis. First, he decapitated a horse and impaled its lopped-off head on a pole. Then he propped open its mouth with sticks to give it wide-grinning jaws, hoping the outlandish apparition would insult and bring bad luck on Od and thwart his immediate efforts. Od was already on his way to meet them when he sighted it from far off, comprehending this unsightly creation, he bade his companions be silent and conduct themselves warily. No one must blurt out any words in case unguarded speech gave a loophole for sorcery. If talk should be needed they must leave him to be their spokesman. A river flowed between Od's party and the vitkis, who, in order to discourage him from approaching the bridge, set up the nidstong with the horse's head at the very edge of the water, on their side. Od, undeterred, walked fearlessly up to the bridge:

20. "May this burden's bad luck recoil on its bearer and ours be the better fortune! Let evil come to evildoers. Let this accursed load break its carrier. Let stronger omens bring us to safety." The outcome happened exactly as he wished, for the neck was immediately shaken free, and the stake fell and crushed the Etin who held it. The whole magical contraption collapsed before the power of a single chant and belied its expectations.

21. Because of the cold in the region, a fire was burning in the hall. It separated the chairs of the jarl, who sat on one side, and his champions, who sat on the other. When Od joined the latter, they emitted blood-curdling cries like howling wolves. The jarl began to restrain their wailing, telling them that their throats ought not to make animal noises, but Od put in that it was dog-like enough for the rest to bark when one had set them going; everyone's habits revealed his true origin and species. Among these Etins, such a reception was regarded as a charming jest, nid-songs as the proper poetry, audacity as wit, and deceit as evidence of a well-developed mind.

22. It was much more shocking to see the jarl and his sister, who sat in the high-seats. They were both young and so beautiful in appearance and so noble in manners that there could be no doubt that these youths were Frey and his sister, Freya. But it was also evident that both were under the influence of Seid. Frey appeared gloomy and troubled. Freya was preoccupied and sunken in dreams. They were enchanted so that they would not be able to use their divine powers. Freya, who had Gullveig herself place a spell on her, had a further harm placed on her. The Etin Grepp, in his attentions, had bound back her hair into a tight knot so that the bunch of locks was held in a twisted mass, a tangled cluster, which no one could unloose except with a knife.

23. The Etins in the hall treated them as if they were the foremost in the place. If Frey said something, they heeded it. The reason for this was that Volund had turned the divine siblings over to them on that condition, and threatened them with harsh retaliation, if this term was not upheld. It only happened once that one of the Etins had behaved insolently toward the young Van. The Etin was Beli, the actual jarl of the clan. Then Frey had pulled a stag's horn from the wall and given Beli his deathblow. All the Thurses wanted to have Freya, but none would venture to approach her. The Grepp who had arranged her theft from Asgard sought to make himself agreeable in her eyes, but she seemed to be unaware of his presence. The nickname by which the Thurses called Freya was Syr, the name of the animal that is the most charming of all creatures in their opinion, and their model of beauty and elegance.

24. Of the days the Alf brothers spent in this manner, it may be said in short that they wished them to be few. From morning until evening there were wild drinking bouts, obscene songs raised by voices howling and barking, assaults, fights, and murders. The Etins had evidently made up their minds that Od and Ull would not come out of there alive. The Grepp who had stolen Freya noticed that her gaze often rested on Od, and became jealous. He sprang from his seat and ran at Od to transfix him with his weapon. But Ull forestalled his attempt with drawn sword and paid him in his own coin.

25. "Kinsmen's service is very valuable when you need help," remarked Od.

26. "In desperate straits you must have good men oblige you," replied Ull.

27. Then Grepp's brothers leapt up snorting and vowed they would wreak vengeance, but Frey then said that Grepp had fallen on his own deeds, and that those who wanted to take his guest's life should do it in an honest

fight. At that, challenge after challenge followed, and duel after duel. Od was ingenious in negotiating favorable conditions for fighting, and the brothers knew to mutually protect one another and to attack together simultaneously. It was as if Egil was in them two-fold, and when armed with Gambantein they were guaranteed constant victory. Nor could the untrustworthy Etins surprise them in their sleep, because one brother always held armed vigil while the other one slept.

28. During all of this, Od never forgot his plan. To have a private conversation with Freya was difficult and would serve nothing because she scarcely seemed to grasp what was said to her. Frey seemed to avoid conversations as well, or cut them short before Od had made his point. But one time, when they were alone, he reminded them that he was the son of Egil, who, along with Volund, was Frey's foster-father, and that they were thus united by the bonds of foster-brotherhood. Frey remarked that Volund and Egil had poorly fulfilled their duties. Od said that he and Ull had come to remedy that and would receive the penalty customary for broken oaths that burdened Ivaldi's clan. They had also come to save the world and the human race, which would be annihilated if the God of harvests were not returned to Asgard. Frey responded that his long captivity among the most wretched of Ymir's descendants and his inability during this time to help humanity, who had believed in his power and performed blots to him, had subjected him to so much indignity and disgrace that he found it better to remain where he was. Od asked if he had forgotten that he had a father who grieved his loss, and who unceasingly searched for him despite difficult dangers. At this, Frey burst into tears, but repeated that he could not follow Od. But he would provide the brothers an opportunity to flee with Freya and he would, if possible, delay and misdirect any pursuit.

29. With this, the Alf brothers contended themselves. One night when the Etins held a wild drinking bout and were dazed senseless or sunken in deep sleep, the brothers left the Etin court, taking Freya with them. They steered a course over the rough waves of the archipelago to the mainland. There, snow-covered fields stretched before them, over which their skis could glide at an arrow's pace, and far away they found a deep wood, which in an emergency could hide them from pursuers. They did not stop before entering the wood, where they decided to rest and prepare a camp for Freya, as best they could. While Ull plaited a shelter of pine-tree branches and prepared a bed of moss beneath it, Od sat beside the Vanadis. The

moon hung above the treetops and shone on her face. Using various incentives, Od attempted to make the girl look at him, but when he had long tried to attract her drooping eyes and nothing happened to accord with his wishes, he abandoned his scheme. He could not bring himself to use her lustfully, for he was unwilling to stain with disreputable intercourse a daughter of divine parentage. So he carried her to bed, and the brothers bade her goodnight.

30. When they looked for her in the morning, she was gone. They searched for her a long time, but in vain. They called, but got no answer. They spent many days anxiously searching. It was the time of year when the nights are long, and so came the evening of the shortest day of the year. They heard bells in the wood and thought that there must be an Etin court in the vicinity. So the brothers went to seek shelter in the hall, from which the bells rang. They came to a glade, bordered on one side by a steep mountain. A herd of goats with tinkling bells made their way towards a door in the mountain. Behind them walked two women, one a Giantess, the other dressed as a goat-maid. When the herd had been driven in, the Giantess opened another door, allowing the glow of the winter-evening sunset to shine in and light her hall. The brothers approached it, and asked the Giantess for lodging for the night. She treated them kindly when she learned that they were Volund's nephews. The brothers saw that the goat-maid was Freya. After she had hurried blindly for a long while through the twisting paths of the wilderness, she chanced to arrive at the hut of the enormous woman of the woods, who assigned her to graze her herd of she-goats.

31. Od and Ull pretended not to recognize Freya, and she seemed to not recognize them. The Giantess was a little suspicious at this point, but was soon put at ease. Over the evening meal, she studied her handsome young guests. She thought most about Od, who was cheerful and full of ideas at the table, and it seemed to her that she could not wish for a better husband. She praised her farm, her herds, and possessions, and asked if it was not tiring to wander the world at length in search of adventure. Od replied that he, as young as he was, had already had enough, and would gladly be a homebound man with a wife and children. Because his clan had breached with both the Gods and human beings, he now traversed the bewildering paths of Jotunheim with his brother, looking for a bride. Nevertheless, he expected little success on his bridal quest, because he did not have an Etin's size or an Etin's character. The Giantess replied that a

little man was still a man, and if Od wanted a shorter wife, she understood the art to make herself as small as he desired. Od said that his errand in Jotunheim was happily accomplished, if he found favor in her eyes. She let him know that he had, and that it would be an honor to be united in marriage with the glorious and celebrated Ivaldi clan. The drinking-vessels were filled to the brim with the beer of the Giantess' court; they talked merrily through the evening—only the goat-maid was silent—and it was agreed that a wedding would be held, as soon as the bride's closest kin had had time to be notified and had arrived at the stronghold. She would go out herself the following morning and invite them. The wedding would be a simple one, with only the eighteen closest Etin clans invited.

32. Long before the sun rose the following morning, the Giantess went out on her errand to distribute invitations to the wedding. Freya once more enlisted Od's help to get free, whereupon he assailed her with these words:

33. "Don't you prefer
to take my advice,
join in a union to
match my desires,
rather than stay here
with this drove
and tend
rank-smelling kids?

34. "Rebuff the hand
of your evil mistress,
take to your heels
from this savage keeper,
come back with me
to the friendly
ships and live
in freedom.

35. "Abandon the animals
in your care,
refuse to drive
these goats,
and return as the
partner of my bed,
a prize to suit
my longings.

36. "As I have sought you
with such eagerness,
turn up your
languid eyes;
it's an easy movement
to raise your
bashful face
just a little.

37. "I shall set you again
in your father's home,
restore you
in happiness
to your tender mother,
once you reveal
your gaze at
my gentle prayers.

38. "Because I have borne you
from the pens of Etins
more than once,
grant the reward
in pity for
my long-lasting,
grueling toils
and relax your rigor.

39. "Why have you taken
   to this crack-brained madness,
   preferring to herd
   a stranger's flock,
   and be reckoned among
   the slaves of ogres
   instead of arranging
   a harmonious,
   sympathetic marriage-agreement
   between the two of us?"

40. Nonetheless, she could not look up to face him, due to the spell cast on her, and continued to preserve the same inflexible habit and kept her eyelids motionless. Od and Ull put on their skis and made their escape with Freya. By that afternoon, they had reached the coast and set out over the Elivagar. Then from behind them rushed a raging wind, which broke its way through the woods, overturning pines, and roared down to the beach and over the waters, so that the Elivagar's waves swelled sky-high. The brothers guessed that it was the bride and the eighteen Etin clans she invited that prepared this parting gift. However, the Galdur that Groa had sung calmed the sea, allowing them to cross safely. Because Od was unable to incite Freya to look at him, even after earning it with a double service, weary with humiliation and grief, he headed home without her.

41. When Od and Ull returned to Ydalir, they found Sif there, preparing for her departure to Asgard and her marriage to Thor.

There they honored their father's death, and, mindful of his riches, pulled his treasure up from the earth and hid it away.

42. Freya took on her falcon-guise, then ranged far and wide as before over the rocky landscape, until she stumbled in her wanderings to Egil's house, where, ashamed of her threadbare, needy condition, she made out that she was the child of paupers. Although she was pale and clad in a meager cloak, Sif observed that she was of high pedigree and having seated her in a place of honor, kept the girl with her, treating her with respectful courtesy. The girl's beauty revealed her divine nature and her telltale features bore witness to her birth. On seeing her, Od asked why she buried her face in her robe, for he knew she was none other than Freya.

43. Od was more sorrowful than glad. He told Sif that he had not gotten a single glance, not a single word from the girl he had rescued from the Etin powers. Sif, who saw that he was in love, bade him to not speak another word about love to Freya. If the Vanadis had concealed feelings for him, Sif would certainly discover it. Otherwise, he must try to forget her; but in any case, it was his duty and his honor to send her back to Asgard, pure and undefiled.

44. At this time, Volund's daughter, Skadi, was staying at Egil's. Sif arranged a pretend

marriage between her and Od, Freya was dressed as the bridesmaid. That night, Freya followed Od and Skadi to the bridal chamber. As he climbed into bed, he gave Freya the lamp to hold. Since the light was nearly out, she was tormented by the flame creeping close to her skin, yet she gave such a display of endurance that she restrained any movement of her hand. She pretended that she felt no annoyance from the heat: the warmth inside her overcame the temperature outside; the glow of her longing heart checked the scorching of her flesh. Finally, as Od told her to take care of her hand, she shyly raised her eyes and turned her gentle gaze to his. Straight away, the pretended marriage became real, and she ascended the nuptial bed as his bride.

45. So that he should not appear to be snatching the maiden's ungranted love prematurely in carnal embraces, he stopped their sides from having contact by placing Gambantein naked between them and made the bed like a tent with divided compartments for himself and his bride. The illustrious Od laid his sword, adorned with gold, between them both: its outer edges were wrought with fire, but within it was tapered with venom-drops. He then gave her the ring called Andvaranaut. Later, he had the Dwarf

named Hornbori to free her hair from the knots Grepp had tied it in.

46. Sif and two other Swanmaids flew north. From Od they now knew the location of the stronghold where Frey was both jarl and prisoner. They flew over the black islands in the archipelago of Beli's clan and saw that the Etins there were in the process of moving. Since Freya had been carried away, and their haunt discovered, they no longer felt safe. They had set boats asea and were on their way with Frey to a more northerly district. The Swanmaids flew farther and spied. They found Skidbladnir, manned by Vanir, lying moored in a bay. Njord sat on a cliff nearby, sorrowful and brooding. Sorcery and mists ever thwarted his search. In the night, Njord had left his camp to continue looking for Frey, when he caught an unusual sound of the air being beaten; stopping in his tracks and looking up, he heard this song from three swans crying above him:

47. "While Frey sweeps the seas
and cuts the rapid tides,
his thrall drinks from gold
and sips milk from goblets.
A slave's happiest condition
is when a royal-born heir
does him homage,
rashly interchanging their estates."

48. Finally, as the birds' voices ceased, a belt fell from the sky inscribed with runes

which interpreted the song: Frey, who had been handed over to the Etins by the Ivaldi sons, was being carried off by one of Beli's kinsmen. He had taken a boat to cross the neighboring coast and was forcing the lad to row as the vessel chanced to pass Njord at the time he was bent on his work of spying. The God hated the thought of the captured youth being made to toil like this and longed to deprive the snatcher of his prey. Frey advised him to treat the Etin to some sharp tirade, assuring him that an attack would work more effectively if he first lashed him with abusive verse. So, Njord began:

49. "If you are an Etin,
    three-bodied and invincible,
    whose head almost
    touches the heavens,
    why does a laughable sword
    stick by your flank,
    a stumpy blade
    gird your great side?

50. "Why do you guard
    your mighty chest
    with a weak weapon,
    careless of your bodily size,
    and only wield
    a puny dagger?
    In a moment I shall
    thwart your impudent attack,
    if you struggle to fight
    with that blunted steel.

51. "As you are a timid monster,
    a lump lacking the proper strength,
    you are swept head-foremost
    like a fleeting shadow,

for your grand,
spectacular figure contains
a craven heart
slippery with fear,
a spirit at complete
odds with your limbs.

52. "The structure of your
    frame is faltering,
    since a tumbledown mind
    lames your fine shape,
    your nature at variance
    in all its parts.
    Henceforth you shall have
    no reward of fame,
    no longer be regarded
    brave and glorious,
    only be numbered
    in the ranks of the unknown."

53. At these words, he lopped off a foot and a hand of the Etin, forced him to flee, and liberated his captive. The pair immediately returned to Asgard, and so Njord had regained his son. The Gods had all of the Swanmaids in their realm, and with Volund dead the powers of the Fimbulwinter were fully destroyed. Another Fimbulwinter would not come until right before Ragnarok.
54. Freya returned to Asgard as well, and when Njord learned that she had married Od, he was very angry, and wished to hang him for debauching his daughter. However, Freya immediately explained in detail how she had been rescued, which brought Od into Njord's favor. Od raised a horg to Freya, made of stones, now that stone has turned to

glass. He newly sprinkled it with the blood of oxen. Od always trusted in the Asynjur.

LXIII. <u>Gambantein</u>

1. Even though Od had bound himself to Freya and the Vanir with matrimonial ties, he still had to perform his duties of vengeance against the Gods for killing Volund, and against Kon for the slaying of his father and insult to his mother. So, armed with Gambantein, he returned to Midgard. There he sought the Etin-jarls who still lived with their clans in Greater Svithjod, and told them that if they did not arm themselves and resist, their time was short. Kon, supported by the Gods, would come with his army and drive them off, back over the Elivagar to Jotunheim, their native land. Then Od traveled to Jotunheim, to the evil and greatly feared Etin-prince Gymir-Aegir, and called the Etin clans living there to battle. He promised them victory, confiding that he owned a sword that their previous jarl, his uncle Volund, had made but never used—a sword which is always attended with certain victory.

2. A vast Etin host, mobilized by Gymir, assembled and marched south with Od as their leader. The danger was great—greater than the Aesir and human beings foresaw—even though the Gods already saw it as so serious that they had to descend and lead Midgard's fylkings. There you could have seen Etins contending with Gods, for on Kon's side fought Odin, Thor, and battalions of deities, divine and human strength joined together in the struggle against Etins. The Gods appeared in armor and on horseback before the eyes of mortals. Thor came with his iron-hammer, and placed himself not far from Kon. Under shield-songs, the armies advanced toward one another. The song of Gymir and his warriors resounded like the wild shriek of an unrestrained storm; the song of Midgard's warriors roared like the sea-breakers. Odin rode before them on his eight-footed horse, with Gungnir in his hand. The armies clashed and the Etins fought wildly, Gymir foremost among them. Odin burst through their battle line with Gungnir, pressing many of Jotunheim's sons beneath the spear's point and Sleipnir's hooves. Tyr and Vidar cut a path with their swords. Where Thor went forth with his hammer, the casualties were great. However, the Etin forces were constantly renewed, and for their part broke through Kon's line.

3. Od, however, clad in a sword-proof tunic, broke through the densest formations of the Gods and offered as much violence as an Alf could to heaven-dwellers. When he swung Gambantein, no fewer of Midgard's warriors fell than did Etins beneath Thor's hammer.

Od sought Kon, who struck out with his bloody club, but until then, he had avoided confronting Od, whose stepfather he was. But when this duel could no longer be put off, he rode to confront his stepson. The club and the sword of revenge met; Kon's favorite weapon, proven in many battles, burst asunder as if struck by a thunderbolt. Gambantein shone like lightning. For every stroke that it rendered, a gleam flashed above the warring throng and all of Midgard. With one stroke, Kon's armor was cleft and he himself wounded.

4. But Thor shattered all the Etins' shield-defences with the terrific swings of his hammer, Mjollnir, calling on his enemies to attack him as much as his comrades to support him. There was no armor that could stand up to his strokes, nor anyone who could survive them. Shields, helmets, everything he drove at with his iron-hammer was crushed on impact, nor were bodily size or muscle any protection. Consequently, victory would have gone to the Gods, had not Od, whose battle-line had bent inwards, flown forward and rendered the hammer useless by lopping off the handle with Gambantein. Immediately they were denied this weapon, the deities fled.

5. During the fight, Kon observed his line giving way and therefore scrambled with Thor to the top of a cliff strewn with rocks. They pried up these boulders and rolled them down on the enemy drawn up on the slopes below. Then Od and his Etin army withdrew, their victory already won. Odin and the other Gods that took part in the conflict were left standing on the battlefield, at least having the honor of being the last ones there. Od avoided a duel with the Asa-majesty; nor would he attack Njord or Frey, since one was Freya's father and the other her brother.

6. Soon Od received word that Kon had died from the wound inflicted on him. Neither healing runes nor Galdur-songs had helped. Hatred's poison lay in Gambantein's edge, the venom of Niflheim's rivers in that blade. Thus Od avenged his father's death and the affront to his mother, Groa.

7. Volund's death, however, still was not avenged. For that to happen, Od would have to wage war on Asgard and slay all of the Gods who had had a hand in his death. He pondered over this fact, cast it aside, and then took it up again. At times, he said to himself that it was his sacred duty, and at times he objected, saying he had already done more than avenge Volund's death. He had restored his uncle's insulted honor and brought the Gods' judgment on the work of the sons of Ivaldi to shame. Could Volund

himself ask for greater redress than Thor, his slayer, having to retreat before his sword?

8. Od disbanded his Etin army, who returned to their homes, proud in victory. They promised to gather anew if ever commanded by his word or signal to do so.

9. In Asgard, however, horror prevailed. It was clear that whoever possessed Gambantein could make himself the ruler of the worlds. Asgard trembled on the point of Od's sword. Yet, he had sent Freya back to the Gods and betrothed himself to her. Could his love not conquer his lust for power? In that case, he would be welcomed in Asgard and recognized by the Gods as Freya's husband. He was neither of Asa- nor Vana-blood, but reconciliation with Ivaldi's clan and the Alfar was desirable for the Gods. If it could be purchased with Od's admission into the Aesir and Vanir clan, with the inclusion of Gambantein among Asgard's treasures, the exchange would benefit Odin and the worlds.

10. Od himself, with his unfathomable intelligence, had achieved wonders surpassing human estimation. Through his deep insightfulness, he had devised recompense for Kon's destruction of his father and bedding of his mother, and with remarkable courage had seized his kingdom from the man who had frequently tried to ensnare him.

11. When Alveig learned of Kon's death, she was grief stricken, and spoke these words:

12. "I shall not sit so happy
in Alfheim,
neither at morn nor night
shall I feel joy in life,
if the prince's beam of light
does not shine over the folk;
if his war-steed,
accustomed to the gold bit,
does not run here under him;
if I cannot rejoice the king.

13. "So had Kon
struck all his foes
and their kindred
with fear,
as from the wolf
the goats run frantic
from the mountain,
full of terror.

14. "So Kon himself
stood among warriors,
as the towering ash
is among thorns,
or as the fawn,
moistened with dew,
that stalks more proudly
than all the other beasts
and its horns glisten
against the sky."

15. A mound was raised for Kon; but when he came to Valhall he was adopted as one of the mighty Gods. A bondmaid passing at evening by Kon's mound saw him riding towards it with many men.

16. "This is only a delusion,

which I think I see,
or the doom of the Gods,
that you, dead men, ride,
and urge on your horses
with spurs,
or has a journey home
been granted to you warriors?"

17. Kon: "It is no delusion,
which you think you see,
nor the end of mankind,
although you see us,
although we urge on
our horses with spurs,
nor has a journey home
been granted to the warriors."

18. The bondmaid went home and said to Alveig:

19. "Come out, Alveig
of Alfheim,
if you wish to meet
the folk-warder.
The mound is open,
Kon has come;
his wounds still bleed:
the prince prays
that you will still
the trickling blood."

20. Alveig entered the mound to Kon and said:

21. "Now I am as glad
at our meeting,
as the ravenous
hawks of Odin [ravens],
when they know of slaughter,
or warm prey
or, dewy-feathered,
see the peep of day.

22. "I will kiss

my lifeless king,
before you set aside
your bloody armor;
your hair, Kon,
is white with frost;
my prince is all wet
with slaughter-dew;
cold and clammy are the
hands of Jarl's son.
How shall I, prince,
make amends for this?"

23. Kon: "You alone are the cause,
Alveig of Alfheim,
that Kon is covered
with the dew of sorrow.
You, gold-adorned woman,
weep cruel tears,
before you go to sleep;
each one falls bloody
on the prince's heart,
ice-cold and piercing,
and full of sorrow,
sun-bright daughter of the south!

24. "We shall surely drink
the Dyrar Veigar,
though we have lost
life and lands.
No one shall sing
a song of mourning,
though on my chest
he sees wounds:
now my bride has
come into the mound,
the daughter of kings,
with us, the dead!"

25. Alveig prepared a bed in the mound:

26. "Here Kon, I have
prepared a peaceful
couch for you,
for the Ylfing's son.
I will lay on your
chest, jarl,

as I did in
my hero's lifetime."

27. <u>Kon:</u> "I now declare
nothing unlooked for,
late or early
at Saevafjol,
since you, Ivaldi's
fair daughter,
sleep in the arms
of a corpse in a mound,
and you are living,
daughter of kings!

28. "It is time for me to ride
on the reddening ways:
let the pale horse
tread the aerial path.
I must go towards the west,
over Vindhelm's Bridge [Bifrost],
before Salgofnir-Gullinkambi
awakens heroes."

29. Kon and his men rode on their way, but Alveig and her women went home. The following evening Alveig ordered her maidservant to hold watch at the mound, but at nightfall, Alveig came to the mound and said:

30. "He would come now,
if he intended to come,
Jarl's son,
from Odin's halls.
I think the hope lessens
of the king's coming,
since the eagles sit
on ash-tree limbs,
and all the folk hasten
to the land of dreams."

31. <u>Maidservant:</u> "Do not be so rash
to fare alone

to the house of Draugs,
daughter of heroes!
All dead warriors
are more powerful
in the darkness of night
than in the light of day"

32. Alveig's life was shortened by grief and mourning.

LXIV. <u>Fjolsvid</u>

1. It was the time of day when the Dwarf Thjodreyrir, who stands outside the door of Delling, the Alf of the rosy dawn, sings the song of awakening over the world and blessing for the Alfar, the Aesir, and Allfather-Odin. It was the time when Yggdrasil drips honeydew, and the horses of the sun, snorting in the morning air, long to be put into their traces and reined.

2. It was the time of year when buds blossom in Midgard's groves and when the carpet that covers the land is a fresh green, evidence that it has just been woven by the Goddesses of vegetation, the Swanmaids. The time of year when the blue sea of air, Ifing or Thund, is so pure and transparent that the longings of men rise higher than the birds are carried by their wings. It was the time that awakens the yearnings of love in all nature.

3. Heimdall, Bifrost's watchman, saw a youth, clad in armor, with a sun-glistening sword at his side, advancing up the bridge

that no one walks without the force of Urd's resolve. His approach was announced to the Aesir, and there was joy in the city of the Gods, because this meant that Od had come, and most certaintly on a benevolent mission, for he resembled a bright spring day.

4. When Odin heard the news of Od's arrival he felt as if he were dreaming. He arose before daybreak to prepare Valhall. He woke the Einherjar, even before the crowing of Gullinkambi. He bade them to get up, to strew the benches, and fill the drinking vessels; he bade Valkyries to bear wine, for a great leader was coming. He looked forward to the arrival of the noble Alf, and it made his heart glad.

5. Bragi: "What is that racket,
as if a thousand men
or some great host were marching?
All the walls and benches are creaking,
as if Baldur were coming
back to Odin's hall."

6. Odin: "Foolish words;
that noise, wise Bragi,
who usually reasons well,
is the sound of Od;
for it is that prince who
comes to Odin's hall.

7. "Sigmund and Sinfjotli [two Einherjar]
quickly rise up
and go to the prince;
therein I bid you,
to see if Od
is more than I had hoped."

8. Sigmund: "Why do you
place hope in Od,
rather than
another king?"

9. Odin: "In the borderland
he raised the reddened
weapon and bore
the bloody sword [Gambantein]."

10. Sigmund: "Why do you
mention his past victory
if you believe
he is capable?"

11. Odin: "From that unwise statement,
I see an old wolf
that has been allowed
in this divine place."

12. Odin went out to the Asgard wall, Gastropnir, in disguise, using the name Fjolsvid. From the ramparts, he saw the leader of the Thurse people [Od].

13. Fjolsvid: "What beast is this,
standing before the forecourt,
near the Vafurfires?
Hurry back hence
along the wet ways,
there is no place for you here, wretch!
Who do you seek?
What do you search for?
Or what, friendless one, do you wish to know?"

14. Od: "What beast is this,
standing before the forecourt,
who does not offer the wayfarer hospitality?
You have lived, it seems,
without honest fame:
but *you* hurry home hence."

15. Fjolsvid: "Fjolsvid is my name;
I am wise of mind,

though not wasteful of food.
You shall never come
within these courts:
so leave now, outlaw!"

16. Od: "Few would turn away
from that which
enchants his eye,
I see estates
reflected in golden halls.
I want to stay here and enjoy this bliss."

17. Fjolsvid: "Tell me, youth,
of whom are you born,
or of what race have you sprung?"

18. Od: "I am called Vindkald,
my father was Varkald,
his father was Fjolkald.

19. "Tell me, Fjolsvid,
that which I ask of you,
and I wish to know:
who holds sway here,
and owns these lands
and treasure-chambers?"

20. Fjolsvid: "Her name is Menglad [Freya],
her mother bore her
with Svafrthorin's son [Njord];
she holds sway here
and owns these lands
and treasure-chambers."

21. Od: "Tell me, Fjolsvid,
that which I ask of you,
and I wish to know:
what is the gate called,
for no mortal has ever seen
such a dangerous creation among the Gods?"

22. Fjolsvid: "It is called Thrymgjoll,
it was made by the three
sons of Solblindi-Ivaldi:
a fetter fastens
every wayfarer,

who lifts it from its opening."

23. Od: "Tell me, Fjolsvid,
that which I ask of you,
and I wish to know:
what is the wall called,
for no mortal has ever seen
such a dangerous creation among the Gods?"

24. Fjolsvid: "It is called Gastropnir,
and I built it
from Leirbrimir-Ymir's limbs;
I have supported it
so solidly that it should stand
as long as the world."

25. Od: "Tell me, Fjolsvid,
that which I ask of you,
and I wish to know:
what are those wolves called,
who pace back and forth,
guarding the tree's foliage?"

26. Fjolsvid: "One is called Gifur-Freki,
the other Geri,
if you wish to know:
they watch the eleven
watchers,
until the Powers perish."

27. Od: "Tell me, Fjolsvid,
that which I ask of you,
and I wish to know:
whether any man
can enter while
those fierce hounds sleep?"

28. Fjolsvid: "They were strictly told
to not sleep at the same time,
when they were given the watch;
one sleeps at night,
the other by day
so no wights can enter, if they come."

29. Od: "Tell me, Fjolsvid,
that which I ask of you,

and I wish to know:
is there any food
that men can get,
so they can run in while they eat?"

30. Fjolsvid: "Under Vidofnir's limbs
lie two wing-bits,
if you wish to know:
that alone is the food
that men can give them,
and run in while they eat."

31. Od: "Tell me, Fjolsvid,
that which I ask of you,
and I wish to know:
what is that tree called
that spreads itself over
every land with its branches?"

32. Fjolsvid: "It is called Mimameid-Yggdrasil;
but no man knows
from what root it springs:
and few can guess
what shall make it fall,
for fire nor iron will harm it."

33. Od: "Tell me, Fjolsvid,
that which I ask of you,
and I wish to know:
what grows from the seed
of that famed tree,
which fire nor iron will harm?"

34. Fjolsvid: "From its fruit,
which shall be borne on fire
to pregnant women,
shall that come out
which was held within;
so it is with the Manna Meotod."

35. Od: "Tell me, Fjolsvid,
that which I ask of you,
and I wish to know:
what is the cock called,
that sits in Vedurglasir-Yggdrasil,
and is all-glittering with gold?"

36. Fjolsvid: "He is called Vidofnir;
he stands in the clear air
on the limbs of Mimameid-Yggdrasil,
he is severely distressed
by swarthy Sinmara's constant sighs,
her, that you have in mind."

37. Od: "Tell me, Fjolsvid,
that which I ask of you,
and I wish to know:
is there any weapon
by which Vidofnir may
fall to Hel-Urd's abode?"

38. Fjolsvid: "It is called Haevateinn,
which Lopt [Volund] forged
down below the Nagates;
Sinmara keeps it
in an iron-chest
secured with nine strong locks."

39. Od: "Tell me, Fjolsvid,
that which I ask of you,
and I wish to know:
will he return alive,
who seeks after
and tries to take the sword?"

40. Fjolsvid: "He will return,
who seeks after,
and tries to take the sword,
if he carries
what few possess,
to Eir of Aurglasir-Yggdrasil [Sinmara]."

41. Od: "Tell me, Fjolsvid,
that which I ask of you,
and I wish to know:
is there any treasure
that men may obtain
to make the ash-colored Giantess rejoice?"

42. Fjolsvid: "You must carry
the bright sickle that lies between
Vidofnir's round-bones to Lud-Grotti,

and give it to Sinmara,
so she will allow you
to have the weapon."

43. Od: "Tell me, Fjolsvid,
that which I ask of you,
and I wish to know:
what is the hall called,
which is surrounded
by wise Vafurfires?"

44. Fjolsvid: "It is called Hyr,
and long has it
trembled on the point of the sword;
this shining house
has from time out of mind
been celebrated among men."

45. Od: "Tell me, Fjolsvid,
that which I ask of you,
and I wish to know:
who made that which
I saw within
the castle wall of the Asmegir?"

46. Fjolsvid: "Uni and Iri,
Ori and Bari,
Var and Vegdrasil,
Dori and Uri,
Delling, the cunning Alf,
is watchman at the gate."

47. Od: "Tell me, Fjolsvid,
that which I ask of you,
and I wish to know:
what is that mount called,
which I see the
daydreaming maid sitting on?"

48. Fjolsvid: "It is called Lyfjaberg,
and long has it been
the joy of the sick and wounded:
each woman becomes healthy,
although she has had a year's disease,
if only she ascends it."

49. Od: "Tell me, Fjolsvid,
that which I ask of you,
and I wish to know:
what are the names
of the women who
sit so pleasantly at Menglad's feet."

50. Fjolsvid: "The first is called Hlif,
the second is Hlifthrasa,
the third, Thjodvarta,
Bjart and Blik,
Blid and Frid,
Eir and Aurboda [Gullveig]."

51. Od: "Tell me, Fjolsvid,
that which I ask of you,
and I wish to know:
do they protect
those who offer to them,
if it is needed?"

52. Fjolsvid: "Every summer
in which men offer to them
at the holy place,
no evil so severe can happen
to the sons of men that they
cannot help them out of their distress."

53. Od: "Tell me, Fjolsvid,
that which I ask of you,
and I wish to know:
is there any man
that may sleep
in Menglad's [Freya's] soft arms?"

54. Fjolsvid: "There is no man
that may sleep
in Menglad's [Freya's] soft arms,
save only Svipdag-Od,
for the sun-bright maid
is destined to be his bride."

55. Od: "Open up the doors!
Let the gate stand wide!
Here you may see Svipdag-Od!
But yet, go learn

if Menglad-Freya
will accept my love."

56. Fjolsvid: "Hear me Menglad-Freya!
A man has come;
go to see the stranger!
The dogs rejoice,
the house is opened,
I think it may be Svipdag-Od."

57. Freya: "On the high gallows
fierce ravens will
tear out your eyes,
if you are lying in saying
that the youth has
come here to my halls from afar."

58. "From where have you come?
Where have you journeyed?
What do your kindred call you?
I must have evidence
of your race and name,
if I am destined to be your bride."

59. Od: "I am called Svipdag-Od,
Solbjart-Egil is my father;
thence the winds drove me on cold ways.
No one may deny
Urd's decree,
however lightly spoken."

60. Freya: "You are welcome:
I have obtained my desire,
a kiss shall follow a greeting.
The sight of one longed for
gladdens most persons,
when one loves the other.

61. "Long I have sat
on my joyous hill,
waiting for you day and night.
And now I have
what I hoped for,
that you, dear youth, have come
again to my halls."

62. Od: "I have longed
for your love,
as you have for me.
Now it is certain,
that we shall
live our lives together."

63. Od and Freya celebrated their lawful wedding in Asgard. As the mund, and as compensation for Volund's failed duties as foster-father, Od gave Gambantein to Frey.

64. Od wished that his half-brother Ull take part in his honor and be adopted into Asgard, since he had participated in his journey to Jotunheim. This wish was granted by Odin so willingly that Thor announced that he and Sif had decided to become husband and wife. Sif, the golden-haired, came to Asgard and brought Ull with her. Od also rewarded his brother with the land their father owned. It is called Ydalir, where Ull has made himself a dwelling. Thor and Sif celebrated their wedding shortly after that of Od and Freya. Together, they had the son named Modi and the daughter named Thrud.

65. Thereafter, a third and then a fourth wedding were celebrated. Idun married Bragi and Auda married Forseti, since Slagfin was Baldur's beloved foster-brother. Consequently, reconciliation was established between the Aesir and Vanir on one side, and Ivaldi's descendants, the finest family of the Alfar, on the other. This reconciliation was

strengthened by the marriage bonds Skadi, Sif, Od, Idun, and Auda had established with the Gods.

LXV. Breidablik

1. Throughout all of the festivities being celebrated in Asgard, Frigga bore a sorrow that grew heavier in contrast to the happiness she held in common with the others. She missed Baldur, her beloved son. She wept in Fensalir for Valhall's woes.

2. Frigga asked who among the Aesir wished to gain all her love and favor by agreeing to ride the Helways to see if he could find Baldur. He was to offer Urd-Hel a ransom if she would let Baldur return home to Asgard. Od, adopted as Odin's son, was the one who agreed to undertake the journey. They caught Odin's horse Sleipnir and led it forward. Odin gave Od a helm and a coat of mail.

3. For nine nights, Od rode through valleys so deep and dark that he saw nothing before he reached the river Gjoll and rode on to the Gjallarbridge. The bridge is roofed with shining gold, and the maiden guarding it is named Modgud. She asked Od about his name and family and said that the previous day five fylkings of dead men had ridden across the bridge, "yet the bridge echoed more under you alone, and you lack the litur

of the dead. Why do you ride here on the Helways?"

4. He answered, saying, "I ride to Hel in search of Baldur. But have you seen anything of Baldur on the Helways?"

5. She replied that Baldur had ridden across the Gjallarbridge, "and down to the north lies the Helways."

6. Od rode on until he came to the wall around Breidablik. There is no place more beautiful. Baldur lives in Breidablik, and no impurity may be there. Delling, the Alf of the rosy dawn and Breidablik's watchman, holds the key to the gate and will not place it in the lock before Baldur and Nanna are to return with Lif and Leifthrasir at the renewal of the worlds. Breidablik's wall was made to be insurmountable.

7. Od dismounted from Sleipnir and tightened the girth. Then he remounted and spurred the horse, which sprang forward, jumping with such force that it cleared the top of the wall without even coming near it. Then Od rode up to the hall. He dismounted and went inside. He saw that Baldur was sitting in the seat of honor. He then stayed there through the night. In the morning, Od rose up. Baldur led him out of the hall, and, taking the ring Draupnir, he sent it to Odin as a token. Along with other gifts, Nanna

sent Frigga a linen veil. To Fulla she sent a gold finger-ring.

8. He then rode to Urd-Hel and asked her to let Baldur ride home with him, telling her of the deep sorrow and the wailing of the Aesir. But Urd answered that a test would be made to see whether Baldur was as well loved as some say: "If all things in the worlds, alive or dead, weep for him, then he will be allowed to return to the Aesir. If anyone speaks against him or refuses to cry, then he will remain in Hel."

9. Then, Od retraced his path, riding into Asgard, where he recounted all that had happened: what he had seen and heard. Next, the Aesir sent messengers throughout the worlds, asking that Baldur be wept out of Hel. All did so, people and animals, the earth, the stones, the trees, and all metals in the way that you have seen these things weep when they come out of the freezing cold and into warmth. As the messengers, having accomplished their task, were returning home, they found a Giantess sitting in a cave. She said her name was Thokk. When they asked her to weep Baldur out of Hel, she said:

10. "Thokk will weep
   dry tears at
   Baldur's funeral pyre.
   Alive or dead the old man's [Odin's]

son gave me no joy.
Let Hel-Urd hold what she has."

11. People believe that the Giantess was Loki Laufeyarsson, who has done most evil among the Aesir.

12. Because of this, Baldur and Nanna have to stay where they are and remain there until the time of the worlds' renewal. Their son, Forseti, has grown up in Asgard and is to some extent a compensation for what the worlds lost through Baldur's departure. He has his father's fair disposition and is more persuasive than any other judge in delicate matters and in settling disputes. The hofs consecrated to him have the highest sanctity. Glitnir is the hall; its pillars are gold, and its roof set with silver. There dwells Forseti throughout all time, and settles all disputes.

LXVI. Alvis

1. Alvis: "They adorn the benches,
   now the bride shall
   make her way home with me;
   this will seem to be
   a hasty match to many:
   they'll rob me of rest at home."

2. Thor: "Who are you?
   Why are you so pale around the nose?
   Did you lay with corpses last night?
   You seem to me to have
   the likeness of Thurses,
   you were not born to have a bride."

3. Alvis: "I am Alvis,
   I dwell in the Underworld,
   I have a house beneath stones.

I have come to visit
the Lord of Chariots [Thor];
let no one break a confirmed promise."

4. Thor: "I will break it;
for as her father I have
the greatest power over the maid.
I was not at home
when you were given the promise,
among the Gods I am the sole giver."

5. Alvis: "What man is this,
who claims power over
the fair, bright maiden?
Few will know you
for your journeys.
Who has adorned you with rings?"

6. Thor: "I am called Vingthor,
I have wandered far;
I am Sidgrani-Odin's son:
you shall not have that young
maiden without my consent,
nor shall you obtain the union."

7. Alvis: "Soon you will give me
your consent,
so I may obtain the union;
I long to have,
and I will not be without,
that snow-white maiden."

8. Thor: "I shall not deny you
the maiden's love,
wise guest,
if you can tell me
all I wish to know
of every world."

9. Alvis: "You can try me, Vingthor,
since you wish to prove
the knowledge of the Dwarf.
I have traveled over
all the nine worlds,
and known every being."

10. Thor: "Tell me Alvis,
for I presume you, Dwarf,
know the urlag of all men—
what do they call the earth,
which lies before the sons of men,
in every world?"

11. Alvis: "It is called Jord among men,
but Fold by the Aesir;
the Vanir call it Vega,
the Etins, Igroen,
the Alfar, Groandi,
the supreme Powers, Aurr."

12. Thor: "Tell me Alvis,
for I presume you, Dwarf,
know the urlag of all men—
what do they call the heaven,
which can be seen
in every world?"

13. Alvis: "It is called Himinn by men;
but Hlymir by the Gods,
the Vanir call it Vindofni,
the Etins, Uppheim,
the Alfar, Fagraroef,
the Dwarves, Drjupansal."

14. Thor: "Tell me Alvis,
for I presume you, Dwarf,
know the urlag of all men—
what do they call the moon,
which men can see,
in every world?"

15. Alvis: "It is called Mani by men,
but Mylin by the Gods,
in Hel they call it Hverfanda Hvel,
the Etins, Skyndi,
the Dwarves, Skin,
the Alfar call it Artali."

16. Thor: "Tell me Alvis,
for I presume you, Dwarf,
know the urlag of all men—
what do they call the sun,

which the sons of men see,
in every world?"

17. <u>Alvis:</u> "It is called Sol among men,
but Sunna by the Gods,
the Dwarves call it Dvalins Leika,
the Etins, Eyglo,
the Alfar, Fagrahvel,
the Asasynir, Alskir."

18. <u>Thor:</u> "Tell me Alvis,
for I presume you, Dwarf,
know the urlag of all men—
what do they call the clouds,
which carry the rains,
in every world?"

19. <u>Alvis:</u> "They are called Sky by men,
but Skurvan by the Gods;
the Vanir call them Vindflot,
the Etins, Urvan,
the Alfar, Vedurmegin;
in Hel, Hulidshelm."

20. <u>Thor:</u> "Tell me Alvis,
for I presume you, Dwarf,
know the urlag of all men—
what do they call the wind,
which widely passes
over every world?"

21. <u>Alvis:</u> "It is called Vind by men,
but Vafud by the Gods,
the wide-ruling Powers call it Gneggjud,
the Etins, Aepir,
the Alfar, Dynfari,
in Hel, Hvidud."

22. <u>Thor:</u> "Tell me Alvis,
for I presume you, Dwarf,
know the urlag of all men—
what do they call the calm,
which lies quietly,
in every world."

23. <u>Alvis:</u> "It is called Logn by men,

but Laegi by the Gods,
the Vanir call it Vindslot,
the Etins, Ofhly,
the Alfar, Dagsevi,
the Dwarves, Dags Vera."

24. <u>Thor:</u> "Tell me Alvis,
for I presume you, Dwarf,
know the urlag of all men—
what do they call the sea,
which men row over,
in every world?"

25. <u>Alvis:</u> "It is called Saer by men,
but Silaegja by the Gods;
the Vanir call it Vag,
the Etins, Allheim,
the Alfar, Lagastaf,
the Dwarves, Djupan Marr."

26. <u>Thor:</u> "Tell me Alvis,
for I presume you, Dwarf,
know the urlag of all men—
what do they call the fire
which burns before men's sons,
in every world?"

27. <u>Alvis:</u> "It is called Eldur by men,
but Funi by the Aesir;
the Vanir call it Vaegin,
the Etins, Frek,
but the Dwarves, Forbrennir,
in Hel they call it Hrodud."

28. <u>Thor:</u> "Tell me Alvis,
for I presume you, Dwarf,
know the urlag of all men—
what do they call the forest,
which grows for the sons of men,
in every world?"

29. <u>Alvis:</u> "It is called Vid by men,
but Vallarfax by the Gods;
Hel's inmates call it Hlidthang,
the Etins, Eldi,
the Alfar, Fagrlimi,

the Vanir call it Vond."

30. <u>Thor</u>: "Tell me Alvis,
for I presume you, Dwarf,
know the urlag of all men—
what do they call Natt [Night],
the daughter of Nor-Mimir,
in every world?"

31. <u>Alvis</u>: "It is called Natt by men,
but Njola by the Gods;
the wide-ruling Powers call it Grima,
the Etins, Oljos,
the Alfar, Svefngaman,
the Dwarves call it Draumjorunn."

32. <u>Thor</u>: "Tell me Alvis,
for I presume you, Dwarf,
know the urlag of all men—
what do they call the seed,
which the sons of men sow,
in every world?"

33. <u>Alvis</u>: "It is called Bygg by men,
but Barr by the Gods;
the Vanir call it Vaxt,
the Etins, Aeti,
the Alfar, Lagastaf,
in Hel it is called Hnipinn."

34. <u>Thor</u>: "Tell me Alvis,
for I presume you, Dwarf,
know the urlag of all men—
what do they call beer,
which the sons of men drink,
in every world?"

35. <u>Alvis</u>: "It is called Ol by men,
but Bjor by the Aesir,
the Vanir call it Veig,
the Etins, Hreinna Log,
but in Hel it is called Mjod,
Suttung-Fjalar's sons call it Sumbel."

36. <u>Thor</u>: "I have never found
more ancient lore

in one mind;
you have been deluded
by trickery, I tell you.
You are above ground at dawn, Dwarf;
now the sun is shining in the hall!"

LXVII. <u>Gerd</u>

1. Gymir-Aegir is the name of the Etin whose wife, Gullveig-Aurboda, came from the family of Bergrisar. Their daughter is Gerd. Gullveig milked Gymir's goats. Frey, son of Njord, had sat one day in Hlidskjalf, and looked over all the worlds. He looked into Jotunheim, and saw there a fair maiden, as she went from her father's house to her bower. When she raised her arms to unlock the door, a light seemed to beam from her arms, both into the air and onto the sea and because of her the whole world brightened in Frey's eyes. Just then, he felt a great love-sickness. He was silent when he returned home. He neither slept nor drank, and no one dared to speak to him. Then Njord sent Od, Frey's servant, and asked him to speak with Frey. Then Skadi said:

2. "Rise up now, Od!
Go and request
to speak to our son;
and ask with whom
the one so wise
is angry with."

3. <u>Od</u>: "I have to fear
harsh words from your son,
if I go and speak with him,
and ask with whom

the one so wise
is angry with."

4. Od: "Tell me now, Frey,
   prince of Gods!
   For I wish to know,
   why do you sit alone
   in your wide hall
   all day long?"

5. Frey: "Why should I tell you,
   young man,
   of my sorrow?
   Alfrodul-Sol shines
   every day,
   but not on my desires."

6. Od: "Your desires cannot, I believe,
   be so great,
   that you can't tell them to me;
   for in early days
   we were young together:
   well might we trust each other."

7. Frey: "In Gymir-Aegir's court
   I saw a maid walking
   whom I long for.
   Her arms gave forth light
   from which shone
   all air and water.

8. "That maid is
   more dear to me
   than any maiden to man;
   yet no one will,
   Aesir or Alfar,
   want us to live together."

9. Od: "Then give me the steed,
   which can bear me through
   the dark Vafurfires;
   and that sword [Gambantein],
   which fights of itself
   against the Etin race."

10. Frey: "I will give you the steed,
    which can bear you through
    the dark Vafurfires,
    and that sword,
    which fights of itself,
    if it is a wise man who owns it."

11. — Od speaks to the horse, Sleipnir:
    "It is dark outside,
    it is time for us
    to ride through frosty mountains,
    over the land of Thurses:
    either we will each return,
    or the dangerous Etin
    shall take us both."

12. Od rode to Jotunheim, to Gymir-Aegir's house, where fierce wolves were chained at the gate of the enclosure that was round Gymir-Aegir's hall. He rode on to where a goatherd, named Eggther, was sitting on a mound, and said to him:

13. "Tell me, goatherd,
    sitting on the mound,
    and watching all the ways,
    how may I get to speak
    with the young maiden
    past Gymir's wolves?"

14. Eggther: "You are either doomed to die,
    or are already dead;
    you will never
    get to speak
    with Gymir-Aegir's
    good daughter."

15. Od: "There are better choices
    than whining
    for him who is prepared to die:
    for one day
    my age was decreed,
    and my whole life determined."

16. Gerd: "What is that sound of sounds,
    which I now hear
    sounding within our dwelling?
    The ground shakes,
    and with it all the house
    of Gymir-Aegir trembles.

17. A serving maid: "A man is outside here,
    dismounted from his horse's back,
    and lets his horse loose to graze."

18. Gerd: "Ask him to enter
    into our hall,
    and drink of the good mead;
    although I fear
    it is my brother's slayer
    who waits outside.

19. "Are you of the Alfar,
    or of the Asasynir,
    or of the wise Vanir?
    Why have you come alone,
    through the leaping flame,
    to visit our halls?"

20. Od: "I am not of the Alfar,
    nor of the Asasynir,
    nor of the wise Vanir;
    yet I have come alone,
    through the leaping flame,
    to visit your halls.

21. "Eleven apples,
    all of gold:
    these I will give you, Gerd,
    to gain your love,
    that Frey shall be
    deemed dearest to you."

22. Gerd: "I will never accept
    these eleven apples
    for any man's desire;
    nor will Frey and I,
    while our lives last,
    both live together."

23. Od: "The ring I will give you,
    which was burnt
    with the young son of Odin.
    Eight of equal weight
    will drop from it
    every ninth night."

24. Gerd: "I will not accept the ring,
    though it may have been burnt
    with the young son of Odin.
    I have no lack of gold
    in Gymir-Aegir's court;
    for I share my father's wealth."

25. Od: "Do you see, young maiden,
    this slender, sign-marked sword
    which I have here in my hand?
    I will sever your head
    from your neck,
    if you do not speak favorably to me."

26. Gerd: "I will never
    be compelled
    to please any man;
    yet this I foresee,
    if you and Gymir-Aegir meet,
    he will eagerly engage in combat."

27. Od: "Do you see, young maiden,
    this slender, sign-marked sword
    which I have here in my hand?
    The old Etin shall fall
    beneath its blade,
    your father is doomed to die.

28. "With Tamsvond-Gambantein I strike you,
    and I will tame you
    maiden, to my will;
    there you shall go
    where the sons of men
    shall never see you.

29. "You shall sit early
    on Ari's perch,
    turned to and longing for Hel;
    food shall be

more loathsome to you,
than the glistening serpent to men.

30. "Fearful to see,
when you go forth;
Hrimnir shall gaze at you,
and all beings stare at you;
you shall become more well-known
than the watchman of the Gods [Heimdall],
if you peer out from your prison.

31. "Topi and Opi,
Tjosul and Otholi,
shall increase your torment and tears;
sit down and I will tell you
of an overwhelming
flood of sorrow, and a double grief.

32. "Tramar shall bow you
to the earth,
in the Etins' court.
You shall crawl each day
to the Hrimthurses' halls
joyless and exhausted;
crying shall be your pastime:
and tears and misery.

33. "You shall forever be bound
to a three-headed Thurse,
or be without a mate.
Let Morn grip you,
let Morn waste you,
you shall be like the thistle
which has thrust itself
on the house-top.

34. "I went to Holt
and to the juicy tree [Yggdrasil],
to get Gambantein,
I got Gambantein.

35. "Odin is angry at you,
the Asa-prince is angry at you.
Frey shall loathe you,
even before you, wicked maid,
shall have felt

the avenging wrath of the Gods!

36. "Hear ye, Etins!
Hear ye, Hrimthurses!
Sons of Suttung-Fjalar,
the Aslidar [Asmegir] themselves,
how I forbid,
how I banish
pleasure from the maid,
joy of men from the maid.

37. "Hrimgrimnir is the Etin
who shall possess you,
down below the Nagates;
there shall the sons of misery,
from the tree's [Yggdrasil's] roots,
give you goats' water.
No other drink
shall you ever get,
neither for your pleasure
or for my pleasure.

38. "Thurse I cut for you,
and three more runes:
longing and madness and lust.
So I will cut them out
as I have cut them in,
if there shall be need."

39. Gerd: "Hail, rather, to you, youth,
and accept a frosty cup,
filled with old mead!
Although I did not think
that I should ever
love one of the Vanir race."

40. Od: "I will know
all my errand,
before I ride home hence.
When will you
hold converse with
the powerful son of Njord?"

41. Gerd: "The grove is named Barri,
which we both know,
the grove of tranquil paths.

There Gerd will grant delight
to the son of Njord,
nine nights hence."

42. Od then rode home. Frey was standing outside, and spoke to him, asking for tidings:

43. "Tell me, Od-Skirnir,
before you take off the saddle,
or fare forward one step,
what have you accomplished
in Jotunheim,
for my pleasure or yours?"

44. Od: "The grove is named Barri,
which we both know,
the grove of tranquil paths.
There Gerd will grant delight
to the son of Njord,
nine nights hence."

45. Frey: "Long is one night,
longer are two;
how then shall I bear three?
Often to me
has a month seemed less
than half a night of longing."

46. Had Gymir-Aegir and his warriors slept so deeply that they did not wake when the ground shook beneath Sleipnir's hooves and the wolves raised their howls? No. Gymir-Aegir saw Od coming; he had long awaited a messenger from Frey. He and Gullveig had conspired between themselves as to how Gambantein, which made Asgard invincible, would come into the Etin's power. Gerd was the fairest maid in Jotunheim, but her white arms could not have shed light over the heavens and the sea without the aid of Gullveig's Seid. Gymir-Aegir had learnt all about Od's good fortune, for his fame preceded him, but when he knew of his arrival, he was afraid that with his profound self-assurance Od would work dire mischief among the Etins. So, he aimed to split him from his wife and unite his own daughter to Od in her stead. To replace his own queen, recently deceased (now reborn and again among the Gods), he desired to marry Frey's sister, Freya, more than anyone.

47. When Od discovered his scheme, he called his comrades together and informed them that his urlag was not yet clear of the reefs. He could see that a bundle was liable to slip if it was not securely tied, and in the same way, if it were not fastened by a chain of guilt, the whole weight of a punishment could suddenly collapse. They had recently experienced this with Frey and perceived how amid the most uncomfortable events the Gods had been on their side and protected their innocence. If they preserved their innocence even longer, they ought to expect similar help under adverse conditions. Od then went home to Asgard to visit Thor.

48. Then, he found Freya, and to test her fidelity asked whether Gymir-Aegir appealed to her, pointing out that it was degrading for

a Goddess to be obliged to share a bed with one of lower birth. Thereupon she earnestly implored him by the holy Gods to say whether this was a ruse or his true thoughts. As he maintained that he was speaking seriously, she replied:

49. "Then you are planning to submit me to the most mortifying disgrace, seeing how deeply you loved me as a maiden and are now going to desert me. Popular report often predicts the reverse of facts; your reputation deceived me. I thought I had married a loyal husband and now, where I had hoped to find absolute faithfulness, I discover someone lighter than the winds." With these words, she dissolved into a flood of tears. Od was happy at his wife's bitterness and shortly, holding her hand close, he said:

50. "I wanted to know the measure of your devotion; only death has the right to sever us. But Gymir-Aegir is scheming to kidnap you and gain your love by theft. When he has managed this, pretend it was what you wished, but postpone the wedding until he has given me his daughter in your place. Once this has been achieved, Gymir-Aegir and I shall celebrate our marriages. In case you should slight the Etin with rather lukewarm looks having me before your eyes, our banqueting halls should be separate, though make sure they share a common dividing

wall. This will be a most effective device for baffling the intentions of your abductor." After this, Od fetched Ull, asking them to join them on their excursion to Gymir-Aegir's halls. He then gave Thor instructions to lurk near the hall with a chosen band of deities, who would lend aid when it was needed.

51. Once nine days had passed, Frey and Gerd met at the grove called Barri. She promised to become his, but only on these conditions, fixed by her parents: Gambantein would be turned over to Gymir-Aegir in the wedding; Od and Freya would appear before him on the appointed day to formally request Gerd's hand on Frey's behalf; Gerd would be adopted into Asgard and have the dignity of an Asynja. Enchanted, Frey would have promised more had Gerd demanded it. He immediately placed Gambantein in her hand.

52. For the Gods, this was a much greater loss than it was a boon for Jotunheim. Volund had not intended for the enemies of the Gods besides the Ivaldi sons' kin to have direct use of the sword, and he had taken careful measures to prevent it. On its blade, with great artistry, he had engraved a depiction of the ancient event when the Hrimthurses were drowned in Ymir's blood. This is why it has been said that Volund's

sword fights of itself against the Etin race. It was to this scene that Od pointed when he showed that blade to Gerd. It illustrated a quality that Volund had hammered into the blade's very essence. If an Etin wields the sword, he surely kills his opponent, but he will kill himself too and with him the entire Etin nation. The Etins knew the quality of this sword, and thus they were as afraid of using it as they were eager to get it out of Asgard, where it was a deposit on the Gods' security. For this reason, when Gerd handed the sword to her father, nothing was more important to him than to guard the sword well and to give it a trustworthy watchman. For this task, he chose his own kinsman, Eggther.

53. When Od arrived at Gymir-Aegir's realm, the Etin declared that he desired to possess Frey's sister, but would give Od his daughter so that he would suffer less regret in yielding his wife to another. It was not unsuitable for the product of an embassy to fall to the ambassador. He was delighted at the prospect of Od as his son-in-law, provided he could claim kinship with Frey through Freya.

54. Od praised the Etin's generosity and approved his idea; he remarked that he could not expect the immortal Gods to confer more on him than this unasked gift. Yet, Gymir-Aegir should first ask Freya's feelings and opinion. She pretended to be gratified at the Etin's flatteries and appeared to consent readily to his request, begging him only to permit Od's wedding to precede her own. If this were allowed to come first, the Etin-jarl's would follow more fittingly, especially since, when she entered into the new contract, she would not feel so squeamish through remembering her former one. In addition, she asserted that there was no point in not jumbling two sets of preparations together in one ceremony.

55. She prevailed completely over the Etin, who warmly commended her requests. His frequent conversations with Od had enabled him to absorb a brilliant set of maxims to delight and invigorate his mind; for this reason, Gymir-Aegir bestowed on him lands in Jotunheim, reckoning that a near relation deserved this favor. Od had brought Sif with him on his travels because of her skill in enchantments; she had pretended to have an eye affliction which necessitated veiling her face with her cloak, so that not the tiniest area of her head could be seen and recognized. When people asked her identity she replied that she was Freya's sister, born of the same mother but a different father.

56. As soon as they reached Gymir-Aegir's hall, they saw that a wedding feast was be-

ing held for his daughter, Gerd. Od and the Etin-jarl took their place at the table in separate rooms divided by a party wall; the interiors were draped throughout with hanging tapestries. Freya was seated next to Gymir, while immediately opposite, on the other side of the wall, Od sat between Sif and Gerd. Amid all the revelry Od stealthily removed a plank from the wall and, unbeknown to the banqueters, opened up a corridor just spacious enough for a person's body to squeeze through. Then, as the feasting progressed, he began to question his intended bride closely, asking whether she would prefer Frey or himself as a husband, stressing that they were probably better suited for one another. When she answered that she could never contemplate a match unless it were sanctioned by her father, he reminded her that she herself would become a Goddess among the holy Gods. This altered all her reluctance, for she was taken by the prospect of such glory. The story goes that Sif offered her a drink mixed with something, which channeled the girl's desires into love for Frey.

57. After the feast, Gymir-Aegir went round to Od's gathering, wishing to make the nuptial hilarity go without a swing. As he left, Freya, acting on instructions, slipped through the wall where the plank had been

withdrawn and took a seat next to Od. Gymir-Aegir was amazed to see her sitting next to him, and asked with some interest how and why she had come there. She replied that she was Freya's sister, and that the jarl was deceived by their closeness in looks. To get to the bottom of this, the Etin swiftly re-entered the banqueting hall, but Freya had returned by the same door and was sitting before the eyes of everyone in her former place. At the sight of her, Gymir-Aegir could not believe his eyes and, completely mistrusting his own powers of recognition, retraced his steps to Od where he found Freya back again as usual in front of him. However often he changed rooms, he came upon the woman in either place. Not merely similar, but identical faces on each side of the wall tortured the Etin with bewilderment. It seemed downright impossible that two beings should so coincide in appearance that they were indistinguishable. At last, the revelry broke up and he escorted his daughter and Od, as is normal after a wedding, as far as their chamber. Then he went off to bed elsewhere.

58. Od allowed Gerd, now destined for Frey, to sleep apart, while, having outwitted the Etin-jarl, he took Freya into his arms, as of old. Gymir-Aegir passed a sleepless night, constantly reviewing the delusive image in

his stupefied, perplexed mind. Not just similar, but identical! From this there entered into his head an unsettled and wavering assumption that he was calling it a mistake when it was something he had actually perceived. At length, it crossed his mind that the wall could have perhaps been meddled with, but when he had given orders for a close examination to be made, no trace was found of any damage. The whole fabric of the room appeared to be sound and undisturbed. In fact, Od, in the early part of the night had fixed the loose plank to prevent his trick from being discovered.

59. Gymir-Aegir next dispatched two spies with orders to penetrate Od's bedroom noiselessly, stand behind the hangings, and listen carefully to everything. They were also instructed to kill Od if they found him with Freya. After entering the chamber stealthily, they hid themselves in curtained alcoves and saw Od and Freya enjoying the same bed, entwined in one another's arms. Thinking the pair were half-dozing, they waited for them to sink into a deeper rest, wishing to lurk there until sound slumber gave them an opportunity to perpetrate the crime. When they heard Od's powerful snores, apparently indicating that his sleep was now more serene, they at once advanced with drawn blades to murder him. As they rushed at him treacherously, Od was awoken and, catching sight of the swords leveled at his head, pronounced his stepmother's name, which she had once told him to utter if he were in danger. Aid for his plight came immediately. His shield, which was hanging high on a rafter, straightaway fell on him and, as if on purpose, protected his unarmed body from the lunges of the assassins. Taking good advantage of his luck, he snatched his sword and sliced off both feet of the nearer cutthroat. With equal vigor, Freya ran a spear through the other.

60. Ull then blew a horn-call to those whose orders were to stand guard nearby, as a signal to invade the hall. When Gymir-Aegir heard it, he believed that it was a sign that the enemy had arrived and fled post-haste in his ship. He traveled to Hlesey, where he built a new hall. His guests were not as fortunate. After the iron-hammer had been broken in two, Thor bore his old hammer of stone. It was not as air-worthy, but it was reliable in battle. Gymir-Aegir's warriors and guests started up. Most of them fled out through the long rows of the mountain-hall. But those who could not escape fell beneath Thor's hammer strikes, or Ull and Od's blows.

61. They returned to Asgard, and Frey celebrated his marriage with Gerd. Together

they had a son named Fjolnir, after one of Odin's names. Od and Freya had the daughters Hnoss and Gersemi, and the son Asmund. Their daughters were so very beautiful, that afterwards the most precious treasures were called by their names.

LXVIII. <u>Fenrir</u>

1. The Gods discovered that Gullveig had once again managed her way into Asgard, and that she was again Freya's attendant, Aurboda. The Aesir gathered for a preliminary tribunal in Valhall to discuss what should be done with her. She stood before them. Odin pointed out that Gullveig had been sentenced to die long ago, that the judgment was permanent, thus still valid, and could not be annulled simply because the evil vala had been reborn into the world. It was the duty of the Gods to execute her when and under whatever guise she appeared anew. A new trial and judgment were not necessary. When Thor heard Odin say this, he sprang up and delivered a deathblow with his hammer, killing the vala for the third time. The Vanir were not present, and when Njord learned what had transpired he said that this was done too hastily, and that he had misgivings about it, which he would reveal after consulting with the Vanir and Alfar. The Gods raised Gullveig on spears, and in Odin's hall, they burned her, three times born oft and again; yet still she lives. It was difficult for the flames to touch her. Loki ate the heart, which laid in the embers, and half-burnt he found the woman's heart, Lopt-Loki was soon with child from the woman, and there came Fenrir among men.

2. Loki traveled to Jotunheim and gave birth to Fenrir by Gnipalund on Thorsnes. Loki bore the wolf with Angerboda-Gullveig. Later Gullveig returned, she was the vala-crone in Varinsey, cunning as a fox, a spreader of lies. She was a mischievous crone, a fierce Valkyrie, hateful and grim in Allfather-Odin's hall. All the Einherjar would fight with each other for her sake, the deceitful woman! In Sagunes, they had nine wolves together; Loki was the father of them all. The old Giantess bore many sons, all in the likeness of wolves, and it is from her that the wolves Skoll and Hati Hrodvitnisson come, who chase Sol and Mani into the Varnwood. When the Gods realized Fenrir was being brought up in Jotunheim, and when the Gods traced prophecies stating that from this great mischief and disaster would arise for them, then they all felt evil was to be expected from him, to begin with because of his mother's nature, but still worse because of his father's.

3. Then Allfather-Odin sent the Gods to seize Fenrir and bring him to him. The Aesir

raised the wolf at home, but only Tyr had the courage to approach it and feed it. But the Gods saw how much the wolf grew every day, and knew that all the prophecies foretold that it was destined to harm them.

LXIX. Folkvig

1. I remember the first folkvig in the world; when the Gods had raised Gullveig on spears, and in Har-Odin's hall they burned her, three times burned, and three times born oft and again, yet still she lives. Shortly thereafter, Njord requested a Thing of the Gods to be called together. The Aesir and Vanir, all with a feeling that something important and fateful loomed, gathered at their holy Thingstead, Glitnir. The Powers all went to their Thingseats, the high-holy Gods to consider thereon: if the Aesir should pay compensation, or if all the Gods should atone with gold.

2. Our ancestors very much loved to fight with weapons, but equally enjoyed contests of argument and reason, of assertions and objections. Thus, the debate that took place between the Aesir and Vanir was detailed and carefully discussed in ancient songs.

3. Njord spoke on behalf of the Vanir. As the God of peaceful commerce, he laid out his words well and with caution, because the matter was delicate and would not turn out well, without minds disposed to mediation.

It was clear that he had consulted with the Vanir and Alfar, and that for the sake of harmony they did not want to challenge Odin's opinion that the judgment passed on Gullveig long ago was still valid. With reason they could entertain doubt, since of course it seemed unclear regarding a being born three times, whether a single judgment pertained to one or all three Giantesses. In regard to Gullveig's wicked deeds, one could say that they were committed by three evil Giantesses or only one. Thus, when doubts were raised on this point, it would have been best to properly examine the case with witness testimony and undertake judgment this time too, and thereby only focus on the deeds that the accused was believed to have committed after her third rebirth.

4. It was also a disquieting matter that Gullveig was killed and burnt in Odin's high-holy hall, which ought not be stained with blood, and where, before the Asa-majesty, everyone ought to feel under the protection of the law.

5. But the real complaint of the Vanir was that when the Aesir had killed Gullveig this time, they had not considered that she was united in bonds of kinship to Gods, primarily the Vanir. The Aesir had killed Frey's mother-in-law. There lay the matter, and it

was this suit that the Vanir and the Alfar now put forth for discussion and settlement.

6. For their part, the Aesir objected, holding that the bonds of kinship between the Vanir and Gullveig were not valid as a defense, since they were a result of one of her all-time worst crimes. No one could doubt that she had striven for bonds of kinship with malicious intent and won them with Seid, this time directed at Njord's own son, the gentle, benevolent Frey, beloved by Gods and men. She had assaulted his senses with such strong sorcery that in Asgard there was no other choice than to watch him waste away and die, or consent to be joined in a marriage that must have been unwelcome to Njord himself. Only then, the bride had to be purchased with Asgard's finest means of defense: Gambantein. This assault had been directed at the Gods and mankind. Thus, Odin expected the Vanir not to take issue with the punishment that Gullveig finally had received, although he could concede that the Aesir had gone about it too hastily.

7. It must have been difficult for Frey to attend this conference, since the love he felt for Gerd was the subject of examinations that could do nothing but vex him. The deliberations had not gone on long before he laid out his and the other Vanir's complaint in the matter. They had decided to demand

weregild from the Aesir for the killing of his mother-in-law.

8. Odin would have probably conceded without hesitation that he and his sons were responsible for the fine, and that he, notwithstanding his high position in the worlds, ought to acknowledge his guilt and give compensation, were it not for the serious danger inherent in such a concession that made it too risky. Among the clans in Midgard all too many would understand the resolution of the lawsuit in such a way that the Aesir could not pay the weregild unless they thought it a crime to have put to death the one who spread the evil runes, invented the evil Seid, and was the origin of all niding acts in Midgard. How then would mankind distinguish between good and evil? Odin, as leader of the worlds, the administrator of the law, and father of humanity, had to view the suit from this standpoint. For that reason, he and his sons would not give the weregild demanded by the Vanir.

9. But likewise it was a holy law, given by Urd and established by Odin, that the death of a kinsman must be avenged by the next of kin, or else weregild given to the party. The Vanir had demanded a fine to keep the peace, since the exacting of revenge would bring great misfortune for all. Certainly, Odin ought to consider that it was a danger-

ous precedent for the humans if the Gods themselves let so sacred a law be broken.

10. The Vanir explained that they could not abandon their demand for weregild. The demand was an unconditional obligation, impossible to set aside.

11. Odin responded that the Vanir had now fulfilled their duty. They *had* demanded weregild. Now another duty obliged them to listen to reason, and, for the sake of the worlds, not leave their Thingseats until it had been agreed that all differences between the Aesir, Vanir, and Alfar had been settled.

12. Here the Aesir and Vanir now seemed to stand firm against one another. But yielding best suited Odin, for Gullveig was justly charged with evil Seid; and, of course, Odin himself had practiced evil Seid when he had sought Rind's favor. The Vanir pointed this out, not to embitter the Asafather, whom they revered, but to move his mind to justice.

13. When Odin heard himself accused of practicing evil Seid, his face changed. He was reminded of a depravity that he could not contest and which also was presumably Gullveig's work, a depravity that he paid for with a son's death.

14. Odin threw his spear over the host of the hof; then came the first war in the world. There alone was Thor swollen with an-

ger—he seldom sits when he hears such things—and the oaths were broken, the words and bonds, every powerful pact between the Powers. Odin left the Thingstead without saying a word, and the Asagods followed him.

15. The Vanir and Alfar remained and deliberated. They did not leave the Thingstead before they had reached a verdict. It was delivered to Odin and worded such that whereas he and Gullveig were guilty of the same crime, the perpetration of evil Seid, and that since Gullveig was justly punished with death, that Odin had tarnished the honor of his divinity by his various lapses from dignity, and decided that he should quit their fraternity. Afterwards, the Vanir and Alfar abandoned their halls in Asgard, and Valgrind closed behind them.

16. Odin sent a message to Mimir, letting him know what had happened and to ask his advice. It was clear, by this breach between the Aesir and Vanir, that the order of the world and the existence of Yggdrasil were once again threatened. Should it come to war between Gods and one or several of them fell, the greatest harm would be done, since each and every one of them is necessary in this age and has his duty to fulfill in the order of things. Mimir promised to seek a compromise, but should he fail and hostili-

ties break out, Odin and his sons should barricade themselves within Asgard and see to its defense, but should do everything in their power to keep from killing any of their former comrades. If the Vanir succeeded in surmounting Gastropnir, Odin should abandon Asgard rather than stain the holy city's grounds with deicide. Hand-to-hand combat within the wall would mean the death of many Gods and the ruin of the worlds. He could foresee that if Odin took this advice, the day would come when the Vanir and Alfar would again honor him as their father and king, and never again pit their will against his.

17. Odin's sons, eager for battle, found this advice difficult to follow, but could not deny its wisdom. And Mimir gave them additional advice that they could accept without being discouraged. This advice was that Loki ought never set foot within Asgard again. Up to this point, Odin had tolerated Loki to uphold his oath to him, made in time's morning. But with such, it is so that one-sided promises given without reservation are always binding; but an oath that invokes a treaty between two or more people is not binding for the one who intends to keep it, if the other or others intentionally break it. In the former case, it was a fetter on the faithful and a license for the faithless to do whatever

he wanted to with the loyal one. The vow that bound Odin to Loki was mutual and, ever since it was made, had been broken almost daily by Farbauti's son [Loki], who had ever aimed to ruin his blodi and his family.

18. Mimir is said to have given the Vanir similar advice, since they too requested his opinion. Along with Odin, Thor, Tyr, Bragi, Vidar, Vali, and Forseti remained in Asgard. Some of the Asynjur remained there as well, but the most prominent were not among them. Frigga believed that her sisterly obligation and her origin among the Vanir demanded that she join them. Therefore, Asgard's queen left her husband and followed her brother Njord. Odin's two brothers, Hoenir and Lodur, took his wife Frigga to themselves. Hoenir is Frigga's father. Freya also followed her brother, Frey, and with her went the host of Einherjar she kept in Folkvang. Both of the Alfar, Od and Ull, chose the Vanir's side, which was to be expected since Od was Freya's husband and Frey's most faithful friend, and since Ull was Od's half-brother and much devoted to him. The whole host of higher and lower Powers that dwelt in Vanaheim and Alfheim took their side and deserted the Aesir. Only Hoenir and Mimir remained true to Odin.

19. Skadi did not follow her husband, Njord, but stayed in Asgard. She and the Vanagod were of different temperaments and had not been able to get along well together. Skadi had dreamt of becoming Baldur's wife, a dream she never fulfilled. Now, she thrived best in the company of Baldur's father, Odin, and more joyfully listened to his words than any other.

20. When the Aesir expressed desire to hear Mimir's thoughts, he, who never forced his counsel on anyone, and remained silent until he was asked, approved of the Vanir's demand for compensation for the death of Gullveig. With this demand they had obeyed a holy law, but he disapproved that they had made no proposal that could signify Odin's well-founded misgivings against providing the weregild. It was of course probable that Gullveig would be reborn again, and again would plot the ruin of the Gods and the world. Would she be allowed to do so under the protection of her family ties to the Vanir, or would they demand compensation for her anew in the event the Aesir executed her for her evil deeds again? Had not the Vanir already given assurance that this was not their intent? And since burning Gullveig seemed to serve nothing, the Vanir could of course propose, that if she ever appeared again, they would join with the Aesir to banish her

from heaven and earth for eternity. The means to carry out such a sentence was not outside the Gods' power. Mimir advised the Vanir to discard the hasty sentence of exile against Odin and take up the proposal for mediation that he had just outlined.

21. The Vanir and Alfar assembled for deliberation. An evil counselor, Loki in disguise, attended, but was not called to speak. It would have been best to have a statement solicited from him, but when this did not happen, he spoke, and although they first heard his voice unwillingly, he laid his words so cleverly and with such great eloquence, that by degrees they made an impression on those who listened.

22. As the Vanir began their Thing, Hoenir, who was the ruler of Vanaheim, pronounced his opinion, approving Mimir's proposal completely and recommending it be adopted. The speech, with which the evil counselor followed, suggested in shrewd and transparently veiled words that while Hoenir was a respected peacemaker, he lacked his own judgment and was merely a tool in the hands of Mimir and Odin. Mimir was described by this speaker as a secret foe of the Gods, who jealously guarded and withheld the mead of the well of wisdom from others and, as the owner of it, possessed a force that should not belong to him, but ought to be in the

Gods' power. He predicted the loss of the Vanir's case and their own ruin, if they would continue to endure such a traitor to the Gods. The one who concealed treasure for a coming age, when he himself expected to be recognized as the ruler of the worlds, should such a traitor have his seat at the center of creation and through Hoenir dictate the Vanir's decision?

23. The Thing ended with another sentence of exile. Hoenir was stripped of his title as Vanaheim's ruler, and this rule was transferred to his brother, Lodur. Njord was appointed to lead the fylkings of Vanir, Alfar, and Freya's Einherjar in war, and if they were victorious, Njord, Frey, Ull, and Od would be jarls in Asgard.

24. The Vanir then took Mimir and beheaded him, then sent his head to the Aesir. Odin took the head, smeared it with herbs so that it should not rot, and sang incantations over it. Thereby he gave it the power that it spoke to him, and revealed many secrets to him. You must know Hugrunes, if you will be a wiser man than every other. Those interpreted, those risted, those devised by Hropt-Odin, from the sap, which had leaked from Heiddraupnir-Mimir's head, and from Hoddropnir-Mimir's horn. Odin stood on a rock, with Brimir's sword [Mimir's head], he had a helm on his head. Then Mimir's head

spoke its first wise word, and uttered true sayings.

25. When Mimir was killed, Urd became the caretaker of Mimisbrunn, as she did during the first Fimbulwinter. But Urd cannot protect or tend the middle root of the tree, Yggdrasil. Yggdrasil's ash suffers greater hardship than the sons of men know of, and when the well of Mimameid-Yggdrasil lost its custodian, the tree began to whither, and by the end of this age, it will take on the appearance of one exhausted by years.

26. Mimir's twelve sons, the great primeval smiths, had shared the care of Yggdrasil with their father. Each one of them had his month of the year, when he had washed the stem of the great ash with the white glimmering waters of the well, poured from the Gjallarhorn, which was Odin's pledge of friendship to them. From full horns, they drank the pure mead from Baugregin-Mimir's well. Saddened by the course of events and weary of beholding the decline after the death of their father, Mimir's sons now withdrew underground to their golden stronghold, called Sindri, which they had built in the northern part of Mimir's kingdom, Natt's native land beneath the shadow of Nidafjoll. Odin-Svafnir and Hoenir, also called Svafrthorin, placed sleepthorns behind their ears, and thus they lay down to

rest for uncounted centuries. In the stronghold are many halls whose walls and benches shine with weapons and other works of art they fashioned. In the innermost hall sleep Sindri and his brothers, clad in splendid garments. The mortals whom Wyrd sometimes allows to enter into the stronghold of Mimir's sons to see this wonder must take care not to touch the sleepers. Those who do are stricken with incurable consumption.

27. Everything around the brothers seems to slumber as well. In the nearest hall stand twelve horses: Sindri's horse Modnir and those of his brothers. They are saddled, as if each is ready for its rider at a moment's notice. Natt cloaks the stronghold in twilight. There, the dins of the World-Mill, Grotti, and Hvergelmir's roaring flood sound like the monotonous lullaby of a waterfall. Now and then, the steps of the Ostaras rustle through the hall as they come to look in on their kin and blow away dust from their garments and weapons. Thus, they shall sleep until Yggdrasil trembles and the world-penetrating blare of Heimdall's Gjallarhorn wakes them for the final battle.

28. Heimdall is reckoned among the Vanir. He did not want to fight his kin or break his allegiance to Odin. Both of the warring groups of Gods agreed that Heimdall should remain outside of their feud and be, as he had until now, the guardian of Bifrost and ruler of the Alf warriors that constitute the garrison of Himinbjorg at Bifrost's northern bridgehead. By necessity, the understanding prescribed that the Etins not take Asgard by force, since this was equally important to the Vanir as to the Aesir. Now that the Gods had divided into opposing camps, it was likelier than ever that the Etins would contemplate such a plan and believe in its success.

29. But, by this arrangement, Asgard itself lost the guardian that requires less sleep than a bird, whose gaze penetrates the depths of night, and whose ears are not eluded by the faintest sound in the far distance. Yet the Aesir themselves believed that this did not reduce their security. The high wall of Asgard, Gastropnir, is insurmountable; only Sleipnir can jump it. Around the wall rushes the broad river that surges down from Eikthyrnir with masses of Vafur-laden water. When the Vafurmist ignites, the river resembles a whirling firestorm shooting bolts of lightning high into the air. This river swirls down with such headlong violence that animals normally lose their strength to keep afloat and are drowned. In all the worlds, there is no horse, other than Sleipnir, that can overcome the river's roaring tide without fatigue, or leap through the Va-

furfires. Asgard's gate, Valgrind, or Thrymgjoll, is a wondrous work of art; it is as if it guards itself and imprisons any intruder who lays hands on it. Its qualities were well known to the Vanir, who had lived in Asgard. However, if its lock were sprung from the inside, it could be opened without harm. The Aesir considered themselves safe within these walls.

30. Odin went out with a great army against the Vanir; but they were well prepared, and defended their land, so that victory was changeable, and they attacked each other. No small tumult arose from Gaut-Odin's heroes when the host's protection went to defend lands against Njord's. All the Einherjar fought with each other; Thor had with Ygg's warriors defended Asgard with might. From Bifrost's southern bridgehead, Njord rode with a great host of warriors from Vanaheim and Alfheim, as well as Freya's Einherjar, up to the extensive territory surrounding Asgard. Odin and his sons watched from Hlidskjalf and the wall as a glittering girdle of weapons formed around their stronghold, yet still a considerable distance from it. There it remained, coming no closer for a long time. But at night, Njord's fylkings of spies, led by Frey, Od, or Ull, crept as closely as the glare of the Vafurfires allowed. They noticed that every night one

of the Aesir rode for a ways in front of and along their outposts, and they observed afterwards that some shining objects moved on the earthwork that joined Valgrind with the drawbridge's exterior brigehead. After many nights' spying, the Vanir came to the conclusion that it was the Aesir's horses, some of which shine, that were being released at nighttime to graze on the shining grass-grown slope of the earthwork once Sleipnir's rider had returned from his excursion. Sleipnir was also let loose to graze with his companions under the watchful eye of the Asagod.

31. This conclusion was correct. So they planned an ambush, and one night they came upon the watchman so suddenly that he could not reach the grazing Sleipnir before one of the Vanir had swung himself up on his back. The Asagod, who heard the Vanir's spears and arrows swishing past him, covered himself with his shield and retreated back across the bridge. When he passed over it, Valgrind opened itself slightly, and at the same time, the bridge drew up and shut again behind the surprised watchman. In this way, Sleipnir came into the Vanir's power and now they possessed the horse that could leap over the Vafurfires and over Asgard's wall. The Vanir did not capture the horses of

the other Aesir, so they rode back to camp in all haste.

32. This event was designed to undermine the Aesir's spirits. However, the loss seemed greater to the Aesir than did the Vanir's prize. Since what could one, or even a few of the Vanir do in the event that they did get inside Asgard's walls on Sleipnir's back? Would they be able to hold out against the Asafather and his brave sons? Certainly not.

33. One dark and stormy night, when the Aesir had gotten up from their drinking table and were making their usual rounds between the castles and Gastropnir, to their surprise, they discovered Sleipnir walking about the courtyard. From this, they drew the conclusion that he had broken loose, sprung out of the Vanir's camp and back over Asgard's wall in order to return to his stall and his companions. Discussing this, the Aesir returned to the drinking table. Njord heard their words from where he stood, cloaked by the dark of night, in the rafters over Valhall's door, beneath the carvings of the wolf and the eagle that decorate its gable. On Sleipnir, he had leapt through the Vafurfires and over the wall. The din of the steed's eight hooves as they hit the ground blended in with the roar of the storm and the surge of the river and thus had gone unnoticed by Valhall's warriors. When they had taken

their seats at the drinking table once more, Njord went to Valgrind. He had commanded his fylkings to advance to the earthwork with the greatest possible silence. With their dark-colored helmets and coats of mail, they looked like a ghost army; not a single weapon jingled during their silent advance. Njord carried his battle-axe, one of the primeval smiths' masterworks, which became the damager of Gaut-Odin's mighty gate. With it, Njord cleaved Herjan-Odin's great gate, Valgrind; broken was the bulwark of the Asaburgh, through combat-foresight the Vanir were able to tread its fields. The gate opened up to the gable and the drawbridge fell over the river, providing a terrible, but safe passage through the Vafurfires. The fylkings of the Vanir and Alfar, with their rulers in the lead, stormed in, trampling the fields that Asgard's wall was meant to protect. They lined the wall, but did not advance towards Valhall. Njord and Frey, Od and Ull and other opponents of Odin waited on horseback for the appearance of the Aesir.

34. Some riders, wrapped in cloaks—Aesir and Asynjur—approached them. Odin rode forth on Sleipnir, and beside him Thor with his hammer. Because of Mimir's advice, Odin relinquished Asgard to the Vanir, who with respect allowed them to pass and

watched the Aesir ride away. Because of all that had occurred, the Vanir ensured that Odin was ousted from his pre-eminence, stripped of his personal titles and worship, and outlawed, believing it better for a scandalous president to be thrown from power than desecrate the character of public religion; nor did they wish to become involved in another's wickedness and suffer innocently for his guilt. Now that the inappropriate behavior of a high deity had become common knowledge, they were aware that those who worship and adore them were exchanging reverence for contempt and growing ashamed of their piety. They saw doom ahead, fear was in their hearts, and you would have imagined that the nid of a single member were recoiling on their heads.

35. So that he would not force them to dispense with public devotion, they banished him and in his stead invested Ull with the trappings of royalty and Godhead. Although they had elected him their leader as a substitute, they bestowed on him full majestic honors, so that he would be regarded as no mere deputy in office, but a lawful inheritor of authority. As he must lack no particle of dignity, they called him Odin too, intending to dispel the stigma to a parvenu by the prestige of his name. Ull established a new religious institution. He asserted that the Gods'

wrath and the profanation of their divine authority could not be expiated by confused and jumbled blots; so he arranged that they should not be prayed to as a group, but separate blots be made to each deity.

36. The Aesir proceeded eastward. Besides their weapons, they carried no treasures other than Draupnir and a golden image, a head with noble features. It was Mimir's head, preserved by Odin's rune-songs, a marvelous feat of workmanship which made it respond to human touch, and which had made it gold. The image spoke when it was questioned, and then Odin heard Mimir's voice and knew Mimir's thoughts. The voice now said that the Aesir ought to proceed eastward to Mannheim, to a district known better by Mimir than to others. Odin dwelt in Mannheim with Skadi, and afterwards married her. Skadi had many sons by him, of whom one was called Saeming. To Asafather-Odin queen Skadi bore Saeming, who dyed his shield in blood. The queen of rock and snow, who loves to dwell in the Underworld, the daughter of the Ironwood, she sprung from the rocks that rib the sea. To Odin she bore many sons, the heroes who won many battles. To Saeming, Jarl Hakon inn Mikla reckoned back his pedigree. After that, Odin proceeded north to where he was faced by the sea, the one which they thought

encircled all lands, and set his son Saeming over the realm which is now called Norway. The kings of Norway trace their ancestry back to him, as do jarls and other rulers.

37. Once Loki had become estranged from Odin, and while he had Mimir's head, Odin did not make any more mistakes, and his counsel is always wise and his deeds always praiseworthy. He had to take two steps before he attained the throne on which he was revered by our folk. He made the first step when he drank from Mimir's well, and made the second when he faced adversity and brought his ond to fruition. Adversity had brought the best gifts: Mimir's words and thoughts.

LXX. <u>Hadding</u>

1. Kon had left behind many sons, the foremost of which were Gudorm, son of Groa and thus half-brother of Od, and Hadding, son of the Swanmaid Alveig, whom Kon had married later on. Hadding was but a small boy when Kon was wounded by Gambantein in Od's hand. He acquired his name because he had an exceptionally rich and handsome head of hair, which he had decided not to cut until he had regained his share of his father's realm. For when Kon had been killed, Od was enriched with the kingdoms of Denmark and Svithjod. Hadding never had a beard, and although he grew up with great strength and was a hero, he resembled a maiden in his younger years. He, with a most auspicious natural growth, achieved the full perfection of manhood even in his first years of youth. He avoided the pursuit of pleasure and zealously exercised himself with weapons, remembering that, as the son of a warrior father, it was his duty to spend his whole life in feats of military excellence.

2. According to tradition, while Od held Denmark, Kon's sons, Gudorm and Hadding, whose mothers were Groa and Signi-Alveig respectively, were shipped off by their guardian, Thor, to Svithjod, to be brought up and protected there by the Etins Vagnhofdi and Hafli.

3. The reason why Thor removed both of Kon's sons was that he feared they would be harmed by Od, who had acquired all of their father's kingdom after his defeat and death, and ruled by means of his jarls. Od could expect that one of the sons, if he reached maturity, would demand blood-revenge on his father's killer. Besides, after his close acquaintance with Od, Thor observed that beneath the surface of his happy, quick, and pleasant personality lay hidden some of his uncle Volund's temperament. Od would not tolerate mention of Kon and it was clear enough that he had transferred the hate he

harbored for Kon to Hadding. In general, the temperament of the Alfar is such that they are friendly and benevolent towards those that do not provoke them, but vengeful and difficult to appease towards all others.

4. At the repeated instigation of his wife, Freya, Od recalled his brother Gudorm from exile. He offered Gudorm and Hadding peace and friendship and promised them regal power among the Teutonic clans. They were, of course, all three united by the bond of brothers: Od was Gudorm's half-brother, Gudorm was Hadding's. Gudorm accepted the offer and, having been promised tribute, Od set him in authority over the Danes. He was given the realm known as Valland, in western Germania. But Hadding preferred revenge for his father to a favor from his enemy.

5. Meanwhile, Loki, who wanted to remain in the good graces of the Vanir and continue the same evil among them as he had perpetrated among the Aesir, decided to find Hadding and betray him to Od. In the meantime, he never grew weary of reminding Od of how much evil Ivaldi's clan had suffered at the hands of the Aesir and Kon, and how Hadding, if allowed to remain alive, would certainly strive to be his bane. Loki's intention was that Od, if he found the boy in his power, would kill him and thereby eternally stain his honor. Thus, Hadding was no longer safe in Vagnhofdi's mountain-hall, but was vulnerable to Loki's snares, since Loki had now discovered where he was hidden. As carefully as Vagnhofdi and his daughter Hardgrepa watched over him, their eyes could not always follow the boy, who longed to escape the mountain court to play in the adjacent meadows and peered at the forest's edge into what was for him a strange new world. Once, as he sat looking out over the wall of the mountain-hall under the watchful eye of Hardgrepa, a wolf with friendly eyes came and asked him if he would not follow and see all the secrets of the forest. Then a horse came and asked if he would not ride around the world and see everything remarkable there. This would have made the boy pine and become dissatisfied with his captivity, and it was his intent to run away when he could.

6. One evening a rider on an eight-footed horse came to Vagnhofdi's court. He was an old, long-bearded man with only one eye. He spoke kindly with Vagnhofdi and Hardgrepa and thanked them for the care they had given the boy. Vagnhofdi set Hadding in the saddle in front of the rider. The boy was delighted to go, but Hardgrepa cried. The rider swung his mantle over and around Hadding and rode away. Hadding

hid, trembling beneath his cloak, but in intense amazement kept casting keen glances through the slits and saw that the sea lay stretched out under the horse's hooves. Being forbidden to gaze, he turned his wondering eyes away from the terrible view of his journey.

7. Shortly before dusk, Sleipnir again set foot on land. Hadding was then in Mannheim, in the land where Mimir had allotted the exiled Aesir refuge and secure abodes. Here he could play in the fields as much as he wanted, and here Tyr trained him in sports, and Bragi in runes and the skaldcraft. Sometimes his forefather, Heimdall, came to see him too, and witnessed his progress in wisdom and strength. When Hadding was old enough to carry weapons, Odin sang protective Galdur over him. After he had refreshed him with the aid of a soothing potion, he told him that his body would become invigorated and strong. He also gave him a drink, delightful to taste, called Leifnir's Fire, which provided Hadding with the same ability that Od had received from Groa's Galdur-songs, the power to loosen bonds and bands with his breath. Odin then demonstrated his prophetic advice by singing:

8. "As you go hence,
    your enemy,

thinking you are fleeing,
will pounce,
to hold you in chains
or expose you to be
mangled and devoured
by wild brutes' fangs.

9. "But you must fill the ears
    of your warders
    with varied tales,
    till, finished with feasting,
    they are captured
    by deep slumber;
    then strike off the shackles
    which bind you, the harsh fetters.

10. "Returning,
    after a brief
    while has elapsed,
    you must rise
    with all your strength
    against a raging beast,
    which loves to toss
    its captives' bodies.

11. "Test your brawn
    against its grim fore-quarters,
    and probe its heart-strings
    with your naked sword.
    Straightway bring your throat
    to its steaming blood
    and devour the feast
    of its body with ravenous jaws.

12. "Then new force
    will enter your frame,
    an unlooked-for
    vigor will come
    to your muscles,
    accumulation of
    solid strength soak
    deep through every sinew.

13. "I shall pave
    the way to your wish,
    weakening the attendants

with sleep,
to snore away
through the lingering dark."

14. While Hadding was staying in Mannheim, a remarkable portent occurred. As he was dining, a woman beside a brazier, bearing stalks of hemlock, was seen to raise her head from the ground and, extending the lap of her garment, seemed to be asking in what part of the world such fresh plants might have sprung up during the winter season. Hadding was eager to find out the answer, and after she had muffled him in her cloak, she vanished away with him beneath the earth. It was by the design of the Underworld Gods that she took a living man to these parts which he must visit when he died. And because he was the first human to make such a journey, Jormungrund is also called Haddingland. First they penetrated a smoky veil of darkness, then walked along a path worn by long ages of travelers, and glimpsed persons in rich robes and nobles dressed in purple; passing these by, they eventually came upon a sunny region, which produced the vegetation the woman had brought away. Having advanced further, they stumbled on a river of blue-black water, swirling in headlong descent and spinning in its swift eddies weapons of various kinds. They crossed it by a bridge and saw two

strongly matched armies encountering one another. Hadding asked the woman their identity:

15. "They are men who met their death by the sword," she said, "and present an everlasting display of their destruction; in the exhibition before you they are trying to equal the activity of their past lives." These were Odin's Einherjar, now in the Underworld because of the exile of the Aesir from Asgard. Moving on, they found barring their way a wall, difficult to approach and surmount. The woman tried to leap over it, but to no avail, for even her slender, wrinkled body was no advantage. She thereupon wrung the head off a cock which she happened to be carrying and threw it over the enclosing barrier; immediately the bird, resurrected, gave proof by a loud crow that it had truly recovered its breathing.

16. Then came the time for Hadding to tread the path life laid out before him. So, he set out on his horse, Skaevad, towards his Wyrd. The goal that he had to strive for was to avenge his father's death and reclaim his portion of power over the Teutonic clans.

17. Among these clans, Kon's name lived on in honored memory, and many wondered what Wyrd had befallen his youngest son, the little Hadding. One rumor had it that he was still alive and one day would appear

among them. Many were displeased by the severity with which Od had treated the friends and foremost comrades of Kon after defeating him. He had exiled them and they went away to the east, to the unknown lands beyond the borders of the Teutonic folk; no one knew exactly where they dwelt or whether they were alive or dead. Among them were Hamal, Kon's foster-brother, and Hamal's sons and relations, who were known by the clan name Amalians. Among them were also some from the Ylfing and Hilding clans, Hildibrand among them, who became Hadding's mentor and friend.

18. When Hadding was equipped to ride away, Odin told him that he should ride westwards through a forest to a place called Maeringaburg where friends expected him. The journey was dangerous and Odin asked if Hadding wanted a companion. He answered that he did not, and he set off alone on his way.

19. The way, as Odin had said, was dangerous. One morning, after an exhausting day's travel, when Hadding woke, he found himself in a mountain cave, bound hand and foot next to a monster, with Loki standing before him. Loki attempted to extort an oath from Hadding to follow him without resistance; should he refuse, he would be thrown to the monster as food. Hadding re-

quested an hour to think about it and solitude to gather his thoughts. Loki left. Then Hadding blew on his bonds and they burst and fell away. He grabbed his sword, gave the monster its deathblow, and, as Odin had advised him to do in such an event, ate its heart. Thereby he became wise and able to understand the speech of animals. When he emerged from the cave, he did not see Loki, only a fylking of warriors fast asleep on the ground. They were horrid and pale as corpses. He later learned that they are called Banings and are brothers to the plague-bringing Leikin, and the sons of Loki and Gullveig. Odin's Galdur-songs accompanied Hadding the entire way to Maeringaburg, and it was these songs that had put the Banings to sleep. Hadding, having found his horse, Skaevad, continued unharmed to Maeringaburg.

20. Hadding was received in Maeringaburg with joy. It was here that Kon's exiled friends and comrades, called the Maerings, had gathered. Here Hadding sat upon the high-seat between Hamal and Hildibrand, and further down the drinking table sat well-tried warriors: Amalians, Hildings, and Ylfings.

21. Some among them went out to the clans that populated eastern Germania to inform them that Hadding lived and had come to

raise a war banner against Od. Thus, they should prepare themselves and their military forces, if they would follow Kon and Alveig's son.

22. Preparations for the campaign demanded time. While they proceeded, a young warrior came riding to Maeringaburg. He said his name was Vidga, son of Volund and Bodvild, Mimir's daughter. He rode on one of the most beautiful horses ever seen by men. His helmet, with its golden-serpent decor, his shimmering coat of mail, his shining sword, his shield whereon tongs and hammer were painted as emblems of his pedigree—all his equipment was the finest and most beautiful work produced by the skill of Volund and the Underworld smiths, treasures from Mimir's treasure-trove. However, at once, he warned that he did not come as a friend. As the descendant of Ivaldi, as the son of Volund, and as a cousin to Od, it was his duty to fight Kon's descendants. Therefore, he challenged Hadding to a life or death duel. Nevertheless, he was invited into the mead hall and entertained there. The heroes saw that he had a pure and true gaze and found more charm in him than in his arrival there, since they feared for Hadding's life. The duel was subsequently held and Hadding fell under Vidga's superior weapon. But, as Vidga raised the sword for the

deathblow, Hamal and Hildibrand stood before him and spoke persuasive words. Vidga then sheathed his sword and extended his hand to Hadding. Thereafter, he remained in Maeringaburg for some time, taking his place at the table beside Hadding, and they became good friends. Once, Hildibrand said to Vidga that he wished this friendship would never end. Vidga responded that Wyrd had laid their lots on opposite sides of a balance. The day would probably come when they would fight on opposing sides; but he made a promise that, even if he fought Hadding's armies, he nevertheless would not raise his sword against Hadding himself. Hildibrand thanked him for this promise, but said nothing of it to Hadding.

23. Word came to Maeringaburg that the east Teutonic clans were ready for battle and that they only awaited Hadding's arrival to depart. When Vidga heard this, he said farewell. He intended to join the clans that supported Od's cause.

24. When Hadding arrived, huge hosts of warriors gathered in east Germania under his standard. Od certainly knew what was transpiring there, but did not want to intervene before Hadding himself had raised the war banner, for then he, Od, would have no blame in starting the feud. He was pleased at

the thought of killing Kon's son on the battlefield, as he had killed Kon.

25. Od descended from Asgard, revealing himself in the Teutonic motherland on the Scandinavian Peninsula and calling its clans, along with Danes and Saxons, to arms. He sent word to his half-brother and tributary king, Gudorm, to gather his military forces and unite them with his own. Many wonderful and large ships were built in which Swedish and Danish fylkings made their way over the sea. Od was first seen among the east Danes, then he betook himself eastward over the sea.

26. The western and eastern Teutonic clans of the Nordic lands were thus at war with one another. Valkyries, shining disir in helmets and mail, were seen riding through the sky. On they came, some from Vanaheim and Asgard, some from Mannheim in the east. Through the skalds that followed his and Gudorm's armies, Od proclaimed that, according to the resolve of divine council, everyone who fell for his cause in the impending battle would be accompanied by Valkyries to Freya's hall, Sessrumnir, to live in eternal bliss. On the other side, through his skalds, Hadding had it proclaimed to the east Teutonic warriors that everyone who fell for his cause would come to Odin and enjoy unending delight in Odin's hall in the Underworld.

27. Around this time, a stranger said to be a prince from a distant land had arrived at Gudorm's court and was received with honor. He was so eloquent, experienced, and wise in counsel that Gudorm placed the greatest trust in him and rarely did anything without consulting him. He called himself Bikki, and when he was not traveling on Gudorm's or his own errands, which frequently happened, he was near Gudorm.

28. Now and then, a man, who seemed much like Bikki when one looked him in the eye, visited Maeringaburg. Like him, he was eloquent, wise in counsel, but underhanded. He said that his name was Blind. Those who got to know him better called him Blind Balewise.

29. Bikki and Blind were, in fact, the same being. In the world of the Gods, he was known as Loki. He was shrewd and patient, and long remembered past insults, was vengeful and very sly. He knew how to use beautiful, sweet-sounding stock phrases. He was malicious and unfaithful, handsome but cowardly. He came to Valland to conduct battles, to provoke the princes, Gudorm and Hadding, against one another, but never reconcile them.

30. Gudorm conferred with him about the impending campaign and Bikki seemed to possess such great insight into warfare that Gudorm gave him a wing of his army to command and made him first among his military leaders.

31. Gudorm and Od's armies united. Now, Hadding's forces marched to face them. Among the clans that followed Od and Gudorm were the Gjukungs, the sons of Volund and Egil's brother Slagfin and thus cousins of Od and Vidga Volundsson. There were Gunnar and Hogni, sons of Gjuki-Slagfin, and Gudrun as well, who was their sister; but Gudorm was not of the Gjukung race, although he was brother of them both. And all were kinsmen of Od Egilsson.

32. From Greater Svithjod came Gudorm's foster-father, Hafli, and the Etin-maids Fenja and Menja, to Gudorm's war host. They would aid the one prince, and overthrow the other, providing Gudorm with help. From Greater Svithjod came Hadding's foster-father, Vagnhofdi, with his daughter, Hardgrepa, clad in warrior's garb, to join his host. Midgard had never before, and has seldom since, seen such great armies as these that were now moblilized against one another. They extended over hill and dale. When they stood in ordered fylkings on horse and foot, their masses of spears resembled an immense field of grain, ripe for harvest, and when the battle came, they broke against one another like breaker against breaker along the seashore.

33. Many battles took place, and it was a long time before a decisive one occurred. The same night the armies clashed, their divine patrons could be seen amid the glittering stars. The Gods favored the prayers of the opponents dividing their exertions, for one side strove for the western Teutons, the other championed those of the east. Over the north and west Teutonic fylkings rode Ull, Njord, Frey, and the Powers of Vanaheim; over Hadding's host could be seen Odin riding with Tyr, Vidar, Vali, and Bragi, as well as Thor among the thunderclouds in his chariot.

34. Od's side then changed their weapons for magic arts and with spells dissolved the sky into rain, destroying the pleasant aspect of the air with miserable showers. Odin, on Hadding's side, met and dispelled the mass of the storm that had arisen with a cloud of his own, and by this obstruction curbed its drenching downpour.

35. So came the decisive battle. Hadding's fylkings were led by Hamal, his foster-brother and field-commader, and on their side it was Hildibrand and the Amalian heroes, with Hildings and Ylfings, as well as

Vagnhofdi and Hardgrepa, who inflicted the greatest casualties. On the other side were Od, Vidga Volundsson, the Gjukungs Gunnar and Hogni, riding on their horses Goti and Holkvir, as well as Hafli, Fenja, and Menja. These battle-maidens from Jotunheim waded through waves of gray-shirted fylkings among broken shields and cleft coats of mail. Thus they went on, so that they were known in conflicts; there they carved, with sharp spears, blood from wounds, and reddened swords. Hardgrepa fought beside Hadding. One host was the other's equal in bravery and disdain for death. All the while, Bikki kept behind the frontline and avoided the tumult of battle. He never drew his sword, no sword, even though his helmet was beaten, and would have been the first to take flight if he had seen his lead falter. Nevertheless, he contributed to the outcome of the battle, since he arranged Gudorm's fylkings with such great skill that his wing broke Hadding's fylkings into disarray by attacking from the side and rear.

36. The great battle ended with the east Teutonic forces broken and fragmented. In scattered groups and pursued by the victors, they retreated, leaving heaps of dead covering the battlefield, their defeat was so thorough that at the end of the battle Hadding was nothing more than a defenseless refugee. This conflict was called the Rabenschlacht by our ancestors.

37. Followed by Hardgrepa, Hadding escaped into the forest, wandering about in the wild for some time. Hardgrepa, the child of Vagnhofdi, tried to weaken his stout spirit by her allurements to love, with repeated assertions that he must pay her the first reward of his bed by marrying her, since she had nursed him in his infancy with particular devotion and had given him his first rattle. She was not satisfied with straightforward persuasion, but also began to sing:

38. "Why does your life
flow by unsettled?
Why wear away
your years a bachelor,
chasing the battle,
thirsting for throats?
Beauty does not
draw your desires.

39. "You are seized
by an uncontrolled frenzy,
but never such as
slides into tenderness.

40. "Dripping with slaughter,
reeking with blood,
you prefer the battlefield
to the bedroom;
no amorous incitements
will refresh that mind
where ferocity never
gives way to leisure.
No time for play
in all your savagery.

41. "While it is irked
by the cult of love's Goddess [Freya],
your hand is not
free from impiety.
Let this hateful stiffness yield,
let a proper warmth inspire you,
tie with me the bond of passion.

42. "For I gave you
the milk of my breasts,
tended you as
a baby boy,
performing all
a mother's duties,
rendering every
necessary service."

43. When he pointed out that the size of her body was unwieldy for human embraces, and the way she was built undoubtedly suggested that she came of Etin stock, she replied:

44. "Don't let the sight of my strange largeness affect you. I can make the substance of my body small or great, now thin, now fat. Sometimes I shrivel at will, sometimes expand. At one moment my stature reaches the skies, at another I can gather myself into the narrower proportions of men." While he was still faltering and hesitating to believe her words, she added this song:

45. "Young man, do not fear
the commerce of my bed;
I change corporeal shape
in twofold manner,
a double law I enjoin upon my sinews,
molding myself in alternating fashion,

shifting my shape at will;
my neck touches the stars and
soars high near to the Thunderer [Thor],
again rushes down and
bends down to human capacities,
pulled away to earth
from the heights of heaven.

46. "Lightly I alter my body by variation,
fluctuating in aspect;
now a tight cramping
bunches my limbs,
now a freedom of height
unfolds them and lets them
touch the topmost clouds;
now squeezed to puny size,
now my pliant knees are stretched,
while my pliant features change like wax.

47. "The Old Man of the Sea [Aegir]
can do as much.
Of uncertain nature,
my two-formed shape
draws in its vast expanse,
only to thrust out,
its unlocked parts,
then roll them in a ball.

48. "Distend, contract, swell out,
shrink, grow rapidly;
immediate transformation
gives me twin conditions,
separate lives;
I become huge
to fight the fierce,
but small to lie with men."

49. With these declarations, she won over Hadding to sleep with her and burned so strongly with love for the young man that, when she discovered that he yearned to return home, she lost no time in accompanying him, dressed like a man, counting it a pleas-

ure to be a party to his toils and perils. They set off together on the journey and, wishing to put up for the night, came, as it happened, to a house where they were celebrating in melancholy manner the Helfare of the master, who had just died. Desiring to probe the will of the Gods by magic, she inscribed runes on wood and made Hadding insert them under the corpse's tongue, which then, in a voice terrible to the ear, uttered these lines:

50. "Let the one
who summoned me,
a spirit from
the Underworld,
dragged me from
the infernal depths,
be cursed and
perish miserably.

51. "Whoever called me
from the lower regions,
one discharged
from life by urlag,
whoever forced me
again to the upper air,
may she die and be sent
to suffer within the dark
mists of Niflhel,
among the gloomy shades.

52. "Hear: beyond intention,
beyond prescription,
I am forced to disclose
bitter information.
As your footsteps bear you
from this dwelling
you will enter the confines
of a narrow wood,
where from all sides

Thurses will plague you.

53. "She who has brought
a dead man from the darkness,
made him look once more
upon this light,
marvelously fastening ties
between soul and body,
luring, pestering a
departed ghost,
shall bitterly weap
for her rash endeavors.

54. "Let the one
who summoned me,
a spirit from
the Underworld,
dragged me from
the infernal depths,
be cursed and
perish miserably.

55. "For a black, pestilent
whirlwind, monster-created,
will thrust its pressure
hard upon your vitals,
and a hand will sweep you by force,
snatching your body,
tearing and cutting
your limbs by cruel talon.

56. "Only you, Hadding,
will survive with your life;
the lower kingdom will not
snatch your ghost away,
nor your heavy spirit
travel to the nether waters.

57. "But the woman,
weighted down by her own offence,
will appease my ashes,
soon become ashes herself,
for causing the backward
return of my wretched shade.

58. "Let the one

who summoned me,
a spirit from
the Underworld,
dragged me from
the infernal depths,
be cursed and
perish miserably."

59. Therefore, when they had built a shelter of brushwood and were spending the night in the aforementioned forest, they saw a hand of enormous size creeping right inside their small hut. Hadding was distraught and cried for his nurse's help. Hardgrepa, unfolding her limbs and swelling to Etin dimensions, gripped the hand fast and held it out for her foster-son to lop off. More pus than blood dripped from its hideous wounds. But later she paid for this deed, for she was slashed by companions of her own race, and neither her special nature, nor her bodily size helped her to escape the savage nails of her assailants, which tore her to pieces.

60. Odin took pity on the lonely Hadding, robbed of his nurse, and sent Heimdall to assist him. Heimdall led Hadding to a place where Hamal and Hildibrand found him again. They conveyed him back to Maeringaburg, where he joined the rest of his companions, who had come away from the battlefield alive.

61. Peace reigned for many years, during which Od's tributary jarls governed Germania. Od himself returned to Asgard, where he lived happily with Freya, and raised his daughters, Hnoss and Gersemi, and their son, Asmund, whom Od appointed king of the north. For thirty years, Hadding remained in Maeringaburg; that was known to many. Gunnar played the harp and sang in these vast halls. After the Rabenschlacht, east Germania had been so short of soldiers that a new generation fit for military service had to grow up and be presented with spear and shield at the Thing before Hadding's banner could fly again.

LXXI. Gudorm

1. These many years, Bikki remained by king Gudorm's side and was his counselor in everything. Of Bikki's—or, to call him by his proper name: Loki's—counsels, it can be said in short that they were designed to thwart every attempt at reconciliation and by means of slander and lies increase the reasons for hostility between the descendants of Kon and those of Ivaldi's sons, so that they would mutually destroy one another. He wanted to prepare the ruin of the Teutonic people, as much as he did their Gods.

2. Gudorm had become a widower, but he had a promising son named Randver, who had just attained his youth. Now the king called his son to talk with him, and said, "You shall travel on an errand of mine to king Jonak, with my counselor Bikki, for

with king Jonak is nourished Svanhild, the daughter of Gudrun; and I know that she is the fairest maiden dwelling under the sun of this world. I would have her above all others as my wife, and you shall go woo her for me."

3. Randver answered, "It is right and proper, fair lord, that I should go on errands for you."

4. Gudrun was the daughter of Slagfin and sister of Gunnar and Hogni. She had been carried to the paternal land of king Jonak on towering billows, and when he saw her he took her in and married her. They had two sons called Sorli and Hamdir. They all had hair black as a raven in color, like Gunnar and Hogni and other Niflungs, descendants of Ivaldi. Jonak had another son, named Erp. Gudrun's daughter Svanhild was brought up there, and she was indeed the most beautiful of all women.

5. Randver set out on his journey, and traveled until he came to king Jonak's abode, and saw Svanhild, which gave them many thoughts concerning the treasure of her goodliness. The next day, Randver called the king to talk with him, and said, "King Gudorm would like to be your son-in-law, for he has heard of Svanhild, and wishes her to be his wife, nor may it be shown that she

may be given to any mightier man than him."

6. The king said, "This is an alliance of great honor, for he is a man of fame."

7. Gudrun then replied, "It is a wavering trust, to trust in luck that does not change."

8. Yet, because of the king's furthering, and all the matters that went therewith, was the wooing accomplished, and Svanhild went to the ship with a goodly company, and sat in the stern beside the king's son. So Svanhild was handed over to Randver. He was to take her to Gudorm. Gudrun sent her daughter, Svanhild, away from the land.

9. Then, Bikki said it was suitable for Randver to marry Svanhild, since he was young, as they both were, whereas Gudorm was old. He said to Randver, "How good and right it would be if you had such a lovely woman as your wife, rather than the old man there."

10. The young people took well to this suggestion. These words seemed good to the heart of the king's son, and he spoke to Svanhild with sweet words, and she to him likewise.

11. So they came ashore and went to the king, and Bikki said to him, "It is right and proper, lord, that you should know what has happened. Though it is hard to speak of, for the tale is one of betrayal, whereas your son

has obtained the full love of Svanhild, nor is she other than his harlot; but you must not let the deed go unavenged."

12. Now, he had given the king many bad counsels, but of all his advice, this was the worst, and still the king listened to all his evil words. So Gudorm called a Thing together, in which Bikki-Loki brought witnesses to testify against Randver. When the case for the prosecution had been fully presented and Randver was unable to support himself with any defense, Gudorm ordered friends to pass sentence on the condemned, for he thought it less impious to delegate the punishment of his son than dispense judgment himself.

13. Woeful deeds arose in that court, at the Alfar's mournful lament; at early morn, men were afflicted with troubles of various kinds, and sorrows were quickened. The decree of the rest was that Randver should be outlawed, but Bikki-Loki did not shrink from voting for the harsher penalty of death, asserting that anyone guilty of such treason must be duly hanged. So that this might not be deemed to proceed from his father's cruelty, he proposed that Randver should be fastened with a noose and stood on a beam which was supported by attendants. As soon as weariness from the weight made them withdraw their hands, they would be as good

as responsible for the young man's execution and clear the king from the bloodguilt of his son. Unless the charges were properly followed by retribution, he asserted, the youth would set a snare for his father's life. To guarantee that Svanhild met a suitably foul death, she must be trampled beneath the hooves of a herd of animals. Bikki said: "For against no other do you have more wrongs to avenge than Svanhild; let her die this shameful death."

14. "Yes," the king replied, "we will follow your advice."

15. The king followed Bikki's advice and had his son led to the gallows. On the way, Randver got his hawk and plucked off the feathers and asked for it to be sent to his father. When he was brought to the gallows, the bystanders held him up on a plank so that he would not be throttled immediately. The harmless cord, straining very loosely at his throat, exhibited merely the appearance of hanging.

16. Gudorm had Svanhild tied tightly to the ground to be crushed beneath the feet of horses. However, she was so lovely, that when she opened her eyes the very beasts cringed from mangling the limbs of such sheer beauty under their dirty hooves. When Bikki saw this, he had a bag drawn over her head, then the herd was driven in and

gouged deep in her body as they stamped all over it. That was Svanhild's end.

17. When king Gudorm saw Randver's hawk, it struck him that just as the hawk was unable to fly and lacked feathers, so his kingdom would be disabled, he being old and having no son. So, he sent someone at top speed to rescue his son from the halter, and asked that his son be delivered from his Wyrd. But during this time Bikki-Loki wrought his will and Randver was hanged, and this was his death.

18. Two young brothers, Imbrekki and Fridla, were the sons of Harlung and were closely related to Kon's clan, the Skjoldungs. It is said that this Harlung was Kon's son outside of his lawful marriage, which would make his sons Gudorm's nephews. At Bikki's instigation, Gudorm captured his nephews and had no hesitation in taking their lives with the noose. Gathering the nobles under the pretence of a banquet, he ensured that they too were dispatched on the same pattern, so that all of the Harlungs royal line was slain.

19. When Gudrun heard of Svanhild's death, she wished to destroy Bikki's counsel, for Gudorm lived for evil. She incited her sons to vengeance for Svanhild. Then I heard tell of dire quarrels, hard words uttered from great affliction, when the fierce hearted Gudrun instigated her sons to slaughter with deadly words. She said to them:

20. "Why do you sit here?
Why sleep your life away?
Why does it not pain you
to speak joyous words?
Now Gudorm has
had your young sister
trampled by horses,
white and black,
on the public road,
with gray and wayward Gothic steeds.

21. "You are not like Gunnar
and the others,
nor as valiant
of soul as Hogni.
You should seek
to avenge her,
if you had the courage
of my brothers,
or the fierce spirit
of the warrior kings."

22. Then Hamdir spoke to his mother:
"We young ones,
acting all together,
will avenge our sister
on Gudorm.
Bring forth the arms
of the warrior kings:
you have incited us
to a sword-Thing."

23. Laughing, Gudrun turned to the store-houses, drew the kings' crested helms from the coffers, their ample corslets, and bore them to her sons. As they were preparing to set out, she provided them with mail-coats and helmets that were so strong that iron could not penetrate them. She told them

what they were to do when they got to king Gudorm's, that they were to attack him at night while he was asleep. Sorli and Hamdir were to cut off his arms and legs, and Erp his head. The young heroes mounted their horses.

24. Then Hamdir,
    the great of heart, said:
    "So the warrior killed
    in the land of Goths
    will no longer come
    to see his mother,
    so that you may drink
    the grave-ale after us all,
    after Svanhild
    and your sons."

25. Then Sorli said—
    he had a prudent mind—
    "Weep for your daughter,
    and your dear sons,
    your dearest kin,
    drawn to the strife:
    you shall have to weep
    for us both, Gudrun,
    who sit here on our steeds,
    fated to die far away."

26. Weeping, Gudrun, Gjuki-Slagfin's daughter, went sorrowing to the forecourt, while her sons went from the court, ready for the conflict. The young men fared over the humid mountains, on highborn steeds, to avenge murder.

27. Erp then said,
    all at once—
    the noble youth was joking
    on the horse's back—

"It is bad for a timid man
to point out the ways."
They said the bastard
was over-bold.

28. They asked Erp
    what aid he could offer.
    "How will the swarthy Dwarf
    be able to help us?"

29. He of another mother
    answered:
    he said that he would
    be able to help his kin,
    as one foot
    to the other
    or, grown to the body,
    one hand to the other.

30. "What can a foot
    give to a foot,
    or, grown to the body,
    one hand the other?"

31. They drew the iron blade
    from the sheath,
    the sword's edges,
    for Hel's delight.
    They diminished their strength
    by a third,
    they caused their young kinsman
    to sink to the earth.

32. Then they shook their cloaks,
    grasped their weapons;
    the heroes were clad in
    wondrous clothes.

33. The ways lay forward,
    they found a woeful path,
    and their sister's son
    wounded on a gallows,
    wind-cold outlaw-trees,
    on the west end of town.
    The raven's food vibrated,
    it was not good to go there.

34. Shortly afterwards, Sorli stumbled, but turned about on his feet, and stood up, then said: "Now I would have fallen, if I had not steadied myself with both feet. It would have been better now if Erp had remained alive."

35. A little while later, Hamdir stumbled, and thrust down his hand to steady himself, then said: "Erp spoke nothing but truth, for now I should have fallen, had my hand not been there to steady me." Then they said they had done evilly with their brother, Erp.

36. And when they got to king Gudorm's at night, while he was asleep, and cut off his arms and legs, he then awoke and called to his men, telling them to wake up. Then Hamdir said: "The head would be cut off if Erp were alive, our brother whom we slew on the way, and found out our deed too late."

37. And when Gudorm did wake with an unpleasant dream in a torrent of swords among bloodstained warriors, there was up-roar in Randver's chief kinsman's [Gudorm's] hall when Erp's raven-black brothers avenged their injuries.

38. Corpse-dew [blood] flowed over the benches with the attack-Alf's [warrior's, Gudorm's] blood on the floor where severed arms and legs could be recognized. Men's ale-giver [king, Gudorm] fell headfirst into the pool mixed with gore.

39. Gudorm's men now fell on them, and they defended themselves well, and were the bane of many men, and iron would not bite them. Commotion was in the mansion; men lay in blood flowing from the Goths' chests.

40. Then Hamdir,
the great of heart, said:
"Gudorm! You did desire
that we come,
the brothers of one mother,
into your burgh;
now see your feet,
see your hands cast
into the glowing fire,
Gudorm!"

41. The god-like,
mail-clad warrior
then roared
as a bear roars:
"Hail stones on the men,
since spears do not bite,
nor the sword's edge or point,
the sons of Jonak."

42. Then Sorli,
the strong of heart, said:
"You did harm, brother,
when you opened that mouth.
Bad counsel often comes
from that mouth.

43. "You have courage, Hamdir,
if only you had sense:
that man lacks much,
who lacks wisdom.

44. "The head would now be off,
had Erp only lived,
our brother bold in fight,

whom we slew on the way,
that brave warrior—
the disir instigated me—
that man sacred to us,
whom we resolved to slay.

45. "I do not think that ours
should be the wolves' example,
that we should contend with ourselves,
like the Norns' dogs [wolves],
that are nurtured,
ravenous in the desert.

46. "We have fought well,
we stand on slaughtered Goths,
on those fallen by the sword,
like eagles on a branch.
We have gained great glory,
though we shall die now or tomorrow,
no one lives till eve
against the Norns' decree."

47. Very soon, Hamdir and Sorli came to be struck by everyone at once with Hergaut-Odin's woman-friend's [Jord-Frigga's, earth's] hard shoulder lumps [stones]. The stones flew thick and fast from every side, and that was the end of their days. Sorli fell there, at the mansion's front; but Hamdir sank at the house's back.

LXXII. Hunwar

1. Now there occurred great events in the world of the Gods. The division between the Aesir and the Vanir had given the Etins hope that they could achieve a great victory. All of their clans united to attack and lay waste to Midgard, and they proposed to Odin that if he assisted them against their common enemy, the Vanir and Alfar, they would assist in returning him to his throne in Asgard. But Odin, who was more concerned with mankind's welfare than his own power and kingship, sought out Frey and told him of the Etins' preparations, and he pledged his help, if they required it. It was sorely needed, since the masses of fylkings that had gathered in Jotunheim and were mobilized, in part, towards Bifrost's northern bridgehead, and, in part, across the Elivagar into Greater Svithjod, were truly enormous. But the combined forces of the Aesir, Vanir, and Alfar struck them back with tremendous casualties. The Elivagar was so full of slain Etin corpses, it seemed as though it had been bridged to make it solid and passable. Furthermore, so extensive were the traces of carnage that an area stretching the distance of a three days' horse ride was completely strewn with Etin bodies. This war, which is known as the Hunwar, so broke the Etins' strength and so devastated their numbers that they will never again be a threat to Yggdrasil or Midgard until shortly before Ragnarok, when a new Fimbulwinter shall occur and the Etin-folk regain their ancient strength. Until then, Thor's hammer is sufficient to hold their growth within certain limits.

2. The Vanir gathered at the Thing and appointed a conference to settle their dispute with the Aesir. Both sides had grown weary of the conflict, and on both sides, they set up a meeting for establishing peace, and made a truce. The Vanir acknowledged that Odin had acted nobly when he had come to their aid, although they had driven him from Asgard. They also realized that they were in the greatest need of the Asafather and his powerful sons' assistance in their battle against Jotunheim.

3. For almost ten years, Ull held the leadership of the divine Thing until the Gods finally took pity on Odin's harsh exile. Reckoning that he had completed a severe enough sentence, they restored him from filthy rags to his former splendor. By now the passage of time had rubbed away the brand of his past disgrace.

4. So, the Aesir were allowed to return to their strongholds in Asgard, and Odin again occupied his throne in Valhall, with the full rights of a father and a ruler. The warriors that had fallen on Hadding's behalf on the battlefield, and to which Odin, during his exile, allotted dwellings and sporting fields in the Underworld, were allowed to accompany him to Valhall as Einherjar and enjoy the life of bliss there.

5. The Vanir were acquitted of all liability stemming from the Asafather's deeds they had disapproved of, and as a sign of this freedom from liability, Njord will, at the fall of the world, return to the wise Vanir, without being bound by his obligations as a hostage. The Vanir considered themselves to have received compensation for Gullveig's death, and should she be reborn and show herself again, she may not be burned, but instead banished to the Ironwood.

6. After Ull had been removed from his office by Odin, he returned to Ydalir. It is called Ydalir, where Ull has made himself a dwelling. As before, one saw Thor and Ull, stepfather and stepson, battle side by side against Jotunheim's inhabitants. Thus, the old bonds were reforged, and everyone was delighted by this.

7. After Odin returned home, he took his wife, Frigga, back. Once Odin had recovered his divine regalia, he shone throughout the earth with such lustrous renown that all peoples welcomed him like a light returned to the universe. There was nowhere in the entire globe which did not pay homage to his sacred power. He banished the Seid as his first act and dispersed the groups of its practitioners which had sprung up, like shadows before the oncoming of his sacred brightness.

8. While the Vanir had been rulers in Asgard, the belief had been established among mankind that the Gods demanded greater offerings than was customary in their forefathers' time, and that blots and prayers devoted to several or all of the Gods at one time did not possess the power to appease and placate. Therefore, every one of the Gods ought to have a separate blot dedicated to them. It was also established that longer prayers and blots that are more abundant would be considered as evidence of greater piety, and thus expected a more willing response to prayers. But Odin let it be known that this was incorrect:

9. "It is better not to pray
than offer too much,
a gift ever looks for a return.
It is better not to send
than blot too much;
so Thund-Odin risted
before the origin of men,
this he proclaimed
after he came home.

10. "Ull's and all the Gods'
favor shall have,
whoever shall look to the fire first;
for the dwelling will be open
to the Asasynir,
when the kettles are lifted off."

LXXIII. Asmund

1. It remained important for the Gods to gather in council. Peace now reigned in the world of the Gods, but the peace in Midgard was threatened by a new feud between Kon's sons. There had to be an end to this brotherly strife, which was to flare up again, now that the clans of east Germania had gathered under Hadding's banner. The Gods let Hadding know that they would not disapprove if he abstained from blood-revenge, which in any case was impossible for a mortal to carry out against an inhabitant of Asgard and a member of the Gods' circle. Hadding went into deliberation with his advisors Hamal and Hildibrand. Blind, who often came to Maeringaburg, took part in the deliberation and said it would be more honorable for Hadding to tell the Gods no; but Hamal and Hildibrand advised him to answer to await Od's decision, and he did so. The Gods asked Od to offer Hadding reconciliation and the share of his father's kingdom due to him; but Od replied that he never renewed a refused offer. The Aesir and Vanir then went to their Thingseats and ordered Od to do just that. But neither their decree nor Freya's tears could persuade him. From Asgard, he proceeded down to the Scandinavian Peninsula, where he commanded his son, Asmund, who was king of the Swedes, to gather his folk and relay word to the Danes and to Gudorm's clans.

2. Shortly thereafter, the Teutonic armies were again mobilized against one another.

The Gods sent the defiant Od a most threatening command to comply with the decision of the lawful world-governing Powers. He refused and sailed eastward with a great Swedish fleet, heavily manned. His expedition was condemned by the Gods. Evil had entered Od. His rise in the world had brought little joy to the Danes, only death and destruction. While still at sea, he was lost. The Gods' wrath had driven him to cast himself into the waters. There, in terror, he realized that he had been transformed into a wyrm. Humiliated and hopeless, he dove down into the deep. The waves of his grief beat him down, for the change in his heart had made him bloodthirsty, his life lost happiness. The Gods hid his Wyrd from Freya.

3. The Swedes must have wondered about the disappearance of their great leader and anticipated a bad outcome of their military campaign. Their fleet was led by Asmund's ship, Gnod, which was capable of carrying three thousand men. Soon, Gudorm's fleet was united with theirs. Bikki followed them too. One night, a tall old man, one-eyed and long-bearded, stepped into Asmund's quarters, as Asmund sat in discussion with Bikki. The old man called himself Jalk [Odin]. He said that if Asmund was not bent on brotherly war and the murder of kin, battle could still be avoided. However, Bikki objected

that if Asmund made peace and marched home, he would break the obligation he had assumed from his father, and it would be seen as a sign of cowardice. As Jalk and Bikki looked upon one another, Odin's sharp eye pierced Loki's with a menacing gaze, which was met with an insolent and mocking stare. Jalk-Odin withdrew. Between themselves, Asmund and Bikki agreed that the latter would orchestrate the fylkings's arrangement and movement, since he had presented himself as an expert in such things. Asmund himself would lead the battle.

4. Then, a great storm, conjured by Odin, threatened Asmund's fleet, for the Allfather did not want him to reach his destination. Asmund's ship, Gnod, sank into the sea and took many men and supplies with it. However, many more were able to escape with their leader to the shore. While coasting towards the battlefield with his fleet, Hadding encountered this storm as well. He then noticed an old man standing on a cliff waving his cloak to and fro to indicate that he wished him to put into land. Though his fellow sailors grumbled that this deviation from their route would be disastrous, he met the old man near the cliff, who said:

5. "What men ride there
on Raefil's horses [ships],

the towering billows,
the wild-tossing sea?
The sail-steeds are bedewed
with salty sweat,
the wave horses will not
withstand the storm.

6. Hamal: "Hadding's men sit
  in the sea-trees [ships],
  a strong wind
  bears us to Hel;
  the steep waves dash
  higher than our prows,
  the roller-horses [ships] plunge:
  who is it that asks?

7. Kjalar: "They called me Kjalar [Odin],
  when I gladdened Hugin,
  young hero,
  and fought battles.
  Now you may call me
  the Man of the Mountain,
  Feng or Fjolnir:
  let me fare with you!"

8. They sailed close to land, and the man came on board. Then the storm abated. Hadding found in him the man to supervise the disposition of his fylkings. The old man was very tall and had only one eye, wrapped in a shaggy cloak, he said that he was skilled in the tactics of war. He offered Hamal, Hadding's general, a most profitable lesson in how to dispose his army in the field. Kjalar-Odin told him that when he was about to make war with his land forces, he should divide his entire battle-line into three fylkings. Each of these he should pack in twenties, but extend the middle section by a further twenty men, arranging them to form the point of a cone or pyramid, and should bend back the wings to create a receding curve on each side. When a rally was held, he should construct the files of each fylking by starting with two men at the front and adding one only to each successive row. Thus, he would set three in the second line, four in the third, and so on, building up the following ranks with the same uniform symmetry until the outer edge came level with the wings. Each wing must contain ten ranks. Again, behind these he was to introduce young warriors equipped with javelins. To the rear of these, he should place a company of older men to reinforce their comrades, if their strength waned, with their own brand of seasoned courage. A skillful strategist would see that the slingers were attached at the sides, who could stand behind the lines of their fellows to assail the enemy with shots from a distance. Beyond these, he should indiscriminately admit men of any age or class without regard for status. The final battalion he ought to separate into three prongs, as with the vanguard, and deploy them in similarly proportioned ranks. The rear, though connected to the foregoing columns, might offer defense by reversing itself to face in the opposite direction. If a sea-battle should occur, he must divide off a sec-

tion of his navy, so that while the main fleet began the prepared skirmish, these other ships could skim round and encircle the enemy vessels.

9. Kjalar-Odin also trained their horses along the seashore, and trained them pretty well. Then Hadding said:

10. "Tell me, Kjalar,
since you know the omens
of both Gods and men;
which omens are best,
if one must fight,
at the swing of glaves?"

11. Kjalar: "There are many good omens,
if men only knew them,
at the swing of glaves,
a faithful fellowship,
I believe, is the dark raven's,
with the armed warrior.

12. "The second is if,
when you have gone out,
and are ready to depart,
you see two fame-seeking
men standing
in the forecourt.

13. "The third omen is,
if you hear wolves
howl under the ash-boughs,
it will announce victory
over helmed warriors,
if you see them before you.

14. "No man should
fight against
Mani's
late shining sister [Sol];
they have victory
who can see clearly

at the play of swords,
or to form the wedge-array.

15. "It is most perilous,
if your foot stumbles,
when you go to battle.
Guileful disir stand
on either side of you,
and wish to see you fall.

16. "Let every man be
combed and washed,
and fed in the morning;
for it is uncertain
where he may be at eve.
It is bad to succumb to Wyrd."

17. They landed at Jutland. Odin then asked if all the warriors in Hadding's camp had arrived. Hamal had asked before and learned that Vagnhofdi was absent. He had received Hadding's message late and was a long way hence from the battlefield, but he hastened to follow. But Kjalar-Odin met him on his way, took him up on his horse, and transported him over water and land so that he, when the battle was hottest and Hadding most needed his help, stood within the bulwark of shields. Thus, it is said that Kjalar-Odin drew Kjalki, which is one of Vagnhofdi's names, as is Vagn.

18. The sun rose and the armies marched towards one another. Shield-songs were raised on both sides; but this time, no God sang under the shields of the north and west Teutons, while Valfather-Odin's voice rang

together with the ringing sound under those of the east Teutonic warriors. As Odin says:

19. "If I am to lead those in battle,
    whom I have long held in friendship,
    then I sing under their shields,
    and with success they fare
    safely to the fight,
    safely from the fight,
    safely on every side they go."

20. Hamal set his fylkings in the wedge-array, and it was he who ordered the contingents of slingers at the sides to drop back into the rear and attached them to the lines of archers. After he had distributed his companies into this wedge formation, he took up his stance behind the warriors' backs. The west's forest of spears formed an elongated square; the east's formed the wedge with shield- and spear-clad sides pointed towards the enemy. Because Odin had taught this formation to Hamal, it is called Hamalt Fylkja, but it is also called Svinfylkja because the front of the formation looks like the head of a boar.

21. The signs had portended, as the battle's outcome proved, that all the Gods, Vanir as well as Aesir, now supported Hadding's cause. Nevertheless, the scales of battle long weighed equally, because Asmund and Vidga Volundsson's courage surpassed that of all others. Fenja and Menja went forth

fiercely as well, but were caught between shields and were led bound from the battle.

22. In the meantime, Asmund, Od's son, sought to engage in battle with Hadding. When he realized that his own son, Henry, whom he loved more than his own life, had fallen fighting courageously, his soul yearned for death, and he hated the sunlight; this was the lament that he composed:

23. "What hero dare
    put on my armor?
    A reeling man needs
    no shining helmet,
    a hauberk is useless
    for one prOstarate.

24. "Am I to exult in war
    with a slain son?
    My towering love for him
    compels me to die;
    my flesh should not
    outlast my child.

25. "I want to grip
    steel in each hand.
    Come now,
    fight with flashing sword-points,
    but no shields to
    cover bared chests.

26. "May the fame of
    our savagery flare;
    we must boldly grind
    the enemy's column,
    let no struggle
    wear us down nor
    the onslaught shatter
    in flight and fade."

271

27. He spoke, put both hands to his hilt, slung his shield, regardless of danger, behind his back, and then drove many to their deaths. Hadding had no sooner cried on friendly powers for help than Vagnhofdi came suddenly riding up to champion his side. Gazing at his crooked sword, Asmund broke out in loud song:

28. "Why do you fight
with crooked blade?
A short sword shall
bring your doom;
or death will come
with the hurled javelin.

29. "You believe that spells
will mutilate
a foe who can only be
vanquished by hand-to-hand;
you grapple with words,
not force,
putting your strength
in magic arts.

30. "Why do you pound
your shield against me,
threaten me with
your impetuous lance,
when you are sullied
and speckled all over
with woeful crimes?

31. "Look how a branded
mark of infamy
has flecked your soul,
your thick blubber-lips,
stinking with villainy."

32. As he shouted these insults, Hadding launched his spear by the thong and transfixed him. Death however had its compensations for Asmund. In his last tiny flicker of life, he wounded his killer's foot, laming him and causing an incurable limp, so that men remembered his overthrow by this small moment of revenge. Thus one received a crippled limb, the other ended his days.

33. Even lamed, Hadding fought on, and pressed forth towards Vidga Volundsson, who is said to have slain several hundred men in this battle with his own hands. But, when he saw Hadding advancing, he leapt on his horse and fled, and when Hadding had overtaken him, he allowed himself to be killed rather than lift his weapon against him. This was in order to fulfill the promise that he had given to Hamal and Hildibrand in Maeringaburg.

34. When the news that Asmund had fallen was known, the white shield was raised, and the enemies extended their hands in peace to one another. At his departure following Hadding's victory, Odin predicted that he would not be destroyed through a foeman's violence, but by a self-chosen kind of death. By avenging his father, Hadding advanced to a high rung of fame and exchanged exile for a kingdom, for he had the fortune to rule his land immediately after he returned to it.

35. Asmund's body was carried in solemn state at a royal Helfare in Uppsala. His wife, Gunnhild, did not wish to survive him, but stabbed herself, choosing rather to follow her husband in death than survive him by living. Their friends, in committing her body to interment, added her remains to those of her husband, for they believed her worthy of his grave-mound when she had preferred to set her love for him above life.

36. When his rival had been removed, all was quiet and Hadding discontinued his warfaring for many years. He was a mild, successfully governing sovereign king, who was known to future generations as Thjod-rek. A long lasting peace followed the world war in Midgard.

LXXIV. <u>Singastein</u>

1. When Od was not heard from, and no one seemed to know anything of his Wyrd, Freya had stayed behind weeping, and her tears are red gold. Freya has many names, and the reason for this is that she adopted various names when she was traveling among strange peoples looking for Od. She is called Mardoll, Horn, Gefn, and Syr. She had taken her falcon guise and flew through all of the worlds in search of her beloved. She finally found him near Singastein, a skerry in the sea, also called Vagasker. As loathsome as the wyrm appeared to her, her love and compassion overcame her loathing, and she remained with the unfortunate one, seeking to console him with her tenderness. She had brought along Brisingamen, which became part of the wyrm's hoard. Whether it was the gleam of this wonderful piece of jewelry, or whether the waves themselves felt joy at having her beautiful face and true heart among them—a beautiful shimmer, the likes of which has seldom been seen since, spread from Singastein across the mirror of the sea. Ever since, Freya has borne the epithet, Mardoll. When the wyrm was awake, she tried to be happy and spoke loving words. When it slept, she could give in to her sorrow, unnoticed, and then Freya wept gold for Od. Hnoss bore her mother's eyelash rain [tears] to Asgard, and the Gods resolved to retrieve Od and forgive him.

2. One day, while Hadding, hot from the scorching sun, was submerging his body in the cool sea-water, he swam after a peculiar monster, dispatched it with numerous strokes, and had its carcass conveyed to his camp. As he was triumphing over this feat, he was accosted by a woman, Freya, who addressed him in these words:

3. "Whether you tread the fields or
set your canvas to the ocean,
the Gods will be hostile to you,
and throughout the whole earth
you shall find the elements of nature

thwarting all your designs.

4. "Dashed on land, tossed at sea,
the perpetual companion of your
wandering shall be the whirlwind;
an inflexible stiffness will
never desert your sails,
if you should seek a roof for your
head it will fall struck by a tempest,
and your herd will perish with cold.

5. "Everything shall be tainted and
mourn the Wyrd of your presence.
Shunned like a noxious itch,
no plague will have ever
been more vile than you.
Such punishment
the Powers of heaven dispense.

6. "For you have killed
with sacreligious hands
a sky-dweller wrapped
in another body:
there you stand,
the slayer of a benign deity.

7. "When you take to the waves
you will feel the frenzy
of the winds upon you;
let loose from their keeper's dungeon;
then Vestri and the rushing Nordri
and Sudri shall sweep to crush you,
conspire together and vie to
shoot forth hurricane blasts,
until with more winning prayers
you appease divine serenity and,
having suffered the earned punishment,
offer placation."

8. Recognizing Freya, Hadding understood that he had killed Od and thus had finally taken revenge on his father's killer. This pleased him, so he refused to pay weregild. Then Singastein's bottom sank down under his feet. The air was black and yellow-green. The earth started to shake as if she were dying. Mountains split from each other to spew fire and flame, others sank down in her womb, and where Jord [Earth] first had fields, she raised mountains thereupon. Singastein, also called Aldland, sank below and the wild waves stepped far over hill and dale, so that all were overwhelmed. Many people were buried in the earth, and many who escaped the fire were killed thereafter in the water.

9. Hadding thus endured unvarying disaster, putting all peaceful places in turmoil by his arrival. Escaping the sinking of the skerry, when he set sail a potent thundercloud arose and engulfed his fleet in a gigantic storm; when he sought shelter after the shipwreck, the house suddenly collapsed in ruins. There was no alleviation for his calamities till he had been able to atone for his wickedness by religious offerings and return to heavenly favor; in order to appease the divinities he did indeed make a holy blot to Frey, Freya, and all the Vanir, who are Od's kinsmen and close friends.

10. When Freya had seen Od hauled, slain, onto the shore and had rushed to place herself in Hadding's path, she had forgotten Brisingamen, leaving it on Singastein. It laid there, illuminating the surrounding area. Lo-

ki, who now stayed near Hadding in invisible form, saw the jewel and came at once with a mind to steal it. It would be good to have as a ransom for his life, since the wrath of all the Gods rested on him, and he knew that Odin no longer felt bound to the oath he swore to him in time's morning. But Heimdall's eyes followed Hadding and saw what went on around him. While Freya spoke to Hadding, a seal crawled up on Singastein and approached Brisingamen. It was Loki in seal-guise. But from the other side, another seal crawled upon the rock toward the necklace. A guise cannot alter the eyes, and Loki recognized his old nemesis, Heimdall, in the eyes of the other seal. Heimdall is called the visitor of Vagasker or Singastein; on that occasion he contended with Loki for Brisingamen. Renowned defender [Heimdall] of the Powers' way [Bifrost], kind of counsel, competed with Farbauti's terribly sly son [Loki] at Singastein. The son of eight mothers plus one [Heimdall], mighty of mood, was first to get hold of the fair sea-kidney [Brisingamen]. I announce it in strands of praise. Heimdall then returned Brisingamen to Asgard.

11. Afterwards, Freya returned to Asgard, where she was received with great joy after her long absence, and was conveyed to Valhall to Odin. Foremost among the Einherjar and closest to the Gods sat Od once again, as young and as handsome as the day he came to Asgard with Gambantein. The dispute between him and the Gods was now settled and his error reconciled. Now he and Freya could again live happily together in Folkvang's hall. Od had been adopted among the Gods by resolution of the divine Thing at Glitnir, and as such greets the mighty heroes as they enter Valhall. He is joined by Bragi, and when a great warrior is to enter the hall, Odin says to them:

12. "Od and Bragi,
    go to meet the prince,
    for a king is coming
    who is considered
    to be a hero,
    here to this hall."

13. Od had a surviving grandson named Hunding, who became king of Svithjod, and with whom Hadding had become united in friendship. Hunding had received a false report of Hadding's end and, thinking to honor the dead, gathered together his nobles. Filling an enormous jar to the brim with beer, he ordered it to be placed amid the guests for their pleasure and, to give a sense of occasion, did not hesitate to adopt a servant's role and play the butler. As he was traversing the palace hall in fulfillment of these duties, he missed his footing, toppled into the

jar and, choked by the liquid, gave up his ghost. Perhaps he was paying the Underworld for appeasing it with spurious Helfare rites, or Hadding for falsely assuming his departure. When he learnt of this, Hadding returned his veneration with a similar courtesy, for, being unwilling to survive the dead man, he hung himself before the eyes of the populace, choosing to go to Valhall through a voluntary death.

The Iron Age

LXXV. Gleipnir

1. The Gods had raised Fenrir in Asgard, but only Tyr had the courage to approach him and feed him. But the Gods saw how much the wolf grew every day and knew that all the prophecies foretold that it was destined to harm them. Then the Aesir devised a plan to make an especially strong fetter. They named it Laeding and brought it to the wolf, inviting him to test his strength against it. As it seemed to the wolf that this test would not require much strength, he let them do as they wished. The first time the wolf stretched the muscles in his legs, the fetter broke. Thus he freed himself from Laeding.

2. Next, the Gods made a second fetter. Twice as strong, it was called Dromi. Again they asked the wolf to test the fetter, telling him that he would become renowned for his strength if such a magnificent forging was unable to hold him. The wolf thought to himself that, even though the fetter was very strong, his strength had grown even more since he had broken Laeding. He also recognized that, to become renowned, he had to place himself in danger, and so he let them put the fetter on him. When the Aesir were ready, the wolf started to twist and beat the fetter against the ground. He struggled with all his might and, using his legs, he snapped the fetter with such force that the pieces flew into the distance. Thus he escaped Dromi. Since then, there has been an expression, when a task is extremely difficult, that one frees oneself from Laeding or breaks out of Dromi.

3. After this happened, the Gods began to fear that they would not succeed in binding the wolf. So Allfather-Odin sent Od-Skirnir, Frey's messenger, down to Svartalfheim, and there he had some Dwarves make the fetter called Gleipnir. It was constructed from six elements: the noise of a cat's footsteps, the beard of a woman, the roots of a mountain, the sinews of a bear, the breath of a fish, and the spittle of a bird. Though previously you had no knowledge of these matters, you now can quickly see the proof that you were not deluded. You must have noticed that a woman has no beard, a cat's movement makes no loud noise, and mountains have no roots. Truly, I say, all you have been told is equally reliable, even though you have no way to test some things.

4. The fetter was smooth and soft as a silk ribbon, yet it was reliable and strong. When the fetter was brought to the Aesir, they heartily thanked the messenger for carrying out his errand. Then the Gods traveled out onto a lake called Amsvartnir, and sent for the wolf to accompany them. They went to an island named Lyngvi, where they showed the wolf the silky band, offering to let him try to break it. They told him that despite its thickness, it was somewhat stronger than it appeared. Passing it among themselves, each tested the band's strength in his hands. No one could pull it apart. Nevertheless, they said that the wolf would be able to break it.

5. Then the wolf answered: "It seems to me that a ribbon like this one, which is so narrow a band, offers no renown even if I break it apart. But if it is made with cunning and treachery, even though it looks unimpressive, then I will not permit this band to be put on my legs."

6. The Aesir replied that he would quickly snap such a narrow, silky band, as he had already broken powerful iron fetters. "But if you are unable to break free from this band, then the Gods will have no reason to fear you, and then we will free you."

7. The wolf answered: "If you were to bind me in such a way that I was unable to free myself, then you would betray and abandon me, and it will be a long time before I received any help from you. I am unwilling to allow that band to be put on me. Rather than questioning my courage, why not let one of you place his hand in my mouth as a pledge that there is no treachery in this offer?"

8. The Gods now looked at one another, realizing the seriousness of the problem they faced. No one was willing to hold out his hand until Tyr raised his right hand and laid it in the wolf's mouth. But when the wolf strained against the fetter, the band only hardened, and the more he struggled, the stronger the band became. They all laughed, except Tyr; he lost his hand.

9. When the Aesir saw that the wolf was truly bound, they took the part that hung loose from the fetter. It was called Gelgja, and they threaded the end of it through a huge stone called Gjoll. They fastened the stone deep down in the earth. Then they took an enormous rock called Thviti and drove it even further down into the earth, using it as an anchor post. As the wolf struggled, he opened his mouth. He gaped horribly, trying to bite them, but they slipped a sword into his mouth. The hilt stuck in his lower gums and the blade in the upper gums, wedging his jaw open. As he growled menacingly, saliva drooled from his mouth, forming the

river called Von. There he remains until Ragnarok.

LXXVI. Hymir

1. Of old the Gods
   made feast together,
   and they sought drink
   before they were sated;
   they shook twigs
   and scryed blood:
   when they found a lack
   of kettles at Aegir-Gymir's.

2. The rock-dweller [Etin] sat,
   glad as a child,
   much like the son
   of Mistorblindi-Fornjot.
   Ygg's son [Thor] looked threateningly
   into his eyes:
   "You shall often hold
   a feast for the Gods."

3. The unwelcome-worded As
   caused trouble for the Etin:
   he quickly thought of
   vengeance on the Gods;
   he told Sif's husband
   to bring him a kettle:
   "in which I may brew
   beer for all of you."

4. The renowned Gods
   found that impossible,
   nor could the exalted Powers
   accomplish this,
   till from trueheartedness
   did Tyr give
   much friendly counsel
   to Hlorridi-Thor.

5. "Eastward of the Elivagar
   there dwells
   the all-wise Hymir,
   at heaven's end.
   My father, fierce of mood,

owns a kettle,
a massive cauldron,
a league in depth."

6. Thor: "Do you know whether
   we can get the liquor-boiler?"
   Tyr: "Yes, friend, we can,
   if we are cunning."
   Quickly they fared forth
   from Asgard that day,
   until they came
   to the home of Ull.

7. They gave the horn-strong
   goats care.
   Then they continued
   to the great hall
   which Hymir owned.
   The youth found his grandam,
   whom he greatly loathed;
   she had nine-hundred heads.

8. But another came forth,
   all-golden and fair-browed,
   bearing the beer cup
   to her son:

9. "Kindred of Etins!
   I will put you both,
   daring heroes,
   under the kettles;
   my husband is often
   greedy towards
   his guests,
   and grim of mind."

10. But the monster,
    the fierce-souled Hymir,
    returned home late
    from hunting;
    he entered the hall,
    the icicles rattled,
    as he came in;
    the thicket on his cheeks was frozen.

11. "Hail to you, Hymir!

Be of good cheer:
now your son
has come to your hall,
whom we have expected,
from his long journey;
and with him fares
the foeman of Hrod,
the friend of man,
who is called Veur-Thor.

12. "See where they sit
under the hall's gable,
as if to shun you:
the pillar stands before them."
The pillar flew into pieces
at the Etin's glance;
first the beam was
broken in two.

13. Eight kettles fell,
but only one of them,
a hard-hammered cauldron,
came whole from the column.
The two came forth,
but the old Etin
surveyed his foe
with his eyes.

14. His heart foretold
much sorrow when he saw
the Giantesses' foeman [Thor]
come forth on the floor.
Then three oxen
were taken,
and the Etin bade
their flesh to be boiled.

15. They cut each one shorter
by the head,
and afterwards bore
them to the fire.
Sif's husband [Thor],
before he went to sleep,
alone ate all of
two of Hymir's oxen.

16. Then Hlorridi-Thor's meal
seemed extremely large
to the hoary friend
of Hrungnir [Hymir]:
"Tomorrow night
the three of us
shall have to live
on what we catch."

17. Veur-Thor said that he would row on the sea, if the bold Etin would supply him with bait: "Go to the herd, if you trust in your courage, crusher [Thor] of rock-dwellers [Etins]. I expect that you will easily obtain bait from an ox." Then Thor quickly went to the forest where he could see a herd of oxen belonging to Hymir, and here an all black ox stood before him. He took the biggest ox, called Himinhrjot. The bane of Thurses [Thor] broke from the beast the high fortress of his two horns [his head], and took it with him down to the sea. Sif's beloved [Thor] quickly brought out his fishing gear to the old fellow. He then told Hymir: "To me, your work seems worse by far, steerer of ships, than if you had sat quietly!"

18. Hymir had already launched the boat. Thor got in and sat down towards the stern. He took two oars and started rowing, and Hymir noticed that he was making some progress. Hymir rowed from the forward bow, and the boat moved quickly. Hymir then said that they had come to the waters where he usually trawled for flatfish, but

Thor said he wanted to row out much further, and they started another bout of fast rowing. Hymir then warned that they had come so far out that to go further was dangerous because of the Midgardswyrm. The Lord of Goats [Thor] told the apes' kinsman [Hymir] to steer the steed of the rollers [boat] out further, for Thor wanted to keep on rowing, and so he did. But the Etin declared that he had little desire to row out further, and by then, he was most unhappy.

19. Finally, Thor pulled up his oars and set about preparing his line, which was very strong, with a hook that was neither weaker nor less firm. The mighty Hymir pulled up two whales by himself on his hook; the son of Odin sat in the stern; Veur-Thor prepared his cast with cunning. The warder of men, the serpent's slayer, fixed the head of the ox on his hook; he cast it overboard, where it sank to the bottom. The foe of the Gods, Jormungand, gaped at the bait, the encircler of all beneath the earth. And it can be said in truth that this time Thor tricked the Midgardswyrm no less than Utgardloki-Fjalar had tricked Thor into lifting the Midgardswyrm with his arm.

20. The Midgardswyrm opened its mouth and swallowed the ox head. Vidir-Odin's heir's [Thor's] line lay by no means slack on Eynaefir's ski [boat] when Jormungand un-

coiled on the sand. The hook dug into the gums of its mouth, and when the serpent felt this, he snapped back so hard, that Ull's relative's [Thor's] fists banged out on the gunwale; broad planks pushed forward. The encircler of all lands [Jormungand] and Jord-Frigga's son [Thor] became violent. The son [Thor] of the father of mankind [Odin] was determined to test his strength against the water-soaked earth-band [Jormungand]. The mighty Thor boldy pulled the serpent, with venom glistening, up to the side. It can be said that no one had seen a more terrifying sight than this: Thor, narrowing his eyes at the serpent, while Jormungand spit out poison and stared straight back from below. Thrud's father [Thor] looked with piercing eyes on steepway's [land's] ring [Jormungand], until the redfish's dwelling [sea] surged over the boat. And the ugly ring [Jormungand], of the side-oared ship's road [sea] stared up spitefully at Hrungnir's skull-splitter [Thor].

21. Just at that instant, Oflugbardi's terrifier [Thor] grabbed his hammer with his right hand and raised it into the air when he recognized the coalfish that bounds all lands [Jormungand]. It is told that the Etin Hymir changed color. He grew pale and feared for his life when he saw the serpent and also the sea rushing in and out of the boat. The

stockily built stumpy one [Hymir] is said to have thought tremendous danger in the goat-possessor's [Thor's] enormous heavy load.

22. As Thor was about to strike the serpent, the Etin, fumbling with the bait knife, cut Thor's line where it lay across the edge of the boat, and the serpent sank back into the sea. The breeze-sender [Etin, Hymir] who cut the thin string [fishing-line] of gulls' Maeri [the sea] for Thor, did not want to lift the twisted bay-menacer [Jormungand]. But the Asagod swung with his hammer and struck the foul head's summit, like a towering rock, of the wolf's [Fenrir's] own brother [Jormungand]. Vidgymnir of Vimur's ford [Thor] struck the ear-bed [head] of the shining serpent [Jormungand] by the waves. The icebergs resounded, the caverns howled, all the old earth was shaken; at length the fish [Jormungand] sank back into the ocean, only to return at Ragnarok.

23. The most mighty fell-Gaut's [Etin's] feller [Thor] made his fist crash on the reed-bed-bone [rock] frequenter's [Etin's, Hymir's] ear. A mighty hurt was that.

24. The Etin was not very glad,
as they rowed back,
so that the powerful Hymir
said nothing,
but moved the oar
in another course.

25. Hymir: "Will you do

half the work with me,
either bear the whales
home to the dwelling,
or bind fast
our goat of the flood [boat]?"

26. Hlorridi-Thor went,
quickly grasped the prow,
and with its hold-water
lifted the water-steed [boat],
together with its oars and scoop;
he bore to the Etin's dwelling
the ocean-swine [whales]
and the curved vessel,
through the wooded hills.

27. The Etin would again
match his might
with the strength of Thor,
for he was stubborn;
he said that none
was truly strong,
however vigorously he might row,
unless he could break his cup.

28. Then Hlorridi-Thor,
when he held the cup,
broke an upright stone
in two;
sitting he threw the cup
through the pillars:
yet they brought it whole
back to Hymir.

29. Until his fair wife
gave important,
friendly counsel,
which only she knew:
"Strike at the head of Hymir,
the gluttonous Etin,
for that is harder
than any cup."

30. The stern Lord of Goats [Thor]
rose on his knee,
and he struck with

all his divine might;
the old Etin's helm-block [head]
remained unharmed,
but the round wine-bearer [cup]
was shattered in pieces.

31. "Fair is the treasure
that is gone from me,
since the cup now
lies shattered on my knees."
Thus the old Etin said:
"I can never say again
'my beer,
you are too hot.'

32. "Now you must see
if you can carry
the kettle
out of our dwelling."
Tyr then tried
to move it twice,
yet each time
the kettle stood fast.

33. Then Modi's father [Thor]
grasped it by the rim,
and his feet sank down
right through the hall's floor;
Sif's husband [Thor] lifted
the kettle on his head,
while about his heels
its handles jingled.

34. They had not fared long
before Odin's son [Thor]
looked back,
to see once more:
he saw the horde
of many-headed monsters
coming with Hymir
from their caves in the east.

35. He set the kettle
down from his shoulders,
hurled Mjollnir
towards the savage crew,

and slew all the whales-
of-the-waste [Etins],
who had pursued
him with Hymir.

36. The mighty one [Thor] came
to the Thing of the Gods,
and had the kettle,
which Hymir had possessed,
now every harvest-tide
the Aesir shall
drink their ale
in Aegir-Gymir's beer hall.

LXXVII. Harbard

1. Thor traveled from eastern ways to the feast of Aegir-Gymir; faring from one of his adventures killing trolls. He came to a strait or sound. On the other side of the sound was a ferryman with a boat. Thor called out:

2. "Who is the youth of youths,
that stands up ahead
by the sound?"

3. Ferryman [Loki]: "Who is that karl's karl,
that calls over
the water?"

4. Thor: "Ferry me across the sound,
then I will feed
you tomorrow;
I have a basket on my back:
in it there is
no better food;
in peace I ate,
before I left the house,
herring and goat-meat,
with which I still feel sated."

5. Ferryman: "Hastily do you praise your meal:
surely you have no foreknowledge;

there is sorrow in your home:
your mother, I believe, is dead."

6. Thor: "Now you say
what seems to everyone
most unwelcome to know—
that my mother is dead."

7. Ferryman: "You do not look like
one who owns three country dwellings,
you stand bare-legged,
and clothed like a beggar;
you do not even have breeches."

8. Thor: "Steer your boat here,
I will direct you
where to land;
but who owns the craft
that you hold by the strand?"

9. Ferryman: "He is Hildolf
who told me to hold it,
a man wise in counsel,
who dwells in Radso sound.
He told me not to ferry robbers,
or horse-thieves,
but only good men,
and those whom I know well.
Now tell me your name,
if you will cross the sound."

10. Thor: "I will tell my name,
although I am an outlaw,
and all my kin:
I am Odin's son,
Meili-Baldur's brother,
and Magni's father,
the Gods' mighty leader:
you may now speak with Thor.
And now I would know
what your name is."

11. Ferryman: "I am called Harbard,
and seldom I hide my name."

12. Thor: "Why should you hide your name

unless you have committed a crime?"

13. Harbard: "Yet, though I may have
committed a crime,
I will nonetheless guard
my life against one such as you,
unless I am doomed to die."

14. Thor: "It seems to me a foul annoyance
to wade across the strait to you,
and wet these eyes;
but I will pay you, trifling boy,
for your mocking words,
if I came across the sound."

15. Harbard: "I shall stand here
and wait for you;
you will find no one stronger,
since Hrungnir's death."

16. Thor: "Now you remind me
of how I fought with Hrungnir,
that stouthearted Etin,
whose head was made of stone;
yet I made him fall,
and sink before me.
Meanwhile, Harbard, what did *you* do?"

17. Harbard: "I was with Fjolvar
five whole winters,
on the island called Algroenn [Midgard];
there we could fight,
and slaughter,
tried many feats,
and mastered maidens."

18. Thor: "How did your women
prove towards you?"

19. Harbard: "We had lively women,
if they had only been meek;
we had shrewd ones,
if they had only been kind;
they twisted ropes of sand
and dug out the ground
into the deep dales:

I alone was superior
to them all in cunning.
I laid with the
nine sisters,
and shared their love
and their pleasures.
Meanwhile Thor, what did *you* do?"

20. Thor: "I slew Thjazi-Volund,
that stouthearted Etin:
I cast the eyes
of Alvaldi-Ivaldi's son
up into the serene heavens:
these are signs of
the greatest of my deeds.
Meanwhile, Harbard, what did *you* do?"

21. Harbard: "I used many wiles
in women's ways with the Myrkriders,
whom I lured from their husbands.
I believed Hlebard-Volund to be
a mighty Etin:
he gave me Mistilteinn,
and I stole his wits away."

22. Thor: "You repaid good gifts
with an evil mind."

23. Harbard: "One tree gets that
which is scraped from another:
in such things each for himself.
Meanwhile, Thor, what did *you* do?"

24. Thor: "I was in the east,
and slew the Etin;
their ill-working women
who went to the mountain;
the Etin horde would have
been great, had they lived,
and not a man left in Midgard.
Meanwhile, Harbard, what did *you* do?"

25. Harbard: "I was in Valland,
and conducted battles,
I provoked princes against one another,
but never reconciled them.

Odin has the jarls
who fall in conflicts;
but Thor the race of Thralls."

26. Thor: "You would divide the folk
unequally among the Aesir,
if only you had the power."

27. Harbard: "Thor has enough strength,
but no courage;
from cowardice and fear,
you were crammed into a glove,
and there forgot you were Thor;
through your terror
you then did not dare
to fart or sneeze,
lest Fjalar might hear it."

28. Thor: "Cowardly Harbard!
I would strike you down to Hel,
if only I could stretch my arm
across the sound!"

29. Harbard: "Why would you
stretch your arm across the sound,
when there is altogether no offence?
What, Thor, did you do then?"

30. Thor: "I was in the east,
I defended the river [Elivagar],
when Svarang's sons [Hrimthurses]
sought to kill me,
and threw stones at me,
though they found little joy
in their success:
they were the first to sue for peace.
Meanwhile, Harbard, what did *you* do?"

31. Harbard: "I was in the east,
and held converse with an Einherja [Idun],
I hovered beside the linen-white one,
and held a secret meeting.
I gladdened the gold-bright one,
and the girl enjoyed the game."

32. Thor: "Full fair was your

woman-finding."

33. Harbard: "Then I was in need
   of your help, Thor,
   when I held the linen-white maid."

34. Thor: "I would have given it to you,
   if I had been there."

35. Harbard: "I would have trusted you,
   had you not betrayed my trust."

36. Thor: "I am no heel-biter,
   like an old shoe in spring!"

37. Harbard: "Meanwhile, Thor,
   what did *you* do?"

38. Thor: "I slew the Berserks brides
   on Hlesey:
   they were most evil,
   they seduced all the folk."

39. Harbard: "It was shameful for
   you to slay women, Thor."

40. Thor: "They were she-wolves,
   and hardly women.
   They crushed my ship,
   which I had secured with props,
   threatened me with iron clubs,
   and drove away Thjalfi.
   Meanwhile, Harbard, what did *you* do?"

41. Harbard: "I was in the war-party
   that came here
   to raise war-banners,
   to redden spears."

42. Thor: "Now you will bring up
   the occasion when you intended
   to offer us an evil lot."

43. Harbard: "That shall be redressed
   with a hands-ring,
   such as arbitrators give,

who wish to reconcile us."

44. Thor: "Where did you learn
   such pointed words?
   I have never heard
   more pointed words."

45. Harbard: "I learned them from men,
   from ancient men
   who live in Heimir's woods."

46. Thor: "You give a good name
   to grave-mounds,
   when you call them Heimir's woods."

47. Harbard: "So I speak of such things."

48. Thor: "Your shrewd words
   will bring you ill,
   if I choose to wade in the water.
   You would howl louder
   than a wolf, I believe,
   if you got a touch from my hammer."

49. Harbard: "Sif has a lover at home,
   you will be anxious to find him:
   it will be more fitting for you
   to put forth your strength on him."

50. Thor: "Your tongue still makes you say
   what seems most evil to me,
   you cowardly knave!
   I believe you are lying."

51. Harbard: "I believe I am telling truth.
   you are traveling slowly:
   you would have arrived long ago,
   if I had ferried you over."

52. Thor: "Harbard, you coward!
   You have held me here too long!"

53. Harbard: "I never thought
   that a ferryman could
   hinder the course of Asathor."

54. <u>Thor</u>: "One advice I will now give you:
row your boat here;
let us cease from threats;
set Magni's father across."

55. <u>Harbard</u>: "Get away from the sound,
the passage is refused to you."

56. <u>Thor</u>: "Then show me the way,
if you will not ferry me
across the water."

57. <u>Harbard</u>: "That is too little to refuse,
it is far to go;
a while to the stock,
and a while to the stone;
then keep to the left,
until you reach Verland [Midgard];
there will Fjorgyn-Frigga
find her son Thor,
and show him his
kinsmen's paths
to Odin's land."

58. <u>Thor</u>: "Can I get there today?"

59. <u>Harbard</u>: "With pain and toil you
may get there while the sun is up,
which, I believe, shall vanish."

60. <u>Thor</u>: "Our talk shall now be short,
for you only answer
with mockery.
I will reward you
for refusing to ferry me,
if we meet again."

61. <u>Harbard</u>: "Just go to where
all the powers of evil may have you."

LXXVIII. <u>Loki</u>

1. Aegir, who is also called Gymir, had brewed beer for the Aesir, after he had obtained the great kettle, as has already been stated. Now Odin raised his face to the Gods' triumphant sons; at that will welcome help awake from all the Aesir that shall enter, to Aegir-Gymir's benches, at Aegir-Gymir's feast. To this feast came Odin and his wife, Frigga. Thor did not come, as he was on a journey in the east, and had been delayed. His wife, Sif, was there, as well as Bragi and his wife Idun. Tyr, who had but one hand, was there; the wolf Fenrir had bitten off his other hand when they had bound him. Besides them were Njord and his wife Skadi, Frey and Freya, Odin's son Vidar, and Urd-Gefjun. Loki was there, and Frey's servants Byggvir and Beyla. Many other Aesir and Alfar were also present.

2. Aegir had two servants, Fimafeng and Eldir. When the Gods had taken their places, Aegir-Gymir had glowing gold brought into the middle of the hall, which illuminated and lit up the hall like fire, and this was used as lights at his feast, just as in Valhall swords are used instead of fire. At this feast everything served itself, both food and ale and all the utensils that were needed for the feast. The place was a great sanctuary. The guests greatly praised the excellence of Aegir's servants. Loki could not endure that, and so he slew Fimafeng. Then the Gods shook their shields, yelling at Loki and drove him away to the forest. Then they returned to

drinking. Loki turned back, and outside he met Eldir. Loki spoke to him:

3. "Tell me, Eldir,
   before you step
   one foot forward:
   what the sons of the
   triumphant Gods speak of
   in their ale-sitting within."

4. Eldir: "The sons of the triumphant Gods
   speak of their weapons,
   and of warlike deeds.
   Of the Aesir and Alfar
   that are here within,
   not one has a friendly word for you."

5. Loki: "I will go
   into Aegir's halls,
   to see the feast;
   I bring strife
   and hate to the Asasynir,
   and will mix their mead with evil."

6. Eldir: "If you go
   into Aegir's hall,
   to see the feast,
   and pour forth hate and mockery
   on the kindly Powers,
   they will throw it back on you."

7. Loki: "You do not know, Eldir,
   that if the two of us
   contend with bitter words,
   I shall be rich
   in answers,
   if you say too much to me."

8. Then Loki went into the hall, but when those present saw who had entered, they were all silent.

9. Loki: "I, Lopt-Loki, have come
   thirsty into this hall

from a long journey,
   to ask the Aesir
   to give me one draught
   of the bright mead.

10. "Why, are you Gods
    so silent, so reserved
    that you cannot speak?
    Give me a place
    and a seat at your feast,
    or tell me to leave from here."

11. Bragi: "The Aesir will never give
    you a place and a seat
    at their feast,
    since they well know
    for whom among beings
    they are to prepare a drink of revenge."

12. Loki: "Odin, do you remember
    when we performed Blodablanda together
    in the early days?
    Then you promised
    to never drink ale
    unless it was offered to us both."

13. Odin: "Rise up, Vidar,
    and let the wolf's father
    have a seat at our feast;
    so that Loki may not
    utter insulting words
    in Aegir-Gymir's hall."

14. Then Vidar arose and poured a drink for Loki, who before drinking said to the Gods:

15. "Hail, Aesir!
    Hail, Asynjur!
    Hail to all the holy Gods!
    Save that one As,
    who sits with you,
    Bragi there on the bench."

16. Bragi: "I will give a horse
    and a sword from my stores,

and the fine with rings as well,
since you wish to show
the Gods your anger,
and provoke them against you."

17. Loki: "You will ever be
in want of horses and rings, Bragi!
Of the Aesir and Alfar
that are present here,
you are the least brave in battle,
and most timid in the play of darts."

18. Bragi: "I know that if I were without,
as I am now within,
the hall of Aegir,
I would have your head
in my hands,
and so punish you for lying."

19. Loki: "You are valiant on your seat,
but your deeds are not,
Bragi, adorner of benches!
Go out and fight,
if you are angry;
a brave man does not sit in thought."

20. Idun: "I beg you, Bragi,
to weigh his kinship,
since he was chosen as wish-son;
and do not speak such
spiteful words to Loki,
here in Aegir's hall."

21. Loki: "Shut up, Idun!
You are the most man-crazy
of all women,
ever since you laid
your finely washed arms
around your brother's [Volund's] bane [Loki]."

22. Idun: "I do not speak to Loki
with spiteful words,
here in Aegir's hall;
I soothe Bragi,
who is inflamed with beer,
for I wish that you not angrily fight."

23. Urd: "Why do you two Aesir
fight with bitter words
within this hall?
Lopt-Loki believes he
has been deceived,
and is urged on by Wyrd."

24. Loki: "Shut up, Urd-Gefjun!
I will now just mention
how you corrupted the mind
of that fair youth [Odin],
who gave you a necklace,
and whom you wrapped your legs around."

25. Odin: "You are raving, Loki!
And have lost your wits,
in calling Urd's wrath on you;
for I believe she knows
the urlag of all men,
even as well as I."

26. Loki: "Shut up, Odin!
You could never fairly
allot men luck in battle:
often you have given
victory to cowards—
those who do not deserve it."

27. Odin: "You know that I give
victory to cowards—
those who do not deserve it?
You were in the
Underworld eight winters,
milking the cows as a maid,
and there bore children:
I think these were womanly ways."

28. Loki: "But, it is said, that you
cast spells like a vala,
once on Samso;
in a vala's guise
you went among the folk,
I think these were womanly ways."

29. Frigga: "You two Aesir should

never speak among men
of what you did in days of yore.
Whatever you have done
in the past should
ever be forgotten."

30. Loki: "Shut up, Frigga!
You are Fjorgyn-Hoenir's daughter,
and have always been man-crazy,
since, Vidir-Odin's wife,
you let Vili-Lodur and Ve-Hoenir
lay in your bosom."

31. Frigga: "Know that if I had,
here in Aegir's halls,
a son like Baldur,
you would not leave
from the Asasynir,
till your fierceness in battle were tried."

32. Loki: "Then, Frigga, do you wish
that I tell you more
of my wickedness?
I am the reason
that you do not see
Baldur riding to the halls."

33. Freya: "You are raving, Loki!
In recalling your
foul misdeeds.
Frigga knows well
the urlag of all,
although she does not say it."

34. Loki: "Shut up, Freya!
Full well do I know you,
you are not free from vices;
of the Aesir and Alfar
who are gathered here,
each has lain as your lover.

35. Freya: "False is your tongue,
and soon you will find
that it will bring you woe;
the Aesir are angry with you,
the Asynjur as well.

You shall go home in sadness."

36. Loki: "Shut up, Freya!
You are a whore,
and filled with much evil;
the gentle Gods caught
you in your brother's arms,
when you farted, Freya."

37. Njord: "Not much harm is there
if a silk-clad woman gets
herself a husband or a lover;
but it is a wonder how a wretched As,
who has borne children,
should enter herein."

38. Loki: "Shut up, Njord!
From here you were sent east
as a hostage to the Aesir;
Hymir's daughters
had you for a urinal,
and flowed into your mouth."

39. Njord: "This was to my benefit,
as I was sent a long way from here
as a hostage to the Gods;
I had a son, whom no one hates,
and is considered foremost among the Aesir."

40. Loki: "Stop, Njord!
Contain yourself within bounds;
I will no longer keep it secret:
it was with your sister, Frigga,
that you had such a son,
hardly worse than yourself."

41. Tyr: "Frey is the boldest rider
of all the exalted Gods
in the Aesir's court:
he makes no maid weep,
nor wife of man,
and loosens all from bonds."

42. Loki: "Shut up, Tyr!
You could never settle strife
between two men;

290

I also must mention
your right hand,
which Fenrir tore from you."

43. <u>Tyr:</u> "I do lack my hand,
you Hrodvitnir-Fenrir,
a sad loss for us both;
nor is the wolf at ease:
he must wait in bonds
until the Gods' destruction."

44. <u>Loki:</u> "Shut up, Tyr!
For your wife once
happened to have a son by me;
not rag nor penny
have you ever been given
for this injury, poor wretch!"

45. <u>Frey:</u> "I see a wolf lying
at the mouth of the river,
until all come into conflict;
if you do not hold your tongue,
you, you niding,
will be chained next to him."

46. <u>Loki:</u> "With gold did you buy
the daughter of Aegir-Gymir [Gerd],
and so gave away your sword:
but when Muspel-Loki's sons
ride over the Myrkwood,
you shall be weaponless, poor wretch."

47. <u>Byggvir:</u> "Had I the ancestry
of Ingunarfrey,
and so honored a seat,
know I would grind you
finer than marrow,
you evil crow,
and crush you limb from limb."

48. <u>Loki:</u> "What little boy is that
whom I see wagging his tail
and eating like a parasite?
You will always be
near Frey's ears,
clattering beneath the millstones [of Grotti]."

49. <u>Byggvir:</u> "My name is Byggvir,
all Gods and men
call me nimble;
and here it is my pride
that Odin's sons
drink ale together."

50. <u>Loki:</u> "Shut up, Byggvir!
You were never able
to divide food among men;
lying in your straw bed,
you were not to be found,
while men were fighting."

51. <u>Heimdall:</u> "You are drunk, Loki,
and have lost your wits.
Why don't you leave, Loki?
But drunkenness
so rules every man
that he does not realize he is rambling."

52. <u>Loki:</u> "Shut up, Heimdall!
For in ancient days
an ugly life was laid out for you:
you will always have
mud on your back,
and wakeful as watch of the Gods."

53. <u>Skadi:</u> "You are merry, Loki!
You will not frolic long
with an unbound tail;
for the Gods will bind you
on a sword's point,
with the entrails of your ice-cold son."

54. <u>Loki:</u> "Know if the Gods bind me
on a sword's point,
with the entrails of my ice-cold son,
that first and foremost,
I was at the slaying,
when we attacked Thjazi-Volund."

55. <u>Skadi:</u> "Know, if first and foremost
you were at the slaying,
when you attacked Thjazi-Volund,

291

that from my dwellings and fields
cold counsels shall
ever come to you."

56. Loki: "Your speech was more mild
to Laufey's son,
when you invited me to your bed;
such matters must be mentioned,
if we accurately
must recount our vices."

57. Then Sif came forward, and poured out
mead for Loki in an icy cup, saying:

58. "Hail to you, Loki!
Receive this cool cup
full of old mead;
for me alone,
among the Aesir,
you know to be blameless."

59. He then took the horn, drank, and said:

60. "So you should be alone,
if you had been strict
and prudent towards your mate;
but one I know
and, I think, I know him well,
who had you from Hlorridi-Thor's arms,
and that is the sly Loki."

61. Beyla: "The mountains quake:
I believe Hlorridi-Thor
is coming from his home;
he will silence he
who here insults
all Gods and men."

62. Loki: "Shut up, Beyla!
You are Byggvir's wife,
and filled with much evil;
never came a greater disgrace
among the Asasynir.
You are a filthy slave."

63. Then Thor came in and said:

64. "Silence, foul wight!
My mighty hammer,
Mjollnir, shall shut your mouth;
I will cleave your shoulder-cliff [head]
from your neck:
then your life will be ended."

65. Loki: "Now the son of Jord-Frigga
has come in:
why threaten so loudly, Thor?
You will not dare do so,
when you have to fight with the wolf:
he will swallow Sigfather-Odin whole."

66. Thor: "Silence, foul wight!
My mighty hammer,
Mjollnir, shall shut your mouth;
I will hurl you up
to the eastern regions,
and no one shall see you again."

67. Loki: "You should never
speak to people
of your eastern travels,
since you hid
in a glove's thumb, Einheri,
and hardly thought you were Thor."

68. Thor: "Silence, foul wight!
My mighty hammer,
Mjollnir, shall shut your mouth;
I, Hrungnir's bane,
shall smite you with my right hand,
till all your bones are broken."

69. Loki: "It is my intention
to live a long life,
though you threaten me with your hammer;
Skrymir-Fjalar's strings
seemed hard to you,
when you could not get at the food,
and, in full health, dying of hunger."

70. Thor: "Silence, foul wight!

My mighty hammer,
Mjollnir, shall shut your mouth;
Hrungnir's bane shall
send you to Hel,
down below the Nagates."

71. Loki: "I have said before the Aesir,
I have said before the Asasynir,
that which my mind suggested:
but I will go out
for you alone;
because I know you will fight.

72. "Aegir, you have brewed beer;
but you shall never
again hold a feast;
flames shall play over
all your possessions
which are herein,
and shall burn your back."

73. Loki payed for his crimes in such a way that he will not soon forget it. With the Gods having become as angry with him as one might expect, he ran away and hid in a certain mountain, then built a house there with four doors so that he could see out of the house in all directions. During the day he often changed himself into a salmon and hid in a place called Franangsforce. He set his mind to discovering what sort of play the Aesir might devise to catch him in the waterfall. Sitting in the house, he took some linen yarn and looped it into a mesh in the way that nets have been made ever since. A fire was burning in front of him. Suddenly, he saw that the Aesir were only a short distance away—Odin having discovered Loki's whereabouts from Hlidskjalf. Loki jumped up and threw the net into the fire, as he dashed out to the river.

74. When the Aesir reached the house, the first to enter was Odin, who had Mimir's head with him. They looked into the fire, and when they saw the outline of the net in the ashes, Mimir realized that it was a device for catching fish. He told the Aesir, and they set to work. They made a net for themselves, copying from Loki what they had seen in the ashes.

75. With the net ready, the Aesir went to the river and cast the net in the waterfall. Thor held one end and all the Aesir held the other, and together they dragged the net. But Loki moved ahead of them and, diving deep, he placed himself between two boulders. As the Aesir pulled the net over him, they realized that something was alive there. They went back up to the waterfall and again cast the net. This time, they weighed it down so heavily that nothing could slip under it. Again, Loki stayed ahead of the net, but when he saw it was only a short distance to the sea, he jumped up over the top of the net and swam back up to the falls. The Aesir, now seeing where he was going, returned to the falls. They divided themselves between the two banks, while Thor waded in the

middle of the river, and then they worked their way down towards the sea.

76. Loki realized that he had two options. He could leap out to the sea, which meant putting his life in danger, or he could once again jump over the net. He chose the latter, jumping as fast as he could over the net. Thor reached out and succeeded in grabbing him, but still the salmon slipped through his hands. Thor finally got a firm hold on it near its tail, and for this reason, salmon are narrow at the end.

77. Loki was now captured, and with no thought of mercy he was taken to Lyngvi, the same cave in Amsvartnir sea where Fenrir is bound. The Aesir took three flat stones and, setting them on their edges, broke a hole through each of them. Then they caught two of Loki's sons, and changed one into a wolf, who then ripped his brother apart. Next, the Aesir took the brother's entrails, and with them bound Loki onto the top of three stones—one under his shoulders, a second under his loins, and the third under his knees. The fetters became iron.

78. Bragi placed a sword with its point in Loki's back as revenge for stealing Idun. Then Skadi took a poisonous serpent and fastened it above Loki so that its poison drips onto his face. But Sigyn, his wife, placed herself beside him from where she holds a bowl to catch the drops of venom. When the bowl becomes full, she leaves to pour out the poison, and at that moment the poison drips onto Loki's face. He convulses so violently that the whole earth shakes—which is what is known as an earthquake. He will lie there until Ragnarok.

79. There lying bound under Hveralund is the one shaped like the insidious Loki. There were Vali's death-bonds twisted, most rigid bonds made from entrails; there sits Sigyn, for her consort's sake, she is not happy. In the land where Loki is bound, the unchanging face of darkness represses any alternation of light. There, through the narrow jaws of the cave lie rows of iron seats covered in slithering serpents. The river Von flows gently over a sandy bed, and upon crossing it one finds a floor sloped downwards rather more steeply. From here is seen a murky, repulsive chamber where Loki lies, hands and feet laden with a huge weight of fetters. There he emits such foul plagues that he seems more loathsome in his present condition than before he was bound. His rank-smelling hairs are as long and tough as spears of cornel-wood. If one of these hairs is plucked, a powerful stench immediately overwhelms those in his vicinity. Similar caves of punishment for Loki's closest kin, called Muspel's Sons, can also be found

within the mountain of the island of Lyngvi in Amsvartnir sea.

LXXIX. <u>Eggther</u>

1. Gullveig had been reborn and was imprisoned by the Gods. She was banished to the Ironwood and constrained there by powerful Galdur until Ragnarok. This Giantess lives to the east, in the forest called the Ironwood, and there fosters the brood of Fenrir. The troll-women who are called Jarnvidjas live in that forest, and hunters and woodsmen must guard against being fooled by sights they see in the wood. Each and every one of Gullveig's relatives can hide in the shade of the spruce or pine and emerge from within to entice men with glamorous charms. From the front, they are lovely to behold, but on the backside, they are as hollow as a trough. They are also called Ividjas.

2. The Ironwood is filled with witchcraft and terrors. The valleys between the dark and wildy jagged, storm-whipped mountains are filled with impassable forests and swamps in which strange, venomous beasts wallow. The unbroken howl of the wind through iron-hard, dagger-shaped leaves of ancient trees fills the heart with fear and confuses the senses. At night, water rushes down from the mountains like a fire-fall, while poisonous flames flicker over the region where no flower thrives.

3. Eggther watches the sword Gambantein until Ragnarok, when Fjalar will come to fetch it for his father, Surt. The sword-guardian devoted himself to magical skills and is an expert hunter. Eggther is a brother of Vidolf, Haki was the best of Hvedna's sons, and Hjorvard-Eggther was Hvedna's father. The sword he watches, Gambantein, is an ancient heirloom, the ideal weapon, one that any warrior would envy.

LXXX. <u>Har</u>

1. Now has been told the events of the Gods and humans during the first ages. The Gods have, just as Embla's descendants, had to learn from experience, and they want nothing more than for their proteges to commit the acquired lessons to memory. Because of this, it is devoutly believed that the Gods are all now worthy of worship: that Odin has become the enemy of all cunning paths, and that Thor learned to restrain his temper, that his hammer can now justifiably bless every promise and treaty. It is devoutly believed that the Gods made mistakes in former times so that they could show their great patience and tolerance towards faulty humans, who seek atonement. Evil ones have less of a right to seek protection behind the Gods' earlier flaws, since even the high-holy ones themselves are prepared to atone for their faults with ruin and death. The most im-

portant thing for the Gods now is to prepare themselves for a dignified fight to the death at Ragnarok, which will crush the evil powers along with them, making way for an uncorrupted world.

2. After the worst proponents of evil were neutralized, harmony prevailed in the world of the Gods and, in the cosmos, all order that is possible during the present period. The much celebrated age of events, known as the Ancient Age, was thereby brought to an end. For the most part, these events had their origin in Loki and Gullveig's intrigues and Jotunheim's rising power. But the power of the Etins was broken for a long time after the end of the Hunwar. Loki lies in chains, Gullveig is banished from Midgard, Odin has Mimir's head and thoughts at his disposal, and, if a dispute arises between clans of Gods or individual Gods, it does not come to the attention of men, because such a dispute is of no consequence to Midgard. Forseti, Baldur's son, settles all such cases. As stated, even the Gods have had a time of learning, which was now complete.

3. The Gods seldom show themselves to men's eyes now. However, the relationship between them is not broken. It is maintained through prayers, blots, and hof-duty, but, before all else, through a life of observing Urd's and the Gods' decrees. Sometimes, it

still happens that when a Teutonic army rides into battle, their seer perceives Odin riding in front of them. More often, his voice is heard in their shield-song. The fylkja that Odin taught Hamal is religiously observed: Teutonic fylkings are always arranged in the form of a wedge, because to them, this fylkja is holy.

4. At times, Odin can be heard traveling through the air followed by the Aesir, Asynjur, and Asgard's wolves, Freki and Geri. Then a storm is in the air, which Odin cleanses of wights of sickness and other harmful beings. If he sees Tunridur doing mischief in the air, he can work so that they will forsake their own forms and their own minds. This event is called Odin's Wild Hunt, as well as Asgardsride, and it takes place at Yule.

5. In the Ancient Age, Odin gave his advice to men, and his words are kept sacred by his followers. These are the words of Har-Odin:

6. All door-ways
   should be looked to
   before going forward;
   for it is difficult to know
   where foes may sit
   within a dwelling.

7. Hail, generous ones!
   A guest has entered:
   where shall he sit?
   He is in much haste,
   who has to prove

himself by the fire.

8. Warmth is needed
   to him who has come in,
   and whose knees are frozen,
   a man requires
   food and clothing,
   who comes over the fells.

9. He who comes to feast
   is in need of water,
   a towel and hospitable invitation,
   a kindly reception,
   if he can get it,
   discourse and answer.

10. The far-traveling wanderer
    is in need of his wit:
    at home all is easy.
    He is a laughing-stock
    who lacks words to speak
    when he sits among the learned.

11. No one should be proud
    of his understanding,
    but rather cautious in conduct.
    When the wise and wary
    come to a dwelling,
    harm seldom befalls the cautious;
    for no man ever gets
    a firmer friend
    than great sagacity.

12. The wary guest,
    who comes to a feast,
    keeps a cautious silence;
    he listens with his ears,
    seeks with his eyes,
    so the wise man observes.

13. Happy is the man
    who obtains honor and
    good reputation for himself:
    less sure is that
    which a man must have
    in another's heart.

14. Happy is the man
    who possesses in himself
    honor and wisdom in living;
    for bad counsels
    have often been received
    from another's heart.

15. No man bears a
    better burden on the way
    than good sense and manners;
    that is thought better than riches
    in a strange place,
    and it gives refuge in grief.

16. No man bears a
    better burden on the way
    than good sense and manners;
    he cannot carry
    a worse provision on the way
    than too much beer-bibbing.

17. For beer is not,
    as it is said,
    good for the sons of men.
    For the more he drinks,
    the less control he
    has of his own mind.

18. The heron of oblivion,
    which steals one's wit,
    hovers over the sumbel.
    I was fettered
    with this bird's feathers
    in Gunnlod's dwelling.

19. I was drunk,
    I was very drunk,
    at that cunning Fjalar's;
    it's the best sumbel
    when each gets home
    retaining sense and reason.

20. A king's children
    should be wise and wary,
    and daring in war;

everyone should be
joyous and generous
until his hour of death.

21. A cowardly man
    thinks he will live forever
    if he avoids the fight;
    but old age will
    give him no peace,
    though spears may spare him.

22. A fool gapes
    when he comes to a house,
    mutters to himself or is silent;
    but all at once,
    if he takes a drink,
    then a man's mind is displayed.

23. Only he is aware,
    who wanders wide
    and has experienced much,
    by what disposition
    each man is ruled,
    who possesses common sense.

24. Do not shun the mead,
    yet drink moderately,
    speak sensibly or be silent.
    None will hold you
    to be uncivil
    if you retire early to bed.

25. A greedy man,
    if he is not moderate,
    eats to his mortal sorrow.
    Often times his belly
    makes a joke of a silly man,
    who sits among the wise.

26. Cattle know
    when to go home,
    and then cease from grazing;
    but a foolish man
    never knows
    his stomach's measure.

27. A miserable man,
    with ill-conditioning,
    sneers at everything:
    one thing he does not know,
    which he should know,
    that he is not free from faults.

28. A foolish man
    is awake all night,
    pondering over everything;
    he is feeble
    when morning breaks
    and matters are still as before.

29. A foolish man
    thinks all who smile at him
    are his friends;
    he does not feel it,
    although they speak ill of him,
    when he sits among the clever.

30. A foolish man
    thinks all who smile at him
    are his friends;
    but he will find,
    when he comes to the Thing,
    that he has few advocates.

31. A foolish man
    thinks himself all-wise
    if placed in unexpected difficulty;
    but he does not know
    what to answer
    if he is put to the test.

32. A foolish man
    who comes among people
    had best be silent;
    for no one knows
    that he knows nothing
    unless he talks too much.
    He who previously knew nothing
    will still know nothing,
    talk he ever so much.

33. He thinks himself wise

who can ask questions
and converse also;
no one can
conceal his ignorance,
because it circulates among men.

34. He utters too many
futile words
who is never silent;
a babbling tongue
often sings to its own harm,
if it is not checked.

35. Do not mock another
who comes among your kin,
although he is a stranger in your home.
Many a one thinks himself wise,
if he is not questioned,
and can sit in dry habit.

36. He thinks himself clever,
the guest who insults guest,
if he takes to flight.
He certainly does not know,
who chatters at the feast,
whether he babbles among foes.

37. Many men are mutually
well-disposed,
yet will torment
each other at tables.
That strife will ever be,
guest will irritate guest.

38. A man should
often take early meals,
unless he goes to a friend's house;
else he will sit and mope,
will seem half famished,
and can inquire of few things.

39. The way is crooked and far
to a bad friend's,
though he dwells by the road;
but to a good friend's
the paths lie direct,
though he is far away.

40. A guest should depart,
not always stay
in one place:
the welcome becomes unwelcome
if he continues too long
in another's house.

41. One's own house is best,
though it is small;
everyone is his own master at home.
Though he possesses only two goats,
and a straw-thatched cot,
even that is better than begging.

42. One's own house is best,
though it is small;
everyone is his own master at home.
He is bleeding at heart
who has to ask
for food at every meal-tide.

43. Leaving his arms in the field,
let no man go
forward a foot's length;
for it is hard to know
when a man may
need his weapon on his way.

44. I have never found a man so bountiful
or so hospitable
that he refused a present;
or so generous
of his property
that he scorned a recompense.

45. Of the property
which he has gained,
no man should suffer need;
for what was intended for the dear
is often spared for the hated;
much goes worse than expected.

46. Friends should gladden each other
with arms and vestments,

as each can see for himself.
Givers and requiters
are friends longest,
if all else goes well.

47. A man should be a friend
    to his friend,
    and requite gifts with gifts;
    men should receive
    laughter with laughter,
    but lying with lying.

48. A man should be a friend
    to his friend,
    to him and to his friend;
    but of his foe
    no man shall
    be his friend's friend.

49. Know if you have a friend
    whom you fully trust,
    and would get good from him,
    you should blend your mind with his,
    and exchange gifts,
    and go to see him often.

50. If there is another,
    whom you trust little,
    yet could get good from him,
    you should speak fairly of him,
    but think falsely,
    and pay a lie for a lie.

51. But of him yet further,
    whom you trust little,
    and you suspect his affection,
    you should laugh before him,
    and speak contrary to your thoughts;
    the gifts should resemble requital.

52. I was once young,
    I was journeying alone
    and lost my way;
    I thought myself rich
    when I met another:
    man is the joy of man.

53. Generous and brave
    men live best,
    they seldom cherish sorrow;
    but a cowardly man
    dreads everything,
    the miser is uneasy even at gifts.

54. In the field I gave
    my garments to
    the two tree-people [Ask and Embla]:
    they seemed heroes to themselves
    when they got clothes.
    The naked man is embarrassed.

55. A tree withers
    that stands on a hill-top;
    neither bark nor leaves protect it:
    such is the man
    whom no one favors;
    why should he live long?

56. Friendship between
    false friends burns hotter
    than fire for five days;
    when the sixth day comes
    the fire cools
    and all the love is ended.

57. Something great
    is not always to be given,
    often little will purchase praise;
    with half a loaf
    and a drained cup
    I got myself a comrade.

58. Little are the sand grains,
    little the wits,
    little the minds of men;
    for all men
    are not wise alike:
    men are everywhere by halves.

59. Each one should be
    moderately wise,
    but never over-wise;

of those men
who know much well,
the lives are fairest.

60. Each one should be
moderately wise,
but never over-wise:
for a wise man's heart
is seldom glad,
if he is all-wise who owns it.

61. Each one should be
moderately wise
but never over-wise:
let no man know his
urlag beforehand;
his mind will be freest from care.

62. Brand burns from brand
until it is burnt out,
fire is quickened from fire:
man becomes
known to man by speech,
but a fool by his bashful silence.

63. He should rise early
who desires to have
another's property or life:
a sluggish wolf seldom
gets prey,
or a sleeping man victory.

64. He should rise early,
who has few workers,
and go to see his work;
much remains undone
for the morning-sleeper:
wealth half depends on energy.

65. A man knows the measure
of dry planks
and roof shingles;
of the firewood
that may suffice
both measure and time.

66. Let a man ride to the Thing
washed and fed,
although his garments are not too good;
let no one be ashamed
of his shoes and breeches,
nor of his horse,
though he does not have a good one.

67. All must be ready,
who will be known as sage,
to question and answer.
Let only one know,
a second may not;
if three, all the world knows.

68. When the eagle comes over
the ancient sea,
he gasps and gapes;
so is a man
who comes among many
and has few advocates.

69. Every wise man
should use his power
with discretion,
for he will find,
when he comes among the bold,
that no one alone is bravest.

70. Every man should be
watchful and wary
and cautious in trusting friends;
he often pays the penalty
from the words
that a man says to another.

71. I came to many places
much too early,
but too late to others;
the beer was drunk,
or not ready:
the disliked seldom hit the moment.

72. Here and there I should
have been invited
if I had needed a meal;

or had hung two hams
at that true friend's
where I had only eaten one.

73. Fire is best
among the sons of men,
and the sight of the sun,
if a man can
have his health
with a life free from vice.

74. No man lacks everything,
although his health is bad:
one is happy in his sons,
one in his kin,
one in abundant wealth,
one in his good works.

75. It is better to live,
even to live miserably;
a living man can get a cow.
I saw fire consume
the rich man's property,
and death stood before his door.

76. The lame can ride on horseback,
the one-handed drive cattle;
the deaf, fight and be useful:
to be blind is better
than to be burnt [on the pyre]:
no one gets good from a corpse.

77. A son is better,
even if born late,
after his father's death.
Memorial stones seldom
stand by the road,
unless raised by kinsman to kinsman.

78. Two are adversaries:
the tongue is the head's bane:
I expect a fist
under every cloak.

79. He welcomes the night,
whose fare is enough,

(short are the yards of a ship),
autumn nights are uneasy;
many are the weather's changes
in a week,
but more in a month.

80. He who knows nothing
does not know
that many a one apes another.
One man is rich,
another poor:
let him not be thought blameworthy.

81. Your cattle shall die,
your kindred shall die,
you yourself shall die;
but the fair fame
of him who has earned it
never dies.

82. Your cattle shall die,
your kindred shall die,
you yourself shall die;
one thing I know
which never dies:
the judgment on each one dead.

83. I saw full storehouses
at Fitjung's sons:
now they bear the beggar's staff.
Such are riches,
as is the twinkling of an eye:
they are the most fickle of friends.

84. A foolish man,
if he acquires
wealth or woman's love,
pride grows within him,
but never wisdom:
he goes on more and more arrogant.

85. Thus it is made manifest,
if you question him on runes,
those known to the high ones,
which the great Powers invented,
and which Fimbulthul-Mimir painted,

that he had best hold silence.

86. The day is to be praised at eve,
    a woman after she is burnt [on the pyre],
    a sword after it is proved,
    a maid after she is married,
    ice after it has been crossed,
    beer after it is drunk.

87. One should chop wood in the wind,
    row out to sea in a breeze,
    talk with a lass in the dark,
    the eyes of day are many.
    Voyages are to be made in a ship,
    but a shield is for protection,
    a sword for striking,
    but a damsel for a kiss.

88. One should drink by the fire,
    slide on the ice,
    buy a horse that is lean,
    a sword that is rusty;
    feed a horse at home,
    but a dog at the farm.

89. No one should place faith
    in a maiden's words,
    nor in what a woman says;
    for their hearts have been
    fashioned on a turning wheel,
    and their breasts were formed fickle.

90. In a creaking bow,
    a burning flame,
    a yawning wolf,
    a chattering crow,
    a grunting swine,
    a rootless tree,
    a waxing wave,
    a boiling kettle.

91. A flying dart,
    a falling billow,
    a one night's ice,
    a coiled serpent,
    a woman's bed-talk,

or a broken sword,
a bear's play,
or a royal child.

92. A sick calf,
    a self-willed thrall,
    a flattering vala,
    a newly slain corpse,
    a serene sky,
    a laughing lord,
    a barking dog,
    and a harlot's grief.

93. Let no one trust
    an early sown field
    nor prematurely in a son:
    weather rules the field,
    and wit the son,
    each of which is doubtful.

94. A brother's murderer,
    though met on the high-road,
    a half-burnt house,
    an over-swift horse
    (a horse is useless
    with a broken leg):
    no man is so confiding
    as to trust any of these.

95. Such is the love of women
    who meditate falsehood,
    as if one drove unroughshod
    on slippery ice,
    a spirited two-year-old
    and unbroken horse;
    or a helmless ship is beaten,
    as in a raging storm;
    or as if the lame were set to catch
    a reindeer in the thawing fell.

96. I now speak openly,
    because I know both sexes;
    men's minds are unstable towards women;
    it is then we speak most fair,
    when we think falsely:
    that deceives even the cautious.

97. He shall speak fair,
    and offer money,
    who would obtain a woman's love.
    Praise the form
    of a fair damsel;
    he gets, who courts her.

98. No one should ever
    wonder at
    another in love:
    a joyous fair litur [image]
    often captivates the wise,
    which does not captivate the foolish.

99. Let no one wonder at
    another's folly,
    it is the lot of many;
    of the sons of men,
    all-powerful desire
    makes fools even of the wise.

100. The mind only knows
    what lies near the heart;
    that alone is aware of our affections.
    No disease is worse
    to a sensible man,
    than to not be content with oneself.

101. I experienced that
    when I sat in the reeds
    awaiting my delight.
    That discreet maiden was
    body and soul to me:
    nevertheless I do not have her.

102. I found Billing's
    lass [Rind] on her bed,
    the slumbering, sun-white maid.
    A prince's joy,
    seemed nothing to me,
    if I could not live with that form.

103. "You must come, Odin,
    closer to evening,
    if you would win the maiden over:
    all will be disastrous
    unless we alone
    should know of such misdeed."

104. I returned,
    thinking to love
    at her wise desire;
    I thought
    I should obtain
    her whole heart and love.

105. When I came next,
    the warriors were
    all awake,
    with lights burning,
    and bearing torches:
    thus was the way to pleasure closed.

106. But at the approach of morn,
    when I came again,
    all the household was sleeping;
    alone I found
    the good damsel's dog
    tied to the bed.

107. Many fair maids,
    when rightly known,
    are fickle toward men:
    I experienced that
    when I strove to seduce
    that discreet maiden:
    that crafty maid
    heaped upon me
    insolence of every kind,
    and I had naught of her.

108. Let a man be cheerful at home,
    and generous towards a guest,
    he should be wise in conduct,
    of good memory and ready speech;
    if he desires much knowledge,
    he must often talk on what is good.
    He is called Fimbulfambi,
    who has little to say:
    such is the nature of the simple.

109. I sought the ancient Etin [Fjalar],
I have now returned:
I got little there by silence;
in many words
I spoke to my advantage
in Suttung-Fjalar's halls.

110. Rati-Heimdall's mouth
made room for my passage,
and gnawed a space in the stone;
above and below me
were the paths of the Etins,
I risked my head so rashly.

111. On the golden seat
Gunnlod gave me
a draught of the precious mead;
for her whole soul
her fervent love,
I later gave her a bad return.

112. I reaped great advantage
from the well changed litur [image]:
few things fail the wise,
for Odroerir
has been brought up
to men's earthly dwellings.

113. It is doubtful to me,
that I could have come
from the Etin's court,
had Gunnlod not aided me—
I won the heart of that good woman,
whom I took in my embrace.

114. The Hrimthurses came
on the following day
to learn of the high union,
in the hall of the high union;
they asked of Bolverk,
were he back among the Gods,
or had Suttung destroyed him?

115. I believe Odin
gave a ring-oath.
Who will trust in his troth?

Suttung is deceived,
his sumbel stolen,
and Gunnlod cries for her lost kinsman!

116. One often hears Thor's chariot in the clouds and sees his lightning bolts, thrown at Bergelmir's descendants. They would become numerous again if he did not decimate them with his hammer. From time to time, he is said to wander in Midgard in human form and oversee the country folk. Thor prefers that man cultivate for the benefit of coming generations, not just his own. He who builds with the thought that his work will only last his life, and he who has no desire to sow a seed or plant a sapling, because he would not enjoy the shade and fruit of the tree, finds no favor with Thor, and misfortune befalls the selfish one and his descendants.

117. All of the Etins who settled in Midgard during the days of the first Fimbulwinter have not returned to Jotunheim. Here and there some are left, particularly in wild mountain districts and deep woods. Sometimes a wanderer can hear the bells of their grazing herds in regions seldom tread by human feet. An unspoken agreement exists between these Etins and their human neighbors: if the neighbor does not bother the Etin or his livestock, the Etin does not interfere with the neighbor or his property. Some-

times, even good will and a willingness to help can exist between them. It often happens, however, that the Etin secretly infringes upon the agreement: that beautiful human daughters are carried away by them; that they delude the sight of a lone traveler and lure him astray from his intended path. In the event the Etins beget a sickly child, they sneak into a human home and lay it in the cradle, carrying away the bright and well-formed human child. Such changelings eat unbelievable amounts. But if the robbed mother is compassionate to the changeling, it may happen that the Etin mother is moved to return the stolen human child, place gold in the cradle, and take the changeling back to the mountains.

118. Although there are many dangerous beings, they are not as numerous as the good-natured and harmless ones. Most have their origin in the seed of life with which Audhumla nourished creation. Everything is alive, although life is of many kinds. Such beings live inside the trees. The old Barnstokks that grow on each homestead have souls sympathetic to the humans whom it has seen born and raised in its shade. If a family dwells on the same land for a long time, and the spirit of the Barnstokk has seen many of the family's children play under its crown and grow up into healthy human beings, then an intimate relationship develops between the Barnstokk and that family. When the latter prosper, the Barnstokk thrives, and in its later years, when it stands without leaves, as if gripped by winter, the people of the house adorn it with multicolored ribbons. Birds never sing more beautifully than in the Barnstokk, and when a person, who has been away at sea or at war for a long time, comes home, then a rustle from its crown greets him and arouses his most cherished childhood memories.

119. Each county has its Barnstokk under which justice is administered, and each clan has its own, where they assemble to confer about war and peace.

120. In memory of the ancient forefather's land, of the graves of the patriarchs, and of the important events that happened in the earliest times on the Scandinavian Peninsula, those clans that dwell south of the sea always pray with their faces turned toward the north.

The Varg Age

LXXXI. Fimbulwinter II

1. The bad time has passed, but there comes another. Jord-Frigga has not borne it and Odin-Wralda has not created it. It comes out of the east, out of the heart of Jotunheim. It shall bring forth so much grief that Jord [Earth] will not be capable of drinking the blood of her slain children altogether. Gloom shall spread over the folk, like thunderclouds over sunlight. Everywhere and always shall guile and power-lust struggle against right and freedom, which shall fall and we with them. Brothers will kill brothers for the sake of greed, and neither father nor son will be spared in the killings and the collapse of kinship. Brothers will become brothers' bane, and blood will spill between sisters' sons. Hardship is in the world, there is much whoredom; axe-age, knife-age, shields are sundered, wind-age, wolf-age, until the world falls into ruin. No man will dare spare another.

2. Hati Managarm will gorge himself with the life of all who die, feasting on the corpses of cowards. He will cause much ruin, and shall certainly, equipped in a troll-guise, rob the moon. He will catch Mani, and will swallow the moon, spattering blood throughout the sky and all the heavens, staining the homes of the Gods. Because of this, the sun will lose its brightness, becoming black for summers thereafter. The winds will turn violent, roaring from all directions, the weather becomes vicious.

3. Then will come the second Fimbulwinter. Snow will drive in from all directions; the cold will be severe and the winds will be fierce. The sun will be of no use. Three of these winters will come, one after the other, with no summer in between. But before that, there will have to be another three winters with great battles taking place throughout the world.

LXXXII. Ragnarok

1. There on a hill the joyous Eggther, Gullveig's watch, will sit striking a harp; by him, in the Ironwood, the bright red cock named Fjalar will crow. Fjalar arrives to retrieve Gambantein for his father, Surt, who shall use it in the conflagration. Gullinkambi, who awakens the heroes with Herjan-Odin, will crow over the Aesir. Another, the soot-red cock in Hel-Urd's halls, shall crow in the Underworld.

2. The whole earth, together with the mountains, will start to shake so that the trees will loosen from the ground, the mountains will fall, and all fetters and bonds will sever and break. Then Garm will bay wildly at Gnipacave, his bonds will break, and the wolf Fenrir will break free. Next will come an event thought to be of much importance. Skoll will capture Sol and offer her to Fenrir. The wolf will swallow the sun and mankind will think it has suffered a terrible disaster. The stars will disappear from the heavens.

3. The Wyrd of creation is forebode by the blare of the old Gjallarhorn. Heimdall stands up and blows with all his strength; he blows loudly with the horn in the air. He wakens all the Gods, who then hold a Thing. Odin speaks with Mimir's head, seeking counsel for both himself and his followers. Mimir's sons spring up, woken from the sleep of ages by the horn's call. Grasping their weapons, they mount their horses to take part in the battle. Their main purpose is to defend Jormungrund's verdant realms from Niflhel's monster-hordes. Yggdrasil's ash quakes where it stands, the old tree trembles, and the Etin gets loose; all are frightened on the Helways, before Surt's spirit [fire] swallows him [the Etin]. Nothing, whether in heaven or on earth, is without fear. Then

Audhumla will be released from her cave in Nidafjoll.

4. Hrym steers from the east and lifts his shield before him. The sea will surge on the land as Jormungand writhes in Etin's wrath and advances up on the land. The eagle screeches, Nidfol tears into corpses. Then it will also happen that the ship Naglfar loosens from its moorings. On the flooding sea, Naglfar comes floating. Gullveig gathers her children for the conflict, then inspires the nidings in Niflhel into action, while giving them weapons. The ship comes from the east, gathering the hosts of Muspel-Loki, who come over the ocean. Loki is pilot. All of Fifl-Loki's sons come with Fenrir, Byleist's brother [Loki] travels with them. The hosts of Muspel-Loki advance until they reach the plain called Vigrid. The Midgardswyrm also goes there. Then Hrym arrives, accompanied by all the Hrimthurses. Vidar's spacious land, Vigrid, is overgrown with branches and high grass, and lies a hundred leagues in every direction. Meanwhile, the Fenriswolf advances with its mouth gaping: its upper jaw reaches to the heavens and the lower one drops to the earth. He would open it still wider, if only there were room. Flames shoot out of his eyes and nostrils. The Midgardswyrm spews out so much venom that it spatters through-

out the air and into the sea. He is terrible and will be on one side of the wolf.

5. Amid this din, the sky splits apart and in ride the sons of Suttung-Fjalar. Surt comes first, faring from the south with the destruction of twigs [fire], riding with flames burning both before and behind him. Then Valtivi-Frey's sword, the magnificent Gambantein, shines like the sun. The sons of Suttung-Fjalar have their own battle fylking, which will meet the Gods at the southern end of Vigrid. I see fire burning, and the earth blazing, many shall suffer the loss of life. The sun will have become a black one, earth will sink into the dark sea, Austri's toil [the sky] will split, all the sea will crash on the fells. The stormy sea ascends to heaven itself and flows over the earth, the sky is split; thence come snows and furious winds, for the Gods are doomed, and the end is death.

6. What is with the Aesir? What is with the Alfar? Jotunheim is in an uproar! The Aesir are at the Thing; Dwarves, the wise ones of the precipice, stand outside the stone doors groaning. The Aesir and all the Einherjar dress for war and advance onto the field. Odin rides in front of them. He wears a gold helmet and a magnificent coat of mail, and he carries the spear called Gungnir. All the holy Gods shall seek the play of swords, to

meet Surt in battle. Bifrost breaks when they cross the bridge, and the steeds shall swim in the flood.

7. Odin goes against the Fenriswolf with Thor advancing at his side. Thor will be unable to assist Odin because he will have his hands full fighting the Midgardswyrm. Hati Managarm advances. He, the worst of monsters, will fight against Tyr. They will be each other's death.

8. Then a second sorrow is at hand for Hlin-Frigga, when Odin fares to fight with the wolf. Then will Frigga's beloved fall. Few may see further than when Odin meets the wolf. Fenrir will swallow Odin, and that will be his death. But immediately afterwards comes Sigfather-Odin's mighty son, Vidar, to battle with his chosen monster. There will the son descend from the steed's back, to boldly avenge his father. He will then stride forward and thrust one of his feet into the lower jaw of the wolf. He wears on that foot the shoe that has been assembled through the ages by collecting the extra pieces that people cut away from the toes and heels when fashioning their shoes. Thus, those who want to help the Aesir should throw these extra pieces away. With one hand, he takes hold of the wolf's upper jaw and rips apart its mouth, then, with his sword in his hands, he will pierce the heart of Hvedrung-

Loki's son [Fenrir], and this will be the wolf's death. Then is Vidar's father avenged. The wolf will devour the father of men [Odin]; Vidar will avenge him: he will cleave his cold jaws in conflict with the wolf.

9. Then comes the strong son of Hlodyn-Frigga, Vidar's brother, Thor, the bane of wolves. Odin's son walks to battle with the serpent. Jormungand comes with frightening suddenness against Thor and blows poison on him. In his rage, Thor will slay the Midgardswyrm. Fjorgyn-Frigga's son will walk nine feet before he must boldly collapse from the poison. The serpent spits on him, and he will fall to the earth, dead. Dead men from Niflhel clear the lands of all people.

10. Loki will battle with Heimdall, and they will be the death of each other. Heimdall cuts off Loki's head, and he himself is struck through by the head, which is grown with spear-like hairs. Frey, Beli's brilliant bane, will fare to the fight with Surt, and it will be a fierce exchange before Frey falls. His death will come about because he lacks the good sword, Gambantein, which he gave to Skirnir-Od. Next, Surt will throw fire over the earth and burn the whole world. The sun is blackened, the earth sinks into the sea. The many stars have fallen from the heavens; fire gushes against Yggdrasil, the flames leap high against heaven itself.

11. What will be after heaven and earth and the whole world are burned? The Gods will be dead, together with the Einherjar and the whole of mankind.

LXXXIII. Gimle

1. A second time the earth will rise up from the ocean, greenery of the eddying fountains, and it will be verdant and beautiful. It is Mimir's and Urd's blessed kingdom. It is the land of the three world wells, home of Hoddmimis Holt and Breidablik, the residence of Baldur, Nanna, and Hod, as well as Lif and Leifthrasir. In this place, Odainsacre, these two people will have hidden themselves from Surt's fire. From these will come so many descendants that the whole world will be inhabited, and from them springs mankind. Cascades fall and the eagle flies over, he who spies fish from the fell.

2. The Aesir meet on Idavoll, where they speak of the immense world-tree; each one is reminded of their remarkable urlag, and Fimbultyr-Odin's ancient runes. They will all sit together and talk among themselves, remembering mysteries and speaking of what had been, of the Midgardswyrm and the Fenriswolf. Then, once again the wondrous game of Tafl is found in the grass; that

which was owned in time's morning by a divine prince, and Fjolnir-Odin's family.

3. Vidar and Vali survive, as neither the flood nor Surt's fire destroy them, and they will inhabit Idavoll. Vidar and Vali will live in the Gods' holy hofs when Surt's fire shall be quenched. To there will come Thor's sons Magni and Modi, and they will possess Vingnir's Mjollnir at the end of the battle. Unsown acres will grow, all evil is remedied, and Baldur returns. He and Hod inhabit Hropt-Odin's victory-home [Valhall], chosen Gods and kinsmen.

4. Then Hoenir is able to choose the lotwood, and the sons [Asmegir] of the two brothers [Baldur and Hod] inhabit the spacious Vindheim. Alfrodul-Sol shall bear a daughter before Fenrir swallows her. This daughter is no less beautiful than she, and the maid shall ride on her mother's course, when the Power's die.

5. There is a hall more fair than the sun, which is called Gimle: there shall the virtuous multitudes dwell, and complete happiness is enjoyed forever. And then shall come, to the doom of the world, the great Godhead [Odin], which governs all. He settles strife, sits in judgment, and lays down laws that will always last. There comes the dark dragon flying from beneath, the glistening serpent, from Nidafjoll. Nidhogg, flying over the plain, bears a corpse on his wings. Now she will descend.

Appendix

The Hugrunes

1. I am the union of fire and ice, where their streams meet. I am energy and have no state. Nothing I grasp, and what have, do not *hold*. I am only I who know and all that I am is that knowing. I am for I know myself to be apart from what I am not.

Selves change: world is eternal. Self reappears, goes about in new forms: self is eternal. World about changes—worlds come and go. I release it and selves change beyond the selves they are. Ginnungagap is eternal, void between fire and ice. It cares not for me nor not-for-me. The Void I have formed; the Void forms me—the Gods both were before and follow too. Conscious became the Void, became first thought and gave first word and it was Odin.

2. Energy goes on, takes new forms. It merges with, emerges from, the play of selves, best tribal minds, the oldest souls. With each living and each dying, they self-merited through successive higher, progression to godlihood. Hugin creates itself best formed mind of tribe, and this goes on, becomes immortal. Ginnungagap is hereby *thought* in minds of Gods and men, and formed thereof and from itself, ancient milk of that first aurochs. Lived much and many, becomes that force compassion, troth in the ways of men. Looked with care upon itself, became Ginnungagap, and it spake, Frigga.

3. Faced stone and storm, the dying and birthing of worlds ere ours was thought to be. Faced with no concern for hurt nor loss, went on, as conscious, went on in all of storms of worlds. Pure courage was born to the Void. Pure ardent valor came to the worlds-before-world and spake the holy spark in darkness, Thor.

Frigga nurtures young shoots of life. Freya is pure beauty and Baldur is pure light. All their own right, self-won, self-determined. Each spake us in the travail of birth. In each cloth tied to bough, in each ale cast from horn, I give to them, and they to me, in turn.

4. Green man Frey came not one great harvestman, nor came he one great swain o'plenty. Long ago, who forestayed Jord's embrace, wrote himself large in the home of Gods. No, ever he grows anew in each fair

312

free-holder, every ardent swain, and bringer of harvest. His is all that lived thus and ever shall. Should none harvest, still he is. Should none love, yet he is. Thought itself too hard a darkness, burst to flame, bright lit, fair and beauteous, Baldur it spake. In the high sun, when the wheel on ground is cut becomes anew, for timeless the Gods and true.

5. Gods give back to me the cycle, time from time. They redeem to me what is forfeit in change from one threadbare cloak to the next. All forgotten here, the Gods beyond change anchor our timeless core. Who opens must sit out his thoughts. Who opens, her shall the Gods speak of time and cause, of life to life renewed. Who sits, renews. Who watches renews. Who cleansed of his own voice hears theirs, renews. And Ask and Embla Odin and Frigga formed, and from the Void gave Hugin and Munin, gave litur too. And the Void moved in smaller ripples and it spake Wunsch. Open is the way to see the Void, open to who reflects it as Gullveig-Ran's daughters' Mani-Knakve's dance.

6. An illness came and took the frail. Lady of small green things helped some, the vitki others. The lady who spun and wove, she never faltered, though it struck about her house. At her stoop she lay unrobed in summer sweat. In the cold day, brisk drove the herd with only a shawl about. In Ostara's cold water was she seen by the men o'weirs.

They came to ask this weft-woman, why never afflicts you? And she told the five purities. I sweat Baldur's gaze but may no return it—this be first. I lay in Sunna's smile and ask that she probe my innards with light, the dark moon chase, this the second. I sit the cold fast water till it is faster than my thought and rumbles out cares for three. Drink I only from skins I fill at the high stony brooks and eat not the day, this every month for four. I sit and ponder, do not do. Once it be wind in rushes—they sweep me clean. Again a brook rushed past and next 'twas leaves before a storm. Last dusk it was a thousand calling frogs. Into the shadow I gaze, where none will look, or to tan grasses, wind-rustled, they sweep me clear. Or in the babble of brook, the play of Sunna's greeting washes my eyes as stone-speech cleanse the ear, and this be five.

7. Opening is active, for the mind I must put aside is active. I take the active urge to be passive, to allow in the knowing of the Powers. Comes only in the active self, then

puts itself aside. The opening I either *do* by act of will, or quite undo by unthinking for the mind I know stands aside the Path of Power. By such paradoxes do I advance, for life is known by precept, but lived by riddle, and so must be thought.

Three states has the life of man, youth, prime, and old—three streams his time, for water comes down divided. One branch 'neath the high sun dry fish, cut peat, and herd to market drive. One branch the tales round fire, the time of Thing, the boy give knife and rope, the girl give loom and ladle, to both to sit, to pray, to grind soot and stir. The third lie still in stream, its course of dreams, of quiet, of fire or moon gazing.

8. Paths of Power yield to the man who stares beyond his own reflected gaze. The inner reckoning, leap beyond the known reflected surface, beckons. The paths open not by act, but by decision. Who has decided he cannot live but in power, that is so. Feasts and draughts arise for who *holds* abundance. Who holds someone sorrows at her loss. Who holds what *should* shall ever regret what *is*. Much a man can hold, but this I know, none may hold the runes. Who holds not, nor expects, he lives in power. Who holds not, nor clutches, nor seizes, is

much given, but little estate will build. Who holds little can little be riven by grief.

9. Never is there time, ere the field be tilled. Never is there time, ere the nets need tying, that I can sit and learn. Never is there time to bend the limb to keep the age-dragged gait away. Act beyond, beyond fatigue. Act beyond, beyond what is not to be worked with, beyond comfort, and beyond known headlands. Who sails beyond creates new charts. If the land comes not here, still is a man richer to have sailed for it. In his voyage shall she send him to a better journey.

Never is there time to strive; yet time must find. Never the man is so busy that he may not stop and look about. Even busy, two in the wharves, one sees the sky, one not. Always one may be aware. I can refrain from too much trencher and too many cups. I can curb the tongue from boast or threat. I can be still and learn, or sit at horg. Even with poor food, even with a humble cottage, much can understand. Even a town sweeper can be of power, and all hear his thought and see his glow.

10. Faith is participation. Faith constructs and creates experience. Like from the mold cheese is taken, thoughts our experiences create, but is also *influential*. Who can hold the image of the higher world will reach it.

He whose logic *deconstructs* experience lives only in his head. Sweet the sleep of the one who tires in striving to know. Sweet is the touch of woman's roundness to man and sweet the hard shoulder of man to woman, but the touch is a moment—no place of full happiness is in this wald.

11. Know the spirit mound is there, is here, and I access it. Do not construct, nor imagine. Stand anew at each threshold, not knowing but at ease with what is not known. Walk briskly in, knowing nothing still, and know the impress of eternity on mind. Calm the heart, calm and deep, the mind which opens to all forms of power. Bliss is in moments, the calm of morning ere the house awakens, waving grain, awaiting the sun's taking off the dew before the scythe, moments are bliss, or it is not at all.

He came to the horg after far trekking to the fiery realm, trading amber. Whereof to consecrate this place, he wot? For I have seen of ewe and fat shoat the folk of robes kill and the notched stone soak. Here they make holy and should we. The gydja gave that to kill and not eat would Vidar and Ull offend. "Consecrate," she said, "this circle, the warrior with his sword motion, the craftsman with her banner, and the brewer with 'is mead. All with her gifts

in mind, this Thor loves best, as keeps the hill. Consecrate thus with your essence given the Gods."

12. Faith is participation. It is choosing not to choose and turning to decide that all is undecided and awaits, eternal journey. It is influential: know that I can journey and all realms of experience are open to my tread. Share with another and they travel also. Believe that what I behold is "just imagination" or "just expectation" and I am moored tight to my own shore. Can or can't, real or imagined: either way I am "right." The can and real are richer and connect me to a deeper journey. Bliss is in moments but the moments are far longer than they seem. Each is endless if one but let it be so.

13. Once smithied, the sword is ever near my grasp. Will becomes reflexive once built. Thor's forge smithies greater evolution. It constructs a higher world by effort's hammer. Then Odin, laughing, releases it all, and I ascend the glass mountain to the Gods.

14. We are reborn;
   self is eternal,
      ever new in new surrounds.
   It is reborn:
      world is eternal.

Itself made by our returning selves.

Truths are created: laws are eternal.
Self is eternal: worlds are eternal:
all are in flux to higher matters bound:
 all need my mind's flight to higher cycles bound.

15. Scarcity, hardship, direst necessity; these were the woodsman's companions. Once his axe struck hoard beneath an ancient oak, as had set there in ancient time. Into a hall, to hold a hall, he took companions. Hungry he acted, though the table high with breads and shields of meat. Why, wot they, of him, pushed away from table? Act ever scarce, he said, pare wanting to the musts and always I'll have enough. Embracing want would never want again.

16. Freedom is a puff of wind. He is not free; the stag who with hoof scrapes beneath the snow for greens. He is not free though I saw him for a moment at the cliff, as if he o'erlooks the valley as lord. It is a moment. It is releasing, and not doing. From impeccable it arises. Who does well worries less than who does poorly his craft. Who does to perfection may then release them, all outcomes great and small. Only the impeccable can release. Only from the perfect arrow's flight, can the archer ere it land, turn his head.

17. Seeking the The Golden Age within, all who do must seek it in their intention. Then it may come to be. Why a Dark Age is thus that most less willing and less able to see. Cleanse sight and hold clear the vision-pure earth, land loved by each, no serfs, all waters clean of hides and wanting little, each is content. Of kings and councils few, and these nearby.

18. Cultivate stillness in reflection. In the business and busyness of life it is not idle, must be thought. Cultivate stillness in all passions, as the Watcher, never judging or reacting. Clear like moon, like lake and still, Heimdall watches over all. Observe detached yet act. For greater truths are in commoner places found. At the wharves and in the commons are greater matters chosen. Wholeness, I know, is facing squarely my situation. Plan that direction to the higher goals, what for the earth and for your folk be good. Further the way where you can. Wholeness is forged from *deciding* and *acting*.

19. Wholeness is *creative* and by intention lives, birthed in the freedom to act, to choose. The Gods leave me free that I may be co-creator. Freedom is momentary. It arises in the impeccable act and releasing

that act from care. Send out my choice, create, detach it from myself. Self goes on: world is eternal.

20. Worlds change: self is eternal, reborn into different matrices that we call 'worlds.' Vision is eternal, beyond time, smallest cell of Ginnungagap, seeking the The Golden Age and my own godlihood, holding the sight. Releasing into being what worlds we have. The seer by knowing knows. The diviner by stave and stone. The man of power holds his vision tightly at the highest reach of self. Released into being his flight is the flight of all whom he touches.

21. Though cozy abed with beloved, each sleeps ever alone. Each is born alone and dies thus, though a foeman with reciprocal strike die too. In all only the Gods accompany us throughout, ever Task-Giver, ever the Bearer of Constitutions, and ever the Tendencies of Breed. Always the Norns and Gods engage each life. The wise keep with them, in turn, while the fool may fear or trivialize, and is ever alone.

22. When choice presents, be kind. Less thought takes the kind man than one of guile, a freer mind and lighter step has he. Easier for self it is to release the higher act.

Be noble, good, kind, where the helping furthers the higher life.

Be passionate but fair, forceful, and quick to scour out sickness. No kindness to the world-destroying serpent, no kindness show to the sun darkening wolf. Act as the talons of the Gods in nature; vermin destroy lest they gnaw the slender thread of food.

23. What the world manifests is what Ginnungagap thought. Its hugur is awakening. The worlds yawn at the cusp of every age. Hugur calls to higher thought, greater knowing. In the scheme of things be kind when you can. When you cannot, be hard, and in either case, be noble.

24. The Galdur is no destination. It is a trackless journey. It is the eyes of the mind, traveled in the attention. It is decision. It is deciding what to *envision*, for what envisions, in some wise comes to be. It is a trackless expanse for the steppe-wanderer, happy for the quest. Whether another arrive or not we cannot know, but journey in joy and without expectation.

25. Self and worlds change: Gods are eternal. Tribe is the medium of transformation. Go to the crossroads and uplift them. In retreats only the self is rested. Through sever-

317

al selves, through the tribe, uplift and detach, struggle to attain higher, release all gains and gain detachment.

Selves are reborn: worlds are eternal. Selves thought beyond the cycle of cause are to godhood born. In passionate involvement cleanse, protect, elevate the tribe. By example of we, the flax-people, will other tribe progress. Self changes; Gods are eternal—heighten the self to seek the realm of Gods.

26. Act passionately with clear vision where you see your way and step lightly where the path ascends in scree. Live fully here, yet live apart. Sustain, achieve, and yet release. Hold tight the moment and shape it intensely, yet give to quiet reflection and release, for matters only the shape of acts, the shape of intentions and the thoughts of souls. Be these high, they know it, to mirror thoughts of Gods. Polish slate to clear act and choose for clear and higher selves to come and may his thought enter every moment. Act for my future selves—be better, higher born: for worlds change; self is eternal.

27. World that is known builds from thought. As seer, it is unlearned, forgotten. As sword wielder, I cut it free. Cleansed of talk, I confront the world. My talk deconstructed, I float without anchor in the eternal. Much is beyond thought. The Galdur has no end, for the Gods are without end and advance also. Cultivate awareness: reach for godhood. There is no truth, but there are truths. What is real we create as do the unseen.

28. Without ideas is drawn by the Norns and inner sight to experience. The gunnar invents in every instant, unencumbered by thought. Without knowing, everything shines anew, every moment. Without knowing, all is lived, not thought into being. Without knowing, all is fresh, and the day's path to stream yet is filled with surprise, with wonder. Patience to the hunter his pursuit, quiet treading. The fisher-folk of silent waves and sun on water see. The gunnar, he by careful moment given, invents each moment, invents his life anew.

29. Impeccable and earnest, warriors come to battle for meaning. Some men of arms but most were in any work but war. Found only battle, urgency, fear, pain, squalor. Found small friend-circles to bind same-chosen hardships and there found meaning.

Still the father threshed, the mother baked. Still the younger carved the wooden bowl and spoon. Filthy and hurt, his pike he hung by fire, hollow his cheeks. What meant, what *known*, the same, the threshing, the pot for water to stream, what meant was how he came again, and that was all. The same place began anew, rich in remembered valor, with the scythe he wend.

30. Eight steps to be godord, yes, but few the journey make. For all there is the eight steps advancing in your state. First, have long sight over many lifetimes, be still and listen, ask her and listen what is not from past fulfilled. Second, live with passionate attainment, for outside reflects within and matters well resolved do bring to peace. Third, do fully the mind apply, yet with full detachment, for never man knows all the winds and currents. Fourth, cultivate noble character, helpful, kind when can be. Fifth, with compassionate bearing, help all ascend upward by example, goad, or teaching. Sixth, make full intention through higher plans and seek their completion. Seventh, cultivate stillness apart and in the core of the business of living. Eighth, create openness to Powers, openness to forces unseen, full know what moves beneath the flux of worlds.

31. At a crossroads camped many diverse men at the summer-high sun. Godi cooked for the lot of them, cleared the vessels and sat. At field's edge apart from camp, he hew the willow branch of creek near road. Strange shapes cut and the plowman said had a glow. "Only cuckoo's day's sun," said a merchant. "With his thoughts, made it thus," offered a maid.

Next morn's light, he stood at hill's edge. Like tree with ancient branches, blown by storm or bent by frost, then still and stared. Glanced over, far to see and said the smoke-meat, "He watches over the shrubs, how silly!" Heard this the houseman's daughter, "No, da, the small ones sport where he does look—canst not see 'em?" And both were right.

At the next road to Uppsala, a miller saw him and remembered as he and son the full sacks wend to market. Another encampment, he sat at water's edge, high sun to's back, and clear the sky. "Feel it tremble," spoke the miller, and fell silent. "But distant cloud-fire," said the son, and both were right. At fire that eve, all knew the godi but none knew his years. The eldest of the market road knew him when a youth—he hoary then, nor whence he came. None could guess—he would not tell, as he to hof wended.

32. Great compassion is a transformation. Freya's tears and Tyr's gripped fist changed

ages in greater and smaller lives. Compassion is power. Great is Heimdall's axe, red-flashing. In superb compassion Thor his great sword wields. Neither from anger, nor from hate does the hawk overfly the field to search for vermin.

Great compassion, like higher love is for the evolved only. Higher life is hardness, the hardness of sea-winters and fields, the forests and squares. In its busyness, its reaching for the world, the higher man overreaches. Who stomachs not the struggle withdraws, deludes from his own I-ness, which thinks itself beyond the world and draws apart. The higher man in struggle is at peace, treats with compassion where is meet and with the talon when is needed.

33. Completeness is the shrouds well tied, the chamber well swept and ordered, and the child full-taught. Wholeness is the spine relaxed, the life well thought, with winter's stores dried and hung.

Fulfillment is the son grown to father, the daughter to mother, and the ship coursing home. Final is the purpled haze of Shedding-time, beech leaf fallen and the warrior's self-known last moment. Completion is the knock released from its grip, the message sealed and sent, the fork behind on the path taken. Hold not to the

doing, nor the making. Create and release, work, plan, prepare, for there is wholeness, but after that, *allow*, and never expect.

34. Grounding is the well fleshed horse a' pastured, the grave-barrow with blue glow, and the stones stood 'neath at four points. Weary but full comes the fisherman home from his trawl and bowman the day's hunt. Complete and whole the warrior without wound from axe field, or the wife, taut-bellied to labors.

35. Fulfilled the pilot who senses the rocks near placid coast or the wayfarer who the highwayman intuits to change his course. Fulfilled the gleaner who knows dry day to harvest. Fulfilled and complete who knows a fellow's needs and fills them—when each for each does, *friend* it is called. Complete is the one with much given to high and noble act, yet needs but little, her shall the Gods fulfill.

36. Beneath waves, within wind, all is motion. Fastness is what I think to see it still and understand. The Gods change, like moon upon waves, we reflect them. Within flux, Ginnungagap called out for order, and it spake Knakve. When its awareness shined upon the sky-sent sons of Heimdall, when

oaks and ashes, speech and mind were given, called they out for order and spake it, Tyr. Beneath, had always been an order, though none divined it, at the heart of storm and birthing of worlds, always the first, Ginnungagap.

37. Before fish are laid to dry is the thought. Before the thatch is laid over is the thought. Silent she weaves between cottages, selling loaves, the Deep-Minded. Between the busyness of life is contemplation. No unnecessary actions, no frivolous occupations, no idle chatter, pleasant but aloof from gossip, erect and alert she goes—who knows her age? The superior woman. Between cottages, between chores, her inner world, the silent marsh at road's edge, silent passes. Between the business is the thought. Before the fire, while others stare like beast, is her contemplation. After linen and wool are on grasses dried in sun before the brook is contemplation. In the hof early and at the stones, with time picked from between the business of life is her meditation. She is not a healer. She is not a seer, but those who seek advice find that she tells well the knots of a man's decision.

38. None should too much hoard: great ownings of some beget great misery by most, and none should have too little. All from the market road, the tavern hour should have, and plenty. From windows should women lean and talk together, and men at shores ere the nets be gathered. By the huntsman's fire is the talk that long endures in ear.

A new road the royal council declared, new markets would bring and great goods from the coast, would all grow in weal. Rather came more beggar and landless merchant, crawled o'er the work camp. And came more brigands to work the road and the toll-takers too. All ended we had less than more. Weal is but for few together banded, the same as chat by nets or hunting's plan. Few to share is weal, for much is not needed, nor by the knobby knees of soulless men. Weal is that done well by few, with few to share and weal is time and talk before late windows and early cups.

39. Another's land wist not, said she from the peaceful land. All councils, unpaid, sit to serve, time given after duties, need no taxes save to build when all have need. They built the quay and some brought bread. Others their carts with sand, some of stone, and some brought rope, did the Frisians. These and their labors given built quay, roads, and hofs. No tax needed they,

nor slaves, nor wars. Great owning creates great dearth and high-paid councils brings the death or armed peasants' sons.

In the peaceful land, all owned roundeal, though all owned different, and none owned another, but only worked *with*. The foldakona, she wove wool and raised her lamp to Frya [Freya]. The augerman with leaves and roots the foaming crock tends. In the peaceful land, each her advantage is yet another's too.

40. Happy he dug barrow as the face flushed pale and blood left more. He was not sad, went to the hill that his mound be seen. "These clothes," he said, "to the wooden maid I give," and waited in the happy hours, though leaves took care, for the death-ship's tide. Feared not the wayfarer of skins and oar the sky stroke or the roiling, coiled beast. Happy he goes to storm and wise, the waves, her daughters' dance—puts out all thought, great ocean mind, was called, eyes gray and deep who said before the hill and he hard climbed, "This voyage but begets another."

41. In the eastern wood, he tracked, was ill and wasted. Sky overshadowed his plan of march and thorns had torn the flesh. On the dry bed he climbed ice-free, a narrow passage, then disputed by bear. Bloodied he smelt, weak he seemed. No way to flee, he threw his life away. His staff he seized and made *pure act* beyond fear, beyond hunger, the huntsman knew fear. He went on and beyond fear lay panic. He moved through panic, came detachment. Released pain, fatigue, and detachment, came he to *resolution*. Drove the wind-broke oak rod deep to innards, not waiting, without the moment's thought. In pure act of resolution he threw his life away and thereby won it.

42. From groans of maid and swain do the shudders of the low chair come. There is a deference to maidly brightness, yet wraps the shuttered gossip about the shuffle footed crone. Strength of bow and staff is first conscripted, first the stout son; foeman's iron will feel. Fine curves of prow cargoes, worms, and scratched at rocks are ruined, so the maid her form brings child, the form to fade. Elder the warrior oozing—scarred and gap-toothed the soothing ale, gone the splendid youth the battle quickly ruined. Only the wit sharpens long past the eyes are dull. Only the hammered hide rings strong long past the arm lifts the smithy's sledge. Mind and soul alone will time alloy.

43. Potter at her fire stared but briefly. White-hot the ox it blew. Away she looked and the black fire saw. Mariner reckoned his way by star and moon, looked upon her and the dark ring saw. Took in the darkness, silent after watch, and sweated out the power. Crewmen cried "moonstruck" or "fool," as warm coasts plied and slapped their arms. He was unbit whom the dark power oozed out, a yew its resin. Alone in the stone-hut the herder saw not his fair face these many weeks, far beneath the maidens' shields. He turned from the fire and warmed the back. He opened to the great eye and the black sun rose.

44. On the voyage bread soured on the spots of rage. In the voyage peas and barley emptied. The one ate of the dew, as others famished, and sat eyes upward, then closed. Rubbed his belly those long days as others perished. Breathed deeply the fogs with ale and water gone, as others from fog huddled. In the cove he walked the surf while others lay and groaned, did Aegir's man.

45. Frey's man at harvest went out with girl-child gathering barley. Bronze-armed and strong, he had scythed: they gathered and tied the sheaves. In a shade of stack he paused to tell her of Gods, of kings, of ships, memories from him flowed whilst she lay her head on his hard shoulder in the late-noon heat.

Freya's dame stoked the hearth, bread baking, while the stout son split wood. A highwayman came as beggar, came to rob. With outstretched bowl he reached the gate over to seize the antlered grip. She without stop split his skull e'en as he seized it.

Happy the maid of valor and the swain of peace. Their young shall prosper and their mated powers increase. Happy the fox who climbs the berry bush when hare is scarce. Well is the wheelwright who hunts the winter marsh. Well is the potter who loaves bakes beside his wares. Pleasing to the Gods is the father who shines on his young like the sun, with play and speech oft given. Pleasing to the Goddesses the mother who takes her lass to haft and steel, to cooperage and thatch. For the Wise One [Odin] says, "Folk are everywhere by halves." And the half lost, must the other one soon learn.

46. Twelve years at rope, sail, and helm, the weathered face made good to mariner's craft, and knew the secret rudder of far routes. Came another to toil at sea, who saw himself at once a leader of crews, but had

not the hard gales and lonely stars for companions.

So came to Thing one who had talked his dream, knew much ere he learned the Gods. The hoary gydja, her knowing came of long hearing and longer recitation, all the ways of Gods and men, for knowledge asks a barter, but the self-important would ever lead the Thing though little knowing. Seven years before the wind a captain makes. Eight steps makes the godi. First, hear of the old ones, know what has gone before. Second, seek solitude in quiet, green places, or in fells and crags to prove runes. Third, journey foodless, sleepless, past the world of men, and seek quiet moment for the voice of Gods. Fourth, return to loom, plow, or flock, doing busy in the ways of men, and seek quiet moment for the voice of Gods. Fifth, act as seer, warrior, caster of the stones of Wyrd, as healer or as scribe. Sixth, reach and bring another to the Thing, godord to train. Seventh, to the world of men apply the Thing-spoken wisdom. Eighth, learn and live the herder's stone hut and the crossroads of men, at once in both and speak the Thing. Seven years the lad to master of the ship and eight who would be master of godly whale-path, the harbors of mind.

47. One walks bent with age soon enough. Bent and broken with care, the warrior is his folk. The lonely border watch, the snows ere short poppies and lupines break the steppe. Bowed with concern the leader, godi, and seer. The knight straightens in the act, like a well-strung bow, he launches cares. Bent ill is the man who shoots not forth his acts. Like a marmot, the face of the man, who, after many years but uses his paws to gather and his teeth to gnaw, full cheeked and beady-eyed the man who lives as squirrel. The knight is neither bent nor rat-faced—is fully formed, be he godi, merchant, or seer—for any can be knightly.

Bent with heavy limbs the oak. Bent with full nuts the oak. Shading, tall standing, robe of Sif, the oak. Knowing has its costs—full hangs the fruits, low hangs the bough. Who does the work of the Gods in Midgard, let ever her head not bow and her back not sag. Lift straight as Sif's shoot and give shelter. For light of step is the rat and light on wind is the noxious weed. One is food for fox or cat and the other trampled by the goat in shade of noble oak.

48. Some at Thing were amber-men and apart they drew. Flocks were fatted and bartered; sons brought flail and spear: apart

they did not age. Like the crag-tree, there from the grandfather's grandfather's tales, they stayed.

Yet all behind, the island fell to sea: dark ones walked and drove skin ships and never they cared for it all. They had no gold, but each gloried in his own glow and in mountain fastness. Their plant withered but the flower in cool, high place endured, seeing only its beauty, changeless before time.

One ages prior had from the crag descended, Rig-Heimdall sired sons of the North. "This mortal vessel I am not," he declared, "and I will return whenever the times have need. Not the self-reflected flower, I go the seed and glow and fruit, life after life. To my shining-ship bear me, when this time is done."

Some transformed, he said, through time, some in the lust of combat, then released; some transform by kindred minds blended to Powers, and, "I transform through you. Though I die many times to be with you. Some for power, some for perfection, some for their amber sheen, but I transform that you transform, as darts against the gathering gloom. Once I was bended at care," said Rig-Heimdall, "then let it go in my best bow's release. In my quietest stealth and bravest position, took

the field of valor. While others held the shield, I held also the sword."

49. At market came the man of power, only a glimpse, to stare, then he fades from sight. Simple lives the vitki and none may know where. His sons upon the hawk's path flown, he tends far borders, rushes, fens. He quickly speaks out his staves, for who have not will envy. Who envy will wound with the tongue or harm with the spear. He finds those who will counsel, does the man of power: none find him, nor is he known to others but as a herder of swine. As the woolen men were about with men-of-arms he reached into his cart, "Mats of rushes! Well-woven mats of rushes!"

50. Others huddled at the storm. She went about in simple thread; hands raised to Erde or Tyr, stood still, tall, proud, palms opened. Others took to shade but in the heat of day she tread slowly. Others made busy in the night, but she gazed to the dark heart at the arch of trees. Others huddled warm, when barefoot in the snow she trekked. Freedom in cold, freedom in hard, freedom is in simple hardships found.

51. The youth thought him mad. He gazed into shadows in the noon slumber of high

summer. In the snow he sat or stood until it melted about. At the marsh he sat, rubbed the juice of roots about to keep biters away, yet stayed and sat. Now and then one sees him. A boy asked of him, why gaze or sit? The hermit answered, "Much do we do between birth and death, and most of it no matter. In all that Grimnir-Odin does, he becomes aware. When he hung upon the tree, he became aware. When he bade Mimir speak, he was aware. Much passes between birth and death. What means any of it, I am not aware?"

But how, asks the youth, is to gaze to be aware? "In each place and force a spirit dwells before me, after me, and always. They show me the world before me and after me. They have shown me our world at the time of hidings, when the people of stones and the people of oaks, when the folk of staves and ravens, are banished, and they show me we shall return again, in the night after the next Sigurd." Now and again, folk see him at marsh or skerry stone and none think him mad.

52. Even among good folk come disputes. Before the Thing may be brought, but first in the common-house before elders. Ere wind bend the trees and rains the field's fair face's smoothness line, much is endured and much more learned. Go thence to elders. If between kin, the common ancestor has gone before, ask always that same from the Living Acre be present; failing this, seek next who dwells behind. If between kins, let each an elder attend and together seek the counsel of the Gods. Should not resolve, the elders looked, godi, gydja, seer, ask to guide their way and make new choice beyond each position. Fails this, then matters wend before the Thing, where Forseti and Odin, Saga-Idun and the Norns sit as matters come to elders of many kin as sit in council wise.

53. She went to the well early to draw for potation of wormwood, for his head was still in his cups, the light of day did wound. She earlier chopped weed, for he could not. He tended not the ox and it feasted bloatweed. No ox to cart, no cart to haul, no eggs to market, though the children took from nest.

In the talk of markets, another ask, how could she suffer thus? The frau quoth, "You must endure. You must be a warrior in life." The gydja, near trading her beads, replied it was false to be a warrior in life 'less first a warrior you be in *choice*. "The warrior's choice first make," saith she, "the good steel to arms, the high ground to hold, the early march on slumbered foe. To fight well who choose poor position is fool more than fighter. Well picks the spearman his ground and the bowman his hillock. Then fight well who must. The stubborn wight an ill-chosen stand may make. For warriors be ignorant or old, but rarely both."

54. Dark was the storm in the east. Dark were the riders, short with horsetail hair. Where they took land are folk as *burnt*. From the horseman keep your daughters, and from the horseman's sons. From the skin house princess, keep your sons, for they go not to streams and drink sour milk.

Where now they trade and farm, are heads like hares, short, swart like elves—beware. Look only to the light of us, the fair browed, whose brows do not meet. Look only to the tall of us, strong going and high minded. Look only to the fair-minded and clever, good at trading stave and equal of temper. Look for the quiet and earnest or the well spoke or sincere. Here seek they maid and swain. Though some be comely too, the dark with dark belong as geese by feathers nest else all is confused.

Once we were all of flax and heather; that was in grandmother's days. Then came from the east in father's time, making the half-dark. Now dark with flax and either with half-dark till neither wood duck nor goose remain.

55. Two brothers were as courted two sisters, both toothsome swains. The Binder held all that he had be it fit or not, but Free Fisted held only were it weal. Binder courted the lass whose bright smile and full form promised strong youths, but her water was foul, for too oft sailed and loved not but her slated face. When tired or fled she, with magic, he by her hair bound her, or stick made to keep her. From Goddess his wish, and bound her fast.

Free Fisted found her sister much the same, and set her free. He slept alone, while Binder made a goodly home for stout children. Often they fought and never was it kempt and never peaceful. Soon they slept apart did Binder and Foul. Free Fisted went long years alone. When he met Fine Spirit, he did not seize her. Though they drew water at the same stream, each smiled, but carried skins apart. They met again and grew to court, to happy home and happy stout child. They prosper at the Mother' hearth, the house in peace.

56. The hooded robed came and we hid in forests to Thing. Dark soldiers they brought from the south so we speak in barns and hid

the two horses amid rushes. From him they stole land, for he would no tax. From him they fined goats, for he would not tithe. Land gone, he settled the vik between the holder's grants.

They would not suffer him to hunt, so weirs and traps he set. Since spring thaws o'er the low hearth flowed, he with sons built on poles, thatched high. The rich taxed his foot upon their trail, so he make float to town. Then skins and fish he brought to market could not sell, be they not blest by the hooded ones, thus he bartered for grain and cloth. Offered they to "save" him, would say at barter; but he wot not and to the Gods was ever true. What they took never he stopped, but made anew. What they dammed he flowed around like waters of first budding. The runes go far now from the land of men, for the new priests are barons and the new kings heavily tax and many

in chains. Those who pray not with them and wot not 1 of 4 their sheep and bushels must with Ull the wild hunt join and pick Frigga's down.

Darkness comes, the carts of cut stone hauled by tax slaves for the hooded ones to build. Runes you shall speak man to man and woman to woman, shall whisper true to grandson brave. Turn to the heath and know it, for beyond this time, Sigurd shall rebirth to us, yet many his dragons and fierce then, say the gydja. Slay he or be slain, the sons of his warriors shall set to the shaven wood again our way. Until then speak it to moon, to heath, to hidden men in places remote. Speak to star and perfect every word where naught hear but whose mind blend with mind. In this time shall speak it oft and truly that in far time it be little changed before it come to birch again.

Glossary

A

Adal (A-dal) "Descendant." One of Jarl's sons with Erna-Drott, a brother of Kon.

Adils (A-dils) "Ruler," "Judge." Another name of Ull.

Aefinrunes (AI-vin-roons) "Eternal Runes." Runes which Heimdall taught humans, believed to be related to religious laws and doctrines.

Aegir (AIG-ir) "The Frightening," "The Terrible." A sea-Etin, identical to Gymir, made to hold a feast in his hall every year for the Gods, near harvest time. With his wife, Ran-Gullveig, he is father of Gerd and the nine Giantesses who are representatives of the waves.

Aegishelm (AIG-is-hehlm) "Terror-Helm." Originally, this was a magical helmet worn to inspire fear in one's foes, probably created by Ivaldi's sons as part of the the Niflung Hoard. It was then worn by Fafnir, and then by Hod, who obtained it from Fafnir's hoard.

Aepir (AIP-ir) "Roarer." The name used by the Etins for the wind.

Aesir (AIS-ir) sing. **As** (AHS) "The Gods." The highest of the divine clans; primarily, though not solely, deities of valor and protection. See As.

Aeti (AIT-i) "Eaten." The name used by the Etins for grain.

Aettarsfylgja (AIT-ars-veelg-ya) "Clan-Fylgja," "Clan-Accompanier." A type of fylgja particularly devoted to the protection of the clan or tribe.

Afi (AV-i) "Grandfather." Husband of Amma and progenitor of the class of Karls or freeborn.

Agnar (AG-nar) "Dreadful-Combatant." 1) A brother of Geirrod. 2) A kinsman of Auda, whom Hild gave victory in battle against Odin's wishes.

Ai (AH-i) "Great-Grandfather." 1) One of the Dwarves who worked under Dvalin-Sindri's guidance. 2) Husband of Edda, progenitor of the class of Thralls.

Al (AL) "Awl." A brother of Brokk, an awl who was used to puncture Loki's lips in order to sew them up.

Aldafather (ALD-a-fah-<u>th</u>er) "The Ancient Father." A name of Odin.

Aldagaut (ALD-a-gout) "The Ancient Goth." A name of Odin.

Aldland (ALD-land) Old Frisian "The Ancient Land," "The Old Land." Identical to Singastein, this land sunk because a celestial being (Od) was slain on it (by Hadding). This sinking represented the end of "The Ancient Time" (Ar Aldr), where the Gods interacted with humans more.

Aldrunes (ALD-roons) "Runes of Earthly Life." The runes taught by Heimdall to humans, believed to be connected to concepts of religious law and doctrine.

Alf (AHLV) "Elf." 1) Name of an Alf, identical to Ivaldi. 2) Alf inn Gamla (the Old) is also an Alf who helped Egil at the battle of Svarinsmound.

Alfar (AHLV-ar) sing. **Alf** (AHLV) "Elves." The third of the Teutonic divine families, who are the Aesir, Vanir, and Alfar. To this can be added the higher clan of the Etins, born of Ymir's arms. The Alfar take on a lower status as demigods when they are born, but this can change. They are the sworn helpers of the Gods, the greatest nature artists and heroes.

Alfarin (AHLV-ar-in) "Fire-Elf." Name of an Etin. Many Alfar and Etins names are related or interchangeable, probably due to the rebellion of Surt's clan.

Alfheim (AHLV-haym) "Elf-Home." The land of the Alfar, located on the eastern edge of Jormungrund. Frey, God of the harvest, received Alfheim as a "toothfee," a tooth-gift, and consequently became ruler over the Alfar.

Alfrik (AHLV-rik) "Elf-Ruler." Another name of Brokk, one of the Dwarves who helped forge Freya's Brisingamen, along with many other treasures.

Alfrodul (AHLV-ruhd-ul) "Elf-Beam." Another name for Sol and Sunna (see).

Alfskot (AHLV-skawt) "Elf-Shot." The arrows used by the Alfar which cause sickness to those who are struck by them.

Algreen (AL-green) "All-Green." Another name of Midgard.

Ali (AHL-i) "Warrior." 1) Another name of Vali. 2) Another name of Od.

Allfather (AL-fah-<u>ther</u>) "The Father of All." A name of Odin.

Allheim (AHL-haym) "Eel-Home." The name used by the Etins for the sea.

Alskir (AL-skeer) "All-Bright." The name used by the Asasynir (here identical to the Asmegir) for the sun.

Alsvart (AL-svart) "All-Black." An Etin.

Alsvid (AL-svid) "All-Swift." 1) One of Sol's horses. 2) An Etin.

Althjof (AL-thyohv) "All-Thief." A Dwarf.

Alvaldi (AL-vald-i) "High-Ruler." Another name of Ivaldi.

Alveig (AL-vayg) "All-Drink," "High Woman." Egil's sister and betrothed, after Groa and Sif are taken from him. Kon, whom she was truly in love with, then takes her from him. She and Kon had many children, and founded many of the most famous clans.

Alvis (AL-vis) "All-Wise." A Dwarf who tries to court Thor's daughter, Thrud, but is tricked by Thor through a series of questions until the sun comes up, which Alvis, as a Svartalfr, is averse to.

Ama (AM-a) "Nuisance." A Giantess.

Amalians (AM-al-i-ans) "Descendants of Hamal." One of the legendary clans of the North.

Ambat (AM-baht) "Maidservant." One of the daughters of Thrall and Thy.

Amgerd (AHM-gerd) "The Gerd (Bride) of Am," "Creator of Darkness." A Giantess.

Amma (AM-a) "Grandmother." The wife of Afi and ancestress of the class of Karls or freeborn.

Am (AHM) "Darkness," "Black." An Etin.

Amsvartnir (AHM-svart-nir) "The Ever-Dark." The sea enveloped in eternal darkness, lying outside Nastrand, in the gulf where the island Lyngvi is located. This is where Loki, Fenrir, and other Sons of Muspel-Loki lie imprisoned until Ragnarok.

An (AHN) "Second," "Other." A Dwarf.

Anar (AHN-ar) "Second," "Other." 1) Another name of Hoenir, also called Fjorgyn, father of Frigga with Natt. 2) A Dwarf.

Andhrimnir (AND-reem-nir) "Spirit-Rime." The cook of Valhall.

Andlang (AND-lang) "Long and Wide." One of the nine heavens.

Andvaranaut (AND-var-a-nout) "Andvari's Gift." A magical ring forged by Volund, which has properties identical to Draupnir.

Andvari (AND-var-i) "Careful One." A Dwarf, probably another name of Egil, who was given Andvaranaut by Volund.

Angeyja (ANG-ay-ya) "She Who Makes the Islands Closer." One of the Etin-maids that turn the Grotti-Mill, the "mill of the skerries," which creates land from Etins' limbs. From this she is also one of Heimdall's nine mothers.

Angerboda (ANG-er-bawd-a) "Grief-Boder." A name of Gullveig.

2) The fourth rune of the Elder Futhark. It represents the Gods, causing it to be linked to ideals of the sacred in the Runelaw.

Ansuz (AN-sooz) Gothic "Asa-God." The fourth rune of the Elder Futhark. It represents the Gods, causing it to be linked to ideals of the sacred in the Runelaw.

Arastein (AR-a-stayn) "Eagle-Stone." The place where Kon rested himself after battling the Swedes.

Arfi (ARV-i) "Heir." One of the sons of Jarl and Erna-Drott, a brother of Kon.

Argjoll (AHR-gyuhl) "Early-Resounding." Another name of Heimdall's Gjallarhorn, used to wake the Gods.

Argud (AHR-gud) "Harvest-God." Another name of Frey.

Ari (AR-i) "Eagle." An Etin, in eagle-guise, who creates wind with his wings. He has his perch in Niflhel.

Arinnefja (AR-in-ehv-ya) "Cooking-Maid." One of the daughters of Thrall and Thy.

Arnhofdi (ARN-huhv-di) "Eagle-Headed." A name of Odin.

Artali (AHR-tal-i) "Teller of Time." The name used by the Alfar for Mani (Moon).

Arvak (AHR-vak) "Early-Waker." One of Sol's horses, the other is Alsvid.

As (AHS) "God." A name of Odin.

Asaburgh (AHS-a-burg) "Asa-Burgh," "Asa-Citadel," "Citadel of the Gods." Another name of Asgard.

Asabrag (AHS-a-brag) "The Foremost As." Another name of Thor.

Asafather (AHS-a-fah-<u>ther</u>) "Asa-Father," "Father of the Aesir." Another name of Odin.

Asagod (AHS-a-gawd) "God of the Aesir." A God of the Aesir clan.

Asasynir (AHS-a-seen-ir) "Asa-sons," "Sons of the Aesir." 1) The sons of Odin, or the Aesir in general. 2) The Asmegir, the humans in Odainsacre that will repopulate the world after Ragnarok, they are the "sons" of Baldur and Hod.

Asathor (AHS-a-thohr) "Thor of the Aesir." Another name of Thor.

Asatru (AHS-a-troo) "Faith in the Aesir." A modern name for the religion of our forefathers, recently established out of necessity. Also called Odinism, Theodism, Irminism, and Forn Sed.

Asbridge (AHS-brij) "Bridge of the Aesir." Another name of Bifrost.

Asgard (AHS-gard) "Court of the Aesir." In its widest meaning, the world in Yggdrasil's upper branches where the Aesir live. In its strictest sense, the area inside Asgard's walls, where Valhall and the other halls of the Aesir are found.

Asgardsride (AHS-gards-rīd) "The Ride of Asgard." Also called Odin's Wild Jagt, it is the hunt in which Allfather-Odin and other Aesir and Einherjar round up demons in the sky. It takes place at Yule.

Asgates (AHS-gayts) "Gates of the Aesir." The gates of Asgard, also called Thrymgjoll and Valgrind.

Asgaut (AHS-gout) "God of Goths." Another name of Odin.

Ask (ASK) "Ash." Mankind's progenitor, fashioned from an ash tree and given life by Odin, Hoenir, and Lodur.

Aslidar (AHS-lid-ar) "Descendants of the Aesir." Another name of the Asmegir.

Asmegir (AHS-mehg-ir) "Children of the Aesir." Lif, Leifthrasir, and their descendants who dwell in Odainsacre under the tutelage of Baldur and Hod until Ragnarok.

Asmund (AHS-mund) "God-Gift." A king in ancient Svithjod, son of Freya and Od.

Asvin (AHS-vin) "Asa-Friend." Another name of Mimir.

Asynja (AHS-en-ya) pl. **Asynjur** (AHS-en-yur) "Goddess." A Goddess of the Aesir.

Atla (AT-la) "The Awful-Grim Maiden." A Giantess, one of the nine mothers of Heimdall who turns the Grotti-mill.

Atli (AT-li) "The Fierce." 1) Another name of Thor. 2) An ancient warrior.

Atridi (AT-reed-i) "Attacker by Horse." Another name of Frey.

Atrid (AT-reed) "Attacker by Horse." Another name of Odin.

Auda (OUD-a) "The Wealthy." A Swanmaid and Goddess of vegetation. Also called Hladgud Swanwhite, sister of Idun (Hervor Alhvit). She was married to Slagfin-Gjuki, then married Baldur's son, Forseti.

Audhumla (OUD-hum-la) "The Hornless Wealth-Cow." The primordial aurochs created out of ice from Ginnungagap, who fed Ymir with her teats and formed Buri by licking the ice or rime of the creation.

Aud (OUD) "The Wealthy." Another name of Njord.

Audun (OUD-un) "Friend of Fate." Another name of Odin.

Aurboda (OUR-bawd-a) "Gold-Liquor." Another name of Gullveig.

Aurgelmir (OUR-gehlm-ir) "Clay-Roarer." Another name of Ymir, who rose up from the melted rime in the mud of Jormungrund. This name is similar to another epithet of his, Leirbrimir "Clay-Etin."

Aurglasir (OUR-glas-ir) "Mud-Glasir." A name for the part of Yggdrasil below ground, related to Glasir (see), which denotes its being covered by the sacred mud of the Underworld, which turns its roots white. See also Vedurglasir.

Aurgrimnir (OUR-greem-nir) "Mud-Grimnir." An Etin.

Aurkonung (OUR-kawn-ung) "Mire-King." Another name of Hoenir, as representative of storks.

Aurnir (OUR-nir) "Rock-Dweller." Another name of Egil.

Aurr (OUR) "Mud." The name used by the "Supreme Powers" for the earth.

Aurvandill (OUR-van-dil) "The One Busy With Arrows." Another name of Egil.

Aurvandilstoe (OUR-van-dils-toh) "Aurvandill's Toe." A star created by Thor from Egil-Aurvandill's frozen toe.

Aurvangaland (OUR-vang-a-land) or **Aurvanga Sjot** (OUR-vang-a SYUHT) and **Aurvangar** (OUR-vang-ar) "The Land of the Clayey Plains." The primeval homeland of the Teutons, the southernmost region of the Scandinavian Peninsula, modern day Skåne.

Aurvang (OUR-vang) "Mud-Field." A Dwarf.

Austri (OUST-ri) "East." One of the four Dwarves who hold up the corners of the sky formed from Ymir's skull.

B

Bafur (BAHV-ur) "Bean." A Dwarf.

Bakrauf (BAK-rouv) "Robber-Bitch." A Giantess.

Baldur (BALD-ur) "The Bright," "The Glorious." The God of summer, justice, kindness, and compassion; son of Odin and Frigga. Husband of Nanna, the moon Goddess.

Baleyg (BAHL-ayg) "Fiery-Eyed." Another name of Odin.

Banings (BAN-ings) "The Destroyers," "The Corruptors." Loki's sons and clan folk.

Bara (BAHR-a) "The Wave," "Billow." One of Aegir-Gymir's daughters with Ran-Gullveig, representative of the wave.

Bari (BAR-i) "The Bearing." A Dwarf.

Barn (BARN) "The Descendant." One of the sons of Jarl and Erna-Drott, brother of Kon.

Barnstokk (BARN-stawk) "Child-Trunk." The ancient Guardian Trees that protect the family, clan, and community.

Barr (BAR) "Barley," "Corn." The name used by the Gods for grain.

Barri (BAR-i) "Pine-Copse." The quiet grove, where Gerd agreed to meet Frey for their wedding.

Baugi (BOUG-i) "Ring." An Etin.

Baugregin (BOUG-rehg-in) "Artisan of Gold Rings." Another name of Mimir.

Beinvid (BAYN-vid) "Big-Bone," "Wide-Bone." An Etin.

Beitur (BAYT-ur) "The Caustic." An Etin.

Beli (BEHL-i) "The Bellower,""The Howler." Ruler of the Etin clan to which Volund surrendered Frey and who received Freya from Gullveig.

Bergelmir (BER-gehlm-ir) "Roaring Bear." Another name of Hrimnir, son of Thrudgelmir and grandson of Aurgelmir-Ymir.

Bergrisar (BERG-ris-ar) sing. **Bergrisi** (BERG-ris-i) "Mountain-Giants." A race of Etins.

Berkano (BERK-an-o) "Birch." The eighteenth rune of the Elder Futhark, generally associated with motherhood. The pictograph or "stave" (*stafr*) is thought to represent a pregnant woman's swollen breasts and belly. The word may be etymologically associated with "Bjarg" (see Bjargrunes below), which is why it is connected to marriage and parenting in the Runelaw.

Berling (BER-ling) "Builder." Another name of Bari, one of the Dwarves who forged Brisingamen.

Berserk (BER-serk) pl. **Berserks** (BER-serks) "Bear-Shirt Wearer." A warrior well known in the ancient North, greatly feared by their enemies, for they would go into a violent battle frenzy that would make them seem invincible.

Bestla (BEHST-la) "Bast-Cord," "Tree-Bark." The primordial mother of the Gods, and first ancestress of the higher Etin clan. With Bur she had the sons Odin, Hoenir, and Lodur. She and her brother Mimir were born from the sweat of Ymir's arm, which was filled with the creative rime he had received through Audhumla's milk.

Beyla (BAY-la) "Milkmaid." Wife of Frey's servant Byggvir, who tends the Grotti-mill's meal, made of the limbs of Etins, and spreads it over the earth.

Biflindi (BIV-lind-i) "Spear-Shaker." Another name of Odin.

Bifrost (BIV-ruhst) "The Trembling Way." The bridge that connects Asgard to Jormungrund, the Milky Way.

Bifur (BIV-ur) "Quaking One." A Dwarf.

Bikki (BIK-i) "Foe," "Opponent." Another name of Loki.

Bil (BIL) "Moment." Another name of Idun.

Bild (BEELD) "Plowman." A Dwarf.

Bileyg (BIL-ayg) "One-Eyed." Another name of Odin.

Billing (BIL-ing) "The Twin (of Delling?)." Lord of the sunset glow. Ruler of the Varns, who protect Sol and Mani from the wolves that pursue them. He is Rind's father and Vali's grandfather.

Bilrost (BIL-ruhst) "Bil's (Idun's) Way." Another name of Bifrost.

Bilskirnir (BIL-skeern-ir) "The Bright-Shining." The name of Valhall before the age of war came.

Bjar (BYAHR) "The Bearing." Another name of Bari, one of the Dwarves who forged Brisingamen.

Bjargrunes (BYARG-roons) "Help-Runes." A class of runic prayers used in healing and childbirth.

Bjart (BYART) "Splendor," "The Shining." One of Njord and Frigga's daughters, a sister and maidservant of Freya.

Bjorgolf (BYURHG-ohlv) "Mountain-Wolf." An Etin.

Bjorn (BYURHN) "Bear." 1) A name of Thor. 2) A name of Hod.

Bjor (BYOHR) "Beer." The name used by the Aesir for ale.

Blain (BLAH-in) "Dark-Hued." 1) A Dwarf. 2) Another name of Ymir, whose limbs were used to create Midgard.

Blak (BLAK) "Black." The name of Hod's horse.

Blapthvari (BLAP-thvar-i) "Chattering-Weapon." An Etin.

Blid (BLEED) "The Blithe." One of Njord and Frigga's nine daughters, a sister and maidservant of Freya.

Blik (BLIK) "The Shining." One of Njord and Frigga's nine daughters, a sister and maidservant of Freya.

Blikjandabol (BLEEK-yand-a-buhl) "Gleaming Disaster." Leikin's bed curtains.

Blindi (BLIND-i) "The Blind." Another name of Odin.

Blind Balewise (BLIND BAYL-wīs) "The Deceptively Cunning." Another name of Loki.

Blodablanda (BLOHD-a-bland-a) "Blood-Blending." A sacred Asatru ceremony where two friends mix their blood in the earth to join together in family bonds.

Blodi (BLOHD-i) "Blood-Kinsman." One who has undergone the rite of Blodablanda with another to join their friendship with family ties.

Blodughofi (BLOHD-ug-hohv-i) "Bloody-Hoof." Frey's horse.

Blodughadda (BLOHD-ug-had-a) "Bloody-Haired." One of Aegir-Gymir's daughters with Gullveig-Ran, who represents the wave.

Blot (BLOHT) "Sacrifice," "Offering." A ceremonial offering to the divine Powers.

Blovur (BLUHV-ur) "The Shining." A Dwarf.

Boddi (BAWD-i) "Head of Household." A son of Karl and Snor.

Bodvild (BUHD-vild) "Warrior Maiden." One of Mimir's daughters with Sinmara, a sister of Natt-Ostara and one of the Ostaras. She was raped by Volund, and consequently had the son Vidga from this.

Bofur (BUHV-ur) "Bean." A Dwarf.

Bogaas (BAWG-a-ahs) "Bow-As." Another name of Ull.

Bokrunes (BOHK-roons) "Book Runes," "Beech Runes." A class of runes, probably used in recording information. In ancient times beech tablets were used to inscribe runes upon and were called "bok," from which we get the word "book."

Bolthorn (BUHL-thawrn) "Bale-Thorn." Another name of Ymir. Cp. Thorn.

Bolverk (BUHL-verk) "Bale-Worker." Another name of Odin, given to him by the Etins.

Bombur (BUHM-bur) "Drummer." A Dwarf.

Borgar (BAWRG-ar) "Defender." Another name of Jarl.

Borghild (BAWRG-hild) "Defending Battle-Maiden." Another name of Drott, mother of Kon.

Bragarfull (BRAG-ar-vul) "Bragi's Cup," "Bragi's Bowl." A vessel of mead on which boasts of past deeds are proclaimed, or oaths to perform future deeds are sworn before drinking.

Bragi (BRAG-i) "The Poet." Son of Odin and Gunnlod, married to Idun.

Bralund (BRAH-lund) "Brow-Grove." The place where Kon was born, possibly modern day Lund.

Brana (BRAN-a) "The Hastening." A Giantess.

Brandingi (BRAND-ing-i) "The Burning." An Etin.

Bratskeg (BRAT-skehg) "Steep-Beard." A son of Karl and Snor.

337

Breidablik (BRAYD-a-blik) "The Far-Shining." Baldur's abode in Mimir's grove, which he shares with Sif, Hod, and the Asmegir until Ragnarok.

Breidurbondi (BRAYD-ur-bohnd-i) "Yeoman." A son of Karl and Snor.

Brimir (BRIM-ir) "Sea," "Sea-Being." 1) A name of Mimir as lord of the fountain ("sea") of wisdom. 2) A name of Mimir's hall that lies near this "sea." 3) A name of Ymir, whose blood was used to create Midgard's sea.

Brimrunes (BRIM-roons) "Sea-Runes." A class of runes used to insure a safe passage at sea.

Brisingamen (BREES-ing-am-en) "The Brising Necklace." Freya's necklace, said to be the most beautiful in all the worlds.

Brisings (BREES-ings) "Fire-Workers." Mimir's sons.

Brokk (BRAWK) "Ruminant." One of the sons of Mimir who created Brisingamen and other treasures for the Gods. Identical to Dainn and Alfrik.

Brud (BROOD) "Bride." A daughter of Karl and Snor.

Bruni (BROON-i) "Bushy-Browed." 1) A name of Odin. 2) A name of Volund.

Brunnacre (BROON-ayk-er) "Bruni's Acre." Volund-Bruni's land in the Ironwood.

Bryja (BREE-ya) "Troll." A Giantess.

Budlungs (BUD-lungs) "Budli's (Danp's) Descendants." A legendary clan of the ancient North.

Bui (BOO-i) "Farmer." A son of Karl and Snor.

Bundinskeg (BUND-in-skehg) "Bound-Beard." A son of Karl and Snor.

Buri (BOOR-i) "Progenitor." 1) Father of Bur and oldest ancestor of the Gods, licked by Audhumla from the ice of creation. 2) A Dwarf.

Bur (BUR) "Son." 1) Son of Buri and father of the Gods through his sons Odin, Hoenir, and Lodur, whom he had with his wife, Bestla. 2) A son of Jarl and Erna-Drott, brother of Kon.

Buseyra (BOOS-ay-ra) "Big-Eared." A Giantess, killed by Thor.

Bygg (BEEG) "Grain." The term used by our ancestors for grain.

Byggvir (BEEG-vir) "Grain-Spirit." Husband of Beyla and distributor of the Grotti-mill's meal as Frey's servant.

Byleist (BEE-layst) "Whirlwind From the East." A storm-Etin, brother of Loki and Helblindi.

Bylgja (BEELG-ya) "Billow." One of Aegir-Gymir's daughters with Gullveig-Ran, who represents the wave.

Byrr (BEER) "Wind." Another name of Volund.

Byrgir (BERG-ir) "Hider of Something." A mead reserve hidden by Surt's son, Fjalar, then retrieved by Ivaldi and taken to Surt, then taken from the Etins by Odin.

Byrgis Argefn (BERG-is AHR-gehv-n) "Byrgir's Harvest-Bringing Goddess." Another name of Idun.

D

Dag (DAG) "Day." 1) Son of Delling and Natt who rides across the sky in his shining chariot drawn by his illuminating steed, Skinfaxi.

Dagaz (DAG-az) Gothic "Day." The twenty-third rune of the Elder Futhark, representing "Day" as the marker of time and a symbol of universal order. For this reason it is connected to our place in this order in the Runelaw.

Dags Vera (DAGS VEER-a) "Day's Haven." The name used by the Dwarves for calm.

Dagsevi (DAGS-ehv-i) "Day's Stillness." The name used by the Alfar for calm.

Dainn (DAH-in) "The Dead." 1) Another name of Brokk, designating him as a representative of death and the afterlife. 2) A hart that feeds on Yggdrasil's leaves.

Danp (DANP) "Bellows Blower." A primeval ruler, father to Jarl's wife and Kon's mother Drott. Danp is the same as Budli, the progenitor of the Budlungs.

Dan Mikillati (DAN MIK-il-aht-i) "Dan the Proud," "The Proud Dane." Another name of Jarl.

Dari (DAHR-i) "The Fortifying." A Dwarf.

Delling (DEHL-ing-r) "The Shining," "The Glittering." The Alf of dawn, father of Dag with Natt. He is the guardian of Breidablik.

Digraldi (DIG-rald-i) "The Fat." A son of Thrall and Thy.

Disir (DEES-ir) "Goddesses." A group of protecting women, female ancestresses, identical to the hamingjas, fylgjas, etc.

Djupan Marr (DYOOP-an MAR) "The Deep Sea." The name used by the Dwarves for the sea.

Dofri (DUHV-ri) "Spear-Thrower." An Etin.

Dokkalfar (DUHK-ahlv-ar) "Dark-Elves." The Alfar of the underground, who are found in many services, including punishing the damned in Niflhel.

Dolgthrasir (DAWLG-thras-ir) "Enemy-Combatant." A Dwarf.

Dolgthvari (DAWLG-thvar-i) "Enemy-Weapon." A Dwarf.

Dori (DOHR-i) "Borer." A Dwarf.

Dorrud (DUHR-ud) "Spear-Fighter." Another name of Odin.

Draug (DROUG) "Outlaw," "One Exiled." A mound-dweller or doppelganger living in a grave or grave-mound. Can be good or evil, depending on their nature before death.

Draug Allvald (DROUG AL-vald) "Ghost Sovereign." Another name of Odin.

Draumjorunn (DROUM-yohr-un) "Dream-Weaver." A name used by the Dwarves for Natt (Night).

Draumkona (DRAUM-kawn-a) "Dream Woman." Another name for the fylgja, who often appears in her favorite's dreams.

Draupnir (DROUP-nir) "The Dropping." 1) A ring forged by Mimir's sons for Odin. Every ninth night it "drops" eight rings of equal value and weight. 2) A Dwarf.

Dreng (DREHNG) "Boy," "Knave." A son of Karl and Snor.

Dresvarp (DREHS-varp) "The Courageous." Another name of Odin.

Drifa (DREEV-a) "Blizzard." Daughter of Snaer.

Drjupansal (DRYOOP-an-sal) "Dripping-Hall." A name used by the Dwarves for heaven.

Dromi (DROHM-i) "Fetter." One of the fetters that Fenrir burst before he was bound with Gleipnir.

Drosull (DRUHS-ul) "Steed" (cp. Yggdrasil). Another name of Skinfaxi.

Drott (DROHT) "Folk-Mistress," "Retinue." 1) Danp's daughter, Jarl's wife, mother of Kon and Hildigir-Hildibrand. 2) A royal court, named after Drott.

Drottins (DROHT-ins) "Folk-Rulers." After Drott, a designation for the highest leaders before they were called "kings" after Kon the Young (Konung= King).

Drottnings (DROHT-nings) "Folk-Mothers." After Drott, a designation of queens.

Drottur (DRUHT-ur) "Loafer." A son of Thrall and Thy.

Drumba (DRUM-ba) "Clumsy." A daughter of Thrall and Thy.

Drumb (DRUMB) "Clumsy." A son of Thrall and Thy.

Dufa (DOOV-a) "Diver." One of the nine daughters of Aegir-Gymir and Ran-Gullveig who represent the waves.

Duf (DOOV) "The Crooked." A Dwarf.

Dulin (DUL-in) "The Reserved." A Dwarf.

Dulsi (DUL-si) "The Proud." Another name of Vilkin, Ivaldi's father.

Dumb (DUMB) "The Dumb." An Etin.

Duneyr (DUN-ayr) "Brown-Ear." A hart that chews on Yggdrasil's leaves.

Durathror (DUR-a-throhr) "Beast of Slumber." A hart that chews on Yggdrasil's leaves.

Duri (DOOR-i) "Slumber." A Dwarf.

Durin (DUR-in) "Slumber." The name of Surt in time's morning, when he was allied with the Gods and Mimir.

Durnir (DUR-nir) "Slumber." Identical to Durin-Surt.

Dvalin (DVAL-in) "The Dormant," "The Sleeping." 1) Mimir's son and one of the most distinguished of the Dwarves artists, identical to Sindri. 2) One of the harts that chew Yggdrasil's leaves.

Dvalins Leika (DVAL-ins LAYK-a) "Dvalin's Playmate." The name used by the Dwarves for Sol (Sun).

Dwarf (DWARF) "Dwarf," "Artisans." The ancient smiths who created objects of fertility and vegetation. These were originally demigods and were not considered to be diminutive of stature.

Dynfari (DEEN-var-i) "Traveling Roar." The name used by the Alfar for the wind.

Dyrar Veigar (DEER-ar VAYG-ar) "Precious Liquids." The purest meads of the Underworld fountains, given to the blessed dead to rejuvenate them and allay any sorrows from their previous life.

E

Edda (EHD-a) "Great Grandmother." 1) Mother of Thrall and ancestress of the class of Thralls. 2) The body of Odinic lore, designated thus to honor the ancestors who passed on the tales.

Eggther (EHG-theer) "Sword-Guardian." A kinsman of Gullveig, who shares her exile in the Ironwood, where she tends her monster herds and guards the Volund-sword, Gambantein, hidden there.

Eggtide (EHG-tīd) "Egg-Tide." The name for May in the Old Norse calendar.

Egil (EHG-il) "Strife." The best of archers. He is Ivaldi's son, Volund and Slagfin's brother, father of Od with his first wife, Groa, and Ull with his second wife, Sif. He was going to marry Alveig after Sif left him for Thor, but he was slain and robbed of her by Kon, who had done this before with Groa.

Ehwaz (EH-vaz) "Horse." The nineteenth rune of the Elder Futhark, related to ideas of friendship and loyalty, which is why it is connected to this in the Runelaw.

Eikin (AYK-in) "Tumultuous." A sacred river.

Eikinskjaldi (AYK-in-skyald-i) "Oaken Shield." A Dwarf.

Eikintjasna (AYK-in-tyas-na) "Gossiper," "Sputterer." One of the daughters of Thrall and Thy.

Eikthyrnir (AYK-theer-nir) "Oak-Stinger." The stag that stands over Valhall.

Eimgeitir (AYM-gayt-ir) "Fire-Goat." An Etin.

Eindridi (AYN-drid-i) "Loner." A name of Thor.

Einherjar (AYN-her-yar) sing. m. **Einheri** (AYN-her-i) sing. f. **Einherja** (AYN-her-ya) "Single-Combatants." Warriors chosen among heroes of our folk to live either in Odin's Valhall or Freya's Sessrumnir.

Einmonth (AYN-muhnth) "Single-Month." The name for March in the Old Norse calendar.

Einvigi (AYN-veeg-i) "Single-Combat." One on one battle between two combatants.

Eir (AYR) "Help." Asynja of healing, Njord and Frigga's daughter, and Freya's sister and maid-servant.

Eirik (AYR-eek) "Higher-Ruler." Another name of Od.

Eistla (AYST-la) "Destroyer." One of Heimdall's nine mothers who turns the Grotti-mill.

Eisurfala (AYS-ur-vahl-a) "Fire-Giantess." A Giantess.

Eitur (AYT-ur) "Poison," "Venom." The drink of the damned, which causes their second death.

Eitri (AYT-ri) "The Venomous." Another name of Sindri.

Eiwaz (AY-vaz) "Yew," "Bow." The thirteenth rune of the Elder Futhark, usually associated with death and dying, leading to its connection to respect for the dead in the Runelaw.

Eldhrimnir (EHLD-reem-nir) "Fire-Rime." The kettle in which Andhrimnir cooks the boar Saehrimnir for the Einherjar.

Eldi (EHLD-i) "Fire-Wood." The name used by the Etins for the forest.

Eldir (EHLD-ir) "Fire-Kindler." Aegir's servant.

Eldur (EHLD-ur) "Fire." 1) The name used by our ancestors for fire. 2) An Etin.

Elhaz (EHL-haz) "Elk," "Defender." The fifteenth rune of the Elder Futhark. It is also called Alciz (AL-keez) and Algiz (AL-giz), a name used to designate Baldur and Hod as defenders of the folk. For this reason, it is connected to such ideas in the Runelaw.

Elivagar (EEL-i-vahg-ar) "Stormy-Rivers." The gulf connecting rivers from the Hvergelmir fountain, by which the Ivaldi clan's home, Ydalir, is located, in Alfheim. This bay, which separates Jotunheim from Midgard, is also called Hronn, Gandvik, and Endil 's (Orvandill-Egil's) Meadow.

Eljudnir (EEL-yud-nir) "Sprayed with Snowstorms," "Damp with Sleet or Rain." Leikin's hall in Niflhel.

Elli (EHL-i) "Old Age." A Giantess, representative of old age.

Ellilyf Asa (EHL-i-leev AHS-a) "The Gods' Remedy Against Old Age." A name for Idun's golden apples, which grow from the World Tree, Yggdrasil.

Embla (EHM-bla) "Mother." The first Teutonic woman, formed by Mimir and Durin from an ash tree, then given life and the divine gifts by Odin, Hoenir, and Lodur.

Endil (EHND-il) "The Opponent." Another name of Egil.

Ennibratt (EHN-i-brat) "High-Browed." Another name of Odin.

Ennilang (EHN-i-lang) "Very Tall." Another name of Thor.

Erde (ERD-eh) Anglo-Saxon "Earth." 1) Another name of Frigga, identical to Jord. 2) An Anglo-Saxon rune honoring Frigga, which is mentioned as a posture (*stada*) in the Hugrunes.

Erna (ERN-a) "The Efficient." Another name of Drott, Jarl's wife and Kon's mother.

Erp (ERP) "The Brownish One." Son of Jonak, brother of Svanhild, Sorli, and Hamdir, killed by his brothers on their way to avenge Svanhild's death.

Etin (EHT-in) Anglo-Saxon "Eater," variant of **Jotun** (YUHT-un) 1) There are two Etin races—the higher born from Ymir's arms, descended from Mimir and Bestla; and the lower born from Ymir's feet, descended from Thrudgelmir. The former are divine and deserve divine honors, the latter are often enemies of the Gods. 2) Name of an Etin.

Eyglo (AY-gloh) "Ever-Glow." The name used by the Etins for Sol (Sun).

Eygotaland (AY-gawt-a-land) "The Goth Islands." A name for the islands of Scandinavia.

Eylimi (AY-lim-i) "He Who Holds the Thorn-Rods (Limar)." Another name of Mani.

Eylud (AY-lood) "The Island Mill." Another name for the Grotti-mill.

Eynaefir (AY-naiv-ir) "Island-Navigator." A sea-king.

Eyrgjafa (AYR-gyav-a) "She Who Creates Sandbanks." One of Heimdall's nine mothers who turns the Grotti-mill. The meal of this mill is used to create land.

F

Fadir (FAD-ir) "Father." Husband of Modir, progenitor of the noble families as father of Jarl and grandfather of Kon.

Fafnir (FAHV-nir) "The Embracer." The serpent killed by Hod to acquire the the Niflung Hoard for the Gods. Later, Christianized stories attributed this to Sigurd.

Fagrahvel (FAG-ra-vehl) "The Fair-Wheel." The name used by the Alfar for Sol (Sun).

Fagraroef (FAG-ra-rurv) "Fair-Roof." The name used by the Alfar for heaven.

Fagrlimi (FAG-r-lim-i) "Fair-Limbed." The name used by the Alfar for the forest.

Fak (FAHK) "Fast." A horse.

Fala (FAHL-a) "Immoral." A Giantess.

Falhofnir (FAL-hohv-nir) "Fal's Fetlocked," "Shaggy Fetlock." Baldur-Fal's horse, who creates fountains by stomping his hooves on the ground.

Fallandaforad (FAL-and-a-vawr-ad) "Pitfall." Leikin's threshold or doorstep.

Fal (FAL) "The Caretaker," "The Defender." 1) Another name of Baldur. 2) A Dwarf.

Farbauti (FAHR-bout-i) "The One Inflicting Harm." An Etin, father of Loki, Byleist, and Helblindi.

Farmagud (FARM-a-gud) "God of Cargoes." Another name of Odin.

Farmatyr (FARM-a-teer) "Cargo-Tyr." Another name of Odin.

Fedja (FEHD-ya) "Tributary." A sacred river.

Fegjafa (FEE-gyav-a) "Wealth-Giver." Another name of Frey.

Fehu (FEH-hu) Gothic "Wealth," "Cattle." The first rune of the Elder Futhark, symbolizing different aspects of wealth, which is why it is connected to this in the Runelaw.

Feima (FAYM-a) "The Shy." A daughter of Karl and Snor.

Feng (FEHNG) "God of Grain." Another name of Odin.

Fenja (FEHN-ya) "Water-Maiden." An Etin-maid associated with the turning of the World-Mill, or the lesser Grotti-mill according to a later saga. She and her sister turn the mill, and are allied with Ivaldi's kin in the great Teutonic wars.

Fenrir (FEHN-rir) "Bog-Dweller," also **Fenriswolf** (FEHN-ris-woolf) "Fenris-Wolf." Son of Loki and Gullveig, bound by the Gods with the fetter called Gleipnir.

Fensalir (FEHN-sal-ir) "Marsh-Halls." Frigga's home in Vanaheim.

Fifl (FEEV-l) "Fool." Another name of Loki.

Fili (FEEL-i) "The One Who Files." A Dwarf.

Fimafeng (FIM-a-vehng) "The Handy." One of Aegir's servants, whom Loki beat to death when he heard of his efficiency and trustworthiness.

Fimbulfambi (FIM-bul-vam-bi) "The Great Fool." The host who does not speak among his guests.

Fimbulsongs (FIM-bul-songs) "The Great Songs." The runes or Galdur-songs.

Fimbulthul (FIM-bul-thul) "Steadily Loud." A sacred river.

Fimbulthul (FIM-bul-thul) "The Great Teacher." Another name of Mimir.

Fimbultyr (FIM-bul-teer) "The Great God." Another name of Odin.

Fimbulwinter (FIM-bul-wint-er) "The Great Winter." There are two "Great Winters": the first took place long ago when Idun, Freya, Frey, and other deities of vegetation were brought into the hands of the powers of frost; when Volund-Thjazi sent violent snowstorms across the worlds. The second will take place right before Ragnarok.

Finn (FIN) "The Finn," "Native of Finland." Another name of Ivaldi.

Finnking (FINN-king) "Finn-King." Another name of Ivaldi.

Fitjung (FIT-yung) "Farmer," "The Wealthy." A man whose sons lost all their wealth.

Fjalar (FYAL-ar) "The Learned." Surt's son who stole some of Mimir's mead to create the Byrgir fountain. Father of Gunnlod. Also called Suttung, Mjodvitnir, Utgardloki, Skrymir.

Fjolkald (FYUHL-kald) "Very Cold." Another name of Ivaldi, grandfather of Od-Vindkald.

Fjolnir (FYUHL-nir) "The Concealer." 1) Another name of Odin. 2) Son of Frey and Gerd.

Fjolsvid (FYUHLS-vid) "Very Wise One." Another name of Odin.

Fjolvar (FYUHL-var) "Glutton." An Etin.

Fjolverk (FYUHL-verk) "Pain-Filled." An Etin.

Fjolvor (FYUHL-vuhr) "Glutton." A Giantess.

Fjorgynn (FYUHR-gen) "Earth." Another name of Frigga.

Fjorgyn (FYUHR-gen) "Earth." Another name of Hoenir, Frigga's father.

Fjorm (FYUHRM) "The Rushing." A sacred river.

Fjosnir (FYOHS-nir) "Stable-Boy." A son of Thrall and Thy.

Flegg (FLEHG) "Cliff-Dweller." An Etin.

Fljod (FLYOD) "Wife." A daughter of Karl and Snor.

Foddik (FAWD-ik) Old Frisian "That Which is Fed." A sacred, perpetual flame, kindled by the Needfire, the friction-fire.

Fold (FAWLD) "Field." A name used by the Aesir for Jord-Frigga (Earth).

Foldakona (FAWLD-a-kawn-a) "Earth-Woman." A type of priestess, or female healer.

Folkmodir (FAWLK-mohd-ir) "Folk-Mother." A ruling woman, similar or identical to a drottning (see).

Folkvang (FAWLK-vang) "Folk-Fields." Freya's realm in Asgard, where she keeps her half of the Einherjar.

Folkvig (FALWK-veeg) "Folk-War." Designates the first civil war, between Aesir and Vanir in heaven, and east and west Teutons (Danes and Swedes) on earth.

Folkvir (FAWLK-vir) "Folk-Warrior." Name of a horse.

Folkwanderung (FAWLK-vand-er-ung) German "Folk-Wandering," "Emigration." The migration that took place during the first Fimbulwinter.

Fonn (FUHN) "Snow-Drift." A son of Snaer, grandson of Kari.

Forad (FOR-ad) "Ruiner." A Giantess.

Forbrennir (FAWR-brehn-ir) "Burner." The name used by the Dwarves for fire.

Forni (FAWRN-i) "The Old." A name of Odin.

Fornjot (FAWRN-yoht-r) "The Ancient Being." An Etin, killed by Thor. Father of Aegir-Gymir (Hler), Kari, and Logi.

Forseti (FAWR-seht-i) "The Presiding." Son of Baldur and Nanna, one of the Ljonar, the divine judges. He inherited Glitnir, the Thingstead of the Gods, from his father.

Fraeg (FRAIG-r) "The Famous." A Dwarf.

Franangsforce (FRAHN-angs-fors) "Franangr's Falls," "Sparkling Falls." A body of water where Loki, in salmon guise, was taken prisoner by the Gods.

Frar (FRAHR) "The Quick." A Dwarf.

Frarid (FRAH-rid) "Fast-Rider." Another name of Odin.

Frekastein (FREHK-a-stayn) "Wolf-Stone." A place where Kon's and Egil's forces collided.

Freki (FREHK-i) "The Greedy." One of Odin's wolfhounds, also called Gifur; the other is Geri. This is also a term for a wolf in general.

Frek (FREHK) "Greedy." The name used by the Etins for fire.

Frermonth (FREHR-muhnth) "Frost-Month." The name for November in the Old Norse calendar.

Freya (FRAY-a) "Lady," "The Dear." Daughter of Njord and Frigga, sister of Frey and Goddess of love and fecundity.

Frey (FRAY) "Lord," "The Dear." Son of Njord and Frigga, brother of Freya and God of agriculture and fertility.

Frid (FREED) "The Fair." A Goddess of beauty in Freya's surroundings, for she is one of her eight sisters and is a daughter of Njord and Frigga.

Fridla (FRID-la) "Friend." Brother of Imbrekki, son of Harlung, who was Kon's son, making Fridla Kon's grandson and nephew of Hadding and Gudorm.

Frigga (FRIG-a) "The Beloved." Daughter of Fjorgyn-Hoenir and Natt. She is our Mother Earth, who birthed ten children with her brother, Njord: Frey, Freya, Hlifthrasa, Frid, Blid, Bjart, Eir, Thjodvarta, Hlif, and Blik. With Odin, her husband, she had Thor, Baldur, and Hod. She is the divine matriarch and Asgard's queen.

Frosti (FRAWST-i) "Frosty," "Frozen." 1) A Dwarf. 2) An Etin.

Frovur (FRAWV-ur) "Ladies." Designation of noblewomen from Freya's name.

Frua (FROO-a) "Lady." Designation of a noblewoman from Freya's name.

Frya (FREE-a) Old Frisian "Lady." Another name of Freya.

Fulla (FUL-a) "Fullness." Frigga's sister, maidservant, and confidante. She is a daughter of Hoenir-Fjorgyn.

Fulnir (FOOL-nir) "The Stinking." A son of Thrall and Thy.

Fundin (FUN-din) "The Founder." A Dwarf.

Funi (FUN-i) "Flame." The name used by the Aesir for fire.

Fylgja (FEELG-ya) pl. **Fylgjas** (FEELG-yas) "Accompanier." Identical to the hamingja, gipte, draumkona, norn, etc. who are mankind's invisible companions and guardian spirits.

Fylking (FEELK-ing) pl. **Fylkings** (FEELK-ing-ar) "Military Unit." A band of warriors.

Fylkja (FEELK-ya) both sing. and pl. "Troop Formation." The means of organizing troops.

Fyrisvellir (FEER-is-vehl-ir) "Fyri Plains" (Fyri= "fjord," a river). Plains near the Fyri river in Svithjod where Jarl was burned on his pyre.

Fyrnir (FEERN-ir) "The Ancient." An Etin.

G

Gafugt Dyr (GAV-ugt DEER) "Slow-Beast." The name Hod gave Fafnir when the serpent asked who he was.

Gaglwood (GAG-l-wood) "Copper Forest," "Bronze Forest." The name of the Ironwood before the corruption brought forth by Gullveig.

Gagnrad (GAG-n-rahd) "Giving Good Counsel." Another name of Odin.

Galar (GAL-ar) "Singer." 1) A Dwarf. 2) An Etin.

Galdur (GALD-ur) "Incantations." The intoning and singing of rune sounds or chants, and the use of runes in spiritual practice in general. In opposition to the Seid, this is the holy art of the Gods.

Galdurfather (GALD-ur-fah-ther) "Galdur-Father." Another name of Odin.

Galdursmiths (GALD-ur-smiths) "Galdur-Smiths." A designation of the Gods, as the authors of the Galdur.

Gambantein (GAM-ban-tayn) "Wand of Revenge." The sword Volund forged which is accompanied by certain revenge.

Gandalf (GAND-ahlv) "Wand-Elf." A Dwarf.

Gandur (GAND-ur) "Wand," "Magic Device." Originally, anything considered to be magical, but later came to specifically designate a wand or staff used for ceremonial purposes.

Gandvik (GAND-veek) "Magic Bay." Another name for the Elivagar.

Ganglati (GANG-lat-i) "Lazy." An Etin, Leikin's manservant.

Gangleri (GANG-lehr-i) "The Way-Weary." Another name of Odin.

Ganglot (GANG-luht) "Slothful." Leikin's maidservant.

Gang (GANG) "The Faring." 1) Another name of Egil. 2) Another name of Ymir.

Gard (GARD) "Court," "Yard." A sacred enclosure or realm.

Gardofa (GARD-rawv-a) "Fence-Breaker." A horse, mother of Gna's horse, Hofvarpnir.

Garm (GARM) "Wolfhound." The wolfhound that howls by Gnipahell, when Ragnarok is immanent and the bound forces of chaos break loose.

Gastropnir (GAST-rawp-nir) "Guest-Refuser." The wall around Asgard, which Odin made from Leirbrimir-Ymir's limbs, probably ground in the Grotti-mill.

Gauksmonth (GOUKS-muhnth) "Cuckoo Month." The name for April in the Old Norse calendar.

Gautatyr (GOUT-a-teer) "God of Goths." Another name of Odin.

Gautland (GOUT-land) "Goth Land." The Old Norse name for Gotland, as well as the original name of Denmark (Denmark).

Gaut (GOUT) "Goth." Another name of Odin.

Gebo (GEH-boh) "Gift." The seventh rune of the Elder Futhark, associated with gift-giving, which is why it is connected to charity and generosity in the Runelaw.

Gefjon (GEV-yawn) also **Gefjun** (GEV-yun) 1) A Goddess, also called Nyhellenia, who helped expose Gullveig when she was spreading her evil Seid in Midgard. 2) Another name of Urd.

Gefn (GEV-n) "Giver." Another name of Freya.

Geigud(GAY-gud) "Gallows-Dangler." Another name of Odin.

Geirahod (GAYR-a-huhd) "Spear-Fighter." A Valkyrie.

Geiravor (GAYR-a-vuhr) "Spear-Goddess." A Valkyrie.

Geirdriful (GAYR-driv-ul) "Spear-Thrower. A Valkyrie.

Geirlodnir (GAYR-luhd-nir) "Inciting Spear-Fights." Another name of Odin.

Geirolnir (GAYR-uhl-nir) "Spear-Charmer," "Spear-Enchanter." Another name of Odin.

Geironul (GAYR-uhn-ul) "Spear-Thrower." A Valkyrie.

Geirrod (GAYR-uhd) "Protection from Spears." An Etin-jarl, father of Gjalp and Greip. He was slain by Thor during the war campaign into Jotunheim.

Geirskogul (GAYR-skuhg-ul) "Spear-Battle." A Valkyrie.

Geirvandill (GAYR-van-dil) "The One Busy With the Spear." Another name of Ivaldi.

Geirvimul (GAYR-vim-ul) "Spear-Teeming." A sacred river, in whose waves weapons roll.

Geitir (GAYT-ir) "Goat-Lord." Another name of Aegir-Gymir. Like the Etin-jarl Beli ("Howler"), who is portrayed as having the head of a dog, Aegir-Gymir's appearance resembles, in one way or another, that of a goat.

Geitla (GAYT-la) "Goat." A Giantess.

Geldur (GEHLD-ur) "Gelding." Another name of Slagfin.

Gelgja (GEHLG-ya) "Fetter." An attachment to Gleipnir, the fetter that bound Fenrir.

Gepides (GEHP-i-des) An ancient clan.

Gerd (GERD) "Maker." Daughter of Gullveig-Angerboda and Aegir-Gymir who became Frey's wife through the aid of Skirnir-Od. Gullveig enchanted Frey with her evil Seid, so she could obtain Gambantein as Gerd's "bride-price" (mund).

Geri (GER-i) "Greedy." One of Odin's wolfhounds. The other is Freki.

Germania (JER-man-i-a) Latin "Land of Germans." The term used to designate the area of Northern Europe inhabited by Teutons.

Gersemi (GER-sehm-i) "Treasure," "The Ornamented." Daughter of Freya and Od.

Gestilja (GEHST-il-ya) "Guest-Maiden." A Giantess.

Gestumblindi (GEHST-um-blind-i) "Disguised Stranger." Another name of Odin.

Gevar (GEHV-ar) "Ward of the Atmosphere." Another name of Lodur.

Geysa (GAYS-a) "Storm-Bringer." A Giantess.

Gif (GEEV) "Greedy." 1) Another name for Odin's wolfhound, Freki. 2) A group of demons that fly in the air. At the Wild Hunt Odin, Thor, Frigga, and a host of Einherjar and other deities go out and cleanse the air of them.

Gilling (GIL-ing) "The Loud." An Etin.

Gimir (GIM-ir) "Fiery," "Jeweled." One of the nine heavens.

Gimle (GIM-lee) "Fire-Shelter," "Gem-Roof." The hall near Urdarbrunn where the blessed dead live after being given the Lofstirr at the Helthing. These people will help populate the world after Ragnarok.

Ginnar (GIN-ar) "Enticer." 1) Another name of Odin. 2) A Dwarf.

Ginnungagap (GIN-ung-a-gap) "The Yawning Chasm." The empty abyss of Chaos, in which cold and warm waves met to create life in the worlds.

Ginnungaheaven (GIN-ung-a-hehv-in) "The Yawning Heaven," "Ginnungr's Heaven." The sky or firmament.

Gipte (GIPT-eh) "Gift-Giver." Identical to the hamingja, fylgja, etc.

Gipul (GIP-ul) "Forward Rushing." A sacred river.

Gisl (GEES-l) "Shining." One of the Aesir's horses.

Gizur (GIZ-ur) "Guesser." Another name of Odin.

Gjallarbridge (GYAL-ar-brij) "The Gjoll-Bridge." The gold-roofed bridge over the subterranean river Gjoll, guarded by Modgud.

Gjallarhorn (GYAL-ar-hawrn) "The Resounding Horn." The horn or horns that are used to drink the holy mead in Jormungrund. It is possible that these came from the slain Audhumla. Heimdall uses the horn, or one of the horns, to wake the Gods, and will blow it aloud to announce the coming of Ragnarok.

Gjalp (GYALP) "Roarer." Geirrod's daughter. At one time she was one of the Giantesses turning the Grotti-mill, for she is accounted as one of Heimdall's mothers. She was killed by Thor.

Gjoll (GYUHL) "The Resounding," "The Loud." 1) One of the Underworld rivers that separates Hel from Niflhel, counted among the Elivagar rivers. 2) The boulder that holds Fenrir, bound by Gleipnir.

Gjolp (GYUHLP) "Boastful," "Braggard." 1) An Etin. 2) A Dwarf.

Gjuki (GYOOK-i) "The Giver." Another name of Slagfin.

Gjukungs (GYOOK-ungs) "Descendants of Gjuki." The clan founded by Gjuki-Slagfin and thus a branch of the Niflungs.

Glad (GLAD) "The Shining." One of the Aesir's horses.

Gladsheim (GLADS-haym) "The Home of Joy." The area inside of Asgard where Valhall stands.

Glaer (GLAIR) "The Bright." One of the Aesir's horses.

Glaevald (GLAI-vald) "The Shining Ruler." Another name of Mimir.

Glammi (GLAM-i) "The Noisy." A sea-king.

Glam (GLAHM) "Two-Faced." An Etin.

Glapsvid (GLAPS-vid) "Seducer." Another name of Odin.

Glasir (GLAS-ir) "The Resplendent." Another name of Yggdrasil, with its golden leaves and golden fruits, born from a golden seed. Cp. Aurglasir, Vedurglasir.

Glasislund (GLAS-is-lund) "Glasir-Grove." The grove where Baldur was born. Cp. Glasisvellir.

Glasisvellir (GLAS-is-vehl-ir) "Glasir-Fields." Mimir's kingdom in the Underworld in which Odainsacre is located. The name is connected to Yggdrasil-Glasir, also known as Mimameid—"Mimir's Tree."

Glaumar (GLOUM-ar) "The Praised." An Etin.

Glaum (GLOUM) "Noisy." 1) An Etin. 2) A horse.

Glaumvor (GLOUM-vuhr) "The Praised." An Etin.

Gleipnir (GLAYP-nir) "Fetter." The fetter used to bind Fenrir.

Glen (GLEHN) "The Shining." Another name of Heimdall.

Glitnir (GLIT-nir) "The Shining Abode." The Thingstead of Asgard. First it was Baldur's then Forseti's home.

Gloi (GLOH-i) "The Shining." A Dwarf.

Gloni (GLOHN-i) "Staring." A Dwarf.

Glora (GLOHR-a) "Faint Light." Thor's foster-mother, wife of Vingnir, both of whom were slain by their foster-son. Also called Hlora.

Glumra (GLUM-ra) "Din." A Giantess.

Gna (NAH) "The Towering." An Asynja, messenger of Frigga. Originally, Gna was a common designation for a Goddess.

Gneggjud (NEHG-yud) "Neigher." The name used by the "Wide-Ruling Powers" for the wind.

Gneip (NAYP) "Cliff-Dweller." A Giantess.

Gnepja (NEHP-ya) "Hunchback," "The Stooping." A Giantess.

Gnipacave (NIP-a-kayv) "The Cave of the Precipitous Rock." Garm howls before Gnipacave, when Loki and Fenrir's bonds burst at Ragnarok.

Gnipalund (NIP-a-lund) "The Grove of the Precipitous Rock." The place where Loki bore his three children: Jormungand, Leikin, and Fenrir.

Gnissa (NIS-a) "Screamer." A Giantess.

Gnitaheath (NIT-a-heeth) "Rock-Heath," "Scree-Heath." The heath where Fafnir brooded over the the Niflung Hoard, when Hod came to kill him.

Gnod (NAWD) "The Rumbling." The ship owned by Asmund.

Godi (GAWD-i) pl. **godar** (GAWD-ar), never capitalized, "He Who Speaks the Godly Tongue," "The Godly," "The Pious." A male priest in the Asatru faith.

Godord (GAWD-awrd) "The Priesthood." Represents the priesthood of the Asatru faith.

Goth-thjod (GAWTH-thyohd) "Nation of Goths," "Nation of Men." The Teutonic folk, the Teutonic nation.

Goi (GOH-i) "Winter Month." 1) The name for February in the Old Norse calendar. 2) A Giantess.

Goin (GOH-in) "Living Deep in the Earth." One of the serpents that gnaws at Yggdrasil's roots.

Goll (GUHL) "The Noisy." A Valkyrie.

Gomul (GUHM-ul) "Ravine." A sacred river.

Gondlir (GUHND-lir) "Wand-Bearer." Another name of Odin.

Gondul (GUHND-ul) 1) Another name of Odin. 2) A Valkyrie. 3) Another name of Gullveig.

Gopul (GUHP-ul) "Chasm," "Ravine." A sacred river.

Gor (GAWR) "Slaughterer." An Etin.

Gormonth (GAWR-muhnth) "Slaughter Month." The name for October in the Old Norse calendar.

Gotaland (GUHT-a-land) "Land of the Geats." A district in southern Svithjod.

Goti (GAWT-i) "The Goth," "Man." 1) Another name of Jarl. 2) Gunnar's horse.

Gotland (GAWT-land) also **Gautland** (GOUT-land) "Land of the Goths." An old name for Denmark, now northern Jutland.

Gotnar (GAWT-nar) "Men." Designates men, or the Tetutonic folk as the progeny of Jarl-Goti.

Grabak (GRAH-bak) "Grey-Back." An serpent that gnaws at Yggdrasil's roots.

Grad (GRAHD) "The Grey." A sacred river.

Grafvitnir (GRAV-vit-nir) "Grave-Wolf." The serpents Goin and Moinn are called Grafvitnir's sons.

Grafvollud (GRAV-vuhl-ud) "Grave-Burrower." An serpent that gnaws at Yggdrasil's roots.

Gram (GRAM) "King," "Prince." 1) Another name of Kon. 2) A son of Kon and Alveig.

Grani (GRAN-i) "Hairy Snout." Sigurd's horse.

Greip (GRAYP) "The Grasping." A Giantess. Gjalp's sister and Geirrod's daughter. At one time she was one of the maids turning the Grotti-mill, since she is counted as one of Heimdall's mothers. She is also the mother of Ivaldi's sons—Volund, Egil, and Slagfin.

Grepp (GREHP) "Grasper." Three brothers with this name were members of Beli's clan when Frey and Freya were in their power, and one of them helped in getting Freya out of Asgard.

Grer (GRER) "Grower." A son of Mimir. One of the artists who created Brisingamen.

Gridarvol (GREED-ar-vuhl) "The Safety Staff." The staff, made of rowan, which Thor used to climb out of the Elivagar on his campaign against Geirrod.

Grid (GREED) "Greedy," "Violence." A Giantess, mother of the Asagod Vidar with Odin.

Grima (GREEM-a) "The Masked." 1) A Giantess. 2) A name used by the "Wide Ruling Powers" for Natt (Night).

Grimling (GREEM-ling) "Mask-Wearer." An Etin.

Grimnir (GREEM-nir) "The Masked One." 1) Another name of Odin. 2) An Etin.

Grim (GREEM) "The Masked One." 1) Another name of Odin. 2) A Dwarf.

Grjotunagard (GRYOHT-un-a-gard) "Courtyard of Rocky Fields." The place where Thor fought Hrungnir, in Jotunheim.

Groa (GROH-a) "Giver of Growth." A Goddess of vegetation, daughter of the Alf ruler Sigtryg, sister of Sif. Mother of Od with Egil and Gudorm with Kon.

Groandi (GROH-and-i) "The Growing." The name used by the Alfar for Jord-Frigga (Earth).

Grotti (GRAWT-i) "Grinder." The World-Mill that turns the sky, grinds Etin limbs for Midgard's soil, creates the Maelstrom, and was the inspiration for the sacred friction-fire.

Grottintanna (GRAWT-in-tan-a) "Gap-Toothed." A Giantess.

Grougaldur (GROH-u-gald-ur) "Groa's Galdur." The Galdur songs Groa sang over Od to aid him in his adventures.

Gryla (GREEL-a) "Nightmare." A Giantess.

Gud (GUD) "God." A Dwarf.

Gudorm (GUD-awrm) "Esteemed by the Gods." Kon and Groa's son, Od and Hadding's half-brother.

Gudrun (GUD-roon) "Rune of the Gods." Daughter of Slagfin, mother of Sorli, Hamdir, and Svanhild, wife of Jonak.

Gullfaxi (GUL-vaks-i) "Gold-Mane." The Etin Hrungnir's horse, who was presented by Thor to his son Magni after Hrungnir's defeat.

Gullinbursti (GUL-in-burst-i) "Golden-Bristle." Frey's boar crafted by Mimir's sons. Also called Slidrugtanni, Hildisvini.

Gullinkambi (GUL-in-kam-bi) "Gold-Comb." The cock in Yggdrasil that wakes the Einherjar in Asgard. Also called Vidofnir and Salgofnir.

Gullintanni (GUL-in-tan-i) "Golden-Toothed." Another name of Heimdall.

Gulltopp (GUL-tawp) "Gold-Tuft," "Golden-Forelock." Heimdall's horse.

Gullveig (GUL-vayg) "Gold-Drink," "Thirsty For Gold." Daughter of Hrimnir and Imd. The thrice born Giantess, origin of the evil Seid. She was called Heid when she went around Midgard teaching her dangerous arts. She was called Aurboda when she was married to Aegir-Gymir. She is now known as Angerboda while she dwells in the Ironwood, awaiting Ragnarok. As the thrice burnt and still living, she bore the name Hyrrokkin—"The Fire Smoked." She is also called Ran, Kalta, and Syrhed.

Guma (GUM-a) "Earthy." A Giantess.

Gungnir (GUNG-nir) "Swaying One." Odin's spear.

Gunnar (GUN-ar) "Warrior." 1) One of Slagfin's sons. 2) Designates a warrior in general.

Gunn (GUN) "Warrior-Maiden." A Valkyrie.

Gunnhild (GUN-hild) "Warrior-Battle-Maiden." Wife of Asmund, mother of Henry.

Gunnlod (GUN-luhd) "The Battle-Inviting." An Etin-maid, Suttung-Fjalar's daughter who helped Odin steal the Byrgir mead from her father.

Gunnthorin (GUN-thawr-in) "Courageous Warrior." A Valkyrie.

Gunnthrain (GUN-thrah-in) "Warrior Threatening." A sacred river.

Gunnthro (GUN-throh) "Warrior-Trough." A sacred river.

Gusir (GUS-ir) "Outpouring." An Etin.

Gydja (GEED-ya) "She Who Speaks the Godly Tongue" "Godly Woman," "The Pious." A priestess of the Asatru faith.

Gylfi (GEELV-i) "King." 1) An Etin ruler who holds lands in Svithjod during the era when Gullveig introduces her Seid into Midgard. 2) A son of Kon and Alveig.

Gylling (GEEL-ing) "The Loud Grating." 1) The key to the Helgates. 2) An Etin.

Gyllir (GEEL-ir) "Golden." 1) One of the Aesir's horses. 2) An Etin.

Gymir (GEEM-ir) "Devourer." Another name of Aegir, husband of Gullveig, father of Gerd and the nine Giantesses of the waves.

H

Hadarlag (HAD-ar-lag) "Hod's Meter," "Battle-Meter." A particular type of verse, in honor of Hod.

Haddingjas (HAD-ing-yas) "The Folk of Hadding." Hadding's troops and kinsmen.

Haddingland (HAD-ing-land) "Hadding's Land." Another name for the Underworld, since Hadding was the first living human to ever visit there.

Hadding (HAD-ing) "The Hairy," "The Fair-Haired." Son of Kon and Alveig; Gudorm's half-brother. His name alludes to his making a vow to not cut his hair until he avenged his father against Od and regained his odal.

Haera (HAIR-a) "Grey-Haired." A Giantess.

Haevateinn (HAIV-a-tayn) "The Sword Pointed to Thrust." Another name of Gambantein.

Hafdi (HAV-di) "Sea-Farer." Son of Thjalfi, husband of Hvita Stjarna.

Haffru (HAV-vroo) "Mermaid," "Ocean-Maid." Designating women of the sea who can be benevolent or cruel. Gullveig and her daughters, the Giantesses of the nine waves, are among the evil ones.

Hafli (HAV-li) "The Seizer." A warrior of Etin birth, Gudorm's foster-father who participates in his struggles.

Hagalaz (HAG-a-laz) Gothic "Hail," The ninth rune of the Elder Futhark. To farmers and other people hail represents disastrous weather, but its ice is also viewed as the active substance of creation, teaching us to recognize the neutrality of natural forces, and of fate. This is why it is connected to such things in the Runelaw.

Hagal (HAG-al) "The Skillful," "Hail." 1) Jarl's friend, Hamal's father, Kon's foster-father.

Haki (HAK-i) "Hook." An Etin, grandson of Eggther.

Hakon (HAK-awn) called **Jarl Hakon** (YARL HAK-awn) or **Hakon inn Mikla** (HAK-awn in MIK-la) "Hakon the Great." Descendant of Odin and Skadi's line through Saeming.

Hala (HAHL-a) "Large." A Giantess.

Halfdan (HALV-dan) "Half-Dane." Another name of Kon.

Half (HAHLV) "Wolf." The one undone by fire.

Hallinskidi (HAL-in-skeed-i) "Ram." Another name of Heimdall.

Hal (HAL) "Man." A son of Karl and Snor.

Hamal (HAM-al) "Wether," "Ram." Son of Hagal, Kon's half-brother on Drott's side. Hadding's confidante, foster-father, and war-general.

Hamalt Fylkja (HAM-alt FELK-ya) "Hamal's Formation." The wedge-shaped battle formation taught to Hamal by Odin.

Hamdir (HAM-dir) "Hawk." One of Svanhild's brothers, son of Gudrun and Jonak. He and his brother Sorli were stoned to death on Gudorm's orders for trying to avenge the killing of their sister.

Hamingja (HAM-ing-ya) "Luck," "Guardian." Female protector assigned to us at birth, to witness for us at the Helthing after death. Also called fylgja, draumkona, norn, gipte, and dis.

Hama (HAM-a) "Guise." A form that can be put on and taken off, changing one's shape. Can usually be detected by the eyes, which remain the same.

Hamskerpir (HAM-skerp-ir) "Thin-Loined." The steed that sired Gna's horse Hofvarpnir with Gardofa.

Hangagud (HANG-a-gud) "God of the Hanged." Another name of Odin.

Hangatyr (HANG-a-teer) "God of the Hanged." Another name of Odin.

Hangi (HANG-i) "The Hanged." Another name of Odin.

Hannar (HAN-ar) "The Skillful." A Dwarf.

Haptagud (HAPT-a-gud) "God of Gods." Another name of Odin.

Haptsoenir (HAPT-sur-nir) "God of Fate." Another name of Odin.

Har (HAHR) "The High One." 1) Another name of Odin. 2) A Dwarf.

Harald (HAR-ald) "Ruler." An ancient warrior.

Harbard (HAHR-bard) "Hoar-Beard." 1) Another name of Odin. 2) A name Loki once assumed in an encounter with Thor.

Hardgrepa (HARD-grehp-a) "The Hard-Grasping." A Giantess, Hadding's companion, daughter of Vagnhofdi, Hadding's foster-father when he was hidden away.

Hardveur (HARD-vee-ur) "Strong-Consecrator." Another name of Thor.

Hardverk (HARD-verk) "Hard-Worker." An Etin.

Harlung (HAR-lung) "The Quick Leader." Illegitimate son of Kon, father of Imbrekki and Fridla.

Harlungs (HAR-lungs) "Descendants of Harlung." A legendary clan of the North.

Harri (HAR-i) also **Herra** (HER-a) "Ruler." A son of Kon and Alveig.

Hati Hrodvitnisson (HAT-i ROHD-vit-nis-sawn) "Hater-," "Enemy-," "-son of Hrodvitnir-Fenrir." The wolf who chases Mani until Ragnarok, when he catches him. Also called Managarm.

Hatun (HAHT-oon) "The High Stead." A royal odal ruled by Kon.

Haugbui (HOUG-boo-i) "Mound-Dweller." The alter-ego or doppelganger of a person, which remains in the grave, or grave-mound after death.

Haug Drottin (HOUG DROHT-in) "Lord of the Mounds." Another name of Odin.

Haugspori (HOUG-spawr-i) "Mound-Raven." A Dwarf.

Haur (HOUR) "The High." A Dwarf.

Haustigi (HOUST-ig-i) "Autumn." An Etin.

Haustmonth (HOUST-muhnth) "Autumn-Month," "Harvest-Month." The name for September in the Old Norse calendar.

Havi (HAHV-i) "The High." Another name of Odin.

Hedin (HEHD-in) "Warrior." Another name of Hod.

Hefring (HEHV-ring) "The Swelling Wave." One of Aegir-Gymir and Gullveig-Ran's daughters who represent the waves.

Heiddraupnir (HAYD-droup-nir) "Reward Dropping," "The Rewarding." Another name of Mimir.

Heidornir (HAYD-awrn-ir) "Cloud Brightness." One of the nine heavens. Also called Vindblain and Hreggmimir.

Heid (HAYD) "Witch," "Sorceress." Another name of Gullveig.

Heidrek (HAYD-rehk) "Heath-Ruler." Another name of Geirrod.

Heidrun (HAYD-roon) "The Clear Stream." The she-goat that stands on top of Valhall, chewing Yggdrasil's leaves. From her udders streams the mead, which fills a large vat, from which the Einherjar fill their drinking horns.

Heimdall (HAYM-dal) "Home-Light" [Hearth-Fire]. God of the pure fire, the friction-fire (which becomes the hearth fire), and guardian of the worlds. Born of nine mothers—the Giantesses who turn the Grotti-mill and created sparks from which he was born. Lodur-Mundilfari is the mill's caretaker and is thus Heimdall's "father." Heimdall blessed the unions of the Teutonic classes, which leads to the appellation "Heimdall's sons" for our folk.

Heimir (HAYM-ir) "Farmer," "Homesteader." An Etin.

Heiptir (HAYPT-ir) "Spiritual Beings." Punishing spirits or maidens of revenge, always female, armed with thorn-rods called limar. They avenge that which has not been avenged.

Hel (HEHL) "The Concealer." 1) Another name of Urd, the Goddess of fate and death. 2) The kingdom of death, the fields of bliss.

Helblindi (HEHL-blind-i) "He Who Blinds With Death." 1) Another name of Odin. 2) An Etin, son of Farbauti and Laufey, brother of Loki.

Held (HEHLD) "Freeholder." A son of Karl and Snor.

Helfare (HEHL-fayr) "Hel-Journey." The ancient designation for a funeral.

Helgi (HEHLG-i) "The Holy." Another name of Kon.

Helgate (HEHL-gayt) "Gate of Hel." One of the gates of Jormungrund, the main one being that which the dead walk through on their way to the Helthing.

Helheim (HEHL-haym) "Hel's Home," "Hel's Realm." Another name for the realm of Hel.

Hellenia (HEHL-ehn-ya) Old Frisian "The Enlightened." Another name of Nyhellenia-Gefjon, given to her by the folk when she came to Midgard to expose Gullveig.

Helregin (HEHL-rehg-in) "Death-Regin," "Death-Smith." An Etin.

Helshoes (HEHL-shooz) "Hel-Shoes." Special shoes blessed and placed on the feet of the dead, aiding them on their journey to the Helthing, signifying our respect for them.

Helthing (HEHL-thing) "Hel's Assembly," "Thing of the Dead." A contemporary designation for the Thing near Urd's fountain, where the dead are judged to determine where they will spend their afterlife.

Helways (HEHL-wayz) "Ways of Hel." The paths in Hel.

Hengest (HEHNG-ehst) Anglo-Saxon "Gelding." Another name of Slagfin.

Hengjankjapta (HEHNG-yan-kyapt-a) "Hanging-Chin." A Giantess, killed by Thor.

Hengjankjopt (HEHNG-yan-kyuhpt) "Hanging-Chin." An Etin.

Henry (HEHN-ree) "The Skillful." Son of Asmund and Gunnhild, grandson of Od.

Heptifili (HEHPT-i-veel-i) "File-Holder," "Filer." A Dwarf.

Herfjotur (HER-vyuht-ur) "Host-Fetterer." A Valkyrie.

Herfather (HER-fah-<u>ther</u>) "Father of Hosts." Another name of Odin.

Hergaut (HER-gout) "Goth of Hosts." Another name of Odin.

Heri (HER-i) "Host." A Dwarf.

Herjafather (HER-ya-fah-<u>ther</u>) "Father of Hosts." Another name of Odin.

Herjan (HER-yan) "War-God." Another name of Odin.

Herkir (HERK-ir) "The Boorish." An Etin.

Herkja (HERK-ya) "Noisy." A Giantess.

Hermod (HER-mohd) "The One Endowed With Martial Spirit." Another name of Od.

Hersir (HER-sir) "Lord." Father of Erna-Drott, identical to Danp.

Herteit (HER-tayt) "Glad in Battle." Another name of Odin.

Hertyr (HER-teer) "God of Hosts." Another name of Odin.

Herules (HER-ul-ehs) "The Ruling Folk." An ancient clan.

Heyannir (HAY-an-ir) "Hay-Making." The name for July in the Old Norse calendar.

Hildibrand (HILD-i-brand) "Sword of Battle." Son of Drott and Hildur, half-brother of Kon, killed by him.

Hildigir (HILD-i-gir) "Battle-Warrior." Another name of Hildibrand.

Hildings (HILD-ings) "Descendants of Hildur." A legendary clan of the North.

Hildisvini (HILD-i-sveen-i) "Battle-Swine." Another name of Frey's boar, Gullinbursti.

Hildolf (HILD-ohlv) "Maiden-Wolf," "Battle-Wolf." The person who gave Loki the boat he had when he confronted Thor on the sound. He may be identical to Volund, or is perhaps a phallic euphemism.

Hild (HILD) "Battle." A Valkyrie who was put to sleep by Odin for granting a warrior victory against his wishes. She married Hod right before his death.

Hildur (HILD-ur) "Battle." Father of Hildibrand with Drott, also called Skat.

Hilmir (HILM-ir) "Prince," "King." A son of Kon and Alveig.

Himinbjorg (HIM-in-byuhrg) "Heaven's Defense." Heimdall's stronghold by Bifrost's northern bridge-head.

Himingloeva (HIM-in-glurv-a) "The Sky-Clear." One of Aegir-Gymir and Gullveig-Ran's daughters who represent the waves.

Himinhrjot (HIM-in-ryoht) "Heaven Trampler." Hymir's ox, slain by Thor and used as bait to catch Jormungand.

Himinn (HIM-in) "Heaven." The name used by our ancestors for heaven.

Himinvangar (HIM-in-vang-ar) "Heavenly-Fields." An odal ruled over by Kon.

Hindarfjoll (HIND-ar-vyuhl) "Deer-Mountain." The mountain where Hild slept when Hod woke her up and took her as his wife.

Hjadningas (HYAD-ning-as) "The Folk of Hedin." Followers of Hod-Hedin.

Hjalmberi (HYAHLM-ber-i) "Helm-Bearer." Another name of Odin.

Hjalmgunnar (HYAHLM-gun-ar) "Helm-Warrior." The warrior promised victory by Odin, but robbed of this by Hild.

Hjalmther (HYAHLM-theer) "Helm-Servant." A warrior.

Hjalmthrimul (HYAHLM-thrim-ul) "Battle-Helm." A Valkyrie.

Hjalp (HYALP) "Help." A rune given to us by Odin to help against strife and cares. Cp. Bjargrunes.

Hjarrandi (HYAR-and-i) "Mail-Coat," "Snarer." Another name of Odin.

Hjordrimul (HYUHRD-rim-ul) "Battle-Sword." A Valkyrie.

Hjorvard (HYUHR-vard) "Sword-Guardian." 1) Another name of Odin. 2) Another name of Eggther, who watches Gambantein until Ragnarok.

Hjuki (HYOOK-i) "Returning to Health." Another name of Slagfin.

Hladgud Swanwhite (LAD-gud SVAN-wīt) Hladgud= "The Necklace Adorned Warrior-Maiden," Swanwhite= "Swan White." Another name of Auda.

Hlaevang (LAI-vang) "Warm-Cheeked." A Dwarf.

Hlebard (LEE-bard) "Wolf." Another name of Volund.

Hledjolf (LEHD-yohlv) "Shield-Wolf." A Dwarf.

Hlefod (LEE-vuhd) "Father of Mounds."Another name of Odin.

Hlefrey (LEE-fray) "Lord of Mounds." Another name of Odin.

Hleidra (LAYD-ra) "Sacred Enclosure," "Lejre." The place where Nyhellenia and Skjold lived together in Zealand.

Hler (LEER) "Roarer." Another name of Aegir-Gymir.

Hlesey (LEES-ay) "Hler's Isle." The home of Aegir-Gymir, where the feast of the Gods takes place, or took place each year. Also where many Etins have lived.

Hlevarg (LEE-varg) "Grave-Mound." A Dwarf.

Hlidskjalf (LID-skyahlv) "Gate-Tower." The Aesir's watchtower where they can view all the worlds, located in Valaskjalf.

Hlidthang (LEED-thang) "Seaweed of Hills." The name used by Hel's inmates for the forest.

Hlif (LEEV) "The Protectress." A daughter of Njord and Frigga, one of Freya's sisters and maidservants.

Hlifthrasa (LEEV-thras-a) "Protecting in Battle." A daughter of Njord and Frigga, one of Freya's sisters and maidservants.

Hlin (LEEN) "The Protectress." 1) Another name of Frigga. 2) One of Frigga's maidservants.

Hljodolf (LYOD-ohlv) "Silent-Wolf." A Dwarf.

Hlodyn (LOHD-en) "Earth." Another name of Frigga.

Hloi (LOH-i) "The Bellowing." An Etin.

Hlok (LUHK) "Battle." A Valkyrie.

Hlora (LOHR-a) also **Lora** (LOHR-a) "The Famous." Thor's foster mother, wife of Vingnir, slain by Thor himself. Also called Glora.

Hlorridi (LOHR-id-i) "Famous Rider." Another name of Thor.

Hlyrnir (LEER-nir) "Twin-Lit." 1) One of the nine heavens. 2) The name used by the Gods for heaven.

Hnikar (NIK-ar) "Spear-Thruster." Another name of Odin.

Hnikud (NIK-ud) "Spear-Thruster." Another name of Odin.

Hnipinn (NIP-in) "Hanging Stem." The name used by those in Hel for grain.

Hnitbjorg (NIT-byuhrg) "Fortification." Suttung-Fjalar's home in Sokkdalir.

Hnoss (NAWS) "Jewel." Daughter of Freya and Od.

Hnossir (NAWS-ir) "Treasures." Here designates the treausures the Dwarves made for the Gods.

Hoddgoda (HAWD-gawd-a) "Hoard of the Gods." A treasure chamber in Mimir's realm, containing many of the divine artifacts.

Hoddmimis Holt (HAWD-meem-is HAWLT) "Treasure-Mimir's Grove." Mimir's grove in the Underworld, where Breidablik is located. Here is where the fewest baleful runes are found. Also called Holt, Mimis Holt, Odainsacre, and Okolnir.

Hoddropnir (HAWD-drawp-nir) "The Treasure-Dropper." Another name of Mimir.

Hod (HUHD) "Battle," "Warrior." 1) One of the Aesir, son of Odin and Frigga, brother and slayer of Baldur, husband of Hild. Also called Hedin and Loddfafnir. 2) A horse.

Hoenir (HURN-ir) "Male Bird." Odin's brother who helped him create the first humans and Midgard. Also called Ve, Aurkonung, and Langifot.

Hof (HAWV) "Temple." A place of worship in the Asatru faith.

Hofvarpnir (HOHV-varp-nir) "Hoof-Flourisher." The horse of Gna, son of Hamskerpir and Gardofa.

Hogni (HUHG-ni) "The Successful." Son of Gjuki-Slagfin, brother of Gunnar.

Holgabrud (HUHLG-a-brood) "Holy-Bride." A Giantess.

Holkvir (HUHLK-vir) "Winner." Hogni's horse.

Hollarwights (HAWL-ar-wīts) "Helpful Wights." A term designating good ghosts.

Holl (HUHL) "Hall." A sacred river.

Holt (HAWLT) "Grove." Mimir's grove in the Underworld.

Horg (HUHRG) "Stone-Altar," "Standing Stones." An altar, called a "stalli" when it is not made of stone.

Horn (HUHRN) "Horn." 1) Another name of Freya. 2) A sacred river. 3) A Giantess.

Hornbori (HAWRN-bawr-i) "He Who Bore Horn's Hair." A Dwarf.

Horr (HOHR) "The Dear." A Dwarf.

Hosvir (HUHS-vir) "The Grey," "Old Man." A son of Thrall and Thy.

362

Hraesvelg (RAIS-vehlg) "Corpse Swallower." An eagle-Etin who creates violent storms.

Hrafn (RAV-n) "Raven." A horse.

Hrafnagaldur (RAV-na-gald-ur) "The Raven-Song," "The Raven's Galdur." The song Hugin sang to Odin announcing the coming of the first Fimbulwinter.

Hrafnagud (RAV-na-gud) "Raven-God." Another name of Odin.

Hrammi (RAM-i) "The Tearer." Another name of Odin.

Hrani (RAN-i) "The Ranter." Another name of Odin.

Hraudnir (ROUD-nir) "Destroyer." An Etin.

Hraudung (ROUD-ung) "The Hasty." An Etin, father of Agnar and Geirrod.

Hreggmimir (REHG-meem-ir) "Storm-Mimir." One of the nine heavens, also called Vindblain and Heidornir.

Hreidgotaland (RAYD-gawt-a-land) "Land of the Eastern Goths." Another name of Jutland.

Hreidgoths (RAYD-gawths) "Eastern-Goths." An ancient clan.

Hreinna Log (RAYN-a LUHG) "Bright-Draught." The name used by the Etins for ale.

Hrid (REED) "The Stormy." A sacred river.

Hrimfaxi (REEM-vaks-i) "Rime-Mane." Natt's horse who grazes on the grasses of Jormungrund and the leaves of Yggdrasil, which are saturated with the sacred mead. From his bit a froth forms that becomes the morning dew, which the bees collect and produce the honey we make our mead from.

Hrimgerd (REEM-gerd) "Rime-Producer," "Hrim's Gerd (Bride)." A Giantess.

Hrimgrimnir (REEM-greem-nir) "Rime-Grimnir." An Etin.

Hrimnir (REEM-nir) "The Frost-Giant," "The Frost-Being." An Etin, father of Gullveig and Hrossthjof. Also called Bergelmir.

Hrim (REEM) "Frost," "Rime." An Etin.

Hrimthurses (REEM-thurs-es) "Frost-Giants." 1) A member of the primordial Etins descended directly from Ymir. 2) Name of an Etin.

Hringhorni (RING-hawrn-i) "Curved-Prow." Baldur's ship, which became his funeral pyre.

Hring (RING) "Ring." A warrior who challenged Jarl and Kon for their kingdom, and was subsequently slain by them.

Hringstadir (RING-stad-ir) "Ring-Stead." An odal ruled over by Kon.

Hringvolnir (RING-vuhl-nir) "Round-Pole Bearer." An Etin.

Hrin (RIN) "Shreeker." A son of Thrall and Thy.

Hripstodi (RIP-stuhd-i) "Spotted." An Etin.

Hrist (RIST) "Shaker." A Valkyrie.

Hrjod (RYOHD) "Coverer." One of the nine heavens.

Hroar (ROH-ar) "Spear-Famous." An Etin.

Hrod (ROHD) "The Famous." An Etin, killed by Thor.

Hrodud (RUHD-ud) "The Swift." The name used by those in Hel for fire.

Hrodvitnir (ROHD-vit-nir) "The Famous-Wolf." Another name of Fenrir, father of Hati Managarm.

Hrokkvir (RUHK-vir) "The Stooping." An Etin.

Hronn (RUHN) also **Hraunn** (ROUN) "Billow," "Wave." 1) Another name of the Elivagar. 2) One of Aegir-Gymir and Gullveig-Ran's nine daughters who represent the waves.

Hroptatyr (RAWPT-a-teer) "God of Gods." Another name of Odin.

Hropt (RAWPT) "The God." Another name of Odin.

Hrossthjof (RAWS-thyohv) "Horse-Thief." An Etin, Hrimnir's son, Gullveig's brother.

Hrotti (RAWT-i) "Springing Rod." The sword Hod retrieved from Fafnir's hoard.

Hruga (ROOG-a) "The Excessive." A Giantess.

Hrund (RUND) "Striker." A Valkyrie.

Hrungnir (RUNG-nir) "The Noisy." An Etin killed by Thor.

Hrungnirsheart (RUNG-nirs-hart) "Hrungnir's Heart." A three-pointed symbol representing the cold, stone heart of Hrungnir.

Hrutmonth (ROOT-muhnth) "Ram-Month," "Hrutr-Heimdall's Month." The name for December in the Old Norse calendar.

Hryggda (REEG-da) "The Sad." A Giantess.

Hrym (REEM) "Frost." A storm-Etin, one of the Etin leaders in Ragnarok.

Hugi (HUG-i) "Thought." Personification of Fjalar's thought, which beat Thjalfi in a race.

Hugin (HUG-in) "Thought." One of Odin's ravens.

Hugrunes (HUG-roons) "Thought-Runes." A group of runes containing wisdom and the skald-craft.

Hugstari (HUG-star-i) "Strategist," "Battle-Thinker." A Dwarf.

Hugur (HUG-ur) "Thought." 1) The Old Norse designation for thought. 2) Another name of Hugin.

Hulidshelm (HUL-ids-hehlm) "Helm of Invisibility," "Secret Helm." 1) The helm that allows one to become invisible. 2) The name used by those in Hel for clouds.

Hunding (HUND-ing) "Son of Hundr," "The Hound." Grandson of Od, king of Svithjod.

Hundla (HUND-la) "Hound," "Dog." A Giantess.

Hundolf (HUND-ohlv) "Wolf-Hound." An Etin.

Hungur (HUNG-ur) "Hunger." Leikin's plate or dish.

Hunwar (HUN-wahr) "The Hun-War." The name of the war the Etins waged against Asgard, while the Vanir reigned there.

Husfreya (HOOS-vray-ya) also **Husfru** (HOOS-vroo) "Lady of the House," "House-Freya." The position of a woman within her home as its caretaker.

Huskarl (HOOS-karl) "House-Karl," "House-Carl." A bodyguard or household soldier of a royal estate.

Hval (VAL) "Whale." An Etin.

Hvatmod (VAT-mohd) "Quick to Anger." Another name of Odin.

Hvedna (VEHD-na) "Roarer." A Giantess, daughter of Eggther.

Hvedra (VEHD-ra) "Roarer." A Giantess.

Hvedrung (VEHD-rung) "Roarer." Another name of Loki.

Hveralund (VER-a-lund) "Kettle-Grove." The place, under which Loki is bound until Ragnarok.

Hverfanda Hvel (VER-vanda VEHL) "Whirling-Wheel." The name used by those in Hel for Mani (Moon).

Hvergelmir (VER-gehlm-ir) "The Roaring Kettle." The well situated on Nidafjoll beneath the Grotti-mill which waters the northern root of Yggdrasil. Its sacred mead gives endurance.

Hvidud (VID-ud) "Gust." The name used by those in Hel for wind.

Hvita Stjarna (VEET-a STYARN-a) "White Star." Wife of Thjalfi's son, Hafdi.

Hviti As (VEET-i AHS) "The White As." Another name of Heimdall.

Hviting (VEET-ing) "The White." A sword given to Jarl.

Hymir (HEEM-ir) "The Miserly." An Etin, married to Tyr's mother, who raised Tyr in his home.

Hyndla (HEEND-la) "Bitch." A Giantess.

Hyrja (HEER-ya) "Slattern." A Giantess.

Hyr (HEER) "Realm of Delight." This is either a hall in Asgard or is another name of Brei-dablik.

Hyrrokkin (HEER-awk-in) "The Fire-Smoked." Another name of Gullveig, the thrice burnt and still living.

I

Idavoll (ID-a-vuhl) "Plain of the Eddies." In time's morning the Gods and Dwarves worked to-gether in Idavoll, crafting tools, forging, constructing, and building. In the renewal of the worlds, the Gods will gather there around Baldur.

Idi (ID-i) "The Lively." Another name of Slagfin.

Idisi (I-dees-i) "Goddesses." Another name of the disir, the female guardians.

Idun (ID-un) "The Rejuvenating," "The Diligent." Daughter of Ivaldi and Sunna, Volund's sis-ter and beloved, mother of Skadi, who later marries Bragi. She carries the apples of youth, which revive the Gods, and she protects the Byrgir mead on the moon.

Ifing (EEV-ing) "The Stirring." Designates the sea of air, also called Thund.

Igroen (EE-grurn) "All-Green." A name used by the Etins for Jord-Frigga (Earth).

Ilm (ILM) "The Pleasant." An Asynja.

Ima (EEM-a) "Sooty." A Giantess.

Imbrekki (EEM-brehk-i) "Battle-Edge." A son of Harlung, grandson of Kon, brother of Fridla, nephew of Hadding and Gudorm. Tricked by Loki, Gudorm had him killed.

Imd (IMD) "Embers (From the Grotti-mill)." One of Heimdall's nine mothers, a Giantess who turns the Grotti-mill. She is also Gullveig's mother with Hrimnir.

Imgerd (EEM-gerd) "Producer of Conflict," "Im's Gerd (Bride)." A Giantess.

Im (EEM) "The Dark." An Etin.

Ing (ING) "King." Another name of Od.

Ingi (ING-i) "King." 1)Another name of Frey. 2) A Dwarf.

Ingunarfrey (ING-un-ar-fray) "Frey, Friend of Kings." Another name of Frey.

Ingwaz (ING-vaz) Gothic "Ing," "Frey," The twenty-second rune of the Elder Futhark. It is also connected to Frey as Ingunarfrey, God of fertility and sexuality, and as such is associated with these concepts in the Runelaw.

Inn Sidskeggja As (IN SEED-skehg-ya AHS) "The Long-Bearded As." Another name of Bragi.

Inn Skjota As (IN SKYOHT-a AHS) "The Swift-As." Another name of Hoenir.

Inn Thogla As (IN THUHG-la AHS) "The Silent-As." Another name of Vidar.

Iri (EER-i) "The Rumor Spreading." A Dwarf.

Ironwood (AH-yern-wood) Situated in the northeastern most regions of Jormungrund, a forest filled with horrors and witchcraft, the haunt of Gullveig, Eggther, Hati, and the rest of "Fenrir's kin," until Ragnarok. Was called Gaglwood before the arrival of Gullveig's Seid.

Isa (EES) "Ice." The eleventh rune of the Elder Futhark, the ice rune. Ice is a symbol of strength and creative power, associating this rune with the ideas of discipline, which is why it is connected to such in the Runelaw.

Isarnkol (EES-arn-kawl) "Ice-Cold Iron." The bellows that cool Sol's horses, Arvak and Alsvid.

Isung (EES-ung) "Iceling," "Child of the Ice." An Etin, kinsman of Greip and Ivaldi's sons.

Ivaldi (EE-vald-i) "The Mighty." An Alf-jarl. With Sunna, daughter of Sol, he fathered Idun, Auda, and Alveig. With the Giantess Greip, he fathered the sons Volund, Egil, and Slagfin.

Ividja (EE-vid-ya) "Forest-Maiden." 1) One of the maidens of the Ironwood, related to Gullveig. See Jarnvidja. 2) Another name of Gullveig herself.

J

Jafnhar (YAV-n-hahr) "Just as High." Another name of Odin.

Jalangsheath (YAL-angs-heeth) "Jalang's Heath." Near Jelling in Denmark, where a ring laid untouched for a long time during the The Golden Age.

Jalk (YAHLK) "Gelding." 1) Another name of Odin. 2) Another name of Slagfin.

Jari (YAR-i) "The Disputing."1) A Dwarf. 2) An Etin.

Jarl (YARL) "Chieftain." 1) Progenitor of the Skjoldunga clan, son of Fadir and Modir, fostered and taught by Heimdall, father of Kon and several other sons with Erna-Drott. Later married Gefjon-Nyhellenia. Also called Skjold, Borgar, Rig II. 2) Designates a chieftain in general, or a member of the noble class.

Jarnglumra (YAHRN-glum-ra) "Iron-Din." A Giantess.

Jarngreips (YAHRN-grayps) "Iron-Gloves." The gloves Thor wears in order to grasp his hammer, Mjollnir.

Jarnsaxa (YAHRN-saks-a) "She Who Crushes the Iron." A Giantess who turns the Grotti-mill, and is thus one of Heimdall's mothers. She is also the mother of Magni with Thor.

Jarnvidja (YAHRN-vid-ya) "Maid of the Iron-Wood (Ironwood)." 1) One of the maidens of the Ironwood, related to Gullveig. See Ividja. 2) Another name of Gullveig herself.

Jera (YEHR-a) "Year," "Harvest." The twelfth rune of the Elder Futhark. It is associated with agriculture and working the land, which is why it is associated with such ideas in the Runelaw.

Jod (YOHD) "The Descendant." A son of Jarl and Erna-Drott, brother of Kon.

Jofur (YUHV-ur) "Prince," "Chieftain." One of Kon's sons with Alveig.

Jokul (YUHK-ul) "Glacier." An Etin.

Jolf (YOHLV) "Horse-Wolf." Another name of Odin.

Jolfud (YUHL-vud) "Bear." Another name of Odin.

Jolnir (YOHL-nir) "The Yule-Being." Another name of Odin.

Jonak (YOHN-ak) "Young Ruler." Husband of Gudrun, father of Svanhild, Erp, Hamdir, and Sorli.

Jor (YOHR) "Horse," A name of a horse.

Jord (YUHRD) "Earth." Another name of Frigga.

Jormungand (YUHR-mun-gand) "The Great Gandur," "The Great Serpent." Son of Loki and Gullveig. He encircles the earth and is so large he has to bite his own tail to fit around it. He will fight with, and be killed by Thor at Ragnarok, but the Asagod will die from the serpent's venom shortly thereafter.

Jormungrund (YUHR-mun-grund) "The Great Ground." The Underworld.

Jormun (YUHR-mun) "The Great." Another name of Odin.

Jorun (YOHR-un) "The Weaver." Another name of Urd.

Joruvellir (YUHR-u-vehl-ir) "The Jara-Plains," "The Sandy Plains." The Aurvangaland's border with the sea, where Ask and Embla were created.

Jotunheim (YUHT-un-haym) "Giant-Home." There are two: one in Midgard located in the far northeast. The other is in Niflhel, where the lower race of Etins go after death.

K

Kaldgrani (KALD-gran-i) "Cold-Mouth." An Etin.

Kalta (KALT-a) Old Frisian "The Secretive," "The Deceptive." Another name of Gullveig.

Kari (KAHR-i) "Wind." An Etin, son of Fornjot, brother of Aegir-Gymir and Logi, father of Jokul.

Karl (KARL) "Freeman." 1) Another name of Odin. 2) Son of Afi and Amma, husband of Snor, progenitor of the class of Karls, the thanes or free class. 3) Designates a member of the free class.

Kefsir (KEHV-sir) "Bastard." A son of Thrall and Thy.

Keila (KAY-la) "Vixen." A Giantess, killed by Thor.

Kenaz (KEHN-az) "Torch." The sixth rune of the Elder Futhark, representing the sacred flame as well as the search for enlightenment, which is why it is associated with such ideas in the Runelaw.

Kerlaugs (KER-lougs) "Tub-Baths." Two rivers Thor must wade over to get to the Helthing near Urdarbrunn.

Kiarr (KEE-ar) "Chieftain." Father of Sif and Groa. Identical to Sigtryg.

Kili (KIL-i) "Arrow-Smith." A Dwarf.

Kjalar (KYAL-ar) "The One Given Offerings." Another name of Odin.

Kjalki (KYALK-i) "Sled," "Sledge." Another name of Vagnhofdi.

Kjallandi (KYAL-and-i) "The Feminine." A Giantess, killed by Thor.

Kleggi (KLEHG-i) "Hay-Giver." A son of Thrall and Thy.

Kleima (KLAYM-a) "The Filthy." A Giantess.

Klur (KLOOR) "The Incompetent." A son of Thrall and Thy.

Kolga (KAWLG-a) "Raging Sea." One of the nine daughters of Aegir-Gymir and Gullveig-Ran, who are representatives of the waves.

Koll (KUHL) "Cold." An Etin killed by Egil.

Kon (KAWN) "The Noble." Also called Konung (KAWN-ung) "Kon the Young," which is the original form of "king." Son of Jarl and Drott, the first Teutonic king, regarded as Thor's son as well and given divine status. He was married to Groa, and with her had the son Gudorm. Then he married Alveig, with whom he had Hadding. He robbed both of these women from Egil.

Kor (KUHR) "Sick Bed." Leikin's bed.

Kormt (KUHRMT) "Protecting One." A river Thor must wade over to get to the Helthing near Urd's fountain.

Kornskurdarmonth (KAWRNS-kurd-ar-uhnth) "Reaping Month." The name for September in the Old Norse calendar.

Kort (KAWRT) "The Short." A horse.

Kott (KUHT) "The Cat-Like." An Etin.

Kraka (KRAHK-a) "Screamer," "Crow." A Giantess.

Kumba (KUM-ba) "Stumpy." A daughter of Thrall and Thy.

Kund (KUND) "Son," "Kinsman." A son of Jarl and Erna-Drott, brother of Kon.

Kveldrider (KVEHLD-rīd-er) "Death-Rider," "Horse-Woman of Death." Evil witches.

Kvikadrops (KVIK-u-drawps) "Poison-Drops," "Life-Drops." The liquids that flowed from the Elivagar into Ginnungagap to mix with the heat flowing from Sokkdalir to create life.

Kynsfylgja (KEENS-veelg-ya) "Kin-Fylgja," "Family-Accompanier." The type of fylgja particularly associated with warding families.

Kyrmir (KEERM-ir) "Screamer." An Etin.

L

La (LAH) "Blood." One of Lodur's gifts to humanity, originally given to the first Teutonic pair, Ask and Embla. Afterwards it is impregnated within the fruits of Yggdrasil, then sent to expecting women. Beyond the idea that La is the sacred life-force that keeps us going, it is also our genetics or family line, passed on through the generations.

Laeding (LAID-ing) "Cunningly Binding." A fetter with which Fenrir was bound, but he broke out of.

Laegi (LAIG-i) "Quiet." The name used by the Gods for calm.

Laerad (LAIR-ahd) "Mead-Tree." Another name of Yggdrasil.

Laeti (LAIT-i) "Motion." Combined with La, "blood," this designates the way a conscious being moves and acts, representing the animal elements as separated from the plant element we were created from. It is one of Lodur's gifts to our people.

Lagastaf (LAG-a-stav) "Drink-Stuff." 1) The name used by the Alfar for the sea. 2) The name also used by the Alfar for grain.

Laguz (LAG-uz) Gothic "Water," "Lake." The twenty-first rune of the Elder Futhark, the water rune, connected to ideas of personal balance and the ability to flow around obstacles in the Runelaw.

Landwights (LAND-wīts) A branch of the Alfar living in Midgard, connected to the land in various ways. Some, like the Tomte, are connected to farms and homes, while others, like the Nixi and Stromkarls, are linked to forests and rivers.

Landvidi (LAND-vid-i) "Wide-Land." Vidar's land where Ragnarok will be fought, identical to Vigrid.

Langbak (LANG-bak) "Long-Back." One of the serpents of Niflhel.

Langifot (LANG-i-voht) "Long-Foot." Another name of Hoenir.

Laufey (LOUV-ay) "Leaf-Isle." Loki's mother, wife of Farbauti.

Leggjaldi (LEHG-yald-i) "Long-Shanks." A son of Thrall and Thy.

Leidi (LAYD-i) "The Sorrowful." An Etin, killed by Thor.

Leifi (LAYV-i) "Deserter." An Etin.

Leifnir's Fire (LAYV-nirs Fīr) "Leifnir's Fire," "The Smeared on Fire." A wonderful potion that can allow one to free themselves from any fetter with their breath.

Leifthrasir (LAYV-thras-ir) "Full of Life," "Desirous of Life." One of the Asmegir, currently dwelling in Mimir's grove, Odainsacre. He will be the progenitor of the next age's human race.

Leikin (LAYK-in) "Plague." A Giantess, Loki's daughter, queen of Niflhel and the wights of disease.

Leipt (LAYPT) "Lightning-Quick." A sacred river, flowing through Hel's fields of bliss, by whose clear, shining waters oaths are sworn.

Leirbrimir (LAYR-brim-ir) "Clay-Brimir." Another name of Ymir.

Leirvor (LAYR-vuhr) "Clay-Vor." A Giantess.

Leita Kynnis (LAYT-a KEEN-is) "Visiting Kinsmen." Designates the trip through Hel one takes, led by their fylgja, to visit their ancestors and learn the history of their family and folk from those who experienced it firsthand.

Lettfeti (LEET-veht-i) "Light-Foot." One of the Aesir's horses.

Lif (LEEV) "Life." One of the Asmegir, the maiden preserved in Mimir's grove, Odainsacre, who shall become the progenitress of the coming world-age's virtuous human race.

Lik (LEEK) "Body." The natural elements that were formed by or grown by Mimir and Durin-Surt into human likenesses, then given life by Odin, Hoenir, and Lodur.

Limar (LIM-ar) "Limbs." Thorn-rods kept by Mani, which the Heiptir use to drive nidings to Niflhel by beating their heals with them.

Limrunes (LIM-roons) "Limb-Runes." A group of runes used in the healing art.

Lindring (LIND-ring) "Serpent-Ring." A designation for an oath-ring in serpent-form, reminding those who make promises of the punishments for breaking them.

Linn (LIN) "Serpent." One of the serpents in Niflheim.

Litur (LIT-ur) "Image," "Countenance." 1) A Dwarf. 2) See Litur Goda.

Litur Goda (LIT-ur GAWD-a) "Image of the Gods." One of Lodur's gifts to humans, a body of finer material existing within the Lik, giving it shape and character which is visible to the eye.

Ljodasmiths (LYOHD-a-smiths) "Song-Smiths." Another name of the Gods, as creators of the Fimbulsongs.

Ljonar (LYOHN-ar) "Peacemakers." The divine (and human) arbitrators and judges who work to settle all disputes. Among the Gods these are primarily Baldur, Hod, and Forseti.

Ljosalfar (LYOHS-ahlv-ar) "Light-Elves." The group of Alfar dealing exclusively with light, or the lighting of the sky, including Dag, Delling, Sol and Sunna, Billing, and even Natt (also called Ostara).

Ljota (LYOHT-a) "The Ugly." A Giantess.

Loddfafnir (LAWD-vahv-nir) "Slow-Fafnir." Another name of Hod.

Lodin (LAWD-in) "Shaggy." An Etin.

Lodinfingra (LAWD-in-ving-ra) "Shaggy-Finger." A Giantess.

Lodung (LAWD-ung) "Cloak-Wearer." Another name of Odin.

Lodur (LOHD-ur) "Fire-Producer." Son of Bur, brother of Odin and Hoenir, with whom he created Midgard and the first Teutons. He is ward of the atmosphere and caretaker of the Grotti-mill. He is father of Mani and Sol, who have the daughters Nanna and Sunna together. Lodur is also called Vili, Mundilfari, and Gevar.

Lofar (LAWV-ar) "The Praised." Another name of Mimir.

Lofdungs (LAWV-dungs) "Descendants of Lofdi." A legendary clan.

Lofn (LAWV-n) "Permission," "Praise." A Goddess, who is said to be good for lovers to invoke whose union is forbidden or otherwise impossible.

Lofstirr (LAWVS-teer) "Lauditory Reputation." The judgment over the dead that grants them access to the blessed realms in the afterlife.

Logafell (LAWG-a-fehl) "Fire-Mountain." This can either be a place where a battle was once fought, possibly a volcano, or it is where the Valkyries come from to visit earth, or it may simply herald their arrival.

Logi (LAWG-i) "Fire." The personification of fire in the service of destruction and as such belongs to Surt's household as Fjalar-Utgardloki's servant. He is a son of Fornjot and brother of Hler-Aegir and Kari.

Logn (LUHG-n) "Calm." The name used by our ancestors for calm.

Logrinn (LUHG-rin) "The Lake," "The Sea." A lake in Svithjod.

Loinn (LOH-in) "Stroller," "Time-Waster." A Dwarf.

Loki (LAWK-i) "Fire," "Destroying Fire." Son of Farbauti and Laufey, adopted into Asgard by Odin. Father of Jormungand, Leikin, and Fenrir, as well as other wolves, with Gullveig.

Loni (LOHN-i) "Lazy." A Dwarf.

Lopt (LAWPT) "The Airy," "Windy." 1) Another name of Loki. 2) Another name of Volund.

Lud (LOOD) "Mill." Another name of the Grotti-mill.

Lund (LUND) "The Grove." The most ancient Teutonic city, the place where Ask and Embla were formed and where Heimdall brought culture to their descendants. Modern day Lund.

Lung (LUNG) "The Quick." A horse.

Lut (LOOT) "The Disgraceful." 1) An Etin, killed by Thor. 2) A son of Thrall and Thy.

Lyfjaberg (LEEV-ya-berg) "The Healing Mount." The hill or mountain in Freya's home, Folkvangr.

Lyngvi (LEENG-vi) "Overgrown with Heather." The island in the Amsvartnir sea where Loki, Fenrir, and other "Sons of Muspel (World-Ruin)" lie bound until Ragnarok.

Lysing (LEES-ing) "The Shining." The sword given to Jarl that Kon obtained, which he killed Hildibrand-Hildigir with.

M

Maeri (MAIR-i) "Sea-Land." A district in Norway.

Maeringaburg (MAIR-ing-a-berg) "Citadel of the Maerings." The place where Kon's friends and comrades, the Maerings, dwelt.

Maerings (MAIR-ings) "Decsendants of Maeri." Kon's friends and comrades in arms, a legendary clan.

Magni (MAG-ni) "The Strong." Son of Thor and Jarnsaxa, brother of Modi and Thrud. He survives Ragnarok with Modi and together they inherit Thor's stone hammer.

Malrunes (MAHL-roons) "Speech-Runes." Runes that can give speech to the dead, especially when they come to the Helthing, where they are otherwise mute.

Mana (MAHN-a) "Moon." A Giantess.

Managarm (MAHN-a-garm) "Moon-Hound." Hati, the Etin in wolf-guise who will swallow the moon at Ragnarok.

Mani (MAHN-i) "Moon." Son of Lodur-Mundilfari and Sol, brother of Sunna and Nanna.

Manna Meotod (MAN-a MEH-o-tud) "The Fate of Men," "Fruits of Fate." The fruits of Yggdrasil after they have been consecrated for the wombs of expecting women.

Mannaz (MAN-az) "Man." The twentieth rune of the Elder Futhark, associated with mankind and our folk. The Gothic form "Mannaz," is related to Kon's name "Mannus," designating him as one of the patriarchs. Because of this, the rune is connected to ideals of our genetic inheritance in the Runelaw.

Mannheim (MAN-haym) "Man-Home." The part of the world where Odin and the Aesir took refuge when the Vanir ruled in Asgard.

Mannsfylgja (MANS-veelg-ya) "Man's Fylgja," "Man's Accompanier." The fylgja of men, the hamingja, norn, draumkona, or dis.

Mannus (MAN-us) Latin "Man." Another name of Kon.

Mardoll (MAR-duhl) "The Sea-Glimmering." Another name of Freya.

Margerd (MAR-gerd) "Maker of Wounds," "Maimer." A Giantess.

Megingjard (MEHG-in-gyard) "The Belt of Strength." Thor's belt, which doubles his strength when he wears it.

Meginrunes (MEHG-in-roons) "Strength-Runes." A group of runes associated with personal empowerment and physical strength.

Meili (MAYL-i) "Gentle," "Mild." Another name of Baldur.

Melnir (MEEL-nir) "Bridle-Wearer." A horse.

Menglad (MEHN-glad) "Necklace-Lover," "Ornament-Lover." Another name of Freya.

Menglodum (MEHN-gluhd-um) "Necklace-Lovers," "Ornament-Lovers." Designates both Frey and Freya.

Menja (MEHN-ya) "Jewel-Maiden." Fenja's sister who helped turn the Grotti-mill during the first Fimbulwinter, which damaged the device and caused the sky to slope.

Menthjof (MEHN-thyohv) "Jewel-Thief." Rider of the horse, Mor.

Middag (MID-dag) "Midday." Another name of Dag.

Midgard (MID-gard) "The Middle-Realm" The centermost portion of the earth-plate, surrounded by the ocean, in which humans reside. Earth.

Midgardswyrm (MID-gards-weerm) "The Midgard-Serpent." Another name of Jormungand.

Midi (MID-i) "The Average." An Etin.

Midjung (MID-yung) "The Average." Another name of Volund.

Midvitnir (MID-vit-nir) "Sea-Wolf." Another name of Fjalar, also called Mjodvitnir.

Mimameid (MEEM-a-mayd) "Mimir's Tree." Another name of Yggdrasil.

Mimir (MEEM-ir) "The Thinker," "Memory." Ymir's son, created from the sweat of his arms with Bestla. The ruler of Jormungrund, keeper of Yggdrasil, guardian of the well of wisdom, Odin's maternal uncle. Husband of Sinmara and father of the Ostaras and the Brisings. He was slain by the Vanir during their war with the Aesir.

Mimisbrunn (MEEM-is-brun) "Mimir's Well." The central well of wisdom, located where Ginnungagap once was, and protected by Mimir. In its waters reaches the central root of Yggdrasil, which is fed by the sacred mead of the well. Also called Son, Bodn, Odroerir, and Kvasir.

Mimsvin (MEEMS-vin) "Mimir's Friend." Another name of Odin.

Minnihorn (MIN-i-hawrn) "Memory Horn." A drink of remembrance, to help one not forget, commonly used in honoring ancestors, but also to retain information.

Mist (MIST) "Mist." A Valkyrie.

Mistilteinn (MIST-il-tayn) "Mistletoe," "Twig of Mistletoe." Besides the plant, this term designates the arrow forged by Volund for Loki, who gave it to Hod, who unknowingly killed Baldur with it.

Mistorblindi (MIST-awr-blind-i) "Mist-Blind," "The Ugly." Another name of Aegir-Gymir's father, Fornjot.

Mjod (MYUHD) "Mead." The name used by those in Hel for ale.

Mjodvitnir (MYUHD-vit-nir) "Mead-Wolf." Another name of Fjalar as the one who stole the mead of Mimir's fountain to create that of the Byrgir well.

Mjoll (MYUHL) "Fresh-Snow." An Etin, son of Snaer.

Mjollnir (MYUHL-nir) "Crusher." The common name for both of the hammers with which Thor appears in the lore. The older hammer, called "Vingnir's Mjollnir" (because Thor inherited it from his foster-father, Vingnir), is made of stone. The newer one, which was iron and was destroyed by Volund's sword, was forged by Sindri.

Modgud (MOHD-gud) "Furious Battler." The Goddess who watches Gjallarbridge, the bridge the dead cross to get to Hel.

Modi (MOHD-i) "The Courageous." Thor's son, brother of Magni who inherits Mjollnir with him after Ragnarok.

Modir (MOHD-ir) "Mother." Wife of Fadir, mother of Jarl.

Modnir (MOHD-nir) "The Courageous." Sindri-Dvalin's horse.

Modsognir (MOHD-sawg-nir) "Mead-Drinker." Another name of Mimir.

Mog (MUHG) "Knave," "Son." A son of Jarl and Erna-Drott.

Mogthrasir (MUHG-thras-ir) "Son of Thrasir (Ymir)." Another name of Mimir.

Moinn (MOH-in) "Moor-Beast." 1) One of the serpents that gnaw at Yggdrasil's roots. 2) A Dwarf.

Moinnsheath (MOH-ins-heeth) "Moinn's Heath," "Moor-Heath." The place where a battle was fought between the Swedes and Danes.

Mokkurkalfi (MUHK-ur-kahlv-i) "Cloud-Calf." A clay-Etin, created by the Etins to help Hrungnir in his battle against Thor. He was slain by Thjalfi.

Mor (MOHR) "The Brown." A horse.

Morgin (MAWR-gin) "Morning." Another name of Delling.

Morn (MUHRN) "Agony." 1) A vaett of disease. 2) A Giantess.

Mornir (MUHRN-ir) "Agonizing." An Etin.

Mundilfari (MUND-il-var-i) "He Who Turns the Mill Handles." Another name of Lodur as caretaker of the Grotti-mill.

Mund (MUND) "Bride-Price." The Asatru form of dowry, paid by the man to the woman or the woman's family.

Munin (MUN-in) "Memory." One of Odin's ravens.

Munnharpa (MUN-harp-a) "Witch." A Giantess.

Munways (MUN-wayz) "Paths of Pleasure." The paths in Hel-Urd's realm of bliss.

Muspel (MUS-pehl) "World-Ruin." Another name of Loki when he brings forth his demonic progeny, "Muspel's Sons," at Ragnarok.

Mylin (MEEL-in) "Mild-Light." The name used by the Gods for Mani (Moon).

Mylnir (MEEL-nir) "The Haltered." A horse.

Myrkmark (MERK-mark) "The Murk-Wood." Another name of the Ironwood.

Myrkrider (MERK-rīd-er) "Murk-Rider." 1) One of the Swanmaids, when they joined Ivaldi's sons in the Myrkwood-Ironwood, and "delighted in guile." 2) A Giantess.

Myrkwood (MERK-wood) "The Murk-Wood." Another name of the Ironwood.

N

Nabbi (NAB-i) "The Acute." Another name of Sindri.

Nagates (NAH-gayts) "Corpse-Gates." The gates of Niflhel.

Naglfar (NAG-l-var) "Nail-Ship." The ship built of dead men's nails, upon which Loki, Fenrir, and Loki's (Muspel's) sons proceed to the battle of Ragnarok.

Naglfari (NAG-l-var-i) "He Who Turns The Nail (The World Nail, *Veraldar Nagli*, which is identical to the Grotti Mill)." Another name of Lodur, as lord of the Grotti-Mill, compare his name Mundilfari.

Nain (NAH-in) "Corpse." A Dwarf.

Nair (NAH-ir) sing. **Nar** (NAHR) "Corpses." Designates the damned; the nidings in Niflhel after they have died their second deaths.

Nal (NAHL) "Needle," "Death-Demon." Another name of Laufey, Loki's mother.

Nali (NAHL-i) "Corpse," "Death." A Dwarf.

Namaeli (NAH-mail-i) "Death-Declaration." The judgment at the Helthing near Urdarbrunn declaring one a niding, damned to spend their afterlife in Niflhel.

Nanna (NAN-a) "The Brave One." A moon-Goddess, daughter of Mani and Sol, sister of Sunna, and wife of Baldur.

Nar (NAHR) "Corpse." 1) A Dwarf. 2) See Nair.

Nastrand (NAH-strand) "Corpse-Strand." One of the places of punishment for the damned in Niflhel.

Nati (NAT-i) "Nettle." An Etin.

Natt (NAHT) also **Nott** (NOHT) "Night." Mimir's daughter with Sinmara. The mother of the Gods. She bore Njord-Aud with Mani-Naglfari, Frigga with Hoenir-Fjorgyn, and Dag with Delling. She has sisters, night-Goddesses, who are twelve in number; one is Bodvild. Natt is also called Ostara, and her sisters Ostaras.

Nauma (NOUM-a) "The Slender," "The Narrow." Another name of Idun.

Nauthiz (NOUTH-iz) "Need," "Necessity." The tenth rune of the Elder Futhark, the rune of need, associating it with such concepts in the Runelaw.

Needfire (NEED-fīr) "The Need-Fire." The friction-fire, made from rubbing two sticks together to form an auger which drills into a softer wood. This friction creates embers that can be kindled into a flame. This is the most sacred fire, inspired from the sparks of the Grotti-mill.

Nefja (NEHV-ya) "Nose." A Giantess.

Nep (NEHP) "Fist." Another name of Mani.

Neri (NER-i) "The One That Binds." Another name of Mimir.

Nid (NID) pl. **Nidar** (NID-ar) or **Nidjar** (NID-yar) "New Moon." 1) A Dwarf. 2) Personification of the new moon, possibly the aforementioned Dwarf.

Nid (NEED) both plural and singular, "Transgression," "Disgrace." A crime against the Gods or folk, a violation of the Norns' decrees.

Nid (NID) "Kinsman." Son of Jarl and Erna-Drott.

Nidafjoll (NID-a-vyuhl) "Nidi's Mountain." The mountain range that separates Niflhel from Hel's realms of bliss, within Mimir's realm.

Nidavoll (NID-a-vuhl) "Nidi's Plain." Part of Mimir's realm where the hall Sindri lies.

Nidfol (NID-vuhl) "Pale-Beak." The eagle who tears into corpses at Ragnarok.

Nidhogg (NEED-huhg) "The Underworld Serpent." An Underworld serpent who gnaws at Yggdrasil's roots and torments the damned in Niflhel. The only known chaotic being to survive Ragnarok.

Nidi (NID-i) "The Underworld Being." 1) Another name of Mimir. 2) A Dwarf.

Niding (NEED-ing) "Criminal." One who has disgraced himself by committing a nid, a transgression of the sacred laws, which can only be countered by compensation.

Nidjung (NID-yung) "The Descendant." A son of Jarl and Erna-Drott, brother of Kon.

Nidstong (NEED-stuhng) "Nid-Pole," "Insult-Pole." A pole raised to declare someone a niding, or to protest a disgraceful act. It traditionally has either a horse's head on it, or an image of the accused in a lewd position.

Niflheim (NIV-l-haym) "Mist-Home," "The World of Fog or Mist." The name for the land of cold in the far north of Jormungrund. Its primordial frost blended with southern elements of warmth, nurtured by the well of wisdom, Mimisbrunn, to create life.

Niflhel (NIV-l-hehl) "Mist-Hel." The forecourt of Niflheim, where Leikin, who works as Urd's servant, administers punishments. Here are the Hrimthurses, wights of disease, demons of torture, and monsters of all kinds.

Niflungs (NIV-lungs) "Sons of the Mist." A designation of Ivaldi's sons and clan.

Niflways (NIV-l-wayz) "Mist-Ways." The paths in Niflheim.

Niping (NIP-ing) "The Dark." A Dwarf.

Nipt (NIPT) "Kinswoman," "Sister." Possibly another name of Urd.

Nixi (NIKS-ee) German "Water-Spirits." A branch of the Landwights, who can be heard striking their harps during storms at sea. A water-sprite, usually in human form or half-human and half-fish.

Njars (NYAR-s) "The Descendants of Neri," "The Binders." Another name of Mimir's sons.

Njola (NYOHL-a) "Darkness." The name used by the Gods for Natt (Night).

Njord (NYUHRD) "The Strong." A Vanagod, Frigga's half-brother with whom she had Frey, Freya, and her eight sisters: Blid, Frid, Bjart, Hlif, Hlifthrasa, Thjodvarta, Eir, and Blik. Njord is Mani's and Natt's son, God of the sea, of wealth, commerce, and seafarers.

Njot (NYOHT) "The Connoissuer." Another name of Odin.

Noatun (NOH-a-toon) "Ship-Yard." Njord's native home in Vanaheim.

Nokkvi (NUHK-vi) also German **Knakve** (NAK-vee) "Ship-Captain." Another name of Mani, who rules the moon-ship.

Nonn (NUHN) "The Daring." A sacred river.

Nor (NOHR) "Sailor." An Etin.

Nordri (NAWRD-ri) "North." A Dwarf, who holds up the northern point of the sky.

Nori (NOHR-i) "Sailor," "Lad." 1) A Dwarf. 2) Another name of Mimir.

Nor (NUHR) "The Slim," "The One That Binds." Another name of Mimir.

Norns (NAWRNS) "The Proclaimers." 1) (Always capitalized) The three Goddesses of fate, Urd, Verdandi, and Skuld who weave the Web of Wyrd, forming the urlag of all things. 2) (Never capitalized) The disir or fylgjas, who attend births and watch over men. The Valkyries, led by Skuld, are also among these lesser norns.

Norvi (NUHR-vi) "The One That Binds." Another name of Mimir.

Not (NUHT) "The Wet." A sacred river.

Nyhellenia (NEE-hehl-ehn-ya) "The New Light." A Goddess, also called Gefjon, a name she shares with Urd. She came to Midgard to expose Gullveig's use of the Seid.

Ny (NEE) "New-Moon." Personification of the new moon.

Nyi (NEE-i) "The Renewed." A Dwarf.

Nyr (NEER) "The New." A Dwarf.

Nyrad (NEER-ahd) "New-Counsel." A Dwarf.

Nyt (NEET) "The Useful." A sacred river.

O

Od (OHD) "Soul," "Soul-Endowed." 1) Hoenir's gift to humans, originally given to Ask and Embla and continued to be delivered to expecting women through the fruits of Yggdrasil. It forms the kernal of human personality, its ego, and its manifestations are understanding, memory, fancy, and will. 2) Egil's and Groa's son, Freya's rescuer and husband, king of the North Teutons, father of Hnoss, Gersemi, and Asmund with Freya.

Odainsacre (OH-dah-ins-ayk-er) "The Acre of the Not-Dead," "The Acre of Immortality." Mimir's grove, the land of the Asmegir, where Baldur, Hod, and Nanna reside.

Odal (OHD-al) "Estate," An estate passed down through generations.

Odin (OHD-in) "The Inspiring." The highest of the Gods. Son of Bur and Bestla, brother of Hoenir-Ve and Lodur-Vili, father of Thor, Bragi, Baldur, Tyr, Hod, Vidar, and Vali. Married to Frigga. He is God of wisdom, music, poetry, victory, wind, inspiration, etc. He owns the horse Sleipnir, the spear Gungnir, the wolves Freki and Geri, the ravens Hugin and Munin, the ring Draupnir, and the hall Valhall. He has over a hundred bynames and epithets.

Odinism (OHD-in-iz-m) "Belief in Odin." The faith of our ancestors, now reborn, which embodies the cultural heritage of Northern Europe. Also called Asatru, Forn Sed, Theodism, and Irminism.

Odlungs (UHD-lungs) "Descendants of Odli." An ancient clan.

Odroerir (OHD-rur-rir) "The Spirit-Rouser." Another name of Mimisbrunn.

Ofdokkum Ognar Ljoma (OHV-duhk-um OHG-nar LYOHM-a) "Black-Terror Gleam." The material with which the Vafurfires are constructed, also called *Vafur*.

Offoti (OHV-voht-i) "Big-Foot." An Etin, whose hound came into the possession of Hod.

Ofhly (AWV-lee) "Sultry." The name used by the Etins for calm.

Oflugbarda (UHV-lug-bard-a) "Strong-Beard." A Giantess.

Oflugbardi (UHV-lug-bard-i) "Strong-Beard." An Etin.

Ofnir (OHV-nir) "The Entangler." 1) Another name of Odin. 2) One of the serpents who gnaws at Yggdrasil's roots.

Ogladnir (OH-glad-nir) "The Unhappy." An Etin.

Oin (OH-in) "The Shy." A Dwarf.

Okolnir (OH-kawl-nir) "The Un-Cold," "The Warm." Another name of Mimir's grove, Odain-sacre.

Okuthor (UHK-u-thohr) "Chariot-Thor." Another name of Thor.

Okkvinkalfa (UHK-vin-kalv-a) "Spindleshanks." A daughter of Thrall and Thy.

Ol (UHL) "Ale." The name used by our ancestors for ale.

Olgefjun (UHL-gehv-yun) "Ale-Giver." Another name of Groa.

Olgefn (UHL-gehv-n) "Ale-Giver." Another name of Idun.

Olg (UHLG) "God of Stormy Seas." Another name of Odin.

Oljos (OHL-yohs) "Lightless." The name used by the Etins for Natt (Night).

Olnir (UHL-nir) "Enchanter." A Dwarf.

Olrunes (UHL-roon-ar) "Ale-Runes." A class of runic prayers used to protect from treachery and poisoned ale.

Omi (OHM-i) "He Who Makes Beautiful Sounds." Another name of Odin.

Ond (UHND) "Spirit," "Breath." Odin's gift to our folk, originally given to Ask and Embla and continued to be delivered to expecting women through Yggdrasil's fruits. It is that which forges our bond with the divine and allows us to participate in workings connected to them.

Ondud (UHND-ud) "The Opponent." An Etin.

Onduras (UHND-ur-ahs) "The Ski-God." Another name of Ull.

Ondurdis (UHND-ur-dees) "The Ski-Goddess." Another name of Skadi.

Ondurgod (UND-ur-gawd) "The Ski-Deity." Another name of Skadi.

Opi (OHP-i) "Hysteria." A vaett of disease.

Ori (OHR-i) "The Raging." A Dwarf.

Ormt (UHRMT) "Tributary." One of the rivers Thor has to wade through on his way to the Helthing by Urdarbrunn.

Ornir (UHRN-ir) "The Quick." An Etin.

Orvandill (UHR-van-dil) "The One Busy With Arrows." Another name of Egil.

Osgrui (UHS-groo-i) "Ash-Heap." An Etin.

Oski (OHS-ki) "Wish-God." Another name of Odin.

Oskopnir (OH-skohp-nir) "The Playground." The plain on which the battle of Ragnarok occurs. Also known as Vigrid's plain.

Oskrud (UHS-krud) "Screamer." An Etin.

Ostara (AWST-a-ra) "Goddess of the Eastern Dawn." 1) Another name of Natt, leader of the Ostaras, wife of Delling. 2) The month of April named after Natt-Ostara. 3) The festival of the spring equinox, named after Natt-Ostara.

Ostaras (AWST-a-ras) "The Goddesses of the Eastern Dawn." Natt's sisters, Goddesses of night and dawn. Cp. Hindu *Ushas*.

Othala (OHTH-al-a) "Estate," "Inheritance." The twenty-fourth rune of the Elder Futhark, associated with inheritance, which is why it is connected to such concepts in the Runelaw.

Otholi (OH-thawl-i) "Restless Anxiety." A vaett of disease.

Owights (OH-wīts) "Undead," "Wights of Undoing." Evil ghosts.

P

Perthro (PER-throh) "Lot-Box," "Dice-Cup." The fourteenth rune of the Elder Futhark, associated with oracles, connecting it to such concepts in the Runelaw.

R

Rabenschlacht (RAHB-ehn-shlakt) German "The Raben Battle." The first battle between Od's and Hadding's armies, where Od was victorious.

Radgrid (RAHD-greed) "Violent-Counsel." A Valkyrie.

Radso (RAHDS-uh) "Union-Isle," "Counsel-Isle," "Sex-Isle." May be an actual island, or part of an insult Loki passed on to Thor.

Radsvid (RAHDS-vid) "Counsel-Wise." A Dwarf.

Raefil (RAIV-il) "The Uprising." A sea-king.

Raesir (RAIS-ir) "Prince." A son of Kon and Alveig.

Raido (RAYD-o) Gothic "Wagon," "Ride." The fifth rune of the Elder Futhark, associated with traveling, which is why it is connected to such concepts in the Runelaw.

Ragnarok (RAG-na-ruhk) "The Twilight of the Gods." The doom of the worlds, the end of this age, or age-cycle.

Ran (RAHN) "Robber." Another name of Gullveig, wife of Gymir-Aegir.

Randgrid (RAND-greed) "Shield-Destroyer." A Valkyrie.

Randver (RAND-veer) "Shield-Warrior." A son of Gudorm, killed by his father for taking his bride-to-be for himself, at Loki's instigation.

Rangbein (RANG-bayn) "The Bowlegged." An Etin.

Rani (RAHN-i) "Divine Strength." Another name of Vali.

Ratatosk (RAT-a-tawsk) "Rati's Tooth." Heimdall's fire-auger, symbolized as a squirrel (which is still a symbol of fire in folk belief), which runs from Yggdrasil's crown down to its roots.

Rati (RAT-i) "The Traveler." Another name of Heimdall.

Raudgrani (ROUD-gran-i) "Red-Mouth." Another name of Odin.

Regin (REHG-in) "The Powerful." Another name of Egil.

Reginleif (REHG-in-layv) "The Mighty." A Valkyrie.

Rekk (REHK) "Warrior," "Hero." A Dwarf.

Rennandi (REHN-and-i) "The Running." A sacred river.

Rifingafla (REEV-in-gav-la) "Mighty-Tearer." A Giantess.

Rig (REEG) "Ruler." Another name of Heimdall, bestowed upon his descendants Jarl (Rig II) and Kon (Rig III).

Rind (RIND) "The Wise." The daughter of Billing, lord of the sunset glow. Mother of Vali, Baldur's avenger, with Odin.

Ristill (RIST-il) "Lady." A daughter of Karl and Snor.

Rognir (RUHG-nir) "Ruler." 1) Another name of Volund. 2) Another name of Odin.

Rosamuda (ROHS-a-mud-a) "Rose-Mouth." A possible successor to the role of Folkmodir after Erna-Drott, which was given to Nyhellenia.

Roskva (RUHSK-va) "The Maturing," "The One Bearing Fruit." Thjalfi's sister, adopted with her brother by Egil, then by Thor.

Rota (ROHT-a) "Creator of Confusion." A Valkyrie.

Rud (RUD) "The Clearing." A sacred river.

Rune (ROON) pl. **Runes** (ROONS) "Rune," "Secret." A group of sacred symbols with many spiritual and practical uses, as well as charms and teachings related to all sorts of topics. The runes act as guides and lessons in matters dealing with aiding others and gaining success in any endeavor. They do so as prayers and songs to the Gods.

Runelaw (ROON-law) "Runelaw." A contemporary reconstruction of ancient Teutonic laws to form a core morality within the Asatru faith.

Rusila (RUS-il-a) "The Raging," "The Red." Ivaldi's mother, queen of the Alfar, also said to be among the Haffrus.

Ryg (REEG) "The Bellowing." A Giantess.

Rym (REEM) "The Roaring." Another name of Thor.

T

Tafl (TAV-l) "Tables." A forerunner of chess, the game of the Gods.

Talhrein (TAHL-rayn) "Decoy-Reindeer." The reindeer used to lure predators, which Volund used to lure the Gods Odin, Hoenir, and Loki.

Tamsvond (TAMS-vuhnd) "The Staff That Subdues." Another name of Gambantein.

Toothfee (TOOTH-fee) "Tooth-Fee." A payment given when a child cuts its first tooth. Frey was given Alfheim as his toothfee.

Tanngnjost (TAN-nyohst) "Tooth-Gnasher." One of Thor's goats that pull his chariot, the other is Tanngrisnir. The goats can be killed, eaten, then resurrected when their bones are consecrated with Mjollnir.

Tanngrisnir (TAN-gris-nir) "Tooth-Grinder." One of Thor's goats that pull his chariot, the other is Tanngnjost.

Thane (THAYN) "Freeman." 1) Identical to one of the Karls, the middle class. 2) A name of one of the sons of Karl and Snor.

384

Thekk (THEHK) "The Welcome One." 1) Another name of Odin. 2) A Dwarf.

Thengil (THEHNG-il) "The Reliable," "Prince." A son of Kon and Alveig.

Thing (THING) "Assembly," "Gathering." A formal gathering where important matters are discussed and debated, disputes are settled, and legal issues resolved.

Thingseats (THING-seets) The judges' seats at the Thing.

Thingstead (THING-stehd) The place where the Thing is held.

Thistilbardi (THIS-til-bard-i) "Thistle-Beard." An Etin.

Thjalfi (THYAL-vi) "Child of the Dyke or Delve." First Egil and Groa's, then Thor's foster-son and companion, Roskva's brother.

Thjazi (THYAZ-i) "The Giant." Another name of Volund.

Thjodnuma (THYOHD-num-a) "Sweeping People Away." A sacred river.

Thjodrek (THYOHD-rehk) "Folk-Ruler." Another name of Hadding.

Thjodreyrir (THYOHD-ray-rir) "Waker of the People." The Dwarf that sings songs of blessing outside Delling's door at dawn.

Thjodvarta (THYOHD-vart-a) "Folk-Warner." A daughter of Njord and Frigga, one of Freya's sisters and maidservants.

Thjodvitnir (THYOHD-vit-nir) "Folk-Wolf." Another name of Heimdall.

Thogn (THUHG-n) "Host-Receiver." A Valkyrie.

Thokk (THUHK) "Thanks," "Gratitude." The being in female guise who refused to cry Baldur out of Hel, most likely Loki.

Tholl (THUHL) "The Still." A sacred river.

Thorin (THAWR-in) "The Daring." A Dwarf.

Thorn (THAWRN) "Thorn." Another name of Ymir, cp. Bolthorn.

Thor (THOHR) "The Thunderer." Son of Odin and Frigga. God of thunder, the farmer's benefactor, protector of Midgard. He wields the hammer Mjollnir against Etins, while wearing the belt of strength, Megingjard, and a pair of gloves, Jarngreips, which aid in his use of the hammer. He is Sif's husband, Magni, Modi, and Thrud's father, Ull's stepfather, and Thjalfi and Roskva's foster-father.

Thorri (THAWR-i) "Black-Frost." 1) An Etin. 2) The name for January in the Old Norse calendar.

Thorsnes (THOHRS-nehs) "Thor's Ness." The site of Gnipalund, the place where Loki gave birth to Jormungand, Leikin, and Fenrir.

Thrall (THRAHL) "Slave." 1) Son of Ai and Edda, progenitor of the class of Thralls. 2) A member of the lower or slave class, the Thralls.

Thrain (THRAH-in) "The Threatening." A Dwarf.

Thrasar (THRAS-ar) "The Furious." Another name of Odin.

Thrasir (THRAS-ir) "Stormer." Another name of Geirrod.

Thridi (THRID-i) "Third." Another name of Odin.

Thrigeitir (THRI-gayt-ir) "Three-Goats." An Etin.

Thriggi (THRIG-i) "The Three-Sided." Another name of Odin.

Thrima (THRIM-a) "Battle." A Valkyrie.

Thrivaldi (THRI-vald-i) "As Strong as Three." An Etin, slain by Thor.

Throng (THRUHNG) "The Slender." Another name of Freya.

Thropt (THRAWPT) "The God." Another name of Odin.

Thror (THROHR) "Inciter of Strife." 1) Another name of Odin. 2) A Dwarf.

Thrudgelmir (THROOD-gehl-mir) "Mighty-Roarer." A Hrimthurse, Ymir's son, born from his father's feet.

Thrudheim (THROOD-haym) "Home of the Mighty," "Thrud's Home." Thor's hall.

Thrud (THROOD) "The Mighty." A Valkyrie, Thor's daughter.

Thrudvang (THROOD-vang) "Plains of the Mighty," "Thrud's Plains." Thor's realm.

Thrund(THRUND) "God of Rising Waters." Another name of Odin.

Thrungva (THRUNG-va) "The Slender." Another name of Freya.

Thrymgjoll (THREEM-gyuhl) "The Loud-Grating." The gate made by Ivaldi's sons for Gastropnir, Asgard's wall. It is also called Valgrind.

Thrymheim (THREEM-haym) "Noise-Home." Volund and Skadi's land in the Ironwood.

Thrym (THREEM) "The Noisy." The Etin who stole Thor's hammer.

Thund (THUND) "The Roaring." 1) Another name of Odin. 2) The sea of air, also called Ifing.

Thunn (THUN) "The Slim." Another name of Odin.

Thurbord (THUR-bawrd) "Arrow-Shield." A Giantess.

Thurisaz (THUR-i-saz) Gothic "Thurse," The third rune of the Elder Futhark, associated with the Etins or Thurses as the great conflicting force against the Gods, which Thor battles courageously. Because of this, it is associated with such concepts in the Runelaw.

Thurse (THURS) "Giant." A designation of the low-born Etins of Ymir's feet.

Thviti (THVIT-i) "Cut to the Ground." The rock anchoring the fetter that holds Fenrir.

Thy (THEE) "Drudge." Wife of Thrall and progenitress of the class of Thralls.

Thyn (THEEN) "Frothing." A sacred river.

Tiggi (TIG-i) "The Glorious." A son of Kon and Alveig.

Tiwaz (TI-vaz) "Tyr," The seventeenth rune of the Elder Futhark. In order to protect the Gods' honor when they bound the wolf, Fenrir, Tyr sacrificed his hand as a pledge. Such an act defines the honorable disposition of the Gods. Seeing as this pledge is connected to oaths given to Fenrir, such concepts are associated with this rune in the Runelaw.

Tjaldari (TYAL-dar-i) "The Trotting." A horse.

Tjosul (TYUHS-ul) "Agony." A vaett of disease.

Tomte (TAWM-teh) "House-Elf." One among the branch of the Landwights connected to houses and farms.

Topi (TOHP-i) "Insanity." A vaett of disease.

Totrughypja (TUHT-rug-hep-ya) "The Slovenly." A daughter of Thrall and Thy.

Tramar (TRAM-ar) sing. **Tram** (TRAM) "Evil Witches." Demons and sorceresses who cause suffering and torment.

Tronubeina (TRUHN-u-bayn-a) "Stout-Leg." A daughter of Thrall and Thy.

Tunrid (TOON-reed) pl. **Tunridur** (TOON-reed-ur) "Night-Hags," "Demons." The evil beings Odin cleanses the air of in his Wild Hunt.

Tveggi (TVEHG-i) "The Two-Sided." Another name of Odin.

Twimonth (TVEE-muhnth) "Second-Month." The name for August in the Old Norse calendar.

Tyhaustur (TEE-houst-ur) "Tyr-Courageous." The type of courage displayed in one who advances to the frontline of combat or adversity without ever losing their courage.

Tyr (TEER) "God." Odin's son, not the original sky-father, but who inherited his father's name. His mother is a Giantess, wife of Hymir. He is the God of war and warriors. **Tyrfing** (TEER-ving-r) "Tyr's Finger." The sword Mimir's sons created and gave to Lodur, trying to mimic Volund's Gambantein.

Tyirings (TEER-ings) "Descendants of Tyr." An ancient clan.

Tyspakur (TEE-spak-ur) "Tyr-Wise." Designates an extremely clever person.

S

Sad (SAD) "The Truthful." Another name of Odin.

Saeg (SAIG) "The Noisy." The pail in which the Byrgir mead was carried.

Saehrimnir (SAI-reem-nir) "Sea-Rime." The boar of Valhall, said to be slain and reborn each day.

Saekarlsmuli (SAI-karls-mool-i) "Sea-Man's Mouth." An Etin.

Saekin (SAIK-in) "Seeker." A sacred river.

Saeming (SAIM-ing) "Son of the Fertility God." Son of Odin and Skadi, probably human since he was born at the time they were stripped of their divinity.

Saer (SAIR) "Sea." The term used by our ancestors for the sea.

Saevafjol (SAIV-a-vyuhl) "Sea-Fell," "Sea-Mountain." The place where Kon was buried after he was slain by Od, where Alveig met his spirit after death.

Saevarstod (SAIV-ar-stuhd) "Sea-Stead." The island where Volund was imprisoned in Mimir's realm.

Saga (SAHG-a) "The Loud," "Carrier of Saeg." Another name of Idun.

Sagunes (SAG-u-nehs) "Saga Ness." The place where Loki and Gullveig bore their wolf brood together.

Salfang (SAL-vang) "Hall-Robber." An Etin.

Salgofnir (SAL-gawv-nir) "The One Crowing in the Hall." Another name of Gullinkambi, the cock in Valhall.

Samendil (SAM-ehn-dil) "The Familiar Foe." An Etin.

Samso (SAMS-uh) "Samr's Isle," "The Dark-Isle." The island where Billing lives with Rind, where Odin went to find a mother for Vali.

Sanngetal (SAN-geht-al) "The One Who Guesses Right." Another name of Odin.

Sangrid (SAN-greed) "True-Destroyer." A Valkyrie.

Seedtide (SEED-tīd) "Seed-Tide." The name for April in the Old Norse calendar.

Segg (SEHG) "Man," "Warrior." A son of Karl and Snor.

Seidberend (SAYD-ber-ehnd) "Seid Workers." Evil sorcerers descended from the Etin Svarthofdi-Surt.

Seidhall (SAYD-hahl) "Seid-Seat." An area consecrated by the powers of Chaos, in which Seid is practiced.

Seid (SAYD) "Sorcery." The black art, founded by Gullveig. It is characterized by mind-control, poisoning, conjuration, and necromancy. It was banned by the Gods after the Folkvig, declared to be harmful to our folk, and blasphemous to our faith.

Sela (SEHL-a) "Woman." A Giantess, sister of Koll, slain by Egil.

Selmonth (SEHL-muhnth) "Mountain-Pasture Month." A name for June in the Old Norse calendar.

Sessrumnir (SEHS-room-nir) "With Many Seats." Freya's hall in Folkvang.

Siar (SEE-ar) "The Panning." A Dwarf.

Sid (SEED) "The Slow." A sacred river.

Sidgrani (SEED-gran-i) "Long-Beard." Another name of Odin.

Sidhot (SEED-huht) "Long-Hat." Another name of Odin.

Sidskeg (SEED-skehg) "Long-Beard." Another name of Odin.

Sif (SIV) "Goddess of Affinity." Daughter of Sigtryg, a Swanmaid, Groa's sister and Egil's second wife, who bore the archer and skier Ull with him. She later became an Asynja and married Thor, with whom she had the daughter Thrud and the son Modi.

Sigarsvellir (SIG-ars-vehl-ir) "Sigar's Fields." An odal ruled over by Kon.

Sigdir (SIG-dir) "Sword-God." Another name of Odin.

Sigfather (SIG-fah-ther) "Victory-Father." Another name of Odin.

Sigmund (SIG-mund) "Victory-Payment," "Giver of Victory." 1) Another name of Odin. 2) An ancient hero, father of Sigurd.

Signi (SIG-ni) "The Blessing." Another name of Alveig.

Sigurhofund (SIG-ur-huhv-und) "Giver of Victory." Another name of Odin.

Sigrun (SIG-roon) "The One Who Knows the Victory Runes." Another name of Odin.

Sigrunes (SIG-roons) "Victory Runes." A group of runes that grant victory in battle or endeavors.

Sigtryg (SIG-treg) "Victory True." 1) Groa's and Sif's father, killed by Kon. 2) Another name of Odin.

Sigtyr (SIG-teer) "Victory-Tyr," "Giver of Victory." Another name of Odin.

Sigtyrsberg (SIG-teers-berg) "Sigtyr-Odin's Mountain." The mountain on which Valhall rests.

Sigurblot (SIG-ur-bloht) "Victory-Sacrifice." The offering made each year for victory in battle or struggle, probably coinciding with Baldag, the Celtic Beltaine, May 1st, the first day of summer.

Sigurd (SIG-urd) "Fated for Victory." A famous hero of the Volsunga clan.

Sigyn (SIG-en) "Victory." Loki's wife who holds a bowl over his face to keep a serpent's venom from dripping onto him. The venom-spewing serpent is a typical punishment for nidings, which the Gods imposed upon Loki for his crimes.

Silaegja (SIL-aig-ya) "Smooth-Lying." The name used by the Gods for the sea.

Silfrtopp (SILV-r-tawp) "Silver Forelock." One of the Aesir's horses.

Simul (SIM-ul) "Brewing Ale," "Mead." 1) The pole on which Hjuki-Slagfin and Bil-Idun bore the pail Saeg with Byrgir's mead. 2) A Giantess.

Sindri (SIND-ri) "Cinders." 1) One of Mimir's most talented artist sons, identical to Dvalin. 2) The hall or smithy where Mimir's sons work, near Nidafjoll.

Sinfjotli (SIN-vyuht-li) "The Sinewy." An ancient hero.

Singastein (SING-a-stayn) "The Old Stone," "The Ornament Rock." Identical to Vagasker and Aldland, this is where Freya stood by Od during his time of exile, where Heimdall and Loki fought for Brisingamen.

Sinhtgunt (SINT-gunt) German "The Nightly Faring Battle-Maiden." Another name of Nanna.

Sinir (SIN-ir) "Strong of Sinew." One of the Aesir's horses.

Sinmara (SIN-mar-a) "Sinew-Maimer." Mimir's wife, mother of Natt, Bodvild, and the other Ostaras.

Sivor (SEE-vuhr) "Burnt-Lip." A Giantess.

Sjofn (SYUHV-n) "Love." An Asynja, concerned with turning men and women's minds to love.

Skadi (SKAD-i) "Shadow," "Scathe." Volund's daughter with Idun, a skier and huntress. She became an Asynja and married Njord. Lived with Odin in Mannheim when he was exiled from Asgard, and had the son Saeming with him.

Skaerir (SKAIR-ir) "Dusk," "Twilight." An Etin.

Skaevad (SKAI-vad) "The Hurrying." The horse of Hadding.

Skafid (SKA-vid) "The Scraper." A Dwarf.

Skald (SKAHLD) "Narrator," "Divinely Inspired." A bard or poet who tells the old tales in verse form or sings the sacred songs.

Skalli (SKAL-i) "Bald-Headed." An Etin.

Skandia (SKAN-di-a) also **Skaney** (SKAHN-ay) "Skåne." The primordial homeland of the Teutonic people.

Skat (SKAT) "Chieftain." Another name of Hildur.

Skatyrnir (SKAT-eer-nir) "Rich-Wetter." The ninth heaven.

Skavaer (SKAH-vair) "The Good-Natured." A Dwarf.

Skef (SKEHV) Anglo-Saxon "Sheaf." Another name of Heimdall.

Skeggbragi (SKEHG-brag-i) "Beard-Bragi." Designates a person with a long beard in connection with Bragi.

Skeggjold (SKEHG-yuhld) "Battle-Axe." A Valkyrie.

Skeidbrimir (SKAYD-brim-ir) "Fast-Galloper." One of the Aesir's horses.

Skerkir (SKERK-ir) "The Noisy." An Etin.

Skerry Grotti (SKER-ee GRAWT-i) "Skerry-Grotti," "The Mill of Skerries." Another name of the Grotti-mill.

Skidbladnir (SKEED-blad-nir) "The Thin-Planked." The ship Ivaldi's sons made for Frey.

Skilfings (SKIL-vings) "Descendants of Skilfr-Skef (Heimdall)." A legendary clan of the North, identical to the Ynglings.

Skilfing (SKIL-ving) "The High-One," "The Skilfing." Another name of Odin.

Skin (SKIN) "Shining," "Gleamer." The name used by the Dwarves for Mani (Moon).

Skinfaxi (SKIN-vaks-i) "Shining-Mane." Dag's horse.

Skipta Litum (SKIPT-a LIT-um) "Exchange of the Litur." A magical practice where two beings can become one another by exchanging their inner-being or litur.

Skirar Veigar (SKEER-ar VAYG-ar) "Clear-Liquids." The meads of the three Underworld fountains combined into one sacred drink.

Skirfir (SKIR-vir) "Skillful Artisan." A Dwarf.

Skirnir (SKEER-nir) "The Shining One." Another name of Od.

Skjaldraras (SKYALD-rar-ahs) "Shield-As," "Shield-God." Another name of Ull.

Skjalf (SKYALV) "Goddess of Fertility." Another name of Freya.

Skjold (SKYUHLD) "Shield." Another name of Jarl.

Skjoldungs (SKYUHLD-ungs) "Descendants of Skjold." The first and foremost legendary clan, descended from the Teutonic patriarchs, Jarl-Skjold and Kon.

Skogul (SKUHG-ul) "Battle." A Valkyrie.

Skoll (SKUHL) "Mockery." A wolf-Etin. Fenrir's son who chases Sol on her path through the sky.

Skram (SKRAHM) "The Frightening." An Etin.

Skrati (SKRAT-i) "Troll." An Etin.

Skridfinns (SKRID-vins) "Ski-Finns." An ancient clan under Ivaldi's rule.

Skrikja (SKREEK-ya) "The Screaming." A Giantess.

Skrimnir (SKREEM-nir) "The Frightening." An Etin.

Skrog (SKRUHG) "The Wolf." An Etin.

Skrymir (SKREEM-ir) "The Large," "Big Fellow," "Boaster." Another name of Fjalar.

Skuld (SKULD) "Debt," "Spinster." One of the high Norns; Urd and Verdandi's sister. She is the leader of the Valkyries.

Skurvan (SKOOR-vahn) "Rain-Hope." The name used by the Gods for the clouds.

Sky (SKEE) "Sky." The name used by our ancestors for the clouds.

Skyli (SKEEL-i) also **Skuli** (SKUL-i) "King," "Protector." A son of Kon and Alveig.

Skyndi (SKEEND-i) "Speeder." The name used by the Etins for Mani (Moon).

Slagfin (SLAG-vin) "The Finn of Stringed-Instruments." Son of Ivaldi and Greip, brother of Egil and Volund. Auda's husband, progenitor of the Gjukungs.

Sleipnir (SLAYP-nir) "The Runner." Odin's eight-legged horse, son of Svadilfari and Loki in mare guise.

Slid (SLEED) "The Fearsome." A subterranean river that flows through Niflhel.

Slidrugtanni (SLEED-rug-tan-i) "Razor-Tooth." Another name of Gullinbursti, Frey's golden boar.

Slungnir (SLUNG-nir) "The Hurling." Ull's horse.

Smith (SMITH) "Smith." A son of Karl and Snor.

Snaefjol (SNAI-vyuhl) "Snow-Fell." An odal ruled over by Kon.

Snaer (SNAIR) "Snow." An Etin, representative of the Fimbulwinter.

Snor (SNUHR) "Daughter-in-Law." Wife of Karl and progenitress of the class of Karls or Thegnar.

Snot (SNOHT) "The Quick." A daughter of Karl and Snor.

Snotra (SNAWT-ra) "The Wise," "The Courtly." An Asynja, said to be wise and to have beautiful manners.

Sokkdalir (SUHK-dal-ir) "The Deep-Dales." Surt's realm in the far south of Jormungrund where the heat of creation issued forth towards Ginnungagap.

Sokkmimir (SUHK-meem-ir) "Mimir of the Deep." Another name of Surt.

Sokkvabekk (SUHK-va-behk) "The Sinking Ship." The name of the moon during its descent.

Sol (SOHL) "Sun." The mother and daughter Goddesses of the sun; both carry all the same names and epithets. To differentiate the two, the mother is here is called Sol, the daughter Sunna.

Solbjart (SOHL-byart) "Sun-Bright." Another name of Egil.

Solblindi (SOHL-blind-i) "Sun-Blind." Another name of Ivaldi.

Solfjol (SOHL-vyuhl) "Sun-Fell." An odal ruled over by Kon.

Solmonth (SOHL-muhnth) "Sun-Month." The name for June in the Old Norse calendar.

Son (SOHN) "Sap." Another name of Mimisbrunn.

Sonar Dreyri (SOHN-ar DRAYR-i) "Son's Blood." The mead of Mimisbrunn, which grants wisdom.

Son (SAWN) "Son." A son of Jarl and Erna-Drott, brother of Kon.

Sonnung (SOHN-ung) "The Loud Youth." Another name of Thor.

Sorli (SUHR-li) "Warrior," "The Armed." Son of Gudrun and Jonak, brother of Hamdir, Svanhild, and Erp, killed by Gudorm.

Soti (SOHT-i) "The Sooty-Black." A horse.

Sowilo (SOH-vil-oh) Gothic "Sun," The sixteenth rune of the Elder Futhark, connected to the sun and to victory. It could also be a rune of Baldur as God of summer and one of the Ljonar—"peacemakers," which is why it is associated with such concepts in the Runelaw.

Sparinsheath (SPAR-ins-heeth) "Sparin's Heath." A place name.

Sporvitnir (SPAWR-vit-nir) "Wolf-Trampler." A horse.

Sprakki (SPRAK-i) "Chatterer." A daughter of Karl and Snor.

Spretting (SPREHT-ing) "The Springing." An Etin.

Sprund (SPRUND) "The Lively." A daughter of Karl and Snor.

Starkad (STAR-kad) "The Strong." An Etin, killed by Thor.

Stigandi (STIG-and-i) "The Leading." An Etin.

Storverk (STOHR-verk) "Strong-Worker." An Etin.

Stromkarl (STRUHM-karl) "Stream-Karl," "River-Sprite." A branch of the Landwights associated with rivers and waterfalls, whose lyre can be heard on summer nights.

Strond (STRUHND) "Strand." A sacred river.

Stuf (STOOV) "The Kicking." A horse.

Stumi (STUM-i) "Pitch-Dark." An Etin.

Sudri (SUD-ri) "South." The Dwarf who holds up the southern point of the sky.

Sult (SULT) "Famine." Leikin's knife.

Sumar (SUM-ar) also **Somur** (SOHM-ur) "Summer." The Etin of summer, son of Svasud.

Sumbel (SUM-bel) "Drinking-Feast." 1) A sacred drinking feast consisting of several rounds or "horns," including the Minnihorn, where ancestors are honored, and the Bragarfull, where deeds are boasted of or oaths are made to partake in future exploits. 2) The name used by Suttung-Fjalar's sons for the mead itself.

Sunna (SUN-a) "Sun." Although both Goddesses of the sun carry this name, here it is used to designate the daughter, rather than the mother (Sol). This is the name the Gods use for the sun.

Surt (SURT) "The Swarthy." Representative of the subterranean fire. In the beginning, he was the Gods' friend and Mimir's co-worker; thereafter he is their enemy. Father of Fjalar-Suttung and jarl of Suttung's Sons. The last possessor of Gambantein, which, when used by Etin hands, causes the subterranean fires to burst loose, bringing forth the world-conflagration. He is also called Durin, Durnir, Svarthofdi, and Sokkmimir.

Suttung (SUT-ung) "Surt's Son." Another name of Fjalar.

Svadilfari (SVAD-il-var-i) "Traveling Misfortune." The horse who sired Sleipnir with Loki.

Svafnir (SVAHV-nir) "Sleep-Inducer." 1) Another name of Odin. 2) One of the serpents gnawing at Yggdrasil's roots. 3) Another name of Hoenir.

Svafrthorin (SVAV-r-thawr-in) "Sleep-Thorn." Another name of Hoenir.

Svalin (SVAL-in) "Cooler." The shield held before Sol, which protects her from the sun's heat.

Svalkaldur Saer (SVAL-kald-ur SAIR) "Cool-Cold Sea." The mead of Hvergelmir, which gives endurance.

Svanhild (SVAN-hild) "Battle-Swan." Daughter of Gudrun, sister of Hamdir, Sorli, and Erp, who was slain by Gudorm at Loki's instigation.

Svanni (SVAN-i) "The Clever." A daughter of Karl and Snor.

Svarang (SVAHR-ang) "The Hard," "The Bad." An Etin.

Svarin (SVAR-in) "The Defender." An ancient warrior killed by Kon.

Svarinsmound (SVAR-ins-mound) "Svarin's Grave-Mound." The place where the great Folk-wanderung began and the return home ended.

Svarri (SVAR-i) "The High-Spirited." A daughter of Karl and Snor.

Svartalfar (SVART-ahlv-ar) "Swarthy-Elves." The Alfar who joined Surt-Durin after his rebellion against Mimir. In this sense the name could also mean "Surt's Elves," although it should be remembered that some remain on the side of good and even help the Gods on occasion. Cp. Svarthofdi.

Svartalfheim (SVART-ahlv-haym) "Home of the Svartalfar." Identical to Surt's Sokkdalir.

Svarthofdi (SVART-huhv-di) "Chieftain of the Swarthy." Another name of Surt.

Svart (SVART) "The Swarthy." An Etin.

Svasud (SVAH-sud) "The Delightful." An Etin, father of Sumar.

Svava (SVAHV-a) "Sleeper." 1) Sol, mother of Sunna and Nanna with Mani. This is also a name of Nanna herself. 2) A Valkyrie.

Svefngaman (SVEHV-n-gam-an) "Sleep's Joy." The name used by the Alfar for Natt (Night).

Sveigdir (SVAYG-dir) also **Svigdir** (SVIG-dir) "The Drinker." 1) Another name of Odin. 2) A name of Ivaldi, which Odin assumed when he stole the mead from Fjalar.

Svein (SVAYN) "Swain," "Youth." A son of Jarl and Erna-Drott.

Sveipinfalda (SVAYP-in-vald-a) "The Veiled." A Giantess.

Svidar (SVID-ar) "The Calming." Another name of Odin.

SVidir (SVID-rir) "The Drinker," "The Wise." 1) Another name of Odin. 2) Another name of Ivaldi.

Svidud (SVID-ud) "The Calming." Another name of Odin.

Svidur (SVID-ur) "The Drinker," "The Wise." 1) Another name of Odin. 2) Another name of Ivaldi.

Svinfylkja (SVEEN-veelk-ya) "Swine-Formation." The wedge-shape battle formation Odin taught to Hamal.

Svipal (SVIP-al) "The Changeable." Another name of Odin.

Svipdag (SVIP-dag) "The Glimmering Day." Another name of Od.

Svipul (SVIP-ul) "Battle." A Valkyrie.

Svithjod (SVEE-thyohd) "Sweden," "Nation of the Swedes." The nation of the Swedes, consisting of Greater Svithjod in the south and Svithjod the Cold (Svithjod the Cold) in the north. It is the land where Ask and Embla were created, and where Heimdall established the first settlement.

Sviur (SVEE-ur) "The Disappearing." A Dwarf.

Svivor (SVEE-vuhr) "The Mocking," "The Shameful." A Giantess, killed by Thor.

Svol (SVUHL) "The Cool." A sacred river.

Svolnir (SVUHL-nir) "He Who Shielded the Sun." Another name of Odin.

Swanmaid (SWAN-mayd) "Swan-Maid." A Goddess of fertility, primarily those who stayed in the Wolfdales with Ivaldi's sons—Idun, Sif, and Auda.

Swanrings (SWAN-rings) "Swan-Rings." The rings given to Ivaldi's sons by the Swanmaids.

Sylg (SEELG) "Swallower." A sacred river.

Syn (SEEN) "Denial." An Asynja. She keeps those out of dwellings who are not meant to enter, and is invoked by defendants at trials.

Syr (SEER) "Sow." Another name of Freya.

Syrhed (SEER-hehd) Old Frisian "Syr's Witch," "Syr's Heid." Another name of Gullveig as the witch who was in Freya-Syr's home.

U

Ud (UD) "The Lover," "Friend." Another name of Odin.

Ulfhednar (OOLV-hehd-nar) "Wolf-Skins." A group of warriors, similar to the Berserks, who fight in Odin's name.

Ulflidur (OOLV-lid-ur) "Wolf-Joint." The point on the wrist where Tyr's hand was bitten off.

Ulfrun (OOLV-roon) "Wolf-Runner," "She Who Rides a Wolf." One of Heimdall's nine Giantess mothers who turns the Grotti-mill.

Ull (UL) "The Glorious." Son of Sif and Egil, Thor's stepson. He is God of the winter hunt, along with his cousin, Skadi. He once held Odin's throne when the Asafather was exiled by the Vanir from Asgard. He is Od's brother and trusted companion.

Uni (UN-i) "The Content." A Dwarf.

Unn (UN) "The Wave." 1) One of the nine daughters of Aegir-Gymir and Gullveig-Ran who represent the waves. 2) A sacred river.

Uppheim (UP-haym) "Upper-Home," "Upper-World." The name used by the Etins for heaven.

Upphimin (UP-him-in) "Upper-Heaven." A name for the sky or heaven.

Uppsala (UP-sal-a) "The Upper Hall," "The High Hall." In Svithjod, a sacred site where the largest Asatru hof once stood.

Ur Age (OOR AYJ) "Primal Age." The first of the six ages, which ends when the Dwarves present golden gifts to the Gods.

Urdarbrunn (URD-ar-brun) "Urd's Well." The southernmost well of Jormungrund, the well of fate, whose mead gives strength.

Urdar Magn (URD-ar MAG-n) "Urd's Strength." The mead in Urdarbrunn.

Urdar Ord (URD-ar AWRD) "Urd's Judgment." The judgment over the dead.

Urd (URD) "Fate," "That-Which-Is." The foremost Norn who feeds the urlagthreads from her well to Verdandi so they can be weaved into the Web of Wyrd. She is the Goddess of fate and death, ruler over Hel and the Helthing near her fountain.

Uri (OOR-i) "The Smith." A Dwarf.

Urlag (OOR-lag) "The Original Law," "Fate," "The Primal Law." The force or principle, created by the Norns, which determines what is and what shall become.

Urlagthreads (UHR-lag-threhds) "Threads of Fate." Threads created from the power of Urdarbrunn which she feeds to her sister Verdandi, who weaves it into the Web of Wyrd, then Skuld cuts it with her sickle.

Urcold (OOR-kohld) "Primeval-Cold." The innate cold nature of Hrimthurses, especially Gullveig, who descended from Ymir, created from the frozen kvikadrops of the Elivagar.

Uruz (OOR-ooz) "Aurochs." The second rune of the Elder Futhark. Because it can be etymologically linked with Uruz, meaning "primal," "original," it can be associated with urlag (*urlagnen* "the original law"), and thus represents this concept in the Runelaw.

Urvan (OOR-vahn) "Water-Hope." The name used by the Etins for the clouds.

Utgardloki (OOT-gard-lawk-i) "Utgard-Loki," "Loki of the Outer Realm." Another name of Fjalar.

Utgard (OOT-gard) "The Outer-Realm." Another name of Sokkdalir, the realm of Surt and Suttung's Sons in the southern end of Jormungrund.

Utiseta (OOT-i-seht-a) "Sitting-Out." A magical or spiritual meditation practice used in Galdur.

V, W

Vadgelmir (VAD-gehlm-ir) "Roaring Water." A sacred river in which liars must wade through with dire consequences.

Vaegin (VAIG-in) "Warmth." The name used by the Vanir for fire.

Vaeni (VAIN-i) "Vänern"= "Hope," "Expectation." A lake in Svithjod.

Vafur (VAV-ur) "Quickness." The substance the Vafurfires and Vafurmists are made from, also called *Ofdokkum Ognar Ljoma*.

Vafurfires (VAV-ur-firz) "Quick-Fires," "Bickering Flames." Flames surrounding fortresses as protection, with lightning bolts that also strike targets, including the earth. They originate from the substance called *Vafur* or *Ofdokkum Ognar Ljoma*. The lightning bolts that strike Midgard occur when Thor strikes the Vafur-laden clouds, causing them to emit these "flames." They are said to be "smart," and never miss their mark. They were implemental in the slaying of Volund-Thjazi and Etins can use them to bring forth destruction.

Vafurmist (VAV-ur-niv-l) "Bickering-Mist." The mist, related to the Vafurfires, and made of the same substance, which is used to protect fortresses.

Vafthrudnir (VAV-throod-nir) "Strong in Entangling (With Questions)." An Etin defeated by Odin in a contest of wisdom.

Vafud (VAHV-ud) "Waverer." 1) Another name of Odin. 2) The name used by the Gods for the wind.

Vagasker (VAHG-ask-er) "Ocean-Skerry." Identical to Singastein and Aldland, where Freya stood by Od in his exile.

Vagn (VAG-n) "Wagon." Another name of Vagnhofdi.

Vagnhofdi (VAG-n-huhv-di) "Wagon-Cheiftain." A warrior of Etin-birth, Hadding's foster-father, Hardgrepa's father.

Vag (VAHG) "Wave." The name used by the Vanir for the sea.

Vaka (VAK-a) "The Wakeful." Feminine form of Vak. The name Odin assumed when he acted as a vala in order to get close to Rind so Vali could be born.

Vak (VAK) "The Wakeful," "The Waking." 1) Another name of Odin. 2) Delling's horse.

Vala (VAL-a) "Seeress." A female diviner or practitioner of the holy Galdur or evil Seid.

Valaskjalf (VAL-a-skyahlv) "The Tower of the Chosen." One of Odin's halls, possibly connected to or identical to Valhall, though it is roofed with pure silver and Valhall gold.

Valfather (VAL-fah-<u>ther</u>) "Father of the Chosen." Another name of Odin.

Valgaut (VAL-gout) "Goth of the Chosen." Another name of Odin.

Valgrind (VAL-grind) "Gate of the Chosen." The gates of Asgard, also called Thrymgjoll.

Valhallagara (VAL-hal-a-gahr-a) "False Valhall." An ancient burgh, owned by Nyhellenia-Gefjon.

Valhall (VAL-hahl) "Hall of the Chosen." Odin's hall in the domain of Asgard called Gladsheim, where his half of the Einherjar live.

Vali (VAHL-i) "Warrior." 1) An Asagod, son of Odin and Rind, who killed Hod to avenge Baldur's death. 2) A Dwarf.

Valkyrie (VAL-keer-ee) "Choosers of the Chosen." The maidens at Odin's or Freya's command, led by the Norn, Skuld, who select warriors on the battlefield to die by weapons and convey them through Hel to Asgard if they are worthy. They also lead warriors who have died from non-violent causes on the paths to Valhall. Once there, they serve mead to those who have become Einherjar.

Valland (VAL-land) "Land of the Chosen." Gudorm's realm in west Germania, where he and Hadding fought.

Vallarfax (VAL-ar-vaks) "The Mane of Fields." The word used by the Gods for the forest.

Val (VAL) "The Dragging," "The Tearing." A horse.

Valtam (VAL-tam) "The Warrior." Another name of Bur, Odin's father.

Valthognir (VAL-thuhg-nir) "Destroyer of Men." Another name of Odin.

Valtivi (VAL-teev-i) "God of the Chosen," "God." Probably originally a name of Odin, but here designates Frey.

Valtyr (VAL-teer) "God of the Chosen." Another name of Odin.

Vanaburgh (VAN-a-berg) "Vanir-Citadel," "Vanir-Burgh." A dwelling of the Vanir, or Vanaheim itself.

Vanadis (VAN-a-dees) pl. **Vanadisir** (VAN-a-dees-ir) "Vanir-Goddess." 1) A name of Freya. 2) A Goddess of the Vanir.

Vanagod (VAN-a-gawd) "Vanir-God." A God of the Vanir.

Vanaheim (VAN-a-haym) "Vanir-Home." The land of the Vanir on Jormungrund's western rim.

Vanir (VAN-ir) sing. **Van** (VAN) "Fertility Gods." Next to the Aesir, they are the foremost tribe of divinities, whose function is primarily focused on the natural order and regulation of the mechanisms of the worlds. They are also deities of peace and love, often invoked in such matters.

Var (VAHR) "Vow." An Asynja, Goddess of promises, whose name is invoked at the wedding, the marriage ceremony. She sees to it that these oaths are kept and punishes those who break them.

Vardruna (VARD-roon-a) "Protective Rune." A Giantess.

Varg Age (VARG AYJ) "Wolf-Age," "Outlaw Age." The age of Ragnarok, which will end with the destruction of the worlds and the subsequent renewal.

Varinsey (VAR-ins-ay) "Varinn's Isle." The place where Gullveig was reborn the final time.

Varkald (VAHR-kald) "Spring-Cold." Another name of Egil.

Varns (VARN-ir) sing. **Varn** (VARN) "Defenders." The warriors of Billing's halls who protect Sol and Mani from the wolves who chase them.

Varnwood (VARN-wuhd) "Forest of the Varns." The forest in Billing's realm where the Varns dwell.

Var (VAR) "The Cautious." A Dwarf.

Vartari (VAR-tar-i) "Lip-Tearer." A thong Brokk used to sew up Loki's lips after the competition of the artists.

Vasad (VAH-sad) "Damp-Cold," "Sleety." Father of Vindloni, grandfather of Vetur.

Vaxt (VAKST) "Grown." The name used by the Vanir for grain.

Ve (VEE) "The Holy." 1) Another name of Hoenir. 2) A sacred shrine or enclosure.

Vedurfolnir (VEHD-ur-vuhl-nir) "The Weather-Bleached." A hawk perched upon the eyes of an eagle sitting in Yggdrasil's branches. The eagle is said to be very knowledgeable, and is probably Odin himself.

Vedurglasir (VEHD-ur-glas-ir) "Weather-Glasir." A name for Yggdrasil's crown, related to Glasir (see), which denotes its exposure to the winds of Asgard.

Vedurmegin (VEHD-ur-mehg-in) "Weather-Might." The name used by the Alfar for the clouds.

Vega (VEHG-a) "The Ways." The name used by the Vanir for Frigga-Jord (Earth).

Vegdrasil (VEHG-dras-il) "Courageous in Battle." A Dwarf.

Vegsvin (VEHG-svin) "Way-Swift." A sacred river.

Vegtam (VEHG-tam) "The Wayfarer." Another name of Odin.

Veidias (VAYD-i-ahs) "The Hunting-As." Another name of Ull.

Veig (VAYG) "Foaming." The name used by the Vanir for ale.

Veig (VAYG) "The Defiant." A Dwarf.

Veratyr (VER-a-teer) "God of Men." Another name of Odin.

Verdandi (VERD-and-i) "That-Which-is-Becoming." Urd and Skuld's sister, one of the three great Norns who weaves the urlagthreads into the Web of Wyrd.

Weregild (VUR-gild) German "Man-Payment." An ancient tradition of offering amends for killing someone.

Verland (VER-land) "Land of Men." Another name of Midgard.

Vestein (VEHST-ayn) "The Westerner." A warrior.

Vestri (VEHST-ri) "West." The Dwarf who holds up the western point of the sky.

Vetmimir (VEHT-meem-ir) "Winter-Mimir." One of the nine heavens.

Vetur (VEHT-ur) "Winter." An Etin, representative of winter.

Veud (VEE-ud) "Shrine Guardian." Another name of Thor.

Veur (VEE-ur) "Watcher of the Shrine (Ve)." Another name of Thor.

Vid (VID) "The Deadly." A sacred river.

Vid (VEED) "The Wide." 1) A sacred river. 2) The field where Ragnarok will be fought, also called Vigrid.

Vid (VEED) "The Far-Seeing." Another name of Odin.

Vidar (VEED-ar) "The Far-Ruler," called **Inn Thogli** (IN THUHG-li) "The Silent." 1) An Asa-god, Odin's son with the Giantess Grid. He will avenge Odin's death at Ragnarok after Fenrir swallows the Asafather. 2) Another name of Odin.

Vidblain (VEED-blah-in) "Wide-Blue." One of the nine heavens.

Vidblindi (VID-blind-i) "Forest-Blind." An Etin.

Viddi (VEED-i) "Wide." An Etin.

Vidfedmir (VID-vehd-mir) "Wide-Embracer." One of the nine heavens.

Vidga (VID-ga) "The Stout." Son of Volund and Bodvild. A hero fighting on the side of the Ivaldi clan.

Vidgymnir (VID-geem-nir) "Wide-Sea." An Etin.

Vidhrimnir (VID-reem-nir) "Foe of Frost." Another name of Odin.

Vidofnir (VID-awv-nir) "The Wide Open." Another name of Gullinkambi.

Vidolf (VID-ohlv) "Forest-Wolf." An Etin.

Vid (VID) "Forest." The name used by our ancestors for the forest.

Vidir (VID-rir) "Weather-God." Another name of Odin.

Vidur (VID-ur) "The Destroyer." Another name of Odin.

Vif (VEEV) "Wife." A daughter of Karl and Snor.

Vifil (VIV-il) "Beetle." An ancient warrior.

Vigglod (VIG-luhd) "Willing to Travel." A Giantess.

Vigg (VIG) "The Toothy." 1) A Dwarf. 2) A horse.

Vigrid (VEEG-reed) "The Battlefield." The field where the Ragnarok battle will be fought, said to be one hundred and twenty leagues in every direction, located in Jormungrund.

Vili (VEEL-i) "Will," "The Willful." Another name of Lodur.

Vilkin (VIL-kin). Ivaldi's father.

Vilmeid (VIL-mayd) "Soothsayer." An Etin, progenitor of evil vitkis.

Vimur (VIM-ur) "The Bubbling." Another name of the Elivagar.

Vin (VIN) "The Delightful." A sacred river.

Vina (VIN-a) "The Delightful." A sacred river.

Vindalf (VIND-ahlv) "Wind-Elf." A Dwarf.

Vindblain (VIND-blah-in) "Wind-Blue." One of the nine heavens, also called Hreggmimir and Hleidornir.

Vindflot (VIND-vlawt) "Wind-Blown." The name used by the Vanir for clouds.

Vindheim (VIND-haym) "Wind-Home." Designates the heavens, where Baldur and Hod dwell after Ragnarok.

Vindhelm (VIND-hehlm) "Wind-Helm." Another name of Ivaldi.

Vindhelms Bridge (VIND-hehlms BRIJ) "Vindhelm's Bridge." Another name of Bifrost.

Vindkald (VIND-kald) "Wind-Cold." Another name of Od.

Vindler (VIND-ler) "The Turner." Another name of Heimdall.

Vindloni (VIND-lohn-i) "Wind-Chill." An Etin, father of Vetur, also called Vindsval.

Vindofni (VIND-awv-ni) "Wind-Weaver." The name used by the Vanir for heaven.

Vind (VIND) "Wind." 1) The name used by our ancestors for wind. 2) An Etin.

Vindslot (VINDS-lawt) "Wind's Lull." The name used by the Vanir for calm.

Vindsval (VIND-sval) "Wind-Chill." An Etin, father of Vetur, also called Vindloni.

Vingnir (VING-nir) "The Strong." An Etin, Thor's foster-father, killed by him. Thor obtained his first hammer, Vingnir's Mjollnir, from him. This hammer is made of stone.

Vingolf (VIN-gohlv) "Friendly-Quarters." Identical to Gimle, Urd's hall in Helheim where the blessed dead live.

Vingrip (VIN-grip) "Friendly-Hold," "Friendly-Grip." An Etin.

Vingskornir (VING-skawrn-ir) "The Mighty in Battle." Hild's horse.

Vingthor (VING-thohr) "The Mighty Thor." Another name of Thor.

Vinili (VIN-il-i) A legendary tribe, the original name of the Longobards.

Vipar (VEEP-ar) "The Trifling." An Etin.

Virfir (VIRV-ir) "The Virulent." A Dwarf.

Vitki (VIT-ki) "Magician," "Seer." A male diviner or practitioner of the holy Galdur or evil Seid.

Vitur (VIT-ur) "Wise." A Dwarf.

Wolfdales (WOOLF-dayls) "Wolf-Dales." The dales in the Ironwood, where Volund, his brothers, and the Swanmaids resided.

Wolfsea (WOOLF-see) "Wolf-Sea." The sea in the Wolfdales, near which the Ivaldi sons and their Swanmaids lived.

Volsi (VUHLS-i) "The Chooser." Another name of Odin.

Volund (VUHL-und) "The Woe-Minded." An Alf-jarl and primeval artist, thereafter the king of the Etins and earth's worst foe. Son of Ivaldi, brother of Egil, Slagfin, and the Swanmaids, husband or lover of Idun, and father of Skadi.

Von (VOHN) "Expectation." The river that flows from the fettered Fenrir's mouth.

Vond (VUHND) "The Tributary." A sacred river.

Vond (VUHND) "Wand." The name used by the Vanir for the forest.

Vor (VUHR) "Awareness." An Asynja, said to be so wise and searching that nothing can be concealed from her.

Vord Goda (VUHRD GAWD-a) "Watchman of the Gods." Another name of Heimdall.

Vornir (VUHRN-ir) "The Cautious." An Etin.

Wralda (RALD-a) Old Frisian "God of the World," "The Old Man." Another name of Odin.

Wunjo (VUHN-yoh) "Joy," "Success." The eighth rune of the Elder Futhark, associated with joy and happiness, which is why it is connected to such concepts in the Runelaw.

Wunsch (VUHNSH) German "Wish." Another name of Odin. Cp. Oski.

Wyrd (VEERD) Anglo-Saxon "Fate," "Destiny." This term is a variant spelling of "Urd," but here represents the concept of fate, manifested as a massive web in the sky, the Web of Wyrd.

Y

Ydalir (EE-dal-ir) "Bow-Dales." Originally Ivaldi's land, south of the Elivagar in Alfheim, where Yset, the fortress of Ivaldi's clan is located. It was passed on to his sons, then finally to Egil's son, Ull.

Yggdrasil (EEG-dras-il) "Ygg-Odin's Steed." The World-Tree born of a golden seed, with golden leaves and fruit. Its trunk and branches are silver.

Yggjung (EEG-yung) "The Terrifying Youth." Another name of Odin.

Ygg (EEG) "The Terrifying." Another name of Odin.

Ylfings (EELV-ings) "Descendants of Ylfr." A legendary clan of the North.

Ylg (EELG) "The Swelling." A sacred river.

Yma (EEM-a) "The Screaming." A Giantess.

Ymir (EEM-ir) "Roarer." The primordial Etin, formed from the rime of Ginnungagap once it was melted by heat. From the sweat of his arms, filled with Audhumla's fertile sustenance, he sired Mimir and Bestla. From his feet came Thrudgelmir. He was slain by Bur's sons for killing Audhumla, and his body was used to create Midgard.

Ymsi (EEM-si) "The Loud." An Etin.

Ynglings (EENG-lings) "Descendants of Yngvi." A legendary clan of the North.

Yngvi (EENG-vi) also **Ynguni** (EENG-un-i) "Warrior," "Prince." 1) Another name of Frey. 2) Another name of Heimdall. 3) Another name of Od. 4) An ancient warrior. 5) A Dwarf.

Yngvin (EENG-vin) "Warrior," "Prince." A member of the Yngling clan.

Yrung (EER-ung) "The Hunter." Another name of Odin.

Ysja (EES-ya) "Sludge." A daughter of Thrall and Thy.

Yset (EE-seht) "Bow-Chalet." The fortress in Ydalir by the Elivagar where the Gods had their outpost against the Etins, entrusted to Ivaldi and his sons. It later became Ull's home, who presumably took up the duty of protecting this borderland.

Yule (YOOL) "Wheel." Representing here the twelve day, thirteen night celebration beginning at the Winter Solstice. It also designates the six-spoked wheel that marks the six ages of the epic, as well as other wheels of time.

Yulefest (YOOL-vehst) "Yule-Fest," also **Yuletide** (YOOL-tīde) "Yule-Tide," The festival or season of Yule or Yule

Index

Introduction

The following terms are cited by passage instead of page number to allow the reader to pinpoint the exact location of any word to be researched. Note the Roman numeral chapters preceding the passage numbers, while terms listed under the abbreviation "Hug." are to be found under the *Hugrunes*. You will note that the *Hugrunes* passages are never cited continuously, as in 4-6, but rather consecutively, as 4, 5, 6. This is because each of the *Hugrunes* are to be viewed as separate in and of themselves, while the main body is part of an ongoing epic chain. Be sure to use the Table of Contents when researching terms, for this will help you more easily find what you are looking for. When citations are numbered 1), 2),etc. these correspond to their various definitions as given in the glossary of the text, and will have each corresponding term next to them.

For example: **Agnar**, 1) Geirrod's brother, XXXII.1 , 2) Auda's kinsman, LII.10.

Also, when researching terms, consider the variant spellings and pluralizations, as shown in the glossary.

A

Adal, XX.83.

Adils, X.13.

Aefinrunes, XX.6, 85.

Aegir, XV.3-6,13, XXII.20, XLIV.4, LXIII.1,LXVII.1,7,12,14,16,24,26,46,48,50-51,53-60, LXX. 47, LXXVI.1,36, LXXVII.1, LXXVIII.1-2, 5-6, 13, 18, 20, 22, 31, 46, 72, Hug. 44.

Aegishelm, L.3, 20-21, 26.

Aepir, LXVI.21.

Aesir, IV.3, V.9,25-26, VI.34, VII.1, X.11,17, XI.10, XII.1,8, XIII.1-2,9, XIV.1, XV.3,7,15, XVI.2,5-6,13-14,16, XIX.2, XX.44, XXII.11,30,47, XXIV.36-38, XXV.3,7,11, XXX.1,7,14,28,31, XXXII.17, XXXIII.2,5,7-8,10,14-16,18, XXXIV.2-3,6, XXXV.5, XXXVI.3-4,16, XXXIII.2,5,7-8,10,14-16,18, XXXIV.2-3,6, XXXV.5, XXXVI.3-4,16, XXXVII.9,22, XXXIX.3, XL.6,9,12-13, XLI.2, XLII.2, XLV.2,17-18,22,LII.9,26,LIII.3,9,14,38,42,50,52,68,76 ,85, LIV.1, LV.1-3,5-6,9, LVI.4,6,8, LVII.1,11, LVIII.38,41,50, LXII.4, LXIII.2,5,9, LXIV.1,3,65, LXV.2,8-9,11, LXVI.11,27,35, LXVII.8,35, LXVIII.1,3, LXIX.1-2,4-8,11-12,16,18,20,24,28-34,36, LXX.5,7,15, LXXII.1-2,4, LXXIII.1,21, LXXV.1-2,4,6,9, LXXVI.3,36, LXXVII.26, LXXVIII.1,4,9,11,15,17,23,29,34-35,37-39,41,58,71,73-75,77, LXXX.4, LXXXII.1,6,8, LXXXIII.2.

Aeti, LXVI.33.

Aettarsfylgja, XIX.20.

Afi, XX.59.

Agnar, 1) XXXII.1,2, 2) LII.10.

Ai, 1) Dwarf, X.3, 2) Edda's husband, XX.45.

Al, XXXIX.6.

Aldafather,V.32.

Aldagaut, V.39, VI.13.

Aldland, LXXIV.8.

Aldrunes, XX.6,85.

Alfar, V.9,25-26, VI.34, X.1-2,6,14,17, XI.10, XII.1, XVI.6,18, XVII.1, XVIII.1, XIX.17, XXVII.5,8-9, XXVIII.4-5, XXXII.22, XXXIII.7-8, XLIII.6,30,35, XLV.1,6, XLVI.4, XLVII.1, L.17, LII.26, LIII.76, LIV.6,9,31, LVII.3, LX.2,22,35, LXII.24,29, LXIII.3,9, LXIV.1,4,46,65, LXV.6,LXVI.11,13,15,17,19,21,23,25,29,31 ,33, LXVII.8,19-20, LXVIII.1, LXIX.3,5,11,15-16,18,21,23,28,33, LXX.3, LXXI.13,38, LXXII.1, LXXVIII.1,4,17,34, LXXXII.6.

Alfarin, XV.13.

Alfheim, X.17, XI.10, XIII.4, XVII.3, XXVII.3-4, XXXII.22, XLIX.3, LXIII.12,19,23, LXIX.18,30.

Allfather, V.35, VII.2, XI.4, XII.3, XIV.8, XVI.5, XXII.45, XXIII.3, XXXVII.20, XLII.5, XLV.1, LIII.31, LXIV.1, LXVIII.2-3, LXXIII.4, LXXV.3.

Alf, 1) Ivaldi, X.7, 2) Alf inn Gamla, LX.3.

Alfrik, XVIII.3.

Alfrodul, XLV.26, LVII.47, LXVII.5, LXXXIII.4.

Algroenn, LXXVII.17.

Ali, X.13.

Allheim, LXVI.25.

Alskir, LXVI.17.

Alsvid, 1) Horse, XI.5, XLV.4, LII.23, 2) Etin, XV.13.

Althjof, X.3.

Alvaldi, LXXVII.20.

Alveig, XIV.20, XVII.1, LX.23-24,26,30,36, LXIII.11,18-20,23,25,29,32, LXX.1-2,21.

Alvis, LXVI.1,3,5,7,9-35.

Ama, XV.14.

Amalians, LXX.17,20,35.

Ambat, XX.56.

Amgerd, XV.14.

Amma, XX.59,61.

Am, XV.13.

Amsvartnir, XXVI.35, XLIV.1, LXXV.4, LXXVII.77,79.

An, X.3.

Anar, 1) Hoenir, X.3, 2) Dwarf, X.17.

Andhrimnir, XXV.7.
Andlang, XI.2.
Andvaranaut, XLIV.19, LIV.12, LXI.4, LXII.45.
Andvari, X.7.
Angeyja,VIII.11, XV.14.
Angles, XLVII.2, LX.19.
Angerboda, XV.10, LXVIII.2.
Ansuz VI.10, XX.16.
Arastein, LX.23.
Arfi, XX.83.
Argjoll, XLV.26.
Argud, XIII.4.
Ari, XXVI.15, LXVII.29.
Arinnefja, XX.56.
Arnhofdi, V.39.
Artali, LXVI.15.
Arvak, XI.5.
As, V.39, VI.10.
Asaburgh, XVI.2, LIII.51, LXIX.33.
Asabrag, XVI.6.
Asafather, XXXVII.8, LIII.92, LVII.1, LXIX.12,32,36, LXXII.2.
Asagod, XXVI.14, XXX.43, LX.17, LXIX.14,30-31, LXXV.22.
Asasynir, 1) Aesir, LXVII.19-20, LXXII.10, LXXVIII.5,31,62,71, 2) Asmegir, LXVI.17.
Asathor, XVI.5-6, XXX.26,32,37, XXXVI.4, LXXVII.53.
Asbridge, XII.8, XXIV.36.
Asgard, V.41, VI.13, XI.8, XII.1-2,5-9, XIII.1,5, XVI.2,5,13,20-21, XVIII.1, XX.104, XXII.1,13,46-47, XXIV.15,37, XXV.3,6, XXVII.9, XXVIII.1, XXXIII.19, XXXV.4, XXXVI.2-3, XXXVII.21-22,27, XL.11-12,15,17, XLI.1, XLIV.2-3,12,14-17, XLVI.4, LI.8,12, LV.2,5-6, LVII.1, LXII.5,23,28,41,43,53-54, LXIII.7,9, LXIV.12,63-64, LXV.1-2,9,12, LXVII.46-47,51-52,61, LXVIII.1, LXIX.6,15-19,23,28-34, LXX.15,25-26,61, LXXII.1-2,4,8, LXXIII.1,LXXIV.1,10-11, LXXV.1, LXXVI.6, LXXX.4.
Asgardsride, LXXX.4.
Asgaut, V.39.

Asgates, LV.5.
Ask, XIX.2-3,5,7,12-13,15,22, XLVI.1, XLVII.2, LIII.42, LXXX.54.
Aslidar, LXVII.36.
Asmegir, XLVI.3-4, LIII.22, LXI.7, LXIV.45, LXVII.36.
Asmund, V.36, LXVII.61, LXX.61, LXXIII.1,3-4,21-22,27,32,34-35.
Asvin, V.9.
Asynja, XIV.1, XVIII.4, XXII.13,46, XXV.6, XXVII.6, XXXIII.15, XXXVII.5, XL.3, LII.9, LIII.3, LXII.54, LXVII.51, LXIX.18,34, LXXVIII.15,35, LXXX.4.
Atla, VIII.11, XV.14.
Atli, 1) Thor, XVI.6, 2) Warrior, X.13, XXI.1, LX.3.
Atridi, X.12.
Atrid, V.35.
Auda, XIV.20, XVII.1, XXVII.10, XLIV.15, XLVIII.1, LII.10,50, LIV.10, LXIV.65.
Audhumla, III.3, IX.1,4, XLVII.1, LXXX.118, LXXXII.3.
Aud, X.17.
Audun, V.39.
Aurboda, XV.3,10, LXIV.50, LXVII.1, LXVIII.1.
Aurgelmir, III.1-2, IX.3, LVIII.29-30.
Aurglasir, LXIV.40.
Aurgrimnir, XV.13.
Aurkonung, V.1, XIX.15.
Aurnir, XV.13, XLIV.6.
Aurr, LXVI.11.
Aurvandill, XXXVI.19.
Aurvandilstoe, XXXVI.19.
Aurvangaland, XIX.2,22, XX.5,12,103, XXI.2, XLVII.2,4-5,7-8, LX.2,4,19.
Aurvang, X.5.
Austri, X.3, XI.1, LXXXII.5.

B

Bafur, X.3.
Bakrauf, XV.14.
Baldur, XII.10, XV.8-13, XVIII.2, XXVI.4, XXXVI.9,11, XL.12,XLVI.4,10, L.1-2,

LI.1,3-5,7-8,10-12, LII.50, LIII.1-3,5-11,22-26,57-59,87-88,92, LV.7-8, LVI.1,3-7,9-10, LVII.1,11-12, LXI.7, LXIV.5,65, LXV.1-2,4-10,12, LXIX.19, LXXVII.10, LXXVIII.31-32, LXXX.2, LXXXIII.1,3. Hug.3-4,6.
Baleyg, V.34.
Banings, XLII.8, LXX.19.
Bara, XV.4.
Bari, X.6,13, XVIII.3, XLVI.3, LX.20-21, LXIV.46.
Barn, XX.83.
Barr, LXVI.33.
Barri, LXVII.41,44,51.
Baugi, XV.13.
Baugregin, XXVI.9, LXIX.26.
Beinvid, XV.13.
Beitur, XV.13.
Beli, X.13, XV.13, XXXVI.14, XL.17, XLII.1, LIII.78, LXII.2-4,23,46,48, LXXXII.10.
Bergelmir, III.2, IX.1,5,6, XV.10,13, XXII.1, LVIII.29,35, LXXX.116.
Bergrisar, XII.8, XV.3, XVIII.2, XXXIV.1,6, XLIV.6, LXVII.1.
Berkano, VI.27, XX.30.
Berling, X.9,13, XVIII.3.
Berserk, V.42, XVI.7, LX.17, LXXVII.38.
Bestla, III.2, IV.4, V.1,6.
Beyla, XIII.4, LXXVIII.1,61-62.
Biflindi, V.36.
Bifrost, XII.8-9, XX.105-106, XXII.1, XXIV.15,36, XXV.3, XLV.9, L.19, LXIV.3, LXIX.28,30, LXXII.1, LXXIV.10, LXXXII.6.
Bifur, X.3.
Bikki, LXX.27-30,35, LXXI.1-2,9,11-13,15-19, LXXIII.3.
Bil, XXXVII.1,3,25.
Bild, X.6.
Bileyg, V.34.
Billing, X.6, XI.4,10,11, LIII.5, LVII.3-4,7-8,10-11, LXXX.102.
Bilrost, L.19.
Bilskirnir, XII.2,6, XXV.10.
Bjar, X.13.

Bjargrunes, VI.4, LII.17,27.
Bjart, XIII.1, XIV.20, LXIV.50.
Bjorgolf, XV.13.
Bjorn 1) Thor, XVI.6, 2) Hod, X.13.
Bjor, LXVI.35.
Blain, 1) Dwarf, X.9, 2) Ymir, XIX.1, LIII.40.
Blak, X.12-13.
Blapthvari, XV.13.
Blid, XIII.1, XIV.20, LXIV.50.
Blik, XIII.1, XIV.20, LXIV.50.
Blikjandabol, XLII.5.
Blindi, V.39.
Blind Balewise, LXX.28-29, LXXIII.1.
Blodablanda, LXXVIII.12.
Blodi, LXIX.17.
Blodughofi,X.12-13, XIII.4.
Blodughadda, XV.4.
Blot, V.1,10,11, XIX.6, XX.40, XXV.29, XXVI.25, XXVII.8, XLIII.1, XLIV.13, LXII.28, LXIX.35, LXXII.8-9, LXXIV.9, LXXX.3.
Blovur, X.9.
Boddi, XX.64.
Bodvild, X.15, XIV.20, LIV.12-13,16,23-24,28,35,38-40, LXI.4, LXX.22.
Bofur, X.9.
Bogaas, XLVIII.2.
Bokrunes, LII.27.
Bolthorn, V.6.
Bolverk, V.34, XXXVII.23, XLV.19, LXXX.114.
Bombur, X.3.
Borgar, XXI.3, XXXVIII.8.
Borghild, XXIX.1.
Bragarfull, XXIV.7, LI.3,9.
Bragi, XXV.3,13, XXXVII.26, XLV.9,16, L.2, LII.24, LXIV.5-6,65, LXIX.18, LXX.7,33, LXXIV.11-12, LXXVIII.1,11,15-20,22,78.
Bralund, XXIX.1,3.
Brana, XV.14.
Brandingi, XV.13.
Bratskeg, XX.64.
Breidablik, XVI.8-9, XXVI.4, XLVI.4, LVI.9-10, LXI.7, LXV.6, LXXXIII.1.

Breidurbondi, XX.64.
Bridal, XXXVII.9.
Brimir, 1) Mimir, X.15, LII.22, LIII.62, LXIX.24, 2) Mimir's hall, IV.3, X.15 3) Ymir, XIX.1, LIII.40.
Brimrunes, VI.5, LII.18.
Brisingamen, XIV.6, XVIII.3, LXXIV.1,10.
Brisings, X.1, XVIII.3, XXXIII.14,16,20, LIV.1.
Brokk, V.9, VI.34, X.3, XVIII.3, XXXV.2-6, XXXIX.1,3,6, XLV.3,13, LX.20.
Brud, XX.65.
Bruni, 1) Odin, V.39, 2) Volund, X.6.
Brunnacre, XLIV.2, LV.1.
Bryja, XV.14.
Budlungs, XX.92, XXI.12, XXIX.2, LX.2.
Bui, XX.64
Bundinskeg, XX.64.
Buri, 1) Bur's father, III.3, V.1, VI.11, 2) Dwarf, X.6
Bur, 1) Odin's father, III.3, V.1, IX.1,3,6, XI.1,6, XIX.2,4,8, XXVI.1, LIII.35, 2) Jarl's son, XX.83.
Buseyra, XV.14, XXXII.23.
Bygg, LXVI.33.
Byggvir, XIII.4, LXXVIII.1,47,49-50,62.
Byleist, XV.7-8, XXIII.1, LIII.75, LXXXII.4.
Bylgja, XV.4.
Byrr, LIV.8.
Byrgir, XVIII.5, XXVIII.2, XXXVII.1,3,7,13,19,21,26.
Byrgis Argefn, XXXVII.25, XL.6.

D

Dag, 1) Delling's son, VI.32, X.13, XI.3-4,10, XLV.24, LII.8, LIII.37, LVIII.12,24-25.
Dagaz VI.32, XX.35.
Dags Vera, LXVI.23.
Dagsevi, LXVI.23.
Dainn, 1) Brokk, V.9, VI.34, X.3, XXXV.2,6, XLV.3,13, 2) Hart, II.8.
Danp, XX.81,90, XXI.2.

Dan Mikillati, XX.90, XXI.2.
Dari, X.9.
Delling, V.26, VI.32, X.6,13,17, XI.3-4,10, XXV.17, XLV.24, XLVI.4, LIII.37, LVII.3, LXIV.1,46, LXV.6.
Digraldi, XX.55.
Disir XIX.18-19,21, XXVI.2,LII.17, LXXI.44, LXXIII.15.
Djupan Marr, LXVI.25.
Dofri, XV.13.
Dokkalfar, XXVI.17,35, XXXV.1, XLV.25.
Dolgthrasir, X.7.
Dolgthvari, X.9.
Dori, X.6, XLVI.3, LXIV.46.
Dorrud,V.39.
Draug, XXII.32, XXIV.13, LXIII.31.
Draumjorunn, LXVI.31.
Draumkona, XIX.19.
Draupnir, 1) Ring, XVI.13, XXXV.3, XLIV.19, LVI.7, LXV.7, LXIX.36, 2) Court, X.7.
Dreng, XX.64.
Dresvarp, V.39.
Drifa, XV.5, XLIV.11.
Drjupansal, LXVI.13.
Dromi, LXXV.2.
Drosull, X.13.
Drott, 1) Danp's daughter, XX.81, XXI.5-7,9-11, XXII.13,15,XXIX.1,7, LX.9, 2) Court, XXI.11.
Drottins, XXI.11.
Drottnings, XXI.11.
Drottur, XX.55.
Drumba, XX.56.
Drumb, XX.55.
Dufa, XV.4.
Duf, X.7.
Dulin, X.9.
Dulsi, XXXVII.24.
Dumb, XV.13.
Duneyr, II.8.
Durathror, II.8.
Duri, X.9.
Durin, X.2,14, XV.13,XVII.1, XIX.1, XXVIII.2-4, LIII.41.

Durnir, XV.13, XXXVII.24.
Dvalin, 1) Mimir's son, V.9, VI.34, X.3,13, XI.4, XVIII.3, XIX.17, XLV.24, L.17, 2) Hart, II.8.
Dvalins Leika, LXVI.17.
Dwarves, V.9,26, VI.34, X.2,14, XI.1,4-5,10, XVIII.1,3, XIX.1, XXVI.17, XXVIII.2,4-6, XXXV.1-2, XXXVII.8,24, XXXIX.4,6, XLV.4,25, XLVII.4, LIII.41,76, LXI.5-6, LXII.45, LXIV.1, LXVI.9-10,12-18,20,22-28,30-31,34,36, LXXI.28, LXXV.3, LXXXII.6.
Dynfari, LXVI.21.
Dyrar Veigar, XXIV.44, XXV.3, XXVI.13, LXIII.24.

E

Edda, XX.45,47,50.
Eggther, XV.13, LIII.67, LXVII.12,52, LXXIX.3, LXXXII.1.
Eggtide, XI.12.
Egil, XV.13, XVII.1,4-5, XXVII.3-4,7-9, XXX.1-3, XXXI.1,3,5-6,9-10, XXXII.5, XXXV.1, XXXVI.19, XL.2,13,15-16,18, XLIII.6-7,27,36, XLIV.4,6,15, XLV.10, XLVII.1, XLVIII.2,XLIX.1,3, LIX.1-3,22,24,LX.3,22-24,34, LXI.1, LXII.8,27-28,42,44, LXIV.59, LXX.31.
Ehwaz, VI.28, XX.31.
Eikin, VIII.2.
Eikinskjaldi, X.5.
Eikintjasna, XX.56.
Eikthyrnir, XII.6, XXV.9, LXIX.29.
Eimgeitir, XV.13.
Eindridi, XVI.6, XXXVI.13.
Einherjar, V.40, XXV.1,5,7-11,15, XXVI.2, XXXII.12, LVIII.40-41, LXIV.4, LXVIII.2, LXIX.18,23,30, LXX.15, LXXII.4, LXXIV.11, LXXVII.31, LXXVIII.67, LXXXII.6,11.
Einmonth, XI.12.
Einvigi, XXI.6, XLIII.28, XLVIII.2.
Eir, XIII.1, XIV.3, LXIV.40,50.
Eistla, VIII.11, XV.14.
Eisurfala, XV.14.

Eitur, XXVI.13.
Eitri, X.9.
Eiwaz, VI.22, XX.25.
Eldhrimnir, XXV.7.
Eldi, LXVI.29.
Eldir, LXXVIII.2-4,6-7.
Eldur, 1) Fire, LXVI.27, 2) Etin, XV.13.
Elhaz, VI.24, XX.27.
Elivagar, I.2,4, III.1, XVII.1-3,5,7, XXVI.12, XXVII.8-9, XXX.4, XXXI.1,3, XXXII.5,9, XXXVI.19, XXXVII.7, XL.13, XLIII.7, XLIV.4, XLV.13, XLVII.1,6, LVIII.31, LX.35, LXII.1,40, LXIII.1, LXXII.1, LXXVII.30.
Eljudnir, XLII.5.
Elli,XXIV.16, XXX.36,41.
Ellilyf Asa, XVIII.4, XL.11, LV.1.
Embla, XIX.2-3,5,7,9,12-13,15,22, XLVI.1, XLVII.2, LIII.42, LXXX.1,54, Hug.5.
Endil , XXXII.5.
Ennibratt, V.39.
Ennilang, XVI.6.
Erde, Hug.50.
Erna, XX.81, XXI.5.
Erp, LXXI.4,23,27-28,34-37,44.
Etin, 1) Giants, III.1-2, V.3,9,37, VI.11,22,34, VIII.6,9,11, IX.1,6, X.1,15, XI.2, XV.1-3,7-8,10-11,15, XVI.1,7,15,19-20, XIX.19, XX.106, XXI.3, XXII.6,11,15, XXV.1, XXVI.17, XXVII.5,9, XXVIII.4, XXX.4, XXXI.1,3,5,10, XXXII.1-4,7,10-12,17-23, XXXIII.5,10,19,23-25,27,29-30,32-33, XXXIV.3-4,6, XXXVI.1-2,4,6-9,12-14,16, XXXVII.7,9-10,19-20,24, XXXVIII.1,XL.9,13,17, XLI.2, XLII.1-2, XLIII.4,7-8,18,20, XLIV.3,5,9,14,20, XLV.13,25, XLVII.1,4,6-7, XLIX.3,L.3,LI.5,7, LIII.4,33,48,62,72,74, LV.22, LVII.3, LVIII.1-2,4-6,8,15-16,19-21,28,30-34,37,42-43,49, LIX.19, LX.4,17, LXII.1-3,18,20-24,27,29-31,38,40,43,46,48-49,53, LXIII.1-5,8, LXVI.11,13,15,17,19,21,23,25,27,29,31,33,35, LXVII.1,9,11,27,32,36,46,50,52-58, LXIX.28, LXX.2,43,59, LXXII.1, LXXVI.2-3,9,12-14,17-18,21-24,26-27,29-

31,35, LXXVII.16,20-21,24, LXXX.2,109,110,113,117, LXXXII.3-4, 2) An Etin, XV.13.
Eyglo, LXVI.17.
Eygotaland, XXVII.1.
Eylimi, XXXVII.27.
Eylud, V.39.
Eynaefir, LXXVI.20.
Eyrgjafa, VIII.11, XV.14.

F

Fadir, XX.67.
Fafnir, L.3-4,7,9,11-13,15-18,22,24-26.
Fagrahvel, LXVI.17.
Fagraroef, LXVI.13.
Fagrlimi, LXVI.29.
Fak, X.12-13.
Fala, XV.14.
Falhofnir, X.11, LIII.2.
Fallandaforad, XLII.5.
Fal, 1) Baldur, LIII.2, 2) Dwarf, X.9.
Farbauti, XV.8, XL.9, LXIX.17, LXXIV.10.
Farmagud, V.39.
Farmatyr, V.35.
Fedja, XXXII.8.
Fegjafa, XIII.4.
Fehu, VI.10, XX.13.
Feima, XX.65.
Feng, V.39, LXXII.7.
Fenja, XXXI.3, XLIV.5, LXX.32,35, LXXIII.21.
Fenrir, XI.9, XV.13, XVI.14,16, LIII.65, LVIII.46-47, LXVIII.1-3, LXXV.1, LXXVI.22, LXXVIII.1,42-43, LXXIX.1, LXXXII.2,4,7-8, LXXXIII.2,4.
Fensalir, XIII.3, XIX.15, LIII.9,59, LVII.1, LXV.1.
Fifl, LIII.75, LXXXII.4.
Fili, X.5.
Fimafeng, LXXVIII.2.
Fimbulfambi, LXXX.108.
Fimbulsongs, V.6, VI.1, XVII.4, XXII.7.
Fimbulthul, I.2, VIII.2.
Fimbulthul, V.8, LXXX.85.

Fimbultyr, V.39, LIII.85, LXXXIII.2.
Fimbulwinter, XLIV.1,14, XLV.2, XLVII.3-5,8, LIV.1, LVIII.44, LX.1,17,20,22, LXII.53,LXIX.25, LXXII.1, LXXX.117, LXXXI.3.
Finn, X.8.
Finnking, XXVII.2.
Fitjung, LXXX.83.
Fjalar, V.37, X.3, XV.13, XXVIII.2-4, XXX.6,12-13,16,18-20,22-24,26,28,30,32,34,36-40, XXXVII.1,7-9,11-12,17,20-24, XLVII.4, LIII.67, LXVI.35, LXVII.36, LXXVI.19, LXXVII.27, LXXVIII.69, LXXIX.3, LXXX.19,109, LXXXII.1,5.
Fjolkald, LXIV.18.
Fjolnir, 1) Odin, V.34, LIII.86, LXXIII.7, LXXXIII.2, 2) Frey's son, LXVII.61.
Fjolsvid, V.34, LXIV.12,15,17,19-54,56.
Fjolvar, LXXVII.17.
Fjolverk, XV.13.
Fjolvor, XV.14.
Fjorgynn, LIII.81, LXXVII.57, LXXXII.9.
Fjorgyn, LXXVIII.30.
Fjorm, I.2, VIII.2.
Fjosnir, XX.55.
Flegg, XV.13.
Fljod, XX.65.
Foddik, XX.96-97, XXII.23.
Fold, LXVI.11.
Foldakona, Hug.39.
Folkmodir, XXII.13,15,22,46.
Folkvang, XIII.5, XXV.6, LXIX.18, LXXIV.11.
Folkvig, LIII.46, LXIX.1.
Folkvir, X.13.
Folkwanderung, XLVII.7.
Fonn, XV.5, XLIV.11.
Forad, XV.14.
Forbrennir, LXVI.27.
Forni, V.39.
Fornjot, XV.3,5,13, XLIV.11, XLV.17, LXXVI.2.
Forseti, LII.50, LXIV.65, LXV.12, LXIX.18, LXXX.2, Hug.52.
Fraeg, X.5.

Franangsforce, LXXVIII.73.
Frar, X.5.
Frarid, V.39.
Frekastein, LX.3.
Freki, V.45, XXV.2,8, LIII.69,73,75,83, LXIV.26, LXXIX.4.
Frek, LXVI.27.
Frermonth, X.12.
Freya, VI.31, XIII.1,4-7, XIV.6, XVIII.3-4, XX.105, XXIV.15, XXV.6, XXXII.20, XXXIII.3-4,9,12-14,23-24,27-29, XXXIV.1,4, XXXVI.3-4, XLII.1-2, XLIV.14, XLVII.3, LIII.48, LV.3, LVI.7, LIX.3,8, LXII.2,5,16,22-24,28-32,40,42-44,46,54, LXIII.1,5,9, LXIV.20,53-57,60,63, LXVII.46,48,51,53-59,61, LXVIII.1, LXIX.18,23,30, LXX.4,26,41,61, LXXIII.1-2, LXXIV.1-2,8-11, LXXVIII.1,33-36, Hug.3,32,39,45.
Frey, X.12-13, XIII.1,4, XVI.2,18, XXVII.4,7-8, XXXV.5-6, XXXIX.1, XL.1,17, XLI.2, XLII.1, XLIV.14, XLVII.3, LIII.78, LVI.7, LIX.3,8, LXII.2,22-23,27-28,46-48, LXIII.5, LXIV.63, LXVII.1,4-5,7,21-22,35,42,45-47,51,53,56,58,61, LXIX.5-7,18,23,30,33, LXX.33, LXXII.1, LXXIV.9, LXXV.3, LXXVIII.1,41,47-48, LXXXII.5,10, Hug.4,45.
Frid, XIII.1, XIV.20, XXXII.6, LXIV.50.
Fridla, LXXI.18.
Frigga, X.17, XIII.1,3, XIV.1,5-6,8,12,14,XVI.3,5,20, XIX.15,18, XXXII.2,20, XXXVI.9-10,13, XLV.23, LIII.2,5-6,9,12,59,78,80-81, LVI.7, LVII.1,11, LVIII.1-2,4, LXV.1-2,7, LXIX.18, LXXI.47, LXXII.7,LXXVI.20, LXXVII.57, LXXVIII.1,29-32,65, LXXXI.1, LXXXII.8-9, Hug.2,3,5,56.
Frosti, 1) Dwarf, X.8, 2) Etin, XV.13, XLVII.4.
Frovur, XIII.6.
Frua, XIII.6.
Frya, Hug. 39.
Fulla, XIV.5, LIII.2, LXV.7.
Fulnir, XX.55.
Fundin, X.5.

Funi, LXVI.27.
Fylgja, XIX.18-21, XXIV.2-3,33,39,45-46, XXV.3, XXVI.3.
Fylking, LX.3-4, LXIII.2, LXV.3, LXIX.23,30,33, LXX.19,25,32-33,35, LXXII.1, LXIII.3,8,20, LXXX.3, LXXXIII.5.
Fylkja, LXXX.3.
Fyrisvellir, XXI.11.
Fyrnir, XV.13.

G

Gafugt Dyr, L.6.
Gaglwood, XXII.8, LIII.67.
Gagnrad, V.39, LVIII.8-18,20,22,24,26,28,30,32,34,36,38,40,42,44,46,48,50,52,54.
Galar, 1) Dwarf, X.9, 2) Etin, XV.13.
Galdur, IV.3, V.46, XX.10, XXVII.8, XL.5, LIII.19, LVII.11, LXI.2, LXII.40, LXIII.6, LXX.7,19, LXXIX.1, Hug. 24,27.
Galdurfather, LIII.16.
Galdursmiths, V.46.
Gambantein, XLIV.20, LIII.13, LIV.12,LXI.4,8,LXII.27,45, LXIII.1,3-4,6,9, LXIV.9,63,LXVII.9,28,34,46,51, LXIX.6, LXX.1,LXXIV.11, LXXIX.3, LXXXII.1,5,10.
Gandalf, X.4.
Gandur, XXII.6, LIII.47.
Gandvik, XXXII.4.
Ganglati, XV.13.
Gangleri, V.33.
Ganglot, XLII.5.
Gang, 1) Egil, XV.13, 2) Ymir, XXXII.6.
Gard, XV.1, XXI.11,XXVI.17,35, XXXI.3, XXXII.2,9, XXXIII.10,24, XXXVII.20, XLIII.27, LIII.39, LVII.8, LXII.1,29-31, LXIV.15,LXVII.7,24,32, LXX.5-6,27, LXXI.13,26, LXXVIII.41, LXXX.113.
Gardofa, XIV.16.
Garm, LIII.17,73,83, LXXXII.2.
Gastropnir, XII.5, LXIV.12,24, LXIX.16,29,33.
Gauksmonth, XI.12.

Gautatyr, V.39.
Gautland, XXVII.1.
Gaut, V.34, XXVII.1, XXXII.3,12, LXIX.30,33, LXXVI.23.
Gebo, VI.16, XX.19.
Gefjon, 1) Nyhellenia, XXII.10-13,15-17,23-25,28,32,34,38,42,44-45,2)Urd, XLV.12, LXXVIII.1,23-24.
Gefn, XIV.6, LXXIV.1.
Geigud, V.39.
Geirahod, XXV.15.
Geiravor, XXV.15.
Geirdriful, XXV.15.
Geirlodnir, V.39.
Geirolnir, V.39.
Geironul, XXV.15.
Geirrod, V.36, XV.13, XXXII.1-3,9,14,19-20,23.
Geirskogul, XXV.15, LIII.56.
Geirvandill, XVII.2.
Geirvimul, VIII.2, XII.7.
Geitir, XV.13.
Geitla, XV.14.
Geldur, XXXVII.6.
Gelgja, LXXXV.9.
Gepides, XLVII.2.
Gerd, XIV.20, LXVII.1,16,18,21-22,24,26,39,41,44,46,51-52,56,58,61, LXIX.7, LXXVIII.46.
Geri, V.45, XXV.2,8, LXIV.26, LXXX.4.
Germania, LXX.4,21,24,61, LXXIII.1.
Gersemi, XIV.6, LXVII.61, LXX.61.
Gestilja, XV.14.
Gestumblindi, V.39.
Gevar, VIII.9.
Geysa, XV.14.
Gifur, 1) Freki, XXV.2, LXIV.26, 2) Demon, IX.2.
Gilling, XV.13.
Gimir, XI.2.
Gimle, IV.4, VII.2, XXIV.9,30,45, XLII.7,LIII.89,LXXXIII.5.
Ginnar, 1) Odin, V.39, 2) Dwarf, X.8.
Ginnungagap, I.1-2,4-6, II.2,III.1, IX.3, XLV.4, Hug.1,2,20,23,36.
Ginnungaheaven, XI.1.

Gipul, VIII.2.
Gisl, X.11.
Gizur, V.39.
Gjallarbridge, XXIV.30, LXV.3,5.
Gjallarhorn, IV.3, XVI.17, XX.106, XXIV.44, XLV.16,26, LIII.53,71, LXIX.26-27, LXXXII.3.
Gjalp, VIII.11, XV.14, XXXII.6,14,19,23.
Gjoll, 1) River, I.2, IV.3, VIII.3, XXIV.24,29-30, XLV.9, LXV.3, 2) Boulder, LXXV.9.
Gjolp, 1) Etin, X.9, XV.13, 2) Dwarf, XV.13.
Gjuki, LXX.31, LXXI.26.
Gjukungs, XL.2, LXX.31,35.
Glad, X.11.
Gladsheim, XII.2, XXV.1.
Glaer, X.11.
Glaevald, XXVI.7.
Glammi, XXXII.13.
Glam, XV.13.
Glapsvid, V.34.
Glasir, XII.2.
Glasislund, XVI.8.
Glasisvellir, IV.3, X.15, XXIV.45, XLVI.3.
Glaumar, XV.13.
Glaum, 1) Etin, XXXII.21, 2) Horse, X.13.
Glaumvor, XV.13.
Gleipnir, XVI.14, XXXII.17, LXXV.3.
Glen, XXXVIII.8.
Glitnir, XVI.8, XXXIX.1, LII.50, LXV.12,LXIX.1, LXIV.11.
Gloi, X.7.
Gloni, X.9.
Glora, XVI.7.
Glumra, XV.14.
Gna, XIV.14,17.
Gneggjud, LXVI.21.
Gneip, XV.14.
Gnepja, XV.14.
Gnipacave, LIII.69,73,83, LXXXII.2.
Gnipalund, XXIII.2, XLII.4, LXVIII.2.
Gnissa, XV.14.
Gnitaheath, L.3.
Gnod, LXXIII.4.

Godi, V.1, XXI.12, II.24,29,31,33,35,37,40-41,43, Hug.31, 46-47.
Godord, Hug.30,46.
Goth-thjod, XXV.15, LIII.56.
Goi, 1) February, XI.12, 2) Giantess, XV.14.
Goin, II.9,XXVI.23.
Goll, XXV.15.
Gomul, VIII.2, XII.7.
Gondlir, V.36.
Gondul, 1) Odin ,V.39, 2) Valkyrie, XXV.15,22, LIII.56, 3) Gullveig, LI.2-3.
Gopul, VIII.2.
Gor, XV.13.
Gormonth, XI.12.
Gotaland, LX.19.
Goths, XLVII.2,4, LX.19, LXXI.24,39,46.
Goti, 1) Jarl, XXVI.1, 2) Gunnar's horse, X.12-13, LXX.35.
Gotland, XXVII.1, XLIII.7,35, LX.19.
Gotnar, XXVII.1.
Gothic, LXXI.20.
Grabak, II.9.
Grad, VIII.2.
Grafvitnir, II.9.
Grafvollud, II.9.
Gram, 1) Kon, XXIX.15, 2) Kon's son, LX.36.
Grani, X.13, LII.25, LIV.9.
Greip, VIII.11, XV.14, XVII.1, XXXI.3, XXXII.19.
Grepp, XV.13, XLII.1-2, XLIII.19, LV.5,LXII.5-6,11,14,16,18,22-24,27,45.
Grer, X.9, XVIII.3.
Gridarvol, XXXII.16,19.
Grid, XV.14, XVI.16, XXXII.12.
Grima, 1) Giantess, XV.14, 2) Natt, LXVI.31.
Grimling, XV.13.
Grimnir, 1) Odin, V.34,36, XXXII.5, XLV.16, Hug.51, 2) Etin, XV.13.
Grim,1) Odin, V.33, 2) Dwarf, X.9.
Grjotunagard, XXXVI.4,7,9.
Groa, XIV.20, XXVII.8-9, XXX.1,XXXV.1,XXXVI.19, XLIII.6-7,10,12,14,16,20,27,34,36, XLIV.14-15,

LIX.1,3,5-7,9,11, LX.22,LXI.2,LXII.40, LXIII.6, LXX.1-2,7.
Groandi, LXVI.11.
Grotti, VIII.1,5-6,10-11, IX.4, XIII.4, XV.10, XVI.1, XX.1, XXVI.12, XLIV.5,7, LIV.1, LXI.7, LXIV.42, LXIX.27, LXXVIII.48.
Grottintanna, XV.14.
Grougaldur, LXI.6.
Gryla, XV.14.
Gud, X.9.
Gudorm, XLIII.36, LIX.3, LXX.1-2,4,25-27,29-32,35, LXXI.1-2,5,8-9,12,16-20,22-23,36-40, LXXIII.1,3.
Gudrun, XLVIII.1, LXX.31, LXXI.2,4,7-8,19,23,25-26.
Gullfaxi, X.12, XXXI.2, XXXVI.1,17.
Gullinbursti,XXXV.6, LVI.7.
Gullinkambi, XXV.11, LIII.68, LXIII.28, LXIV.4, LXXXII.1.
Gullintanni, XX.105.
Gulltopp, X.11, XX.105, LVI.7.
Gullveig, XV.3,10,14, XVI.12,20, XXII.1,5,7-8,11,13-16,19-20,23,47, XXIII.1, XXV.1, XXVI.2, XXXII.5,20, XLII.2-3, XLIV.3,XLV.1, XLVI.1, LI.2, LIII.5,46, LX.17, LXII.5,22,LXIV.50, LXVII.1,46, LXVIII.1-3, LXIX.1,3-6,12-13,15,20, LXX.19, LXXII.5,LXXIX.1, LXXX.2, LXXXII.1,4, Hug.5.
Guma, XV.14.
Gungnir, XXXV.1,5, LII.25, LXIII.2, LXXXII.6.
Gunnar,1) Slagfin's son, X.13, XLVIII.1, LXX.31,35,61, LXXI.4,21, 2) Warrior, Hug.28.
Gunn, XXV.15,22, LIII.56.
Gunnhild, LXXIII.35.
Gunnlod, XV.14, XXXVII.7-9,13-14,16,19-20,23,26, LXXX.18,111,113,115.
Gunnthorin, XXV.15.
Gunnthrain, VIII.2.
Gunnthro, I.2, VIII.2.
Gusir, XV.13.
Gydja, Hug.11,46,52,53,56.

Giantess, VIII.6,X.1, XV.10,14, XVI.6,15-16, XVII.1, XXIV.42, XXVI.17, XXXI.3,9, XXXII.6-7,12,19, XXXVI.18, XLV.14, XLVII.6, LIII.65,67,77, LVIII.32, LX.17-18, LXII.30-32,LXIV.41, LXV.9,11, LXVIII.2, LXIX.3, LXXVI.14, LXXIX.1.

Gylfi, 1) Etin, XXII.11-12,47, 2) Kon's son, LX.36.

Gylling, 1) Key, XXIV.18, 2) Etin, XV.13.

Gyllir, 1) Horse, X.11, 2) Etin, XV.13.

Gymir, XV.3,13, XXII.20, XLIV.4, LXIII.1-2, LXVII.1,7,12-14,16,24,26,46,48,50-51,53-60, LXXVI.1,36, LXXVII.1, LXXVIII.1-2,13,46.

H

Hadarlag, XVI.11.

Haddingjas, X.13.

Haddingland, XVI.17, LXX.14.

Hadding, LX.36, LXX.1-7,14,16-24,26,29,31-37,49,56,59-61, LXXII.4, LXXIII.1,4,8,17,21-22,27,32-34,36, LXXIV.2,8-10.

Haera, XV.14.

Haevateinn, LXIV.38.

Hafdi, LX.19.

Haffru, XV.3, XVII.1.

Hafli, XV.13, LXX.2,32,35.

Hagal, Hamal's father, XXIX.13.

Hagalaz VI.18, XX.21

Haki, X.13, XV.13, XXXVI.11, LXXIX.3.

Hakon, LXIX.36.

Hala, XV.14.

Halfdan, XXIX.10, XLIII.1.

Half, XV.6.

Hallinskidi, XX.105.

Hal, XX.64.

Hamal,XXIX.13, XLIII.7,9,11,13,15,17,28, XLVII.8, LXX.17,20,22,35,60, LXXIII.1,6,8,17,20,33, LXXX.3.

Hamalt Fylkja, LXXIII.20.

Hamdir, LXXI.4,22-24,35-36,40,43,47.

Hamingja, XIX.18-19, XXIV.3, LIII.14, LVIII.49.

Hama, XXIV.11.

Hamskerpir, XIV.16.

Hangagud, V.39.

Hangatyr, V.39.

Hangi, V.39.

Hannar, X.5.

Haptagud, V.39.

Haptsoenir, V.39.

Har, 1) Odin, V.33, LIII.46,95, LXIX.1, LXXX.5, 2) Dwarf, X.7.

Harald, X.13.

Harbard 1) Odin, V.36, L.8, 2) Loki, LXXVII.11,13,15-17,19-21,23-25,27-31,33,35,37,39-41,43,45,47,49,51,53,55,57,59,61.

Hardgrepa, XV.14, LXX.5-6,32,35,37,59.

Hardveur, XVI.6.

Hardverk, XV.13.

Harlung, LXXI.18.

Harlungs, LXXI.18.

Harri, LX.36.

Hati Hrodvitnisson, XI.9, XV.13, LVII.3, LXVIII.2, LXXXI.2, LXXXII.7.

Hatun,XXIX.8.

Haugbui, XXIV.13-14.

Haugspori, X.7.

Haur, X.7.

Haustigi, XV.13.

Haustmonth, XI.12.

Havi, V.39.

Hedin, XXXII.17.

Hefring, XV.4.

Heiddraupnir, LII.21, LXIX.24.

Heidornir, XI.2.

Heid, XV.10,XXII.6,13,23, LIII.5,47.

Heidrek, XV.13, XXXII.20.

Heidrun, XXV.9.

Heimdall,VI.34, VIII.11, XII.8, XV.10, XVII.2, XX.1,4-10,12,33,37,40-41,43,91-93,95-96,98,103-106, XXI.3,12-13, XXII.2,7,13,22,30,38, XXIV.44, XXIX.11, XXXIII.16, XXXVII.11,19,21, XXXVIII.3,6-8, XLV.9,11,14,16,20, XLVII.5,LIII.32,55,71, LVI.7, LX.2,35, LXIV.3, LXVII.30, LXIX.28, LXX.7,60,

LXXIV.10, LXXVIII.51-52, LXXX.110, LXXXII.3,10, Hug.18,32,36,48.

Heimir, LXXVII.45.

Heiptir, XI.8, XXVI.3, XXXVII.27, LIII.121.

Hel,1)Urd,XXIV.1-2,19-21,47, XXVI.3,31, L.25, LIII.18,68, LIX.13, LXIV.37, LXV.2,8,10, LXXI.31,LXXXII.1, 2) Kingdom, VIII.3, XVI.17, XXI.13, XXIV.1-3,11-12,15,17-18,28,33,45, XXV.1,16, XXVI.13,34, XXXII.22, XXXVII.27, XLII.6, XLIII.15, XLV.11, L.14, LIII.15,21,24,77, LVII.12, LVIII.43, LXV.4,8-9, LXVI.15,19,21,27,29,33,35, LXVII.29, LXXIII.6, LXXVII.28, LXXVIII.70.

Helblindi, 1) Odin, V.33, 2) Etin, XV.7-8.

Held, XX.64.

Helfare, XXIV.15,32, XXXI.7,9, LI.6, LVI.6-7, LX.34,LXX.49, LXXIII.35.

Helgi, XXIX.15.

Helgate, I.1, XXIV.18,36.

Helheim, I.3,5-6, II.2, III.1, XX.40.

Hellenia, XXII.26.

Helregin, XV.13.

Helshoes, XXIV.4,11,28.

Helthing, XXIV.4,15-16,30,33, XXV.3, XXVI.2,LII.20.

Helways, XXIV.18, LIII.72, LXV.2-5, LXXXII.3.

Hengest, XXXVII.6.

Hengjankjapta, XV.14, XXXII.23.

Hengjankjopt, XV.13.

Henry, LXXIII.22.

Heptifili, X.5.

Herfjotur, XXV.15.

Herfather, V.39, XXV.8, LVIII.2,40.

Hergaut, LXII.47.

Heri, X.8.

Herja, XXV.15.

Herjafather, V.39,47, LIII.54.

Herjan, V.33, XXV.11,15, XLV.16, LIII.56,68, LXIX.33,LXXXII.1.

Herkir, XV.13.

Herkja, XV.14.

Hermod, V.47, XXV.3.

Hersir, XX.81, XXI.5.

Herteit, V.34.

Hertyr, V.39.

Herules, XLVII.2,4.

Heyannir, XI.12.

Hildibrand, XXI.9, LXX.17,20,22,35,60, LXXIII.1,33.

Hildigir, XXI.9, LX.5-6.

Hildings, XX.92, XXI.9,12, XXIX.6, LX.2,5, LXX.17,20,35.

Hildisvini, XXXV.6.

Hildolf, LXXVII.9.

Hild, XXV.15,20, LII.1,10,12,31,49, LIII.56, LVII.12.

Hildur, XXI.7-10.

Hilmir, LX.36.

Himinbjorg, XX.105, XLV.26, LXIX.26.

Himingloeva, XV.4.

Himinhrjot, LXXVI.17.

Himinn, LXVI.13.

Himinvangar, XXIX.8.

Hindarfjoll, LI.15, LII.2.

Hjadningas, LII.49.

Hjalmberi, V.33.

Hjalmgunnar, LII.10.

Hjalmther, X.13.

Hjalmthrimul, XXV.15.

Hjalp, V.12.

Hjarrandi, V.39.

Hjordrimul, XXV.15,20.

Hjorvard, 1) Odin, V.39, 2) Eggther, LXXIX.3.

Hjuki, XXXVII.1,3.

Hladgud Swanwhite, XXVII.10.

Hlaevang, X.7.

Hlebard, LXXVII.21.

Hledjolf, X.9.

Hlefod, V.39.

Hlefrey, V.39.

Hleidra, XXII.46.

Hler, XV.3.

Hlesey, LX.17, LXVII.60, LXXVII.38.

Hlevarg, X.9.

Hlidskjalf, XII.3, XXII.10, XLIV.2, XLV.10, LXVII.1, LXIX.30, LXXVIII.73.

Hlidthang, LXVI.29.

Hlif, XIII.1, XIV.20, LXIV.50.

Hlifthrasa, XIII.1, XIV.20, LXIV.50.

Hlin, 1) Frigga, LIII.78, LXXXII.8, 2) Maidservant, XIV.12.

Hljodolf, X.8.

Hlodyn, LIII.80, LV.23, LXXXII.9.

Hloi, XV.13.

Hlok, XXV.15.

Hlora, XVI.7.

Hlorridi, XVI.6, XXX.2, XXXIII.8-9,15,32, LXXVI.4,16,26,28, LXXVIII.60-61.

Hlyrnir, 1) One of Nine Heavens, XI.2 , 2) Heaven, LXVI.13.

Hnikar, V.34, XLV.19.

Hnikud, V.35.

Hnipinn, LXVI.33.

Hnitbjorg, XXVIII.4, XXXVII.7,11,24.

Hnoss, XIV.6, LXVII.61, LXX.61, LXXIV.1.

Hoddgoda, XXVI.4.

Hoddmimis Holt, XLVI.5, LVI.9, LVIII.45, LXXXIII.1.

Hoddropnir, LII.21, LXIX.24.

Hod, 1) Odin's son, XVI.11-13, XXXII.17, XL.12,15-17, L.1-3,5,8,10,12,14,16,18,21,23-26, LI.1-9,11-14,17, LII.1-3,5,7,10,12,28,30,47,49, LIII.24-25,58,87-88,93,96-97,99-101,103-106,109-116,118-119,121-122, LVI.1-2,4-5,LVII.11-12, LXXXIII.1,3, 2) Horse, X.13.

Hoenir, V.1,41, IX.3, X.17, XIII.1,9, XVI.3-4, XIX.3,13,15-18, XL.4,6,8-10, LIII.43,88, LV.3, LXIX.18,22-23,26, LXXVIII.30, LXXXIII.3.

Hof, VI.26, XIII.2, XX.40,105, XXII.32, XXIV.41, XXVI.2, LIII.38,51, LVIII.38,51, LXV.12, LXIX.14, LXXX.3, LXXXIII.3, Hug. 31,37,39.

Hofvarpnir, XIV.14,16.

Hogni, X.13, XLVIII.1, LI.14, LII.1,49, LX.3,LXX.31,35, LXXI.4,21.

Holgabrud, XV.14.

Holkvir, X.13, LXX.35.

Hollar Voettir, XXIV.12.

Holl, VIII.2.

Holt, XLVI.3-4,6,9, LVI.9, LXVII.34.

Horg, VII.1, XIII.1-2, XX.40, LIII.38, LVIII.38, LVIII.38, LXII.54, Hug.9,11.

Horn, 1) Freya, XIV.6, LXXIV.1, 2) River, LIX.13, 3) Giantess, XV.14.

Hornbori, X.5, LXII.45.

Horr, X.9.

Hosvir, XX.55.

Hraesvelg, XV.11,13.

Hrafn, X.13.

Hrafnagud, V.39,45.

Hrammi, V.39.

Hrani, V.39.

Hraudnir, XV.13.

Hraudung, XV.13, XXXII.1.

Hreggmimir, XI.2.

Hreidgotaland, XXVII.1, LX.19.

Hreidgoths, LVIII.12.

Hreinna Log, LXVI.35.

Hrid, I.2, VIII.3.

Hrimfaxi, XI.4, XLV.23, LVIII.14.

Hrimgerd, XV.14.

Hrimgrimnir, XV.13, LXVII.37.

Hrimnir, XV.10,13, XVI.20, XXII.1, XXXII.20, LIII.5, LXVII.30.

Hrim, XV.13.

Hrimthurses, 1) Type of Etin, III.1-2, IX.2,6, X.18, XII.8, XV.1,10, XVIII.2, XXVI.1,17, XXXI.1,3, XXXIV.1, XXXVII.7,9,23, XXXIX.4, XLIV.20, LVIII.33, LXI.6, LXVII.32,52, LXXVII.30, LXXX.114, LXXXII.4, 2) Etin, XV.13.

Hringhorni, XVIII.2, L.2, LVI.6,8.

Hring, XLIII.37, LX.3.

Hringstadir, XXIX.8.

Hringvolnir, XV.13.

Hrin, XX.55.

Hripstodi, XV.13.

Hrist, XXV.15.

Hrjod, XI.2.

Hroar, XV.13.

Hrod, XV.13, LXXVI.11.

Hrodud, LXVI.27.

Hrodvitnir, XI.9, LXXVIII.43.

Hrokkvir, XV.13.

Hronn, 1) Elivagar, VIII.3, XXVI.12, 2) Aegir's daughter, XV.4.

Hroptatyr, V.26, XI.10, LVI.7.
Hropt, V.38, XXV.2, XLV.23, LII.21, LIII.87, LVII.4, LXIX.24, LXXXIII.3.
Hrossthjof, XV.10,13, XXII.1, LIII.5.
Hrotti, L.26.
Hruga, XV.14.
Hrund, XXV.15.
Hrungnir, XV.13, XXXI.2, XXXVI.1-14, XXXVII.15, XLIV.6, LXXVI.16,20, LXXVII.15-16, LXXVIII.68,70.
Hrungnirsheart, XXXVI.7.
Hrutmonth, XI.12.
Hryggda, XV.14.
Hrym, XV.13, LIII.74, LXXXII.4.
Hugi, XXX.19,21-22,39.
Hugin, V.45, XXXVII.8, XLV.3, LXXIII.7, Hug.2,5.
Hugur, Hug.23.
Hugstari, X.8.
Hugrunes, VI.8, LII.21, LXIX.24.
Hulidshelm, 1) Helm, LXI.6, 2) Clouds, LXVI.19.
Hunding, LXXIV.13.
Hundla, XV.14.
Hundolf, XV.13.
Hungur, XLII.5.
Hunwar, LXXII.1, LXXX.2.
Husfreya, XIII.6, XX.68.
Huskarls, XXIX.9.
Hval, XV.13.
Hvatmod, V.39.
Hvedna, XV.14, LXXIX.3.
Hvedra, XV.14.
Hvedrung, XV.13, LIII.79, LXXXIII.8.
Hveralund, LIII.60, LXXVIII.79.
Hverfanda Hvel, LXVI.15.
Hvergelmir, I.2, II.2, III.1, IV.2,6, VIII.1,5, XVII.2,5, XX.3, XXV.9, XXVI.12,17, XXVII.3,5,7, XXXVII.9, LIV.1, LXIX.27.
Hvidud, LXVI.21.
Hvita Stjarna, LX.19.
Hviti As, XX.105, XLV.14.
Hviting, XXI.5.
Hymir, XV.13, XVI.15, XL.11, LXXVI.5,7,10-11,15-19,21-25,28-29,34-36, LXXVIII.38.

Hyndla, XV.14.
Hyrja, XV.14.
Hyr, LXIV.44.
Hyrrokin, XV.10,14, XXXII.23.

I

Idavoll, VII.1-2, X.2,15, XI.3, LIII.38,85, LXXXIII.2-3.
Idi, XV.13, XXXII.4, XLIV.6.
Idisi, XIX.19.
Idun, XIV.2, XVII.1,6, XVIII.4, XXVII.6,XXXVII.1,3,5,25, XL.6,11, XLI.1-2,XLIV.14-15, XLV.6,8, XLVII.1, LIV.6,10, LV.1-4, LXIV.65, LXXVII.31, LXXVIII.1,20-22,78, Hug.52.
Ifing, XI.2,8, XII.8,LVI.6,8,LVIII.16, LXIV.2.
Igroen, LXVI.11.
Ilm, XIV.20.
Ima, XV.14.
Imbrekki, LXXI.18.
Imd, VIII.11, XV.10,14.
Imgerd, XV.14.
Im, XV.13.
Ing, 1) Od, VI.31.
Ingi, 1) Frey, XLI.2, 2) Dwarf, X.9.
Ingunarfrey, LXXVIII.47.
Ingwaz VI.31, XX.34.
Inn Sidskeggja As, XXXVII.26.
Inn Skjota As, V.1.
Inn Thogla As, XVI.16.
Iri, X.6.
Ironwood, XXII.8-9, XL.19, XLI.1, XLIV.1,15, XLIX.1,3, LI.2-3, LIII.65, LV.23, LXIX.36, LXXII.5, LXXIX.1-2, LXXXII.1.
Isa, VI.20, XX.23.
Isarnkol, XI.5.
Isung, XXXI.3.
Ivaldi, X.8,18, XII.5, XVI.18, XVII.1-5,7, XVIII.1,4, XXVII.2-7, XXXI.1,3, XXXV.1,5,XXXVII.1-2,6,11,15,18,24,27, XXXVIII.1-3, XXXIX.8, XL.1-3,13,15,17-18, XLIII.6-7, XLIV.1,15-16, XLV.2,6,XLVII.4,6, XLVIII.1, XLIX.1,

L.3, LII.50, LIV.6,10, LV.5, LXII.28,31,48, LXIII.7,9,27, LXIV.22,65, LXVII.52, LXX.5,22, LXXI.1,4, LXXVII.20.

Ividja, 1) Ironwood maiden, LIII.33, LXXIX.1, 2) Gullveig, XV.10, XXII.8, XLV.1.

J

Jafnhar, V.36.

Jalangsheath, XX.92.

Jalk, 1) Odin, V.36, LXXIII.3, 2) Slagfin, XXXVII.6.

Jari, 1) Dwarf, X.5, 2) Etin, XV.13.

Jarl, 1) Kon's father, XX.75-76,78,82,84,87,90-92,96-97,103, XXI.1-3,5,7,10-13, XXII.1,11,13,46-47, XXVII.1, XXIX.6,10-11,13-14, XXXVIII.8, XLIII.27,37, XLVII.5,7-8,LX.2-3,22-23,36, LXIII.22,30, 2) Chieftain,V.1, VI.13, XI.10, XIII.1, XVI.18, XXI.3, XXII.41, XXIV.7, XXV.3,24, XXVIII.4, XXIX.4,7,9-10, XXXVII.24, XXXVIII.5, XLIII.6, XLVII.4-5,9,LIII.5, LX.2-3,22-23, LXII.1,18,21-23,46, LXIII.1,26, LXVII.54,56-58, LXIX.23,36, LXX.3,61, LXXVII.25.

Jarnglumra, XV.14.

Jarngreips, XVIII.2, XXXII.20.

Jarnsaxa, VIII.11, XV.14, XVI.6, XXXVI.16.

Jarnvidja, 1) Ironwood Maiden, XXII.8, LV.23, LXXIX.1, 2) Gullveig, XV.10, XXII.8.

Jera, VI.21, XX.24.

Jod, XX.83.

Jofur, LX.36.

Jokul, XV.5,13, XLIV.11.

Jolf, V.38.

Jolfud, V.39.

Jolnir, V.39, XXXII.18.

Jonak, LXXI.2,4-5,41.

Jor, 1) Horse, X.12

Jord, X.17, XIV.1, XXXII.20, XXXIII.1, XXXVI.9-10,13, LXVI.11, LXXII.47, LXXIV.8, LXXVI.20, LXXVIII.65, LXXXI.1, Hug.4.

Jormungand, XXIII.1-3, LIII.74, LXXV.19-22, LXXXII.3-4,9.

Jormungrund, II.1-2,5, IV.1,V.3,45, XI.4,10, XII.8, XIII.1, XV.11, XVIII.5, XIX.19, XX.1,106, XXII.8, XXIV.1,9,15,17-18,28-29, XXVI.1,13,17, XXVIII.1, XXXVII.8, XLIV.1,3,5, XLV.25, XLVI.1, LVI.9, LXX.14, LXXXII.3.

Jormun, V.39.

Jorun, XLV.15.

Joruvellir, XIX.2, XX.43, XLVII.2,4.

Jotunheim, VI.34, IX.2,6, XV.1-2, XVI.1,7,15,19, XVII.2,7, XXII.1,5,8,11,47, XXIII.2, XXIV.17, XXVII.3,5,9, XXXI.3, XXXII.17, XXXIII.7,13-14,21-22,27,29, XXXIV.4,6, XXXVI.1,3,6, XXXVII.7,9,26, XL.10,13, XLII.4, XLIII.3, XLIV.1,4, XLIX.3, LI.2-3, LIII.39,76, LV.3, LVI.8, LX.4, LXII.1-2,4,31, LXIII.1-2, LXIV.64, LXVII.1,12,43,46,52,55, LXVIII.2, LXX.35, LXXII.1-2,6, LXXX.2,117, LXXXI.1, LXXXII.6.

Jutland, XXVII.1, LX.19, LXXIII.17.

K

Kaldgrani, XV.13.

Kalta, XXII.14,24.

Kari, XV.3,5-6,13, XLIV.11.

Karl, 1) Odin, V.39, 2) Afi's son, XX.61,63, 3) Freeman, XX.65,91, XXIX.11, LXXVII.3.

Kefsir, XX.55.

Keila, XV.14, XXXII.23.

Kenaz, VI.15, XX.18

Kerlaugs, VIII.4,XXIV.36.

Kiarr, XXXV.1.

Kili, X.5.

Kjalar, V.36, LXXIII.7-11,17.

Kjalki, V.36, LXXIII.17.

Kjallandi, XV.14, XXXII.23.

Kleggi, XX.55.

Kleima, XV.14.

Klur, XX.55.

Kolga, XV.4.

Koll, XV.13, XXXI.5-6,9.

Kon, X.13, XX.83,85,88-89,96, XXI.11, XXVII.1, XXIX.1,8,10-15, XLIII.1,7,13,15,18,23,27-29,32,34-37, XLVII.5-10, LIX.3, LX.2-6,16,22-24,34-36, LXI.1-4, LXIII.1-3,5-6,10-11,13-15,17,19-20,22-23,26-27,29, LXX.1-3,5,17,20-22, LXXI.1,18, LXXIII.1.

Kor, XLII.5.

Kormt, VIII.4, XXIV.36.

Kornskurdarmonth, XI.12.

Kort, X.13.

Kott, XV.13.

Kraka, XV.14.

Kumba, XX.56.

Kund, XX.83.

Kveldrider, XLII.6.

Kvikadrops, I.4, III.1, LVIII.31.

Kynsfylgja, XIX.20.

Kyrmir, XV.13.

L

La, XIX.2-3,13-14, XXIV.9, LIII.43.

Laeding, LXXV.1-2.

Laegi, LXVI.23.

Laerad, XXV.9.

Laeti, XIX.2-3,13-14, LIII.43.

Lagastaf, 1) Sea, LXVI.25, 2) Grain, LXVI.33.

Laguz, VI.30, XX.33.

Landwights, XXVIII.5.

Landvidi, XVI.16.

Langbak, XXVI.23.

Langifot, V.1, XIX.15.

Laufey, XV.7, XXXIII.19,21, XLV.16, LXXVIII.56.

Leggjaldi, XX.55.

Leidi, XV.13, XXXII.23.

Leifi, XV.13.

Leifnir's Fire, LIX.15, LXX.7.

Leifthrasir, XXVI.4, XLVI.5, LVI.9-10, LVIII.45, LXV.6, LXXXIII.1.

Leikin, XV.14, XXII.6, XXIV.16,18, XXVI.18, XXXII.23, XLII.4-8, XLVI.7, LIII.47, LXX.19.

Leipt, I.2, VIII.3, XXVI.4.

Leirbrimir, IX.3,XII.5, LXIV.24.

Leirvor, XV.14.

Leita Kynnis, XXIV.46.

Lettfeti, X.11.

Lif, XXVI.4, XLVI.5, LVI.9-10, LVIII.45, LXV.6, LXXXIII.1.

Lik, XIX.13, XXIV.9.

Limar, XI.8, XXVI.3,32, XXXVII.27, LII.32.

Limrunes, VI.6,8, LII.19.

Lindring, XLIV.19.

Linn, XXVI.23.

Lister, XXXII.19,22.

Litur, 1) Dwarf, X.4, 2) Litur Goda, XIX.14, XXIV.9-11,31,XXXVII.22, LXXX.98,112, Hug.5.

Litur Goda, XIX.2-3,13, XXIV.9, XXVI.14, LIII.43.

Ljodasmiths, V.31.

Ljonar, XL.12.

Ljosalfar, X.17, XI.2,10-11.

Ljota, XV.14.

Loddfafnir, LIII.96-97,99-101,103-106,109-116,118-119,121-122.

Lodin,XV.13.

Lodinfingra, XV.14.

Lodung, V.39.

Lodur, V.1,41, VIII.9,11, IX.3, X.17, XI.5, XIII.1,4,XIX.3,13-15, XX.1, XXVI.14, LIII.43, LIV.12, LVIII.23, LXIX.18,23, LXXVIII.30.

Lofar, X.8.

Lofdungs, LX.2.

Lofn, XIV.8.

Lofstirr, XXIV.40,45, XXVI.13.

Logafell, XXV.17, LX.23.

Logi, XV.3,5-6,13, XXX.18,39.

Logn, LXVI.23.

Logrinn, XXII.11.

Loinn, X.9.

Loki, XV.3,7-10, XVI.12-13,20-21, XX.105, XXII.1, XXIII.1-2, XXIV.6, XXVI.18, XXX.1-2,4,17-18,39, XXXII.2-6, XXXIII.2,5,8,10,12,19,21, XXXIV.2,4,6, XXXV.1-2,5, XXXIX.1-2,4-7, XL.4,6,8-11, XLI.1, XLII.3-4, XLIV.15,17, XLV.9,16,20,

XLIX.2, LIII.9,13,30,60,75,79, LV.2-4,9,LVI.1,3-4, LVII.1, LXV.11, LXVIII.1-2, LXIX.17,21,37, LXX.5,19,29, LXXI.1,12-13,17, LXXIII.3, LXXIV.10, LXXVII.3, LXXVIII.1-2,5,7-9,12-14,17,19-26,28,30,32-34,36,38,40,42,44,46,48,50-54,56-58,60,62,65,67,69,71,73-79, LXXX.2, LXXXII.4,8,10.

Loni, X.5.

Lopt, 1) Loki, XV.7, XXIII.1, XXXII.3, XL.11, XLII.3, XLV.9, LXVIII.1, LXXVIII.9, 2) Volund, LXIV.38.

Lud, LXIV.42.

Lund, XIX.11,XX.8.

Lung, X.12.

Lut, 1) Etin, XXXII.23, 2) Thrall's son, XX.55.

Lyfjaberg, XIII.5, LXIV.48.

Lyngvi, LXXV.4, LXXVIII.77.

Lysing, XXI.5-6,9, LX.5-6.

M

Maeri, LXXVI.22.

Maeringaburg, LXX.18-20,22-23,28,60-61, LXXIII.1,33.

Maerings, LXX.20.

Magni, XVI.6, XXXVI.15-16, LVIII.51, LXXVII.10,54, LXXXIII.3.

Malrunes, VI.7, XIX.5,XXIV.8,38, XXV.3, LII.20, LVII.12.

Mana, XV.14.

Managarm, XI.9.

Mani, X.17, XI.1,5-6,8-9, XVI.10,13, XVII.6, XXIV.36, XXVI.3, XXXVI.9, XXXVII.2-3,5-6,25-27, XXXVIII.3,8, L.1-2, LI.1,5, LIII.36,121, LVI.6, LVII.3, LVIII.22-23, LXI.4-6,8, LXVI.15, LXVIII.2, LXXIII.14, LXXXI.2, Hug.5.

Manna Meotod, II.3, XVI.20, LXIV.34.

Mannaz, VI.29, XX.32.

Mannheim, XLV.24, LXIX.36, LXX.7,14,26.

Mannsfylgja, XIX.20.

Mannus, XXIX.15.

Mardoll, XIV.6, LXXIV.1.

Margerd, XV.14.

Megingjard, XVIII.2, XXXII.11, LX.35.

Meginrunes, LII.27.

Meili, XXXVI.9, XL.9, LXXVII.10.

Melnir, LX.3.

Menglad, LXIV.20,49,53-56.

Menglodum, LIX.8.

Menja, XXXI.3, XLIV.5, LXX.32,35, LXXIII.21.

Menthjof, X.13.

Middag, XI.3-4, LIII.37.

Midgard, IX.2,4,6, XI.4,6,10-11,XV.2,15, XVI.1,20, XIX.3,8,19, XX.1,4, XXI.12, XXII.1,5-6,10, XXIV.3,5,9,16,44, XXV.29, XXVII.3,5-7, XXVIII.1,5, XXIX.13-14, XXXI.10,XXXIV.1,XXXVII.9, XLIII.7,27, XLIV.3-4,10,13,16,18, XLV.13,24, XLVI.5, XLVII.1,4,6,10, LIII.35, LX.1-2,36, LXIII.1-3, LXIV.2, LXIX.8, LXX.32, LXXII.1, LXXIII.1,36, LXXVII.17,24,57, LXXX.2,116-117, Hug.47.

Midgardswyrm, XXX.40,42, XXXII.3, LXXVI.18-20, LXXXII.4,7,9, LXXXIII.2.

Midi, XV.13.

Midjung, XV.13, XL.11.

Midvitnir, XXVIII.4, XXXVII.20.

Mimameid, IV.3, LXIV.32, LXIX.25.

Mimir, III.2, IV.3-4, V.3,6,8-9,30,43, VI.1,34, IX.2, X.2,8,10,14-15,17-18, XV.13, XVI.13,17, XVII.4, XVIII.1-3, XIX.1,19, XX.10,106, XXII.7, XXIV.30,44-45, XXVI.4,7,9, XXVIII.1-4, XXIX.4, XXX.4, XXXII.12, XXXVII.1, XXXIX.1, XLIV.3,14, XLV.5,7,19, XLVI.1,3,5-6,9, L.1, LII.21-22, LIII.41,53,62,71, LIV.1,9,11-12,14-17,22,29,34,36-38,40-41, LVI.9, LVIII.49, LIX.19, LX.20, LXI.4-7, LXVI.30, LXIX.16-18,20,22,24-26,34,36-37, LXX.7,22, LXXVIII.74, LXXX.2,85, LXXXII.3, LXXXIII.1, Hug.51.

Mimisbrunn, I.4, II.1-2, IV.3,6, V.3,40, X.10, XX.3, LIII.31, LXIX.25.

Mimsvin, V.39.

Minnihorn, LII.12.

Mist, XXV.15.

Mistilteinn, LIII.13, LVI.4, LXXVII.21.

Mistorblindi, LXXVI.2.
Mjod, LXVI.35.
Mjodvitnir, V.37, X.3, XXVIII.4.
Mjoll, XV.5, XLIV.11.
Mjollnir, XVI.7, XVIII.2, XXX.2,9, XXXII.21-22, XXXIII.31, XXXIV.6, XXXVI.12,14, LV.5, LVI.6,LVIII.51,LXIII.4, LXXVI.35, LXXVIII.66,68,70, LXXXIII.3.
Modgud, XIV.20,XXIV.30, LXV.3.
Modi, XVI.6, LVIII.51, LXXVI.33, LXXXIII.3.
Modir, XX.67,71.
Modnir, X.13, LXIX.27.
Modsognir, XIX.1, LIII.41.
Mog, XX.83.
Mogthrasir, XIX.19, LVIII.49.
Moinn, 1) Serpent, II.9, 2) Dwarf, X.8.
Moinnsheath, LX.4.
Mokkurkalfi, XXXVI.7,15.
Mor, X.12-13.
Morgin, X.13, XI.3.
Morn, 1) Vaett, IX.2, XXVI.18, LXVII.33, 2) Giantess, XV.14, XXXII.11.
Mornir, XV.13.
Mundilfari, XI.5, LVIII.23.
Mund, LII.49, LXIV.63.
Munin, V.45, XXXVII.8, Hug.5.
Munnharpa, XV.14.
Munways, XXIV.46.
Muspel, XXIV.6, XXXV.5, LIII.75, LXXVIII.46,79, LXXXII.4.
Mylin, LXVI.15.
Mylnir, LX.3.
Myrkmark, LV.23.
Myrkrider, 1) Swanmaid, XLIV.16, XLIX.2, LXXVII.21, 2) Giantess, XV.14.
Myrkwood, XXII.9, XLIV.15, XLIX.1, LV.23, LX.3, LXXVIII.46.

N

Nabbi, XXXV.6.
Nagates, XXIV.9, XXVI.12-13,15, LXIV.38, LXVII.37, LXXVIII.70.

Naglfar, XXIV.6, XXXV.5, LIII.74, LXXXII.4.
Naglfari, X.17.
Nain, X.3.
Nair, XXVI.3,14,36.
Nal, XV.7, XLV.16.
Nali, X.5.
Namaeli, XXIV.40, XXV.3.
Nanna, X.17, XIV.20, XXVI.4, XXXII.7, L.1, LI.1-5, LII.50, LIII.2, LVI.6,9-10, LXI.7, LXV.7,12, LXXXIII.1.
Nar, X.3.
Nastrand, XXVI.2,24,35-36, LIII.63.
Nati, XV.13.
Natt, VI.32, X.15-17, XI.3-5,10, XIII.1, XIV.18, XXV.17, XLV.7, LII.8, LIII.37, LIV.1, LVIII.13,24-25, LIX.18, LXVI.30-31, LXIX.26-27.
Nauma, XLV.8.
Nauthiz, VI.19, XX.22, LII.15.
Needfire, XX.4,40, LX.19.
Nefja, XV.14.
Nep, LVI.6.
Neri, XXIX.4.
Nid, 1) Dwarf, X.9, 2) New Moon, XI.3, LVIII.24-25.
Nid, XXIV.3,8, XXVI.34-35, XLVI.1, LXII.21, LXIX.34.
Nidafjoll, I.2, IV.2, VIII.1, IX.1, X.18, XXVI.12, XL.2, LIII.91, LIV.1, LXI.5,7, LXIX.26, LXXXII.3, LXXXIII.5.
Nidavoll, X.15.
Nidfol, LIII.74, LXXXII.4.
Nidhogg, II.2,7,10, XXVI.15,19,21,23-24, LIII.60,91, LXXXIII.5.
Nidi, 1) Mimir, XXVI.9, LIII.62, 2) Dwarf, X.3.
Niding, XXIV.3,39, XXV.1,3, XXVI.2-3,35, XLII.5,8, LX.16, LXIX.8, LXXVIII.45, LXXXII.4.
Nidjung, XX.83.
Nid, XX.83.
Nidstong, LXII.19.
Niflheim, I.2,6, II.2, IV.2, IX.2, X.18, XV.1, XVII.4, XX.106,XXII.1, XXVI.1-2, XXVII.3, XXXVII.8, XLII.5,

XLIV.1,3,5,16, XLV.26, LIV.1,9, LXI.5-6, LXIII.6.

Niflhel, XXIV.16,45, XXV.1,3, XXVI.1-2,12-13,15,17-19, XXXIV.6, XLII.8, XLIII.15, XLIV.20, LIII.15, LVIII.43, LXX.51, LXXXII.3-4,9.

Niflungs, XXVII.3, XL.2, L.3, LI.6, LXXI.4.

Niflways, LIX.18.

Nine Vices, XXII.7.

Nine Virtues, XX.36.

Niping, X.3.

Nipt, LII.8.

Nixi, XXVIII.7.

Njars, X.1, LIV.1,9,29,38.

Njola, XLV.26, LXVI.31.

Njord, X.17, XIII.1-2,4,8, XVI.2-3, XVIII.2, XXVII.4, XXXIII.23, XXXV.5, XL.3-4,12-16, XLII.2, LV.8,11, LVIII.38, LXII.3,48,53-54, LXIII.5, LXIV.20, LXVII.1,40-41,44, LXVIII.1, LXIX.1,3,6,18-19,23,30,33, LXX.33, LXXII.5, LXXVIII.1,37-40.

Njot, V.39.

Noatun, XIII.2, XVI.2, XXXIII.23, LV.8,11.

Nokkvi, XI.8, XXXVII.26, Hug.5,36.

Nonn, VIII.3.

Nor, XV.13.

Nordri, X.3, XI.1, LXXIV.7.

Norway, LXIX.36.

Nori, X.3.

Norns, 1) Goddesses of Fate, IV.4-5,V.3, VII.2, XX.11,15,26,35, XXIV.2,42, XXV.14,XXVIII.4,7, XLII.7,XLIII.32, XLV.1, XLVII.10, L.15, LI.17, LII.25, LIII.92, LVII.2, LIX.9, LX.15, LXI.1, LXXI.45, Hug.21,28,52, 2) Fylgjas, XIX.17,18, XXVI.3, XXIX.2,10, L.16-17.

Nor, LXVI.30.

Norvi, XLV.7.

Not, VIII.3.

Nyhellenia, XXII.10,13,15-16,22-25,30,32,36-38,40-42,44-46.

Ny, XI.3, LVIII.25.

Nyi, X.3.

Nyr, X.4.

Nyrad, X.4.

Nyt, VIII.3.

O

Odainsacre, XVI.8, XLVI.3,5,9, LVI.9, LVII.12, LXXXIII.1.

Odal, XVI.2,15, XVII.3, XIX.15, XX.77,90, XXII.24-25, XLIX.3, LXII.16.

Odin, II.6, V.1-4, V.9,11,26,30,38-40,42-44,46-47, VI.1-2,34, VII.2, IX.3-4,6, XI.4,10, XII.2-3,5,10, XIII.1,5-6, XIV.1, XVI.2-3,5,8,11,13-21, XVII.6, XIX.3,5-7,13,16,22,XX.39,41,104, XXII.2,10,34,38,45,47, XXIII.3, XXIV.2,13,15,18,38,44, XXV.2,4-9,11-16, XXVI.2,14,XXVII.1,XXVIII.1, XXXII.5,12,18,20, XXXIII.22,34, XXXIV.7, XXXV.5-6, XXXVI.1-2,4,10,13,18, XXXVII.8-9,11-15,18-26, XXXIX.1, XL.1-6,9,12, XLII.5, XLV.1,9-10,16-19,22-23, L.8, LI.1,12,16,18, LII.5-6,10,20-21, LIII.2,5,14-16,18,21,23-24,26,28-32,43,51-58,68,71,78-80,85-87,90,93, LV.10, LVI.4,6-7, LVII.1,3,6-7,9-12, LVIII.1-3,5-6,8,40-41,52,54-55, 64, LXIII.2,5,9,21,30, LXIV.1,4-6,9,11-12,64, LXV.2,7,10, LXVI.6, LXVII.23-24,35,61, LXVIII.1-3, LXIX.1-4,6,8-9,11-20,22,24,26,28,30,33-37, LXX.15,18-19,33-34,60, LXXI.47, LXXII.1-4,6-9, LXXIII.3-4,7-9,17-18,20,34, LXXIV.10-11, LXXV.3, LXXVI.19-20,34, LXXVII.10,25,57, LXXVIII.1,12-13,24-27,30,49,65,73-74, LXXX.1-5,103,115, LXXXI.1, LXXXII.1,3,6-9,LXXXIII.2-3,5, Hug.1,5,13,45,51,52.

Odlungs, LX.36.

Od, 1) Freya's husband, XIX.2-3,13-14,16, XXIV.9,13-14, LIII.43. 2) Hoenir's gift, V.47,X.13, XIV.6, XXV.3, XXVII.8, XLII.2, XLIII.34,36, LIII.48, LIX.1,3-5,8,10,22,24-27, LXI.1-8, LXII.1,4-5,8,12,15,17,19,21,24-25,27-29,31-32,40-46,54, LXIII.1-10, LXIV.3-4,6-

8,12,14,16,21,23,25,27,29,31,33,35,37,39,41 ,43,45,47,49,51,53-56,59,62-65, LXV.2-3,6-7,9, LXVII.1-4,6,9,11-12,15,20,23,25,27,40,42-44,46-47,49-61, LXIX.18,23,30,33, LXX.1-5,17,21-26,31,34-35,61, LXXIII.1-2,22, LXXIV.1,8-13, LXXV.3, LXXXII.10,

Odroerir, II.2, IV.3, V.6, XLV.2, LXXX.112.
Ofdokkum Ognar Ljoma, XII.6, LI.15.
Offoti, XV.13, XL.17.
Ofhly, LXVI.23.
Oflugbarda, XV.14.
Oflugbardi, XV.13, LXXVI.21.
Ofnir, 1) Odin, V.38, 2) Serpent, II.9.
Ogladnir, XV.13.
Oin, X.9.
Okolnir, IV.3,X.15, LIII.62.
Okuthor, XVI.6, XVIII.2, XXX.1,16.
Okkvinkalfa, XX.56.
Ol, LXVI.35.
Olgefjun, XXXVI.19.
Olgefn, XXXVII.25, LV.2.
Olg, V.39.
Oljos, LXVI.31.
Olnir, X.9.
Olrunes, VI.3, LII.15,27.
Omi, V.36, XLV.22.
Ond, V.2, XIX.2-3,13-14,16, XXIV.9,13-14, XXVI.14, LIII.43,LXIX.37.
Ondud, XV.13.
Onduras, XLVIII.2.
Ondurdis, XXVII.6, LV.10.
Ondurgod, XXVII.6, XL.10.
Opi, IX.2, XXVI.18, LXVII.31.
Ori, X.6, XLVI.3, LXIV.46.
Ormt, VIII.4, XXIV.36.
Ornir, XV.13.
Orvandill, XVII.5, XXXI.5-6.
Osgrui, XV.13.
Oski, V.36.
Oskopnir, L.19.
Oskrud, XV.13.
Ostara, 1) Natt, X.16, LIV.1, 2) April, Hug.6, 3) Spring Equinox.
Ostaras, X.1, LIV.1-2, LXIX.27.

Othala VI.33,XX.36.
Otholi, IX.2, XXVI.18, LXVII.31.
Owights, XXIV.12.

P
Perthro, VI.23, XX.26.

R
Rabenschlacht, LXX.36,61.
Radgrid, XXV.15.
Radso, LXXVII.9.
Radsvid, X.4.
Raefil, LXXIII.5.
Raesir, LX.36.
Raido, VI.14, XX.17.
Ragnarok, II.3, IX.1, XVIII.4, XXIV.6, XXVIII.4, XXXVII.27, XLVI.5, LIII.30, LVII.3,12, LXII.53, LXXII.1, LXXV.9, LXXVI.22, LXXVIII.78, LXXIX.1,3, LXXX.1.
Ran, XV.3-4,10, Hug.5.
Randgrid, XXV.15.
Randver, LXXI.2-3,5,8-9,12-13,15,17,37.
Rangbein, XV.13.
Rani, LIX.11.
Ratatosk, II.7.
Rati, XXXVII.19, LXXX.110.
Raudgrani, V.39.
Regin, X.4, XLV.10, LV.4.
Reginleif, XXV.15.
Rekk, X.9.
Rennandi,VIII.2.
Rifingafla, XV.14.
Rig, XX.6,43-44,46,48,57,60,66,70,73,87,95,98,103, XXI.3,12-13.
Rhine, VIII.2, XLVII.10.
Rind, XIV.19, XLV.23, LIII.5,26, LVII.3,9-11, LIX.11, LXIX.12,LXXX.102.
Ristill, XX.65.
Rognir, 1) Volund, XXXII.5, XL.9, XLV.10, LII.23, 2) Odin, V.39.
Rosamuda, XXII.15.

Roskva, XIV.20, XXVII.8, XXX.1,3-4,43, XXXVI.15.
Rota, XXV.14.
Rud, LIX.13.
Rune, II.6, IV.3-4, V.5,8-9,23,43,45-46, VI.1,9,11,X.18,XI.5,XII.8, XVI.13,XX.8,77,85,87,XXII.5,32,XXIV.38-39,XXVI.26, XXVII.8, XXIX.12, XXXIV.7, XXXV.5, XXVII.26, XLIV.20, XLVII.5, XLVIII.2, LII.11,20, LIII.19,85,95,121, LVII.2,9,12, LVIII.42-43, LX.35, LXII.48, LXIII.6, LXVII.38, LXIX.8,36, LXX.7,49, LXXX.85, LXXXIII.2, Hug.8,46,56.
Runelaw, XX.11-12.
Rusila, XVII.1.
Ryg, XXXII.22.
Ryg, XV.14.
Rym, XVI.6.

S

Sad, V.34.
Seedtide, XI.12.
Saeg, XXXVII.3,21-22.
Saehrimnir, XXV.7, XLV.19, LVIII.41.
Saekarlsmuli, XV.13.
Saekin, VIII.2.
Saeming, LXIX.36.
Saer, LXVI.25.
Saevafjol, LXIII.27.
Saevarstod, LIV.14,17, LV.1.
Saga, XIV.2, XXXVII.25, Hug.52.
Sagunes, LXVIII.2.
Salfang, XV.13.
Salgofnir, XXV.11, LXIII.28.
Samendil, XV.13.
Samso, LVII.3, LXXVIII.28.
Sanngetal, V.34.
Sangrid, XXV.15,20.
Segg, XX.64.
Seidberend, XV.10.
Seidhall, XXII.6.
Seid, XXII.3,6-8,31, XXIII.1, XXV.1, XXXII.5, XL.5, XLIV.3-4, XLVI.1, LIII.47,

LVII.10, LIX.23, LXII.18,22, LXVII.46, LXIX.6,8,12-13,15, LXXII.7.
Sela, XV.14, XXXI.9.
Selmonth, XI.12.
Sessrumnir, XIII.5, XVIII.3, XXV.6, XLII.1, LXX.26.
Siar, X.7.
Sid, VIII.2.
Sidgrani, V.39, LXVI.6.
Sidhot, V.35.
Sidskeg, V.35.
Sif, XIV.20, XVI.6, XXVII.8, XXXIII.25, XXXV.1,5, XXXVI.3, XLIV.15, XLVIII.2, XLIX.1,3, LIV.10, LIX.1-4,24,26-27, LXII.41-44, LXIV.64-65, LXVII.55-56, LXXVI.3,15,17,33, LXXVII.49, LXXVIII.1,57, Hug.47.
Sigarsvellir, XXIX.8.
Sigdir, V.39.
Sigfather, V.35, LIII.79, LXXVIII.65, LXXXII.8.
Sigmund, 1) Odin, V.39, 2) Sigurd's father, V.47, LXIV.7-8,10.
Signi, LX.26, LXX.2.
Sigurhofund, V.39.
Sigrun, V.39.
Sigrunes, VI.2, LII.14.
Sigtryg, 1) Groa's father, XXVII.8, XXXV.1, XLIII.6-7,14,26-28,35, XLIV.15, 2) Odin, V.39.
Sigtyr, V.39, XII.2.
Sigtyrsberg, XXV.2.
Sigurblot, XIX.6.
Sigurd, X.13, Hug.51,56.
Sigyn, XIV.20, XV.9, XVI.21, XL.10, LIII.61, LXVIII.78-79.
Silaegja, LXVI.25.
Silfrtopp, X.11.
Simul, 1) Pole, XXXVII.3, 2) Giantess, XV.14.
Sindri, 1) Mimir's son, V.9, VI.34, X.3,13,15, XI.4, XVI.13, XVIII.3, XIX.17, XXXV.2-3,6, XXXIX.1-3,7-8, XL.1, XLIV.3,19, XLVII.4,L.17, LIII.62, LIV.1, LXIX.26-27, 2) Hall, X.15, LXIX.26.
Sinfjotli, LXIV.7.

Singastein, LXXIV.1,8,10.
Sinhtgunt, LIII.2.
Sinir, X.11.
Sinmara, X.1, XIV.20, LIV.1,11,13,41, LXI.4,8, LXIV.36,38,40,42.
Sivor, XV.14.
Sjofn, XIV.7.
Skadi, XIV.20, XXVII.6, XL.3,9-10, XLIV.3, XLVIII.1, LV.1,6,9-11,16,21-23, LXII.44, LXIV.65, LXVII.1, LXIX.19,36, LXXVIII.1,53,55,78.
Skaerir, XV.13.
Skaevad, X.13, LXX.16,19.
Skafid, X.7.
Skald, V.47, XXV.13, XXXVII.25-26, LXX.26.
Skalli, XV.13.
Skalmold, XXV.15.
Skandians, XLVII.4.
Skat, XXI.7-10.
Skatyrnir, XI.2.
Skavaer, X.9.
Skef, XX.5,98.
Skeggbragi, XXXVII.26.
Skeggjold, XXV.15.
Skeidbrimir, X.11.
Skerkir, XV.13.
Skerry Grotti, VIII.1.
Skidbladnir, XXXV.1,5, LXII.3,46.
Skilfings, XVII.2, XX.92, LX.2,36.
Skilfing, V.38.
Skin, LXVI.15.
Skinfaxi, VI.32, X.13, XI.4, LVIII.12.
Skipta Litum, V.43.
Skirar Veigar, XXIV.44, XLVI.4, LIII.22.
Skirfir, X.7.
Skirnir, LXVII.43, LXXV.3, LXXXII.10.
Skjaldraras, XLVIII.2.
Skjalf, XIV.6.
Skjold, XXI.2-3,5,7,10, XXII.46, XXVII.1, XXIX.6,10,13.
Skjoldungs, XX.92, XXI.2,12, XXVII.1, XXIX.2,10, LX.2,36, LXXI.18.
Skogul, XXV.15, XLV.19, LIII.56.
Skoll, XI.7, LVII.3, LXVIII.2, LXXXII.2.
Skram, XV.13.

Skrati, XV.13.
Skridfinns, XXVII.2.
Skrikja, XV.14.
Skrimnir, XV.13.
Skrog, XV.13.
Skrymir, XV.13, XXX.6,8-10,12,14, LXXVIII.69.
Skuld, IV.4, XXV.14,16, LIII.45,56.
Skurvan, LXVI.19.
Sky, LXVI.19.
Skyli, LX.36.
Skyndi, LXVI.15.
Slagfin, XV.13, XVII.1,4,6, XXVII.3-4,7,10, XXXII.4, XXXVII.1,3,6, XL.13, XLIV.4,6,15, XLVIII.1, XLIX.1,3, LI.6, LII.1,50, LXIV.65, LXX.31, LXXI.4,26.
Sleipnir, X.12, XXXIV.7, XXXVI.1, XL.5, LI.18, LII.23, LIII.15, LXIII.2, LXV.2,7, LXVII.11,46, LXIX.29-34, LXX.7.
Slid, I.2, VIII.3, XXVI.17, LIII.62.
Slidrugtanni, XXXV.6, LVI.7.
Slungnir, X.13.
Smith, XX.64.
Snaefjol, XXIX.8.
Snaer, XV.5,13, XLIV.11.
Snor, XX.63.
Snot, XX.65.
Snotra, XIV.13.
Sokkdalir, I.3, XI.1,5, XXVIII.4, XXX.4, XXXVII.7-9,11,21.
Sokkmimir, V.37, XXXVII.20,24.
Sokkvabekk, XIV.2, XXXVII.25.
Sol, Sun Goddesses, X.17, XI.1,5-7,9-10, XIV.18, XVII.1, XXXVIII.4, XLV.23,26, LIII.35-36, LVII.3, LVIII.22-23,47, LXV.17, LXVII.5, LXVIII.2, LXXIII.14, LXXXII.2, LXXXIII.4.
Solbjart, LXIV.59.
Solblindi, X.9, XII.5, LXIV.22.
Solfjol, XXIX.8.
Solmonth, XI.12.
Sonar Dreyri, IV.6, XX.3.
Son, XX.83.
Sonnung, XVI.6.
Sorli, LXXI.4,23,25,34,42,47.
Soti, X.12.

Sowilo VI.25, XX.28.
Sparinsheath, LX.3.
Sporvitnir, LX.3.
Sprakki, XX.65.
Spretting, XV.13.
Sprund, XX.65.
Starkad, XV.13, XXXII.23.
Stigandi, XV.13.
Storverk, XV.13.
Stromkarl, XXVIII.7.
Strond, VIII.3.
Stuf, X.12-13.
Stumi, XV.13.
Sudri, X.3, XI.1, XXXII.20, LXXIV.7.
Sult, XLII.5.
Sumar, XV.12-13.
Sumbel, 1) Drinking feast, XXXVII.16, XLV.18, LXXX.18-19,115, 2) Mead, LXVI.35.
Sunna, X.17, XIV.20, XVII.1, XXVII.6, XXXVII.2, XXXVIII.1,3,5,7-8, LIII.2, LXVI.17, Hug.6.
Surt, V.37, X.2, XV.10,13, XIX.1, XXVIII.4, XXX.4, XXXVII.21,24, L.18, LIII.41,72,77-78, LVIII.17-18,50-51, LXXIX.3, LXXXII.1,3,5,10, LXXXIII.1,3.
Suttung, XV,13, XXVIII.4, XXX.16, XXXVII.11-12,22-23, LXVI.35, LXVII.36, LXXX.109,114-115, LXXXII.5.
Svadilfari, XXXIV.2,5-6.
Svafnir, 1) Odin, V.38, LIII.5, LXIX.26, 2) Ivaldi, II.9, 3) XVI.4.
Svafrthorin, LXIV.20, LXIX.26.
Svalin, XI.5.
Svalkaldur Saer, IV.6, XX.3.
Svanhild, LXXI.2,4-5,8-11,13,16,19,24.
Svanni, XX.65.
Svarang, XV.13, LXXVII.30.
Svarin, XLIII.35, LX.25.
Svarinsmound, XLIII.6, XLVII.4, LX.22,35.
Svarri, XX.65.
Svartalfar, X.17, XXXVIII.6.
Svartalfheim, LXXV.3.
Svarthofdi, XV.10.
Svart, XV.13.

Svasud, XV.12-13, LVIII.27.
Svava, XXV.15.
Svefngaman, LXVI.31.
Sveid, XXV.15.
Sveigdir, 1) Odin, V.39, 2) Ivaldi, XXXVII.15,24.
Svein, XX.83.
Sveipinfalda, XV.14.
Svidar, V.39.
SVidir, 1) Odin, V.37,XXXVII.20, 2) Ivaldi, XXVII.15.
Svidud, V.39.
Svidur,1)Odin, V.37, XX.41, XXVII.1, XXXVII.20, 2)Ivaldi, XXVII.1-2, XXXVII.15.
Svinfylkja, LXXIII.20.
Svipal, V.34.
Svipdag, LXIV.54-56,59.
Svipul, XXV.15,20.
Svithjod, XVII.2, XX.41, XXI.3, XXII.6,10-11,47, XXVII.1-2, XXXII.18, XXXVII.1,6, XLIII.6,36, XLIV.11, XLVII.2, LX.9, LXIII.1, LXX.102,32, LXXII.1, LXXIV.13.
Sviur, X.5.
Svivor,XV.14, XXXII.23.
Svol, I.2, VIII.2.
Svolnir,V.39, XXXVI.10.
Swanmaid, XLIV.15-16, XLVII.3, XLVIII.1, XLIX.1, LIV.6, LIX.2, LXII.46,53, LXIV.2.
Swanrings, XLIV.15.
Sylg, I.1, VIII.3.
Syn, XIV.11.
Syr, XIV.6, LXII.23, LXXIV.1.
Syrhed, XXII.13.

T
Tafl, XVI.13, XVIII.4, XX.83, LIII.39,86, LXXXIII.2.
Talhrein, XL.6.
Tamsvond, LXVII.28.
Toothfee, XIII.4, XXVII.4.
Tanngnidr, XXV.15.
Tanngnjost, XVIII.2, XXVII.9.

Tanngrisnir, XVIII.2, XXVII.9.
Thane, 1) Freeman, X.12, XX.101, XLV.17, 2) Karl's son, XX.64.
Thekk, 1) Odin, V.33, 2) Dwarf, X.4.
Thengil, LX.36.
Thing, V.36, XIV.11, XIX.2, XX.39, XXIV.2,4-5,36-39,41,44,47, XXV.3, XXVI.2, XXXIII.15, XXXIX.3, LII.20,33,50, LIII.3,9,LIII.42,76,98, LV.2, LVI.1, LVII.12,LX.2-3, LXIX.1,22-23, LXX.61, LXXI.12,22, LXXII.2-3, LXXIV.11, LXXVI.36, LXXX.30,66, LXXXII.3, Hug.7,46,48,52,56.
Thingseats, XI.3, XIX.1, XXIII.1, XXIV.38, XLII.2, LIII.37,40,48,50, LXIX.1,11, LXXIII.1.
Thingstead, XXIV.33, XXV.16, XXXIX.1, LXIX.1,14-15.
Thistilbardi, XV.13.
Thjalfi, XXVII.8, XXX.1,3-4,19-22,39,43, XXXII.5,11-13,16-17,21-22, XXXVI.8,15-16, XLVII.1, LX.17-19,35, LXXVII.40.
Thjazi, XV.13, XLIV.3,6, LV.22, LXXVII.20, LXXVIII.54-55.
Thjodnuma, VIII.3.
Thjodrek, LXXIII.36.
Thjodreyrir, V.26, X.7, XI.10, LXIV.1.
Thjodvarta, XIII.1, XIV.20, LXIV.50.
Thjodvitnir, XII.8.
Thogn, XXV.15.
Thokk, LXV.9-10.
Tholl, VIII.2.
Thorin, X.4.
Thorn, XXXII.4,11,19.
Thor, XVI.6-7,16, XVIII.2, XXIV.36, XXVII.9, XXIX.11,XXX.1-13,15,23,25,27-29,31,33-38,42-43, XXXI.1, XXXII.2-7,9,11-14,16-23, XXXIII.8-10,15-16,18-20,25,32, XXXIV.3,6, XXXV.1,5-6, XXXVI.1,3-19,15, XXXIX.6, XL.11-12, XLII.3,5,7,27, XLIV.3, XLVII.6, LIII.49,80, LV.2,5,10, LVI.6, LX.4,17,23,35, LXI.3-4, LXII.41, LXIII.2-5,7, LXIV.64, LXVI.2-4,6,8,10,12,14,16,18,20,22,24,26,28,30,32,34,36, LXVII.47,50,60, LXVIII.1,LXIX.14,18,30,34, LXX.3,33,45,

LXXII.1,6, LXXVI.2,4,6,11,14-23,26-28,30,33-34,36, LXXVII.1,4,6,8,10,12,14,16,18-20,22-30,32-34,36-40,42,44,46,48,50,52,54,56-58,60, LXXVIII.1,60-61,63,65-68,70,75-76, LXXX.1,116, LXXXII.7,9, LXXXIII.3, Hug.3,11,13,32.
Thorri, 1) Etin, XV.5,13, XLIV.11, 2) January, LXVI.35.
Thorsnes, XXIII.2, XLII.4, LXVIII.2.
Thrall, 1) Ai's son, XX.50,54,91, 2) Slave, XV.10, XXIX.11, XL.15, LIV.38, LXII.47, LXXVII.25, LXXX.92.
Thrain, X.4, XLV.3.
Thrasar, V.39.
Thrasir, XXXII.20.
Thridi, V.33, XXXII.4.
Thrigeitir, XV.13.
Thriggi, V.39, XXXVII.26.
Thrima, XXV.15.
Thrivaldi, XV.13, XXXII.23.
Throng, XXXII.20.
Thropt, V.39.
Thror, 1) Odin, V.36, 2) Dwarf, X.4.
Thrudgelmir, III.2, IX.5, XV.13, LVIII.29.
Thrudheim, XVI.6.
Thrud, XIV.20, XVI.6, XXV.15, XXXII.20, LXIV.64, LXXVI.20.
Thrudvang, XVI.6, XXVII.9, XXX.42, XXXVI.19.
Thrund, V.38.
Thrungva, XIV.6.
Thrymgjoll, XII.5-6,9, LXIV.22, LXIX.29.
Thrymheim, XLIV.2, LV.1,11,21-22.
Thrym, XV.13, XXXIII.6-7,9,12,23,26,31-32.
Thund, V.11,33, LXXII.9, XII.8, LVI.8, LXIV.2.
Thunn, V.39.
Thurbord, XV.14.
Thurisaz VI.12, XX.15
Thurse, Etins, XV.13,15, XIX.7, XX.42, XXXIII.6,12,23,26,31-32, XLIII.20, XLIV.5, XLV.1, LIII.29,39, LXII.23, LXIV.12, LXVI.2, LXVII.11,33, LXX.52, LXXVI.17.

Thviti, LXXV.9.
Thy, XX.53-54.
Thyn, VIII.2.
Tiggi, LX.36.
Tiwaz VI.26, XX.29.
Tjaldari, X.12.
Tjosul, IX.2, LXVII.31.
Tomte, XXVIII.6.
Topi, IX.2, XXVI.18, LXVII.31.
Totrughypja, XX.56.
Tramar, IX.2, XXVI.18, LXVII.32.
Tronubeina, XX.56.
Tunrid, V.21, LXXX.4.
Tveggi, V.39.
Twimonth, XI.12.
Tyhaustr, XVI.14.
Tyr, 1) Odin's son, XVI.14-15, XIX.19, XL.6,12, LII.14, LXIII.2, LXVIII.3, LXIX.18, LXX.7,33, LXXV.1,8, LXXVI.4,6,32, LXXVIII.1,41-44, LXXXII.7, Hug.32,36,50.
Tyrfing, LIV.12.
Tyirings, XLVII.2.
Tyspakur, XVI.14.

U
Ud, V.33.
Ulflidur, XVI.14.
Ulfrun, VIII.11, XV.14, XLV.26.
Ull, X.13, XXXII.20, XXXV.1,XXXVI.10, XLVIII.2, LIII.5, LIX.1,4,22-24,26, LXI.1, LXII.1,4,24,26,28-29,31,40-41, LXIV.64, LXVII.50,60, LXIX.18,23,30,33,35, LXX.33, LXXII.3,6,10, LXXVI.6,20, Hug.11,56.
Uni, X.6, XLVI.3, LXIV.46.
Unn, XV.4.
Uppheim, LXVI.13.
Upphimin, XI.4,10.
Uppsala, XXI.11, LXXIII.35, Hug.31.
Ur Age, XVII.1.
Urdarbrunn, I.3, II.2,5, IV.4-6, XX.3, XXIV.36-37,44, XXV.16, LIII.44,94.
Urdar Magn, IV.6, XX.3,6.
Urdar Ord, XXIV.40, XXV.16.

Urd, IV.4, VII.2, XIV.4, XIX.17-18, XXII.28, XXIV.1,3,16,18,30,32,36,40, XXV.16-17, XXVI.4, XLII.6-8, XLIV.14, XLV.2,9,11-12,15,20,L.25, LIII.1,31,45,52,68, LIV.1, LIX.2,12, LXI.6, LXIV.3,37,59, LXV.2,8, LXIX.9,25, LXXVIII.1,23-25, LXXX.3, LXXXII.1, LXXXIII.1.
Uri, X.6, XLVI.3, LXIV.46.
Urlag, IV.4, VI.31, VII.2, XIII.3, XIX.2,17-18, XX.33, XXII.3, XXIV.1,46, XXIX.2, XLIII.30, XLIV.15, XLIX.1,LI.14,LIII.31,42,45,47,85, LVIII.38,40,42,LX.15, LXVI.10,12,14,16,18,20,22,24,26,28,30,32,34, LXVII.47, LXX.51, LXXVIII.25,33, LXXX.61, LXXXIII.2.
Urlagthreads, IV.4, XXIX.3, LXI.4,8.
Uruz, VI.11, XX.14.
Urcold, XV.3, XLII.3.
Urvan, LXVI.19.
Utgardloki, XXX.13,16,18-20,22-24,26,28,30,32,34,36-40,42, LXXVI.19.
Utgard, I.3,XXVIII.4, XXX.4,13.
Utiseta, V.43.

V,W
Vadgelmir, XXVI.33.
Vaegin, LXVI.27.
Vaeni, LX.2.
Vafur, XII.6, LXIX.29.
Vafurfires, XII.6, XXIV.7, XLIV.20, XLVI.4, LI.16, LII.2,10, LV.5, LXIV.13,43,LXVII.9-10, LXIX.29-31,33.
Vafurmist, XII.6, LXIX.29.
Vafthrudnir, XV.13, LVIII.1-3,6-7,9,11,13,15,17,19,20-43,45,47,49,51,53,55.
Vafud, 1) Odin, V.38, 2) Wind, LXVI.21.
Vagasker, LXXIV.1,10.
Vagn, LXXIII.17.
Vagnhofdi, V.36, LXX.2,5-6,32,35,37, LXXIII.17,27.
Vag, LXVI.25.
Vaka, LVII.8.
Vak, 1) Odin, V.38, 2) Horse, X.13.

Vala, XV.3,10, XXII.6, LIII.18,22-30,47, LVII.8, LIX.2, LXVIII.1-2, LXXVIII.28, LXXX.92.

Valaskjalf, XII.3.

Valfather, V.35, XVI.16, LIII.14,32,55, LXXIII.18.

Valgaut, V.39.

Valgrind, XII.5, LXIX.15,29-31,33.

Valhallagara, XXII.13,23.

Valhall, VI.13, XII.2, XIX.6, XXIV.28, XXV.1-3,5,7,9-11,13-14,16, XXXII.4,12, XXXVI.3-4, XXXVII.8, XLV.17, LI.3, LIII.12,31,59,87,93, LVII.1,12, LXIII.15, LXIV.4, LXV.1, LXVIII.1, LXIX.33, LXXIV.11,13, LXXVIII.2, LXXXIII.3.

Vali, 1) Asagod, XIV.19, LIII.26,61, LVII.11, LVIII.51, LIX.11, LXIX.18, LXX.33, LXXVIII.79, LXXXIII.3, 2) Dwarf, X.9.

Valkyries, XVI.6, XXIV.15,18,31, XXV.3,14-18,20,23,26-27, XXXVI.12, XLV.1, XLIX.1, LII.10, LIII.56, LVI.7, LX.23, LXIV.4, LXVIII.2, LXX.26.

Valland, LXX.4,29, LXXVII.25.

Vallarfax, LXVI.29.

Val, X.12-13.

Valtam, LIII.21.

Valthognir, V.39.

Valtivi, LIII.77, LXXXII.5.

Valtyr,V.39.

Vanaburgh, XVI.2.

Vanadis, XIV.1,6, LXII.29,43.

Vanagod, XIII.9, LXIX.19.

Vanaheim, XI.11, XIII.1, XVI.2-3, XX.4,104, LVIII.39, LXIX.18,22-23,30, LXX.26,33.

Vandill, XV.13.

Vanir, V.1, VI.34, X.17, XIII.1,9, XIV.1,14, XVI.2, XX.1, XXXII.6, XXXIII.16, XL.4,XLII.2, LII.26, LIII.7,51, LVIII.39, LXII.23,46, LXIII.1,9,65, LXVI.11,13,19,23,25,27,29,33,35, LXVII.19-20,39, LXVIII.1, LXIX.1-3,5-12,15-16,18,20-24,28-34,LXX.5, LXXII.1-2,5,8, LXXIII.1,21, LXXIV.9.

Var, XIV.9, XXXIII.31.

Vardruna, VI.12, XV.14.

Varinsey, LXVIII.2.

Varkald, LXIV.18.

Varns, XI.11, LVII.3.

Varnwood, XI.7, LIII.2, LXVIII.2.

Var, X.6, XLVI.3, LXIV.46.

Vartari, XXXIX.6.

Vasad, XV.12.

Vaxt, LXVI.33.

Ve, 1) Hoenir, V.1, LXXVIII.30, 2) Shrine or enclosure, V.1.

Vedurfolnir, II.6.

Vedurglasir, LXIV.35.

Vedurmegin, LXVI.19.

Vega, LXVI.11.

Vegdrasil, X.6, XLVI.3, LXIV.46.

Vegsvin, VIII.3.

Vegtam, V.39, LIII.21,23,25,27-28.

Veidias, XLVIII.2.

Veig, LXVI.35.

Veig, X.4.

Veratyr, V.39.

Verdandi, IV.4, LIII.45.

Weregild, XL.2, LVI.5, LVII.2, LXIX.8-11,20, LXXIV.8.

Verland, LXXVII.57.

Vestein, X.13.

Vestri, X.3, XI.1, LXXIV.7.

Vetmimir, XI.2.

Vetur, XV.12.

Veud, XVI.6.

Veur, XVI.6, LXXVI.11,17,19.

Vid, VIII.3.

Vid, I.2, VIII.2.

Vid, LXVI.29.

Vidar, 1) XVI.16, XLV.17, LIII.79-80, LVIII.51,53, LXIII.2, LXIX.18, LXX.33, LXXVIII.1,13-14, LXXXII.4,8-9, LXXXIII.3, Hug.11, 2) V.39.

Vidblain, XI.2.

Vidblindi, XV.13.

Viddi, XV.13.

Vidfedmir, XI.2.

Vidga, LIV.41, LXI.4,8, LXX.22-23,31,35, LXXIII.21,33.

Vidgymnir, XV.13, LXXVI.22.

Vidhrimnir, V.39.
Vidofnir, II.11, XXV.11, LXI.4, LXIV.30,36-37,42.
Vidolf, XV.10,13.
Vidur, V.39.
Vidir, V.39, XLV.9, LXXVI.20, LXXVIII.30.
Vidur, V.39.
Vif, XX.65.
Vifil, X.13.
Vigglod, XV.14.
Vigg, 1) Dwarf, X.9, 2) Horse, X.12.
Vigrid, LVIII.18.
Vikings, XXXII.12, XXXVIII.5.
Wild Hunt, LXXX.4.
Vili, V.1, LXXVIII.30.
Vilkin, XVII.1.
Vilmeid, XV.10,13.
Vimur, XXXII.9-10, LXXVI.22.
Vin, VIII.2.
Vina, VIII.3.
Vindalf, X.4.
Vindblain, XI.2.
Vindflot, LXVI.19.
Vindheim, LIII.88, LXXXIII.4.
Vindhelm, XXV.3, LXII.28.
Vindkald, LXIV.18.
Vindler, XX.105.
Vindloni, XV.12.
Vindofni, LXVI.13.
Vind, 1) Wind, LXVI.21, 2) Etin, XV.13.
Vindslot, LXVI.23.
Vindsval, XV.12-13, LVIII.27.
Vingnir, XV.13, XVI.7, XXXVI.13, LVIII.51, LXXXIII.3.
Vingolf, IV.4, VII.2, XXIV.30,45.
Vingrip, XV.13.
Vingskornir, LI.17.
Vingthor, XVI.6, XXXIII.1, LXVI.6,9.
Vinili, XLVII.2.
Vipar, XV.13.
Virfir, X.7.
Vitki, LXII.19, Hug.6,49.
Vitur, X.4.

Wolfdales, XXII.9, XLIII.6, XLIV.15-16,18-19, XLV.6, XLVIII.1-2, XLIX.1, LIII.13, LIV.1,9, LV.1,23, LIX.1.
Wolfsea, XXII.9, XLIV.2, LV.1.
Volsi, V.39.
Volund, X.6, XV.13, XVI.18, XVII.4-5, XVIII.4, XXVII.3-4,6-7, XXXIX.2,8, XL.1-6,9-11,13-14,17, XLI.1, XLIV.2-4,6,12-13,15,17-20, XLV.10, XLVII.1, XLVIII.1, XLIX.1, L.3, LII.23, LIII.13, LIV.2,5,8-10,12,15,24-25,28-32,37,39-41, LV.1,3-6,10-11,22, LIX.2,LX.1, LXI.4,8, LXII.1,4,23,28,30,44,53, LXIII.1,7, LXIV.38,63, LXVII.52, LXX.3,22,31, LXXVII.20-21, LXXVIII.21,54-55.
Von, VIII.3, XXVI.7, LXXV.9, LXXVIII.79.
Vond, VIII.3.
Vond, LXVI.29.
Vor, XIV.10.
Vord Goda, XX.105.
Vornir, XV.13.
Wralda, XV.39, XIX.3, XXII.34, LXXXI.1.
Wunjo, VI.17, XX.20.
Wunsch, Hug.5.
Wyrd, IV.4, IX.1, XX.93, XXVI.3, XXXI.7,XXXIV.4,XXXV.5, XLIII.16,34, L.15, LIII.71, LIV.17,21, LX.4,21, LXI.1,4, LXIX.26, LXX.16-17,22, LXXI.17, LXXIII.2,16, LXXIV.1,5,LXXVIII.23, LXXXII.3, Hug.46.

Y

Ydalir, XVII.3, XXVII.3-4,8, XL.5,13, LIX.1, LX.24, LXII.41, LXIV.64, LXXII.6.
Yggdrasil, II.1-4,7,9-11, IV.3-4,6, X.11, XII.1-2,6,10, XIII.7, XVI.20, XVIII.4-5, XIX.2,12-13,15,18, XX.2, XXII.7, XXIV.36,44, XXV.2,9, XXVI.4, XXVII.6, XXVIII.1, XXXIX.1, XLIV.14,16, XLV.6, XLVII.3, LIII.31,44,72,82, LIV.41, LXIV.1,32,35-36,40, LXVII.37,LXIX.16,25-26, LXXII.1, LXXXII.3,10.
Yggjung, V.39, XLV.18.

Ygg, V.38, XXVI.2, XLV.17, LI.16, LIII.18, LVII.10, LVIII.5, LXIX.30, LXXVI.2.

Ylfings, XVII.2, XXI.12, XXIX.5, LXIII.26, LXX.17,20,35.

Ylg, I.2, VIII.3.

Yma, XV.14.

Ymir, III.1-3, V.1,3,6, IX.1,3-6, X.1-2, XI.1, XII.5, XV.4,10,13,XVI.1, XIX.1,XXVI.17, XXXII.4,6,11,19,LIII.34,40, LVIII.21,28-29,32,LXII.28,LXIV.24, LXVII.52.

Ymsi, XXXII.4.

Ynglings, XVI.2, XX.92, XXI.11, LX.2,36.

Yngvi, 1) Heimdall, XX.92, 2) Warrior, XXI.11, LX.3, 3) Dwarf, X.7.

Yngvin, XXI.11.

Yrung, V.39.

Ysja, XX.56.

Yset, XVII.3, XXVII.8-9, XXX.4,XXXI.10, XL.5.

Yule, XXVIII.6, LXXX.4.

Yulefest, XIX.2,11.